AIMEE SEMPLE McPHERSON

AIMEE SEMPLE McPHERSON

*And the Making of Modern Pentecostalism
1890–1926*

Chas. H. Barfoot

LONDON   OAKVILLE

Published by
UK: Equinox Publishing Ltd., 1 Chelsea Manor Studios, Flood Street, London
SW3 5SR
USA: DBBC, 28 Main Street, Oakville, CT 06779

www.equinoxpub.com

First published 2011

British Library Cataloguing-in-Publication Data
A catalogue record for this book is available from the British Library.

ISBN   978 1 84553 166 9 (hardback)

Library of Congress Cataloging-in-Publication Data

    Aimee Semple McPherson and the making of modern Pentecostalism,
1890-1926/ Chas. H. Barfoot.
        p. cm.
        Includes bibliographical references and index.
        ISBN 978-1-84553-166-9 (hb)
        1. McPherson, Aimee Semple, 1890-1944. 2. Evangelists–United States–
Biography. 3. International Church of the Foursquare Gospel–Clergy–Biography.
5. Pentecostal churches–History. 6. Pentecostalism–History. I. Title.
        BV 3785.M28B37 2009
        289.2–dc22
        [B]
                                                        2009009279

Printed and bound by CPI Antony Rowe, Chippenham, United Kingdom

If personality is an unbroken series of successful gestures, then there was something gorgeous about … [her], some heightened sensitivity to the promises of life, as if [she] were related to one of those intricate machines that registers earthquakes ten thousand miles away. . . .It was an extraordinary gift for hope, a romantic readiness such as I have never found in any other person and which it is not likely I shall ever find again.

—F. Scott Fitzgerald
The Great Gatsby

America . . . is a fabulous country, the only fabulous country; it is the only place where miracles not only happen, but where they happen all the time.

—Thomas Wolfe
Of Time and the River

It was an age of miracles … It was an age of excess.

—F. Scott Fitzgerald
Echoes of the Jazz Age

With a heart full of gratitude, this book is dedicated to a quartet of Barfoots who have filled my life with love.

Howard and Nora,
Parents and Preachers

Sarah Jeanne,
Loving Circle of Life Daughter

Jeanette Marie,
Lover, Life Partner, and Lion Tamer

TABLE OF CONTENTS

PREFACE

Precious father, loving mother, fly across the lonely years
And old home scenes of my childhood in fond memory appear.

In the stillness of the midnight echoes from the past I hear,
Old-time singing, gladness bringing from that lovely land somewhere.

Precious memories, how they linger, how they ever flood my soul;
In the stillness of the midnight, precious, sacred scenes unfold.
—J.B.F. Wright
"Precious Memories"

Sing me back home with a song I used to hear
Make my old memories come alive
Take me away and turn back the years
Sing me back home before I die.

—Merle Haggard
"Sing Me Back Home"

By the rivers of Babylon, there we sat down, yea, we wept when we remembered Zion…How shall we sing the Lord's song in a foreign land?
—Psalm 137

I suspect that my reason for writing this book originated in the great agricultural heartland of northeastern Montana. The seeds for this project were planted, long before I was born, in that great windswept plain and took root there in the shortgrass prairie. It is a rather remarkable piece of level land that stretches forever—or at least as far as the eye can see. This vast plain was created when great glaciers moved southward from arctic Canada, forcing the Missouri River along with it. It is a land shaped as much by defeat as it is by dreams.

On this land, in view of the Bear's Paw Mountains where the warm Chinook winds blow, is where General Nelson Miles overtook the Nez Perce, who were fewer than forty miles from reaching sanctuary in Canada.

This land was the battlefield where Chief Joseph surrendered, offering up his most memorable speech: "Hear me, my chiefs. I am tired; my heart is sick and sad. From where the sun now stands, I will fight no more forever."[1]

This land was cowboy country—the place where Charley Russell settled down to work in his log cabin studio and where, at times, he traded his Western works of art for whiskey.

Ultimately, it was the land that James J. Hill and the Great Northern Railway took over and renamed as the "Hi-Line." At the turn of the century, thousands of homesteaders, many of them European immigrants, packed their cardboard suitcases, took the train to the Hi-Line and stepped off onto their fields of dreams.

Among the many homesteaders arriving on the Hi-Line was my maternal grandmother, Inga Larsen, from Norway. In addition to her homesteading, she eventually took title to Lot 8, Block 13, in Havre, the largest town on the Hi-Line, located in Hill County—named after James Hill—in the state of Montana.

On May 9, 1913, Inga Larsen from Norway married Karl Lager from Sweden. Karl immigrated to the United States on September 17, 1908, traveling in steerage (third class) on the vessel *Saxonia* of the Cunard line, arriving at Boston. Eight months later Karl was a farmer on the Hi-Line. Soon he was working for "Yem" Hill as a fireman on the Great Northern Railway, a job he kept until his death in 1941.

Five months after Karl and Inga's marriage, which was officiated by a Lutheran pastor, the first of seven children arrived. On St. Patrick's Day, 1917, Nora Josephine Lager, my mother, was born. Everyone said how special Nora was, owing in part to her being the first of Karl and Inga's daughters to live beyond childhood.

On some unknown day, most likely when my mother was a young girl, Inga Lager had a religious conversion. She traded in her Old-World Lutheranism for the new, modern American religious movement called Pentecostalism. Inga Lager's conversion was profound and had far-lasting consequences. Karl Lager quit drinking and became a God-fearing, church-going deacon. Family lore and legend has it that he was aided and assisted in his decision by Inga chasing him around the dining room table and breaking a chair over his head. Four of Karl and Inga's seven children went into the ministry, including my mother. And apparently no one was more responsible for this religious conversion so much as a young woman revivalist by the name of Aimee Semple McPherson. Because of Aimee Semple McPherson's influence, by the time that Karl and Inga's sixth child was born in 1927 she was appropriately named Aimee, after my grandmother's favorite preacher.

In the fall of 1935, Karl and Inga's oldest living daughter, Nora Josephine Lager, rode the rails of the Hi-Line out of Havre and headed for the Central Bible Institute in Springfield, Missouri, to begin training to become a Pentecostal evangelist, much like her role model, Aimee Semple McPherson. A striking Scandinavian beauty with blue eyes and blond hair, Nora Lager was also a gifted writer and speaker. Prior to her graduation from high school, she won numerous awards for both her speaking and writing abilities.

Howard and Nora Barfoot, radio evangelists in Wolf Point, Montana, 1941 (author's collection).

After returning for a short stay in her hometown in 1940, Nora Lager once again took the Great Northern east from Havre, this time headed to North Dakota. In the far northwestern corner of the state, just miles from the Saskatchewan border, she held a revival in Crosby for a newly arrived young minister from Canada. The evangelist's most significant convert was none other than her host pastor. On August 1, 1940, the Reverend Nora J. Lager and the Reverend Howard M. Barfoot were married. After their marriage in Havre and honeymoon in Glacier National Park, they returned to Montana to co-pastor Pentecostal churches with the Assemblies of God, first in Wolf Point and later in Miles City. Despite a successful radio ministry on KGCX in Wolf Point and a good church in the seat of Custer County, the lonesomeness of the prairie and plains eventually became too much for the young preachers.

By the time I was born, on April 24, 1949, on a Sunday at 9:46 a.m.—one minute late for Sunday school—my parents were starting a new church from scratch in Yakima, Washington. After twelve years in Yakima and four years in Anacortes, they finally arrived at their final church, their dream church—Bethel Temple in Los Angeles—after some hard time spent in exile, pastoring a home mission church in West Covina, preaching funerals in La Puente for the Viet Nam war dead, and performing janitorial duties at a factory in East Los Angeles. Bethel Temple was the first Anglo church established directly from the Azusa Street Mission and the mother church of their denomination, the Assemblies of God, in Southern California.

T.S. Eliot once wrote "the end of all our exploring will be to arrive where we started."[2] These words proved prophetic for my mother. On January 19, 1983, she was killed in a tragic car accident on the mean streets of Los Angeles. Her cause of death, "multiple blunt force trauma," was pronounced at the Queen of the Angels Hospital. Her funeral was held in Bethel Temple, a church my father pastored for twenty-two years. Upon my father's retirement in 1994, the Queen of the Angels Hospital and the proceeds from the sale of Bethel Temple were merged into the ministry of Angelus Temple, the church Aimee Semple McPherson founded in Echo Park, only a few blocks away from Bethel Temple.

Twenty years after my mother's death, almost to the day (always falling around Martin Luther King's holiday), I conducted my father's funeral in the very spot where Aimee Semple McPherson had preached and where her own elaborate funeral was held in 1944. Perhaps the strongest evidence of the power and influence of Aimee Semple McPherson over my grand-mother's and mother's lives was discovered a year after my father's death. One day, while going through his extensive library, I found an old, battered briefcase. On one of its worn leather sides, barely legible, were the initials *NJL*. Upon further inspection, I realized it had belonged to my mother when she was a traveling evangelist, before she met and married my father. I am sure it must have been one of the few possessions she took with her from home with when she entered the ministry. After sixty-some years in storage, it finally yielded its secrets. Its contents were few and meager, yet very meaningful for my mother. I found several of her sermons, tried and true, and I am sure they were used over and over again as she traveled from town to town. There were letters from my father, promising his undying love. In both their handwritings were his and her lists of the names and addresses of people they had invited to their wedding. There were birthday and Christmas cards from their first parishioners. And then there they were—sermons and pamphlets written by Aimee Semple McPherson. There was even a larger tract written by Aimee that assured her Pentecos-tal constituents that her kidnapping in 1926 had really happened. If Sister Aimee had converted my grandmother from Lutheranism to Pentecostal-ism, she had also provided a role model for my mother to follow.

Merle Haggard once wrote in a country song, that "the roots of my raising run deep."[3] My own spiritual roots were formed, in large measure, by my Norwegian, homesteading grandmother from the high, wide, and handsome plains of Montana. Out on those wide-open spaces she, too, experienced her own share of defeat, as well as dreams that came true. She lost two children but then raised two nieces when her sister died from complications due to childbirth. She lost a husband at an early age to Lou Gehrig's disease but gained two sons-in-law who were Pentecostal preachers. She sold a car to help build a new church but lived comfortably in her house until the day she died.

Thomas Wolfe was also a theologian of sorts when he wrote, "We are the sum of all the moments of our lives—all that is ours is in them: we cannot escape or conceal it."[4]

The older I become, the more interested I am in how I was spiritually formed and in my religious roots. Even through denominational divorces and remarriage (Assemblies of God, Presbyterian, Congregational, Non-Denominational, and, forever, a "closet" Episcopalian—I have multiple religious belongings) remaining scraps and fragments of how I met the "holy" still survive and surface from deep down within me. Perhaps Soren Kiekegaard said it best, when he wrote that "Life must be understood backwards; but…it must be lived forward."[5]

I know that my spiritual journey is far from unique and peculiar. I am hardly some sort of Pentecostal "prodigal." In the most recent extensive survey by the Pew Forum on Religion and Public Life exploring the shifts taking place in the United States' religious landscape today, it is observed that "More than one-quarter of American adults have left the faith in which they were raised in favor of another religion—or no religion at all.

> If change in affiliation from one type of Protestantism to another is included, roughly forty-four percent of adults have either switched religious affiliation, moved from being unaffiliated with any religion to being affiliated with a particular faith, or dropped any connection to a specific religious tradition altogether.[6]

Despite the fact that the majority of my students are around my daughter's age, I also realize that my spiritual journey resonates with at least some of them, especially those who are Native American Christians and the "Lost Boys of the Sudan." Together, we share in the larger world of Christianity but still stubbornly and proudly lay claim to our various tribal identities and attachments that shaped much, if not all, of our childhoods. Colorful, old-fashioned characters still lurk and loom large in our memories from another, more pre-modern world. Ancestral spirits, once embodied as grandparents and spiritual matriarchs and patriarchs, seem forever with us. My strongest bonds of attachment and affection as well as my sense of personal identity, have come from my birth, and subsequent spiritual formation, as a Pentecostal. How I met the "holy" can never be expunged, forgotten, or altered. Like Sandra Scofield, it too has taken me, "a long time to understand that my memories largely shape the meaning of my life."[7]

Over the years I have learned to cherish those precious memories of my childhood identity, hold them close to my heart, and integrate them with the person I am today. I make it through occasional dry spells of "spiritual homelessness" by recalling the immortal lines from the eloquent Henry Van Dyke, given to a divided Presbyterian church so long ago:

> Something to learn and something to forget:
> Hold fast to the good, and seek the better yet:
> Press on, and prove the pilgrim hope of youth
> That creeds are milestones on the path to truth.[8]

I will never forget the colorful God of my tribal identity and the equally meaningful, old songs of Zion. Unlike the god of mainline modern America, our God visited us frequently, especially all day Sunday, in downtown rented Teamster halls or storefronts and in tent meetings out on the fairgrounds. Who could ever forget such a God, a God who, as the most popular Pentecostal evangelist of my childhood put it:

> Was Father to the orphan,
> Husband to the widow,
> To the traveler in the night,
> He is the Bright and Morning Star,
> To those who walk in the lonesome valley,
> He is the Lily of the Valley,
> The Rose of Sharon and
> Honey in the Rock?[9]

Pentecostalism, an orphan daughter of American religion, had many a prophesying daughter in its genesis. There was, however, only one "Sister Aimee." Over the years, she, even more than the movement she helped to mother in its infancy, remains a prisoner of the caricature of that tradition that has, by now grown grotesque. Some of us raised in this tradition feel about her much the same way Sir Elton John felt about Marilyn Monroe, as expressed in his posthumous tribute to her:

And I would have liked to have known you,
  but I was just a kid.
Your candle burned out long
before your legend ever did.[10]

Despite a spate of recent biographies, Aimee Semple McPherson remains imprisoned by caricature. Although she has been rediscovered in recent years, her reputation, standing, and place in history has hardly improved since the first major scholar wrote about her, four decades ago. In his groundbreaking work, which was published appropriately in the *Journal of Popular Culture* in 1967, the esteemed historian from Brown University, William G. McLoughlin, correctly observed:

> History has done a double injustice to Aimee Semple McPherson. On the one hand it continues to mouth the distorted picture of her as the colorful exhibitionist described in the trite phrases of the yellow press: 'the titian-haired whoopee evangelist,' 'the Mary Pickford of revivalism'… and 'the Barnum of religion.' And on the other hand it perpetuates the Menckenesque evaluation of her motives and character expressed in the sophisticated liberal journals of the 1920s like the *New Republic*: 'She is a frank and simple fraud, somewhat like Texan Guinan, but more comical and not quite so cheap.' The psychologists of religion explain her simply as a neurotic. The sociologists see her as a climatic phenomenon evolving out of the endemic quackery and semi-moronic church clientele of Southern California. The cynical accept her as 'a smart operator' who mixed sex, personality, and salesmanship with the old-time religion, 'made a fast buck' and then had the bad luck to get caught in a secret lovenest [*sic*]. The serious students of history and religion dismiss her with a smile as a quaint and typically bizarre sport of the Harding Era.[11]

Sadly, forty years after McLoughlin's article appeared in print, many serious students of history and religion are still dismissing "Sister Aimee" as a smart operator who made a fast buck and got caught in a "secret lovenest [*sic*]."

On the eve of 2007, *The Atlantic* asked ten eminent historians to answer the question: Who are the most influential figures in American history? The responses from the historians generated its cover story for December 2006, "The 100 Most Influential Americans of All Time." Needless to say, Aimee Semple McPherson was among the missing, not surprisingly, as one of the historians, Mark Noll, a professor at the University of Notre Dame, projected that "politics would dominate the final list," and that there would be "little room for religion."[12] However, religious figures such as Martin Luther King, Jr. (8), Joseph Smith (52), Brigham Young (74), Jonathan Edwards (90), and Lyman Beecher (91) all made the list.

And it wasn't the case that few women were represented. "The Top 100" included the following women: Elizabeth Cady Stanton (30), Susan B. Anthony (38), Harriet Beecher Stowe (41), Eleanor Roosevelt (42), Margaret Sanger (51), Jane Adams (64), Betty Friedan (77), Margaret Mead (81), and Mary Baker Eddy (86). But no "Sister Aimee," even though the distinguished historian of the West Ferenc Morton Szasz wrote that "During the mid-1920s, it would have been no exaggeration to say that Sister Aimee was the most famous American woman of her day, a position she held until the appearance of Eleanor Roosevelt....Moreover, unlike many western clerical figures, her fame has persisted....Contemporaries termed her a 'national institution,' and later historians have labeled her an 'American phenomenon.' "[13]

Why, then, the absence of Sister Aimee? Several of the historians stated rather precisely what they were looking for when they comprised their lists of influential Americans. David M. Kennedy, a Pulitzer Prize-winning author and a Stanford professor "looked for...'originals'—that is, people who laid the foundations for enduring institutions or cultural practices or ways of thinking."[14] Doris Kearns Goodwin, another Pulitzer Prize winner, looked for "great public figures who made it possible for people to lead expanded lives—materially, psychologically, culturally, spiritually."[15] Still another Pulitzer Prize-winning author and historian at Brown University, Gordon S. Wood, paid attention to "peculiar personalities...who were ideally suited for the moment."[16] Aimee, again, not only met, but exceeded, such criteria. Why then her absence among this list of influential Americans?

During Aimee's era, as Warren Susman suggests, personality replaced character as the essential ingredient for success in the culture. Character, the earlier virtue, Susman argued, was "either good or bad." With personality, however, one was either "famous or infamous."[17] And Aimee Semple McPherson, with her abundant charm and charisma, her overflowing personality, was both. First, she became famous (1890 through 1926) and later she became infamous (1926 through 1944). Rarely has an American life been so fractured, ripped apart, and torn in two. Aimee Semple McPherson lost her place in history, in the years since her death, because her infamy transcended and overshadowed her earlier rise to fame and prominence. In 2007, a PBS special on "Sister Aimee" carried the following subtitle, "Saint or Sinner?" Even the late John Updike managed to get in on Aimee's recent resurrection by noting in *The New Yorker* that her name is "a rather comical run of syllables" that only "resonates faintly now."[18] Worse yet, the most recent biographical attempt of her life, published by Harvard University Press, paints her as a fundamentalist and as the mother of Jerry Falwell's and Pat Robertson's religious right.[19] This is hardly a rehabilitation of her reputation. More than ever before, Aimee Semple McPherson remains a prisoner of her infamous caricature; a cartoon figure from the past that has been relegated to endless, merciless reruns.

The thesis that Aimee was somehow the founding matriarch of the religious right who resurrected a so-called "Christian America" has three major fault lines running through it. By seeking middle-class Protestant mainline support and approval for Pentecostalism, Aimee did buy into American popular culture—and many times uncritically. If Pentecostalism began as a lower-class protest movement, preaching, in H. Richard Niebuhr's words, "A Christ Against Culture," it was transformed by Aimee's ministry into a much more middle-class, accommodating movement, offering the more acceptable "Christ of Culture" instead. By the start of the Second World War, Pentecostalism, especially in southern California, had morphed into the latest and newest version of American civil religion. Pentecostalism, in this regard, was hardly unique. It had simply joined forces with the larger evangelical mainstream—with America's folk religion.

By relaxing its tension with the surrounding southern California culture, Aimee's brand of Pentecostalism was also able to complete the "sect-church cycle" by the start of the Second World War. Again, this transformation was not unique to Pentecostalism. The movement, as a whole, had simply followed in the religious wake and well-worn path of its Methodist stepparent. Ethnic and racial separation and segregation would continue, education would replace evangelism, bureaucratic, priestly roles would supplant charismatic, prophetic ones, and men eventually would elbow the women preachers out of the newly formed, suburban pulpits dotting the American landscape. Although Aimee at first welcomed the church-like changes in the movement, she spent her final years fighting vehemently against their inevitable drift and direction. Before her death, she had not only rediscovered and recaptured her Pentecostal roots, but she was doing her best to preserve their uniqueness and identity in her own denomination.

Finally, from 1926 through 1944, Aimee's life was very much lived "like a candle in the wind, never knowing who to cling to when the rain set in."[20] Vulnerable, lonely, often depressed, and continually searching for new beginnings, she was susceptible to various schemes and plans that she thought would move her ministry beyond the consequences of her summer of 1926. Founding her own denomination was not enough; she remained convinced that there were still more worlds for her to conquer.

The desire to reclaim her earlier fame led Aimee to form a partnership in 1934 with Guido Orlando. "Guido Orlando," observed the *New York Times* in his obituary, was "a flamboyant press agent, charlatan and bemedaled publicist for dozens of the wish-to-be-famous."[21]

"I have been called the most evil man in the world as well as the world's greatest con man and the greatest public relations wizard," declared Orlando, in an unpublished autobiography. "There is a good deal of truth in all of these. The fact is that one talent feeds the others."[22]

The problem with Guido Orlando, who stood all of five feet, five-and-a-half inches tall in his elevator shoes and who looked like he had just stepped out of the cast of Little Caesar, was that he was precisely the type of man from whom her mother, Minnie Kennedy, had done her best to protect and shield her daughter. Dubbed "the king of contacts" by Franklin Roosevelt, he was the man to whom Aimee turned in the 1930s to resurrect her career and to re-open closed doors. Orlando, who claimed he'd been Valentino's "mouthpiece," made Greta Garbo a legend, and been the one who got the pope to sell ladies' hats, had an abundance of ideas for Aimee. He would make her one of the top vaudeville acts of the day. He booked her at the Capitol Theater on Broadway. He even lit up her name in lights on the theater's marquee. He secretly met with William Randolph Hearst, hoping to make a deal with Marion Davies, whom he wanted to play the lead role in Aimee's life story.

Orlando's most ambitious project for Aimee, however, was his "Save America from Communism" campaign:

> The Save America from Communism project was something I had dreamed up that would keep Aimee before the public. By combining her religious zeal with a hatred for Communism, I decided, she would appeal to many people. She would begin to win acceptance from large numbers of Americans who had never heard her before and ultimately she would win back the huge following she had had before her mysterious disappearance.
>
> I began by taking her to a group of smaller cities along the Eastern Seaboard, then shifted my campaign toward the larger cities like Philadelphia and Washington. In each city, I promoted her appearance by getting her interviews, pictures and the usual things.[23]

Ever hungry for headlines, Orlando even proposed the preposterous idea of a political ticket featuring Huey Long for president and Aimee Semple

McPherson for vice president. "When I broached... [this] idea to Aimee... she was equally enthusiastic. The twin platforms of fighting the Reds and Huey's plan for redistributing the wealth so that it elevated the common man were an unbeatable combination, she said excitedly."[24]

Aimee's Canadian birth prevented such a coalition in the first place, but even if it hadn't, she quickly learned that she would lack significant support. William Randolph Hearst summoned both Orlando and Aimee to his Manhattan office and delivered the grim news that he would support neither their movie proposal nor their "Save America From Communism" campaign.

"If I backed you," Hearst informed Aimee, "every crackpot in America would be after me. I don't regard you as a crackpot, Mrs. McPherson, but you must agree that you are very controversial."[25] In Hearst's eyes, Aimee was damaged goods.

As so many of her other relationships had, Aimee's and Guido's partnership broke apart and dissolved. Prior to his death, Orlando gave me his memoirs and unpublished manuscripts. His concluding paragraphs in the chapter on Aimee are most instructive, especially concerning the notion of Aimee as the foundress of the religious right:

> Her obituaries predictably stressed the more lurid and notorious aspects of her career. They made her sound like some Mata Hari of the church. Nothing could be further from the truth. She was a simple country girl who had powerful longings to be loved and an equally powerful desire to preach and help the poor and lonely. She was not a bigot, she did not pry into peoples' private lives, she did not conduct any right wing crusades as did so many of the clergy who disliked her. She was in all the time I knew her incapable of malice toward anyone.
>
> When I think of her now, I like to think of the day I put her in the ring with the broken down pug who portrayed the devil. I smile as I think of Aimee chasing him around the ring and then, having demolished him for good, turning to the rapt audience and yelling triumphantly, "ALL RIGHT, EVERBODY, GET OUT THOSE BILLS!"[26]

"If Aimee Semple McPherson is ever to receive her due," wrote William McLoughlin, in 1967, "it will be necessary to evaluate more carefully the three distinct claims to historical fame and respect which her defenders have tried (so far in vain) to make for her":

> In the first place...she ought to rank with Mary Baker Eddy and Joseph Smith as the founder of a uniquely American denomination which...

has become firmly established not only in the United States but around the world as a flourishing religious home for thousands of sincere, generous, hard-working Christians….the International Church of the Foursquare Gospel has outlasted the captious questions about its founder and has grown steadily in size, wealth, and respectability…Her second claim to fame lies in the astounding personal accomplishments of her own lifetime. It is too often forgotten that Mrs. McPherson, who was raised on a small farm near Ingersoll, Ontario, who never graduated from high school, and whose missionary husband died a month before her first child was born in Hong Kong in 1910, managed almost single handedly [sic] to establish and direct a million-dollar religious enterprise (complete with Temple, radio station, Bible College, publishing house, branch churches, and overseas missionary settlement) before she was forty years old.. . . . And third, however she may have mispublicized [*sic*] herself…(she had) the courage and the humility to laugh not only at the foibles of the world but at her own shortcomings. She was, in short, a real and honest woman, not a fraud, a clown, a hypocrite, or a mercenary charlatan.[27]

Finally, McLoughlin rightly suggested that "No one can begin to understand Aimee until he understands the first…years of her life."[28] And that is precisely what this book is all about: the famous Aimee Semple McPherson, not the abbreviated, infamous Aimee—the one who briefly emerged for the final third of her life.

In October 2006, the Pew Forum on Religious and Public Life (with generous support from the John Templeton Foundation) released their path-breaking, ten-country, cross-national survey of Pentecostals: *Spirit and Power*. The report's preface gave the following reasons for such a survey:

Religion…is reshaping the world's social and political landscape. Despite predictions of religion's demise…we have been witnessing the growing power of religion…Talk of 'secularization' and of a 'post-religious' society has given way to a renewed recognition of religion's influence in people's social and political lives. This re-emergence of 'public religion' is happening throughout the world and across religious traditions— from Islam and Hinduism to Buddhism and Judaism. Christianity, the world's largest religion, is no exception.

Within Christianity, Pentecostal and related renewalist or Spirit-filled movements are by all accounts among the fastest growing. Only a century after the movement's birth, the major strands of Pentecostalism now represent at least one quarter of all Christians, ranking second only to Catholicism in the number of followers. In direct and indirect ways, Pentecostal beliefs and practices are remaking the face of world

Christianity. In Latin America, for example, Pentecostals now account for approximately three-in-four Protestants.[29]

In the survey's summary, the authors especially note the fact that, "Despite the rapid growth of the renewalist movement…relatively little is known about the religious, political and civic views of individuals involved in these groups."[30]

No one was more important in the formation and rise of modern Pentecostalism than Aimee Semple McPherson. As a young woman in her thirties, she took the movement out of its back-alley storefronts and upper-room missions and gave it a solid, middle-class appeal when she placed it on a mighty boulevard in Los Angeles, just south of Sunset Boulevard and next to Hollywood itself. She was a preacher and teacher; actress and author; administrator and healer, but more importantly, she was a molder and a mother to the movement in its infancy. By ingeniously uniting as one both the sacred and secular, she became the movement's most glamorous symbol of success and its most visible spokesperson. An innovative and charismatic leader, she charted the course and blazed the trail for the movement's future.

To learn more about this most significant movement of the past century, as well as about women in revivalism, divine healing, religion in the West (California and Los Angeles), it was necessary at times to trade in a telescope for a microscope. Along the way this book borders on micro-history in its tedious attempt to recover the forgotten people of Pentecostalism— back when the movement was still considered something of an "orphan daughter of religion," and long before it morphed into "a mighty man," second only to Catholicism in its market share of Christianity.[31]

In 1996, Duke University historian Grant Wacker made a very perceptive point about the study of Pentecostalism: "No one, to my knowledge, has tracked the mainline Protestant culture's perception of Pentecostals before World War II, or the way that secular journalists and academics viewed them—on those rare occasions when they did."[32] This, too, is a major theme that runs through this book. It may come as somewhat of a surprise and a shock to my readers as to how accepting and open the mainline Protestant churches and the secular culture were, especially to Aimee's unique brand of Pentecostalism, prior to her disappearance in 1926.

I grew up with the same religion and in the same region where "Sister Aimee" preached for two decades. My own Pentecostal and Southern California roots help to explain why I have attempted, and at times felt compelled to tell her story. Aimee's story, in a way, is my story, our common "myth" long gone but now preserved by memory. And despite a Princeton professor's remark that I "hailed from the land of fruits and nuts," I believe more than ever that those memories are worth preserving. As Peter Berger reminds us, "Society, in its essence, is a memory. [And] through most of human history, this memory has been a religious one."[33]

Similarly, Robert Bellah contends that a religious community, more than anything else, is a "'community of memory,' one that does not forget its past." And also, "In order not to forget that past, a community is involved in retelling its story…and in so doing, it offers examples of the men and women who have embodied and exemplified the meaning of the community."[34]

It is my belief that no one embodied and exemplified the meaning of classical Pentecostalism better than Aimee Semple McPherson. This then is her story and the story of the movement she shaped and symbolized. And, to the best of my ability, I have made every effort to tell "our" story as truly and honestly as possible. Timothy L. Smith, in his careful and competent history of the Nazarenes, offers some sound advice when writing about one's own religious history: "Those who write the story of their own family, church, or nation must chasten both mind and emotion at every turn in the road, lest their history become mere propaganda—a tale spun out to influence the present by distorting the past."[35]

"A successful biographer," wrote Allison Silver, "somehow transcends his own being in order to comprehend the life of his subject and illuminate it as from within."[36] No early Pentecostal leader was more colorful, controversial, or more formative to the movement than was Aimee Semple McPherson. To attempt to recreate this complex and driven woman's life, after more than a half century of her absence, is only made possible by attempting to enter into her own inner self-understanding and by attentively hearing her "voices" and seeing her "visions."

In David Martin's words, we become "interested in how believers structure their worlds in their own words."[37]

"We historians have not done enough to let our subjects speak in their own voices," observed Richard W. Fox, when writing about the Beecher-Tilton scandal. Fox proposes a historiography of attentive "listening…to hear what the tellers are saying about their selves, their relationships, their culture."[38]

To really hear what the tellers are saying, I frequently use quotations. It is a method about which I am unrepentant, believing, as Walter Hollenweger does, that selective quotations are "more important than my interpretation"[39]

"In the long run," wrote Henry F. May, "I believe, the historian is most like an artist, and history is irreducibly a kind of literature. However careful and ingenious and innovative his accumulation of facts, the historian must finally strive to present them in a way that engages the reader's emotional and aesthetic response as well as his intellectual assent."[40]

When writing a religious biography, one could not improve upon the advice John Bunyan gave the reader in *The Pilgrim's Progress*: "O then come hither, and lay my book, thy head and heart together."[41]

Chas. H. Barfoot
Arizona State University
Tempe, Arizona

ACKNOWLEDGMENTS

Now that my ladder is gone,
I must lie down where all ladders start,
in the foul rag-and-bone shop of the heart.

                              —William Butler Yeats
                         "The Circus Animals' Desertion"

As an empty-nester Baby Boomer, I recently discovered that strange things can still occur in your remaining years, especially after your parents are no longer with you physically. Rather unexpectedly, I became soul-naked again in my fifties. While most of my generation began turning their thoughts toward retirement, I began thinking instead of restarting an unfinished, encore career. By far the hardest part of the passage was letting go of all the carefully created ladders and scaffolding I had erected, over the decades, to reach the various passes and summits of my dreams. Where would I be, I wondered, without all those strategically-placed props that somehow, in the process of preventing my falling, had come to symbolize, even to define my existence? I left the safety net of the ministry, which was something I could never do either as a young father or to my father in his old age. My wife and I together let go of the big house on the hill that overlooked the golf course and faced the mountains that the Conquistadors thought looked like cathedrals, let go of the yacht in San Diego harbor, and let go of many miscellaneous toys my church had begrudged my having in the first place. Although my ordination vows had never included poverty, it was still very much expected of a mainline minister. "At least don't live any better than your average parishioner," ran their reasoning. Pentecostals, of course, have had no such problems with their preachers! Their ministers are the community's symbol of success. We kept the ten-year-old Tahoe, and my wife surprised me with a "one for the road" farewell gift of a one-hundreth anniversary Harley-Davidson Road King Classic, a symbol of a new life on two wheels. But this was no easy exit off the fast freeway of life, no smooth transition into semi-retirement. Not every passage, I learned, is a rite of passage. Life can be squeezed dry, hand wrung out of ritual itself. Worse, we had no mile-markers indicating the distance to our next destination. Fortunately, we found a new life a hundred miles up the highway from Tucson, in Tempe, Arizona.

In the spring of 1978, after moving from Harvard to Berkeley, I signed a book contract with HarperSanFrancisco for a religious biography of Aimee Semple McPherson. Needless to say, those were heady salad days that stretched into long nights for a twenty-something, ex-Pentecostal preacher boy. Recently, Al Silverman has argued that this was "The Golden Age of Great American Book Publishers"—those two decades before "the great 'bookmen' stepped aside and the bottom-liners of business took over."[1] I needed no such convincing at the time, and neither did my editor. Every night was a cause for celebration, with me playing Scott to his Max. When it came to books in religion, HarperSanFrancisco was the only game in town. Mercifully, when my modest advance ran out, my editor moved me in-house, with an office and all its perks and parties. For close to two years, I lived and breathed the rarified air of printer's ink. It was as valuable an education as any Ph.D. program. I was struck then, as I am now, by how terribly old-fashioned—despite all the latest technology—bookmaking remains. The best in the business, the Porsches of publishing, are still the stellar, small boutique houses slowly turning out their individualized, high-end, hand-made products. Even book sales are generated from old-fashioned word of mouth.

On November 1, 1983, a cold, grey, rainy, Berkeley morning, my daughter Sarah Jeanne was born. Her arrival at Alta Bates Hospital was a day of reckoning for her father. For the last twenty-six years, I have dated my life from her arrival on that cold bleak morning. Since the job market in the academic world of the 1980s seemed strangely suited only for the so-called "gypsy scholars," my thoughts turned toward ordination and ministry; something I had put on the back burner for years. Compared to the alternatives the ministry appeared attractive, even giving off the illusion of a stable profession.

For the next twenty years I preached, pastored, and put up with petty church politics: "My circus animals were all on show,/ those stilted boys,/ that burnished chariot,/ lion and woman and the Lord knows what."[2] I started several churches from scratch, and there were moments in that career trajectory when it seemed that endless rungs were attainable on the ministerial ladder of success. I was unwilling, however, in my father's words, "to pay the price." The voice of experience informs me today that the professorship—not the pastorate—is the one true privileged profession. I believe it was naïve on my part to think I could write a biography of a major ministerial figure without having served some hard time there myself. Simply having been the son of preachers was a poor substitute for the real thing. My years in the church not only helped raise a family, but deepened my understanding and appreciation for what Aimee endured, especially in the final fractured third of her life and ministry.

While my writing continued as labor-intensive, weekly, manuscript sermons, (something Pentecostals didn't require), Aimee sat, neglected, in a box on my study floor, never making it to a library or bookstore shelf. Adding insult to injury, the venerable house of Harper itself was sold in 1987 to a bottom-liner. Even my bookmen—both my editor and publisher that I had worked so long and closely with and who had made the wise decision to allot two volumes to Aimee's life—eventually left the house. Since I had been the first researcher allowed into church archives, it was not a pleasant time for me, in the 1990s, when I first began noticing other Aimee biographies appearing in print. Like an ex-junkie swearing off a bad addiction, I would wistfully look at their jacket covers, daring myself to sneak a peak. With a sudden rush of adrenalin, I would pop open their spines, scan a paragraph or two, and then slam them shut, saying to myself, "I still have my story, it hasn't yet been told!" In the end, all we really have are our stories. Hopefully, they get a chance to be heard, if not preserved, before we pass. Our stories not only save us, as James Carroll suggests, but they remain as our final footprint on the planet, long after we are gone.

In 2004, I sat down, like a child at Christmas, with my "Aimee box"—sat back down on the floor where all ladders start. It was as if that box was my one prized possession left in life. As my muse and mistress, Aimee had been quietly whispering to me for years. She was now loudly clamoring to be heard, to end her twenty-year exile and captivity, to finally climb out of her cardboard container. Thankfully, I was able to start sifting through the first half of her life, again, in the Department of Religious Studies at Arizona State University. My transition from theology to religious studies was long-overdue and should have been made in a post-Harvard move to Santa Barbara, instead of to the seminaries perched atop "Holy Hill" in Berkeley. The study of religion today, in a post-9/11 world, can no longer be divorced from or separated from the university as if it were an unwanted stepchild. Not only does the discipline need its own, recognized department, it must also be free from any entanglement or association with any religious body or organization.

One hundred and twenty years ago, Daniel Dorchester, one of America's first religious historians, published his major tome, *Christianity in the United States*. In his preface, Dorchester observed the following about his long endeavor:

> For over a dozen years the subject was studied for the author's personal satisfaction…The mental exercise…and the difficulties encountered in

the task need not be here related. The work, sometimes intermitted for months and twice for several years, amid other heavy duties, though never out of thought, has constantly broadened and matured.[3]

Like Dorchester's history, my subject, too has never been far from thought or out of mind. But what I am most grateful for is that, in the past four years at Arizona State University my understanding of Aimee and Pentecostalism has also broadened and matured.

Despite the solitary confinement of the act of writing, there have always thankfully been for me those "other voices" in the "other rooms of my life." The following friends, colleagues, and mentors have helped, sustained, and guided me more than they know during this strange, thirty-year saga. Unfortunately some of them, like my parents, are no longer physically with me to celebrate and share in Aimee's resurrection. My deep appreciation for their conversation and influence extends to the following: Roy M. Carlisle, Clayton Carlson, Eugene Clay, Chas S. Clifton, Harvey Cox, Raymond L. Cox, Robert C. Cunningham, Don Dayton, Charles Emerson, Barbara Hargrove, Jack Hayford, Dean R. Hoge, Walter J. Hollenweger, Kathleen McGrory, William G. McLoughlin, Rolf K. McPherson, Moses Moore, Marie Augusta Neal, Byron Nease, Jacob Neddleman, Douglas J. Nelson, Guido Orlando, Mary Paci, Richard Quebedeaux, Dotson Rader, Dan Ramirez, Herb Richardson, John Rose, Roberta Star Semple Salter, Jerry Sheppard, Janet Simonsen, Russ Spittler, Henry Stevens, Leta Mae Steward, Ferenc Szasz, Bob Trennert, Wayne Warner, Jim Washington, Mark Woodward, and Thomas F. Zimmerman.

Thankfully, most of us who write also teach. I feel fortunate to teach across traditional disciplines, spending my time in religious studies, humanities and the arts, and social and behavioral sciences. My trinity of chairs at Arizona State University—Joel Gereboff, Duane Roen, and Nick Alozi—have not only been equally supportive of my teaching, travel, and research, but they also have been more friends than bosses. Ultimately, of course, my students are my final jurors. They are the ones who find and fill my classes, and they are the ones who selected me for a distinguished teaching award in the past year. I am indebted to their enthusiastic responses to my attempts to tell old stories in new and different ways: "What can I but enumerate old themes?"[4]

Finally, of course, my deepest thanks and appreciation belong to Janet Joyce and Equinox, the best in the business, for saving Aimee from her fate on the floor of that rag and bone shop of [my] heart.

Nothing happens, no loss, it's still a strange pageant…
Yet the books will be there on the shelves, well born.
Derived from people, but also from radiance, heights.[5]

—CHB

CHAPTER ONE

An Answered Prayer: Aimee Elizabeth

For this child I prayed; and the Lord has granted me the petition that I made to him.

I Samuel 1:27

Aimee Elizabeth Kennedy was born on a Canadian farm in the fall of 1890. In Los Angeles, California, half a century and four years later to the day, the world she so loved bade her an extravagant good-bye. Modern America paid its final respects to its most spectacular woman evangelist ever, the new religious movement of Pentecostalism to its most illustrious prophesying daughter, the Foursquare denomination to its foundress, and everyone else, in Aimee's own autographic phrase, to their "Sister in the King's Glad Service." Despite a rather short physical timespan, Aimee had a rich and remarkable spiritual life: baptizing forty thousand converts, establishing four hundred branch churches, and creating 178 mission outposts around the world. And more importantly, her work did not end with her passing. It not only endured, it thrives today, with more than eight million members and sixty thousand churches.

No glamour queen's funeral of Hollywood's golden years rivaled the emotional farewells on that sad day in October 1944. Sister Aimee's service was no mere funeral, no fond farewell; rather, it was a glamorous recessional for the end of an era. An era—an age—that is best described as the great "in-between" years. America itself was "in-between." In between a foreign policy that dictated strict isolation, and one that not only sought to police the world, making it "safe for democracy," but also one that, by splitting the force of nature upon two cities in Japan, shattered and remade the world in its own image. America was in between the two wars it chose to identify by numbers: in between Versailles and Pearl Harbor. Americans themselves were in between the excesses of the Jazz Age's prosperity, and the Depression with its poverty—the time of "Brother, can you spare a dime?" American Protestantism was in between the two polarities it termed *modernism* and *fundamentalism*. The American landscape itself was in between, where home life became suburban on new plots of ground, lying somewhere in between the thriving cities and the fading farms. And Aimee Semple McPherson became a symbol of this age, precisely because she herself was "in between." Commanding the glamorous center of American revivalism, Aimee was in between the two Billys—Billy Sunday and Billy Graham— the two dominant male professional evangelists of the twentieth century.

"We seem to have fluctuated between headaches," Isabel Leighton wrote. "During these throbbing years we searched in vain for a cure-all, coming no closer to it than the aspirin bottle. Hence: The Aspirin Age."[1]

The era's prophet, F. Scott Fitzgerald, protested, claiming, "It was an age of miracles, it was an age of art, it was an age of excess."[2]

As are the rest of us, Aimee Semple McPherson was a prisoner of the period in which she lived and toiled. Unlike the vast majority of us, however, her work transcended time and is actually thriving today. To be mother of a modern religious movement and the foundress of a successful American denomination is an accomplishment few individuals have achieved in American history. Her story begins more than a century ago, in the Canadian countryside when the world appeared more whole, more unified. But a new era, a fragmented age, was lurking around the corner, waiting to make its appearance and transform a Canadian farm girl into an American household word. "Sister Aimee," as she would fondly be called, did not just become the symbol of popular American religion during those often fluctuating and chaotic years. She also would be looked upon as a cure-all, a healer, a mother, a molder and shaper, and even more importantly, as a shepherdess of the most dynamic movement of Christian faith in the twentieth century.

The only child of James and Mildred (Minnie) Kennedy, Aimee Elizabeth was born, with the assistance of a midwife, in an upstairs bedroom of the family farmhouse on October 9, 1890, in the township of Dereham, Ontario. Her arrival was perceived more as an "answered prayer" than the routine birth of a child. Destiny for the family, especially for Aimee's mother, seemed ever-present from the beginning. Minnie, a young, childless woman, prayed the prayer of Hannah of Old Testament times to conceive a child "as unto the Lord." Unlike most mothers who prayed that their offspring "for the Lord" would be male, Minnie Kennedy prayed that she would have a daughter—a daughter who could be what she herself might have been, had she been given a real choice in life. Aimee represented hope in her mother's life—vicarious hope, and hope from a distance—but nevertheless hope all the same. Hope that would begin to build in such proportions for Minnie that she soon became convinced that this daughter of hers, "born as unto the Lord," would someday resemble her very own role model, Evangeline Booth, daughter of Salvation Army founder William Booth. Apart from Aimee Elizabeth, the Salvation Army was Minnie Kennedy's one true love. She retreated as often as possible to this fledgling religious movement, escaping her (perceived) "prison life" on the farm.

William Booth had often declared that in his "Army," his "best men were women" and the best of these women was his own daughter, "Commander Eva," as she was called. At age thirty-one Eva was appointed leader of the rapidly advancing Salvation Army in Canada. Little did Minnie Kennedy realize at the time that this small infant of

Minnie Kennedy, mother of Aimee Semple McPherson (used by permission of the International Church of the Foursquare Gospel, Heritage Department).

hers—her answered prayer and source of hope—would in full maturity bear an uncanny resemblance to the Canadian commander's high, dramatic style. Eva rode on horseback daily to her headquarters in Toronto, with a red cape flying from her shoulders and a red hat perched on her head. She "loved vivid colours and martial music, she was enthralled by pageantry and giant procession." [3]

Minnie's husband, James Morgan Kennedy, was fifty-six when Aimee Elizabeth was born. He lived well into the 1920s and died at age ninety-three, at the end of the decade of his daughter's most spectacular success. At the height of her fame, Aimee was to refer to her father, fondly, as a "wonderfully interesting character." Although the inimitable "Ma," "Minnie," "Mother"' Kennedy would later share countless headlines and news stories with her daughter, James would remain a shadowy background figure, a question mark of a person for the curious, but his effect on his daughter was critical. His contemporaries described him as a "handsome, powerful man with a flaming red beard; a hero to boys and the envy of his juniors." [4]

3

Minnie Pearce was James' second wife, and Aimee was the child of his late middle age and thus was always something special to him. With his first family already grown and married, he gave to Aimee Elizabeth a special kind of fatherly warmth and tenderness usually reserved for a grandchild. Young Aimee would neither have to compete with siblings nor with her father's ambitions for his attention. James was always available for Aimee and joyfully so. He would sometimes break the monotony of long days by leaving his plow in mid-furrow to search for his "Beth"—sometimes "Babs"—always "Betty" in times of stress, and show her a fallen robin's nest or a buttercup in spring. He showed her the unfolding of the seasons as could only be known by one who toiled daily with nature. While Minnie sought to shield her daughter—her vicarious "hope"—James sought to expand and enlarge his daughter's life. He exposed Aimee early on to vigorous outdoor activities such as horseback riding and ice-skating, while resisting Minnie's desire for real or imaginary protections. Almost every night, after the farm chores had been completed, James would still have time for Beth and would, more often than not, turn up the kerosene lamps and entertain his special daughter with a "hand-shadow show of rabbits, birds, and elephants that danced across the kitchen wall to her delight."[5]

By temperament, James was an earthy man. Aimee as an adult would be torn always between the earthiness of her father and the enlarged piety and shrewdness of her mother. By middle age, Aimee would become more like James and less like Minnie. Although she normally thought of her father as conservative, she also described a different temperament upon relating a scene when he became provoked:

> He would burst forth! "By the lightning set free! By the great horn-spoon!" And then wax more and more eloquent. Just when he reached the "Blast his eyes" stage, the door of the back porch would open and the feminine constituency of our household would storm: "James Morgan Kennedy" (he was Jim at all other times) "have you lost your mind?" "No!" "Then hush up, hush!" "All right, all right," he steamed, cooling off like water embers. [6]

The earthy James, the post-middle-aged and hyper-indulgent father, liberated the dramatic imagination of his beloved Beth. With her mother, Aimee was oriented towards goals to be attained, hopes to be nurtured. But with her father, she could give herself to things larger than life: the freedom of fantasy, the joy of pretending, and the world of make-believe. In her father's world, all things were possible—dancing rabbits, birds, and elephants appearing across a kitchen wall were proof of that. Tending to one hundred acres of rolling farm land, five miles outside the market town of Ingersoll, Ontario, James Morgan Kennedy was known as a skillful farmer. But his interests extended beyond local farming concerns. He subscribed to the *Montreal Star* and discussed world events with fellow farmers in his kitchen. He was also known as a good carpenter and a master bridge builder. At some point in his life, he acquired a reputation for being the only man who could bridge a bottomless swamp. Legend had it that, while other men tried in vain to bridge a boggy stretch of land between Salford and Ingersoll, only James had succeeded, inventing a pontoon bridge that floated planks on the water. His daughter was also to become a bridge builder, and she would always display her father's practical originality, especially when it came to meeting human need.[7]

James was a descendent of a Kennedy clan from the Scottish Isles, and becoming a minister was a trait that ran in the family. His father and grandfather were said to have been Methodist preachers. Though it was Minnie who indoctrinated Aimee with Bible verses and stories, James was also devout in his faith. While Aimee was growing up, he served his local Methodist congregation both as church organist and choirmaster. Religious faith came easily and naturally to him, like the unfolding of seasons, and was not something to be labored at or forced upon another. Significantly, it was James, not Minnie, who took Aimee to the mission where she received the conversion experience that altered the course of her life. And it was James who showed his "Beth" the beauty of musical expression of the faith on the small pump organ in the family parlor, and had her playing hymns as soon as her feet could reach the pedals. Little is known about James' former family or about the eventual failure in later years of this, his second marriage. We know that to him Beth was special, and to her he was endlessly interesting—a person larger than life.

Aimee's relationship with her mother was the opposite of the one that she had with her father. It was not free and easy; rather, it was based upon essential survival needs they had of one another. When Aimee authored her first book at age twenty-nine the first chapter one was entitled "My Mother." Their relationship—always intense—was perceived by both women as being more spiritual than physical. On the very first page of her spiritual autobiography, Aimee attempted to define that relationship:

It is because the words, 'Before I formed thee, I knew thee, and before thou camest forth I sanctified thee,' are so true in my life, that I must

5

begin my testimony, by taking you back some twenty years before I was born. Our lives are like a great loom, weaving many threads together, and the first threads of my life are inseparably woven about my dear Mother. It is with her, therefore, that the story of my life really begins. [8]

Mildred Pearce's ancestry was English, and, as did her husband's it also included ministers. Her maternal great-grandmother moved from England to Canada, where Minnie was born. An uncle was the compiler of the Clark School Books. Her church background, like that of James, was Methodist. But the early life of Minnie Pearce remains largely a mystery.

Two events occurred when Minnie was twelve that changed her life forever. One day she heard of a strange "Army" that was coming to town to take "prisoners for the King." Persuading her mother to go with her, Minnie discovered the Salvation Army. Both she and her mother readily embraced the new religious movement—Mrs. Pearce because it happily reminded her of the joy and spontaneity of early Methodism.

But shortly after this event, Minnie Pearce became an orphan. Aware of her impending death, her mother made arrangements with a Salvation Army captain and his wife, who had served as what she called her "spiritual parents," to take care of her young daughter after her death. For at least two years, Mildred Pearce's home was in the Salvation Army quarters in a distant town. The religious impact of those years, accompanied by utter loneliness, would never be erased, either for Minnie or her offspring. Illness eventually prevented Minnie from remaining in Salvation Army quarters and forced a change of environment.

Answering a newspaper ad for a live-in nurse, Minnie Pearce, age fourteen, met her future husband, James Morgan Kennedy. At that time he was married to a woman who was an invalid. When James' wife died a few months later, Minnie stayed on in his employ as a housekeeper. James and Minnie were married not long after this. At the time of their marriage, Minnie was a girl of fifteen, and James was a fifty-two-year-old man. The union of the aging farmer and the young housekeeper created no small stir within the village community, but it was soon recognized that the new Mrs. Kennedy was very much her own person: a girl who had been early-matured by hardship and who possessed a strong and determined temperament.

Being both bold and fearless in personality, Minnie made no attempt to hide a growing disdain for the routine of life on a farm. To escape her mental boredom and to satisfy her restless spirit, she rejoined her former spiritual comrades in the Salvation Army, and soon became a junior sergeant major in its ranks, and the superintendent of the Sunday school. She was also placed in charge of fund drives, work for which she proved to have an abundance of talent. Later in life Aimee would interpret her mother's marriage to James in a spiritual manner:

> Then it was, while weak in body, depressed in spirit, and mourning over the loss of a mother's sympathetic hand, that she married, hoping to be able to continue her work for God. But amidst the strenuous and unaccustomed duties of heavy farm work, she was compelled to acknowledge that she was caught in the devil's net, helpless as far as active service was concerned, and must largely devote herself to the manifold cares of life and home…My mother's pathway, in those days was hedged about with difficulties. Shorn of her usefulness, fettered by circumstances, she truly did grind in the prison house.[9]

The ray of hope that finally penetrated Minnie Kennedy's "prison house" came while she pondered the scriptures one day, struggling for clues to the meaning of her life. In her less-than-systematic study of scripture, she discovered the story of Hannah. From the Old Testament narrative, Minnie read that the central character, Elkanah, was married to two women: Hannah and Peninnah. The bitter irony was that despite Elkanah's stronger love and affection for Hannah, she remained barren, while Peninnah, the less-loved, bore him children. Out of desperation, so the story went, Hannah promised God that if she received grace to bear a "man-child," he would be "lent unto the Lord as long as he lived." Hannah then approached Eli, the priest, with her dilemma and novel proposal; however, she was quickly dismissed as drunk since she was "praying silently; only her lips moved, but her voice was not heard." To convince Eli that she was sober, Hannah argued that her strange condition had resulted not from "wine or strong drink" but from "a sorrowful spirit." Hannah then left Eli the priest with a promise to go in peace, for the God of Israel, he said, had heard her petition.[10]

In her child-like simplicity of faith, when she was perhaps only eighteen years of age, Minnie prayed the petition of Hannah, with the exception that for her the promised child should be a daughter, one who could fulfill what she had felt to be her own life's calling, purpose, and mission. The answer to this prayer, Aimee Elizabeth, never learned of her mother's prayerful petitions until adolescence, when she was plagued with religious doubts. Every maternal move, however, taught young Aimee Elizabeth that her life was meant to be different from all others. Intuitively, she sensed that she was being groomed for a mission divined by her mother's spiritual vision.

"Creativity is born in the family's cradle," argues Margaret Morgan Lawrence, "and it is born in the inner world of parents before the child is born.

Parental expectations, Lawrence concludes, can also lead to either creativity or psychopathology. [11]

Three weeks after Aimee's birth, Minnie's plans for her daughter were put in motion by attending a Salvation Army Jubilee. Three weeks after that, Mrs. Kennedy formalized her spiritual/maternal vision for her daughter before the same Christian community. There had been considerable disagreement within the Kennedy family as to when and where this solemnization should occur. Both James and Aimee's namesake aunt, Elizabeth, cautioned Minnie to remain patient and wait until Aimee was

Aimee Semple McPherson as an infant, 1890 (used by permission of the International Church of the Foursquare Gospel, Heritage Department)).

older, rather than risk pneumonia from the chill of a Canadian fall. They also attempted politely to persuade Minnie that a Methodist Church was more appropriate for the occasion than the bleak barracks of the Salvation Army. They expressed serious reservations about the child being exposed to this radical, new-fangled sect. A child, they reasoned, should obtain Christian nurture in surroundings more dignified than one that sported drums, flags, tambourines, and pageantry. James especially, perhaps because of his descent from Methodist ministers, disapproved of the Army's militant earnestness, its appeal to the riff-raff, and its extreme unpopularity—the latter evidenced by members being greeted with buckets of blood whenever they passed beneath the slaughterhouse windows while attempting to hold street services.

Minnie's persistence won out, foreshadowing times to come. At one and one-half months of age, bundled in cashmere, Aimee Elizabeth Kennedy lay cradled on the first crude bench of a Salvationist's barracks, five horse-drawn miles from home, awaiting her dedication. The solemnization was accompanied by the crackling of logs from a red baseburner and the enthusiasm kindled by a Salvationist band, replete with tambourines. Given her parent's differing religious preferences, it was literally true, as Aimee mused years later, that she had grown up with one foot in the Methodist church and the other in the barracks of the Salvation Army. Both traditions would surface in eclectic and creative ways in her later ministry.

Aimee Kennedy's childhood resembled that of other farm children, except for being an over-protected only child. She had an insatiable curiosity about how everything worked. Later, in her Angelus Temple, Aimee would recall with fondness those childhood years on the farm, and the stories struck a responsive chord with many a former Midwestern farmer. A favorite memory of life on the farm, and one that was guaranteed to bring the house down with laughter, described the time she dyed her father's snow-white hair and beard bright blue while attempting to wash them for him in the kitchen sink, (while Minnie, of course, was gone). Since James was soon to be on his way to a meeting with the town mayor, he had little time to rid himself of his new hair color. Due to his beloved Beth's assistance, James was known as "Bluebeard" for some time to come.

Aimee's insatiable curiosity about how things worked often prompted her to climb to the top of anything that aroused her attention. As an example of this, she once related,

> I don't think there was a tree in our part of the country that I didn't go to the top of when I was a girl. I used to go to the top of the barn and walk the ridge pole. When father was shingling…I would put a rope around my waist and sit on top of the barn, thinking I was holding him, while he was on the sides of the roof shingling. I would go to the top of the windmills. One time my mother came out in horror; saw me at the very top of a high windmill. She didn't dare scold me until I got down.[12]

Aimee's bold behavior carried over into her later ministry. A contemporary of Aimee's characterized her ministry by its daring quality. "She was daring in everything she undertook and had a fearlessness in her ministry which has rarely been equaled."[13]

Aimee had little use for conventional childhood toys and playthings: "I didn't care for dolls. I would rather have a live mouse than a make-believe doll. I liked real things: the lambs, cattle, horses [she had her own horse, Flossie], cows, even the tamed black pigeon I had [Jenny], were always friends to me."[14]

Her biggest challenge with "real things" came, one day, in the form of her father's new stud colt. Aimee set out to break him for riding, although everyone had clearly and repeatedly been warned to leave the young stallion alone. The result was a broken ankle, a half-broken-in colt, and Minnie and James both rushing to Aimee's side. "Mother arrived first," remembered Aimee, "though she was three times as far away as father."[15] Even as a grown, mature woman, Aimee counted on her mother to be her rescuer. This well-worn pattern of behavior, established in childhood, would continue well into the 1920s. In time, Minnie would become not only a stage mother but also prove to be her daughter's best business manager. When Minnie's rescuing finally ceased, it had devastating consequences for Aimee's ministry.

Aimee enjoyed and thrived on the rigorous out-of-doors environment of farm life as much as her mother detested it. In time she became a swift skater, a strong swimmer, played hockey as the boys did, and found her freedom on a bicycle—that wonderful new invention created five years before her birth. She took pride in being able to turn a somersault forty-two times without stopping. It was this energetic childhood in the Canadian countryside that provided the physical strength she would later use to set up and pull down her tents when she was a wandering American revivalist.

Aimee's personality and temperament as a child was affectionate but determined, programmed for inevitable conflict. She was by nature a caregiver—a role where it is extremely difficult to feel successful. Not only does the caregiver live for those she is attached to, but maintaining her self-esteem is dependent on the object of her attachment's continuing need for her. Aimee's caregiver tendencies showed up early in her life. "I was always a great little nurse. Anybody sick within a mile, I would go and nurse them. I seemed to have a natural tendency to be around sick folks and help them."[16]

Young Aimee's caregiving extended beyond the real world, into the land of pretend and make-believe. She spent many of her play hours in the maple sugar bush, in "the woods," to be among trees, mulberry bushes, elderberries, and bulrushes. Whenever she entered the "woods," they seemed to become for her an enchanted forest where magically trees and plants for hours became her playmates and charges. As the goddess of her green-garden, make-believe world, she experienced both a sense of omnipotence and "a soft spot in my heart for the underprivileged and the maimed."[17]

Playing amid the ladies' slippers, jonquils, violets, and wild roses, she discovered,

They all seemed vested with a human voice. Now and then… I would spy one that seemed more faded than his fellows. Plucking it out, no sooner had I cast it on the ground than the whole woods would seem to break out into derisive laughter: "A-ha…a-ha! You have been rejected! You are too sick…too old…too faded…she has cast you aside to die… A-ha! A-ha!" Stopping dead in my tracks, I would return, search out the cowering and shamed little sister, pick her up, kiss her expiring lips and place her in the very center of my bouquet and soothe: "There! There! You're the sweetest of the lot!" A chagrined sigh would come from the forest; and triumphantly we would proceed on our homeward way. "A-ha! You've failed." "No! No! She loves me'"—the drooping blossom would cry joyously. "See…I am honored above all, and receive the greatest consideration."[18]

Like that other simple farm girl, Joan of Arc, Aimee heard voices—even voices in nature seeming to seek pity and care. Those voices would never leave or forsake her. They were with her as a child, when she created for her schoolmates a make-believe Salvation Army. And they were with her as an adult, when she was healing the sick and helping to shape a new religious movement. The role model she inherited from her mother was Commander Eva in her flamboyant cape, on horseback with a military air. The model she adopted for herself, however, was that of Grace Herseley Darling—a heroine and caregiver—who had saved lives as well as souls.

Grace was the daughter of William Darling, keeper of the Longstone Lighthouse in the Farne Islands. On the morning of September 7, 1883, the luxury steamship *Forfarshire* ran aground on rocks in view of the lighthouse. Thinking that there might be survivors in the wreckage, Grace and her father managed to row a coble, their open fishing boat, through treacherous seas to the stricken ship. With daring, strength, and skill, Grace and her father saved the survivors. For her act of courage, Grace received nationwide fame and, along with her father, received a gold medal from the Humane Society. Subscriptions of money were collected for the two of them. Despite her instant fame and celebrity, Grace chose to live the rest of her brief life alone, as the keeper of the lighthouse. It was more than a coincidence that, when America's mainline churches were in wreckage, Aimee created churches that she called "lighthouses."

Like many only children, Aimee was able to wield influence over her peers. Due to the unpopularity of her mother's religious affiliation, Aimee was taunted by her classmates as the "fire and blood lassie." Aimee soon found a creative solution: converting her persecution to a form of play. Appro-

Aimee playing "Salvation Army lassie" as a girl (used by permission of the International Church of the Foursquare Gospel, Heritage Department).

priating her teacher's red tablecloth, tacking it to a long pole, and borrowing a dishpan and a spoon, Aimee, with makeshift flag and drum, intermittently issuing orders, was soon leading her classmates in marching about the schoolyard singing Salvation Army songs. "It ended up by their not teasing me anymore," she later recalled, "because it was lots of fun to play Army."[19]

Aimee's leadership extended itself also to mischief. "I was always the one to suggest playing 'hooky' and the others would come…around me. I would suggest sliding down the stairs, and the others came scooting after. I was the one to suggest putting a crow-bar through the gymnasium lock, and the rest came along."[20] Aimee's early play, whether it was "healing" deformed flowers in the maple sugar bush, banging a dishpan loudly as a Salvation Army lassie, or simply playing "hooky" from school, was the source of her creativity. Studies of creative adults establish that the sources from which they draw creativity go back to and are linked with "childhood play" and "early delight with nature."[21]

The creative individual, as an adult, periodically plunges deep within—back down to the fantasy of childhood—back to where it all began. As children grow older, according to this theory, "they often lose the skill to dip into their own stories of pleasure and fantasy."[22]

To fully develop his or her creative potential in adulthood, it is necessary that a child, growing into adulthood, preserves and keeps alive his or her sense of wonder from earlier experiences. The personal interest of a caring and knowledgeable adult is crucial in maintaining this sense of wonder as the child matures. For Aimee, the crucial caring adult in her creative development was James, her doting father.

The significance of James and Aimee's relationship cannot be underestimated. With Aimee, James could allow his real self to safely show, could be more emotional, even vulnerable; something he dared not be with Minnie. More importantly, in Aimee's time, it was the father who represented the outside world: the first contact with society. James, the farmer, the earthy man of the soil, prepared his "Babs" well for her later encounters with the real world.

In her classic text, *Writing a Woman's Life*, Carolyn G. Heilbrun accurately depicts a woman's relationship with her mother as "inevitably complex," but also observes that, "The relation with the father will be less complex, clearer in its emotions and desire, partaking less of either terrible pity or binding love."[23]

In the nineteenth century, *Routledge's Manual of Etiquette* referred to a girl's mother as "that truest and most loving of friends." In one passage, Routledge wrote,

> Fortunate is the daughter who has not been deprived of that wisest and tenderest of counselors—whose experience of life…whose anxious care and appreciation of her child's sentiments, and whose awakened recollections of her own trysting days, qualify and entitle her above all other beings to counsel and comfort her trusting child, and to claim her confidence. Let the timid girl then pour forth into her mother's ear the flood of her pent-up feelings. Let her endeavor to distrust her own judgment, and seek hope, guidance, and support from one who, she well knows, will not deceive or mislead her. [24]

The loss of a mother at an early age—Minnie's deprivation—would not befall Aimee. Minnie would be Aimee's truest friend and best counselor. Aimee would be her mother's greatest gift and a possession she could never fully relinquish to God, husbands, or congregations. Their future separation and estrangement would occur because of Aimee's lack of timidity and her increasing desire to trust her own instincts and judgment.

Both her parents supported their daughter's education, unusually so for their place and time in history. In her class picture at Number Three Dereham School, Aimee is captured as an eager schoolgirl, situated front and center, prominently displaying the school sign. After a falling out with her teacher, James Kennedy, ever the indulgent father, leased land in another school district adjoining his property, so that his Beth would be able to transfer to Number Two Dereham School. Aimee did well there. "I passed the examinations at the head of my class, and came in second for the scholarship offered the one making the highest grades in the collegiate [high school]

Aimee's childhood homes in Ontario (used by permission of the International Church of the Foursquare Gospel, Heritage Department).

entrance examination."[25]

In her autobiography, perhaps unaware of the marital discord between her parents or choosing to ignore it, Aimee was able to provide the caption of "childhood's happy home" beneath the picture of the family farm. Because her childhood home had indeed been a happy one for her, she would place a special emphasis upon the importance of the child in her ministry. But one childhood wish, a longing, went unfulfilled. It was always mentioned in an often-repeated sermon entitled "Rebekah at the Well." "I always wished I might have a brother. Sometimes I used to think how wonderful it would be to have a big brother to take me places. Mother would not let me go with very many people when I was a girl."[26]

Reflecting on her youth, Aimee recalled ironically,

> Everything went well until it was learned that I had some little talent for elocution. The distance to the barracks [the Salvation Army branch where her mother was actively engaged in service] being great, and the churches seeming much more popular, I began going to the Methodist church where my father had formerly been a choir leader. Once invited to take part in their entertainments, I was soon received in other churches and appearing on the programs the country round.[27]

"Childhood's happy home" came to an abrupt end for Aimee with her enrollment in high school, her attendance at the local Methodist Church, and her increasing worldly popularity.

Aimee's high school attendance served a hardship on the Kennedy family in that it left more work for her parents. She was freed from daily farm chores to make her nearly ten-mile round-trip commute between the farm and Ingersoll by train, horse and buggy, and sleigh and snowshoe. Perhaps because early marriage seemed an appropriate substitution for an education, records of the Ingersoll Collegiate Institute indicate that male students outnumbered females by more than two to one.

The Ingersoll Collegiate Institute, originally built in 1874, was a two-and-a-half story, square, brick building with four classrooms. By 1886, the school had met the necessary educational requirements to attain the status of a collegiate institute. Requirements for the school's enhanced standing included the employment of four teachers who were considered to be specialists, the building of a gymnasium, and the purchase of laboratory equipment for the teaching of science. And it was in that science classroom that an unfathomable gulf opened for Aimee between her childhood faith and her newly acquired learning. When she matriculated, the Institute employed a faculty of six and reported a student body of approximately one hundred and sixty. It was rated "first class" and ranked "very high on the list of similar institutions throughout the province." Within several years it was considered "one of the finest secondary schools in Ontario."[28]

"My future and educational prospects looked promising," declared Aimee. "No effort or labor was counted too great upon the part of my parents to send me to school, and indeed it was no little matter for them— ten miles to be covered each day on the train or with horse and cart over country roads with their mud, rain or snow."[29]

The Ingersoll Collegiate Institute opened up a new world for young Aimee, a world she at first shrank from but then embraced, then ultimately came to symbolize. Like others of her time, Aimee in her cutter, crossing through the snow, was leaving her rural past behind forever. She was heading for the Jazz Age, where she would become a dazzling symbol of a renewed religious vitality. It was not the family farm, it was the market town of Ingersoll that held for Aimee both the promise and fear of the future. As an adult, Aimee would muse, "I never would have stayed on the farm; if it had not been one thing it would have been... another."[30]

For James Kennedy and Minnie Kennedy, life would never be the same either. A child from a farming family could literally lead one or both parents out of the rural past and into the modern age. And an educated child was their one hope for the future—their interpreter of the ever-new and bewildering, increasingly industrialized and urbanized, twentieth-century world. Leaving behind "childhood's happy home" in the rural past, Aimee found her emergence into the modern age accompanied by spiritual conflict that would remain her constant traveling companion throughout the next three decades. Even as her world grew international in scope, her ceaseless conflicts would eventually trouble her soul and exhaust what had once seemed to be an inexhaustible supply of surplus energy.

A seemingly unavoidable conflict of those in-between years—one that would scar a generation and transform a Canadian farm girl into an American household word—was an emerging conflict between the scientific theory of evolution and the Biblical faith of creation. The question was new and personally troubling to Aimee. The boundary lines, like an autumn's day, were clear and crisp, battle lines firmly drawn, enemies recognizable and well-defined. One seemed required to choose between being a believer or an infidel, especially if they possessed the whole-hearted temperament of a young Aimee Kennedy.

Recalling the major struggle of her late adolescence and early adulthood, she would confess,

> Through the teaching of evolution in my high school, I almost became an atheist. I shudder to think of it. Had it not been that, through the preaching of an evangelist, I was converted and convinced that there really is a God in Heaven, I might have been on the atheistic lecture platform today...I was like a soldier caught in the midst of a poison gas attack without any mask...At the age of seventeen I considered myself forever through with the church, the Bible, faith and Christianity. I was going to live my life as I pleased. I wanted to enjoy the pleasures of the world, to turn what talents I possessed toward a career on the stage,... so many people who said they were Christians seemed to always be so long-faced and sad about it, that I hoped if ever I did become a Christian it would be when I was too old to find any zest in living.[31]

Prior to her skepticism, Aimee had spent considerable time visiting churches in the Ingersoll area, especially the Methodist, Presbyterian, and Baptist churches. Because she had earned a reputation for elocution, winning gold and silver medals from the local chapter of the Women's Christian Temperance Union, area ministers eagerly enlisted her speaking and dramatic ability—often in Irish dialect—for comic monologues for fund-raising, oyster suppers and strawberry festivals. Asked whether the host minister wanted something sacred or secular for the parishioners, the preferred response was invariably for the latter.

"As I recited," Aimee recalled, "...the audience would laugh and clap and laugh again until the tears came to their eyes ...The praise and applause of the people was very alluring to some of us younger ones, and we often talked together of going on stage, arguing that the church was giving us a good training …and that … there was not much difference whether a play or a concert was given in the church or at the theatre."[32]

The perceived, eroding forces of education and secularization were straining Aimee's relationship with her mother. Struggles ensued over such things as attending the college ball:

> When I brought home the engraved invitation card, Mother flatly refused her permission for me to go, and it took a great deal of pleading and coaxing to gain an unwilling consent. My dress and slippers were purchased, and I went to my first dance radiantly happy on the exterior, but I knew that Mother was sad and praying alone at home. It seemed to be a very proper affair, however. My first dancing partner was the Presbyterian preacher. Other good church members were there—surely Mother must be mistaken or a little old-fashioned in her ideas. How lovely it all seemed, the orchestra, the flowers, the attention paid me, the fine clothes and the well-appointed luncheon![33]

It is doubtful that any of her schoolmates went through the enormous emotional upheavals, between Christian nurture and secular education, that Aimee experienced from ages fifteen through seventeen. Like most charismatic religious leaders who develop a strong following, Aimee was showing a special sensitivity to the stresses of her time. Sensing that her daughter was moving in a much different direction from that which she intended, Mrs. Kennedy revealed to Aimee for the first time her prayerful petition for her at her birth. It was to no avail.

Aimee remembered encountering her mother on their steep cellar steps, and asking, "'Mother, how do you know there is a God?'…Her every attempt at explanation, I met with the learned words of those books and the superior twentieth-century wisdom of my seventeen summers—books and wisdom which left mothers and Bibles far behind…here all superstructure that Mother had built was coming down with a crash."[34]

Not content to learn the theory of evolution from a high-school textbook, Aimee studied at the local library, reading Ingersoll, Darwin, and Payne. Their discovery represented "a millstone of destruction of everything that had been built up through these years…I had never thought about part of the Bible being true or part of it being false. To me a person was true or false; a book was true or it was a lie. Either the Bible was God's Word, inspired, every word of it true to me; else it was undependable. I would have to disbelieve some part of it, and I couldn't tell where to end; so I would end by disbelieving it all."[35]

Aimee never mentioned the effect of her disbelief upon her father.

A theatrical Aimee who was convinced that she could do "as much work for God on the stage as in the pulpit" (used by permission of the International Church of the Foursquare Gospel, Heritage Department).

But Aimee was acutely sensitive to her mother's distress. "This was a dreadful blow to Mother. She had sacrificed everything to send me to high school, was getting along on the big farm without me."[36] In one of many attempts to appease her mother, Aimee agreed to ask her questions about faith—and her doubts about it—in a letter to the *Family Herald and Weekly Star*, Canada's leading newspaper, which was published in Montreal. Her letter to the editor was signed, "A perplexed school girl." Written in innocence and reflecting both an extreme awareness of her mother's feelings and a questioning, probing intellect, Aimee's letter asked the newspaper's readership what she should believe in and what she should do, now that she could no longer reconcile her Christian upbringing with her education. The attempt proved futile, except that her quest for an answer generated further questions that enlarged the scope of her awareness.

"Arguments both for and against the book and its teachings were brought out... [my letter] brought in, I believe, thousands of letters. The papers were full of it. Bishops wrote, archaeologists wrote, geologists wrote. They told me what they thought. Out of them all there was only one that said, 'little girl, stick to your Bible.' "[37] Her science teacher as well as her Methodist minister failed in their attempts to solve and settle her doubts. Her minister, Aimee thought, was not only condescending but evaded the questions. "The more I read and observed the lives of Christians," she wrote, "the more skeptical of the reality of God I became…I looked for the hypo-crites, and picked them out above all the good people….Oh, I must know the truth—was there anything in religion?"[38]

Her father's Methodist church was also dark and depressing. "We had those big walnut pews….'Hark, from the tombs a doleful sound, how tedious and tasteless the hours' was sung, and I thought, 'Oh, I hope I don't get religion until I am old. I do want to have a good time before I die. I hope I don't get religion and be so sad and long-faced.' "[39]

It was apparently right before or during his daughter's disillusion-ment with organized religion that James' own growing religious disaffec-tion occurred. In any event, James shared little of his wife's concern over Aimee's religious well-being. Whatever spiritual direction his Babs sought seemed to be fine with him. Unlike Minnie, he did not translate religious conflict into a life-or-death matter.

In a final attempt to achieve some spiritual resolution and to restore domes-tic tranquility with her mother, Aimee agreed to visit various churches with Minnie, discern their doctrinal differences, and ultimately join the one which best suited her interests. When both mother and daughter visited a Salvation Army revival meeting, Minnie Kennedy feared that all was lost. It had been some time since they had been to a Salvationist meeting together, and Minnie felt as embarrassed as Aimee felt vindicated when the service opened with an "entertainment." Portraying a black minstrel, an officer was entertaining the congregation with a skit. After the service ended, there was an altar call, in which members of the audience were urged to come forward and pledge their lives to Jesus. Lingering back by the door at the rear of the hall, Aimee was approached for conversion by three people: the evangelist's daughter, his wife, and finally the evangelist himself. To their dismay, and to her mother's, Aimee fought back, affirming the teachings of evolution over those of biblical faith. During the long drive home, Minnie Kennedy wept bitterly, perhaps not so much out of humiliation in front of fellow Salvationists as out of a sense of failure in her spiritual mission with her daughter, whom she had promised God to lend unto the Lord as long as she lived. All along, she had never doubted that her child had a spiritual destiny in the world, especially since her own life had been self-described as one that was shorn of usefulness, fettered by circumstances, and spent grinding away in the prison house of life on the farm. Suddenly her deepest hope seemed defeated.

Aimee later described her reaction to her mother's tears as follows: "Con-science-stricken, and shamed for grief, I fled to my room to think things over. I certainly loved my mother; to cause her grief and sorrow was the last thing in this wide world which I wished to do—and yet—and yet."[40]

Later that evening, after un-harnessing their horse, Aimee went again to her room. She turned the key and opened the window, keeping the light off and her coat on. She knelt at the window sill and gazed out over apple trees bathed in winter ice, sparkling now "like ten million diamonds." On the ground, the crust of the snow sparkled. Above, the moon seemed to be sailing toward her from the eastern sky; the stars were reflective. Taking hold of a comforter to dull the winter chill, she began to be conscious of the nearness of a presence. Feeling the seed of faith beginning to take root, she reasoned with her heart regarding Christian faith. "Suddenly, without stopping to think, I threw both arms impulsively out of the window and, reaching toward heaven, cried: "Oh, God!—If there be a God—reveal yourself to me! The cry came from my very heart. In reality, a whisper was all that came from my lips—but just that whisper from an honest, longing heart, was enough to echo through the stars and reach the Father's throne."[41]

Within twenty-four hours of that event in December 1907, Aimee Elizabeth Kennedy found not only an answer to her prayer but her life's work as well. Future detours of doubt would be brief.

During this time, Aimee wrote an article for the local newspaper arguing that since the churches were empty and the theatres full, the theatre was now the place to reach the crowds with "good morals." She was rehearsing for a benefit concert that would raise money for children in Japan. She not only conceived the idea of the concert, she also wrote all the recitations and dialogues, in an effort to prove that she could do "as much work for God on the stage as in the pulpit."[42]

The day after the fateful Salvation Army meeting with her mother, James Kennedy, the ever-doting father, picked up his Beth at school to drive her to rehearsal. Riding down Main Street in the family cutter in mid-December thinking about the previous night's experience and the onrush of Christmas, Aimee turned briefly to her left and discovered a large, storefront with a sign stating that full gospel services, with meetings every night, and all day on Sunday, were held there. This was a place she had heard about, a place where weird things occurred, where people rolled around in the aisles and spoke in strange "tongues." Outsiders called these people "Holy Ghosters" or "Holy Rollers." She asked her father to take her there some evening so she could witness the events for herself. James suggested that they could go the following evening while en route to her play rehearsal at the town hall. The next evening, while sitting with her father in the second-to-last row of the storefront mission, several things caught Aimee Kennedy's curious and critical eye. The first was the apparent lack of wealth and status of the parishioners:

> They seemed to be a very ordinary lot of people; none of the wealthy or well-known citizens of the town were there and dressed as I was with the flowers on my hat, a gold chain and locket and rings on my fingers, I felt just a little bit above the status of those round about me, and looked on with an amused air as they shouted, danced and prayed…At all these things I giggled foolishly, not understanding it and thinking it all very laughable…The mail-man, whom I knew well, lifted his hand as he sang. So did the dry cleaner and I giggled with amusement.[43]

What impressed Aimee, however, was the intense spirituality of the parishioners, in contrast to that of the members of the older, more established churches. "There were no announcements of oyster suppers or Christmas entertainments or sewing circles, there was no appeal for money. Not even a collection was taken. It was just God, God, God."[44] Above all else, however, it was Robert Semple, the preacher, an ex-Presbyterian now turned Pentecostal evangelist, who captured her rapt attention:

> Soon a tall young man, (six-feet-two) rose to his feet on the platform and taking his Bible in his hand, opened it and began to read. I could not help admiring his frank, open, kindly face, the Irish-blue eyes with the light of heaven in them, and the bushy hair, one brown curl of which would insist on falling down close to his eye no matter how often he brushed it back with his fingers. As he spoke with earnest zeal I took him in from head to foot.[45]

The attraction Aimee felt was immediate and complex: it was both physical and spiritual. A very young, determined Aimee Kennedy would soon marry the handsome Pentecostal preacher. Tragically, she would lose him after only two years and one week of marriage, but her devotion to him and the cause he represented she carried with her to her grave. In a short amount of time, Aimee Kennedy's life was radically altered and changed by her encounter with Robert Semple. The rest of her life could be viewed as a living memorial to the former boilermaker from Magherafelt, Ireland, who not only became her devoted husband, but her spiritual mentor, brother in the faith, and faithful friend.

In many ways, Robert Semple was the incarnation of Aimee's fondest childhood hope: that wonderful big brother, who at the height of his youthful brawn would unlatch the gate of the family farm and carry her forth

Aimee and Robert Semple, her devoted husband and spiritual mentor ((used by permission of the International Church of the Foursquare Gospel, Heritage Department).

into the modern world. Robert was to become Aimee's *everything*, her only real-life prince, her handsome lover, her constant friend, and her elder brother. He was the man to carry on for her where the other one, her father, left off. In the drama that was to be Aimee's life, only three men would play supporting roles: James, Robert, and a forthcoming son. All other men were only bit players in her one-woman show. There would be no future, permanent *other* waiting in the wings for the exhausted religious actress when the lights mercifully went out. As she herself so often said, she went home alone and kissed her shoulder goodnight. Her permanent *other* would exist only in memory, slowly changing with the passing of the seasons from faded stills of black and white to a living portrait composed of rich and vivid hues.

While it might have been Robert's handsome appearance that captivated Aimee that first night in the storefront mission, which he had cleaned and furnished himself, it was his message that effected her conversion. Robert's words, for Aimee, "flowed like a river, searched like a light…burned like a fire, piercing, convicting, wooing…on and on they flowed; words that brought me from darkness unto light and catching me up on the mighty bosom of that tide, swept me clear from a quiet Canadian farm…then 'round the world and back again…mighty words, soul-shaking words… they were God-given.' "[46]

The one word that Aimee remembered above all others was *repent.*

Robert preached a gospel that demanded strict separation from the world. "It was as though he drew a straight line down the center of the universe, placing God on one side and the devil on the other. That man made a real difference between a sinner and a saint—between a worldling and a Christian."[47]

Aimee, seemingly very worldly at the time, wondered whether or not someone had told the evangelist that she was present, "so vividly did he picture my own life and work."[48]

After a brief salvation message, Robert expounded on the Pentecostal doctrine of the baptism of the Holy Spirit, whose evidence, he taught, was the "speaking in other tongues." When he had finished this doctrinal part of the sermon, he himself began to speak loudly in a strange language. This caught Aimee by surprise, for part of the immediate attraction she had felt for Robert had stemmed from his conservative, reserved manner. When he got up to preach, she could not help noticing that he seemed different, far removed from "the antics going on with the congregation." Now the unintelligible words issuing from Robert seemed to be claiming that she was "a poor, lost, miserable sinner."[49]

> No one had ever spoken to me like this before. I had been petted, loved and perhaps a little spoiled. Now, God was telling me the truth!. ..My haughty pride had vanished; my soul had been stripped bare before the Almighty—I knew there was a God. I wondered, humbly, how I could have ever looked down upon these dear people and felt myself better than they...they were saints, I was a sinner.[50]

Leaving the storefront mission early, returning to her questioning state of mind, Aimee left uncertain; not yet converted. Long and hard, she pondered all that she would be required to give up in order to become a Pentecostal: dancing, novels, the theatre, and worldly music. The one thing she found herself unwilling to surrender was her gift for elocution. "Yet I knew that I could not be a Christian and recite those foolish Irish recitations and go through those plays and dialogues."[51] For three days her struggle intensified:

> At the end of the third day, while driving home from school, in the family cutter, I could stand it no longer...not pausing to consider what anyone—preachers, entertainment committee, school friends—would think or say, I threw up my hands and cried aloud out of the depths of my soul's despair: "Oh Lord God, be merciful to me, a sinner!" Immediately the most wonderful change took place within my soul! ...Suddenly

without effort or apparent forethought I found myself singing that old, familiar hymn:

> Take my life and let it be
> Consecrated, Lord, to Thee;
> Take my moments and my days,
> Let them flow in ceaseless praise!
> Take my hands and let them move,
> At the impulse of thy love,
> Take my feet and let them be,
> Swift and beautiful for Thee.
> Take my lips and let them sing,
> Always, only, for my King![52]

Her conversion was complete. Aimee recalled, "It has always been typical of me not to make any half-way decisions; to believe entirely in a certain thing or not accept it at all. The same was true of my conversion... I burned my rag-time music, the jazz of that day, burned my dancing slippers and gave up all ambition to be an actress. It was the Bible, the hymn book and a life of Christian service for me from then on."[53]

Converted or not, Aimee would always retain her curious and critical nature. Her personality, in the final analysis, would neither be altered by Pentecostal ecstasy discovered in a storefront mission nor by the eloquence of the handsome Robert Semple. As a persuasive actress and preacher, she would have no equal. And the force of her persuasion would come from the fact that Aimee always preached first to herself, attempting to find answers for the questioner deep within; when she preached to others, she was really preaching to believe herself.

Aimee's conversion to Pentecostalism was propitious, in that it harmoniously united her secular and sacred ambitions into one single purpose. Aimee would not only become an inspiring actress and gifted preacher, she would also become this new religious movement's most visible symbol. And she would influence and mold the young movement as no one else would do, during its most colorful, controversial, and formative years.

Aimee's Pentecostal conversion experience did little to relieve the tensions with her mother. In some ways it only heightened them, for in a theological sense, Minnie was like the *many who were called,* but her answered prayer, Aimee Elizabeth, had become one of the *chosen few.* This was a development that Minnie Kennedy could never fully accept and—consciously or not—would later seek to sabotage.

CHAPTER TWO

Romance and Religion: Mrs. Robert Semple

I did the work in the meetings as a little organist, dusted, sang, while my husband was the preacher...and he would stand on the platform, impressively preaching in the blazing glory of his message, [while] I would sit in the audience and pray and offer encouragement...I had been content to do the things a wife should attend to.

—Aimee Semple McPherson
The Bridal Call

Minnie Kennedy did not take well to her daughter's newly found faith, and even James wagered that it would only last two weeks. Although Aimee rejected her part in the forthcoming Christmas play and pageantry, Minnie was still rather unnerved by it all. Two events occurring in one day prompted Minnie to issue Aimee an ultimatum. First, when Aimee was at school, she replaced the novel hidden inside of her algebra and geometry books with a New Testament. Soon after the replacing of the book, the high school principal sent Mrs. Kennedy a letter stating that her daughter was in danger of failing. That same day, several Salvation Army officers called on Mrs. Kennedy to warn her about Pentecostalism, which was, they said, a false and fanatical movement.

Fearing all the talk circulating about Aimee's conversion to an unacceptable faith, Minnie gave her daughter the ultimatum: if she could not stay away from the mission, she should stay away from school. It was a difficult choice. But as Aimee said later, providence itself intervened. The following day, while taking the train to school because of heavy snowfall, Aimee had to walk past both the storefront where Robert Semple was preaching and the house of a woman who attended the mission—the woman she would soon turn to as spiritual mother. Immediately, the conflict arose between going to school or seeking the "second blessing"—what Pentecostals called "the Baptism of the Holy Ghost"—the ecstatic experience of speaking in other and unknown tongues; the same activity she had earlier ridiculed at the mission—the activity which was providing the new religious movement with its most salient feature. Again, Christian nurture won out over secular education, as Aimee decided to spend the day in prayer, seeking this strange, new spiritual gift with her new found spiritual mother. Snowed-in by a storm, Aimee spent the night and the following day there in search of this strange "gift." She read in Matthew's gospel about how "the Kingdom of Heaven suffered violence and the violent take it by force." She felt she herself must now "storm Heaven" before her gift could be received. True to her later style in her subsequent ministry and most similar to Robert Semple's, while kneeling beside a Morris chair she recalled,

> A quietness seemed to steal over me, the holy presence of the Lord to envelop me. The voice of the Lord spoke tenderly: "Now, child, cease your strivings and your begging; just begin to praise Me in simple, child-like faith, receive the Holy Ghost"…All at once my hands and arms began to shake, gently at first, then violently, until my whole body was shaking under the power of the Holy Spirit…My tongue began to move up and down and sideways in my mouth. Unintelligible sounds as of stammering lips, and another tongue… began to issue from my lips… Then suddenly, out of my innermost being flowed rivers of praise in other tongues as the Spirit gave utterance (Acts 2:4)…[1]

Aimee had received, according to Pentecostals, "the Baptism of the Holy Spirit," the experience that would later become the second article of faith in her "Foursquare Gospel."

Immediately afterward, two other spiritual-mystical events occurred whose impact was even more profound. Continuing in prayer, she received a vision. The world appeared as ripe with wheat. In her vision, she witnessed the wheat transformed to "human faces" and the leaves transformed to "human hands stretched up." Aimee then received her calling, a theological calling that was very precise and well-defined.

> He placed in my hand a sharp, two-edged sickle—the Word of God—and in my heart these words: "Go gather in the grain, but ever remember that thy sickle is given thee for the cutting of the wheat. Many reapers, alas, use the sickle rightfully for a few brief hours, then turn to cut and slash their fellows. None other can wound so deeply, for none have so sharp a weapon. Apply thyself to the task before thee. Cut but the wheat, and gather precious sheaves."[2]

Aimee would never forget the caution and the warning that accompanied her calling. Often the target and butt of ridicule in her early ministry for being a Pentecostal woman evangelist, it was characteristic of her ministry that she never fought back. The call to a theological task, however, was bewildering and confusing to Aimee, who was still very young, being only seventeen years old at the time.

> At first it seemed too astounding and impossible to be true that the Lord would ever call such a simple, unworthy little country girl as I to go out and preach the Gospel, but the call and ordination were so real that, although later set apart and ordained by Saints of God, the memory of my little bedroom, flooded with the glory of God as He spoke those words, has always been to me my real ordination.[3]

The timing could not have been better for Aimee, for it gave her a great chance to be successful. As with early Christianity itself, Pentecostalism recognized the equality of women in the ministry in its first prophetic stage of evolution. In its infancy, the movement understood ecstatic experience chiefly through Biblical accounts of prophetic figures.

Three factors accounted for the equality of women in the early Pentecostal ministry and defined the difference between ministers and laity: the receiving of a divine call; the confirmation of that call, through a recognition of charisma by the community; and the community's eschatological belief that they were experiencing the "latter rain of the Holy Spirit" (Joel 2:23)[4], in which your "sons and daughters will prophesy" (Joel 2:28).

Biblical accounts of the prophets were powerful rhetorical models by which women such as Aimee could and would lay claim to pastoral roles in prophetic Pentecostal communities. The calls of Moses, Gideon, Isaiah, Jeremiah, and Ezekiel share common features: the divine confrontation, the introductory word, the commission, the objection, the reassurance, and the sign. As for objections, Moses protested that he was inept at speaking, and Jeremiah complained that he was too young. Women Pentecostal ministers, including Aimee, objected to the call on the grounds that they were women. But looking to Biblical portraits of the prophets, they could find reassurance and a reconfirmation of their call, in spite of gender. Like Aimee, however, many would endeavor in their early ministry to test their calling and to seek additional signs, frequently putting their health at peril. For Aimee, it took a hospital bed and the termination of a second marriage before she was fully persuaded and convinced of the genuineness of her earlier call to ministry.[5]

Aimee's new spiritual mother, a poor housewife with a large family, was by now providing something resembling a spiritual half-way house for Aimee away from the farm. It had become the spiritual counterpart to the

Ingersoll Collegiate Institute, which was only two short blocks away. Aimee would later describe her spiritual mother's home as a "shrine of blessing to me."[6] This home was where Aimee was spiritually formed and where Robert Semple proposed marriage. Robert Semple had also been at the house when Aimee received her baptism.

Downtown at the mission, Aimee's ecstatic experiences continued throughout the weekend. She remembered her friends and schoolmates visiting the storefront and standing on the seats to witness her activities on the floor.

> One man was so scandalized to see me lying on the floor that he got up and left the meeting, and going to the telephone called my Mother.... He said, "You had better come into town and see to that daughter of yours, for she is lying on the floor in the mission, before all the people, chattering like a monkey."[7]

As always, when she perceived her daughter was in danger, Minnie Kennedy arrived quickly on the spot. Aimee remembered hearing her mother "scolding me more severely and saying more harsh things than she ever had in my life."[8] Attempting to enlist James' support, Minnie claimed that the Pentecostals had Aimee "under their influence, hypnotized, mesmerized her or something."[9]

The mother-daughter conflict over Aimee's conversion experience and call to ministry would eventually resolve itself over time, with Minnie losing the theological battle with her daughter and, at least in an outward fashion, identifying herself with Pentecostalism. In her heart of hearts, however, it is doubtful that the inimitable Ma Kennedy was ever truly anything other than one of General Booth's officers in the Salvation Army. Minnie longed for the day when her prayer would be answered and Aimee Elizabeth too, would become one of the general's "best men."

Aimee's conversion to Christianity and subsequent call to a Pentecostal ministry only further fueled her own inner conflict between affection and ambition. And Aimee was left alone to resolve it. Robert Semple, an itinerant evangelist, had moved on to Stratford for yet another Pentecostal campaign. Although services continued on in the Ingersoll mission, and Aimee dutifully attended them, they undoubtedly lacked the warmth Robert's presence had brought. In an attempt to sustain the fervor that Robert Semple had created, cottage prayer meetings were formed in the home of Aimee's spiritual mother. Despite her new spiritual setting and surroundings, ambition was compelling Aimee to think once again of moving outside her all-too-familiar village environment. A move would, however, bring the loss of the affection she so desperately needed and depended upon, unless, of course, she found someone new, living outside her increasingly small universe.

Her inner voices reminded her, "There is your mother to be considered. You are an only child, her only comfort and object of affection in this world. Surely you would not consider leaving her out there in the country all alone, after all that she had done for you?"[10] Her internal voices remained strangely silent about her father's feelings.

Aimee's small world was soon invaded once again by Robert Semple. "He continued to encourage and instruct me in the Lord by many long letters, all of which were filled with scriptures and food from God's store-house."[11] Two months after her conversion, while attending the sick children of her spiritual mother, Aimee saw Robert again. It was not a meeting by chance or by accident, since Aimee knew in advance of Robert's intentions. She simply volunteered her services to her spiritual mother, knowing it would be the first house the Reverend Mr. Semple would visit upon his return to Ingersoll. Upon hearing Robert restate his desire to go to China as a missionary and especially his need for a "helpmate," Aimee suddenly realized her role:

> Here was the visible answer to the call. Here was the loving human hand sent to unlatch the gate of opportunity and guide my steps into that shining path and start me well upon the way…My girlish heart suddenly began to pound against my ribs—like a caged tropical bird beating its wings against the bars that kept it from the golden, mellow sunlight of a South Seas Island Paradise. Everything else in the world around me seemed to melt and fade out of focus. Love—triumphant, powerful and elemental—was surging and taking possession of me like a young giant set free, while faith, satisfying and serene, seemed to engulf me like a pleasant, restful dream. Then it was I realized that I was in love. I was happy. Months passed like hours.[12]

While piously solemnizing their marital engagement through prayer, Aimee experienced yet another vision so hauntingly accurate of her future that it would become something of her official spiritual portrait: forever frozen in time; incapable of being altered or changed:

> While on my knees, with closed eyes and throbbing heart—(why, this was the very room in which I had received my baptism!)…the room seemed filled with angels who lined either side of a golden, sunlit path

of life that stretched away into the vista of the future…and there was I, walking hand in hand with Robert! I opened my eyes, the picture faded… quickly I closed them again. There was the same pathway, but this time there was only one figure. I was walking steadily into the light, as before, but I was alone! I did not know the meaning of that picture then; and even if I had understood fully, I would still have whispered "yes" to God![13]

Alone. Aimee's heavenly vision, in time, would turn into the hellish nightmare of reality. Aimee's whispered yes to God was also a simultaneous yes to Robert—the loving human hand sent to unlatch the gate of opportunity—the hand that set free a caged tropical bird beating its wings against the bars that kept it from a South Seas Island Paradise. Despite her short, two-year marriage, one of Aimee's earliest and most abiding theological tenets was that romance and religion went hand in hand. Had she not found God through Robert Semple? Aimee would struggle throughout her life with her repeated attempts to reunite the physical with the spiritual. She would be without peer as a Christian minister in modern America who was attempting to connect the sacred with the profane. And only by such attempts would she ever feel whole again; a real person.

By midsummer 1908, the Reverend Mr. Semple summoned the courage to approach Minnie Kennedy (not James) to ask for Aimee's hand in marriage. Aimee remembered the encounter with Robert being "straight forward" and "manly" and her mother declaring that the "sunshine," "laughter," and "music" would disappear with her daughter from the house. Aimee also remembered a probing, fatherly conversation she had later with James, regarding her decision to marry an itinerant Pentecostal evangelist.

"This man you are marrying, Aimee…he seems wonderful, but has he any money?"

"Shame on you, Dad! Of course not! He's a preacher," she answered.

"Has he a salary?" he persisted.

"No…he is an evangelist and as such, trusts the Lord and the people he serves," she replied.

"W-Well, I hope it will turn out all right," Aimee remembered him saying, blaming her father's concern on his Scotch blood.

"Scotch blood is the finest in the world," he flamed. "It's not stingy. It's just practical. Who is going to buy your clothes and food?"

Aimee's final response to her father's concerns was that she would "pray about the matter."[14]

Turning a corner and disappearing up the stairs of the family farmhouse,

James quickly ended both his fatherly concerns and his active role in his beloved Bab's life.

Eight months after the handsome Irish evangelist's efforts had ended in Ingersoll, the local newspaper noted that Aimee Elizabeth Kennedy and Robert J. Semple were married, on August 12, 1908, at "Kosy-Kot, the charming country home of Mr. and Mrs. James Kennedy, near Salford."[15]

Despite her daughter's conversion experience and decision to marry a Pentecostal evangelist, Minnie Kennedy tightly controlled the religious setting of the event, much as she had her daughter's first religious rite of passage at birth, with the newspaper noting that "the domestic event," having been looked forward to with intense interest by a large number of young people, "was conducted according to the beautiful service of the Salvation Army…in the presence of about fifty guests."[16]

The newspaper account further noted that the bride was neatly attired in a white silk gown "trimmed with real lace" and was "very popular in the community around Salford and Ingersoll [and that] she is also a gold medalist in elocution, and has always been a cheerful contributor at local entertainments when requested to assist on the program." Robert was noted for being formerly engaged in business and having recently taken up mission work "with gratifying success."[17]

Their honeymoon, beginning in a ribboned bridal carriage drawn by two horses, extended over a two-year intensely pietistic idyll and ended at the Happy Valley Cemetery, in Hong Kong, China, with Robert's death, which was due to "hemorrhagic dysentery, and exhaustion."[18] He was twenty-nine years old when he died, and six weeks later his only child, a daughter, was born. The two short years with Robert were in actuality the totality of Aimee's theological training, her seminary, and her spiritual apprenticeship. "He was my Bible School. He taught me the word of God and he was always speaking of the Kingdom of God and things pertaining to the Lord."[19]

A rather subdued Aimee was known during these two years as "Sister Semple." She noted, "I did the work in the meetings as a little organist, dusted, sang, while my husband was the preacher…And he would stand on the platform, impressively preaching in the blazing glory of his message, I would sit in the audience and pray and offer encouragement…I had been content to wash the dishes and cook and do the things a wife should attend to."[20]

The beginnings for both were meager. Home was no longer on rolling acres of farmland, but was instead three barren rooms in central Stratford, Ontario, surrounded by smoking factories and foundries. Aimee was a housewife learning to cook and clean for the first time. Robert was a boiler-maker in a locomotive factory by day and a moonlighting pastor for a poor mission by night. Robert and Aimee, desiring to enter full-time evangelism in order to raise money for their forthcoming missionary endeavors, moved from Stratford to London, Ontario. Pentecostalism was new to the city and provided Robert with fertile ground. Living with someone whom they called a "spiritual sister," they began to hold meetings in her parlor until it was outgrown. At a larger house, attendance grew until more than a hundred converts within a year's time had experienced the Pentecostal teachings as taught by Robert Semple. From these humble beginnings, Aimee recalled, "a large, thriving, centrally located Pentecostal mission has been built on one of the main streets."[21] "Sister Semple" by now had attained a growing consciousness about too many Pentecostal missions existing in back alleys and out-of-the-way places. She would later seek with much success to put her style of Pentecostalism on Main Street.

Pentecostalism in the United States was now in its golden glow. In the wake of the Azusa Street Revival in Los Angeles, under the leadership of the African-American exhorter William J. Seymour, the movement, still largely interracial and non-denominational, was flourishing in many major cities and was especially strong in the Midwest. The Reverend Owen Adams, who had gone to Canada directly from the Azusa Street Mission in Los Angeles, was the man who had converted Robert Semple to Pentecostalism. The East End Mission in downtown Toronto quickly became Canada's very own Jerusalem and Azusa Street. It was here that Robert Semple claimed his own personal healing of tuberculosis and renewed his calling to preach the Gospel. It was also the place where Robert "tarried and received the baptism in the Spirit during the earliest days of…the…Mission."[22]

After attracting worldwide attention for at least four years, the Azusa Street Revival was beginning to fragment, both racially and theologically. A former Baptist preacher by the name of William H. Durham had come to Los Angeles from Chicago. His heavy emphasis on *grace*, as opposed to *works*, was fueling the flames of one of the first theological controversies confronting the infant movement.

Durham's controversial new doctrine, "The Finished Work of Calvary," promised complete sanctification at the time of conversion. This new teaching denied the traditional Wesleyan view that saw sanctification as a second, separate experience of grace following conversion. Durham not only held up the Wesleyan view for ridicule but proclaimed his "Finished work of Calvary" [was] "the very germ and life of [the] Gospel" itself and that, apart from his teaching, "there is no other gospel."[23]

An eyewitness to his later work in Los Angeles summarized the impact and influence his teaching was having on Pentecostalism as follows: "His word was coming to be almost law in the Pentecostal missions, even as far as the Atlantic Coast"[24] At the height of Durham's influence in the struggling Pentecostal movement, "The Lord," wrote Aimee, "began to impress [sic] us that we were to go to Chicago, Illinois, to attend the meetings of Brother W. H. Durham."[25] Minnie Kennedy, who by now had started to worry about how her daughter would manage financially while married to a itinerant Pentecostal preacher, provided "the fare and necessary expenses" for her daughter and son-in-law to travel to the United States and be instructed by this important leader of the fledgling movement.[26]

Durham's Chicago North Avenue mission, furnished with curtains and a seating capacity for two hundred people, was a critical, pivotal place for the spiritual direction and formation of the Semples. Two events alone attest to this fact. First, both Robert and Aimee on January 2, 1909, were ordained with the Pentecostal movement through the Full Gospel Assembly, with its general offices located at 943 North Avenue, Chicago. Secondly, during the time spent with Durham, Aimee experienced the Pentecostal teaching of "divine healing," which would later become the third cardinal doctrine of her own Pentecostal denomination. Summarizing those months in the Windy City, Aimee was to recall, "Oh, the teaching and the deepening, and the experiences that were ours in the little North Avenue Assembly, where we worshiped for several months, have meant so much in the years which followed." [27]

Durham's role in the successful birth of the Pentecostal movement as a whole was an important one. A tall, attractive man, he was thirty-six years old when he met the Semples. He died three years later in Los Angeles of tuberculosis. In addition to his North Avenue Mission in Chicago, Durham rented a large building in Los Angeles with room for one thousand people. At the time of his death, he saw his mission at Seventh and Los Angeles Streets as "the headquarters for a nationwide organization of the Pentecostal movement."[28] Durham's influence was considerable. In addition to creating ten other missions in Chicago, he had a strong following among Italian Pentecostals and those who, like Robert Semple, came from a "reformed" theological background. Several Pentecostal denominations trace their origins directly to Durham.[29]

Thus, the theological roots of Aimee Semple McPherson's subsequent International Church of the Foursquare Gospel were laid in Durham's North Avenue Mission. Like the Assemblies of God, the Foursquare denomination would emerge primarily from a "reformed" rather than a "holiness" background.

Robert Semple, perhaps because of his reserved temperament and Presbyterian Church background, did not manifest in Chicago many of the spiritual gifts that classical Pentecostals were claiming to receive. Aimee was much more desirous of experiencing them than Robert was. She always remembered her first experience with the Pentecostal teaching of divine healing, which alone in coming years would make her ministry famous. After breaking her ankle in Findley, Ohio, during a visit to a Pentecostal mission there, her inner voice spoke to her and said, "If you will wrap the shoe for your broken foot and take it with you to wear home, and go over to [the] North Avenue mission to Brother Durham and ask him to lay hands on your foot, I will heal it."[30]

After Durham prayed, Aimee testified, "I suddenly felt as if a shock of electricity had struck my foot. It flowed through my whole body, causing me to shake and tremble under the power of God. Instantaneously, my foot was perfectly healed."[31] Aimee was subsequently bothered when onlookers expressed doubt over the genuineness of her healing. Another spiritual gift Aimee was to receive during her Chicago visit was the "gift of interpretation," the spiritual ability to translate into English a message spoken in other tongues.

A member of the North Avenue Mission remembered both the founding minister and his young apprentice. Durham, she recalled, was "tall and attractive," while Aimee was remembered for teaching Sunday school. She was also, the member recalled, a "fervent young woman" and "quite a preacher."[32] While at Durham's mission Aimee had clearly begun to come into her own, emerging out of her beloved Robert's large and overpowering spiritual shadow. In 1910, after their Chicago apprenticeship had ended, both Robert and Aimee sensed it was time to go to China. With "no earthly board behind us, no organization to lean upon," the Semples learned, within two weeks, that their source of support would come "by the dear Saints of God, not by the rich, but by the poor."[33]

William Durham had, however, solicited funds for the young couple. In his monthly periodical published in December 1909, he noted: "Brother and Sister Semple will leave for China in January, God willing. Offerings for their traveling expenses can be sent to Pastor Durham, 2836 W. North Avenue."[34]

Early on, Aimee was to learn that a hallmark of the fledgling Pentecostal movement, a "people's religion," was its followers' willingness to respond financially to perceived need:

We find, all over the country in our meetings that the rich and near-rich will come to us and say: "Oh, I am so sorry that I am not in a position just now to give something. My money is tied up and I am so situated that I am not able to do much now; how I wish I could." And while they are humming and hesitating over it, the poor step up, and with a glad light in their eyes, grip our hands with a hearty: "God bless you. Here's a dollar or here's five or ten," as the case may be. "Oh, I only wish it were more, but I will have more when next week's pay envelope comes in. How proud I am to have this privilege!"[35]

Unlike the Protestant mainline churches with their featured "princes of the pulpit" and endowments gained at the expense of the Industrial Revolution that enabled them to move "uptown" in American society, Pentecostalism, much like Catholicism, was a "downtown" movement—an organization comprised of the urban poor, the immigrants, and the rising lower middle class. Pentecostal missionary exploits such as the Semples' as well as Aimee's own subsequent ministry came neither from powerful church boards nor from the rich, but rather from humble folk whose hearts had been touched by the missionaries' potential and promise. Through their donations they experienced vicariously the missionaries' own participation in active Christianity.

When the Semples said good-bye to a large Italian congregation that had been founded through Robert Semple's ministry, the parishioners responded to the young couple with a "green handshake" that provided the funds for their fares to China. After a good-bye visit to the Kennedy farm, the Semples then set sail for Northern Ireland so that Robert could introduce his young bride to his family before their voyage to China. Leaving from St. John, New Brunswick, the Semples left Canada with the added knowledge that they were in the process of becoming parents.

Like the horse and buggy and the cutter in the snow on the farm, the *Empress of Ireland*, (which later sank with one thousand victims), opened up an ever-increasingly new world for the young missionary bride. Having never seen an ocean or traveled before on water, Aimee felt consternation at the rough seas and turbulent storms of the North Atlantic while also experiencing sickness associated with her pregnancy. Robert, her source of strength, helped to provide some inner calm, and soon the Canadian winter and the North Atlantic crossing disappeared, and the lush, spring-green countryside of England came into view. Leaving Liverpool for Belfast, the Semples conducted a three-week revival in that city before reaching Robert's hometown of Magherafelt and his family of seven. At the conclusion of the meetings in Belfast, the Semples received an invitation from the Lord

Mayor to visit him at City Hall, where they were presented with the key to the city. "I was awed," recalled Aimee, "with his pompous robes, golden chains and gleaming medals. Robert stood very straight and tall among the crowd that had gathered on the marble steps for the ceremony."[36]

Aimee remembered Magherafelt, a town twenty miles outside of Belfast, as being "quaint . . . lying among emerald hills, bottomless lakes, and winding roads."[37] She was as taken by her new surroundings and family as she was with the local folklore and folktales which accompanied them. She enjoyed being treated as "one of the family, in that quaint glorious stone house among the shamrocks next to her father-in-law's general store."[38]

She enjoyed hearing the endless yarns about cities long buried under deep green lakes and about how fairies danced in eternal circles, and learning that her recently acquired name, *Semple*, had originally been *d'Paul*, or "of Saint Paul." It was, however, an Irish folktale of an enchanted forest of beautiful trees that impressed itself upon Aimee more than anything else during her stay. The tale told of a long-ago, enchanted forest, where if one entered it through the surrounding tall trees, one discovered a charmed circle where no foe could enter. One was safe from every ill—or so the story went—in the green grass of that forested circle.

In the spring of 1937, when controversy, family squabbles, and lawsuits were threatening to destroy her ministry forever, she would use the Irish legend as the basis for a sermon entitled "In the Center of God's Will." It would mark a new level of maturity in her personal dealings and insecurities, as well as in her theological understandings and development. The serenity and security she felt with the Robert Semple family during their stay in Magherafelt undoubtedly prompted this remembrance for her in her later years.

Robert's mother, upon her son and daughter-in-law's departure, received a "spiritual witness," an intuitive warning, that she would never see her son again. While waiting in London for their Orient-bound boat, the Semples visited some thriving Pentecostal services being held in various parts of the city. During this London stay, Aimee received a vision that the Christian church had entered into "the dispensation of the Holy Spirit." While there she also for the first time preached a sermon before a congregation. Addressing "fifteen thousand spectators," the prepared sermon "evaporated," and "the Spirit of God took over."[39]

It would be almost a decade before Aimee Semple, alone, would again address such a crowd. Although alone in the future, she would never be without an audience, and, in time, she would be more at home with a congregation of five thousand people than she would be with five friends in a parsonage. Her spiritual impact, like her temperament, would be in the form of "all or nothing."

Slipping out of a London wharf accompanied by the singing of the Pentecostal saints, Robert and Aimee Semple set sail for the land of China—Robert's dream destination, which had, to some extent, created and enhanced their romance. The crossing of the seas was somewhat poetical to Aimee. "Skirting the edge of the Bay of Biscay, we sailed on to Gibraltar, then in through the blue, sunlit waters of the Mediterranean, to the Suez Canal, and on into the Red Sea, through which the Children of Israel had been led dry-shod."[40] En route the Semples gathered good reports of the growing and flourishing Pentecostal movement in such ports of call as Egypt, India, Ceylon, and Malta.

Twenty-four years later, while revisiting China without Robert, Aimee, with the increased awareness brought on by age and insight, recollected earlier memories of that maiden voyage to her first mission field. "Robert and I had stood on just such a deck as this and viewed the land wherein we expected to spend the balance of our lives. Precious few dollars were ours. No prearranged home awaited us or the 'little one' whom we were soon to welcome."[41]

"Home" for Aimee, on this first voyage to China, was simply being in Robert's arms. A true romantic who would never again find the tenderness and warmth that she experienced with Robert with any other man, she spent the long hours of the ship's passing in a form of play with the sober and serious Robert Semple. "Smiling up into the serious face beneath the white cork helmet, immaculate white linen enfolded me. 'My home is in your arms, Robert,' I said. 'I need none other.' "[42]

After encountering a typhoon, their ship berthed at the harbor of the mountain that was Hong Kong, arriving a decade after the Boxer rebellion. In 1910, Hong Kong was a gaily bannered city, elongated in opposite directions between the mountains and the sea and offering to the Semples all the complexities that were associated with a cross-cultural experience.

"When in the Occident," Aimee recalled, "one sees the Orient through rose-hued glasses, considering largely the romance, travel, picturesque scenes, cherry blossoms, lotus and magnolia, delicately painted vases and tea served in frail chinaware on teakwood tables inlaid with ivory and mother-of-pearl. These things were in evidence, but for Robert and me, life in China was to be a very grim reality."[43]

Bewildering as a foreign culture could be to a newly married, ex-Canadian, nineteen-year-old farm girl, Aimee did not rest easily or sit idly by. She remembered both her early stress and Robert's quick humor—an intuitive devise he readily employed when times were hard.

A missionary's wife who spent time with the Semples in their early days in Hong Kong remembered how loving and supportive Robert was of Aimee. At times Aimee would long to return home, but always Robert was there to provide assurances that everything was going to be all right. "She [Aimee] wanted to go home," recalled the missionary, "and he [Robert] would say, 'come here'; he'd sit in the chair and hold out his arms to her and he'd say, 'come home,' to her." Aimee, however, remained "fussy and figety."[44]

This missionary's wife, who often saw Robert as he walked to town, noted his exceptional character. "If you ever saw a man full of the Spirit of God, you saw one when you saw Robert. He was the most precious child of God I ever saw. His life spoke just as he walked to town but he would walk so quietly, you could tell he was thinking about heavenly things more than the earthly…I never saw anybody just quite like him. He was the most saintly person I ever saw."[45]

While Robert's missionary passion led him to foreign-language study and prayer, Aimee, in addition to learning Chinese, concerned herself with the practical matters of running a household. The reality of the heat and unsanitary conditions imposed themselves rudely and harshly upon her fairyland concept of missionary home life. Aimee discovered a row of empty flats offered at a "ridiculously low figure." Because the Semples were non-European, the reason for the vacancies soon became apparent. They were considered to be haunted. Undaunted, Aimee selected the "most airy of the lot." The flat itself opened upon a court of a Hindu temple, and the overhanging balcony jutted above a well-worn path to the international burial grounds that were named "Happy Valley." Her most vivid recollection of living there was that of being curled-up in a hammock that Robert had hung for her while rats roamed underneath, accompanied by "the eternal monotone of temple tom-toms and chanting priests. Visually, innumerable [funeral] processions past [*sic*] my portal."[46]

Aimee, however, at the outset of her missionary endeavors, revealed a marked sensitivity to the cultural differences that separated Westerners from the Chinese. Rapidly, her stereotype of the Chinese as "lowly, truck gardening people" was transformed to an appreciation of them as "quick-minded, serious students and keen of perception."[47] Aimee repeatedly sided with the Chinese in their contempt for the Americans in their country and their association of America with Christianity.

Happy Valley Cemetery fulfilled another function for the Semples. It soon became a free place for leisure and reflection:

When the steaming humidity of the day would be too much, we would trudge up there, sit on the grass and drink in each breath of fresh air, and admire the surroundings, such wealth and profusion of flowers... At times I found it a lovely place to walk amid the quiet green, away from the hard glare of daylight, a haven where angel statues spread their marble wings above me. Little did I think that the dear form which upheld me in its strong arms during most of my walks would rest one day in the near future amid this beauty.[48]

Whether or not it was because Robert had a premonition of his imminent death, he did tell his expectant wife, four months earlier, that he seriously doubted he would ever return to America. His concerns were immediate, pragmatic, and somewhat prophetic, as evidenced by his self-understanding of his ministry. "Just think," Robert told Aimee, "every third baby born in the world is Chinese. One third of the world's population is Chinese, every third funeral is that of a Chinese. What a mighty task lies before Christianity and the Church of Christ...I believe that when the master comes, I will rise to meet him from Chinese soil, my arms laden with yellow pearls won for Him here."[49]

After a month or two of work in Hong Kong, Robert felt called to minister in the Portuguese settlement of Macao, an island at the mouth of the Canton River, opposite Hong Kong. Leased by the Portuguese in 1557, Macao, on the western bank of the Pearl River estuary in southwestern China, was the oldest permanent European possession in the Orient. Its total land area covered six square miles, and the Chinese accounted for about ninety-five percent of its population. On this small island, in a new mission station, Robert realized more success, having made "some promising Christian converts."[50]

The heat, and the "unmentionable methods" by which the Chinese fertilized their gardens forever interrupted their lives together. "I was not warned, until too late," wrote Aimee, "of the danger of eating lettuce, celery, tomatoes, and other vegetables and fruits uncooked."[51] Malaria raged, and they were both stricken with the Eastern fever. Between bouts of high fever, followed by intervening chills, they stumbled across the floor caring for each other, with the caregiver being the one who felt the strongest at the given moment. Removed by missionary friends from their island of tragedy, they were taken back to the city from where they started. They were then transported to the English Hospital of Matilda, built especially for missionaries, where care was given free of charge. Robert, the weaker one, made the ascent to the hospital with the use of a stretcher and jogging coolies; Aimee by funicular railway. She would later remember separate wards for men and women, her separation from Robert, white sheets and enamel beds, and a doctor's interrogation about her husband's prior diet. On August 12, 1910, Robert and Aimee celebrated their second wedding anniversary through an exchange of notes carried by a kindly nurse.

At the end of a week in the hospital, the physician in charge allowed Aimee to visit her husband. She found him white and thin, his eyes bluer and larger than she had ever seen them, his fingers between the pages of his well-worn Bible; the one she remembered seeing in his hand on the night she first met him. They talked in whispers. Robert mentioned his concern about her being left alone. Aimee recalled that while she was talking to him, in a comforting way, and "attempting to dispel the fear and doubt in his heart and mind, a gray look seemed to slowly overshadow his face. It was as though some great, gray bird had flown across the sky outside the window and thrown its shadow upon him."[52] A nurse intervened, feeling that Robert was weakening.

They said goodnight. Aimee remembered his saying that he would see her in the morning. She, returning to the women's ward, tried in vain to sleep, but was staring into the darkness while listening to the irregular breathing of the other women patients. A terrible premonition swept over her. Around midnight, a bright light burned through the window that she knew to be beside Robert's bed. The night nurse walked down the corridor that connected the two wards. Aimee was summoned to her husband's bed. When told he was "sinking fast," she remembered reasoning, "Death—O, surely not; it couldn't be....I had never seen anyone die. I was not yet twenty years of age, and a way out here on the opposite side of the globe from the Mother who had always shielded and protected me from every wind that blew."[53]

Robert died: neither his wife's fears of abandonment and aloneness nor the attending physician's heroics were able to save him. Aimee collapsed on the floor, rising later to kiss, for the last time her husband's forehead. Biblical words came to mind, she said, "The Lord giveth and the Lord taketh away"[54] Strong and bitter words, hardly words of comfort and consolation.

She was sent back to bed and woke the next day from a fitful sleep. Had it all been just a bad dream? Soon a nurse appeared in her room and pulled down the shades. But the nurse could not hide the sounds of men bearing a burden. "I knew it was the body of my husband—and each footfall seemed as a stone falling on my wounded heart. How could I stand it here, with Robert gone—friendless, penniless, tired?"[55]

CHAPTER THREE

Going to Nineveh by Way of Tarshish: A Pentecostal Prophetess

Now the word of the Lord came to Jonah…saying, "Go at once to Nineveh, that great city, and cry out against it"…But Jonah set out to flee to Tarshish from the presence of the Lord. He went down to Joppa, and found a ship going to Tarshish: so he paid his fare and went on board to go with them to Tarshish, away from the presence of the Lord.

—Jonah 1:1-3

The Christian churches have never denied that the gifts of the Spirit are poured out on men and women alike. But in the second and third centuries rising Episcopal power struggled to suppress the autonomous power of prophets. The historical ministry of bishops, as keepers of the keys and discerners of spirits, claimed the right to judge and control the occasional ministry of prophets and prophetesses. It routinized the power of the Spirit as automatically transmitted through apostolic succession and thus illegitimized any prophecy not under Episcopal control.

Nevertheless, the phenomenon of independent prophets and prophetesses does not disappear from popular Christianity…In the left-wing sects of the Reformation is a new appearance of groups who define the free prophetic Spirit as the true author of Christian ministry….The Spirit is no discriminator among persons on the basis of gender but can empower whomever it will. 'Ministry is proven by its gifts, not by its credentials.'

—Rosemary Radford Ruether

Religious traditions that place a strong emphasis on the "word" as the source of divine authority have been described as particularly masculine in orientation, whereas those that privilege the more mystical elements of religious faith, like that of personal revelation, are seen as more feminine.

—Susan Juster

Have you ever had," asked Aimee, "a secret tucked away in the closet of your Christian experience which you shrank from exposing to the sunlight of public gaze and criticism—a spot... where somewhere on your spiritual anatomy [was] so sore that the very thought of its being touched by a curious, probing finger made you wince?"

> A certain period of your life which you would a little rather not have generally known or discussed,...Have you, in telling your experience, been tempted to take a hop, skip and a jump over deviations from the straight and narrow path of God's best and perfect will for you? Have you felt like leaping over and omitting, when telling your Christian experience, the things which should have been omitted in real life?—Well, that has just been my case exactly.[1]

That is how Aimee chose to interpret the next six years of her life, without Robert, and, to a certain extent, as she perceived it, without God. Of her years alone and of her subsequent second marriage she seldom spoke other than to say they were years of "backsliding"—years on the boat going to "Tarshish" instead of heading toward "Nineveh"— which was ultimately, for her, Los Angeles.

Following Robert's burial, held in the afternoon of August 19, 1910, exactly one week after their second wedding anniversary, Aimee received a letter from two sisters in the Pentecostal movement in Chicago who had felt led a month earlier to put sixty dollars in an envelope and send it to her. Their unexpected funds paid the burial expenses for her missionary husband. No lasting memorial was erected for Robert at the time, but Aimee's early preaching became something of a living memorial to his memory.

Years later, when Angelus Temple was built, the stained-glass window nearest the altar—the Gethsemane window—had Robert Semple's name upon it; a continual reminder to Aimee of her tall, handsome, Irish evangelist with a heart of gold. Before her later audiences in Angelus Temple, she would recall in story form his presence and power upon her life. To all who attended, it was obvious and apparent that the torch of her love for Robert would follow her to the grave. No subsequent love would ever be described by Aimee as "triumphant, powerful and elemental...surging and taking possession of me like a young giant set free."[2] As in her earlier vision, she would continue walking steadily into the light, but she would walk alone. It was the most bitter irony of her life that her love was lavished only upon congregations at a safe distance and that for the majority of her life when the lights went out, she went home alone.

Five weeks after Robert's death, on September 17, 1910, as a "hurricane was shrieking its cry of loneliness over the storm swept city as if in tune with the empty desolation in my own heart,"[3] Aimee, a nineteen-year-old widow, gave birth to her first child in the same hospital in which her husband had died.

Her daughter was named Roberta Star because, Aimee said, "like the star of sunrise my child was born to me…. My star of Hope rose in the East, harbinger of a new day, messenger of joy and peace. I named her Roberta Star Semple—Roberta in memory of my husband; Star because it was as such she came to shine from out of my darkened sky, bringing a new meaning to life and to a lonely heart something for which to hope."[4] When Roberta Star was six weeks old, Aimee took her to visit her father's grave. She carefully placed Roberta on Robert's grave and then she knelt down at his graveside as if it were an altar and began weeping and seeking answers.

The missionaries were no longer helpful. The men, especially, talked of "tight budgets," her "lack of experience," and how China was "no place for a lone woman with a child."[5] And the missionary wives would glance at Roberta—"just a wispy mite of a thing," weighing four pounds at birth, and tell Aimee to "take your baby and go home—where she'll have a better chance to live in a healthier climate."[6]

She was surrounded at the altar of Robert's grave by many smaller gravesites, all bearing silent testimony that sudden death was no respecter of age. She began speaking to Robert's grave, hoping beyond all hope that his once-guiding wisdom would come forth and help her unlock her new prison door. Finally, at Happy Valley, she began to sense some direction and after having received money from Minnie, she then shortly set sail for San Francisco on the *Empress of China*.

One of the last recollections a missionary's wife in China had of this young widow was of Aimee bundling up Roberta and taking her along with her to a missionary home, and then throwing herself across a bed and sobbing, "My Robert, my Robert."[7] As Aimee began to sail home with Roberta, two other lives were waiting to converge with her on the East Coast, in New York City, and together they would form an irregular triangle of persons destined to make modern American religious history. One was her mother, Minnie Kennedy; the other was a twenty-year-old man from Providence, Rhode Island: Harold Stewart McPherson.

Harold McPherson was born May 5, 1890, in Providence. William Stuart McPherson, Harold's father, was from Nova Scotia. William had immigrated as a young man to the United States and had worked as a fisherman until the high seas of a terrifying storm persuaded him of the value of different work. In Providence, on solid ground, he worked as a meat packer. Annie Hamlett, Harold's mother, was born in 1865. Her father, Henry H.

Harold Stewart McPherson (used by permission of the International Church of the Foursquare Gospel, Heritage Department).

Hamlett, was an inventor by trade and built the first merry-go-round and Ferris wheel, known as a "Fang-Dang-Go," in America after seeing a photograph in a German newspaper. Some of his later creations were put on permanent display in a New England museum.

Life was rather uneventful for Harold, the second child of the McPherson family, until the financial panic of 1907. When he was seventeen, he quit school to help support his family. He quickly found work for the *Saturday Evening Post* as a salesman. Saving two and a half cents for every copy he sold at five cents, Harold soon had four hundred regular customers, his own sales crew, and was selling more than two thousand copies each week. Impressing the "right people at the right time" with his potential, Harold left the *Post* to become a "runner," delivering checks between city banks for a clearing house.[8]

Meeting Aimee Elizabeth Semple was for Harold McPherson an act of God. Perhaps what led to a temporary bond of kindred spirits and their union of marriage was their common experience of conversion through revivalism. Like Aimee, Harold had a conversion experience while listening to an evangelist. In 1907, the evangelist Gypsy Smith visited Providence to hold a week of revival meetings. Harold along with a friend attended the meetings and said, "That day a most wonderful thing took place in both our lives. We were both saved and a short time later we joined and were baptized in the Pearl Baptist Church."[9]

After his marriage to and divorce from Aimee, Harold would show up in the newspaper pages from time to time as the ex-husband of the famous woman evangelist. His caricature, hardly flattering, was usually that of a "worldly" grocery clerk. Harold had, in fact, considered the ministry as a vocation and, more likely than not, his problems with his future spouse were more related to differing temperaments and Aimee's continued devotion to Robert than to his lack of religious conviction.

Long before he met Aimee, Harold, along with his friend Wesley Lowrey, had become "very interested and active in church work [by] becoming personal workers in visiting the sick in hospitals and Sunday School work."[10]

They made plans to enter the ministry together. The normal practice at that time, for those who had experienced conversion during exposure to revivalism and consequently wanted to become ministers, was to attend a bible school to receive practical ministerial training. Their plan was to attend the William Jewel College Bible School in Missouri to receive this training.

But as was to occur for the remainder of his life, destiny intervened, and Harold began his life's journey as a background figure. "My friend, Wesley Lowrey, went at the appointed time but a sudden sickness and operation to my mother caused me to put my plans aside for a short time till Mother recovered. This took a much longer [time] than was expected. I finally gave up this opportunity [Bible school], drifting back into secular life."[11]

Drifting back into secular life to obtain money for doctor bills led Harold to the Narragansett Hotel in Providence. As a bellman he made "fantastic tips from the flamboyant show business personalities who came to town— often as much as fifty dollars a night."[12] Soon he was promoted to night manager.

Seeking medical specialists in New York City for his mother, Harold moved the family there from Providence in the summer of 1910 and found work at the Belmont Hotel on 42nd Street. After meeting Mr. Kuhn, the inventor of the "Kuhn Checking System," Harold next became the checker comptroller at Callazzi's Restaurant: "an elegant brownstone mansion with many private dining rooms and a fashionable clientele" located near 23rd Street and Fifth Avenue.[13] Harold found housing, renting a first-floor walk-up: a "big parlour apartment" with "three good clean likeable fellows" on the corner of 13th Street and Sixth Avenue."[14] He recalled getting together after work with his roommates: "We all enjoyed singing all the popular songs of the 1900s, the Good Years."[15]

And it was here where he was destined to meet Aimee, and then forever after their divorce be known as "Aimee's ex-husband," owing to the fact that Aimee never reverted back to "Semple," or "Kennedy," but kept Harold's surname as her own for the rest of her life.

Minnie Kennedy, now forty, moved to New York City in the fall of 1910 to begin what she thought of as her "real life"—with the Salvation Army and without James. After Aimee left the farm, Minnie had decided to work full-time for the Army, at least full-time for most of each year. Except for the harvest time, James no longer really needed her. Since she felt that her real life had only been interrupted by marriage and farm chores, Minnie in mid-life was ready to begin again.

The Army's pioneer "lassies" whom Minnie had known as young girls, before she had met and married James, were now "important officers and officials at the National Headquarters in New York. Through correspondence, 'her sisters' encouraged her to join their ranks again, knowing that she would 'be wonderful at organization work.'"[16] Minnie agreed, and, so three lives converged in the winter of 1910: Minnie from the Ingersoll farm, Harold from Providence, and Aimee Elizabeth from Hong Kong.

Aimee remembered returning home from China feeling that she resembled

> a wounded little bird, and my bleeding heart was constantly pierced with curious questions from well-meaning people who could not see the will of God in our call to China, and who felt that there must be a mistake somewhere, either in Robert's sudden death or my return home. I could not answer them, not being able to see the will of God in all this myself....Oh! How I longed for someone who would understand or put their arms about me and help me at this critical moment of my life, and this was just the time that the Lord permitted those I loved best to seem to draw aside the arms that had been before so strong and dependable, causing a little curtain of reserve to drop between us, leaving me on the outside with my baby...It was just at the time of my greatest perplexity, when I had begun to lose out spiritually and wander away from the Lord, and was longing to make a home for the baby, that I married again.[17]

Aimee, through her omission, spoke volumes about her second marriage to Harold McPherson.

Coming home on the *Empress of China*, Aimee discovered the kindness of strangers through the generosity of the ship's passengers—a characteristic of future parishioners. Explaining their gifts given to her and to Roberta, she contended, as she would with the building of Angelus Temple, that, "These people gave those little gifts not because I had asked them—which I had not—but because God had touched their hearts and shown them the need."[18] Her ability to touch the heart was already becoming apparent. From San Francisco, she crossed the bay by ferry to Oakland and then took the train, which she described as "thundering East." All Aimee recalled was the "ceaseless clicking car wheels" asking the eternal "What'll you do? What'll you do? ... Yes, what would I do? Where would I take up the broken threads of my life? This one thing I knew—God had his hand on my life, and would direct my path!"[19]

Aimee rather aptly would describe her life to her students and parishioners as one made up of "valleys and peaks." No other "valley" experience would compare with the six years spent after leaving the Happy Valley Cemetery, the years before her own ministry began. It was by far her longest and deepest "valley experience," her time alone without Robert, without God, and without direction. "The loom of life seemed then to be but a tangled maze whose colorings had suddenly plunged from mountain tops of sunlit glory to the depths of a seemingly endless valley of bewildering gloom."[20] It was also at this time that she lost a sense of warmth and support from the church. Its telltale scar upon her life would be her ability to have an influence upon the unchurched, which was, in fact, in many ways her most significant contribution to the history of American Christianity.

Going east on the train, Aimee did not know where to settle. She shuffled between Chicago, where Robert's friends were, and New York City, where her mother lived. New York finally won out, possibly due to the convenience of having her mother there to help tend to Roberta's needs. And Chicago was full of memories—memories of Robert.

Minnie Kennedy once again took charge of her daughter's life, providing structure along with firm affection. She turned the spacious front room of her apartment over to Aimee and her granddaughter. She announced that there was to be no moping about—that God had a purpose for Aimee's life in New York City, as well as in China. In just a week's time, Aimee—in a borrowed Salvation Army uniform—was serving lunch at a midtown Manhattan rescue mission and, along with her mother, caring for her baby. In January 1911, Aimee was transferred to a new job with the Army—this time to the theater district on Broadway—to collect money for the organization between the acts of the plays. On Sundays, Minnie and Aimee attended Salvation Army worship services together.

Aimee's relationships with her mother and daughter were, however, not enough. She longed for something, and someone, more. The void that Robert had filled returned. The theater district was an especially lonely place. She and Robert had gone to China as independent Pentecostal missionaries; now she was working for an organization that served the religious needs of her mother better than it did those of her own. The army was too regimented, too disciplined, too formal for one of Aimee's temperament, but for Minnie it was a perfect match.

Aimee felt more alone than ever: "Night after night I watched all the elegant young couples arrive at the theater arm in arm, laughing gaily and departing after the show, happy in each other's company. The whole world seemed to move two by two."[21] Aimee's aloneness on cold winter nights in deserted theater lobbies accounted for her ability in later years to relate to the loneliness rampant in the boom years associated with the growth of

Los Angeles, the kind of loneliness that author John Fante described in his book *Ask the Dust* in the following way: "Faces with the blood drained away, tight faces, worried, lost. Faces like flowers torn from their roots and stuffed into a pretty vase, the colors draining fast."[22]

Aimee's loneliness also left her vulnerable and open to the possibility of meeting someone outside the ranks of the Salvation Army. And while she was in that receptive state, she met Harold Stewart McPherson.

Harold, in later years, recalled to Roberta how he met her mother:

> Coming home one evening it was raining and I stood on 6th Avenue awaiting the rain to abate a little. I was on the corner…looking at the brown house where I lived with…three boys …when out of the heavenly blue I heard a sweet voice say, "Would you like to share the protection of my umbrella?" And before one could say Jack Sprat, your mother and I were walking on a cloud in the rain south down 6th Avenue as if we had known each other all our lives. She told me about your father having come to Canada.[23]

When Harold met Aimee, she still wore Robert's wedding band. Immediately attracted to her, Harold was greatly relieved when he learned that she was a widow.

Aimee's romance with Harold was not as impetuous and as blinding as the one with Robert had been. Robert had changed and challenged her life; Harold would accompany her life and do it well. What the relationship lacked in intensity was compensated for by Harold's consistency. Night after night, after Callazzi's closed, Harold would rush uptown on the subway and appear in the shadows of the theater lobbies, watching over her while she extended her tambourine to solicit contributions. To Harold, she seemed sadly and oddly out of place. He was impressed by her dignity and charm. He found himself wanting to provide care and protection for her. When the final crowds had left the theater lobbies, Harold, at a discreet distance, followed Aimee home, unaware that her Salvation Army uniform was protection enough. Life with Aimee, for Harold, would always be lived at a distance. Early on in their courtship, however, he was convinced he could close the gap.

When Harold finally mustered the courage to tell Aimee of his intentions toward her, she was startled. With her sense of independence, having traveled halfway around the world unescorted and unprotected, she didn't feel that she needed Harold for anything except as an antidote for her loneliness. She finally agreed to let him see her safely home. It was weeks before Harold asked her out for an actual date. It was an offer Aimee couldn't refuse. Choosing the night of the first full moon, Harold suggested that they go ice-skating in Central Park. Aimee accepted and for the first time in months felt like a youthful woman—alive and radiant—no longer just a distressed, penniless, missionary widow.

Bashful and fearful, Harold allowed the music of the era to subtly convey his intentions to Aimee:

> I was afraid I would lose her if I told her how deeply I cared…it was actually Tin Pan Alley that came to my rescue. The songs in 1910… said everything I dared not say; I was smart enough to let them say it for me. We skated to "Let Me Call You Sweetheart," dined to the music of "I'm Falling in Love with Someone." Even the newsboys we passed whistled "I Want a Girl Just Like the Girl that Married Dear Old Dad." It was a good year for bashful young men. There were other songs, of course—like "Alexander's Rag Time Band" and "Come Josephine in My Flying Machine"—but they were not the ones I hummed in her ear as we skated in the moonlight, and I waited for the right moment to declare my feelings.[24]

Aimee responded to it all with an unequal measure of acceptance, guilt, and confusion. She enjoyed the world-famous Hippodrome, enjoyed viewing the spectacular stage shows with live camels, desert sandstorms, and the shimmering, spangled girls that vanished, seemingly forever, into the stage water. With Harold, she saw the *High Hat Harry* actors at the Broadway Automat after their performances, "resplendent with silk hats, velvet capes and silver-headed canes." It was a new and exciting urban world unfolding before "country girl Aimee."[25]

Roberta, years after her mother's death, and by then a mature woman herself, perceptively analyzed this period in her mother's life that Aimee herself found difficult to explain, other than to say she was "backslidden" and "at a very low ebb, spiritually."

> She was dazzled by the bright lights of Broadway, the gaiety of the theater crowds, the silken gowns of the beautiful women so different from the drab, practical costumes of the farm wives and missionaries she knew. She thrilled to the excitement of this new world.
>
> Yet she was distressed. How could she be almost "actually happy?" Was she drifting away from her dedication to God and his work? She had pledged herself to carry on Robert's unfinished work; now she was actually frittering away her free time on frivolous pleasures! Was she backsliding; was she disloyal to Robert's memory; had she any right to be so carefree, even for a few hours?

Confusion and guilt overwhelmed her. If God had a plan for her, why didn't He show it to her…open a door of real service? Soliciting for the Salvation Army did not seem enough; there must be more. What was God's plan for the rest of her life? All she knew for certain was that she was alone, penniless, with no money of her own, and a small baby to somehow support. Robert was gone; Harold was here, kind, friendly and devoted. Could she be responding to his quiet affection? How could she be so disloyal? Perhaps this is part of what she had meant when, many years later, she told her congregation at Angelus Temple, "I was at a very low ebb, spiritually."[26]

Part of the problem for Aimee had nothing to do with Harold McPherson. It was the beginning of her own struggle, which only by midlife did she master, to reconcile her sense of spirituality with a secular culture. Like Moses fleeing Pharaoh's burning Egyptian sands, so early Pentecostals sought to escape the threat and menace of American secular culture. Sectarianism and other worldliness dominated their world view. Aimee, more than any other figure in the movement, sought to reconcile and bring together in her temple both the sacred and the profane. Ironically, years later, after Angelus Temple was built, Sarah Comstock in *Harper's Monthly Magazine* would mention the similarities between Aimee's temple in Los Angeles and the Hippodrome in New York City.[27]

Aimee would fight for the rest of her life for a delicate balance between the flames of fanaticism in Pentecostalism and the cold formalism of mainline Protestanism. Religion, according to Aimee, should be joyous and warm having an effect upon secular culture, not retreating from it. Since her own theological vision had not yet emerged, she had fallen victim while living in New York City to what her mother and organized religion thought about how she should conduct herself. In reality, it was her "low ebb, spiritually."

Harold's increasing dilemma with Aimee had much to do with his expectations as her future husband. Like the majority of men of his generation, Harold envisioned a woman's role as simple and uncomplicated: she was to be a wife and a mother while he maintained the traditional role of provider. But he also knew that Aimee was different. She was special, and he knew that he was reluctant to share that specialness if it infringed upon his privacy. Just as an actress or other public figure did, Aimee would, in time, become more comfortable in front of five thousand people—until the lights went down and she went home alone again.

Neither Minnie nor Harold were willing to accept her in this role. Her future son with Harold, Rolf, was the only person to successfully bridge that divide. He would, with grace and the maturity of years, take up where Robert Semple left off. Robert and Rolf were Aimee's most stabilizing influences. Fittingly, they bracketed her ministry: one at the beginning of it; the other seeing her through to its conclusion.

Help for Harold in his courtship of Aimee came unexpectedly from Minnie Kennedy herself. This is what Aimee made reference to when she wrote, "and this was just the time that the Lord permitted those I loved best to seem to draw aside the arms that had been before so strong and dependable."[28] Minnie's help for Harold came in the form of her disapproval of him, which proved to Aimee that only Harold really cared. Promenading on Fifth Avenue with Harold on her arm and Roberta in the baby carriage, Aimee began to believe that they did in fact make a handsome couple, though she never made mention of Harold's quiet good looks.

Every day Harold consistently reminded her that her whole life was ahead of her and that she could not remain alone and unprotected forever. Resolving the conflict by recounting Harold's virtues, Aimee finally convinced herself, if not her mother, that Harold was the one for her. It was a reluctant survival decision, free of the joy and spontaneity that accompanied the decision to be with Robert. It also carried with it a stipulation that would ultimately lead to Aimee and Harold's separation and render their union asunder. Aimee's conversion experience with Robert had changed and channeled her life. She knew that she could never discard that or put aside her sense of being called. When Aimee said yes to Robert, she also said yes to God, so she stipulated to Harold that, "if God ever calls me back into His service, you must agree never to stand in the way."[29]

Harold promptly agreed, perhaps with smug confidence that this peculiar obsession of Aimee's would simply go away, especially with the joy and comforts of the home he intended to provide. They were both twenty-one years of age and breaking into the realities of America's growing urban culture and sophistication together.

Wisely, Harold suggested elopement for their wedding. Aimee selected Chicago because she "had good friends there."[30] Boarding the train, Harold refrained from asking too many questions, content to know that he had finally won the woman of his dreams. Nothing else really mattered to him at the time.

It was a strained and strange wedding. Instead of riding in a beribboned horse-drawn bridal carriage with parental blessing, Harold, Aimee, and Roberta were runaways on a Chicago-bound train. They arrived exhausted and located a minister through the telephone directory, seeking his sanctioning of their vows. In short order, through a modest ceremony in the parsonage parlor, Aimee Semple became, on February 28, 1912, Aimee Semple McPherson: both a future household recognized name and an American citizen. Harold located a bright, furnished apartment and a job that paid well. Aimee contacted her Chicago friends. Immediately, they insisted that she come back to the mission. They wanted to see Robert's baby daughter. They wanted to hear all about her prior missionary work in China.

Harold didn't object at first, but the demands increased. Before he knew it, Aimee was involved in church work three or more nights a week. She was playing the piano, teaching Sunday school, and telling the women of the mission what *not* to send to missionaries. She was careful to point out that missionaries didn't need "worn out clothes," because they "have enough of those already."[31]

Harold began to resent eating hurried dinners so that Aimee could rush off to church. He purchased a wicker baby stroller for Roberta with the hope that the three of them would use it for Sunday-morning outings in the park. Aimee felt guilty about missing church, so Harold decided it was time for a drastic course of action—a move back East. If Aimee started spending time with his mother and his sister, he was convinced that she would become "normal" and settle down into being Mrs. H.S. McPherson, instead of a missionary-evangelist's wife. Harold had high hopes when they visited Minnie Kennedy in New York, especially when she finally extended her blessing at a more formal wedding ceremony. But Aimee was becoming more and more miserable:

> Disturbed and troubled in my heart... I turned again to the world, endeavoring to stifle my longings ...It was such a relief to be able to stay away from the meetings...I was torn between the two conflicting forces. Some of the saints saw me backsliding and drifting into the world... When my husband received an invitation from his mother to come to her home in Rhode Island, I was willing to consent to board the boat in my endeavor to flee unto Tarshish from the presence of the Lord.

Providence, Rhode Island, was "Tarshish." The years that she and Harold spent there were her most unhappy and unproductive years. Like Roberta, who arrived after her father's death, so Aimee's only son, Rolf, came after his mother's near-death experiences in Providence. Like his half sister before him, his birth not only proved redemptive for his mother, he was also the sole survivor of their union together.

For a time, the couple lived with Harold's parents. This arrangement was short-lived, with Aimee briefly noting the outcome in this way, "Seeing my unhappy, melancholy state, my mother-in-law advised us to rent and furnish a home of our own, saying that the work would occupy my mind and keep me from thinking so much about myself…With the help of our parents and our own earnings, a well-furnished home was made, containing all that heart could wish…"[33]

Although life materially was much better with Harold McPherson than it had been with Robert Semple, the young couple had it none to easy, and Aimee returned to New York City and the Salvation Army to augment Harold's income.

> When Harold's money ran short, I went to New York…as a solicitor for the Salvation Army. Dutifully I walked the beat between Columbus Circle and the Battery…Restaurants and bars where tipsy men gave liberally became my hourly haunt while soaking my blistered feet, I counted the receipts of the day…[being permitted to keep half for the needs of her family and] I continued this means of augmenting our livelihood, until shortly before my son, Rolf McPherson, was born.[34]

On March 23, 1913, Rolf Potter Kennedy McPherson was born. He was for both parents their only son. His parents were twenty-two years of age, and his father's occupation was listed as "clerk" upon his birth certificate. The certificate also listed Harold's parents' address as the home address. It was after Rolf's birth that the McPherson family moved to their own house, at 10 Foster Street, with a convent on the other side of the street, which seemed to Aimee to be a glaring reminder that she was neglecting her calling.

Rolf's birth, at Dr. Potter's Hospital in Providence, was a difficult one. He did not breathe at first and was plunged into alternate tubs of hot and cold water until from the shock he cried and so lived. Aimee encountered medical problems with the delivery, "which eventually led to an operation which made it impossible for her to have any more children."[35] That summer, Harold leased a house at the shore with another couple. While the men commuted to work, the women were free to enjoy their children and the ocean. Aimee played with the children, swam in the ocean, and strolled the beach, but she "seemed oddly moody and restless."[36] Harold's mother assured her worried son that Aimee was only going through what she called the "post-baby blues" and that when Aimee regained her strength, everything would be fine.

Aimee tried her best to snap out of her depression. Married life was becoming much the same as her New York experience. The church bells across the street, ringing hourly, were of no help, only a continual reminder that she, Aimee, had been dedicated to God for a special purpose and a life of service. She knew it was not to be found in mopping floors and dusting furniture, just as it had not been found in theater lobbies soliciting money for the Salvation Army. Aimee threw herself into household chores with a whole-hearted vengeance:

> A dozen times a day, I would look into my mirror, tearfully, and take myself to task for my restlessness. "Now see here, this will never do! What right have you to fret and pine like this? Just see those shining, pol-ished floors, covered with soft, thick rugs. Just look at the richly carved mahogany parlor furniture, and the big comfortable beds…Why aren't you glad to have a home like this for the babies, as any other mother would? This is what you wanted." Time after time I would try to shake off the lethargy and depression which engulfed me by keeping as busy as possible. Such a fever of restlessness came upon me that it seemed as though I must wear the polish off the furniture by dusting them so often.[37]

Years later, Aimee remembered how dutiful and attentive Harold had been to both her and to the children. "My husband, showing no partiality between the two [Roberta and Rolf], trotted about the house and garden bearing one baby on each shoulder. As for me, I was a constant problem." The noise of the tea kettle bothered her, the "little ones" were implored to talk in whispers, and "the sunshine was an unbearable torment; so I lived behind closed shutters and drawn blinds."[38]

Aimee had far more material comfort with Harold than she had ever had with Robert. But the sense of having a spiritual purpose and plan was missing. She started excusing herself from the inner spiritual demands upon her life on the grounds that she was a woman, a mother, and a wife. "Oh, Lord, You know that I cannot go. Here are the two babies and here is the home, and here is the husband, who has not the baptism [the Pen-tecostal teaching of the Baptism of the Holy Spirit as evidenced by glos-solalia] and is not even seeking it. I will work here in the local mission, and that will do." Aimee's bargaining with God didn't work. "The answer still came back, clear from heaven: 'Go! Do the work of an evangelist; Preach the Word! The time is short; I am coming soon'"[39]

She knew her calling was clear and precise. But where would she fit in? With what church? As a woman? Harold at this point had become reli-giously lackadaisical. She found herself feeling as alone as ever before, but with the added burdens and responsibilities of two small children and a husband. She found some solace in her attendance of the High Church ser-vices at St. Stephen's Episcopal Church in Providence. It is very likely that her love for and adoption of ornate vestments in her later ministry, entirely out of place among the Pentecostal clergy, was acquired during her visits to St. Stephen's. After Angelus Temple was built, Aimee conceded that the Episcopal Church was for her "the most perfect in the world."[40]

She was impressed with its openness to divine healing. She regretted that it made no allowance for women ministers. And she was convinced that she was called to preach. "Oh, don't you ever tell me that a woman cannot be called to preach the Gospel," she wrote years later. "If any man ever went through one-hundredth part of the hell on earth that I lived in, those months when [I was] out of God's will and work...they would never say that again."[41]

Like Jonah going to Tarshish, she needed a whale to get her to go to Nineveh. Her "whale" came in the form of sickness, surgical operations, and near death. It was the final decision in her bargaining with God. "I wonder if Jonah had nearly as rough a passage as I did when he ran away and disobeyed God. His trip was not as long as mine anyway...That great white whale, the operating table, had thrown me up on the shore...Foolish and impossible as the idea might seem, I was going to strike out for Nineveh, without a moment's hesitation."[42]

Her right to leave her wifely duties to become a Pentecostal preacher actually made sense to the socially conservative Pentecostals, because they would, like she, compare her experiences as a housewife to those of Jonah's drowning in the sea. Her sickness and the operating table corresponded with God's enigmatic whale by means of which the prophetess came to terms with her call. Aimee in this regard was already becoming a role model for other women to follow. As did hers, their stories would often require a sign to confirm they had a true calling, as with the Biblical prophets. In many cases, sickness and being near death became that sign.

Being a woman was no longer a good excuse to deny a religious calling, any more than had been Moses' lack of eloquence or Jeremiah's youth and inexperience. The structure of the emerging American Pentecostal movement was still flexible enough that it provided a welcoming place for its "prophesying daughters."[43]

"A marked feature of this 'latter day' outpouring is the Apostolate of women," declared an editorial in *The Weekly Evangel* in 1916. "If a woman gave birth to our Lord, why not [sic] her daughters take part in this great work? Men have hypocritically objected to women making themselves conspicuous in pulpit work... They did not push themselves to the front, God pulled them there. They did not take this ministry on themselves; God put it on them."[44]

In the spring of 1915, after three years of marriage to Harold, Aimee, alone one night and believing God was calling her back to ministry, telegraphed her mother for money. "At eleven o'clock [I] bundled my two babies inside [the taxicab] while the chauffeur piled the two suitcases on top, and away we sped to catch the midnight train for home and mother. To make a new start and begin all over again it seemed the most natural thing in the world to go back to the starting place from which I had set out before."[45]

Since her mother was back with James on the farm, it was back to Ingersoll, Ontario, that Aimee went, back to where seven years earlier she had said yes to God and yes to Robert. Shortly thereafter, Aimee Semple McPherson, the most famous woman minister of the twentieth century, began her ministry in her homeland of Canada. The beginning of her ministry was humble and hard.

CHAPTER FOUR

Tents and Tabernacles: Camping in Canaan's Happy Land

For I have not lived in an house…but have gone from tent to tent, and from one tabernacle to another.

—I Chronicles 17:5

I have left the land of bondage with its earthly treasures,
I've journeyed to a place where this is love on ev'ry hand;
I've exchanged a land of heartaches for a land of pleasure,
I'm camping, I'm camping in Canaan's happy land.

—E.M. Bartlett
"Camping in Canaan's Land"

For two years I have lived in a tent without even a board floor…(and) slept on a soldier's cot… That tent was my world. It meant far more to me than this temple means to me. That tent was my earthly all…It was my church.

—Aimee Semple McPherson
The Bridal Call

At Everybody's Tabernacle, Everybody's welcome,
Come and find the Savior there.
Your ev'ry need He'll meet for you,
for spirit, soul and body too,
In answer to believing pray'r.

—Unknown
"Everybody's Tabernacle"

As much as Harold Stewart McPherson loved his wife, he was incapable of comprehending the intensity of her calling and "her overwhelming sense of destiny."[1] Harold had not heard Aimee's inner voices. Her leaving devastated him. He gave notice to his employer and went to Canada in pursuit of his wife and two children. Arriving at the Kennedy farm, he found Rolf and Roberta, but no Aimee. "She's gone to a camp meeting in Berlin [now Kitchener]," Minnie told him, when he asked where Aimee was.[2]

Harold spent the night on the farm and found a new Aimee the next

Harold and Aimee, "camping in Canann's happy land (used by permission of the International Church of the Foursquare Gospel, Heritage Department).

day. She was as radiantly alive as she had been when they had first skated together under the full moon in Central Park, and she showed no sign of conflict about what she had done: about having left him and their marriage behind.

His wife's role in the Pentecostal camp meeting was a modest one. Aimee had arrived feeling spiritually out of sorts. "Instead of going to the platform of the big tent, that afternoon, I preferred to sit in the audience. I felt cold, out of the center of sunshine from the open heavens—not quite worthy."[3] After the sermon, she prayed at the altar, seeking forgiveness for her backslidden state. She felt it would take both time and effort, but more quickly than she had expected she sensed a state of forgiveness—a state she felt was confirmed when she began to ecstatically speak in other tongues. She knew then, beyond all doubt, that she was back "In the King's Glad Service."

Aimee asked the camp's evangelist, after the initial meeting had ended, what she could do to help in the services. Though she had never been domestically inclined, she nonetheless soon found herself, in her silk dress, staring at a mountain of dirty dishes in the sink in the cooking tent. "That couldn't be a stack of soiled dishes! Not that high! But it was! A mammoth pile in cold water, filmed with grease. And washing dishes was my pet aversion! But I was looking for something to do and here was plenty of it."[4] "Can you play the piano?" was the next question, and Aimee, with her rolling arpeggios, was soon adding new zest to the old hymns.

And when the male minister lost his voice and couldn't speak loudly enough to preach, Aimee filled in, making eleven converts at the end of the service. Near the end of her life, Aimee recalled that momentous moment in time:

> And thus it was that I preached my first sermon as an independent evangelist. I do not remember the text of the message. But I do recall that some eleven souls made their way to the altar....As I saw them coming down the aisles, such a wave of exultation swept over me that I was weak and dizzy from the sheer joy and glory of it....Standing there and looking down through swimming eyes at those first...converts, I did not know that they were but the advance guard for hundreds of thousands who would follow in their steps throughout the years of my life-long ministry.[5]

From the back of the tent Harold took it all in from a safe distance. When Aimee's voice rang out vibrant with inner fervor, he knew in a strange way that he had lost her forever. He did what he thought he had to, what he felt was his only recourse. He left, and on his way home he passed by the Kennedy farm, picked up Rolf, bribed the hired hand, and with his son went back to Providence. Aimee was frantic, especially when she began receiving letters with messages such as, "Come back home and act like a normal woman."[6]

Her response was, "If you love me, come and talk to me. I've tried to walk your way and failed...now you come and try my way. God has called me, and I must follow. If you love me, come and bring Rolf. We'll talk." Harold loved her; he came to her, and he brought Rolf.[7]

Aimee had moved on, this time with the certainty that there were "plenty of jobs to do in the King's Glad Service."[8] The camp evangelist's wife had asked her to assist in their forthcoming campaign in London, Ontario. At the close of the London meetings, she was also invited to conduct Bible meetings in a little hall called Victory Mission in Mount Forest. There were healings and conversions, but the best thing that happened for Aimee was when, "right in the midst of one of the meetings...my husband landed with his suitcase, to attend the meeting. So changed was I, so radiantly happy, so filled with the power of God and unction of the Holy Spirit, that he had to admit that this was indeed my calling and work in life. Before many hours had passed, he himself had received the baptism of the Holy Spirit, spoke in tongues and glorified God."[9]

Aimee's start at Mount Forest in August 1915 was small and meager, but it clearly established her ability to draw a crowd. She had been invited in the first place because none of the well-known male ministers, the "good preachers," would consider coming to such a small place as Victory Mission.

"A doll's church" is what Aimee thought when she first viewed the mission, situated between the bank and the print shop, on the town's only street. "As I stepped inside, I saw only a dozen chairs before a tiny platform…that afternoon, I worked diligently in my room, rather excitedly, preparing the first sermon of my first campaign!"[10]

That night, Aimee preached to two people and ten empty chairs. After the third night, this time with the attendance of two preachers and a congregation of two people, Aimee courageously asked her host pastor where the people were.

"This is it," she was told.

"That won't do," said Aimee, "I am going to get a crowd."[11]

Aimee had no idea how to get a crowd. But the budding actress intuitively remembered her mother's Salvation Army street meetings. She had, however, never seen anyone hold a street meeting alone, and once again, she was alone. Taking a chair from the mission as her only prop, Aimee went to the main street corner of Mount Forest, a block from the town hall, stood on it and began to pray. "Almost instantly, I heard approaching footsteps, then voices."[12]

The crowd that gathered wondered what was wrong with her. Was she in a trance? "At length, a curious finger poked me," remembered Aimee, "and I opened my eyes quickly. There was my crowd!…'Quick! Quick! Come with me!' Chair in hand, I fairly flew up the street, with the wondering crowd trailing close behind. Into the mission hall I sped, warning the usher as I hurried to the platform: 'As soon as the place is full, shut the doors; don't let anyone out!' I launched at once into my sermon, and I'm happy to say, no one tried to leave."[13]

The following night, the mission was filled to capacity, with many turned away. The farmers donated their lanterns to hang in the trees so that Aimee, preaching from her host's front porch, could see and be seen by the crowds that had gathered on the lawn.

Not only was Aimee's ability to get a crowd demonstrated at her first meeting in Mount Forest, but also her early attitude toward the financing of such endeavors. "At the end of my first week I was reminded that I had taken no collection. The next night I timidly took one. It was sixty-five dollars. I sat up almost all night watching it, I was so proud of it."[14]

Aimee's offering had been designated for her personal needs, but, as she would often do in the future, she used it for what she called "the Lord's work"—buying a used tent in a bag—a mistake she was never to make again.

After her solo debut at the Mount Forest meeting, Aimee and Harold decided to stay together, becoming independent Pentecostal evangelists. Together, they went back to the Kennedy farm at Ingersoll to share their plans with Minnie. Minnie, as always, was concerned with the practicality of such endeavors. She wanted to know if any church had invited them. Because the answer was no, Minnie proceeded with more interrogating questions, never receiving what she considered to be satisfactory answers. All she was told about their planning related to their proposed division of duties: that Harold would set up the preaching tent, while Aimee's task would be to prepare her sermons. They told her they would sleep on the road, in a smaller tent.

Minnie quickly declared that Roberta would stay with her, since "she was too frail for a gypsy kind of life."[15] Reluctantly, Aimee and Harold agreed that it would be easier with only one child.

"What about money?" asked Minnie.

"God will provide," Aimee answered.

"And a lot of hard work, Harold, mark my words," retorted Minnie.[16]

Together with Rolf they set out as independent Pentecostal evangelists. While Aimee studied and practiced preaching sermons, Harold began to learn all he could about tents, carpentry, block-and-tackle methods for hoisting heavy items, freight rates, and the best way to move a tent from one town to the next.

The couple went back to Providence in September 1915, "to dispose of our little store of earthly goods."[17] There they purchased a new 40-x-80-foot Gospel tent. Because it wasn't quite ready, they pitched their old tent on a bluff on June 1, 1916, overlooking Narragansett Bay because, Aimee insisted, "the breeze would be cool and the view magnificent!"[18]

With such a campsite selection, Aimee's early efforts at evangelization in America nearly became a complete fiasco. The bluff had more than gentle breezes. Strong winds blew across its surface from time to time, and on the third night of their ten-day meetings, the tent went down in a storm and was badly ripped. Together Harold and Aimee repaired the rips and tears, only to see the tent go down the following night. Once more, they sewed it back together, and once more the wind toppled it—this time beyond repair. Harold became discouraged and declared it was useless to try again. At that point, Harold decided to give up on evangelism.

"He had taken a position and returned to secular work," wrote Aimee, "but I knew that hundreds would be there for the night meeting. I could not manage that big tent alone, so with the help of a little boy, in the heat of the noon hour, we set to work."[19] Stringing ten camper tents end-to-end, Aimee successfully sheltered her first American audience with a canvas covering ten feet wide by one hundred and twenty feet long. She began her ministry in America with the feeling that "the enemy was still testing my faith and endeavoring to draw me back from the work, but thank God, my feet were kept from slipping…many precious souls wept their way to Jesus' feet and received the blessed Holy Spirit, the comforter whom Jesus sent."[20]

The truth is that if Aimee had not begun her ministry when she did, it is very likely that her impact upon the formative stages of the Pentecostal movement would have been lost forever. In four short years she would establish herself as the most visible woman minister in the largest Anglo-Pentecostal denomination. Had she remained in Providence as a dutiful housewife and mother, all would have been lost. Her sense of timing was critical for her success.

Leaving Providence, Aimee, once again alone, set out for Massachusetts, holding two meetings: one at the Montwaitee Camp Grounds in Framingham, and the other at the Holiness Camp Grounds on Onset Bay, Cape Cod. Near the end of the Montwaitee meeting, Aimee wrote that the Lord spoke to Harold in Providence "in three dreams, calling him to leave his secular work in the plant where he was employed and come and assist me with the tents."[21]

At the Onset Bay meeting, where the new tent was pitched for the first time, it appears that Pentecostalism was competing against other religious movements of the time, with Aimee noting that, "the war against spiritualism, Christian Science, and demon powers was hot and heavy."[22]

While still at Onset Bay, and while contemplating shipping her tent south for the winter, the word "corona" came to Aimee's mind. Since she was already contributing to various Pentecostal magazines, she thought the concept had something to do with the obtaining of a typewriter. A few days later, she received a letter from someone she described as a "Pentecostal saint," who was living in Corona, Long Island, New York. The unknown sister asked Aimee to "come at once to Corona…Revival clouds are ready to burst upon our heads. 'The Lord hath need of thee!' "[23]

Setting out for New York and finding this person she thought of as a "sister in the faith," Aimee was startled and surprised. Not only was the sister the only Pentecostal believer in the immediate area—she was also black. "Upon first arrival this seemed a most discouraging field. No one but this precious colored sister was known to have received the baptism of the Holy Spirit according to Acts 2:4....though everyone else doubted my call, I knew that God had sent me."[24]

The call to Corona was providential. Two events occurring in Corona would mark her later meetings: Aimee had both her first interracial meeting and her first experience as a healer. Aimee and her new found sister in the faith walked for blocks, attempting to rent a storefront or hall for the meetings. Nothing was available. The minister of the Swedish Methodist Episcopal Church, upon hearing that a lady evangelist was in town, consented to let his church be used for open meetings during the week.

Aimee noted the outcome:

> The second night the church was filled to the door, though church members had been warned by their ministers to keep away from the Pentecostal people and have nothing to do with those folks who talked in tongues. Just one week from the day [after the] meetings were opened, the break came. A Sunday school teacher from one of the large churches, a man whose sound Christian standing had been known for years, was the first to receive the baptism. The wife of a leading citizen was the second and when the altar call was given, scores from the audience, which was made up entirely of church members, gathered about the altar.[25]

Aimee, ever sensitive, felt somewhat uncomfortable. Knowing that area clergymen had warned their congregations that Pentecostalism was only "hypnotism," she refrained from any physical action. "I was very careful not to lay hands upon, or speak to the seekers, but prayed by my own chair earnestly."[26]

Ultimately, the minister who had most warned his congregation against her not only attended the service but also offered his larger church for her evangelistic efforts. The church "was packed from pulpit to the door and far out into the street. The windows had been opened, and the people stood on boxes or ledges, looking in."[27] Several clergymen from the area sat behind her on the platform. "I took one more hurried glance at the dignified clergymen who, it seemed to me, sat like human interrogation marks at the very thought of a woman preaching the Gospel, and launched into my message."[28]

Aimee's messages were always ones of simple Christian faith that Jesus Christ, in the early twentieth century, was still the same, yesterday, today and forever. She preached the doctrines of a conversion experience, the Baptism of the Holy Spirit, the second coming of Christ, and divine healing, all of which would later become the cardinal theological tenets of her "Four-square Gospel." She would, rather quickly, become known in her ministry as a faith healer. It was not a role she felt comfortable with or one that she actively sought. If anything, she shrank away from its demands. The Corona meeting was her first experience with her strange new gift.

A young woman from a Catholic family, who was severely crippled with rheumatoid arthritis, was carried to one of Aimee's meetings in a taxicab. Supported by crutches and by friends, the woman was brought forward to the front of the church at the end of the service:

> A gasp of pity rippled over the entire assemblage, as eyes were focused upon the procession. Now, I had no experience whatsoever in praying for the sick. Indeed, very little…had been said or done about this great doctrine…yet in my sermons I had constantly proclaimed Jesus Christ to be the same Healer He was in days of old…but oh, I did wish then and there that I could have begun with someone who looked a bit more mendable than this poor little thing…the eyes of the people looked first at the young lady and then at me; and I, God help me, felt my face flushing more each moment…Then I prayed for her healing, telling her to lift her hands and praise the Lord…Slowly her head began to turn, and then the chin lifted as she gazed heavenward. In a moment she was to her feet! Clinging hand over hand to the chancel rail she began to walk as the limbs straightened.[29]

Years later, Aimee would recall, "Whether it was because I had until this time never seen such a sight, I know not; but to this day the healing of that young lady seems to me one of the most mighty miracles I have ever known."[30]

When her meetings in Corona were over, Aimee left behind a thriving Pentecostal church, something that was repeated virtually everywhere she preached. Setting out from Corona by faith, much as Abraham had done, and "not knowing where she was going," Aimee became intrigued one day watching the wild geese flying south for the winter. Their flight over the Long Island Sound provided an answer: like "the birds of the air," she too would head south in the winter and travel back to the north in late spring. She could still utilize her new canvas cathedral in a warmer climate. "Must we, then, be left behind to hibernate for the winter? Must the white wings of the tent remain folded until next summer?"[31]

The "saints at Corona" with their "love offerings" provided the necessary funds for the tent to be shipped to Florida, where Aimee had been "called to preach among the poor and to those who had not yet heard the message of Pentecost."[32]

When Aimee wrote her first book, she ended a chapter entitled the "Corona Campaign" and then began the next chapter with a recounting of her tent meetings in Jacksonville, Florida, titling that chapter "The Gateway to the Lower South." Aimee did not recount for her readers the hardships and struggles while traveling from Corona to Jacksonville. The gaps in her stories were testimonials of her indefatigable optimism.

The year of 1916 was not a good one for the McPherson family. Harold, back with Aimee for the final time, drove the car south over roads that were rutted, slippery, and muddy. The trip from New York to Florida took more than five days, even for the most experienced of drivers. There were few bridges en route, and it was a seller's market for the farmers who ferried the drivers across the swamps, streams, and rivers. Sometimes only trestles for trains spanned the gaps over water, and automobiles crossed over on flatbed cars. Directions were often discerned only by locating local landmarks.

During that harsh winter of hardship Aimee and Harold slowly grew closer. Harold felt useful and productive, "the captain of the ship for perhaps the first time in his marriage."[33] Each night, Harold pitched camp alongside the road while Aimee cooked a simple dinner. After Rolf was asleep, they often walked arm-in-arm down country roads.

When they arrived in Jacksonville, Harold handled the practical matters, such as finding a centrally located lot, obtaining the necessary permits from the city's mayor and fire chief, and unpacking and setting up the tents. While Aimee was preparing her sermons, Harold was purchasing lumber, installing electricity, constructing benches and a pulpit, printing handbills announcing the meetings, and paying boys to distribute them. His efficiency worked well in Jacksonville. Everything was ready a day ahead of schedule, and there was exactly five cents left in the budget.

Crowds gathered. They were a strange mix of locals and tourists, all curious about hearing a woman preacher. Aimee would emerge out of the sleeping tent dressed in her best black dress, wearing with it a stiffly-starched, small, white lace collar.

This was the same style of clerical dress that the "little lame English-woman," A. Maude Royden, who was considered to be "one of the six great preachers of the world," wore in the pulpit. Miss Royden's clerical garb in the early 1900s was described as being a "white collar on a plain black dress with a small cap above as dark as her hair."[34] Aimee would soon alter her pulpit attire, becoming known as "the woman in white." Her explanation for the change was simply that she would rather look like "God's dove" than "God's crow."[35]

Both of the original black and white outfits were purchased as maid's uni-

James Morgan Kennedy with Harold, Aimee, and Rolf, St. Petersburg, Florida, 1916 (used by permission of the International Church of the Foursquare Gospel, Heritage Department).

forms.[36] Such simple, unadorned uniforms, of course, suppressed any hint of sexuality. Like the earlier women preachers of Methodism before them, most Pentecostal women ministers viewed themselves as *sisters* or *mothers* to the church. Harry Stout's fine depiction of Methodist maternal pastors is equally applicable to Pentecostalism's prophesying daughters:

Most renounced the world… Insofar as the language of sexuality or love appeared at all, it tended to be as metaphor for the believer's "marriage" to Christ. Female Methodists…evidenced a loyalty to the cause of revival that was so monolithic as to place all—joy and affections—including the family—in a secondary role.[37]

Harold was always at the back of the tent when his wife, more the "Bride of Christ" than his own bride, walked across the sawdust to her homemade pulpit. Behind the pulpit she became a different woman; she belonged to no one except God and yet to everyone, both at the same time. The rich, throaty voice spoke in everyday, conversational English. Biblical characters came alive. Tourists and locals alike were transformed into one homogeneous, worshiping congregation. When Aimee's real work began, Harold's had already ended. Like a stage manager, his work for the day was done when Aimee appeared behind the pulpit. Only on rare occasions would Harold venture to the front of the tent, usually to join Aimee in a duet she had written to the tune of "Brighten the Corner Where You Are." While living in Florida, Aimee kept Harold at a distance, just as she had when they were in the deserted theater lobbies in New York City. There was a chasm between them that Harold could never bridge until they were on the road again.

Despite being the star attraction in their ministerial team, Aimee never took Harold's work for granted. Writing to her followers, Aimee reminded her readers of the role of her husband, whom she referred to in her writings as "Brother McPherson." "The lumber is made by Brother McPherson into platform and seats, tables and benches… He often stays up all night to complete the work, so that no time need be lost, for Jesus is coming soon and everyday means souls for the Master."[38]

Aimee's congregations were always enthusiastic but for the most part poor. The tin collection cups' failed many times to provide enough money for supper. Buttons were always part of the nightly collection. On such occasions as these, Harold would go fishing, returning later with his own offerings for the family.

Aimee was aware from the beginning of her ministry that as a woman preacher she was somewhat of a novelty:

> At the time when I began my ministry, women were well in the background of life in Canada and the United States. Women in business life and before the public eye were the exception to the rule. Men largely monopolized their activities outside the home. Still they reasoned: If the Lord chooses a woman to attract those to Himself, who otherwise might not have come, who among us should question the wisdom of God?[39]

Recognizing her novelty as a minister, Aimee also quickly concluded that the popular evangelism techniques of the day "were too archaic, too sedate, too lifeless to capture the interest of the throngs. The people wanted to hear, not only of the Christ of 1900 years ago…but of the living, vitalizing, empowering Christ of today."[40]

Florida was attractive to both Aimee and Harold. Aimee attempted to describe the winter Eden to her readers back home. She wrote about "the beautiful tropical foliage," the "wonderful orange groves," and the "sunshine and flowers." But more than anything else, "Florida," Aimee declared, "is the meeting place of thousands of tourists who flock there from all over the world."[41]

Aimee had begun to realize that if she reached the tourists, her message would travel farther while she herself journeyed less. Left unmentioned in her various descriptions of Florida was the fact that Jacksonville had earned the title of "The Winter Film Capital of the World." From 1908 through 1918, more than thirty film companies had established studios in town. Jacksonville seemingly had it all: a warm climate, exotic locations, excellent rail service, and a surplus of cheap labor. The first motion picture made in Technicolor was filmed on location in Jacksonville in 1917. During Aimee's visits to the city, she was made aware of the increasing unrest of the town's conservative residents. More often than not, their newly discovered life in Eden was disrupted by make-believe car chases, bank robberies, and even an occasional riot. In 1917, a newly elected mayor vowed to tame the ever–expanding and growing movie industry. Most studios simply packed up and moved to southern California, the newly created West Coast version of earthly paradise, which was more than hospitable to evangelists and movie-makers alike. Aimee too soon began hearing the clarion call of Los Angeles. Hollywood was there, but so was the fabled Azusa Street, the "new Jerusalem" of American Pentecostalism. After they parted ways, Harold chose to remain in the East Coast Eden of Florida, while his former wife, mother-in-law, step-daughter, and son made their long trek west—a type of pilgrimage made holy by their preaching and healing as they journeyed southwest—crossing vast deserts to the Promised Land of Southern California.

From Jacksonville, the McPhersons traveled to Tampa, Durant, and St. Petersburg. In Tampa, Aimee noted that the tent "was packed to the farthest corner, many standing and more turned away."[42]

The United States was on the brink of World War I, and Pentecostalism was soon to thrive under war conditions. At St. Petersburg, Aimee decided that a new approach was in order. The city was celebrating Mardi Gras, and Aimee quickly decided to enter the parade. Her parade entry took the form of a white sheet—a luxury of camp life—covering a wooden frame with the shape of a tent that was mounted on the car they called the "Gospel Automobile." The writings on the sides of the car-mounted tent read: "Jesus is Coming Soon" and "I am going to the Pentecostal Camp Meeting, are you?" Aimee wrote, "Concealing a baby organ under the tent, I sat beneath it out of sight of the crowd, and the Lord shut the policeman's eyes so that we could slip into the grand parade of cars and get the full length of Main Street with our advertisement...that night the tent was packed, and we had no more trouble getting crowds."[43]

From St. Petersburg, the McPhersons traveled to Savannah, Georgia, sending their tents ahead on the railroad. In Savannah, when Aimee learned that the United States had entered World War I, she established a network with her followers that would last until her death in 1944. In June 1917 she became the editor of her own monthly Pentecostal periodical, *The Bridal Call*. On the cover of the periodical was a drawing of Christ coming in the clouds with angels for his "bride"—a symbolic representation of the church. The motto was taken from the Song of Solomon: "Rise up my love, my fair one, and come away." (No one would ever use the bridal mysticism of the Pentecostal movement with greater zeal than did Aimee Semple McPherson.) Brother and Sister H. S. McPherson were listed as editors of the periodical, and F. A. Hess was named as its publisher. Aimee was specific as to the paper's purpose: "the Lord has opened the way to edit this

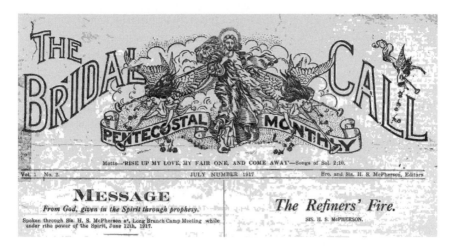

An early Bridal Call *"banner," emphasizing the "bridal mysticism" of Pentacostalism (used by permission of the International Church of the Foursquare Gospel, Heritage Department).*

simple little 'Bridal Call,' which we are praying God will make a blessing to all with whom it comes in contact. We are fully persuaded that Jesus is coming soon, and long to spread the Gospel and take advantage of every means of telling the world of his nearness."[44]

Her first theological and doctrinal formulations appeared in its pages, as well as her critique of the established mainline Protestant churches for their perceived lack of spirituality. "Just left-over scraps of morality, church-going, socials, big suppers in the basement, of earthly food instead of heavenly, X-mas trees, social gatherings, and half-hearted, empty profession."[45] Aimee quoted a chorus that provided a theme song of sorts for the fledgling Pentecostal movement. "Jesus has a table spread, where the saints of God are fed. He invites his chosen people come and dine; with his manna he doth feed, He supplies our every need, O it's sweet to sup with Jesus all the time. He who fed the multitude, turned the water into wine, to the hungry calleth now come and dine."[46]

Daniel N. Maltz, an anthropologist, has studied the bridal mysticism of Pentecostalism and has developed five characteristics of the bride of Christ metaphor that was so widely used in the movement. "Being a bride implies possessing a relationship that (1) unites two individuals into a larger whole, (2) is sexual and intimate, (3) is pure and legitimate, (4) is expressed from a female point of view, as opposed to the relationship of a bridegroom to his bride, and (5) is active in the sense that a bride is *in the process of becoming* a wife."[47]

"The [image of the] bride of Christ," states Phyllis Mack, "was no longer that of the chaste virgin, but the expectant wife, prepared for sexual union with the bridegroom."[48]

By the fall of 1917, *The Bridal Call* had introduced its readers to the major tenets of the Pentecostal faith, as interpreted by Aimee—tenets which would later become collectively known as the "Foursquare Gospel." "We endeavor to set forth in simple words that all can understand, the plain message of Salvation, the Baptism of the Holy Ghost, Divine Healing and the Soon Coming of Jesus."[49]

Despite an abundance of Pentecostal periodicals appearing at the same time, a simple comparison with the many others readily confirms the unique stamp Aimee's personality added to everything she touched. More importantly, she ignored the movement's growing controversies and doctrinal differences. The message of *The Bridal Call*, said Aimee, "was not to be one of controversy, fighting, great wisdom or eloquence, but simply what its name implies—a call to the bride to prepare for her heavenly Bridegroom."[50]

Aimee's paper was a labor of love for her followers. It was written on a second-hand typewriter in the backseat of the Gospel Auto while traveling over rutted roads. Its circulation began with two to three thousand copies sent out per month and increased rapidly. In her own inimitable, folksy style, it was "the last invitation to the Marriage of the Lamb."[51] For her emerging followers, it was a continuous link with "their Sister."

The summer of 1917 was a pivotal one for Aimee's ministry. She prepared a booklet entitled *The Personal Testimony and Life of Sister H.S. McPherson*, which she described as "containing her photograph, and telling of her Infidelity [loss of faith], Conviction, Salvation, Holy Ghost Baptism, Healing and Calling." The publisher noted that Aimee's testimony and life story "was having quite a sale and we are nearly out of finished copies."[52] More importantly, the summer's events marked Aimee's desire to settle down and make her ministry permanent and less transient.

The Savannah publisher of the first three issues of *The Bridal Call,* who had donated his services for free, decided, "not to go on [doing so]."[53] Aimee, in what later proved to be an extremely decisive move, journeyed back to New England and secured the services of Samuel G. Otis, superintendent of the Christian Workers Union, to be her next publisher.

Samuel Otis had formerly been employed in secular business and had no thought of going into publishing when he felt called to look "over the field to see which was the most spiritual undenominational paper [being] published and selected *The Christian,* which was published by H. L. Hastings of Boston."[54]

The Christian became something of a spiritual template for Otis' growing calling with Christian publishing. Otis began publishing his own periodical, which he called *Word and Work*, deriving the name from Colossians 2:17, "Whatever you may do in Word or in Work, do all in the name of the Lord." After becoming a Pentecostal himself in 1906, he correspondingly changed the emphasis of his monthly periodical.

Otis' headquarters were at Montwaite, in Framingham, Massachusetts. Montwaite itself was owned by the Chautauqua Association and was only used a few days each year. The Chautauqua Association was born out of the fervor of early Methodist camp meetings. The Methodists by 1811 held at least four hundred camp meetings scattered throughout the country and situated at such places as Chautauqua, New York; Oak Bluffs, Massachusetts; and Ocean Grove, New Jersey. The early days of such meetings were full of "frenzied excitement." The early ecstasy, however, soon dissipated, and the "grounds were policed, admittance was restricted, crowds were carefully controlled, and the meetings became much more sober, dignified, and orderly."[55] By the 1830s, the camp meetings had become "an occasion when the faithful gathered to combine an annual outing with an opportunity to listen to inspirational addresses."[56] Ultimately, with upward mobility and secularization, the Methodist camp meeting locations were transformed into conference centers or summer resorts.

In 1912, Otis moved his printing presses to Montwaite. The Chautauqua camp came equipped with a large tabernacle, three dormitories, and a dining hall and chapel. The former Methodist site quickly became an important center for the growing Pentecostal movement in New England. The Pentecostal movement at Montwaite, much like earlier Methodism, met with severe local opposition.

Otis wrote to his subscribers in April 1915, telling them, "We have held the fort here as best we could, amidst discouragements and opposition and persecution, and testings on every line. God alone knows what we have been through, and were it not for the fact that we know He sent us, we would have run away many times."[57]

In the summer of 1917, Aimee made Otis her publisher and Montwaite her home base. Serving as a contributing editor for Otis' *Word and Work*, along with Dr. F. F. Yoakum, who was later to found the Pisgah faith home in Los Angeles, Aimee established something of a headquarters for her ministry in New England. Over the next two years, *The Bridal Call* more than tripled its monthly circulation, increasing it to approximately ten thousand copies being sent out, due to its mailing list being able to include the existing *Word and Work* subscribers.

> For the next two years…in summer and in winter, north or south, I worked by day and dreamed by night in the shadows of the tent. I watched my tents as a mother watches her only child; I could not bear to be out of sight of them. They were the entire world wherein I lived, breathed, and had my being. I slept on a soldier's canvas cot in a little tent beside the big one myself and two children *[sic]*; and as I slept, I sometimes stroked the side of the cot and felt that I, too, was a soldier upon the battle ground of the Lord."[58]

Her dreams kept her going. For two years, she traveled up and down the East Coast, perfecting her preaching style, deepening her commitment to Pentecostalism, and pitching her tent as far north as Washburn, Maine, in the summer, and as far south as Key West in winter.

Known in later years in Angelus Temple for her flamboyant, entertaining "illustrated sermons," Aimee in the summer of 1917 introduced drama, for the first time, in her sermon at her meeting in Washburn. Through the influence of Otis and the Montwaite camp meetings, Pentecostalism had taken root in northern Maine. "One night a drama was all worked out in the Spirit, showing forth the ten Virgins, going first with white robes to meet the Bridegroom…This was only one of the many wonderful messages and dramas worked out in our midst which were beyond description."[59]

Before leaving Maine for Florida, Aimee was ordained for a second time by Nelson J. Magoon, an independent Pentecostal pastor and railroad engineer. Through connections made at Montwaite, Magoon and his wife moved to Washburn in 1915 and rented a small, vacant Mormon church on Main Street. Magoon's church grew rapidly, and in the summer of 1917 Aimee pitched her tent in the parking lot behind his new church. For unknown reasons, Magoon laid his hands on Aimee and ordained her as an evangelist. When she made application for ordination with the Assemblies of God in 1919, she noted that she had been ordained by both William Durham in Chicago and by Nelson Magoon in Washburn. It is quite possible that her second Pentecostal ordination occurred because Aimee felt she had backslid; felt that she had, metaphorically speaking, gone to Tarshish instead of Nineveh, after her first ordination eight years earlier with Robert Semple.

Purchasing a second Gospel Auto in the fall of 1917, the McPhersons headed south again for their second Southern campaign. Perhaps feeling a need to align herself more closely to the mainstream of the ever-increasing Pentecostal movement, Aimee was officially ordained on September 4, 1917 by the newly formed General Council of the Assemblies of God.

Aimee sensed a momentum growing with her meetings but she admitted that, "It has meant self-sacrifice, and in our reports we endeavor to picture the sunny side, to encourage the many who live far from [the] meetings, but fail, perhaps, to show the other side, where sometimes in driving rains, we find our sleeping tents ankle deep in water, our bedding wet, where we struggle to cook on smoky oil stoves and not yet keep [sic] singing and smiling, fighting the good fight of faith."[60]

In reality there was at times no smoky oil stove to cook over but only a box of crackers and a quart of milk or a single can of corn for dinner, eaten huddled inside their Gospel Auto while the rain whipped against the isinglass curtains. Aimee's desire to live life as a traveling evangelist was nothing more than a strange obsession as far as Harold was concerned. After preaching again in Jacksonville and Tampa, they headed for Miami. Attempting to travel lightly, they shipped their small sleeping tents ahead of them while they crossed through the wilderness of the Okeechobee Swamp. The fifty-mile trip took more than three days. They slept in various places on the way—inside the car, in a vacant shack, and in an empty railroad station—arriving at Palm Beach on Christmas Eve. Harold created a palm-branch shelter on the deserted beach, and after Rolf had been put to sleep in the sand, his parents decorated a nearby shrub with trinkets and gifts for the boy to discover on Christmas morning. For Aimee, it was the necessary price she had to pay for preaching. She found comfort in the scripture that said that, "The birds have nests and the foxes have holes, but the Son of Man has no where to lay his head." For Harold, this was simply the beginning of the end.[61]

The meetings in Miami and in Key West were a success. Aimee reported that, "To the first meeting thronged the rich and fashionable in their automobiles and fine clothing. A tent meeting was a novelty. They came to be amused, but many remained to weep and pray."[62]

Aimee's concerns extended beyond the spiritual needs of the middle class, as was demonstrated when she said, "Because of the strong racial feeling, the dear colored people did not feel free to attend the white meeting. The Lord put such a love in my heart for the colored race that it was impossible for me to pass one of them on the street without such floods of love welling up in my heart…thus it was that after the white camp meeting we moved our equipment to the other side of town amongst these precious people."[63] The ability Aimee possessed to cross denominational lines blurred racial boundaries as well. In Key West, while holding a "colored camp meeting," she found that, "it was impossible to keep the white people away. So for the first time in the Island, the white and colored attended the same place of worship and glorified the same Lord side by side. We arranged seats for the white people at the sides, reserving the center for the

Two views of Roberta's interracial baptism (used by permission of the International Church of the Foursquare Gospel, Heritage Department).

colored people, but so interested became the people in the meetings that reserve was a thing unknown."[64]

Aimee was perhaps the first evangelist in modern America to hold integrated revival meetings in the South.

Key West was also full of soldiers and sailors active in World War I, and they too, Aimee noted, "thronged to our tent every night," as they would to her temple during World War II.[65]

On March 11, 1918, Aimee gave her readers the first overt clue that her marriage had ended. To her faithful followers she wrote,

> At present I am very weak in my body, and have to hang on to God for strength for each meeting. Please pray for me, saints, that I do not fail God…Brother McPherson has gone on ahead arranging other meetings, so I am alone, playing, leading, singing, preaching, and praying at the altar, besides our monthly magazine *The Bridal Call* to prepare. Under this heavy strain it is only the power of God that can keep. Pray also that the Lord will supply our needs, in such a manner that the colored people, and the poor, the maimed, the halt, the blind in all these highways and hedges may have this Gospel preached unto them that his house may be full. I feel my weakness and utter dependence upon God as never before, as I look out over the sea of hungry faces, crowds still increasing, hundreds unable to obtain seats. Pray saints…yours in the King's Glad Service, Sister H.S. McPherson.[66]

Only Aimee and Harold knew what caused the break-up of their marriage. Harold, even after Aimee's death, made no comments about it. He would mention, from time to time, that he "always loved her."[67] By the July issue of *The Bridal Call*, only one name appeared on the masthead as editor—"Sister Aimee Semple McPherson"—a name that in time would blaze in neon in the Southern California night and would dominate the

NATION-WIDE
PENTECOSTAL

CAMP MEETING

TO BE HELD AT

PHILADELPHIA
PA.

July 21 to September 1, 1918

Brother and Sister H. S. McPherson. Evangelists.

All Day Meetings.   Pentecostal Prayer Meetings.   Old Time Power and Glory

The Lord has been laying upon the hearts of many of His children the longing for a grand gathering together of Spirit filled saints and workers from far and near for a definite time of prayer and praise, and the edification and upbuilding of His waiting people.

A SPECIAL INVITATION. Let those hungry for God's best, come.. If you are seeking for Salvation, for the Baptism of the Holy Spirit according to Acts 2:4; if you are coveting earnestly the best gifts, and longing to go on to perfection; if you are seeking healing for your body; if the oil has languished or leaked out of your vessel; if the new wine is dried up and you are longing for a refilling—COME and unite with us at this time for a definite outpouring of God's Spirit.

BEGIN PRAYING NOW for these meetings. ADVERTISE IT FAR AND WIDE through all the Pentecostal friends and assemblies of your acquaintance. Write us for handbills for distribution.

SEND US A LIST OF ALL NAMES AND ADDRESSES OF PENTECOSTAL ASSEMBLIES, FRIENDS AND WORKERS, that we may extend to them a personal invitation to this meeting.

Speakers and workers to be invited from all parts of the U. S. A. and Canada. We are believing for a time of real heart searching, and humbling before God; a time of spiritual uplift and blessing. Unceasing prayer will be made from this time forth to this end.

ALL THINGS IN COMMON, free tents and cots for all as the Lord provides. We also hope to have meals on free will offerings plan as in the Word after Pentecost they dwelt together and no man called aught that he had his own, but they did eat their meat with gladness and singleness of heart praising and glorifying God.

LIVING TENTS, with electric lights, and with or without board floors, may be obtained. Dining Tent accommodations.

Further information may be obtained by addressing Elder Jas. R. Greig, 906 Filbert St., Philadelphia, Pa., or Brother H. S. McPherson, Montwait , Framingham, Mass.

An announcement for the Nation-Wide Camp Meeting, the turning point in Aimee's ministry (used by permission of the International Church of the Foursquare Gospel, Heritage Department).

secular press.

In March 1918 Harold took a smaller tent and set off to go preaching on his own. "Perhaps he hoped," speculated Roberta, "that if he were successful, she would come and join him. If she were to become the preacher's wife, things might be different. The need to be one's own man must have been overwhelming. Or, he may have felt that when Aimee discovered how much she needed him, how important he really was, she would call him back."[68]

But she did not. Instead, as before in her times of trouble, she called her mother. "God had called her daughter…and now her daughter was calling her."[69]

Minnie, almost forty-eight years of age, did not hesitate—she arrived in Key West to do her duty to God and her daughter. Minnie brought with her the invaluable organizational knowledge she had acquired from her work with the Salvation Army in New York. In Florida, at her daughter's side, she organized a Sunday school and the choirs, and she took over the mounting correspondence with converts from earlier meetings. As Roberta recalled, "Harold was replaced, almost without effort."[70]

Aimee was now preoccupied with her preparations for the forthcoming event entitled the "Nation-Wide Pentecostal Camp Meeting," which was to be held in Philadelphia from July 21 through September 3, 1918. This one meeting would solidly establish her as Pentecostalism's most illustrious prophesying daughter. The time of tents would soon be over. Auditoriums and tabernacles would take their place, followed in time by churches. Aimee was twenty-eight years old and entering the most productive years of her preaching ministry.

Seven years later, Aimee would recall, for the *Bridal Call* readers, her apprenticeship in her early evangelistic efforts. Much of her success, she perceived, resulted from having stayed focused, committed to her cause, and not finding contentment easily.

> As I look back over the years to those times of our early beginning, I wonder whether the dauntless courage and positive refusal to be beaten, or be content with the few when we might be reaching the many, has not had a great deal to do with the success of the present work. When I see ministers and workers content to sit and talk to a half-filled church or to empty pews, I often look back with pardonable pride to those strenuous days and the courage with which we set forth."[71]

Roberta also was able to recall the hardships of "those strenuous days… Often I would wake up and find the wind howling and Mother gone from the bed beside me. I was only seven but I would follow her up into the wind and rain and I would find her with a sledge hammer in her hand driving the stakes, pulling guy ropes, pulling the tent into position. Drenched to the skin, she would come in and climb into a damp bed, for the tent we slept in leaked. I remember sleeping with an umbrella over my bed and big *[sic]* wash tub on Mother's bed."[72]

There was for Aimee an inherent joy to all of the hardships, however, for, like the chorus of early Pentecostalism, she had "left the land of bondage with its earthly treasures, [and had] journeyed to a place where there is love on every hand; [she had] exchanged a land of heart aches for a land of plea-sure, [and she too, was] camping,…camping in Canaan's happy land."[73]

CHAPTER FIVE

Mother and Daughter en route to the Promised Land

> But Ruth said, "Do not press me to leave you or to turn back from fol-
> lowing you! Where you go, I will go; where you lodge, I will lodge; your
> people shall be my people, and your God my God. Where you die, I will
> die—there will I be buried."....So the two of them went on until they
> came to Bethlehem. When they came to Bethlehem, the whole town was
> stirred because of them.
>
> —Ruth 1:16-17, 19

Camping in Canaan's land was made easier and somewhat happier for
Aimee because she was reunited with her mother and daughter. Minnie
Kennedy remembered two things about this time: how long the trip was
from Florida to Pennsylvania, and the "heavy heart" her daughter had
when, "after hours of pleading [Aimee] had realized that the arm of flesh
[Harold] had failed and [that Aimee] must go on alone except for the babies
and I [*sic*]."[1]

The mother-daughter relationship never worked better than it did in
the years between 1918 and 1923. Aimee was visionary, Minnie was practical, and together, using common sense, the two women were able to make
modern American religious history. Between 1918 and 1923, Aimee and
her mother crossed the United States eight times, conducting thirty-eight
revivals in major cities. Their meetings usually began in tents and tabernacles, occasionally moved into churches, and finally ended being held in
theaters and auditoriums—places where both mother and daughter seemed
to feel more at home. During these years, Minnie, along with hundreds of
others, was able vicariously through Aimee to live out her grandest religious
aspirations.

When Minnie left New York, she packed lightly. A typewriter—a possession Minnie had only recently acquired—took preeminence in the continual repacking of the Gospel Auto, and it contributed significantly to her
daughter's expanding success.[2] After Aimee was asleep, Minnie would rise
in the night and with two fingers type letters "to all of our friends whose
addresses we had, telling them of the coming camp meeting and of our
need of a tent."[3]

Mother and daughter: Aimee Semple McPherson and Minnie Kennedy (used by permission of the International Church of the Foursquare Gospel, Heritage Department).

At the time, Aimee's "two great horrors of…life were that of the tent being torn by a gale, or being mildewed in shipping from being packed damp."[4] It was time for a new tent, a larger one, and Minnie, ever the practical one and the best business manager her daughter ever had, put her Salvation Army experience to work and from Florida to Pennsylvania solicited for a tent fund for the forthcoming camp meeting in Philadelphia.[5]

The Nation-Wide Camp Meeting in Philadelphia was scheduled for July

21 through September 3, 1918, under the auspices of the United Apostolic [Pentecostal] Assemblies of Philadelphia, Pa. The meetings had been advertised since January 1918 by Otis' publishing concerns and other Pentecostal publications. Pentecostal "saints and seekers from all over the United States and Canada" were invited in much the same way that the military advertised for recruits: "If God wants you at this Camp Meeting, we want you. On this basis you are invited."[6]

Tents for the event rented for two dollars per week for dormitory style and $2.25 per week for a 7 x 9, "with fly and light accommodating two." For $3.75 per week, or $17.50 for the season, a 7 x 9 came with a floor.[7]

"During our stay in Philadelphia," wrote Aimee, "Mother had insisted that a floor be laid in my sleeping tent. This was the first time in all my tent work that I had anything but the bare ground as a floor, summer or winter."[8]

This was no ordinary camp meeting for the infant movement of Pentecostalism. The rapidly multiplying Pentecostal missions had combined in love and humility to work together in unity. All Pentecostals were invited regardless of difference of views. All side issues and nonessentials were to be laid aside. The meetings were advertised for those seekers and saints who were coveting the best spiritual gifts, longing to go on to perfection, seeking healing for their bodies, and for those wanting a refilling of the oil that had leaked out of their vessels. The forty days and nights in Philadelphia were to be a time of all-day meetings, all things in common, all in one accord in one place, praising and glorifying God. Perhaps more than anywhere else, Philadelphia was the one place for Pentecostals to finally bind up the wounds and heal the divisions that had followed in the wake of their 1906 Azusa Street Revival in Los Angeles. The featured evangelist was Sister H.S. McPherson, the dynamic half of the Brother and Sister Harold Stewart McPherson evangelistic revival team, soon to be better known in North America as Sister Aimee or simply as Aimee Semple McPherson.

A committee consisting of James R. Greig, Hank Simokat, and Herbert Dingee—men whom Aimee would later refer to as "pirates"—made all the arrangements, another first for her meetings. She had only to preach. The smaller sleeping tents were already standing on a "beautiful hill" where for Aimee "earth and Heaven seem to meet."[9] It was a Pentecostal vision of a camp-meeting heaven, and the streets on the grounds bore names like "Glory Avenue," "Heaven Street," and "Amen Boulevard."

The immediate task at hand for mother and daughter upon their arrival in the city was to locate and select a new tent for the meeting—no easy matter during World War I, as the government had appropriated all tent-

Aimee's dream "tabernacle-tent" erected where "earth and heaven seemed to meet," Philadelphia, 1918 (used by permission of the International Church of the Foursquare Gospel, Heritage Department).

making concerns for war purposes.

Aimee was still convinced that her meetings would continue to be held in tents. "Two years of constant and practical service with a big tent, 40 x 80 feet with 3,200 square feet, has convinced us beyond the shadow of a doubt that this means of preaching the Gospel gives us a freedom and a power to reach the masses that never enter a church or a mission door, and of traveling into territory that could not be reached in any other way."[10]

According to Aimee, providence again intervened. She soon learned that a tent made from the best United States Army duck material had been sewn in the city by a local manufacturer for some Philadelphia churches that were sponsoring a large, forthcoming, city-wide, evangelistic meeting. The scheduled evangelist became ill because, Aimee claimed, he "refused the Light, [and] took a stand against the outpouring of the Spirit. His tent, fully ready for use and now lying in "an attic store-room of a downtown building" quickly became Aimee's.[11] Upon further inspection, Aimee declared it was exactly what she had in mind:

> After two years' experience, I had my own ideas of the kind of tent I wanted, its size, shape, seating capacity, texture, and make: one that would shed the rain, be mildew-proof, well roped and guyed, arranged with block-and-tackle system of lowering and raising. Where could such

a tent be purchased? When we arrived in the city of our summer's work, there was the very tent of my dreams and prayers, in an attic store-room of a downtown building, all tied up in bags, poles and stakes complete, ready for erection. Hallelujah![12]

The merchant contended that Aimee's dream tent was worth $2,500, due to the war, but could be purchased for $1,800. A bit more shrewd this time, after having purchased her first tent—from another Pentecostal evangelist—and then discovering, too late, that it had been rolled up in its bag in such a way as to hide the fact that it was full of holes, Aimee held out for $1,500, and "at first they would not accept this, [but] as the man stood in the door and read the sign, [on the Gospel Auto door that said] Judgment day is coming, get right with God,' his face became thoughtful and he said he would let us know later, and of course, Father opened the way."[13]

The white, billowy "tabernacle-tent," as Aimee termed it, was soon standing on the grounds at 34th and Midvale Avenue where "earth and heaven seem to meet."[14]

The area was an ethnic neighborhood and at least seventy-five percent Roman Catholic. That notwithstanding, two thousand chairs were placed in the tent and were filled an hour before the service began. During the service, as an eyewitness described it, "all around the tent they stand ten, fifteen deep, in profound attention for an hour and a half or two hours. Crowds composed of every nationality; all the Protestant denominations, and the Roman Catholics, with a good sprinkling of clergy and a large crowd of non-church attendants."[15]

Through it all, Aimee led the diverse worshipers, despite repeated disturbances by roving gangs of local youths, intent on inflicting their own brand of religious persecution upon the "fanatics" who occupied "their" hill. Automobiles on the grounds had licenses bearing California and Florida registration tags.

New sleeping tents were ordered and another dormitory tent erected. On the second Sunday of the meetings it was determined, by the counting of raised hands, that thirty-five states were represented. When the attendees were polled to determine the various nationalities present at the camp meeting, "people who had been born in Italy, Russia, Lithuania, Germany, Sweden, Poland, Finland, Holland, Canada, Ireland, England, Egypt and Wales responded."[16]

Since the police were preoccupied with a race riot in the center of the city, Minnie turned into "a first-class sleuth. While I conducted the meetings inside," said Aimee, "she [Minnie] was outside standing guard, lest an attempt be made upon the large tabernacle tent with its hundreds of people inside."[17] Despite Aimee's feelings of "opposition," the religious participation was ecstatic and enthusiastic.

These spiritual manifestations would continue on in Aimee's meetings until a later campaign—an independent and undenominational meeting in Baltimore, Maryland. To the accompaniment of a brass band, snare drum, and tambourines, the camping congregation would sing, together, a growing Pentecostal favorite:

> Victory! Hallelujah, what a thought!
> Jesus, full salvation brought.
> Victory! Victory!
> Let the power of sin assail,
> heaven's grace can never fail.
> Victory! Victory!
>
> Shout your freedom everywhere,
> His eternal peace declare,
> Victory! Victory!
> Let us sing it here below
> in the face of every foe.
> Victory! Victory!
>
> Yes, Victory! Hallelujah,
> I am free, Jesus give me Victory.
> Glory, Glory, Hallelujah,
> He is all in all to me.[18]

The singing would swell into a crescendo until the majority of the congregation were on their feet, some dancing while others shouted. Then, like a gentle rain on a thirsty, spring afternoon, the singing became more diminuendo; still heavy, but more hushed. Ethnic accents blurred; sopranos, altos, tenor, and bass had all become one, and they were now singing harmoniously, as they described it, "in the spirit." And for a brief lapse of time, they were no longer standing on the hill at Midvale and 34th but were in heaven, singing one of its anthems. Some would fall to the sawdust, "slain in the spirit," while others spoke out in loud, unintelligible words, which they called "speaking in other tongues." Often times, especially at the close of the meetings, the demarcation line between the earnest and the mockers had disappeared. All had become as one, sharing the heightened awareness that comes through mystical, spiritual transcendence. In that electrically charged atmosphere, the sick "of all denominations," were brought forward for prayer and "divine healing."[19]

The ecstasy extended also to the children. Not only were they allowed to freely participate in the Pentecostal services, they even at times controlled the meetings as they had done at the old Azusa Street Mission in Los Angeles. "Another little tot of six years, suddenly filled with the power, began to dance in a pretty, childish way. Sister McPherson, led by the Spirit, placed the little one on the altar rail, and for twenty minutes the little girl preached Jesus to a multitude who came to look upon God's work."[20]

By the end of the meetings, both a Baptist and an Episcopal clergyman were reported to have attended, and another group of people—the "unchurched"—also attended. The volume of that category of individuals continued to grow under Aimee's ministry and would in and of itself help to make her ministry famous. "In personal conversation with the people about the tent, we also find there is a large number who have no church home whatever, and many who have never been to church. These are a surprised and interested body of people upon whom God is also moving mightily."[21]

For perhaps the first time in her fledging ministerial career, Aimee's meetings also attracted press coverage. Less than a month after the camp meeting began, the *Philadelphia Public Ledger* declared in its headline that "OLD-FASHIONED METHODISM OUTDONE AT PENTECOSTAL CAMP-MEETING." "Shouting, dancing and leaping with religious ecstasy, babbling in strange tongues or falling into a trance, in which… they remain for hours," the *Ledger* reported. "Members of the Nation-wide Pentecostal Camp-Meeting Association—who have been given the name of 'Holy Rollers'…are holding services daily in a large tent at Thirty-fourth street and Midvale avenue. Crowds numbering from 1,000 to 10,000 persons flock to the big tent nightly….It is the first nation-wide Pentecostal meeting that has been held in the Atlantic States."[22]

"We have no doctrine," the paper quoted Aimee as saying, "We more nearly represent an old-time Methodist camp-meeting than anything else."[23]

The article also reported that "five clergymen of evangelical churches" had "received the baptism" and had become participants themselves "in the strange rites." "I don't know what will happen to them," Aimee said, "when they go back to their own churches."[24]

The article concluded by describing the lifestyle of this new version of old-fashioned Methodism. "The Pentecostal people abstain from theatre-going, profanity, smoking, intoxicating liquors and even roller-skating.

Many of them give one-tenth of their incomes to religious work, and their preachers receive no remuneration."[25]

Ma Kennedy would soon erase that final feature of Pentecostalism forever. Penniless Pentecostal preachers would quickly be a thing of the past, and Aimee, as so many of the movement remembered, would be the first evangelist to "put the cost in Pentecost."

The Philadelphia meeting was a turning point, both in Aimee's personal life and in public ministry. Eight years later, before a crowded courtroom in Los Angeles, Aimee would tell the court and ultimately the world through subsequent newspaper releases that the 1918 Nation-Wide Camp Meeting in Philadelphia marked the beginning of her success. In Philadelphia her meetings reached new heights, with somewhere between eight to ten thousand people in attendance. In Philadelphia Aimee experienced her new theological calling, which prompted her exodus from the East Coast and her journey to the Promised Land of Los Angeles. More than anything else, however, Philadelphia in 1918, was "one great big stretch of middle class."[26] This was the place where Aimee experienced ministerial success and public acceptance for the first time on a grand scale. What occurred first in Philadelphia was soon to be repeated in major cities across the country. Philadelphia set the pattern for her ministry in Los Angeles, where she would reach the middle-aged of the middle class from the Middle West.

As a result of her growing reputation from the Philadelphia meetings, invitations began to pour in, and at the age of twenty-eight Aimee was soon barnstorming America as everybody's "Sister in the King's Glad Service." Having to sleep on deserted Florida beaches would soon be over; needing to raise fallen tent poles in tropical storms would be relegated to being only a recurring nightmare. Sister Aimee, like the movement she represented, had begun to take hold in American culture. A third force, distinct from both mainline Protestantism and Catholicism, was beginning to emerge in American religious life, and Sister was rapidly becoming its most colorful personality and persuasive preacher. Aimee would provide for the movement itself a wider acceptance, bringing it into the mainstream of evangelicalism, while she herself became associated with the popular culture of Southern California and Los Angeles.

On a hot September afternoon near the conclusion of the meetings, Harold Stewart McPherson, anxious about Aimee's welfare, showed up unannounced. Standing on the shady side of the preaching tent, Harold absorbed his wife's message. Roberta, who had just turned eight, would always remember that there was "something strange" in the way "Daddy Mack" just "stood there.[27]

"I sensed in that intuitive way children sometimes have [that] he seemed alone, forlorn."[28]

At his bidding, Roberta found Rolf for Harold, and while he tightly clenched his son's small hand, Roberta took a coin he gave her, bought an ice cream sandwich sold by a vendor on the grounds, and continued to glance now and then, at her stepfather. She overheard Harold asking a passer-by "if there was anything he could do to help?"[29]

The answer came back, polite but firm: "Why no, Brother, everything has been taken care of. But thank you for asking."[30] Again for Harold, as when he first met her, life with Aimee was to be lived at the edge—at a safe distance:

> The next time I returned, Harold was gone. I did not see him for over forty years, [but] I was haunted by the remembrance of the odd way he had 'just stood there' in the shadow of the big tent, quietly holding little Rolf's hand and listening to his wife's magnetic voice as she preached about God's everlasting love. I think that on that hot September day in 1918 Harold realized he had lost Aimee forever, and realized, too, that she would never be out of his heart completely. Aimee would fulfill her dream, he knew without him *[sic]*. But he could not have imagined that in two years, she would be known from coast to coast as the "Female Billy Sunday," and that in just five years, she would dedicate her own church, seating over five thousand persons in Southern California. Of what had happened to Harold after that day, I knew almost nothing...he remained a blank space in my family history book.[31]

Their final separation occurred just as strangely as their first one, and all the ones in between. Minnie had never been of any help to Harold. As in most marital separations, however, only Harold and Aimee really knew what occurred that day, and they themselves were perhaps incapable of understanding what really had happened, given their ages and the circumstances under which they had married. What is known is that Harold was the one who filed for their divorce, charging desertion. It was only after their divorce had been finalized and Angelus Temple had been built that Aimee gave her version of what had happened to the marriage to her followers:

> My companion had arrived [in Philadelphia] and for a few hours my hopes ran high, only to be dashed to the ground. To the very last moment I hoped and prayed, cried and pled for help and companionship; but to no avail. Even after the car was packed and ready to start, we waited, praying, pleading—it seemed impossible otherwise. Sick at heart, weary

with the long mental strain of these personal affairs, in addition to the tremendous work of the campaign, I reluctantly set forth.

The one who had sworn to stand by me, and whom I needed now more than I ever needed one who would understand and help, had failed me, had taken the greater proportion of the money which I did have, through the little love offerings of a few friends, and had gone to Florida on a fishing trip. Who was there to turn to but the little mother? God bless her! She saw my eyes red with weeping. She saw with an aching heart, the smiles which I kept for the world; but she also saw the pillow wet with tears as she would slip into my tent at night to find that I had at last dropped to sleep from sheer exhaustion. You know, an evangelist can never have any troubles or worries. She must always smile for the world. Her tears must be between her and the Lord.

Up to that time my mother had not realized that she was to stay with me any length of time in the work. She had considered her campaigning as more or less temporary; but now, more and more she realized my need. She could see that the one who should have helped [Harold] had shirked his responsibility and she stepped in. The people were not blind. They could not help but see what conditions were. All of this time we had been praying earnestly for harmony to be restored; but to our horror, we discovered that our friends were praying for deliverance. She [Minnie] took upon her own dear shoulders all the responsibility of business arrangements, securing of camp grounds, renting of buildings and preparation of advertisements. Together we put over great revival campaigns, for which other evangelists would require great organizations and months of preparation.[32]

Harold had wanted a wife. Aimee had wanted another Robert Semple. Destiny in that regard was cruel to them both. "A flamingo in a chicken coop," is how an earlier biographical attempt summarized Aimee's relationship with Harold.[33] Aimee was not meant to be just another woman, just one man's wife. Both she and her mother were clear about that. And Minnie would go to any extreme in the future to protect Aimee—her "promise" born to her, the promise of a vicarious life—that had let her out of her own self-described "prison house" twenty-eight years ago.

At the height of Aimee's fame, every so often an enterprising reporter would find Harold and write about the "ex" in Aimee's life. Almost always Harold was casually dismissed as a "grocery clerk or candy salesman." After that hot September afternoon of their last parting, Harold had tried to remain in the ministry. For a time he assisted an evangelist named John Ashcroft, the grandfather of the United States attorney general of the same name in George W. Bush's first term. Ashcroft's son would later play an important role in education with the Assemblies of God. "But it wasn't the same," he later told Roberta, "and I just sort of drifted away."[34] While Aimee was steadily building her ministry, with the help of her mother and devoted followers, Harold foundered for a few years, trying to find himself.

Roberta later recalled that her stepfather over the years "had prospered with good years, and done better than most men when times were bad."[35] He flourished, as Aimee did, during the boom years of the 1920s and eventually founded his own business—the Ocala Candy Company—in Florida. Harold married again twice, and in his eighties he retired to Titusville, Florida, where at long last he was finally reacquainted with Rolf and Roberta, who frequently visited him in his final years. He spent his remaining years true to his reserved nature and quiet temperament "content at last to grow roses, pick oranges from his own backyard trees, and become active again in church work."[36]

Harold died on July 18, 1978, at the age of eighty-eight—thirty-four years after Aimee's passing. His two-paragraph obituary appeared in the local Titusville newspaper, the *Star Advocate*, in contrast to the four-page Associated Press obituary for Aimee. His third wife, Pearl, two daughters, one son, and six grandchildren survived him. His son Rolf, by then the leader of Aimee's world-wide denomination and the living proof of Aimee and Harold's love, preached at his funeral. Harold carried with him to his grave in his own quiet way a small flame for Aimee, much as she had carried the same in her own inimitable style for Robert Semple.

The Nation-Wide Camp Meeting ended on a Sunday evening, with the city police estimating the crowds to be between eight to ten thousand people. Aimee, ever the visionary one, heard her "heart throb, 'Los Angeles! Los Angeles!'"[37]

Minnie, ever practical, suggested that Aimee go on ahead, leaving the two children with her in the East. Aimee, however, appropriated for herself, her mother, and the children, the Old Testament promise and commandment originally given to Abraham: "Get thee out of thy country unto a land that I will show thee."[38]

Aimee felt that it was a theological exodus—"a going out. We have preached up and down the eastern coast, from the Canadian border to the farthest boundaries of Florida; yet our real call to preach the Gospel in every state has not been fulfilled. The gates of the nation swing wide before us! We must make this trip by auto, that we may scatter the Gospel seed as we go."[39]

Aimee's reflection after the camp meeting was that she and her mother "together...put over great revival campaigns, for which other evangelists would require great organizations and months of preparation"[40] Practicality and originality were combined in the mother-daughter twosome. Mistakes made were not repeated. An intuitive genius was quietly at work in the acceptance and rejection of various calls to minister. Aimee was, as she termed it, "being led of the Spirit." And those who knew her best always maintained that her dependence upon the Spirit "would continue to grow throughout her lifetime," despite her detractor's contentions that she succumbed early on to "worldliness" in Los Angeles.[41]

"We had been in the hands of pirates, acting under the name of a financial committee, and had received only a mere pittance, such as would not have been proffered to a pianist, so we were broke as far as that meeting was concerned," wrote Aimee, regarding the financial remuneration for the summer-long camp meeting.[42]

In a letter addressed to her, dated the September 25, 1918, a committee member wrote that he had issued her a check for two hundred dollars. "We hope to get together and get another settlement soon. There is [*sic*] still considerable outstanding pledges."[43]

The letter mentioned in passing Harold Stewart McPherson. Apparently, however, no funds were forthcoming, as Aimee recalled that, "The only thing we received were their little love gifts pressed into our hands as they bade us good-bye. It seemed that those who were most anxious to have us come were the least concerned about making any monetary provision now."[44]

Just as a new tent had been in order for the Philadelphia meeting, so a new Gospel Auto was determined to be necessary for the forthcoming journey west. After Aimee sold her present car, for "almost as much…as I had originally paid…I returned home in such an incredibly short time as to astonish even my mother, triumphantly driving a new car which I had taken out on trial."[45]

The new Gospel Auto was quickly "adorned with the standard six-inch gold letters [spelling out that] 'Jesus is coming soon. Get ready!' and 'Where will you spend eternity?' " The Pentecostal saints in Los Angeles would remember always the arrival of the evangelist in a long, black, seven-passenger Oldsmobile that had "made it all the way from the East Coast."[46] The Oldsmobile was advertised in the newspapers at the time as a car with "power, speed, [and] grace [where] beauty of line and finish go hand in hand with the virtue of economy" and that driving one of them was the "ideal way to tour."[47]

The idea of taking such a trip in the first place probably originated for Aimee out of the interest in the growing movie-making capital of the West,

Hollywood. Reflecting on the journey much later, she recalled, "The transcontinental auto trip was not common then… and especially [not] for lone women. It [the trip] had been made by a movie star for advertising purposes, but had never been made by a lady evangelist."[48] Aimee was, in fact, one of very few women of the time to ever attempt a transcontinental auto trip without the assistance of a man.

The fall of 1918 was spent in smaller meetings in the Northeast in preparation for the forthcoming cross-country journey. Throughout the month of September, a chain of meetings was held in Connecticut and Massachusetts.

Minnie's organizational genius had clearly begun midway through the Philadelphia meetings, in response to the growing number of requests for Sister to come and minister. In the September 1918 issue of the *Bridal Call*, four conditions for Sister Aimee's coming meetings were put forth by Minnie:

> [First] before writing, inquire first the fare on the train to your town from Montwaite, Framingham, Mass., (one of the most central places in New England…being half way between Boston and Worcester)…Also state whether you are able to meet this fare, etc. Second: Let us know whether you can secure or rent a suitable building in which to hold these meetings. Also whether your faith covers this expenditure. Third: What advertising facilities have you. Fourth: Population of the town. Also state whether any there have [the] baptism [of the Holy Spirit]; if so, about how many…This work is run on faith lines, no salary, no earthly board behind us, but we have a Heavenly Board [Father, Son and Holy Ghost] Hallelujah![49]

The influenza epidemic of 1918 was raging throughout the country and affected Aimee's scheduled meetings in the fall. The October *Bridal Call* noted, "Meetings in general have for a few weeks been stopped over the country on account of the prevailing epidemic."[50] Otis' publishing concerns were cut back when his printer became ill and his infant daughter died. The flu touched Aimee directly when Roberta fell ill during her meeting in New York. It was a sure sign, to Aimee, that "God was leading her West—to a more permanent habitation unto the Lord."[51]

By October 1918, Minnie's organizational strategy had been put into operation for Aimee's New York meetings. A sponsoring minister and his wife originally let Aimee hold her meetings at their Pentecostal mission, with the first meeting being held on October 3. The Pentecostal mission meetings were quickly overcrowded, so the sponsors decided to rent the larger Harlem Casino to host Aimee's meetings. Aimee, her mother, and her children were given lodgings at a nearby hotel. The Harlem Casino was located at 100 West 116th Street, at the corner of Lenox Avenue, which was at the time a section of Manhattan with a large Jewish population. Aimee wrote about the facilities to her followers, noting, "There could not have been a better location for a Pentecostal Convention in New York City than the Harlem Casino, which is easy of access by subway, elevated, surface cars and buses. The hall seated some seven hundred people."[52]

Besides speaking in several established churches in New York City, Aimee was also invited to speak daily at the businessmen's noon-day meeting, held at the John Street Methodist Church. A reporter for Otis' *Word and Work* took note of the occurrence: "They have given her liberty to preach the baptism of the Holy Ghost with the Bible evidence speaking in tongues, and as this meeting is largely attended by Christian workers and ministers, doctors of divinity, a wide area is being reached and these meetings are truly as a stone dropped in calm waters, sending ripples far and wide in all directions."[53]

The last of a set of meetings reaching from Montwaite to New York was completed at New Rochelle. The meetings, Aimee noted, were without "one discordant note...one unkind word or criticism or tale-bearing."[54] Doctrinal differences would divide much of the Pentecostal movement throughout the 1920s. Aimee, more than any other Pentecostal leader, would stress unity in the movement and shy away from doctrinal disputes. In announcing her forthcoming transcontinental meeting in Tulsa, Oklahoma, which was "beginning on or about November 10, 1918," Aimee admonished the Pentecostals to "drop all differences and non-essential issues, and come with one accord to wait upon the Lord."[55]

At New Rochelle, both Aimee and Roberta were stricken by the raging influenza epidemic of 1918. When Roberta, her "star of hope," developed double pneumonia while "staying in the furnished rooms without heat or home comforts," Aimee wrote, "I yearned for a little home where I could care for her properly."[56]

Praying for her daughter as Roberta hovered near death for two days, Aimee not only felt an assurance that her life would be spared but also that "the Lord...also poured balm upon my troubled heart by saying: 'I will give you a little home—a nest for your babies—out in Los Angeles, California, where they can play and be happy and go to school and have the home surroundings of other children. You fixed a home once before out of My will [with Harold McPherson], and it was taken away; now I will give you a home in My will.' "[57]Roberta Star's near-death experience was, for Aimee, the final, sure sign that God, indeed, was leading her west.

For years the influenza epidemic of 1918 was overlooked in the telling of American history. It was equally overlooked and ignored for its contribution to the rise of global Pentecostalism. Not only did Aimee's career as a faith-healing evangelist skyrocket in its wake, one could quite easily make the case that, just as the 1906 earthquake in San Francisco served as a catalyst for the Azusa Street Mission in Los Angeles, the pandemic of 1918 similarly served as an impetus for the wide acceptance of divine healing in global Christianity.

Even World War I did not come close to causing the casualties of the flu epidemic. While the war claimed an estimated sixteen million lives, some fifty million people worldwide were killed by the deadly virus. More people died in 1918 than in the four years—1347 through 1351—of the Black Death (the bubonic plague). Science simply was at a loss and could not identify the disease that struck so quickly and savagely, defied both treatment and control, and indiscriminately ravaged all age groups. During that time, school children would skip rope at recess to a rhyme the disease had inspired:

> I had a little bird,
> Its name was Enza.
> I opened the window,
> And in-flu-enza.[58]

The flu was rampant in both urban and rural areas, eventually infecting twenty-eight percent of all Americans. It struck America in two successive waves. Kansas and various military camps were hit first in the spring of 1918. The second and deadlier wave arrived in Boston in September. At New Rochelle, Aimee and her family were less than two hundred miles from the plague's new epicenter. The deadly virus claimed two hundred thousand lives in the month of October alone, the same month that Roberta was stricken. Ironically, the year 1918 would go down in American history as a year of peace and also of extreme suffering and death. At year's end, both events were noted in an article in the *Journal of the American Medical Association*:

> 1918 has gone: a year momentous as the termination of the most cruel war in the annals of the human race; a year which marked, the end at least for a time, of man's destruction of man; unfortunately a year in which developed a most fatal infectious disease causing the death of hundreds of thousands of human beings. Medical science for four

and one-half years devoted itself to putting men on the firing line and keeping them there. Now it must turn with its whole might to combating the greatest enemy of all—infectious disease.[59]

In 1918, the First World War and the influenza epidemic both contributed to the success of Aimee's career as a Pentecostal evangelist. Not only was there a shortage of healers in the land, but there was also, due to the war, an equal shortage of preachers. The following year, in July 1919, the *Latter Rain Evangel*, a Pentecostal periodical, took note of Aimee's increasing visibility. Although many Pentecostal preachers were pacifists, the article attempted to explain to its readers the reason for Sister Aimee's ever-expanding ministry. "The war has demanded many of our young men and it seems as if the Lord is now making use of the ministry of His handmaidens who are given to Him for His work. May the Lord give us many more like our dear sister."[60]

With the flu epidemic still raging in the Southwest, Aimee received a telegram from the host minister of the scheduled meetings in Tulsa, advising her to postpone coming because "All churches are closed" and "it is not safe for you to be abroad in the land."[61] Aimee ignored the telegram and listened to her inner voices instead. "Fear not, do not lose a single day," they told her. "Go at once, and the day you arrive the ban will be lifted and the churches open."[62]

Not wasting a day, the Gospel Auto left Camden, New Jersey, on October 24, arriving in Tulsa, Oklahoma, on November 10. Minnie had by this time fully accepted the journey west and was beginning to finally comprehend her daughter's sense of destiny and self-understanding. Mother and daughter kept a travel log of the journey, and in 1926, while her daughter was in the Holy Land on her first "real vacation," Minnie would share her insights regarding both her daughter and the trip west with *The Bridal Call* readership. Minnie realized now more than ever that her daughter's spiritual mission was difficult to categorize. And it would never fit in with the standard way of doing things. Their trip was but one more example of that. "Sister McPherson has been called of God," said Minnie, "out of the regular, accepted routine and has to go her way alone. It is not always the soft-carpeted, chicken dinner-strewn pathway that leads from obscurity to world prominence. As a matter of fact, it is usually quite the opposite."[63]

Arriving in Tulsa, Aimee wrote to her followers, "Well, Hallelujah! The Lord took us through the swollen river bottom without mishap…In all these 1500 miles we have had but two slight punctures and absolutely no engine trouble."[64]

The river that overflowed its banks swamped the road and at times

The famous Gospel Auto that brough Aimee to Los Angeles in 1918. The seven-passenger Oldsmobile was advertised as "the ideal way to tour" (used by permission of the International Church of the Foursquare Gospel, Heritage Department).

washed over the fenders of the Gospel Auto and covered the floor boards. But no matter. Aimee in an old discarded Army leather jacket, Minnie in a bearskin coat, and Rolf and Roberta huddled together under the warmth of a lap robe continued their journey west. Aimee and the growing band of Pentecostal believers were reliving biblical days. They were not so much living in twentieth-century America as they were living in both the Old and New Testament times. Like the Children of Israel, they were traveling to a "promised land." Rivers had to be crossed on hand-propelled ferries, but had not God opened the Red Sea for his children? This was for them the "latter rain," God's final dispensation, the age of the Holy Spirit, as evidenced by speaking in other tongues or as Aimee so aptly said in the title of her first book, *This Is That* (a reference to Acts 2:16-18). Aimee had no sense at the time that she would make American religious history; rather, she was convinced that she was an active participant in the ongoing of biblical history. Even her son's earliest recollections were the stories from the Old Testament. "We felt," remembered Rolf "like the children of Israel."[65]

Arriving in Tulsa, Aimee immediately began to spiritualize the Southwest. It was like arriving in the Promised Land itself. Her travel log reveals her thoughts:

> At noon, looking across the great stretches of prairie, the city of Tulsa, great oil center, came into view, and as we saw the skyline, the buildings and the paved streets…it seemed as though that must be the way it will be when a soul is nearing Heaven, coming up the last lap of the journey,

the beautiful city, with its walls of jaspers looming just before no more deep ruts or ditches to be avoided, but smooth streets that are paved with gold; no more camping by the way in the darkness, for there will be an eternal day that shall never fade away.[66]

Aimee would write to the scattered Pentecostal saints, "We realize that we are in the center of God's will and His smile is upon us."[67] "The Center of God's Will" would become a familiar theme in her ministry. She would later even write a song about it. Her use of the expression not only reflected a growing optimism about her min-

Maria Woodworth Etter, an early role model for istry but her coming to terms as
Aimee (used by permission of the Flower Pente- well with her marital separation.
costal Heritage Center). For Aimee, like so many Method-

ist leaders before her, an unhappy and unfulfilled personal life seemingly became the prerequisite for finding God's will.

An obvious disappointment for Aimee in her trip west had been her stop over in Indianapolis. Indianapolis was the home of Mrs. Maria Woodworth Etter, at the time the most prominent woman evangelist in Pentecostalism. Beginning in the Holiness movement, by 1918 Mrs. Etter had been preaching for forty years. She had her own tabernacle, the Woodworth Etter Tabernacle, located at 2112 West Miller Street. She was a pioneer in Pentecostalism and in many ways something of a role model for a young Pentecostal woman minister such as Aimee. She dressed in white and had authored several books, which Aimee's first greatly resembled stylistically. She was widely known for her spiritual abilities in "divine healing." She had even helped to establish Pentecostalism at Aimee's first home base, Montwaite, until disorder broke out from religious persecutors. The Framingham police were called in to quell the disturbance, and Mrs. Etter and her associates were charged in the district court that they had "intended to cheat and defraud, falsely pretended to be able to cure and heal persons afflicted with cancer, tuberculosis, deafness, blindness and leprosy." The judge later dismissed the case, and Mrs. Etter returned to the Midwest.[68]

Aimee's similarities with Mrs. Etter ended here. Their temperaments were wholly different. Etter was aloof and rigid, lacking the warmth of Aimee's personality. She was also considerably older. Aimee mentioned in her travel log "For years I have been longing to meet this dear sister and have been talking about it more and more in recent months. I have longed to hear her preach and be in just one of her meetings." Her subsequent meeting with Mrs. Etter proved a disappointment as it was noted only in passing with the attached comment that "there were only a very few at the meeting."[69]Maria Woodworth Etter's day had come and gone while Aimee Semple McPherson's was just beginning.

Aimee's "inner voice" had proven to be accurate about going to Tulsa: "That very day the ban [because of the influenza] lifted and the churches opened, and though tired in body, the Lord helped us to enter right into the next meeting, where we found the church, seating some 700, well filled, and the shouts and 'Glorys' of the saints filling the tabernacle."[70]The services were held at the Assembly of God Tabernacle and hosted by the Reverend S.A. Jamieson, a former Presbyterian minister and superintendent of home missionary work for his denomination in northern Minnesota. A convert to Pentecostalism through his wife, Jamieson attended various Pentecostal camp meetings after leaving the Presbyterian Church and eventually started the Pentecostal work in Dallas. Jamieson's attention was called to Mrs. McPherson's work like growing numbers of others "through her writings, which displayed her faith and consecration, and after reading her periodical, *The Bridal Call,* we were convinced that she was the person who, through the Spirit, could wake up to our privileges in Christ Jesus."[71]

Jamieson and the "Tulsa saints" were not disappointed. Jamieson's subsequent testimonial added strength to the wide reputation Aimee earned following the Philadelphia camp meeting, "It seemed the very moment she placed her hands on some of the sick ones the disease took its flight…We have been at a spiritual banquet during the stay of our Sister McPherson.[72]

The Gospel Auto was put to good use during Aimee's time in Tulsa. "Having secured one of the best corners in the city, the top of the auto was put down, and singers, with their musical instruments, filled the car; … Illustrated charts were hung from a stand, these charts drew crowds from all about."[73]Aimee and her Gospel auto were most effective, whether it was at the Tulsa Iron Works for noon-time meetings or downtown at night. Always an "altar call" was given with the penitents kneeling at the running board for a makeshift altar.

At the conclusion of the Tulsa meetings, Aimee wrote to her faithful readership, "[We will] resume our journey to Los Angeles, California in which state we expect to spend the balance of the winter...We would also be pleased to hear from as many of the saints as possible living along the coast of California who are interested in...revival meetings."[74] The address Aimee gave her readership was in care of Pastor W. W. Fisher, 125½ South Spring Street, Los Angeles, California.

Aimee's arrival in Los Angeles was to be propitious. Religion and society would never intersect any better at any time. Pentecostalism had originated in Los Angeles; however, in recent years it had fragmented racially and doctrinally. With Aimee's assistance it was about to be reborn and take root in American culture, ready to leave its attics and missions for the good part of the town and the "right side of the tracks." Los Angeles also was about to be awakened from its slumber as a sleepy overgrown "Midwestern" town. It was not until the years following World War I that "the old Pueblo stepped out on the 'Big Time' circuit, and definitely took her place among America's metropolitan cities."[75] The value of building permits rose from twenty-eight million dollars in 1923, placing Los Angeles third in the nation following New York and Chicago. The flood of population that inundated Southern California and Los Angeles during the early 1920s was comparable only to the extraordinary growth of Chicago immediately after the Civil War. "Conservatively estimated, the city's population grew at the rate of 100,000 per year. By the end of 1923, its total had reached 900,000."[76] "Nearly every newcomer was the seeker of a home. And, in 1923 more buildings were started or completed than ever before in a single year: 800 mercantile buildings; 400 industrial buildings; 60 hotels; 130 schools; 130 warehouses; 700 apartment houses; and 25,000 single and double dwelling houses."[77]

It was also in the same year, 1923, that "Sister Aimee" would open the doors to Angelus Temple, providing a spiritual home for the new arrivals. In the process her name would forever be linked with the City of Angels and the area "South of Tehachapi" known as "Southern California Country." Carey McWilliams, chronicler of the new land, summarized it best when he wrote of Aimee's future relationship with Los Angeles: "In Los Angeles she was more than just a household word. She was a folk hero and a civic institution; an honorary member of the fire department; a patron saint of the service clubs; an official spokesman for the community on problems grave and frivolous."[78]

Approaching Los Angeles just before Christmas of 1918, Aimee allowed the Gospel Auto to coast down the grade from the mountain passes to San Bernardino. "After the prairies, plains, deserts, and mountains this seemed like a new world...we were in the land where thousands of acres were

filled with nothing but beautiful fruit trees, oranges, lemons, grapefruit,…
hanging in abundance."[79] Both Aimee and Minnie appropriated for themselves the Old Testament text of Joshua 6:16: "Shout, for the Lord hath
given you the city."[80]Even though he was only a young boy, Rolf never
forgot the sensation of the Gospel Auto "suddenly dropping down into
the bowl of Southern California. It seemed like a great oasis stretching out
forever. It was filled with fruit trees and crops were growing in the fields."[81]
Aimee's young son too could make the identification of Southern California as their new place of promise. Their days of wandering in the wilderness like the children of Israel would soon be over. "The fragrance of the
orange blossoms welcomed us," wrote Ma Kennedy, "as they welcome all
who come over the mountains, through the desert, to this land of golden
sunshine."[82]

Despite her boldness in appropriating Old Testament passages for her
family and forthcoming ministry in California, Aimee, was also briefly paralyzed by the sudden fear of being "a stranger in a strange land."

> The enemy rose up and began to accuse me of my unworthiness and
> pointed out that we were coming as strangers into a strange land, and
> had nothing but a few letters of invitation. As we arrived at the home
> of Brother and Sister Blake, however, they ran to open the gate to admit
> our car. I think it was the biggest gate I have ever seen, and as it rolled
> back so smoothly on its hinges, God spoke to me and said, "Just like this
> I will open the big hearts of my people to you, and swing wide the door
> of California before you!"[83]

Prophets and prophetesses, like the pioneers, have always moved westward
and with increasing success. At the age of twenty-eight Aimee discovered
that in Southern California revival meetings could be conducted not on a
seasonal but on a year-round basis. Soon the door of not only California
but the entire country would indeed "swing wide" before her.

CHAPTER SIX

Los Angeles

To many a newcomer, Los Angeles is a Promised Land. It amazes and delights him, and thaws him out physically and spiritually. There is a heady fragrance in the air, and a spaciousness of sky and land and sea that give him a sense of freedom and tempt him to taste new pleasures, new habits of living, new religions....And because the array of things to do and see is so dazzlingly different from everything he has known, his curiosity is always whetted, his appetite never sated. He feels a certain strangeness that is at once exhilarating and disturbing, and that he had not known in his native place back East.

—*Los Angeles: A Guide to the City and Its Environs*

This strip of coast, this tiny region, seems to be looking westward across the Pacific, waiting for the future that one somehow sense, and feel, and see. Here America will build its great city of the Pacific, the most fantastic city in the world.

—Carey McWilliams
Southern California Country, 1946

Los Angeles is not a city that dwells on the past. It's the city of the future, free of traditional thinking—the city of reinvention and second chances...In the "Land of Sunshine," pretty Midwestern girls become movie stars, and immigrants shed their Old World names. Everyone seems to come from somewhere else, unfettered and free to start over in a land without history. Or so it seems.

—Louise Publols

Los Angeles matured...by covering up places, people, and histories that those in power found unsettling. Los Angeles became a self-conscious "City of the Future" by whitewashing an adobe past.

—William Deverell

El Pueblo de Nuestra Senora la Reina de los Angeles de Porciuncula was founded September 4, 1781. The city of Los Angeles, the town of Our Lady the Queen of the Angels, from its earliest beginning has had in a sense "a spiritual history," since religious rites were part of its earliest

Sketch of the village of Los Angeles in the 1850s. The central plaza was located at the present intersection of Sunset and Main. View is toward the east from Bunker Hill to the Plaza Church. The village was built "on a gentle slope...about twenty miles from the sea and fifteen from the mountains, a most lovely locality" (used by permission of the Security Pacific National Bank Collection/Los Angeles Public Library).

makeup. Contrary to popular misconceptions, Los Angeles, unlike many major American cities, did not simply spring up from a crossroads, a fort, or just happen. Following its days as an Indian village, it was a Spanish colonial settlement, a Mexican provincial capital, and finally a Yankee boomtown.

In its first stages of evolution, Los Angeles was an Indian village called Yang-na. Over the Southern California land were several score *rancherías*, villages, of fifty to more than one hundred persons each. "The Gabrielino, rather than the distinctively American Indian...resembled the Alaskan and Aleutian tribes which crossed from Asia when that continent and North America joined."[1] Contemplative and philosophical, the Gabrielino were at ease with the mystical and supernatural as well as the material. They believed in one God, "the maker and creator of all things, whose name was held so sacred among them, as hardly ever to be used; and when used only in a low voice."[2]

Spanish explorers penetrated to the California coast as early as 1542. The name *California* was supposedly derived from a Spanish novel. In the novel there existed an imaginary island called California, which was rich in pearls and gold and peopled with black Amazon women who were robust of body and passionate of heart. They were ruled by a queen, Califia, who was both beautiful and warlike and was supposedly leagued with pagan princes against the leaders of Christendom.[3] And as George P. Hammond has so astutely noted, "the search for the fabulous always accompanied the settlement of the southwest."[4]

Not until 1769, however, did Spain move to occupy its most remote frontier provinces. The Portola expedition of 1769, four years before the Boston Tea Party, was sent forth from Baja (lower) California to establish a mission in Alta (upper) California. The Spanish governor of the Californias, Don Gaspar de Portola, and his men were the first Spanish to pass through the Los Angeles area and to come into contact with the Indian village called Yang-na. Los Angeles at first appeared to the Franciscan priest Juan Crespi, the chief chronicler of the trip, as a "delightful place among the trees on the river,"[5] and as "a beautiful, fertile plain blooming with wild roses."[6] The area was discovered on one of the most holy days of the Catholic year, August 1, the day of Jubilee of Our Lady of the Angels of Porciuncula. Originally granted by the Pope to the church of Our Lady of the Angels at Poriuncula in Italy, "it was finally extended to every Franciscan 'wherever he may erect an altar' on that day."[7] The holy day lasted from August 1 to sunset on August 2 and "whosoever confesses and receives sacrament is granted plenary remission of his sins in this world and the next."[8]

Father Crespi's diary describes both days and the naming and description of the future city:

> This day was one of rest [and] to celebrate the jubilee of Our Lady of Los Angeles de Porciuncula. We said Mass and the men took communion…We set out from the valley in the morning…we entered a very spacious valley, well grown with cottonwoods and elders, among which ran a beautiful river. We halted not very far from the river, which we named Porciuncula. Here we felt three consecutive earthquakes….This plain where the river runs is very extensive. It has good land…and is the most suitable site of all that we have seen for a mission, for it has all the requisites for a large settlement.[9]

"The delightful place among the trees on the river" that had all the needed "requisites for a large settlement," followed the pueblo plan of colonization under the new governor of California, Don Felipe de Neve. The head of the first families were required to fit the following description: "The head or father of each family must be a man of the soil, *Labrador de exercicio*, healthy, robust, and without known vice or defect."[10] In Mexico only twelve of the twenty-four families originally requested were secured, with one family never making the trip at all. Of the adults of the eleven first families of Los Angeles, their nationality broke down as follows: "two Spaniards, one mestizo, two negroes, eight mulattoes, and nine Indians."[11] On September 4, 1781, as the American Revolution was ending on the other side of the continent, Los Angeles was founded. Forty-four persons with an escort of soldiers and priests left San Gabriel for the founding of the new pueblo.

It was not until 1784, three years after its founding, that the new pueblo had its own chapel. Those desirous of attending church previously had to journey to San Gabriel. After the small adobe church on the plaza was erected and services held, the visiting padres who conducted the mass complained about the lifestyle of the parishioners. Subsequently four of the families were expelled from the community "as useless to the Pueblo and to themselves."[12] For forty years, from 1781 to 1821, Los Angeles remained a Spanish *pueblo*. In 1790 the first census of the fledgling community was taken—also the year of the first federal census in the United States. The census revealed twenty-eight men and one hundred forty-one persons total. In nine years the racial and ethnic breakdown had changed considerably: Europeans, l; Spaniards, 72; Indians, 7; mulattos, 22; and mestizos, 30. The *pueblo* at the close of the century had seventy families and three hundred fifteen people, "and thirty small adobe houses either grouped about the Plaza or clustered nearby."[13]

Despite the missionaries' complaint at San Gabriel that the new pueblo was preoccupied with "fast horses, strong drink and loose women," the settlers had managed to produce more horses and cattle and grain than any other community in Alta California.[14] By the year 1800, horses and cattle numbered 12,500 and there had been a harvest of 4,600 bushels of wheat. At the same time, "Washington, D.C. remained unincorporated, Philadelphia still being the capital of the nation. Cleveland, Indianapolis, Wilmington, Memphis, Minneapolis, Tampa, Kansas City, Seattle, Houston, and Omaha had not come into existence."[15]

Visitors to the old Spanish *pueblo* of Los Angeles were rare. In 1805 the *Lelia Byrd* anchored at San Pedro, the first American vessel to defy Spanish law prohibiting trade with foreign ships. The master of the ship carried back to the United States a glowing account of the wealth of California as well as a cargo of hogs and sheep. In 1818 Joseph Chapman, re-baptized José, was captured as a pirate and became the first English-speaking settler. Held prisoner, Chapman, owing to his knowledge of the scientific felling of trees, was later released and set to work. He built the first successful water grist mill to be operated in California, supervised the construction of a schooner for the padres and erected the church, since remodeled, that still stands facing the plaza, the Church of Our Lady of the Angels.

In the spring of 1822, word reached the *pueblo* that Mexico had won its independence from Spain. California became Mexican territory and the flag flying above the plaza changed from Spanish lion to the Mexican eagle and serpent. The Mexican nation was, however, a much less effective overlord than Spain, and its rule lasted only half as long as the Spanish era. During the interlude the missions were secularized (1834-1837) and the *rancho* period began. The result was that "more American traders, miners, and adventures drifted in, embraced the Roman Catholic religion, married Mexican heiresses and became Yankee dons. During the storied rancho period all of southern California was held under the virtual feudal sway of a handful of Mexican cattle barons—Pico, Figueroa, Sepulveda, Bandini, and others."[16]

When Sir George Simpson passed through California on his 1841 trip around the world, he found its trade in the hands of foreigners, mostly from the United States. Five years later, after Texas had become part of the Union, an often-quoted speech attributed to Governor Pio Pico warned Californians about the "hordes of Yankee emigrants."

> They are cultivating farms, establishing vineyards, erecting mills, sawing up lumber, building workshops, and doing a thousand other things which seem natural to them, but which Californians neglect or despise. What then are we to do? Shall we remain supine, while those daring strangers are over-running our fertile plains, and gradually out-numbering and displacing us? Shall these incursions go on unchecked, until we shall become strangers in our land?[17]

On January 18, 1847 the Stars and Stripes went up in the plaza, replacing the Mexican eagle and serpent. The *Californios*, like the earlier Indians, had indeed become strangers in their own land. From 1850 to 1870 the old *pueblo*, a nondescript village of fewer than than three housand inhabitants, was transformed into a Yankee boomtown. With the discovery of gold in 1849, San Francisco and the Mother Lode country exploded. Los Angeles, four hundred miles to the south, was somewhat stimulated by the Gold Rush because of an insatiable market for southern California cattle, but its population grew to a total of only 5,614 by 1870. During this time it dropped from being the largest city of the state to just another town. Several cities, including Grass Valley in the north, were larger. Compared to San Francisco, now the largest city west of the Mississippi, Los Angeles was a mere village.[18]

During these years of transition *La Estrella de los Angeles*, or *The Los Angeles Star*, printed half in Spanish and half in English, complained that the civic conscience had fallen so low that "her bowels are absolute strangers to sympathy, when called upon to practically demonstrate it."[19] Los Angeles' vigilantes, known as "Rangers," lynched four times as many as the more well-known vigilantes of San Francisco. Those driven out of that city soon found their way south to Los Angeles.

Mainline Protestant missionaries made an early unsuccessful attempt to convert both the growing village's Catholics and "heathens." Soon after their arrival, they abandoned Los Angeles as hopeless. What had taken root in Northern California failed to flourish in the South. The Methodists arrived in 1853, the Presbyterians in 1854, and the Episcopalians in 1857, who erected the first Protestant church building in the city, St. Athanasius Episcopal Church, located on the southwest corner of Temple and New High streets. However, as a later report of the city indicated "All three ministers left for more hopeful fields."[20]

The Methodist minister, the Reverend James W. Brier, who arrived in Los Angeles by oxcart, had been determined to "preach the Resurrected Christ" and to establish a Sunday school for the children of American migrants. In three months time he left. His reason for leaving was his inability to adjust to the "spiritual hardness of heart" among his would-be parishioners. The Reverend James Woods, the Presbyterian minister, concluded after his brief tenure, "The name of this city is in Spanish the city of the angels, but with much truth might it be called the city of demons."[21] Before he left Los Angeles, Woods noted in his diary (1854–1855) the moral character of the town, the general lack of religion, and the already emerging eclecticism of the meager religious faith that was present:

> While I have been here in Los Angeles only two weeks, there have been ... eleven deaths, only one of them a natural death—all the rest by violence. There is...no interest felt here upon the subject of religion—it is like the valley of dry bones, scarcely any professors of religion...Paid a visit to Dr. H. He is certainly unbalanced in mind. He has religion, socialism, Swedenbergeanism *[sic]* all mixed up together.[22]

In the spring of 1859 the Reverend George F. Pierce, the Methodist bishop of Georgia, made an overland stage journey with his family from San Antonio, Texas, to San Francisco. Expressing the common disdain most Protestants had for the strong Catholicism of California, Pierce nevertheless marveled in his diary regarding the solid advances it had made as well as the natural beauty of Los Angeles.

> Let Protestantism ponder the example. Shall a corrupted Christianity outvie a purer, more spiritual system? ...Catholic priests came, toiled,

suffered, died, and left … decaying monuments of their heroism…out of 2,464 traveling preachers and 5,117 local preachers, all sons of Wesley— I cannot get ten to go to California to preach the everlasting Gospel!!!…. Now we come upon a scene of enchantment—Los Angeles…To us it was like a magical creation. Aladdin's lamp could hardly have conjured up a brighter, more unexpected scene…It is an old place, revised, enlarged, modernized. Spain has left her footprints, but young America will soon have left no vestige of her presence except the grape-vine.[23]

In 1860 a geological survey was made of California. William H. Brower, a member of the team from Yale University graphically described Los Angeles at the time of the Civil War:

Los Angeles is a city…nearly a century old, a regular old Spanish-Mexican town…The houses are but one story, mostly built of adobe or sun-burnt brick, with very thick walls and flat roofs. They are so low because of earthquakes, and the style is Mexican.….Here is a great plain, or rather a gentle slope, from the Pacific to the mountains. We are on this plain about twenty miles from the sea and fifteen from the mountains, a most lovely locality; all that is wanted naturally to make it a paradise is water, more water…The weather is soft and balmy—no winter, but a perpetual spring and summer. Such is Los Angeles, a place where every prospect pleases and only man is vile….Here let me digress. This southern California is still unsettled. We all continually wear arms—each wears both bowie knife and pistol.…Fifty to sixty murders per year have been common here in Los Angeles, and some think it odd that there has been no violent death during the two weeks that we have been here.…I have been practicing with my revolver and am becoming expert.[24]

It was as "Los Diablos" that Los Angeles in 1871 made front-page news across the country. After the accidental killing of a white man by a Chinese, a mob of five hundred lynched eighteen innocent Chinese and looted Chinatown. "The town," as one report noted, "was shocked into sudden sobriety."[25] The lawlessness of the period was more than just a result of the Gold Rush days. The old *pueblo* was experiencing culture shock in its transition to a Yankee boomtown, especially in the efforts to accommodate Spanish customs to American law. Compounding the problem was the treatment some two thousand Indians received living in squalor and poverty just off the Plaza in "Nigger Alley." Fortified with liquor on Saturday and Sunday nights, they would be dragged off in an unconscious state to a corral and on Monday morning be auctioned off as slaves. For a week's work they would receive only a dollar or two with part of the payment in brandy. "This condition of affairs lasted until the Indians were all dead, and they went out rapidly under such a hideous system."[26]

Through the efforts of four Sacramento merchants—C.P. Huntington, Charles Crocker, Mark Hopkins, and Leland Stanford—the Southern Pacific Railroad reached Los Angeles in 1876. The Santa Fe came in 1885, leading to bitter rivalry:

> Immediately one of the bitterest railroad rate wars in history broke out. The Santa Fe reduced the fare from the Mississippi Valley from $100 to $95. Passengers scurried from one railroad office to the other to obtain the latest bargain. At the height of the hostilities, the fare dropped to $15, then to $5, and for one day in the spring of 1866, the Santa Fe advertised "Kansas City to Los Angeles for a dollar!" Train after train rumbled into Los Angeles, packed to the doors, and the first and gaudiest of its real estate booms was under way.[27]

No one has captured the transition of Los Angeles from a sleepy Mexican village into a booming Yankee city better than the historian Leonard Pitt. "When the first railroad started running in southern California…shuttling back and forth from Los Angeles to San Pedro, vaqueros," Pitt noted in his *The Decline of the Californios*, "would gleefully race their horses against the locomotive. They won the short sprint, but…lost in the long haul."

> The civilization represented by the locomotive was bearing down on them slowly but with irresistible force….as many as three and four coach trains descended on the city each day, depositing in 1887 alone more than 120,000 tourists…These developments… "the most extravagant in American frontier experience" …sealed the coffin of the old California culture….What started out as a "semi-gringo" town…became practically overnight a booming Yankee commercial center and the best-known place in the entire West….The most elemental change lay in the chopping up of the ranchos into farms and towns…the eroded claims of the original claimants washed away steadily and flowed into the hands of the newcomers—financiers, railroad developers, town promoters, cooperative colonizers, and irrigation companies.[28]

The old pueblo's population swelled from twelve thousand to fifty thousand in a little more than two years time. Lots around the plaza sold at one thousand dollars a front foot, and subdivisions were laid out from Santa Monica to San Bernardino, a distance of seventy miles. Full-page advertisements in the newspapers beckoned for potential newcomers:

He or she
that hesitates is lost
an axiom that holds good
in real estate, as well
as in affairs of the heart.
Selah![29]

With the first population boom, the *Los Angeles Times* warned its readers that the town was no place for "dudes, loafers, paupers; those who expect to astonish the natives, those afraid to pull off their coats, cheap politicians, business scrubs, impecunious clerks, lawyers, and doctors."[30] Attempting to rid Los Angeles of its backward and lawless reputation, *The Times* also assured the rest of the country that "Los Angeles people do not carry arms, Indians are a curiosity, the gee string is not a common article of apparel here, and Los Angeles has three good hotels, twenty-seven churches, and 350 telephone subscribers."[31]

The Yankee rush to the West, and Los Angeles in particular, was for many more than just greed and quick opportunism. With the railroads also came a health rush. Ads from Los Angeles asking the following questions soon began appearing in the nation's newspapers:

Aren't you tired of the doctoring and nursing,
Of the sickly winters and the pocket pills—
Tired of sorrowing and burying, and cursing,
At Providence and undertaker's bills?[32]

An editorial in the *Los Angeles Daily News* in January of 1869 declared that, "the great desideratum, a genial and healthful climate, constitutes the chief attraction."[33] One physician in Los Angeles in 1873 remarked that he had never seen in any other state so much suffering from pulmonary diseases as he had found in southern California. "Oh! What a lot of coughing, suffering mortals are coming here! Many too late. One man died in sight of the harbor."[34] Even the area's irreverent journalists jested about the city's main attraction at a convention in 1886.

I thought I came here to die. Alas, when I left home I had but one lung and it almost gone. I couldn't speak above a whisper, and had no appetite. I have been two weeks in Pasadena, have three lungs, can roar like a descending avalanche, ate three mules for breakfast, and am going to try it for another week.[35]

By the 1890s the sick "had become as typical as palm or orange tree. A tuberculosis patient described the result in Los Angeles:

> At every street corner I met a poor fellow croaking like myself. I strolled into the Plaza, there to imbibe the exhilarating effects of a community with broken lungs in all stages, and the inspiring comfort of a vocabulary like this: "Well, how do you feel today?" "Did you have a good night?" "Are you trying any new medicine?" "O, the pain in my side is very bad." "Do you cough much now?".... On the streets and in the trolleys or at the post office, where they invariably awaited cheering letters from home, one could meet these desperately ill yet courageous people with their "hollow eyes and still more hollow cough"[36]

Due to a serious housing shortage and the lack of new hotels, the cities of San Diego and Santa Barbara early on drained off the first health seekers that came to Los Angeles. By the turn of the century, however, at least one-fourth of those who had established homes in the Los Angeles area had come for health reasons. The medical science of the time recommended the move to a sunny, dry climate for various respiratory ailments. Thus, "Los Angeles acquired a reputation as the 'One-lunged Tourist Town' and the young women complained in their diaries of being unable to find a suitor who was all of one piece."[37] "The true Californian," declared Will Irwin in 1906, "lingers in the north; for southern California has been built up by 'lungers' from the East and middle West and is Eastern in character and feeling."[38]

"Arabs of the Southwest" is how John Cowan described the health seekers living in tents sprouting up in Redlands and San Bernardino: "There are tents in front yards and back yards, in vacant lots, by country roadsides, on farms and ranches, in secluded canyons, in deep recesses of the forests, far out upon the deserts, and away up in the mountains. They are the camps of the Arabs of the Southwest—a forlorn, homeless and almost hopeless multitude of wanderers, chasing the phantom, Health."[39]

As the nineteenth century was coming to a close and just as the health rush to southern California reached its zenith, the Reverend Dwight L. Moody visited the region in one of his last evangelistic campaigns. Preaching in Pasadena's Tabernacle, the famous evangelist surveying his temporary congregation remarked, "How we cling to life. Thousands (are) here in California seeking health, bearing loneliness, homesickness, heartache and separation from dear ones, all that they may add a few years to life's span. Soon this audience will have passed from earth."[40] Moody, soon to die himself, felt that the many health seekers sitting before him in Southern

California "should be preparing themselves for the coming life rather than spending precious earthly time on their physical problems."[41] Unlike the evangelicalism of Moody, a new religion born in Los Angeles at Eastertide in 1906 would attempt to address both concerns.

By the 1915 Panama-California Exposition in San Diego, Southern California was not only touted as the "playground of the world" but also as a place for "spiritual uplift." The sacred and profane came together harmoniously in Southern California, especially during the decade of the 1920s, when the "Garden of the World" had become the new "Garden of Eden.""Spiritually this Southland is particularly blest," read a brochure. "The moral and religious tendencies of the people are especially worthy of note and throughout the land...are numerous houses of public worship from the unpretentious 'meeting house' to the towering temples of the affluent...The delightful climate, the picturesque scenery, the birds and fruits and flowers, all combine to create an atmosphere of culture which permeates...in this well-named 'Garden of the World.' "[42]

Many again heeded this new call to Los Angeles, none more than those from the Middle West. "On the road to old L.A., Where the tin-can tourists play and a sign says 'L.A. City Limits' at Clinton, Iowa."[43] They not only heard the call, they kept coming, especially in the 1920s. Mildred Adams wrote,

> Like a swarm of invading locusts, migrants crept in over all the roads... they had rattletrap automobiles, their fenders tied with string, and curtains flapping in the breeze; loaded with babies, bedding, bundles, a tin tub tied on behind, a bicycle or baby carriage balanced precariously on the top. Often they came with no funds and no prospects, apparently trusting that heaven would provide for them...They camped on the outskirts of town, and their camps became new suburbs[44]

The typical newcomers, this time, for the most part were "the middle-aged from the middle class of the Middle West."[45]

The development of transcontinental automobile travel had much the same relationship to the boom of the 1920s that completion of the Santa Fe line had to the boom of the 1880s. The resultant migration into Southern California between 1920–1930 has been characterized "as the largest internal migration in the history of the American people...most of them came directly to the City of Los Angeles which reported a population increase of 661,375 or a gain of 143.7% for the decade. Eight new cities were created in Los Angeles County during this ten-year period...During the forty-year period 1900 to 1940, the population of the region increased 1,107%, while the population of Los Angeles increased 1,535.7%, by comparison with an increase of 172 percent in San Francisco."[46]

The chain reaction set off by the real estate boom, motion-picture production, oil strikes, and the tourist trade of the 1920s was to Southern California what the Gold Rush had been to Northern California. The greatest increase occurred between 1920 and 1924, when at least one hundred thousand people a year poured into Los Angeles alone. The results of the unparalleled urban growth were often devastating, as Carey McWilliams noted in his classic work, *Southern California Country.* "Millions of dollars in new income poured into Los Angeles, undermining the social structure of the community, warping and twisting its institutions…For Southern California the decade was one long drunken orgy, one protracted debauch."[47]

Protestantism had failed miserably when it first appeared in the City of the Angels. The railroads changed all that, however, and created a Protestant boom for the city along with the real estate boom:

> With the beginning of the seventies [1870s], Los Angeles changed rapidly from a virtually barren Protestant religious field to a luxuriant pasture for any and all beliefs… Churches as well as real estate subdivisions mushroomed all over town; no less than forty were erected in the booming eighties and many more in the nineties.[48]

By 1881 Los Angeles was known as "a City of Churches"—for the most part, Protestant. By the following year, the Roman Catholic Church was only one of seven denominations and comprised only two-fifths of the church-going population.[49]

Protestantism and religion in general came to full bloom in Los Angeles, however, only with the migration following World War I. As a result, religion would be forced to compete with leisure and the other forms of entertainment. *The Guide to the City* noted that for the newcomer, "There is a heady fragrance in the air; and a spaciousness of the sky and land and sea that give him a sense of freedom and tempt him to taste new pleasures, new habits of living, new religions."[50] And it was this "sense of freedom" to "taste new religions" in the wake of the war that bothered the older Protestant Angelenos the most. Writing in 1921, John Steven McGroarty claimed that "Los Angeles is the most celebrated incubator of new creeds, codes of ethics, philosophies and near philosophies and schools of thought, occult, new and old."[51] McGroarty worried that his city was becoming a home and haven of "freak religions" that lured "people pale of thought."[52] By the

1930s the "new religions" were solidly entrenched in Los Angeles.

"When a survey of churches was taken in the 1930s, almost all of those in San Francisco were listed as either Protestant or Catholic. In Los Angeles, 147 of the churches were Catholic, 836 were Protestant and 850 were recorded as 'other.'"[53] *The Guide to Los Angeles* could legitimately state that "the multiplicity and diversity of faiths that flourish in the aptly named City of the Angels probably cannot be duplicated in any other city on earth… Orthodox creeds prosper side by side with numerous fanatical movements. There are rites and philosophies to suit all tastes."[54]

At the dawn of the twentieth century, Los Angeles was positioned to become not only the premier city on the West Coast, but the nation's next "shock city"—"a place that fully captures the period's emerging metropolitan trends and points to a new future."[55] By 1930 the city had realized its dream with a population of 1,238,084. America's "shock city" of the twentieth century had been created "by constructing a massive aqueduct system; annexing lands to the east, west, and south of its original borders; developing a harbor; building a massive infrastructure including roads and rail line; instituting the nation's first zoning laws, and fostering financial investment."[56] Far harder to measure but very real nevertheless were the spiritual and health seekers, all the newcomers who viewed Los Angeles as nothing less than their very own slice of Eden, like "a friendly island, not without promise of fine hours on a further day."[57]

CHAPTER SEVEN

Azusa Street and Aimee of the Angels

"He listened inside himself as if something by an unknown composer, powerful and strange and strong, was about to be played for the first time....He strained to hear it, knowing only that music was beginning, new music that he liked and did not understand....this was new and confusing, nothing one could shut off in the middle and supply the rest from an old score."

—F. Scott Fitzgerald
The Last Tycoon

Just as the nineteenth century was turning into the twentieth...two powerful and interrelated American cultural expressions—one musical and one religious—came to birth....Try as they have at times to deny their common parentage, jazz and Pentecostalism belong together. Each sprang from the obscure underside of the society. Each first appeared in one of the great polygot cities of America, jazz in New Orleans and Pentecostalism in Los Angeles. Each was despised and ridiculed at first, but both then went on to become major vehicles through which...the Universal Spirit with a distinctly American accent—would reach virtually every corner in the world...Just as white musicians sought out the French Quarter dives where the blacks were playing jazz...at Azusa Street...white people flocked into a black church, and they were welcomed....Both jazz and Pentecostalism stand as powerful reminders that who we are as Americans—though we often try to deny it—is a direct result of the unique mixture of black and white which has shaped us.

—Harvey Cox
Fire From Heaven

California irreligious? No!...the Abrahamic soul may still find its Canaan in the west, beside the waters of the world's last Mediterranean...Perchance our Moses is not born, our David still unnamed, our Elijahs and Elishas, our Isaiahs and Hosesas, and Jeremiahs are yet to come. But the spirit of a happy and holy inspiration broods over our land, and the world of tomorrow shall not only get its Commerce by way of the Golden Gate, but forth from our city of Saint Francis, and our city of the Angels there shall go the songs and prophecies of the world's best faith.

—Robert Whitaker, "Is California Irreligious?"
Sunset Magazine, 1906

Is not this the land of Beulah,
Blessed, blessed, land of Light,
Where the flowers bloom Forever,
And the sun is always Bright?
> —favorite chorus of Bishop William Joseph Seymour

The preacher is the most unique personality developed by the Negro on American soil.
> —W.E.B. DuBois

In 1906 Los Angeles had the highest level of religious diversity in the country.[1] On April 18 of that year the *Los Angeles Times* not only introduced the "newest religious sect" in a city already known as a hothouse incubator of them, but one that by a century later would be transnational, global, and the most dynamic representative of the Christian faith. America's gift to Christianity may have been Puritanism and Methodism but it was on the Pacific Coast, "on the edge of the last sea of history," at Azusa Street in Los Angeles, California where global Pentecostalism was birthed. "WEIRD BABEL OF TONGUES" screamed the headlines of the *Los Angeles Times*. "NEW SECT OF FANATICS IS BREAKING LOOSE." "WILD SCENE LAST NIGHT ON AZUSA STREET."

> Breathing strange utterances and mouthing a creed which it seem no sane mortal could understand, the newest Religious sect has started in L.A. Meetings are held in a tumble-down shack on Azusa Street, near San Pedro Street...Colored people and a sprinkling of whites compose the congregation, and night is made hideous in the neighborhood by the howlings of the worshipers...They claim to have "the gift of tongues" and to be able to comprehend the babel.
>
> Such a startling claim has never yet been made by any company of fanatics, even in Los Angeles, the home of almost numberless creeds... An old colored exhorter, blind in one eye, is the major-domo of the company...One of the wildest of the meetings was held last night and... which continued in "worship" until nearly midnight. The old exhorter urged the "sisters" to let the "tongues come forth"' and the women gave themselves over to a riot of religious fervor. As a result a buxom dame was overcome with excitement and almost fainted.[2]

The *Los Angeles Herald*, showing a bit more restraint than the *Times*, observed,

The Stevens African Methodist Episcopal Church, later known as the Asuza Street Mission (used by permission of the Flower Pentecostal Heritage Center).

> There were all ages, sexes, colors, nationalities and previous conditions of servitude. The rambling old barn was filled and the rafters were so low that it was necessary to stick one's nose under the benches to get a breath of air.[3]

A Los Angeles minister not only attempted to describe the new religious meetings to his congregation but predicted the fate and future of the new sect: "with odor more or less tainted…they rant and dance and roll in a disgusting amalgamation of African voodoo superstition and Caucasian insanity, and will pass away like the hysterical nightmares that they are."[4]

If Los Angeles matured, as William Deverell claims, "by whitewashing an adobe past,"[5] so Pentecostalism matured by whitewashing its African-American past. The fabled Azusa Street Mission owes its genesis to two African-Americans: one, a former slave; the other, the son of former slaves.

Before the advent of the railroads, when the old pueblo entered an unprecedented period of lawlessness during its transition to a Yankee boomtown, it was often referred to as "Los Diablos." Yet as one early account of the future city noted, "Like orchids in a swamp, some of Los Angeles' most useful institutions, nevertheless, took root in this dark era of the city's history."[6] One person who was convinced that the growing town of "Los Diablos" was only temporary was a slave in search of freedom.

Biddy Mason had begun her trek toward freedom in Mississippi, slowly walking across the continent behind her Mormon master's wagon train.

She entered Los Angeles from Salt Lake City in 1851. Since California had entered the Union as a "free state"—without slavery—Mason was able to achieve her freedom in a Los Angeles courtroom. As a newly freed slave Biddy Mason then hired on as a "confinement nurse" to a doctor at the wage of $2.50 a week. Through her incredible survivor skills, thrift, and savings, she was able to purchase a prime piece of downtown property. By 1891, the property was worth two hundred thousand dollars.[7] A white resident said of Biddy Mason that she "left to her family and heirs a handsome fortune. But greater than this, she left behind a legacy, a life of a splendid, God-fearing Christian woman doing His work in deeds of relieving and aiding the poor, particularly those of her own color."[8] Indeed she did.

In 1872 the first African Methodist Episcopal Church was organized in Biddy Mason's home. Funded by Mason through its lean years, Stevens African Methodist Episcopal Church was finally built at 312 Azusa Street in 1888. Mason had earlier purchased the land for two hundred fifty dollars in 1866.[9] In 1904 the church followed black migration patterns and moved to Eighth and Towne streets, changing its name to First African Methodist Episcopal. It stood as a "magnificent architectural landmark" and was "an important place in black Los Angeles....Most Afro-Angelenos called it 'Eighth and Towne'...the building and the space it occupied...stood for something more than just another church."[10] Little did the former slave Biddy Mason know that the church's first building at 312 Azusa Street, a project she helped to found and fund, would become even more famous than the "magnificent architectural landmark" at Eighth and Towne. By 1906, 312 Azusa Street would become the Mecca for the miraculous—the New Jerusalem of modern Pentecostalism.

"The last twenty-five years of the nineteenth century," according to Timothy E. Fulop "have appropriately gone down in African-American history as 'the Nadir.'"

> Disenfranchisement and Jim Crow laws clouded out any rays of hope that Reconstruction had bestowed in the American South...The civil, political, and educational rights of black Americans were greatly curtailed, and lynching reached all time highs in the 1890s...The Nadir was accompanied by a cacophony of black voices seeking to make sense of the history and destiny of African Americans. One strand of these voices proclaimed in song, sermon, and theological treatise that the millennial reign of God was coming to earth.[11]

It was during "the Nadir" in 1890 that W.E.B. DuBois also wrote powerfully and prophetically:

Back of this still broods silently the deep religious feeling of the real Negro heart, the stirring, unguided might of powerful human souls who have lost the guiding star of the past and are seeking in the great night a new religious ideal. Some day the Awakening will come, when the pent up vigor of ten million souls shall sweep irresistibly toward the Goal, out of the Valley of the Shadow of Death, where all that makes life worth living—Liberty, Justice and Right—is marked "For White People Only."[12]

Another powerful and prophetic voice during the Nadir belonged to an African-American preacher, the Reverend Francis J. Grimke. Born to a black mother who was enslaved by his white master father, Grimke by the age of ten had become a runaway slave. Captured several years later, he was confined to a Charleston workhouse, where he almost died. Despite provisions made for him in his father's will, his jealous white half-brother continually sought to have him enslaved like his mother. Sold to a Confederate army officer, Grimke survived the Civil War and through the generosity of whites moved north after the war. Through an amazing turn of events, Francis Grimke met and "formed close family ties with two of his father's sisters, his white aunts, Sarah and Angelina Grimke, of antislavery fame."[13] While in the North, Grimke also was "instructed and respected" by his white professors at both Lincoln University and Princeton Theological Seminary. "From Charleston jail to Princeton Seminary, from betrayed brother to beloved nephew, from slave to prominent cleric: the trajectory of Grimke's own life," observed Albert Raboteau, "contradicted despair."[14]

During one decade alone, between 1889 and 1899, some 1,240 black men and women were lynched in the United States. One of the most notorious lynching was of Sam Hose, a black man accused of assault and murder. On Sunday, April 28, 1899, two thousand whites gathered as a mob outside Atlanta not only to lynch Hose but also to burn him alive. "According to the newspapers, local whites celebrated the atrocity as a festive occasion."[15] Less than two months later on June 4, 1899, the Reverend Francis J. Grimke mounted his pulpit at the fashionable Fifteenth Street Presbyterian Church in Washington, D.C. to preach the first of a three-part series of sermons on lynching.

On the eve of a new century, race relations, the preacher told his congregation, were deteriorating instead of improving. Worse yet, argued Grimke, "how could the American church 'with 135,667 preachers and more than 2,000,000 church members permit this awful, black record of murder and lawlessness?' "[16] "How could it be," asked Grimke, that at the dawn of a new century when slavery itself had ended, "blacks were still 'a weak and defenseless race' at the mercy of a 'Negro-hating nation?' "[17] Despite the despair of the dire conditions, the preacher became prophetic, however, when he viewed the future and the coming of a new century.

> Christianity shall one day have sway even in Negro-hating America; the spirit which it inculcates…is sure, sooner or later, to prevail. I have, myself, here and there, seen its mighty transforming power. I have seen white men and women under its regenerating influence lose entirely the caste feeling.…Jesus Christ is yet to reign in this land. I will not see it, you will not see it, but it is coming all the same. In the growth of Christianity, true, real, genuine Christianity in this land, I see the promise of better things for us as a race.[18]

Out on the bayous of the great Mississippi delta in Centerville, Louisiana, population 500, a black baby boy was born on May 2, 1870, in the middle of "the great night" of the Nadir. He was destined, it seemed from birth to become in DuBois' words, "the guiding star" of "a new religious ideal" and destined, it seemed, to usher in, according to Grimke's words, a "true, real, genuine Christianity…even in Negro-hating America."[19] On that day in a place "almost untouched by the passage of time," William Joseph Seymour became the son of Simon and Phyllis Seymour, former slaves, freed only four and a half years before.[20] The area had been developed by fortune hunters seeking "white gold" found in the sugar cane fields of the Louisiana bayou. With the white fortune hunters came their black slaves, who worked the fields some eighteen to twenty hours a day come harvest, in one of the hottest, most humid areas on earth. "Backs bent and bodies groaned while machetes flashed in the sun, slashing and severing the wiry two-inch fibrous stalks just above the earth. Such labor in the killing heat demanded superhuman strength, and the slaves had it."[21]

As young William grew up among the sugar cane fields he too "soon shouldered a man's burden."[22] Becoming strong and husky, Seymour learned to read and write when the day's work was done. Despite the story circulating in Louisiana that a master who gave the Bible to his slaves was "not fit to own a nigger," young William had one.[23] Although he was baptized a Catholic, young Seymour's church quickly became, in Albert Raboteau's memorable words, "The 'Invisible Institution' in the Antebellum South."[24] Only four and a half years had separated him from a sentence of slavery. Despite his hard work as a youth, stories of former slaves like Minnie Fulkes rang true in his heart.

Lord! Lord! Baby, I hope you' young fo'ks will never know what slavery is, an' will never suffer as yo' foreparents. O God! God! I'm livin' to tel' de tale to you,' honey. Yes, Jesus, you've spared me. [25]

Not only did young William believe "Jesus had spared him," he also believed Jesus had given him a purpose that would take him far beyond the "delicate Spanish moss" and those "massive white oak trees" of his humble childhood home. A sensitive…youth…he "experienced…visions and early in life began to look for the apocalyptic" and millennial return of his Jesus."[26]

In 1895, when William Seymour was twenty-five, he rode the rails out of the rural South to a Northern city long associated with the Underground Railway. Indianapolis, Indiana, at the time was considered a "progressive city." Local citizens exercised their bragging rights by proclaiming their railroad station the largest in the world and that their inter-urban lines radiated "outward for forty miles like spokes of a wheel."[27] Soon Seymour found one of the more desirable jobs available to him—being a waiter in a large downtown hotel's restaurant. It was also a job where he met whites and "where people spoke to one another across the color line."[28] Like his job, his choice of a church also enabled him to worship across the color line. Seymour rejected the Bethel African Methodist Episcopal Church (the denomination founded by Richard Allen), seven blocks closer to his residence, for a Northern Methodist Church, today's United Methodist Church. Seymour's vision of racial harmony, however, was short-lived. By 1900 when "racial attitudes hardened in Indiana" Seymour moved on, this time to Cincinnati, Ohio, another center for the famed Underground Railroad.[29]

For the next two years, from 1900 to 1902, things came together for William J. Seymour in Cincinnati. More than anything else he found a spiritual home and he finally heard, himself, the unmistakable call to preach. His journey toward ministry began when he finally, reluctantly, gave up on the Northern Methodist Church because of its increasing segregation and formality. He became attracted instead to the ministry of a former Methodist evangelist, Martin Wells Knapp. Knapp's nightly meetings, held in the downtown Revivalist Chapel, also included black people. "Seymour responded enthusiastically to the ministry of Knapp who represented the original fervor and racial inclusiveness of Methodism."[30] After contracting typhoid fever, Martin Wells Knapp, Seymour's friend and mentor, died at age forty-eight. It was not without some sort of strange irony that in the middle of the "Nadir," in what W.E.B. DuBois called "the great night" and in William Seymour's own personal darkness, he discovered the local ministry of the "Evening Light Saints." "The movement reached out vigorously to include black people. It was a singing, happy faith of radiant Christians who believed that the "evening light" [or last spiritual outpouring] of Zechariah 14:7 was given to the "saints" [or believers] just before the close of history."[31]

In 1901, at the end of the Nadir, one of the Evening Light Saints had the courage to publish a book, *Is the Negro a Beast? A Reply to Charles Carroll's Book Entitled The Negro a Beast.* The author urged that racial prejudice be eliminated and argued that black people were descendents from great past civilizations. "Amid rising national racism this was the last major effort of any Christian group to secure fair treatment for blacks or fellowship with them."[32]

Douglas Nelson, a theologian who studied with Walter Hollenweger at the University of Birmingham astutely summarized the theological attractiveness that the Evening Light Saints must have had for Seymour:

> The "saints" followed John Wesley to teach the experience called "sanctification"....Black people traditionally experienced the Spirit as more important for Christians than many whites realized. For a black person the experience of holiness differed profoundly, constituting strength to triumph over social oppression and injustice rather than a strictly personal or individual matter. Wesley taught the need for sanctification in a social context not always followed by Americans. Among the "saints" Seymour found interracial welcome which enabled him to receive the experience.[33]

In the racial darkness of the time Seymour readily responded to the light and warmth he felt from the "saints." It was within this nurturing, holiness, millennial offshoot of Methodism that Seymour experienced the call to preach. Like so many preachers before him, Seymour tested his calling. And just like so many others it also took an intervening disaster, a Jonah experience, to convince him of the reality of his calling. For Seymour it was smallpox, the "most contagious disease of the time," and often fatal among blacks.[34] After suffering for three weeks he survived, but like Jacob wrestling with his night angel, Seymour too was left with a permanent reminder of his struggle—facial scarring and the loss of vision in his left eye. "Smallpox dramatically changed Seymour's life. He grew a beard to cover his facial disfigurement but never again served tables in any expensive white restaurant; his left eye remained impaired with a small, partial, opaque covering."[35]

Seymour now realized he had been summoned to a much higher calling following his illness. From now he would help prepare God's table for the great eschatological banquet he knew was soon to occur—"the joyful feast for the people of God." And he knew that the people of God would come from the east and the west, from the north and the south, until all were gathered around the table. He just did not know quite yet where and when it would all happen. As a traveling evangelist with the Evening Light Saints, Seymour returned to the South, stopping in Texas to look for relatives separated by slavery. "Finding family in Houston he made his home there."[36] In July and August, 1905, evangelist Charles Fox Parham, the founder of the Apostolic Faith Movement, held meetings downtown in the large Bryan Hall. Every evening Parham and his team put on a parade on Main Street wearing spectacular clothing from the Holy Land while carrying a large banner that read—APOSTOLIC FAITH MOVEMENT. "Newspapers provided much favorable publicity, and large crowds attended."[37] Some of the black people who attended Parham's meetings sat "segregated in the rear."[38] One of the black women attending was Lucy F. Farrow, pastor of a black holiness church and also a niece of the famous African-American abolitionist Frederick Douglass.[39] Parham offered Lucy Farrow a position as governess in his family if she would return with him to Kansas after the Houston meetings. Not only did Lucy Farrow accept Charles Parham's offer, but she asked her friend William Seymour to be the "supply pastor" of her church. Seymour served as the interim minister until her return in late October.

As the "supply pastor" of Lucy Farrow's holiness church in Houston, Seymour met a Sunday visitor from Los Angeles, Mrs. Neely Terry. Upon her return to Los Angeles, she in turn gave a glowing account of Seymour to her fellow worshipers and to the church's leader, Mrs. Julia Hutchins. When Lucy Farrow returned to Houston from Kansas, she was a different person. She relayed to her friend Brother Seymour how she had received the gift of the baptism of the Holy Ghost and had spoken in "unknown tongues" in Parham's home. She was convinced "this gift of the spirit" was part of the millennial hope they had been seeking.

In January1906, when Parham announced the beginning of a short-term Bible study course to be held in Houston, Seymour, ever the spiritual seeker, showed interest. With Parham expressing his concerns for racial attitudes in the city, "a compromise was reached that ...allowed Seymour to set just outside the classroom beside the door which Parham left ajar. In this manner Seymour attended classes every morning."[40] Two things captured Seymour's interest in this former Methodist minister. The first was his millennial vision—that these were indeed "the Last Days." The second thing

Charles Fox Parham considered himself "the origi-nator of the Apostolic Faith movememt for the res-toration of primitive Christianity" (used by permis-sion of Flower Pentecostal Heritage Center).

that attracted him to Parham was his teaching about "divine empowerment through the gift of the spirit." "There was 'some-thing' manifested by glossolalia still beyond him. He became a seeker of that yet to be attained spiritual reality even though this quest conflicted with (the) 'saints' belief.' "[41]

Since Parham only provided for segregated seating in his public meetings and had prohib-ited interracial mingling at the altar afterwards, Seymour never received "the gift of the spirit" under Parham's hands. What he did receive from Parham, however, was just as beneficial.

"Mother Cotton," a black woman and an early leader in Pentecostalism, recounted how Seymour went to Los Angeles: "Sister Terry later returned to Los Angeles where she immediately went out on Santa Fe to the little Nazarene group, and told Sister (Julia) Hutchins (the pastor of the congregation) about the 'very godly man' she had met in Houston. Right away interest was stirred and the group invited the Holiness preacher, Brother Seymour, to their little church."[42]

A woman who traveled with Charles Parham remembered the generosity of Seymour's new spiritual mentor:

> Seymour didn't have a penny to his name. He never had any money...You never got money in those days for anything you did. It was all free... everybody did it for nothing and you took what you got and liked it. But Dad Parham did something that I've never seen another preacher do. He always had a light jacket that he would put on and it had two big pockets, you know, and those pockets were always jammed full of money and he would instead of putting people on a salary—he'd just hand them a roll of bills. He paid them, you know, just personally, out of these two pockets. And so Seymour received the call from the Lord to go out to Los Angeles and he'd never been there and he was a colored man...but he had nothing so Dad Parham bought him a suit, paid his fare and sent him out to L.A.[43]

For whatever reason, Seymour never mentioned this financial help. Perhaps Parham himself did not want it known. The first time Seymour wrote about going to Los Angeles he simply stated, "It was the divine call that brought me from Houston, Texas, to Los Angeles...The Lord sent the means."[44] After his subsequent break with Parham, however, the story is told that "the saints in Los Angeles" provided for his move west by "sending his fare."[45] When Sarah Parham wrote her husband's biography in 1930, she noted, "Early in the spring of 1906, Mr. Parham made up his [Seymour's] car fare and we bid him God's speed to the western coast."[46]

In *Bound for Freedom: Black Los Angeles in Jim Crow America*, Douglas Flamming writes that Los Angeles in 1906 was "a city called heaven for people of color."[47] One thing was certain; no other American city was growing as fast as Los Angeles. At the turn of the century the city had a population of 102,479 which included 2,131 black persons. By 1906, "relatively little racial segregation...afflicted Los Angeles. Downtown hotels and restaurants served black people and interracial contacts and friendships were the rule rather than the exception. Los Angeles became the first American city to utilize black fireman and policeman."[48] From 1900 to 1920 black migration to Los Angeles multiplied more than sevenfold. In their attempt to break a strike by Mexican construction workers, the Southern Pacific Railroad recruited two thousand blacks to the city in 1903. The following year "hundreds of Negroes in Texas" left for Los Angeles, where they believed there was "no antagonism against the race."[49] When William J. Seymour sat segregated outside the door in Parham's Bible School in Houston, he too must have heard through the grapevine about that wonderful "city called heaven for people of color."

The earliest black newspapers in Los Angeles sought early on to get the word out to the people of the East. "With regard to Los Angeles and the condition of its colored citizens, there is no place in the United States," claimed the *Weekly Observer*, "where moral and intelligent colored people are treated with more respect than they are in Los Angeles, by all classes."[50] By the turn of the twentieth century blacks living in Los Angeles saw the South as "the ultimate example of what the nation should not become— and idealized the West as both a place and a metaphor."[51] Black Los Angeles was also heavily Texan, "and increasingly, Houston sent black Texans westward."[52] And so on February 22nd, when William Seymour's train arrived in Los Angeles, that "luxuriant pasture for any and all beliefs," he must have carried with him the conviction that this was the one place in America where he, too, could introduce his millennial vision of the "latter days" and the "New Jerusalem."

In 1906 the "city called heaven for people of color" numbered some 230,000. Between 1900 and 1910 about 5,500 blacks moved into Los Angeles "along with large numbers of Mexicans and Japanese."[53] Los Angeles as a whole was fairly well integrated, as the earliest black residents were spread throughout the city.[54] There were, however, in 1906 several small areas where the population was predominately black. One small cluster centered on a semi-industrial area composed of livery stables, a tombstone shop, and a lumber yard. This was perhaps "the original black area of Los Angeles."[55] A major street in the area was Azusa Street. "Azusa Street was only one block long, intersecting busy Spring Street on the west, and dead ending at the rear of the railroad freight terminal on the east. Beyond the terminal flowed the Los Angeles River, and across the river Azusa Street continued for one more block."[56] In 1888 the first black Christian church in Los Angeles, Stevens African Methodist Episcopal Church, was built at 312 Azusa Street. As the new century dawned, a second cluster of black families formed to the south and east, bounded by Maple Avenue, Olympic Boulevard, and Central Avenue.[57] This newer cluster formed alongside the railroad tracks of the Santa Fe line, where lots cost between two hundred and five hundred dollars. Homes were built between Santa Fe Avenue and Mateo Street. "Stevens African Methodist Episcopal Church moved with the migration to 8th and Towne in 1904, changing its name to First African Methodist Episcopal Church."[58] After its former building at 312 Azusa Street was vacated, it was used for storage. "Nearby saloons and less desirable activities gave the location a skid row flavor." [59]

In 1913 Hugh Macbeth, a recent African-American graduate of Harvard Law School, visited Los Angeles for the first time. He quickly relayed his impressions of the city to his wife back East. "Come and dwell in God's country," Macbeth wrote his wife.[60] One reason Los Angeles was a "city called heaven" and "God's country" was because by 1910, thirty-six percent of Los Angeles' black families owned their homes. Black home-ownership rates anywhere else rarely hit ten percent "and none exceeded 15 percent."[61] Touring the city in 1913, W.E.B. DuBois told the readers of his monthly magazine that black Angelenos were "without doubt the most beautifully housed group of colored people in the United States."[62] "Many homes were lovely," notes Douglas Flamming, "especially compared with what blacks were accustomed to back East." The city's bungalows and Spanish-style stuccos fit nicely with the climate, which made just about any house look good. "And the lawns were an embarrassment of green, studded with palm trees, yuccas, jacarandas, and an endless variety of flowering plants and vines."[63]

When William Seymour arrived in "God's country" with his millennial hope and vision still intact for a new religious ideal, he was met by his enthusiastic congregation "and nightly meetings began immediately at 9th and Santa Fe." This location, where the second cluster of black families had formed, had been secured by the church's leader, Julia W. Hutchins. A year earlier, at the historic Second Baptist Church (the first black Baptist Church in Los Angeles), Hutchins had been expelled from the congregation for advocating the teachings of the holiness movement. Moving around Los Angeles, from tents to homes, with the eight families who accompanied her, she was finally able to lease a small mission hall at Ninth and Santa Fe. With increasing attendance, this small interracial band of holiness believers began looking for a pastor. This was Seymour's first church in Los Angeles and was almost his last. His first few sermons covered a broad range of topics. But then Seymour zeroed in on the spiritual gift of "glossolalia," preaching that "it should be part of every believer's experience," even though he himself had not experienced it.[64] Julia Hutchins, as "the church mother," was incensed and called in the leader of the Southern California Holiness Association, who warned Seymour "not to preach any further along those lines."[65] Seymour remained convinced of the reality of the spiritual gift he had yet to receive and remained unrepentant. By the fifth night, the church mother padlocked the door of the mission against him, even refusing him his room at the mission. Seymour soon found himself without a pulpit, even "without a place to stay, and little money." Fortunately for Seymour, a church family, Edward and Mattie Lee, took him in. Every evening they would pray together, and soon their nightly prayer meetings attracted visitors.[66]

In mid-March the growing cottage prayer meeting was moved two blocks "to the larger home of Richard and Ruth Asberry at 214 North Bonnie Brae Street."[67] One historian of Pentecostalism placed the Asberry residence "in downtown industrial Los Angeles."[68] This of course perpetuates the "poor black mythology of Azusa Street" while in reality the Asberrys were homeowners in a racially mixed and socially dynamic neighborhood. "Bonnie Brae in 1900 and 1910 consisted of black homes interspersed among white, with clusters of each trading off from one street to the next. This pattern of racially and ethnically mixed neighborhoods was typical for the city in this period."[69] The prayer services continued to grow in the new house church, still composed mainly "of black people and a sprinkling of white visitors."[70] On Monday, April 9, 1906, the house was crowded with black people before the service began. No whites were present. Seymour selected Acts 2:4 for his text for the evening: "And they were all filled with the Holy Ghost, and began to speak with other tongues, as the Spirit gave them utterance." The first person to speak in "other tongues" was Jennie Evans Moore, who owned the house across the street. Moore had been a resident of Los Angeles since 1895, when she arrived from Austin, Texas, to be with her relatives, the Asberrys and Neely Terry. From April 9th to the 12th there were "days of exuberant celebration for Seymour's black prayer group of wash women, cooks, laborers, janitors, and railroad porters, who [were] joined by huge crowds of black and white alike, surrounding the house. The wooden front porch collapses under the strain but no one is hurt, and it is soon repaired."[71]

On the final night of the three-day marathon Seymour finally received his own baptism of glossolalia. Fittingly, it came to him while he was praying next to his prayer partner, who happened that night to be white. "A broad smile wreathed his face…he arose happily and embraced those around him….It is…perhaps highly significant that Seymour found the release he was seeking not in an all black group but side by side with a white man."[72] At long last, as a seeker "in the great night" of a new religious ideal, William Joseph Seymour had experienced his awakening. More than anything else that evening Seymour had been baptized with love and had received a new social vision. Like Peter on the original day of Pentecost, Seymour was convinced that he too was "living in the last days" and that the gift of the spirit was now being poured out "upon all flesh."

> Your sons and your daughters shall prophesy…your young men shall see visions…your old men shall dream dreams. Even upon my slaves, both men and women…I will pour out my Spirit…before the coming of the Lord's great and glorious day.[73]

With his "latter day" gift of the spirit Seymour championed one doctrine above all others: "there must be no color line or other division in the church of Jesus Christ because God is no respecter of persons. He resolutely refused to segregate or Jim Crow the movement."[74]

In the early morning hours of April 13 the Bonnie Brae band of black believers recognized that their days (and nights) as a house church were over for good. Larger quarters needed to be secured. Since some of them had been the original members of the first black church in the city, Stevens African Methodist Episcopal Church, they remembered that the old building at 312 Azusa Street was still standing. "The name 'Azusa' comes from an ancient village of the American Indian Shoshone tribe, originally near Los Angeles, and means 'blessed miracle.' "[75] The Azusa Mission would over time become a worldwide legend and a Mecca for the miraculous. But when Seymour's band of prayer partners took it over on April 14, 1906, they found it a wreck and a mess. "The ravages of time had set in with a vengeance during the three years of its vacancy. A fire had broken out, destroying much of the upper sanctuary. The remaining upper part had been partitioned off into tenement apartments while the downstairs with its dirt floor had been turned into livery stable." "Barn like," it seemed to capture the essence of "Bethlehem's manger."

> Amid the debris they cleared space downstairs to seat about a hundred persons, laying redwood planks across nail kegs, old boxes, and odds and ends of chairs. This…represented a long tradition in black Christianity, backless pews being preferred by the slaves because they allowed "room to pray"…Two large wooden shoe crates were placed one on top of the other and covered with cotton cloth to make the pulpit—appearing to be "worth about fifteen cents to a junk man." They scattered sawdust all over the dirt floor.
>
> Seymour designed an unusual seating arrangement. He placed the pulpit in the center of the room with altar in front of it, serving as a bench for persons to use following the invitation. The pews formed a circle surrounding the pulpit and altar—all on one level. This plan reflected the "oneness in equality" Seymour envisioned. Worshippers gathered in a new way completed equal in the house of God…not a collection of individuals looking over the back of many heads simply to the clergy or choir but an intimate whole serving one another. This unconventional seating plan revealed Seymour's conviction that events transpiring at Azusa Mission were different, unique, and revolutionary.[76]

After the Azusa Mission was cleared, cleaned, and the circular seating arrangement created by Seymour, initial services were held April 14, 1906, a Saturday night. The next day was appropriately Easter Sunday. On Tuesday night, April 17, a reporter from the *Los Angeles Times* attended the service. The next morning his sensational account appeared on page one of the paper's second section.

Wednesday, April 18, the day the sensationalized story of the Azusa Street Mission appeared in the *Los Angeles Times*, was also the day of the great San Francisco earthquake. Hitting at 5:12 a.m., it was over in a minute. Most of proud San Francisco lay in rubble, while much of what was left standing quickly burned to the ground in the firestorm that followed. The devastation seemed unbelievable when the final numbers were tallied: three hundred thousand out of four hundred thousand were left homeless, and ten thousand were dead. "The San Francisco earthquake was surely the voice of God to the people on the Pacific Coast," wrote one Anglo minister, "who printed thousands of 'earthquake' tracts for distribution and who was one of the first white converts to the mission."[77] As early as 1730, John Wesley in a famous sermon declared that God himself was the author and sin the moral cause of earthquakes. Still others felt that this particular awful destruction had been prophesized at the mission. As the sociologist Earl R. Babbie rightly observed, "Particularly in the West, the nature of the external forces operating on man has been understood as divine."[78] California was easily both Eden and Paradise Lost, the Promised Land and an apocalyptic nightmare.

One week after the *Times* article and the San Francisco earthquake, the Azusa Mission was crowded. There were three services, every day of the week: morning, afternoon, and evening. They often merged and ran continuously. The largest crowds gathered on Sundays from seven in the morning until midnight. The mission was only forty feet by sixty feet, a total of 2,400 square feet; yet, some seven hundred fifty to eight hundred persons overflowed the inside, while four or five hundred stood squeezed together on the board sidewalk that surrounded the structure.

In his third and final family memoir, *The Prince of Frogtown*, the Pulitzer Prize-winning writer Rick Bragg vividly and unforgettably describes both the sin and salvation found in his dirt-poor southern Appalachian mill village. "In a place where machines ate people alive, faith had to pour even hotter than blood."[79] And the one faith that poured "hotter than blood" like a runaway redemptive river overflowing its boundaries and blotting up the town's blight was none other than Pentecostalism. Bragg's beautiful description of the movement's mission days is a universal one, applicable not only to his hometown of Jacksonville, Alabama, but the Promised Land of Los Angeles, and all those many other long-forgotten leased storefronts scattered across America, found somewhere in between the fabled Azusa Street Mission itself and those tucked away anonymously, hidden for a half-century, like spiritual moonshine, in the mist-shrouded mill towns of the Appalachian mountains.

> The Holy Ghost moved invisible, but they could feel it in the rafters, sense it racing inside the walls. It was a real as a jag of lightning, or an electrical fire.
> The preacher stood on a humble, foot-high dais, to show that he did not believe he was better than them…He preached…of the end of the world, and it was beautiful…

It had no steeple, no stained glass, no bell tower, but it was the house of Abraham and Isaac, of Moses and Joshua, of the Lord thy God. People tithed in Mercury dimes and buffalo nickels, and pews filled with old men who wore ancient black suit coats over overalls, and young men in short-sleeved dress shirts and clip-on ties. Women sat plain, not one smear of lipstick or daub of makeup on their faces…Their hair was long, because Paul wrote that "if a woman have long hair, it is a glory to her, for her hair is given her for a covering."

The congregants' eyes were shut tight.

"Do you feel the Spirit?" the Reverend shouted.

Their hands reached high.

"Can you feel the Holy Ghost?"

They answered one by one, in the light of the full gospel.

"Yeeeeessss.'"

Then, as if they had reached for a sizzling clothesline in the middle of an electrical storm, one by one they began to jerk, convulsing in the grip of unseen power. Others threw their arms open wide, and the Holy Ghost touched them soul by soul.

Some just stood and shivered.

Some danced, spinning.

Some leapt high in the air.

Some wept.

Some of the women shook their heads so violently that their hair came free and whipped through the air, three feet long. Hairpins flew.

The Ghost was in them now.

They began to speak in tongues.…the congregation leaned in, to hear the miracle. It sounded like ancient Hebrew, maybe a little, and other times it sounded like nothing they had heard or imagined. They rushed to the front of the church and knelt in a line, facing the altar, so the preacher could lay his hands on them, and…make them whole.

One by one, they were slain in the Spirit, and fell backward, some of them, fainting on the floor. The services could last for hours, till the congregants' stomachs growled. "If it's going good," [one] said, "why switch it off?" [80]

If "The time was ripe," as David Martin suggests, "for Pentecostalism to pick up Methodism's 'unfinished task,' " the time was equally right to reunite body and spirit in Protestant worship.[81] "In moving to a position of prominence and acceptability in the urban east, the Methodist church," claims Troy Messenger, "eschewed an engagement of the body in spiritual exercises."

Achieving respectability in the city meant not only banning the whiskey seller from the perimeter of the campgrounds but also forbidding the disrobing of women in the ecstasy of hymn singing and the spectacle of men on all fours barking the devil up a tree. By mid-century, (nineteenth) evidence of conversion and perfection in holiness was claimed by faith, even if no tangble physical sensation accompanied that transformation.

At the same time increasingly separated from the spirit in respectable worship, it was undergoing a similar fragmentation from other spheres of life. The rise of industrial capitalism meant that the body was forced to assume a respectability at work that paralleled the respectability of the pew.[82]

Frank Bartleman, the author of the "earthquake" tract and an early participant at Azusa, took special notice of the mission's racial and ethnic diversity: "The place was packed out nightly. The whole building, upstairs and down, had now been cleared and put into use. There were far more white people than colored coming. The color line was washed away in the blood."[83] Other early participants at this mission supported Bartleman's claims. "There were no differences in race or color," said Lawrence Catley, "everybody was somebody."[84] Catley also claimed that the Azusa Mission was much more than a place like jazz nightclubs or speakeasies where whites came and went. "Azusa was an interracial assembly—not just whites and blacks sitting together, but real oneness. Even as late as 1910 the two races could be found eating, sitting, and praying together."[85] A former Methodist minister from the South summed it up this way: "I, being southern born, thought it a miracle that I could sit in a service by a colored saint of God and worship, or eat at a great camp table and forget I was eating beside a colored saint, but…God was worshipped in love and harmony."[86]

Seymour's religious periodical, *The Apostolic Faith*, early on noted the mission's diversity: "Multitudes have come. God makes no difference in nationality, Ethiopians, Chinese, Indians, Mexicans, and other nationalities worship together….The people are all melted together…made one lump, one bread, all one body in Christ Jesus. There is no Jew or Gentile, bond or free, in the Azusa Street Mission….He is no respecter of persons or places."[87]

One historian has developed a data base of five hundred individuals who attended the mission from its beginning in 1906 to 1909. Of these five hundred individuals, forty-five percent were African-American; forty-five percent were Anglo-American and ten percent were "other," mostly Mexican-Americans.[88]

The interracial harmony of Pentecostalism, especially among whites and blacks was not limited to Los Angeles, either. As early as 1908, headlines appeared in the *New York Times* announcing that "HOLY GHOSTERS WIN WHITES AND NEGROES."

"For more than a year," the *Times* reported, "whites and negroes" have been 'holding daily meetings'" at a Mission "at 325 West Forty-first Street." "Last night," the *Times* noted, "when the mission service began...the room was thronged with men and women of all ages, white and black, all sitting together."[89]

As the Azusa Mission garnered headlines and gathered multitudes, there were also equal amounts of opposition. Just two months after the mission opened, the Los Angeles Church Federation attempted to have it shut down by complaining to the city that it was creating "a public disturbance." The Los Angeles Police Department surveyed neighboring businesses but failed to find enough opposition to support the complaint.[90] The mission had obviously grown enough to threaten those in the established churches. In Rick Bragg's memorable phrase, "Biblical scholars turned their noses up, calling it hysteria, theatrics, a faith of the illiterate."[91] But the real opposition to both Seymour and the mission came four months later in the unlikely form of Seymour's newest spiritual mentor. The man with the "two big pockets...full of money" who had "bought him a suit, paid his fare and sent him out to Los Angeles"—none other than Charles Fox Parham.

During the formative period of the mission from April to September, Seymour "received only marginal" attention from Parham due to his mentor's own "energetic efforts in the Midwest."[92] At some point during his time in Los Angeles Seymour had written to Parham requesting ministerial credentials with his Apostolic Faith Movement. After having severed his relationship with the Evening Light Saints, Seymour "received his credentials in July." [93]

One month later, in August, Seymour formed "a board of twelve to supervise the mission, ordain ministerial and missionary candidates, and issue credentials."[94] The stage either knowingly, or unknowingly, had been set for a showdown during Parham's visit in late October. In the excessive energy and drama of a new religious movement, sudden shifts in leadership seem to spontaneously occur. None were more surprising than the Parham-Seymour shift in leadership.

The first few months of *The Apostolic Faith*, the mission's periodical, show nothing but deference to Parham and acknowledge him as the movement's leader. The very first issue of September 1906 emphatically states, "Bro. Charles Parham...is God's leader in the Apostolic Faith Movement...This work began about five years ago last January...under the leadership of Chas. Parham...in Topeka, Kan."[95] The September issue includes a short letter from Parham stating his joy and plans to be with them: "I rejoice in God over you all, my children, though I have never seen you; but since you know the Holy Spirit's power, we are baptized by one Spirit into one body. Keep together in unity till I come…to meet and to see all who have the full gospel when I come."[96]

The October issue of *The Apostolic Faith* was even stronger in its praise of Parham:

> All along the ages men have been preaching a partial Gospel.…God has from time to time raised up men to bring back the truth to the church. He raised up Luther to bring …the doctrine of justification by faith. He raised up…John Wesley to establish Bible holiness…Then he raised up Dr. Cullis who brought back…the wonderful doctrine of divine healing. Now He is bringing back the Pentecostal Baptism to the church.
>
> God laid His hand on a little crippled boy [Parham] and healed him.… He has since been in evangelistic work over the United States, seeing multitudes saved, sanctified and healed.…He was surely raised up of God to be an apostle of the doctrine of Pentecost.
>
> This Pentecostal Gospel has been spreading ever since, but on the Pacific coast it has burst out in great power and is being carried from here over the world. We are expecting Bro. Parham to visit Los Angeles in a few days and for a mightier tide of salvation to break out.
>
> Before another issue of this paper, we look for Bro. Parham in Los Angeles…He, with other workers, will hold union revival meetings in Los Angeles and then expects to go on to other towns and cities, and will appoint workers to fill the calls that shall come in.[97]

If Pentecostalism hatched into worldwide proportions in the spring of 1906, it had incubated some six years earlier and fifteen hundred miles eastward in Topeka, Kansas. "If Seymour was the populist leader of the Apostolic Faith movement, Charles Parham was its spiritual elder."[98] Charles Fox Parham, remembered as being bright and club-footed and formerly one of the youngest ordained Methodist ministers in the country, became by some accounts a father to the movement when one of his students, Miss Agnes Ozman, spoke in "other tongues" at Bethel College, a Bible school in Topeka. Parham laid his hands on her and prayed that she would receive the New Testament gift. One account offered the following description of what occurred: "With resignation, he (Parham) laid hands on her and asked God to baptize her in the Holy ghost. Suddenly, a halo of light formed around her head, and a stream of exotic words poured out of her mouth. For three days, Agnes Ozman spoke nothing but Chinese!"[99]

Parham and his band of followers did not fare well following the ecstatic experiences. Newspaper reporters, journalists, and some scholars descended upon the school pejoratively known as "Stone's Folly"—a former two-story mansion on Topeka's outskirts that was elaborately constructed but never finished due to a lack of funds. Once the novelty died down, Parham and his group were subjected to repeated ridicule by organized religion and the press, as well as charges about sexual misconduct by the leader. Sporadic revivals continued to occur throughout the Middle West in the early 1900s despite the accusations and the dire financial conditions of the itinerant traveling group. In revival meetings in El Dorado Springs, Missouri, and in Galena, Kansas, in 1903, Parham gained more credibility and a measure of respectability through stories of remarkable healings occurring under his ministry. Finally, re-establishing a Bible school at a rented building at Fifth and Rusk streets in Houston, Parham met the pupil who would give world-wide dimensions to the fledgling movement in Los Angeles.

Charles Fox Parham was as complex as he was controversial. He may have been homosexual. He certainly was a racist. Yet to those who knew him best he presented a light, even a loving side. "Dad Parham," as he was affectionately called by one itinerant who traveled with him, was remembered as

> One of the nicest little fellows you ever met in your life. He was little, you know. He was short. He was nice looking. Always well dressed. Smart as a cricket. Comical as I don't know what…He'd keep people in splits, not by just meeting with them personally, but from the pulpit…he'd have his own sayings and all…that was a brilliant man, he was a brilliant man.
>
> He went through a great deal of persecution. He's got fifty marks on him from being beat up for preaching on the street…They just beat the tar out of him for street meetings…Course it got so that there were a lot of campaigns and they wouldn't let them do that, you know, the law wouldn't let them do it but…he was attacked. And he carried a big lump on his neck where somebody hit him with a crowbar or something and he carried it to his grave and he died young.
>
> He was a grand preacher. He was very fiery. Comical as they make them…never at want for words. It is what you would call a "dapper little fellow." He was very charming…and He had an answer for everybody and he'd turn everybody's sorrowfulness into a joke. He was kind and good to everybody.
>
> I'll tell you what he was a hundred percent against—organization. He was against organization. He didn't want God's power organized…He never wanted to sell the gospel. He never took up an offering but he was never without money. His pockets were always full of money.[100]

Still another of his contemporaries remembered Parham as being "a personable, gifted, accomplished, original and forceful thinker, as well as a vivid, magnetic personality with superb, versatile platform ability, he always held his audience in the curve of his hand.[101]

Prior to visiting Seymour and the mission, Parham had received reports from friends in Los Angeles who were both critical and concerned about the "black influence at Azusa."[102] Coming fresh from successful meetings in Houston and Zion City, Illinois, Parham assumed he would take over the mission as it rightful leader and bring an end to "white people imitating unintelligent, crude negroisms of the Southland, and laying it on the Holy Ghost."[103]

> A clash of monumental proportions ensued…It did not take Parham long to assess the situation…(He) worked his way through the crowds to the front, greeted Seymour,…took the pulpit delivering a stinging rebuke, beginning with the declaration, 'God is sick at his stomach,' and going on to explain that no self-respecting God could stand for such animalism. This approach alienated the Azusa congregation which did not accept his leadership, resulting in Parham's departure to open a rival campaign, at the socially respectable Women's Christian Temperance Union Building, lasting until December.[104]

The contrast between Parham and Seymour extended far deeper than their skin color. An early Azusa street participant and leader noted that Parham "became puffed up, declared himself the progenitor of the movement, and would strut around with a high silk hat like a dictator."[105] With Parham there was also "the absence of the spirit of love." Seymour, on the other hand, was seen as "meek and humble, and could preach love….It was the wonderful character of…[Seymour] whom God had chosen that attracted the people to keep coming to this humble meeting."[106]

Although Charles Fox Parham failed in his bid to take over the Azusa Mission and reform Seymour of his "crude negroisms," he continued to the day he died to condemn them at every opportunity in the strongest possible terms. Charles Parham remained a racist and a Ku Klux Klan sympathizer. According to his theology "the color line had not been washed away in the blood." He preached in his sermons that "the word Saxon" was a derivation of Isaac's sons: "The Saxon conquest of Great Britain and today…with the United States…proves the Scriptures: they were to be the 'head and not the tail of nations'…while the heathen,--the Black race, the Brown race, the Red race, the Yellow race, in spite of missionary zeal and effort are nearly all heathen still."[107]

What Parham witnessed at Azusa Street only served to add more poison to his already venomous pen, as he continued to attack his fellow "Christian heathen." He left no doubt, either for his readers about what "mission" he was describing: "Men and women, whites and blacks, knelt together or fell across one another; frequently, a white woman, perhaps of wealth and culture, could be seen thrown back in the arms of a big 'buck nigger,' and held tightly thus as she shivered and shook in freak imitation of Pentecost. Horrible, awful shame!"[108]

In one of the final chapters of a book he wrote, Parham set out to show the difference, between himself and the followers of Seymour, whom he called "spooks."

> O, how many, instead of giving the Holy Spirit his legitimate use in their lives, have used that power to gratify their spiritual sensuality for 'feeling's;' and the groveling surrender of most missions to fleshy, magnetic sensations has disgraced the work the world over... "Pentecost" is on trial for its very life...To illustrate: A Free Methodist preacher of Los Angeles...visited the Azusa Street Mission and was seized with a spook...Such forces are a prostitution of spiritual power...I have seen meetings where all crowded together around the altar, and laying across one another like hogs, blacks and whites mingling...our public services should be for the edification of the church, not to get worked up into an animalism creating magnetic currents tending to lust and free love.[109]

Charles Fox Parham, whose ancestry extended back to colonial Pennsylvania, would live out the rest of his days as an enigma to the very movement he helped to found. The General Council of the Assemblies of God, the largest Anglo Pentecostal denomination to emerge from the movement, would banish his name for years in the repetition of the mythology of their origins. A close ministerial colleague of Parham's who later joined the Assemblies appeared to be his chief accuser in the sexual misconduct charges—something that may have been rooted in professional jealousy and rivalry rather than ministerial ethics. "Dad Parham" would continue on with his message, however, as a traveling tent evangelist preaching to two thousand to three thousand people at a time. And after his tents were folded, he would leave new Pentecostal churches in their wake. The Kansas State Historical Society noted in 1928 that "A New York statistician has given Mr. Parham credit for the conversion to Christianity of fully 2,000,000 persons through his personal appeals and through the medium of ministers who have loyally followed his teachings and example."[110]

For the rest of his life Parham billed himself as "the originator of the Apostolic Faith movement, for the restoration of primitive Christianity."[111] Parham remained convinced that "the people wanted the old-time religion."[112] He felt "that the world needed the restoration of primitive Christianity, with all its gifts and graces" so much so that "he was moved to leave the narrow confines of the modern pulpit to preach everywhere the 'New-Old Way.' "[113] Preaching the "new-old way" had also helped to bring Parham financial rewards much greater than Methodism. In an address given in Wichita on November 31, 1913, Parham said "Permit just a word of reminiscence":

> When I first took this way I was getting from $500 to $700 a year in a Methodist pulpit; I now get from $5,000 to $7,000 a year. I had the confines of a pastorate, with a lot of theater-going, card-playing, wine-drinking, fashionable, unconverted Methodists; now I have a world-wide parish, with multitudes to preach the gospel message to…I had but a small pretense of a home then; later I was the possessor of more property.[114]

On June 2, 1926 the *Baxter Springs Citizen* noted, "The Rev. Charles F. Parham, senior minister of the Apostolic Faith and original preacher and teacher of all Full Gospel movements, will be honored here next Sunday for the 20th consecutive year in celebration of his birthday anniversary. Similar affairs held in (the) past few years drew crowds of from 1,000 to 2,000 people, and the evangelist has been showered with letters and telegrams of congratulations, as well as with gifts of all kinds."[115]

On January 29, 1929 Charles Fox Parham died in the bedroom of his large house, a converted brewery in Baxter Springs that was always full of family and friends forever praying for the return of his health and the continuation of his ministry. Despite a severe winter snowstorm, "twenty-five hundred people attended his funeral held in the local Baxter Springs theater."[116] A pulpit-shaped monument provided by his followers capped his gravestone. A simple inscription served as a final reminder that Charles F. Parham was the "Founder of the Apostolic Faith Movement."[117]

Back when William Seymour had been "a sensitive youth" in bayou country, before he rode the rails out of the South for interracial freedom, he had begun to have visions. Those experiences continued throughout his life; however, he rarely shared them with anyone else, preferring to keep his visions to himself. After his break with Parham, he felt emboldened to share a remarkable dream he experienced just before the opening of the mission. He shared his dream with his congregation and also with "a sensitive youth" much like himself. He dreamed, he said, of a vast forest. Small fires soon broke out, spreading until they merged and then began to consume the forest with one solid wall of flame. In his dream he saw a preacher rush to the fire with a wet gunny sack, striving in vain to quench it but the flames only leaped higher spreading beyond the preacher's reach. To the young man who reminded him of himself he turned and confided, "Frankie, son, this teaching is meant to spread over the entire earth."[118]

After the break with Parham was officially made, the Azusa Street Mission's periodical never mentioned him by name again. Referring to Seymour's vision, the November issue of *The Apostolic Faith* did note that "a brother had a vision of fires springing up…A preacher was trying to put it out with a wet gunny sack, but it was evident there was no use fighting it. Our God is marching on. Hallelujah. The man with the wet gunny sack is here, also, but his efforts only call attention to the fire."[119]

The editors of the mission's periodical subtly noted the shift and change in leadership. "No church or organization is back" of the mission, they declared. "The Holy Ghost is the leader."[120] They also observed that when "travelers from afar" try to find "their way to the headquarters at Azusa Street," they are often asked, "O, you mean the Holy Rollers" or "It is the Colored Church you mean?" The writer of the article identified "headquarters at Azusa Street" thus: "In the vicinity of a tombstone shop, stables and lumber yard (a fortunate vicinity because no one complains of all-night meetings) you will find a two-story, white-washed old building. You would hardly expect heavenly visitations there, unless you remember the stable at Bethlehem.[121]

"A leading Methodist layman of Los Angeles" was quoted as saying that "scenes transpiring" at the Mission "are what Los Angeles churches have been praying for years." The layman concluded that he was happy that the revival had not come to his church, the First Methodist Church, or "any church in this city." But because it happened "out in the barn…we might all come and take part in it. If it had started in a fine church, poor colored people and Spanish people would not have got it."[122]

Not so subtle, however, was the change in the name of the movement. No longer was it just "The Apostolic Faith Movement"; it was now "The Pacific Apostolic Faith Movement." The new Pacific Apostolic Faith Movement also went on record by stating "We are not fighting men or churches… 'Love, Faith, Unity' is our watchword."[123]

In the final month of its most eventful year, the Azusa Street Mission reported, "Many are asking how the work…started and who was the founder." Again, as during the previous month, Parham's name was purposely omitted. "The Lord was the founder," stated the mission, adding that He was also "the Projector of this movement." "Projector," of course, was the title Parham had appropriated for himself. "There is no pope," continued the editorial, "we are all little children….This work is carried on by the people of Los Angeles that God has united by the precious blood of our Lord Jesus Christ and the power of the Holy Spirit." Seymour's role in the life of the Mission was then described and defined, biblically: "Bro. Seymour is simply a humble pastor of the flock over which the Holy Ghost made him overseer, according to Acts 20: 28. Each mission will be united in harmony, having its own pastor simply that the Holy Ghost shall appoint."[124] It was obvious to the saints at Azusa Street, at least, that the Holy Ghost had appointed William Joseph Seymour to be pastor of the mission—and not Charles Fox Parham.

For the next two years the flame William Seymour ignited at the Azusa Street Mission spread to more than fifty nations. Unfortunately, what Charles Fox Parham set in motion with the first racial division would also continue. Over the years the color line appeared even at the Azusa Mission as the whites left, following their various preachers to other competing missions. By 1911 there were at least eleven other missions in Los Angeles, the largest being the Upper Room Mission. "Seymour and the Azusa miracle gave birth to the Pentecostal movement in a transformation of prevailing white American racial attitudes of exclusiveness, now the movement began to conform to these attitudes."[125]

In less than two years time an internal feud, also involving race, rocked Azusa Street. Seymour, perhaps unknowingly, was responsible. It even made Charles Parham's visit seem tame by way of comparison. It would signal the beginning of the end for Seymour's and the African-American influence at the Azusa Street Mission.

This most damaging challenge to Seymour's leadership at the mission erupted soon after he and Jennie Evans Moore were married on May 13, 1908. Moore, the first person to speak in "other tongues" at the cottage prayer meetings on North Bonnie Brae Street, "was strikingly beautiful and known for her intellect and elite status among the black people."[126] Edward S. Lee, Seymour's first benefactor in Los Angeles, the one who had taken him in when he had no place to go after being locked out of Julia Hutchin's mission at Ninth and Santa Fe, performed "the quiet ceremony."[127] Interestingly, when applying for her marriage license, Jennie Moore answered the question regarding race with "Ethiopian." It is very possible that Jennie Moore, known for her intellect as well as her beauty, gave Ethiopia as her ancestral home because it was tied in with eschatological beliefs in African-American religious traditions about an inevitable "African redemption."

The "redemption of Africa" is a phrase that had wide currency during the nineteenth century among Afro-Americans who supported the missionary movement as well as among Black Nationalists. They based their hope upon a Biblical prophecy…Psalms 68: 31, "Princes shall come out of Egypt and Ethiopia shall soon stretch forth her hand unto God." (When the Ethiopians defeated the Italians at the Battle of Adowa in 1896 the event was widely interpreted as the beginning of the fulfillment of the prophecy).[128]

In *A Fire in the Bones*, Albert J. Raboteau notes that this passage from the Psalms, "without doubt the most quoted verse in black religious history," was elaborated in greatest detail by two black theologians of the late nineteenth century:

Theophilus Gould Steward and James Theodore Holly moved the interpretation of Psalms 68:31 to a new global perspective. Both men insisted that the psalmist had predicted a special role for the darker races in the millennial phase of history, the end time….a new and final age of a raceless and peaceful Christianity would begin, in which the darker, non-Christian peoples of the world (Africans, Indians, Chinese) would hear and accept the pure gospel of Christ, undefiled by Anglo-Saxon prejudice. "The crowning work of the will of God is reserved for the millennial phase of Christianity when Ethiopia shall stretch out her hands directly unto God"…Steward and Holly pushed the interpretation of Psalms 68:31 as far as it could go in explaining human history—all the way to the millennium….In this new age, it will be the destiny of those who were oppressed but did not oppress, those who were enslaved but did not enslave, those who were hated but did not hate, to realize the gospel on earth.[129]

It is quite possible then that Jennie Moore believed even more strongly than her husband did that "Negroes were not only the chosen people" but that they would bring about "the restoration of Ethiopia's ancient glory."[130] And the Azusa Street Mission is where this "new age" would finally be ushered in. Jennie Moore promptly left her home at 217 North Bonnie Brae Street, and "the Seymours moved into a modest upstairs apartment at Azusa Mission."[131] "An unexpected crisis developed immediately. Criticism of Seymour erupted from a small but influential group at the Mission…. this was the turning point of Seymour's influence and worldwide spread of the Pentecostal movement from Azusa Mission."[132]

The Reverend Ernest S. Williams served as the general superintendent of the Assemblies of God from 1929–1949. Passing on October 25, 1981 at age

Brother W.J. Seymour and his wife, Sister Jennie Moore Seymour *(used by permission of Flower Pentecostal Heritage Center).*

ninety-six, Williams was remembered by his denomination as "a spiritual giant, a prince of God, and a father in Israel."[133] Born in San Bernardino, California, on January 7, 1885, Williams grew up in a poor but "holiness-believing" family.[134] Returning to Los Angeles from Denver in the fall of 1906, Williams visited the Azusa Street Mission at the request of his mother. Just prior to his ninety-second birthday, Williams reminisced about the mission and its leadership. "The work began among...a group of colored people. [It] was furnished very crudely, very crudely. But the white people, the white people went there. I received the Baptism at Los Angeles at Azusa Street. I had a wonderful experience in God."[135]

Not only did Ernest S. William's mother get her son to the mission but she was also responsible for introducing the future leader of the "small but influential group" that undercut William Seymour's influence. "My mother said to Mrs. [Florence] Crawford, 'I would like to take you where the Lord is working...but I don't think you would like to go to that neighborhood.' And she replied, 'I'll go anywhere if I can get to the Lord.' She really was a leader by birth."[136] Obviously, Mrs. Williams was well aware of Crawford's deep racial prejudice. Both she and her husband had "looked down on anyone who even spoke to a colored [*sic*] person, unless he was a servant."[137]

Soon Florence Crawford, "a leader by birth," was one of Seymour's associates and a close personal friend of Clara Lum, secretary of the mission and co-editor of the newspaper. "As co-editor...of *The Apostolic Faith*, Crawford was second only to Seymour in the number of signed articles found in its pages. She was [also] instrumental in distributing the periodical."[138] Within six months of her first visit to the mission, Florence Crawford was appointed state director for the fledging movement.

As an eighteen-year-old granddaughter of Oregon pioneers, Crawford had journeyed south to Los Angeles in 1890 in a personal quest for health and to escape a youthful marriage. "As a child she had been injured in a collision with a horse-drawn carriage and had suffered debilitating bouts of spinal meningitis and tuberculosis. Later she would recall that she had migrated to the 'sunny south,' Los Angeles, out of sheer desperation."[139] By the end of her first year in Los Angeles, Florence had married Frank M. Crawford and was a mother the following year. Crawford, raised an atheist, converted to Christianity "while dancing in one of the city's ballrooms."[140] She became convinced she had heard "the voice of God" on the dance floor piercing "through the glitter and glamour."[141] "After God saved me," she wrote, "I...launched into...prison work, and the prison work was my life."[142] For five years, from 1900–1905, Crawford was involved with Los Angeles prisoners and "other local reform organizations."[143] After accompanying Mrs. Williams to the Azusa Mission in April 1906, she underwent yet another change in lifestyle. "The jewelry went off my hands and the flowers and feathers out of my hat. I began to dress in modest apparel and live the life."[144] She would soon be out the door of her marriage to Frank Crawford as well. Her restless spirit also quickly chafed under Seymour's spiritual leadership. Perhaps eager to have her own ministry and to be free of both a husband and a male spiritual mentor, Florence Crawford, the movement's best example of a "biblical feminist," went up the coast to Oakland and then to Portland, "and she brought the Pentecostal message to them and it was accepted."[145] Part of the problem for Crawford was polity. "Seymour had begun to institute a number of small, but significant, changes to the government of the...Mission that would limit the level of leadership to which...a woman could ultimately rise."[146] The movement as a whole would later adopt these changes that gave their women ministers "limited liberty." Pentecostalism in general would limit their prophesizing daughters only to prophetic roles, while the priestly functions of the church would be reserved exclusively for males. In her move north Crawford was also "the only one of the early...leaders that actually ruptured her relationship with Pastor Seymour in the first year...of the revival..."[147] "She seems to have thought she could, in essence, lead a coup d'etat that would effectively unseat William J. Seymour, relocate the center of the revival in Portland, and lead that revival into the future."[148]

After Seymour's marriage to Jennie Moore in May of 1908, Clara Lum, who was editor of Seymour's newsletter, took the mailing list...and abruptly moved to Portland, Oregon. There she joined ... Florence Crawford, and they started their own paper."[149] Seymour's decision to marry Jennie Moore sent Clara Lum packing for Portland and Florence Crawford for two possible reasons. In some of the early photographs of the mission leadership, Clara Lum is seen sitting next to Seymour on his left-hand side. In addition to serving Seymour as his stenographer and secretary, there very well may have been a romance or at least hope for one between the two:

> The late Bishop Ithiel Clemmons reports a conversation he had with Bishop Charles H. Mason...He claimed that Mason had told him Clara Lum had fallen in love with Pastor Seymour and had sought a proposal of marriage from him. Seymour had come to Mason for his advice. Mason had cautioned him against marrying a white woman, given the state of race relations in the United States at the height of the Jim Crow era. As a result, Seymour, who wanted to marry, had chosen Jennie Evans Moore.[150]

Whether jilted or not, Clara Lum turned to Florence Crawford for solace and support. And more than anything else, Florence Crawford herself was dead set against the institution of marriage. Despite getting married at "Mrs. Crawford's home...in 1900 and eleven," although not by her, Ernest Williams slowly, carefully remembered her harsh stance on the subject:

> She was opposed to marriage. She was married herself and I kinda think married more than once but that isn't supposed to be noted... made known. Once when she was a young woman. (The first one) was a rancher, a grain rancher. After (her) baptism they separated. It wasn't a happy situation I don't think. But that's too private for me to talk about it...She did some hard things...I don't know that I should talk too much about some of those things...Some dear people really separated through her influence. Wives, that she would come in between them and their husbands. She was really quite a strong influence in those days....And anybody that didn't take her position was dis-fellowshipped and she was very severe in it... that shows her domination. They weren't even to visit their relatives, that didn't believe this way."[151]

Actually Florence Crawford had been "outed" long before Ernest Williams mentioned her marriages. Forty-one years earlier, in 1935, *Time* magazine not only noted that "'Mother' Florence Louise Crawford, 63, ... [was] twice married and the mother of two," the article also made public her views on marriage and sexual relations. "'Mother' Crawford," claimed

Time, "owns…a big white house where she boards and trains promising young Apostolic ministers. When they marry, iron-willed 'Mother' Crawford throws them out. She advocates celibacy, recommends continence among married folk, was chagrined when her two children married. Stern, dowdy in dress, 'Mother' Crawford lavishes affection only on her kennel of Pomeranian dogs which she takes along, like yapping cherubim to camp meetings. "[152]

From their headquarters in Portland, Oregon, Crawford and Lum controlled all "22 subscriber lists for the paper. Twenty lists represented Los Angeles and the surrounding towns…The other two lists were the national and international lists, crucial for the life of the paper."[153] The newly married Seymours even traveled to Portland in hopes of retrieving the crucial mailing lists. They arrived back in Los Angeles empty-handed. Publishing at least one more issue of *The Apostolic Faith* on his own, William Seymour sought to set the record straight:

> I must for the salvation of souls let it be known that the editor is still in Los Angeles … and will not remove "The Apostolic Faith" from Los Angeles without letting subscribers and field workers know. This was a sad thing to our hearts for a worker to attempt to take the paper which is the property of the Azusa Street Mission to another city without consent, after being warned by the elders not to do so.[154]

"With the passing of the newspaper from Seymour and Azusa Mission," as Douglas Nelson correctly notes, "an era ended at Los Angeles. The Pentecostal movement changed decisively from one of interracial equality characterized by unity to one of white domination separated into divisions."[155]

Like most new religious movements, Pentecostalism attracted outside opposition and persecution as well. The persecution in Los Angeles was the strongest from 1906 to 1916. A participant described what occurred:

> Many of us were thrown in jail. Others were horsewhipped, clubbed, or stoned and seriously injured, or even killed…The persecution to two of three Holy Ghost-filled Catholic Priests was unbelievable. Both were killed. One was pursued and caught between Long Beach and Los Angeles, stripped naked, and slashed with boat oars until his body looked like chopped liver. His stomach was ruptured in many places. Rushed to the hospital on the crest of Alpine Street in Los Angeles, he died before medical attention could be administered… Unfortunately, all the opposition to us Pentecostals… was not from ill-educated hoodlums. Much of it came from ministers of established churches, reluctant to accept that anyone of that day could have been baptized in the Holy Spirit. [156]

On September 9, 1910 the *Los Angeles Times* gave the movement a stinging rebuke after three "Holy Rollers" had starved themselves to death following a long bout of fasting and prayer. In an editorial on "Frenzied Religion," the *Times* claimed,

> We have had frenzied finance, frenzied politics, frenzied muck-raking, frenzied journalism—frenzy…in every walk of life: but surely religion… should be conducted along sane and spiritual lines. Religion was never intended to drive its devotees to insanity or suicide.
>
> The originator of this new cult was a one-eyed negro…He claimed, among other things, to possess the "gift of tongues"…His church service consisted of rolling, leaping and other varieties of sensational gymnastics calculated to work on the feelings of the morbidly inclined.
>
> Now, a prophet may have a dark skin, may be minus an optic…be an expert roller or a veritable bouncing ball. Yet all this should not be taken as proof positive of divine inspiration, and any man who uses such performances for the wrecking of human lives and the overthrow of human reason becomes a fit study, not for the psychologist, but the police court.
>
> Religious freedom is guaranteed to all citizens of the republic. It is to the interest of every religious body which values this privilege to take care that this freedom is not abused. This right was intended to safeguard faith, not frenzy.
>
> As for the so-called Holy Rollers, they have a right to their beliefs, whatever those beliefs may be, so long as they practice them without disturbing the public peace or violating the canons of established decency. Public worship in our churches should be dignified, elevating, reverent. With this reservation, a citizen may worship whatever god he chooses; may be a follower of Christ or Mohammed, Confucius, or Buddha, or even a one-eyed negro.[157]

The opposition to Pentecostalism by the organized church in its Azusa Street days points out its uniqueness as well as its failure to be integrated within the later movement of fundamentalism. Although the majority of Pentecostals were fundamentalist in lifestyle, quickly adopting the negative holiness code of no smoking, drinking, dancing, theater attendance, and so on, the great debates of fundamentalism were absent in the movement. Fundamentalism indeed would later become the largest opponent of the young movement, since "speaking in tongues" did not fit within its dispensational schema of interpreted Biblical events, and more often than not, it was simply dismissed as "demon possession." Protestant liberalism, on the other hand, sought to explain the phenomenon as "deviant psychological behavior." Pentecostalism and its later second cousin of fundamentalism were almost opposing theological movements, despite the fact that they shared twin cultural attitudes and lifestyles. Viewing both movements from a distance, "it was easy to lump them together."[158] Pentecostalism, however, as perceived by the fundamentalists, was "a threat to evangelical orthodoxy."[159]

In many significant ways, Pentecostalism had more in common with Roman Catholicism than it did with conservative evangelical Protestantism. "Not long after the Pentecostals appeared on the scene, one stern Princeton Presbyterian naysayer declared that because they believed in contemporary miracles they were just as bad as Catholics." The quest for spiritual transcendence through "extraordinary religion," the mystical union with Christ as the Bridegroom of the church, the emotional versus the rational appeal, the female mystical imagery, the nurturing, collective community of a people's religion is much more intertwined with Catholic roots than it is to the reaction of the "ordinary religion" of conservative Protestantism during the late teens, 1920s, and 1930s of the twentieth century. Many of the early converts to Pentecostalism were from Roman Catholic backgrounds, and revivalism flourished within Catholicism during much of the formative period of Pentecostalism. Both movements appealed to the same constituency—the urban lower middle class, "the lower two-thirds" of the country—and recent immigrants. In lifestyle, early Pentecostals were fundamentalist, while in worship behavior and patterns they were more mystical/Catholic. The reception of Pentecostalism in later years at Catholic and Episcopal institutions helps to confirm this thesis. It is doubtful that Pentecostalism will ever be accepted at existing centers of fundamentalism such as Dallas Theological Seminary, Southwestern Baptist Theological Seminary, or Bob Jones University. Harvey Cox rightly sees Pentecostals as "populist mystics" and claims that they "have more in common with Saint Catherine of Sienna than with John Calvin."[160] Cox also cites recent sociological analyses that suggest that Pentecostals, especially in Latin America, "might better be understood as a mutation not of evangelical Protestantism but of popular folk Catholicism."[161] Similarly, the Mexican religious historian Jean-Pierre Bastian sees Pentecostals as "Catholics without priests."[162] Walter Hollenweger is also in agreement:

> Pentecostals consider themselves to be heirs of the reformation. They do not realize that many of their deeply felt convictions belong to catholic popular religion....Most of this owes more to Thomas Aquinas than

to the reformation. A Catholic in France or Latin America who converts to Pentecostalism does not change his religion, but only his organization....Pentecostalism is strongest in Catholic cultures.[163]

Classical Pentecostalism represented, then, more a social and spiritual revolt against "cold formalism" and the loss of spiritual transcendence than a rational doctrinal or dogmatic defense of historic Christianity in collusion with recent scientific thought. Pentecostal spokespersons confirm this:

> Azusa's revolt was a climactic war against the perversion of biblical Christianity. It was not inherently a conflict of doctrines, methods, administration, denominational idiosyncrasies and the like. It did not concern itself with the various schools of the theological conflict. It was a fundamental revolt against an institution system.[164]

Hollenweger further argues that a major contribution of Pentecostalism to global Christianity and the Church Universal has been "their emphasis on experienced religion":

> The main focus of early Pentecostal critique was not diluted theology but withered piety. The problem lay not in wrong thinking so much as in collapsed feeling. Not the decline of orthodoxy but the decay of devotion lay at the root of the problem. It was not that the church was liberal but that it was lifeless. What was needed was not new arguments for heads but new experiences for hearts. Fundamentalists and neo-orthodox theologians mounted arguments. Pentecostals gave testimony. One can therefore not range Pentecostalism simply among the fundamentalists, even more so since fundamentalists have been and are the most bitter opponents of Pentecostalism.[165]

Of course every religious movement has its own internal spectrum of conservatives and liberals, and, ironically, it was doctrinal disputes that finally dissolved the Azusa Street Mission after its three-year history of continuous revival. An early eyewitness recounted the outcome: "I was thirteen when Azusa Street closed, three years after it opened. My parents saw the end coming. Pastor W. J. Seymour and the man who often substituted for him, Pastor William H. Durham, had deep differences in doctrine."[166] The doctrinal differences between Seymour and Durham also led to a further racial splintering of the movement since Seymour was black and Durham white.

Durham's two theological contributions to the movement have remained with the majority of Anglo-Pentecostals to this day. Russ Spittler has said that it is something of an accident that the Assemblies of God are not known as "Durhamites." Durham not only repeatedly emphasized that glossolalia was the "evidence" of the baptism of the Holy Spirit, he also ended, at least for the white Pentecostals, the holiness teaching that "sanctification" after "salvation" was a "second definite work." Durham's teaching, which split the Azusa Street Mission, was commonly known as the "Finished work of Christ on Calvary." Durham argued thus:

William H. Durham (right) and his associate Harry Van Loon (author's collection).

> When I saw the absurdity of such teaching, (the second definite work) so far as it refers to cleansing the heart from sin, I began to write and speak against the doctrine that it takes two works of grace to save and cleanse a man. I denied and still deny that God does not deal with the nature of sin in conversion…Therefore, through our identification with Him, who is our Savior and Sanctifier, we are both saved and sanctified.[167]

In February of 1910 William Durham came to Los Angeles, "the great Pentecostal center, to deliver his message, and amidst persecution and opposition of every kind, God baptized hundreds in the Spirit in a few months, and established an assembly of over six hundred people who stand for the truths of the finished work of Calvary, and the baptism in the Holy Spirit."[168]

An early participant in the Azusa Street Mission had by the latter part of 1907 begun to notice "some friction and with it, a decline of the Spirit." Matters came to a head, however, when Seymour visited Chicago and at the same time Durham came to Los Angeles filling the pulpit at the mission for Seymour. An eye witness observed the following:

> When Pastor Seymour left for Chicago for a special meeting, Pastor Durham took over the pulpit. Then a second, great outpouring of God's

Holy Spirit took place. It was such a tremendous revival that it was called the 'second Azusa outpouring.' Every night humanity jammed the Azusa Street Mission. Hundreds we turned away. It was clear that a larger building was necessary. Pastor Seymour returned and saw that even greater crowds were attending the Durham meetings than his own. Although he might have denied it, he regarded Pastor Durham's spectacular rise as King Saul did that of young David. Like King Saul, he began making mistakes. The most grave was chaining and padlocking the Azusa Street Mission door shut. Pastor Durham was not too upset. The time for a break was overdue. Durham and his elders rented a new location.—two stories of a building on the northeast corner of Seventh and Los Angeles Streets.[169]

For at least two years, 209 East Seventh Street became the major Pentecostal center in Los Angeles, although there were already at least three other spinoffs from the Azusa Street Mission existing at the same time, the most notable being Elmer Fisher's Upper Room Mission on South Spring Street. An eyewitness recorded both the significance of the new mission for the movement and its growth elsewhere and subsequent opposition:

> By this time, Pentecost was a going concern and Pentecostal churches, thanks to the Azusa Street and Seventh and Los Angeles Street Holy Spirit revival began opening in most major cities of the world. It had to be so, for the Pentecostal could find not even a finger or toehold in established churches.[170]

For his beliefs and new doctrine Durham attracted both verbal and physical abuse. A young woman attempting her own version of an exorcism attacked Durham with her large hat pin, hoping to dispel his "demonic" views. Even an almost-forgotten Charles Parham attempted to move into the Durham spotlight of controversy. From his home in Kansas the "projector" of Pentecostalism called for a special sign from heaven itself. "If this man's doctrine is true," declared Parham, "let my life go out to prove it, but if our teaching on a definite grace of sanctification is true, let his life pay the forfeit."[171] Less than a year later, on July 7, 1912, William H. Durham, secretly suffering from pulmonary tuberculosis, died, or as his followers put it, "fell asleep in Jesus." Durham was only thirty-nine years old at the time of his death. Needless to say, Charles Fox Parham felt vindicated.

What William Durham managed to accomplish in his short but influential life was to bring an end to the Methodist impulse and Wesleyan theological tradition in much of Pentecostalism. After Durham's pivotal career, the majority of the movement adopted more of a theological hybrid model that reflected Reformed and Wesleyan theology. Far from dying out, the Wesleyan influence was no longer paramount. It was simply subjugated to the much stronger Reformed position. Yet a century after his demise-some "sanctified" Pentecostals are still attacking Durham's "Finished Work Doctrine."

Recently, the president of a small Pentecostal Bible school sought to educate his flock about Durham's doctrine:

> This doctrine declares that sanctification can never be obtained in this life, only in the next. There is only one basic problem with "The Finished Work Doctrine" and that is, THERE IS NO BIBLE FOR IT. "The Finished Work Doctrine" is something concocted by man and his own fleshly desire. Just as the Roman Catholic Church devised Purgatory, many Pentecostals have devised "The Finished Work Doctrine."
>
> I can and will tell you that there has never been a genuine revival in the land without people believing in the doctrine of Sanctification. [172]

After William Durham's death, the second major doctrinal dispute to fragment the infant movement occurred at the first "worldwide" Pentecostal camp meeting in the Los Angeles area, held at the Arroyo Seco, where the Pasadena Freeway enters Los Angeles at Avenue 60. Pentecostal camp meetings at Arroyo Seco began the summer of 1907 and continued sporadically until 1920. They were born out of necessity following the first summer at the cramped and overflowing Azusa Street Mission where "it was necessary to stick one's nose under the benches to get a breath of air."[173] The saints would be so "taken up with sitting at the feet of Jesus that they lost track of the time and would sit there in the heat, wiping the perspiration from their faces."[174] The May 1907 issue of *The Apostolic Faith* (that by now had a monthly circulation of forty thousand) announced that "we expect to have a grand camp meeting in Los Angeles, beginning June 1, and continuing about four months."[175] It was to be a "grand camp meeting" indeed. The "grove of sycamore and live oak trees near Hermon" was selected because it adjoined the city limits and was only "several miles from the center of town." The fare on the electric cars which ran every seven minutes was only five cents. And it was just three blocks from where the South Pasadena or Church of Angels cars stopped to the camp meeting. A "tabernacle" with a seating capacity of one thousand people was also advertised. The camping grounds in the grove were free. "The air is fresh with the sea breeze which comes in from the distant ocean, and there is plenty of good water." The best selling point for the Pentecostal saints, however, was the fact that "you can pray there as loud as you like. There are wooded hills all about which we expect will ring with the songs and prayers of the saints and shouts of new born souls." *The Apostolic Faith* announcement failed to mention that on top of the wooded hills there was the Free Methodist community of Hermon. Because the wooded hills did "ring with the songs and prayers of the saints and shouts of new born souls," often tents were slashed and guy ropes cut in the middle of the night. The Free Methodists were blamed for most of the harassment, although at least one resident was converted by her new noisy neighbors:

> A woman who lived in... [the] settlement, was told the meetings were of the devil. As the music and shouts of praise wafted up to her Hermon home, she thought to herself, "so that is the devil, well the devil has some sweet singers." She attended the meetings and received the baptism in the Spirit.[176]

R. J. Scott, a businessman who organized the camp meeting on fifteen leased acres, reported that the saints who first visited the "grove of sycamore and live oak trees" exclaimed, "Why, this is a happy place, we would rather be here than even at Azusa Street." The secular press also took notice of the "happy place," observing that "the Holy Rollers' tents extend along both sides of the arroyo for a distance of perhaps half a mile. There are hundreds of them."[177] The most scandalous thing about the tents of "the Holy Rollers," according to the press, was the fact that "in them live negroes and whites, side by side," and that there were "hundreds of little children, scores of them already obsessed by this curious mental disease, masquerading as religion."[178]

The children had not been forgotten but had carefully been planned for by the camp meeting organizers. The very first announcement stated, "There will be a separate tabernacle for meetings for the children with services daily, so it will be a children's camp meeting as well as a grown up people's meeting. There will be competent workers to teach and to help them spiritually. We expect it to be a time of salvation among the children. Mothers' meetings are also planned for."[179]

The Arroyo Seco was both an earthly and a heavenly home, a bridge between the reality of Los Angeles and the promise of the millennial New Jerusalem:

> The move to outdoor spaces indicated "a rejection of traditional space" identified with a "social order" in which many of the participants held the least desirable locations....implicit in the move out of the church and

civic centers is a rejection of the order imposed by those institutions....
Worshiping under a brush arbor, campers marked themselves as pilgrims, temporary residents moving mythically with the ancient Israelites
from one home to the next.[180]

By mid-summer 1907 the *Los Angeles Times* reported on the activity of the
"Holy Ghosters" and "Rollers" in the Arroyo Seco. In just over a year's time
it was obvious that there were at least three things occurring with the young
movement. First, even in "their campaign for souls in...the woods," persecution still plagued the movement. "Loud Prayers Stir Protest," declared
the headlines, "Fervor of 'Rollers' Makes Highland Park Howl." "Loud
praying at the big camp meeting of the 'holy rollers'...is keeping Highland
Park awake at nights," observed the *Times*. "Reports have been made at
the health office in...City Hall that the camp is becoming so crowded that
there is a likelihood of an outbreak of disease among the band of religious
enthusiasts."[181]

Despite the announcement that the camp meeting would conclude
by October 1, the *Times* also reported that "some of the brothers" were
hopeful that "they will be deeded land in the Arroyo on which to establish permanent headquarters."[182] The desire for permanence was influenced
by two factors. First, "the work... [was] growing faster" than the "brothers" thought it would since it had been founded "about a year and a half
ago."[183] The second factor was due to the desire "for the establishment of
a seminary for the training of 'tongues' missionaries." "Highland Park,"
concluded the *Times,* "fears that the loud praying is to become a fixture in
the landscape."[184]

Finally, after just a year and a half it is quite possible that racial segregation was slowly beginning to occur. Contrary to earlier published reports
about Negroes and whites living "side by side," the *Times* reported that
"One part of the camp ground is given over to Negroes, many of whom are
from Southern States. They conduct their own restaurant."[185] Even more
telling, however, was the reporter's observation that although the Apostolic Faith Movement had been founded by William Seymour, "Seymour
is gone now, and R.J. Scott [who was Anglo] of Winnipeg, Man., where a
large branch has been established, is in charge of the local work, as well as
of the big camp meeting."[186]

A month later, the *Times* announced another change in the movement's
leadership. "A white woman has been the leader, and her lieutenant has
been a colored man, but Mr. Trotter in his talk yesterday intimated...that
he is now the leader."[187] Actually it was "iron-willed Mother Crawford's, "a

leader by birth," final attempt at taking over the movement's leadership in Los Angeles. Since her husband, Frank, a local real estate agent and developer, had arranged the Arroyo Seco lease for the camp meeting, Crawford had been privy to the planned meeting even though she had spent the past year in Portland. In July 1907 Crawford was summoned back to Los Angeles by authorities because her daughter required medical attention. It was during her short stay in Los Angeles that the *Times* noted the shift in the movement's leadership to "a white woman" and a "Mr. Trotter."

> She took the opportunity to attend the 1907 camp meeting then in progress. Will Trotter, a longtime friend with whom she had worked during her years of rescue work, had just been fired from his position as director of the Union Rescue Mission in Los Angeles because he announced at the camp meeting that he had spoken in tongues and would now identify with the Apostolic Faith movement. Crawford and Trotter undoubtedly shared notes and spoke of the future.[188]

For whatever reason, Mother Crawford and Will Trotter failed in their bid to take over the local leadership. It is very likely that both their temperaments were in sharp contrast with Seymour's humble nature and that they failed to win and unite the hearts of their followers. "Trotter, in his opening prayer," observed the *Times,* "prayed fervently that if any one was present for the purpose of criticizing, his tongue might be paralyzed."[189] By summer's end, "Crawford and her daughter, Mildred, and Trotter and his family had all moved to Portland. While Crawford would later claim that the formal break with Seymour did not take place until nearly 1908, by September 1907 it was essentially complete."[190]

During the summer of 1907 the camp meeting at the Arroyo Seco was plagued with more than potential leadership changes. The young movement also faced a continuing crises experienced since its founding as to who could rightfully claim membership. In an article entitled, "In Grip of the Holy Rollers," a reporter for the *Times* noted, "At the meeting…a woman threw herself on the floor in the throes of spiritual 'ecstasy' and cried at the top of her voice: 'I want a man! I want a man!' "[191] Not only had Charles Parham, the self-appointed projector of the movement, sought to purge the Azusa Street Mission from its "crude negroisms," he also sought to rid the movement of its animalism that created "magnetic currents" that led "to lust and free love."[192]

Perhaps the movement's strongest threat came from the spiritualists who early on were attracted to the mission. Seymour himself singled them out and labeled them as "Counterfeits." Because of their presence in Pentecostalism, the movement was quickly identified with "free loveism." It was guilt by association. "Free loveism," as Mel Robeck explains, "was originally intended as a liberation movement for women. It gave them the freedom to choose their sexual partners as well as the freedom to submit to or decline their husbands' requests for marital sex....While not all spiritualists were free lovers, nearly all free lovers were spiritualists. The presence of known 'spiritualists' at the Azusa Street Mission...may have led to the accusation being lodged against the Mission."[193]

"One visit to the...(Arroyo Seco) is enough to disgust any thoughtful person," concluded the *Los Angeles Times* reporter. "The more light of day that is turned upon it, the less people will have to do with it, even though they be plain folk with little education, biblical or otherwise."[194]

Six years later, however, in the spring of 1913, R.J. Scott once again sponsored a camp meeting that sought to accommodate some five thousand persons, reflecting the growing interest and magnitude of the movement. As in Aimee Semple McPherson's Philadelphia tent meeting, a tent city was erected with street names such as "Praise," "Glory," and "Hallelujah" avenues. Many of the Pentecostals who moved into the tent city at the Arroyo Seco stayed on after the meetings for economic reasons until a winter flood permanently moved them out. "People came from around the world to take part in it...two thousand attended the opening service. William J. Seymour received no special invitation, nor was he seated on the platform. Those leading the movement around the country and in Canada now received pride of place."[195]

The featured evangelist was a woman—Mrs. M.B. Woodworth Etter— who had a reputation as a "healing evangelist" and whom Aimee had stopped to see in her first transcontinental trip. Despite the fact that Mrs. Etter was so ill herself "that she sometimes had to be carried up onto the crude, unfinished, pine platform," there was, according to an observer, "nothing sickly, pale, or weak about her ministering."

> Once her equally ill husband joined her, she raised her small hands and the power of the Holy Spirit electrified us all. A series of healing miracles thrilled the entire audience...Hundreds were saved. Many, sitting on wooden folding chairs or kneeling at the crude wooden altar, received the baptism of the Holy Spirit.[196]

According to Frank J. Ewart, Durham's assistant minister at the Seventh and Los Angeles Street Mission, who became the pastor following Durham's death, those who had come to the camp meeting "were restless, inquisitive, and on the tip-toe of expectancy."[197] The mood of expectancy was further heightened during the month-long meetings when a sermon from Jeremiah 31: 32 was given, assuring the crowd that God was about to perform a "new thing" in their midst. The "new thing" emerged out of the baptismal pool near the large tent, at which the Canadian evangelist R.E. McAlister in an exhortation "pointed out that the apostles baptized not in the triune formula but in the Name of the Lord Jesus Christ."[198] This "new revelation" gave rise in time to "oneness Pentecostalism," a schismatic movement that emerged within the larger Pentecostal fellowship. This movement was also known as the "New Issue," "Jesus Only," "Jesus Name," "Oneness," "Christian Monotheism," and "Christo-Unitarianism."[199] Ever since the founding of the Azusa Street Mission, where dance preceded dogma in their spiritual lives, Pentecostals had become addicted to new experiences and revelations. As one Apostolic Faith preacher put it, "A preacher who did not dig up some new slant on a Scripture, or get some new revelation to his own heart ever so often; a preacher who did not propagate it, defend it, and if necessary, be prepared to lay down his life for it, was considered slow, stupid, unspiritual."[200]

By the spring of 1915 the "'new movement' was spreading like wildfire from mission to mission, assembly to assembly, until it became the issue of the day within the new fellowship."[201] Ewart became an early leader of the new movement and left the Seventh and Los Angeles Street Mission to set up a tent in Belvedere, as did Franklin Small, Andrew D. Ursham, and Garfield T. Haywood—a popular black preacher of non-Holiness persuasion who carried with him large members of the non-holiness black Pentecostals into the movement.[202] The new theological conflict made Durham's theological arguments seem tame by comparison. It erupted into a kind of theological civil war, dividing friends and families and ultimately the church and their leadership. It became a major rift within the movement that even time has not been able to heal.

The best understanding of both the Durham and Ewart controversies has come from Allen Clayton who has rightly argued that "the piety of the early Pentecostal movement was characterized by an emphasis on Jesus:

> It was this Jesus piety that lay at the bottom of both the Finished Work and the Oneness controversies. Ewart's revelation…gained wide acceptance because it resonated with this piety.…the unchecked emphasis on Jesus in the devotional life of early Pentecostalism was the major cause of both this division and the earlier one over sanctification.[203]

One could make the argument that the final nail in the coffin to the Azusa Street experiment occurred in April 1914 when "mostly white men from the American plains and Ozarks—especially, Missouri, Kansas, Arkansas and Texas…gathered together [and] sought to impose doctrinal and social order on the chaotic world of early Pentecostalism."[204] Converging on the local opera house in Hot Springs, Arkansas, several hundred loosely affiliated Pentecostal preachers and faith healers gathered not only to decry denominationalism but also to "disapprove of all unscriptural methods, doctrine and conduct."[205] The newly created organization, known as the General Council of the Assemblies of God, "developed over the next decade from a loose confederation of believers into a full-fledged denomination that initially sought and then later demanded social and theological orthodoxy."[206] More than anything else, however, the creation of the Assemblies of God proved H. Richard Niebuhr something of a prophet when he wrote, "Denominationalism in the Christian church is such an unacknowledged hypocrisy….It represents the accommodation of Christianity to the caste-system of human society….The division of the churches closely follows the division of men into the castes of national, racial, and economic groups. It draws the color line in the Church of God."[207]

"As Pentecostalism turned respectable," observed Martin Marty, "it also became increasingly segregated." [208]

Vivian Eilythia Deno in her groundbreaking work of the first two decades of Pentecostalism accurately assesses and summarizes the actions taken by what would become Anglo Pentecostalism's largest denomination.

> As the early conventions [of the Assemblies of God] sought to root out doctrinal heterodoxy, especially those who espoused "Jesus only" beliefs, these same conventions also sought to eradicate social heterodoxy in the forms of female pastors and interracial fellowship. In doing so, they tied what had once been a socially radical message of faith to a thoroughly conventional if not reactionary social order of female and racial subordination." [209]

It was no mere coincidence either that in May 1914, one month after the infamous Opera House gathering in Hot Springs, William Joseph Seymour revised the Azusa Mission's articles of incorporation and constitution. He obviously perceived an organized racial threat to the movement and a possible hostile take over of the mission itself, and his revisions made clear that the Apostolic Faith Mission would not only be carried on "for the benefit of the colored people" but that "the people of all countries, climes, and nations shall be welcome."[210] Like Richard Allen before him,

Seymour accepted the designation of "bishop," and the by-laws provided that the offices of bishop, vice-bishop, and trustee were to be "people of color." "Seymour...sought to insure that Azusa would remain true to its original purpose, and not be taken over by white people who did not understand or accept that purpose."[211] Despite Seymour's protective and preventative measures, his earlier instincts about a hostile takeover of the mission proved to be prophetic. And it provided, in Mel Robeck's memorable phrase, a "sordid ending to an otherwise brilliant story."[212]

After Seymour's largely unnoticed death in 1922, Jennie Seymour attempted to carry on the work of her husband with the remaining faithful few. In 1930, a white man, Ruthford D. Griffith, a self-proclaimed Coptic priest and bishop, showed up and insisted "that the congregation's leader should be a man....He forced the smaller Seymour party to worship upstairs, while he took the main sanctuary as his own. He announced that he was the new bishop of the Mission and proceeded to take control."[213]

In January 1931, the growing tension between the two worshipping and warring congregations—one upstairs, one downstairs; one white, one black—"exploded into an argument that reduced both parties to throwing hymnals at one another. Police were called; the mission padlocked."[214] The fate of the spiritual birthplace of Pentecostalism was finally determined by a secular court in June of 1932. The court found in favor of Mrs. Seymour, but it was too little, too late. By then the old barn-like building had been reduced to rubble, and the remaining group of African-Americans had "moved back to the Asberry home on North Bonnie Brae Street, where the revival and the mission had been born twenty-six years before."[215] "It was said that they were scattered as sheep without a shepherd."[216]

Jennie Evans Seymour died like her husband on this side of the Jordan, having only seen the land of promise from afar. Even the Assemblies of God turned down an opportunity to buy what remained of the Azusa Street site, saying they were "not interested in relics."[217] In the quest for upward mobility, one did not need reminders of humble origins. After foreclosure proceedings by Security-First National Bank were finally approved following a two-and-a-half-year battle in the courts, 312 Azusa Street, the place of promise and Mecca for the miraculous, once seen "to have been annexed to heaven" and "the habitation of legions of the heavenly host," remained for years nothing more than a barren downtown city parking lot.

Two other major revivals occurred in Los Angeles, both in 1918, before Aimee came to town. The first occurred in early 1918 and was referred to as the Ice Palace Revival, held at the former ice-skating rink located downtown at Tenth and Broadway. It was sponsored by Arthur Osterberg, who had helped to transform the Azusa Street Mission from a "stable" to a "church." It featured the Persian evangelist Andrew D. Ursham, who was by now part of the "New Issue." The final major Pentecostal revival before the advent of Aimee Semple McPherson was the second "World-Wide" Camp Meeting held at Arroyo Seco in the summer of 1918.

Los Angeles, as the birthplace of modern Pentecostalism, was in many ways leaderless in that regard for several years until Aimee Semple McPherson drove into town in her black Oldsmobile just before Christmas 1918. One observer's sentiments were echoed by many :

> When the Pentecostal Church needed a standard-bearer, Aimee Semple McPherson burst upon the scene...Many ministers in a spiritual depression got a lift from the bottom of the valley to the top of Mount Everest... Aimee Semple McPherson was many things...including perpetual motion and seeming omnipresence. She was in so many cities to preach that she appeared to violate the physical law of being limited to one place at one time. Thousands of souls were introduced to Christ by her. [218]

When Aimee first visited Los Angeles, her home base was at Victoria Hall at 222 South Spring Street. Warren Fisher was the pastor of the mission, and it represented about the fourth major independent Pentecostal revival in Los Angeles during the chaotic years following William Durham's death. The most established Pentecostal work in the city at the time was Bethel Temple, the mother church of the newly formed General Council of the Assemblies of God in Southern California.

Before her meeting at Victoria Hall Assembly began in December 1918, Aimee astutely noted, "There are thirty (Pentecostal) assemblies...in Los Angeles, and more than four thousand saints who have the baptism of the Holy Spirit in this city, which has been such a beacon light for Pentecost the world over during the last twelve years."[219] Much later she would write more:

> This hall, we were told, had been almost empty. The dear pastor had been preaching in his shirtsleeves to about a dozen people...Here, in the "City of angels," where the Pentecostal power had so wonderfully fallen...on Azusa Street, we learned that several doctrinal differences had gotten the eyes of many off the Lord and that there was a dearth in the land.[220]

Attending Aimee's meetings at Victoria Hall "as one among many" was none other than Bishop William J. Seymour.[221] Greeting a former member of the mission, Seymour in a rare personal comment said "that he had not been feeling completely well; his heart had been hurting him."[222] Four years later, on September 28, 1922, Seymour suffered one last "sudden attack of severe pain to his heart."[223] Dead at age fifty-two, William Joseph Seymour had nevertheless been to the mountaintop and like Moses had seen the Promised Land from a distance. While he had performed "signs and wonders" in Egypt, it remained for Aimee alone, the movement's Joshua, to lead her people to the place that Bishop Seymour so often sang about, "to the land of Beulah, Blessed, blessed, land of light. Where the flowers bloom forever, and the sun is always bright."

When Luke as a historian took note of the Christian church's first Pentecost at Jerusalem, he recorded that outside observers "were amazed and perplexed, saying to one another, 'What does this mean?' "[224] A century after America's own upper-room experience at the New Jerusalem in downtown Los Angeles, skeptics and scholars alike are still asking the same question about the new Pentecost born at the dawn of the twentieth century. Bishop William Joseph Seymour and the barn-like "Bethlehem manger" of the old Azusa Street Mission have, of course, transcended time itself, having long ago entered the rarified world of myth and legend. Yet the question of meaning still persists into a new century, especially as Pentecostalism becomes the dominant expression and manifestation of Christianity in the global South.

The question of meaning of the Azusa Street myth is partially answered by a socio-theological understanding of the movement's origins. Roger Bastide was born into a Protestant family on April 1, 1898, at Nimes, France. With the soul of a poet, Bastide studied theology before discovering sociology of religion. After publishing two works in his area of expertise, Bastide went to Brazil, where in 1938 he was made a professor of sociology at the University of Sao Paulo. Returning to Paris in 1954, Bastide wrote his doctoral thesis at age fifty-nine and finished his academic career at the Sorbonne. Recently the work of Roger Bastide has been rediscovered.

The "sacred" is the central concept in Bastide's sociology of religion. The sacred can either burn "hot," creating a rupture and critical force in society, or it can also become "cold," generating social solidarity instead. What is universal about the sacred, according to Bastide, is that it has these two sides, the "savage sacred" and the "tamed sacred." The "savage sacred" is "ritual wild." It burns "hot" outside institutions and is beyond all boundaries and standards. The "tamed sacred" or "domesticated sacred" runs "cold" and is the domain of the "established official organizations" such as the historic Christian churches or even the Bible.

Roger Bastide's sociological distinction of the "savage sacred," "ritual wild," and the "tamed" or "domesticated sacred" is complimented by Harvey Cox's theological understanding of Pentecostalism. Cox sees in Pentecostalism "a kind of primal spirituality that had been all but suffocated by centuries of western Christian moralism and rationality."[225] "Pentecostals have not prospered in the twentieth century simply by blending into its cosmopolitan ethos," claims Cox. "They succeed by criticizing that ethos and by suggesting an alternative to it." Cox's "primal spirituality," functions just like Bastide's "savage sacred" by creating a rupture and critical force in society itself. Like Bastide's "savage sacred," Cox's "primal piety" or "primal spirituality" reconnects emotions and ideas, religion and healing. "By embracing ecstatic praise, visions, healing, dreams, and joyous bodily movement, Pentecostal worship" Cox concludes, "lured anarchy into the sacred circle and tamed it.

> It tapped into a raging underground sea of raw religious feeling and turbulent emotion and gave it shape and expression. In the history of religion…the conflict between Order and Chaos is deeper than the rift between Good and Evil. The Pentecostals sensed this and boldly made that struggle a part of their liturgical life.[226]

The taming dialectic of the "savage sacred" and its transformation into the "tamed sacred" not only describes the ministry of Aimee Semple McPherson, it also helps explain the making of modern Pentecostalism in the Americas and in the global village. Perhaps the best definition of Pentecostalism to date is found in the simple statement by David Martin that the relatively new global face of Christianity "brings together the most ancient and the most modern"[227] In other words, under the big top tent of Pentecostalism are found at long last the lamb of the miraculous and the lion of modernity lying down together in peace. Amanda Porterfield picks up this duality of Pentecostalism in her *Healing in the History of Christianity*.

> Much as Christianity's effectiveness as a healing cult facilitated its spread throughout the far flung Roman Empire in late antiquity, healing performances enable Pentecostalism to grow in many parts of the early twenty-first century world.
>   At the same time, the modern character of Pentecostalism is evident in its depictions of the Holy Spirit as a force of energy analogous to electricity and high speed communications.[228]

Porterfield, like Harvey Cox, before her, also discovers the true ancientness of Pentecostalism in all its many global manifestations. Its ancient character is found in something more than even the early practice of Christian healing. It is something more primal, older still than Christianity, itself. It is found in an adaptation of shamanism, humanity's original spiritual practice. Shamans were humankind's first healers and therapists, their first showmen and storytellers. "In Seoul and other cities in South Korea," notes Porterfield, "Pentecostalism fuses evangelical Protestantism with indigenous forms of shamanic healing. In the United Kingdom, Pentecostalism attracts immigrants from the Caribbean and other regions where spirit possession and shamanic healing are well known."

> Pentecostalism resonates with experiences of shamanic healing associated with indigenous cultures while at the same time promoting a strict behavioral code that enables migrants from rural areas to reorganize their lives and cope with the poverty, disease, loneliness and other stresses of urban life.[229]

Shamans, the "shock absorbers of history," and Pentecostal faith healers have been rediscovered, even rehabilitated in recent years.[230] Both were long discounted and discarded as socially marginal shadowy figures, hucksters who used sleight of hand and hypnotism to fool their followers for personal gain. The majority opinion from America's Protestant mainline was that the only miracle that occurred across the tracks from them, out in those tents pitched on county fairgrounds, was the parishioners' separation from their money. Not only have anthropologists been in the vanguard of tracking Pentecostalism as it travels from country to country, culture to culture, and city to city, they have also rescued shamanism from oblivion. As one anthropologist observed in 2004, "The shaman has been largely rehabilitated, to become a talented psychotherapist and dramaturge, serving a community's needs for reassurance, explanation and social adjustment with flair and insight."[231]

Earlier on in her ministerial career Aimee, like her father, was a master bridge builder between "the most ancient" and "the most modern." Slowly but surely, in her attempt to "fish for whales," to bring Pentecostalism into the Evangelical mainstream, she transformed the "savage sacred" into the "tamed sacred," but in the end "the most ancient" appeared to lose out to modernity and especially to the popular culture associated with the rise of Southern California.

CHAPTER EIGHT

The Beautiful Woman in White

When I am in California I am not in the West. It is West of the West. It is just California.

—Theodore Roosevelt

All of this land and this sea belongs to you. All of California. There is no California, no Los Angeles, no dusty streets, no cheap hotels, no stinking newspaper, no broken, uprooted people from the East, no fancy boulevards. This is your beautiful land with the desert and the mountains and the sea. You're a princess, and you reign over it all.

—John Fante,
Ask the Dust

The analyst of California is like a navigator who is trying to chart a course on a storm; the instruments will not work; the landmarks are lost; and the maps make little sense.

—Carey McWilliams

Here the city lights out shine the moon...
Sometimes when the wind blows you can
See the mountains,
And all the way to Malibu,
Everyone's a star here in L.A. County,
You ought to see the things that they do!

—David Frizzell,
"You're the Reason God Made Oklahoma"

Please come to LA to live forever...
I live in a house that looks out over the ocean
And there's some stars that fell from the sky
Livin' up on the hill
Please come to LA.

—Dave Loggins
"Please Come to Boston"

Los Angeles has five major industries—oil, aviation, motion pictures, citrus fruits and Aimee Semple McPherson. The last name is probably the most spectacular.

—*PIC Magazine*

A imee at Victoria Hall was remembered by those present as being "very good looking and she dressed always in a white uniform."

> She had her hair always fixed rather nice and a little bit on the high side…
> sermons were very effective, she first of all used very down-to-earth lan-
> guage,…not that preacherish or pastorish way,…and she made it so clear
> just come to Jesus, …he will heal you, he will baptize you, he will save
> you…it naturally appealed to a common type of person very quickly, not
> only to them, but it gave a quick entrance and she would always have
> her altar calls and there would always be dozens up at the altar call…and
> her dress was rather long—maybe it was the style at the time—I would
> say probably just a little, maybe six inches above her shoe-top,…I think
> she was a little bit plump, a little bit plump…I'm sure she took weight
> off afterwards. You know, probably more conscientious of it then, but
> she was a little bit robust, not, not so it was objectionable, but that is the
> impression that you got…and Rolf was in knee pants…and Roberta was
> at that time, I recall, somewhere around ten years old…I remember Rolf
> in a sailor suit the kinda suit that had a collar, you know, that goes down
> the back, always looked neat, and …she came out in an Oldsmobile and
> the Oldsmobile has "Where will you spend eternity?" on the side[1]

When asked how Aimee was different from other Pentecostal evangelists of the the same period, a person remembered, "She was younger and a woman. She was an attractive woman, and this, I think, is where it stands out. You just loved to look at her. And she had such a nice way about her and she seemed just to love everybody and people would come up to be prayed for and she would hug them…that's where she seemed to differ from what I see, sometimes now, she just loved the person…now this is just an impression."[2]

Her pianist, Minnie Draper, a young woman of sixteen years of age at the time recalled, "Well, there's no comparison whatsoever, [with other evangelists of the time]. She was a most marvelous, articulate, beautiful [woman]… how she could bring the Word of God out and full of the power and of course you know, there weren't too many women evangelists in those days and she just shone like a star, the Lord used her—especially in healings…She was magnetic, you couldn't help but love her."[3] Still another recalled "Aimee's charisma, personal charm, physical attractiveness, liquid

Aimee (in white) and a Gospel band at Victoria Hall (author's collection).

fluency with words, and her rare ability to present the gospel in simple terms." [4]

Victoria Hall Assembly, also known as the Central Pentecostal Church of Christ, was located at 225 South Spring Street—a good location in a good part of town—in fact the best part of the emerging metropolis. The street was so named because it was the nickname of a beautiful woman— the granddaughter of Portola's scout—who was affectionately called *La Primavera* (springtime). When a young army lieutenant named Ord made the first survey of Los Angeles and attempted to straighten out the old *pueblo,* he gave the street the scout's granddaughter's affectionate name.[5] With the growth of the metropolis, Spring Street became the "Wall Street of the West;" the birthplace for the first public school, the first multiple-story office building, and the largest and finest hotel in Los Angeles, the Alexandria. It was also home to the first brewery, the first terminus for the arrival and departure of transcontinental stage coach lines, and the first city hall, city jail, and fire station. It was as an early report of Los Angeles declared: "The pacemaker and spinal column for the present largest metropolis of the Pacific Coast."[6]

Victoria Hall had emerged out of the 1913 World-Wide Camp Meeting held at the Arroyo Seco. It was only about a block away from yet another Pentecostal mission, the Upper Room Mission, located at Second and Spring Street, where the Reverend Elmer Fisher was the pastor. Victoria Hall was simply a large hall with some smaller side rooms over a downstairs print shop. Early Pentecostals, whether by accident, design, or because the rents were low, seemed to always end up in "upper rooms." Victoria Hall gave the appearance as having been used as a lodge sometime in its history. Roberta remembered Victoria Hall as "a quaint, plain, homey place with devout people."[7]

The *Los Angeles Times* took notice in early 1919 of the religious fervor occurring in the downtown section of the city noting

Aimee, her mother, and her children in the Promised Land of Southern California (used by permission of the International Church of the Foursquare Gospel, Heritage Department).

that, "Evangelists Move in Where Burlesquers Once Reigned: Bars are Bible Halls."[8] The article attributed the religious renaissance to the post-war days and compared the tenants with the previous ones:

> The growth of religious thought and evangelism in Los Angeles has been noticeable during the past year. Gospel tents, gospel missions, evangelistic meetings and religious conclaves of varied character have been seed sown in the wake of the war. Now former bar-rooms are Bible Halls; the men of God have moved in where the burly burlesquers formerly did obeisance to the great god Bel…Outside, the forty-horse-power lithographs of burly ladies" in bursting tights have gone, we know not where, and in their places there appear the sedate features of evangelists from this, that or the other place…So it goes, new wines of salvation in old barrels of

damnation; and the devil on the run.[9]

The thriving Pentecostal missions in the "old barrels of damnation" were also in close proximity to Los Angeles' fledgling theatrical district. During the booming 1880s, traveling theater troupes visited the area, putting the city on the nation's theatrical map as being good for shows "direct from New York" and for "regular one-week stands."[10]

Warren W. Fisher, the pastor at Victoria Hall Assembly, was a business-man of at least sixty years. He was reported to have been wealthy—"almost a millionaire"—owning a building on the corner of Fifth and Hill streets and paying out of pocket all the bills and expenses related to the mission. As a result of Warren Fisher's generosity, appeals for offerings were almost nonexistent at Victoria Hall.[11] Dr. Finis Ewing Yoakum, who had started Pisgah home in Pasadena and whose publication, like Aimee's *Bridal Call*, was published by the Christian Worker's Union at Montwaite in Framing-ham, Massachusetts, also used the building in the afternoons for "healing and deeper-life ministries." Yoakum, despite having "the most socially sig-nificant outreach of the entire movement," remains something of a Pen-tecostal mystery man.[12] He had arrived in Los Angeles like so many before him in search of health. Once "a prominent brain surgeon" and a "pro-fessor at Gross Medical College," Yoakum had suffered a severe injury from a traffic accident in Denver. In Los Angeles "he experienced dra-matic healing through prayer." Following his healing, Dr. Yoakum began a remarkable ministry of social outreach which grew to include a large complex of activities:

> Pisgah home in Pasadena which welcomed and treated many sick persons and social outcasts, serving 18,000 free meals each month, Pisgah Ark for expectant unwed mothers, Pisgah Gardens, 18 mountain acres for tuber-cular patients amid fruit and vegetable gardening, and Pisgah Grande, a 3,200 acre mountain ranch and farm producing food for the poor.[13]

In addition to Dr. Yoakum's "deeper life" afternoon meetings, itinerant Pentecostal evangelists also held nightly meetings at Victoria Hall because Warren Fisher was "quite an old man—and he was a terrible preacher... (who) would go all over the place."[14] No evangelist for Fisher had ever "packed out" Victoria Hall until Aimee Semple McPherson came to town. She quickly relayed the results of her meetings to her followers:

> The large hall, seating six hundred and fifty, was quickly filled to its utmost capacity, and Sunday afternoon, ...school room doors were

opened wide, it was impossible to accommodate the throngs, many of who sat on the floor and stood in the aisles and the hallways, while scores stood for hours on the wide steps leading up to the hall as far as they were able to hear the message, even though they could not see anything within.[15]

It was perhaps the most demonstrative meeting of all Aimee's meetings, even eclipsing the Nation-Wide Camp Meeting in Philadelphia.

> Never have we seen the glory of the Lord fall in a more remarkable way... At last night's meeting there must have been more than one hundred and fifty slain under the mighty power of God...Missionaries, evangelists, preachers, workers and seekers are here from the world over...Never have I personally witnessed such a melting down and breaking to pieces of formality and stiffness, such hunger and yieldedness to the Spirit... Some of the other assemblies and pastors have closed their meetings and are coming right in with this revival, the Lord having given them the witness that this is the move of God.[16]

To the accompaniment of her young pianist, who remembered playing "until her fingers bled," and who, according to those who were there, "hit every key on the keyboard,"[17] Aimee introduced to the Pacific Coast a growing Pentecostal favorite picked up in the East that not only summarized her meeting but reflected the protest of the growing Pentecostal movement:

> When David danced before the Lord
> The ark was coming up the road,
> His wife despised him in her heart,
> The ark was coming up the road.
>
> I do believe without a doubt,
> The ark is coming up the road,
> God's Children have a right to shout,
> The ark is coming up the road.
>
> Sing on, pray on, we're gaining ground,
> The ark is coming up the road.
> The power of God is coming down,
> The ark is coming up the road.
>
> It's coming, Hallelujah.
> The ark is coming up the road.
> It's coming, Hallelujah,
> The ark is coming up the road.[18]

Another Pentecostal song of protest Aimee undoubtedly enjoyed singing while at the mission was number thirty in the paperback song book *Victorious Songs as Sung by the Victorious Saints at Victoria Hall Assembly*. The song reflected their new found common identity:

> I long ago left Egypt, for the promised land,
> I trusted in my Saviour and to His guiding hand,
> He led me out to vict'ry through the great red sea,
> I sang a song of triumph, and shouted I am free.
> You need not look for me, down in Egypt's sand,
> For I have pitched my tent far up in Beu-lah land.[19]

Aimee would preach from forty to forty-five minutes, and those who heard her said they could have listened to her for two hours. They also clearly remembered the role of her mother in the meetings. While her daughter was preaching, Minnie would sit with the rest of the congregation "and she would just go right along with Aimee's message, every word Aimee would say, she would say it, whisper it, you know, just like she was preaching with her."[20] The differences in styles and temperament of mother and daughter were also readily noticeable to the "saints" at Victoria Hall. "Ma Kennedy," as she was getting to be known, was always "a different story" in contrast with her daughter's charm. She was remembered as being "money-minded…she ran everything and everybody and her daughter, too, and her daughter just had a little bit of money she'd give her for spending money. She held that bag, the money and she'd stay up all night counting money…I guess she thought she had to be that way to be a good manager, but she had her little daughter under her control, very much, but Aimee, she submitted, …somebody had to take care of her."[21] Another echoed the same sentiments stating: "She [Ma] was very dominant. She did all the business—all the arranging—they all had to deal with 'Ma' Kennedy."[22]

In defense of the "demonstrations" going on in Victoria Hall, Aimee wrote an editorial for her *Bridal Call* readers entitled "What about these manifestations?—Dancing, Shouting, Falling Prostrate under the Power, Speaking in Tongues, Interpretation." Her answer was simple at the time; however the questions of how many manifestations and where and why they should occur would plague her throughout her ministry.

> Take down your shining tea kettle that has stood so long, filled with cold water, on the shelf, quiet, cold and orderly enough to please any church member; put it over the hot flame, keep it there a few moments, and the first thing you know it will just be obliged to break forth into singing;

If you do not like manifestations, dear preacher, turn the gas or power off and you will not be bothered with the manifestations very long, your particular kettle will soon sit still enough and cold enough to suit even your most rigid ideas of propriety and order.

We repeat that where there is power there is a manifestation of that power,[23]

By the end of her first month in the "modern Jerusalem" of Los Angeles, Aimee reported back to her Pentecostal readership about "a mighty hunger" for a return of the "old-time power." Despite "the many divisions and the growing coldness...of the four thousand who have the baptism of the Holy Ghost in this city"... (there is), sensed Aimee, "a mighty hunger...to bring back the old-time power of Azusa Street days... (to) this wonderful city, which, as a modern Jerusalem, once held aloft the beacon light of Pentecost, which shone the world around..."[24]

The "physical manifestations" at Victoria Hall also seemed to have had a healing and unifying effect upon the fragmented Pentecostal veterans and warriors from Azusa Street:

A demonstrative Aimee bringing back the "old time power" of Asuza days (used by permission of the International Church of the Foursquare Gospel, Heritage Department).

> Many who were here say that they have traveled the world over the last twelve years; since the latter rain began to fall, and that they have seen great revivals, but all declare that they never saw a revival like this, and all agree that it outshines the wonderful days of old Azusa Street, of which they all speak with rapt faces; such a unity and melting together of workers, such a laying aside of quibbles and hairsplitting doctrines.[25]

The Azusa Street veterans were very clear from their long days and nights spent at the mission that "dance," for them, had clearly preceded "dogma."

In the wake of the revival, various doctrines and dogma threatened the unity and oneness participants had earlier experienced. "If God's people would only come together," wrote one of them, "and forget about doctrines….Doctrines…have their proper place in the gospel plan but that overpowering, drawing power of the love of God must come first.[26]

The first two months of 1919 were momentous ones for Aimee. She was suddenly thrust into a leadership role in the birthplace of modern Pentecostalism, filling a vacuum that had existed since William Durham's death. Her East Coast apprenticeship had prepared her well for this role, and she felt more than ever that she was especially in Los Angeles, that she was "in the Center of God's will"; yet with genuine humility she stood in awe of what was occurring as evidenced by correspondence with her followers who by now had reached ten thousand paid subscribers.

> There was never a time that I felt my own helplessness and insufficiency, my utter dependence upon God, as I do now, having been led from the Atlantic to the Pacific to deliver the simple …message that the Lord has given me for this hour…In the natural it seems so amazing and almost unbelievable that… I could be of any assistance to these learned, scholarly patriarchs in the Pentecostal movement…I realize perhaps more than at any other time in all my life that I am in the center of His will, and am being led unerringly by Him who said, 'I will take a worm to thrash a mountain, the weak things and things that are to confound the mighty and things that are.'
>
> Again asking the prayers of all God's dear children, I am, the least of all saints, Sister Aimee Semple McPherson.[27]

The Reverend Fisher's brother-in law, G.S. Blake, secretary of Victoria Hall, also remembered as a "man of money," announced to the assembly,

> It remained for this child of the King to cross the continent and come thousands of miles to answer these prayers and groaning of the saints to get the people together for another awakening…letters of inquiry are received every day concerning the meetings…In all we have never seen such wonderful meetings, which are kept in the Spirit by the Lord.[28]

The attendance was so great at Victoria Hall from those coming in "from the surrounding country" that the Reverend Fisher and Mr. Blake rented the largest auditorium they could find in the city, the nearby Philharmonic Auditorium at Fifth and Olive Streets. Seating thirty-five hundred, it was leased for one hundred dollars for three hours time. This auditorium, at the center of Los Angeles' theater district, had previously been under different names the home of the city's first professional stock companies.

On Sunday, January 12, 1919, Aimee preached to "nearly 3,000 for over an hour with the Gospel message" in the Philharmonic. It marked a turning point in her ministry as significant as the Nation-Wide Camp Meeting in Philadelphia. It was the first time she preached to a non church, largely secular crowd, and she loved it. Her ministerial priorities in her evangelistic efforts suddenly began to shift and to change. She found herself asking the question, "Why fish for minnows, when you can fish for whales?" She was now reaching people who did not ordinarily go to church, and immediately her priorities began to shift to reach "the sinner, instead of the saint." And Los Angeles, more than anyplace else, afforded the perfect opportunity. Winter in California was the time of the tourist, and so she reasoned, "Instead of going from place to place, why not stay put in one place, especially a place such as Los Angeles, where so many visitors come and go on their vacations?"[29] The crowds would continually change yet, she could remain settled in one place and raise her children.

The auditorium appealed far more to her than did the missions and the upper rooms of various halls. She noted its "rows of galleries, the orchestra pit and the great rostrum."[30] She included two photographs of the building in her first book. She was convinced that the Pentecostal message belonged in such a place and would be better received outside of basements, attics, storefronts, and missions. The call to reach those outside of Pentecostalism was especially compelling, since the movement had fragmented so badly and doctrinal differences ran deep. Her calling was not to nurse the wounds of the seasoned Pentecostal veterans who mainly comprised the Pentecostal movement in the city. As one account stated, "They were largely called and prepared for years, from the Holiness ranks, and from the mission field… They had been burnt out, tried and proven. They were largely seasoned veterans."[31] Aimee's vision to "fish for whales instead of minnows" would take many forms in her ministry. It would also prove to be very controversial for the Pentecostal movement. In 1918, however, she had provided a much needed unifying effect upon the fragmented movement in Los Angeles.

So great was Aimee's acceptance within Pentecostalism that she was immediately invited to hold a week's meetings at Bethel Temple following her service at the Philharmonic. Bethel was the mother church of the future Assemblies of God of Southern California, the most staid and established Pentecostal work in the city. The Reverend George N. Eldridge, pastor of Bethel Tempe and a former Methodist minister, reported the results:

> After a simple message from the word and an earnest altar call, sinners and believers were on their way together to the basement...Ere long the floor was covered with the slain of the Lord and many workers, evangelists and missionaries were passing from one to the other, praying with the rejoicing over those who were coming through to their baptism.[32]

After Bethel Temple it was back to Victoria Hall, where the meetings ended on February 14, 1919 with Aimee noting that the "revival... is not expected to stop, but to go on until Jesus comes. Night after night the hall was packed, and often our hearts were made sad by the sight of the scores being turned away, oft-times an hour before the schedule time for services."[33]

It was also during this time that one of Victoria Hall's most famous spiritual seekers began attending the Sunday afternoon meetings. A Presbyterian from Placentia and a Pomona College graduate, where he had been president of his class and captain of a championship football team, Charles Fuller began sneaking away from his Presbyterian church to attend the Pentecostal mission, "seeking deeper spiritual truths and a closer walk with God."[34] Long after Fuller Theological Seminary had been established, Daniel Fuller wrote about his father's visits to the mission. Aimee was never mentioned, but she was ministering there at the time of Fuller's visits and had undoubtedly placed Victoria Hall on the religious map for spiritual pilgrimages in Los Angeles. Daniel Fuller also made it clear that his famous father seemingly had more in common spiritually with the minister of the established mother church of the Assemblies of God, Bethel Temple, than he did with the independent mission of Victoria Hall:

> On some Sunday afternoons, [in February 1919]...the Fullers would go to a little mission...called Victoria Hall. Charles Fuller...received much help from...this mission. On other Sunday afternoons they would go to Bethel Temple where a Dr. Eldredge was pastor. A number of people spoke in tongues there, and Charles Fuller thought that he should seek this gift. But he never spoke in tongues. Some years later he had Dr. Eldredge come out to his church in Placentia to preach. Taking him back to the train station after the services were over, Charles was still concerned that he had not received the gift of tongues and he talked to Dr. Eldredge about it. The older man put his hand on his shoulder and said, 'Charlie, what you need to seek is the Giver, not the gifts.' God settled the whole matter for him right then and there. He saw in a flash that Christ had dispersed His gifts sovereignly to His people, and that he had received not the gift of tongues but of expository evangelistic teaching. Thereafter he was content simply to exercise this gift.[35]

Fuller Theological Seminary, long a theological home for Pentecostals seeking a seminary education, perhaps owes that particular role to its namesake founders' spiritual searches at the upper room mission on South Spring Street.

Victoria Hall provided for Aimee the acceptance and first taste of permanence she had known since starting her ministry. As the traveling evangelist-woman in white, she posed for a picture on the platform with her co-workers at the "upper room" mission. With the women of the mission holding songbooks and the men their Bibles, the group also displayed their musical instruments ranging from a snare drum, violin, trumpets, and tambourine to a bass drum. All posed by a rear platform door with a partially open transom window with a naked light fixture managing to catch the corner of the camera's eye. Pentecostal placards decorated the door frame:

THE COMING OF THE LORD DRAWETH NIGH

JESUS IS COMING—LOOK AND LIVE

This was a scene which could have been easily duplicated in literally thousands of struggling Pentecostal missions across the country. This scene also would bear little or no resemblance in a few short years to what the press would dub "Aimee's Temple"—a concrete-and-steel domed-amphitheater which would rival the movie palaces of Hollywood for the attention of the Southern California tourists. The woman in the starched white uniform would no longer sit on a stiff wooden chair on a humble mission platform. In her temple she would open an upper balcony door, descend down a long concrete ramp with billowy clouds painted overhead carrying at least one bouquet of red long-stemmed roses, and be bathed simultaneously by the glare of a spotlight and the hush of a capacity house crowd. In the temple, stained glass would replace clear glass transom windows, and ornately carved throne-like pulpit chairs—a gift from the gypsy tribes to their "Sister"—would take the place of the oaken spindle-back bargain-store specials. Instead of placards scattered about a door frame, a scrolled inscription above the pulpit read, "Jesus Christ, the Same, Yesterday, Today, and Forever."

A religious response to the combined forces of industrialization, urbanization, and immigration, Pentecostalism was a most modern American religious movement seeking to duplicate New Testament Christianity and the supernatural days of the apostles. Pentecostalism was transformed by Aimee into a practical, spectacular form of Christianity, a spiritual movement utilizing the most advanced secular forces.

The rise of Pentecostalism closely paralleled the growth of Hollywood, perhaps to the dismay of both. Despite the obvious differences, their growth and style has been remarkably similar. Like the movies which emerged out of the sun-drenched California countryside in 1906, with its large open-air spaces and back lots, Pentecostalism emerged out of the industrial section of Los Angeles in the same year and came complete with its own vaude-villian days of the camp-meetings and Chautauqua circuit. Both settled down together, one forming studios and theaters; the other tabernacles and temples. Both were fueled with high energy and drama sustained by the flames of controversy. Over the years both movements kept a remarkable even pace, becoming mature and sophisticated through the use of technology and the mutual discovery of the ultimate personal medium—television. And Aimee Semple McPherson, like no other Pentecostal evangelist of "people's religion" before or since, would be able to blend the secular with the sacred. It is little wonder then that with the passing of time the Hollywood stars would discover the magnetism of Sister Aimee. She would become the personal pastor to the Pantages family, the spiritual counselor to a troubled Jean Harlow, and dedicate a beautiful baby girl born in the charity wing of the Los Angeles General Hospital "as unto the Lord"—long before Hollywood changed her name from Norma Jean Mortensen to Marilyn Monroe.[36] A young Anthony Quinn would blow his saxophone in the temple band and preach the Foursquare Gospel on Los Angeles street corners.[37] Charlie Chaplin would himself suggest the proscenium arch—the backdrop for "Sister's" pulpit and the housing for the red velvet curtain which would rise on her subsequent illustrated sermons and sacred operas. [38]

It was Victoria Hall, an independent mission, that would also provide for Aimee's physical needs in contrast to the established Assemblies of God church, Bethel Temple. Alone, as with Robert, she would time and again learn that her source of support would come "not from the rich, but from the poor." On a Sunday evening in the mission hall after her meetings at Bethel Temple had ended, her dreams for permanence came to pass.

> For many months, as I have been traveling from place to place, carrying my two little children (Roberta, a little over eight and Rolf, six,) with me, I have felt the ever growing need of some little home for the children… where I could have a home address for my large correspondence, and from whence the children could go to school and have a little of the home life and child-time memories which is the privilege of every little one. Being taken from city to city, house to house, and meeting to meeting—sleeping in tents or on the floor of the automobile, or in people's

homes, as the occasion provided, they have known little or nothing of what it means to have a home, place to play and go to school, or call their own…He was in some miraculous way or other going to open the way for me to have a home for them here in California. I did not know, and do not even yet see fully how or through what channel the completion of their house is to be brought about.[39]

At the Sunday evening service at the mission, a "working girl who owned four lots" interrupted the meeting by declaring: "The Lord shows me that I am to give a lot to Mrs. McPherson…I am not called to preach the Gospel, while she is, and by giving the land that the little ones may have a home and she may be free to come and go in the Lord's work, I will share in her reward."[40] A brother sprang to his feet, saying, "Yes, and I will help dig the cellar. Others chimed in with: Yes, I will help lay the foundation; I will do the lathing; I will do the plastering; I will furnish the dining room, and so it went on until even the little canary bird was promised. A lady promised rose bushes. Now the canary and the rose bushes touched my heart and caused me to shout more than all else, for small as the incidents may seem, I could see God, for the canary and the rose bushes were the two things the children had asked for beyond all else. The Heavenly Father had not forgotten."[41]

"The house that God built" meant much more to Aimee than the typical Southern California stucco bungalow sprouting up in the emerging suburbs of Los Angeles preceding the housing boom and population explosion of the 1920s. She remembered and reflected about her days with Harold McPherson and how they struggled together in vain to have a home in Providence, Rhode Island:

> Away back yonder, when out of the will of God, how I had struggled to get a little rented flat furnished, and what misery I had gone through, but now God is Himself planning a home which would be our own, a home given and built by the saints, where every tap of the hammer drove nails of love into the building and into our hearts.[42]

It was also "through the love and consecration of the dear saints at Victoria Hall that the Lord has opened for us a large, light store on the street floor of the same building to be used as our publishing house."[43] Aimee made this first announcement to her *Bridal Call* readership in March 1919, noting that the office of "the Western edition of *The Bridal Call* "would also fill orders for our tracts and latter rain literature at nominal prices, thus avoiding the two weeks delay of writing to the eastern office."[44]

"The house that God built"—no small bungalow (used by permission of the International Church of the Foursquare Gospel, Heritage Department).

In June 1919, her former publisher, Samuel G. Otis, superintendent of the Christian Workers Union at Montwaite, summarized his working relationship with Sister Aimee to *The Bridal Call* subscribers:

> In the summer of 1917 our dear Sister Aimee S. McPherson came to us saying she had started the paper, *The Bridal Call,* and had issued three numbers, and that her printer had decided not to go on…We took all risks of making it pay if she would interest as many as possible to subscribe and would take a number of copies at the low price of one cent each…She was pleased with this plan and so we have since then been printing ten thousand and sending *The Bridal Call* to all of our subscribers, which increased the circulation of *The Bridal Call* from about three thousand to ten thousand a month. Last winter we were attacked with the 'flu' and for a time it looked as though we were going down,…our papers were not out on time nor in good condition and our dear Sister became discouraged, started a Western edition of *The Bridal Call* and now, as her home is in Los Angeles, California, she feels it would be better that *The Bridal Call* be issued from her home address, 125 1/2 So. Spring St., Los Angeles, California. She had advanced the price from 50 cents to $1.00 a year…We feel sad to have our dear Sister leave us and take on the great load of running a publishing work, and we will pray that God will give her wisdom from above and bless her labors in helping to get a bridal company ready for the soon coming of the Bridegroom, our Lord Jesus Christ.[45]

In the spring of 1919 Aimee's work showed its first signs of evolving out of Los Angeles. Due to the generosity of the Victoria Hall "saints," both a residence and an office were gladly and promptly created for their "Sister in the King's Glad Service." Over the next two decades Aimee would become synonymous with the rise of Los Angeles and Southern California as she planted the seeds of Pentecostalism up and down the Pacific Coast and back and forth across the Middle West. Things were finally starting to come together. The fears and worries of just a few months ago were quickly departing.

During the winter of 1919 the secular press discovered Aimee. It was the beginning of a never-ending and at times strained but yet enduring love affair that continued until the last camera flash and banner headline of the evangelist's death and graveside ceremony at Forest Lawn. By the mid-1920s reporters would be assigned the "Temple Beat," and intramural temple feuds would rival those of national and international importance in the Los Angeles Dailies. In the era of "yellow journalism" "Aimee stories" abounded, always alternating her between the roles of heroine and villain and transforming her into popular folk culture. "Aimee" became a household word as much as "Amos 'n' Andy." Few Hollywood stars ever received as much media exposure as the woman in white—Sister Aimee. Her handsome face, the sensitive eyes, the husky, vibrant voice and the ever-present energy seemed ideally suited for glossy photographs and newspaper ink. Such stories would serve well the burgeoning newspaper networks and emerging conglomerations such as the Hearst Empire.

The discovery of Aimee by the secular press once and for all placed her outside the narrow bounds of Pentecostalism and helped to create the first taste of public acceptance for the movement as a whole. By the May 1919 issue of *The Bridal Call*, Aimee attempted to explain her "experience with the press."[46] She recalled her difficulty in Los Angeles "to reach the real heart of the public, that men and women in shops and homes might know of the meetings and hear the burning message which the Lord has laid upon our hearts in these last days."[47] The "brethren" at Victoria Hall had advertised in the daily newspapers her special meetings at the Temple Auditorium. Aimee noted the outcome: "When the Temple Auditorium was engaged in Los Angeles, the brothers paid thirty and forty dollars for each little two-column advertisement in the daily papers, and then it was put away back on one of the advertising pages."[48]

Aimee's desire to "reach the real heart of the public ... [the] men and women in shops and homes" made her in American religion what A.P. Giannini with his innovation of "branch banking" was for banking and what Henry Ford putting "the nation on wheels" was to the auto industry. It was an appeal primarily to the common people largely neglected with the disruption of urbanization who yet composed in popular parlance "the lower two-thirds" of the American population by the time of the Depression and the Franklin Roosevelt administration. By the end of the Second World War, "the lower two-thirds" had been re-established as the strong, solid, middle-class backbone of the country. Pentecostalism, with its strict demands upon its members, greatly assisted their ascent in upward mobility. Household money that once went for vice and "worldly entertainment" now went for God and family. Americans are practical and pragmatic. They like things that work, including their religion.

"In larger industrial communities," observed the American church historian Winthrop Hudson, "the working-classes tended to be impervious to the message and ministry of the churches. It was not that the churches had 'lost' these people; they never had most of them."

> The churches were well attended. Costly and imposing edifices were… built to match the increasing prosperity of their clientele, and congregations vied with one another to possess the tallest steeple as a symbol of wealth and prestige. Pipe organs were installed, paid soloists were employed, and the preachers were polished orators who ranked in status with the most substantial citizens….preachers—men like Henry Ward Beecher…in Brooklyn, Phillips Brooks…in Boston …Russell Conwell in Philadelphia…were figures of national prominence …every city boasted eloquent preachers who could hold their congregations spellbound and who were regarded with deference and respect. Furthermore, the most influential leaders of business and society—Jay Gould, J. Pierpont Morgan, John D. Rockefeller…and many others—were prominent churchmen, active in religious enterprises and frequently Sunday school teachers.[49]

The Boston Brahmin and prince of the pulpit Phillips Brooks once remarked, "I like working men very much and care for their good, but I have nothing distinct or separate to say to them about religion."[50]

The rift between labor and business greatly affected the Protestant church. With the tremendous increase in the wealth of the nation resulting in an improved economy, the existing churches became more and more concerned with the middle and upper middle classes as their members rose into these groups. As Protestantism became more exclusive, the poor became more neglected. Thus, as Sydney Ahlstrom noted, the increase of wealth "created a serious cleavage in city population in relation to religious affiliation. The people who could afford churches were well churched; those who could not were unchurched—and hardly cared, or even regarded church people as their economic oppressors." [51]

As early as 1899 *The American Journal of Sociology* took note of "The

Workingman's Alienation from the Church." Reasons for the workingman's alienation from most churches were given as "too much theology and not enough plain gospel truth in the sermon. This theology is beyond the comprehension of the workingman. He has no interest in it....The church has...no sympathy with the masses. It is a sort-of fashionable club where the rich are entertained and amused, and where most of the ministers are muzzled by their masters and dare not peach the gospel of the carpenter of Nazareth."[52]

Even the Methodist Church after 1830 distanced itself from the common person and its revivalist past. "Heart religion," it seemed, was fast disappearing. The essence of Methodism, however, as James C. Deming and Michael S. Hamilton demonstrate "relocated into the holiness and Pentecostal movements ... [of] the mid-nineteenth and early twentieth centuries."[53] "The simplication of preaching" itself was for one Pentecostal participant one of the marked miracles of the Azusa Mission. "For fifty years the American people have been cursed with head, and starved for heart preaching. Many churches have demanded of their ministers a classical education before ordination, and have made little or no demands of them along spiritual lines. It has been all head and no heart."[54]

Ma Kennedy, ever the shrewd business woman and practical genius, also came up with her own novel solution to advertising her daughter's meetings in Los Angeles and reaching "the real heart of the public." Approaching city merchants, Mrs. Kennedy offered her services to freely address their bills with the stipulation that a circular announcing her daughter's forthcoming meetings be enclosed with the billing. It was a trade-off many merchants found difficult to resist.

Upon Aimee's return to Victoria Hall, "the telephone rang, reporters and city editors called up, sometimes two or three in one afternoon. Coming into the hall one afternoon we found two reporters sitting on the steps who refused to move until they had an interview. (And not only did they interview us, but finding us a very poor subject, they got our books and every other available source of information.)"[55]

It was, of course, precisely the opposite. The press quickly discovered that Aimee was indeed a very good subject. Reporters and editors were quite intrigued by the young woman in white, mother of two children, who had just recently made a transcontinental auto trip without the assistance of a man. This was a new kind of modern woman who had tied petticoats and sweaters around the car tires to give more traction when the wheels wouldn't move and had learned how to unthaw a frozen radiator. A woman reporter inquiring about her ministry asked if she wasn't something like

Billy Sunday. "Oh, no!" Aimee replied, "Nothing like that. Both my work and personality is totally different. After a few more questions they took their departure."[56]

The following morning the *Los Angeles Times* broke the story about the young revivalist woman in white dubbing her "The Female Billy Sunday." Aimee's new found celebrity made her uneasy:

> When the *Los Angeles Times* was placed in our hands, we stood there for a moment rooted to the spot, for there under my name, appeared, in glaring letters—"The Female Billy Sunday!" I hoped no one outside California would see it, but the newspaper syndicates caught up the name and flashed it across the continent, reporting not only our meetings, but our Gospel Auto, ocean to ocean, tract-distributing trip. Several friends in Massachusetts, Oklahoma, New York, Illinois, and other places, cut the clippings from their local papers and mailed them to us. Each time the letters came we would say—"Oh, what will the saints [Pentecostals] think?" Evidently the Lord wanted me to die out a little more to the opinions of people, and took this way of humbling one.[57]

Aimee's musings of, "Oh, what will the saints think?" reflects not only an astute awareness and sensitivity of her brothers and sisters in the faith, but it would remain a recurring, troubling question throughout her ministry. She was really at her best, as she would discover within a year's time, outside the bounds of all organized religion, attempting to reach and convert the largely secular and unchurched portion of the population. This alone would make her unique in American Revivalism. She was rapidly becoming for the unchurched less a "preacher" and more their "Sister."

At the time of Aimee's meetings in San Francisco two months later, the *San Francisco Examiner* in a two-column story complete with a picture of an exuberant Aimee announced to the Bay Area that the " 'Female Billy Sunday' Arrives. Plans to Redeem Sinful San Francisco." Aimee resented the nickname even though it helped to create her growing fame: "We requested them to please leave off the nickname, pleading that we detested the word 'female,' and that, with all respect to Billy Sunday our work was on a totally different plane and of a different character than his. Nothing yet, [May, 1919] however, has moved them from this addition to my name."[58]

It is further possible that Aimee resented the Billy Sunday identification and connection because Sunday had earlier snubbed and rejected her. According to historian William G. McLoughlin, both Sunday and Aimee once held simultaneous revivals in Tampa, Florida. "Sunday refused to allow Mrs. McPherson to sit on the platform during his campaign in Tampa."[59]

Homer Rodeheaver ("Rody"), Bill Sunday's talented chorister and Aimee's close personal friend (used by permission of the International Church of the Foursquare Gospel, Heritage Department).

Homer Rodeheaver ("Rody"), Sunday's talented and devoted chorister, however, supposedly escorted Aimee "to the bathing beaches." In time Rody and Aimee became close personal friends, often swimming together at Rodeheaver's home at Winona Lake, Indiana. Rodeheaver would also assist Aimee in Angelus Temple from time to time. And it was Rodeheaver who would introduce Aimee to her third and final husband, David L. Hutton.

Ma Kennedy was more accepting of the comparison, realizing that it had at least provided some good free advertising. "We could recognize no similarity in the personality or message of the two evangelists. Yet, looking back, we know that this was one of the 'all things' which so often God has sent into our lives."[60]

When the *Los Angeles Times* discovered Aimee and dubbed her the "female Billy Sunday," the newspaper still noted the activities of the "real" Billy Sunday. The story appeared however, in part three, page two of the Sunday edition"

> The same old "Billy Sunday" spoke the other night at the Metropolitan Opera house in Philadelphia, with the characteristic gestures, picturesque phrases and militant manner…Pathos and humor, sarcasm and invectives were used by "Billy" in bringing his points to bear on the audience. But he did not omit the contortions and gymnastics that have made him one of the most picturesque of American evangelists. [61]

A minister who had extensive experience in the revivals of both Billy Sunday and Aimee Semple McPherson provided the clearest perspective on the two evangelists and their differing temperaments when he recalled, "She [Aimee] was more just down to earth, and love and compassion but he'd [Billy] come up there, you know, with his breaking chairs, hell fire and things, you could just see the fire burning, you know." [62] As Jon Butler perceptively points out in his *Softly and Tenderly Jesus is Calling: Heaven and Hell in American Revivalism 1870-1920*, "The theological division with Evangelicalism…directly affected revival preaching on heaven and hell. A type of hellfire sermon served as a vehicle for fundamentalist vindictiveness."[63] This was also the perceptive difference between the female mystical piety of Pentecostalism and the athletic, muscular manhood of fundamentalism: "Billy Sunday was driving….Aimee was disarming. Sunday's traditional form of evangelical revivalism with its wholesale denunciations and high-pressure tactics was also quickly losing much of its appeal with the advent of radio and motion pictures whose methods of communication were exactly the opposite."[64]

"While she believed in heaven and hell, mother put the emphasis on heaven," recalled Roberta. "She had a tender touch. She inspired people and gave them hope. Everyone was important."[65] "Who cares about old Hell, friends?" asked Aimee in a famous sermon. "Why, we all know what Hell is. We've heard about it all our lives. A terrible place, where nobody wants to go. I think the less we hear about Hell, the better, don't you? Let's forget about Hell….What we are interested in…is Heaven and how to get there!"[66] "God's sheep," preached Aimee, "are tired of being beaten. They are bruised and sore. They wince before threats and blows, but oh, how they respond to the call of LOVE!"[67] As the picture of the "female Billy Sunday," a woman preacher in white, began appearing in newspapers across America in late 1918 and early 1919, a caption taken from one Aimee's sermons announced, "We are not going to a funeral—we are going to a wedding."[68]

Although Billy Sunday would not achieve the apex of his evangelistic career until the spring of 1917, the poet Carl Sandburg for one had tired of Billy's antics a good two years earlier. In a poem addressed "To Billy Sunday" Sandburg wrote in the fall of 1915:

> This Jesus guy was good to look at, smelled good, listened good. He threw out something fresh and beautiful from the skin of his body and the touch of his hands wherever he passed along.
>
> You, Billy Sunday, put a smut on every human blossom that comes in reach of your rotten breath belching about hell-fire and hiccupping about this man who lived a clean life in Galilee…
>
> Go ahead and bust all the chairs you want to. Smash a whole wagon load of furniture at every performance. Turn sixty somersaults and stand on your nutty head. If it wasn't for the way you scare women and kids, I'd feel sorry for you and pass the hat….
>
> I'm telling you this Jesus guy wouldn't stand for the stuff you're handing

out. Jesus played it different. The bankers and corporation lawyers of Jerusalem got their sluggers and murderers to go after Jesus just because Jesus wouldn't play their game. He didn't sit in with the big thieves.

I don't want a lot of gab from the bunkshooter in my religion.

I won't take my religion from a man who never works except with his mouth and never cherishes a memory except the face of the woman on the American silver dollar.

I ask you to come through and show me where you're pouring out the blood of your life.

I've been in this suburb of Jerusalem they call Golgotha, where they nailed Him, and I know if the story is straight it was real blood ran from his hand and the nail-holes, and it was real blood spurted out where the spear of the Roman soldier rammed in between the ribs of this Jesus of Nazareth.[69]

Like the Jesus in Sandburg's poem, Aimee, unlike Billy, was "good to look at" and was giving out "something fresh and beautiful," a "wedding" not a "funeral." And unlike Sunday who had only worked "with his mouth," Aimee had literally poured out everything she had. "This girl," Aimee wrote of herself, "preached outdoors and in churches, dance halls, theatres, prize fight rings and under all manner of circumstances and conditions that would have broken the heart and courage of many a strong man."[70]

While Sunday scorned the "new methods," Aimee made them work for her. Aimee's style was always "soothing and warming and the very essence of simplicity."[71] Julia Budlong captured the essence of Aimee's appeal when she observed "Mrs. McPherson, wheedling, cajoling, admonishing, 'kidding,' her vast audience is like a mother with a numerous brood."[72]

Despite their obvious differences, Billy Sunday not only helped to set the Los Angeles stage for Aimee's acceptance, he created a national one for her as well. Following his ten-week crusade in New York City from April to June 1917, attended by one and a half million people and considered to be the zenith of his evangelistic career, Sunday journeyed west to Los Angeles for his first California campaign. In reality Sunday's career may have peaked two years earlier in Philadelphia, the year of Carl Sandburg's poem. Homer Rodeheaver claimed in his *Twenty Years With Billy Sunday* that "We all felt that the greatest single meeting was the Philadelphia campaign in 1915."[73] Sunday himself even mentioned the event in Los Angeles noting "In Philadelphia one night we had 22,000 people in the tabernacle...and 45,000 standing on the outside."[74] "It was generally true," remembered Rodeheaver, "that the Billy Sunday campaign in the average community was the biggest thing the local churches ever had undertaken. For many years he would not accept an invitation unless all the churches united in the call....He wouldn't go to a city where some of the churches were on the side lines if other cities were waiting with a united front. The Catholic churches were not included, and sometimes the Episcopalians were not in sympathy.[75]

Los Angeles did not disappoint Billy Sunday. His meetings were sponsored by the ministers of the Church Federation of Los Angeles representing some "248 Protestant Evangelical churches" and like many another American city were most likely "the biggest thing the local churches ever had undertaken." More than seven hundred ministers had met with Sunday's advance man at the First Methodist Church in final preparations for the meetings. The Los Angeles organization of the Sunday campaign with twenty-some

Billy Sunday in Los Angeles (used by permission of the Herald-Examiner Collection/Los Angeles Public Library).

separate committees also oversaw the construction of the specially created "Sunday Tabernacle" at Twelfth Street and Grand Avenue.

> Few cities then had public buildings large enough to hold the crowds anxious to hear Mr. Sunday, and even when a fair-sized auditorium was available the stage platform would not accommodate the great choirs; there Mr. Sunday had tabernacles constructed in most of the larger and smaller cities where he preached. The seating capacity ranged from five to six thousand in the smaller cities to between sixteen and twenty thousand in Philadelphia, Boston, New York and Chicago. Platforms were built to seat as many as two thousand singers.[76]

Again, Los Angeles came through for the former ball player turned evangelist. After two months, the revival meetings came to a close on October 28, 1917. "Members of the Sunday party," observed the *Los Angeles Times* "stood on the platform, a farewell song was sung, Billy offered the farewell prayer and benediction, and then a mighty cheer arose from the 16,000 persons there assembled."[77]

Despite his ringing endorsement from the *Los Angeles Times*, achieving twenty thousand "trail hitters," and receiving a twenty-thousand dollar love offering for his work in Los Angeles, two city columnists were critical of Sunday's methods. In a column titled "Grouchy Remarks About Billy Sunday," Harry Carr noted that when Sunday "says 'darn,' kicks over chairs, shakes his fists, throws imitation fits, crawls around the stage on all-fours and cuts up other capers is neither here nor there. That's just baseball.... To a baseball fan, Billy's alleged-to-be-sensational gymnastics are old stuff. But, oh, Bill! That trail-hitting."[78] It wasn't Sunday's baseball gymnastics that Harry Carr had a problem with. It was rather Sunday's "trail-hitters," his converts or lack of them, that posed the problem:

> But Great Sticks—to quote one of Bill's wicked words...Most of the sinners who hit the trail were pious and flat young ladies from the choir. No lady sinner can be convincing who is without curves. I never saw such a pious-looking gathering in my life as the sinners who hit the trail. They looked like a graduating class of a Bible Institute, and my belief is that they were. Not a sinner wept. They all came by, grinning.[79]

In other words, it was Harry Carr's belief that a Sunday crusade was nothing more than a "re-circularization of the saints." Carr's observations also seem born out by the data gathered on the Los Angeles "trailhitters." Of the 18,824 reported conversions, only 1,274 converts reported no religious identification or affiliation. The vast majority of the "pious-looking... sinners who hit the trail" all had major Protestant denominational affiliation: 4,471 Methodists, 2,711 Presbyterians and 1,989 Baptists.

Alma Whitaker, a young woman columnist for the *Times* who would later follow Aimee very closely, also noted Sunday's audience and his increasingly outdated appeal in her own "Kittenish Comment on Billy Sunday."

> Billy Sunday impressed me as the small boy who had learnt some new, naughty words. As a man of God, he can come right out in the open and say 'em so all can hear; but under more youthful circumstances he would have muttered them joyously to himself behind a tree.
>
> His tongue just slithers with delight as he points a disconcerting finger at his vast and sweltering audience, made up largely of nice, respectable gray-haired, shirt-waisted women with copious fans and motherly bosoms, and declares: "You women that gossip about your neighbors, that pick a woman to pieces behind her back, you are a lot of old hags, I tell you."
>
> And then, while their faces express every conflicting emotion under the sun, as they mop their sweating brows with hopelessly inadequate

handkerchiefs, he tosses them a radiant, beaming smile of such infinite good humor—and a belated titter spreads through the tabernacle and one can almost hear them saying with motherly tolerance, "Oh, now, ain't he the naughty boy?"

For one of Billy Sunday's most ingratiating traits is his boyish delight in being very shocking and getting away with it....We go to hear Billy because he shocks us in the name of goodness, accuses us of sins we never knew existed, gives us the thrill of being suspected of a gay and sinful dogginess that our neighbors would cynically deny, and altogether provides us with all the excitement of sin by proxy which the vast majority of us would never dare to sample direct.[80]

The developing movie industry in Hollywood also showed interest in the campaign, and Sunday not only played baseball with handsome "movie star Douglas Fairbanks, but held personal conferences with 'America's Sweetheart,' Mary Pickford and, the most widely visualized personality, Charlie Chaplin."[81] Both Chaplin and Pickford recounted their private experiences with the evangelist for the newspapers. "I was swept off my feet," wrote Charlie Chaplin. "I had known that I was to meet him and had tried to think of some nice things to say. But I just could not talk. I had a bad attack of stage fright. He put his arm around my shoulder and then I felt sure that he was going to ask me about my soul. But he did not. He asked me to join the family in his dressing room. I followed him in, still dazed.

> There was nothing artificial about the man or any of his family—there was no grand stand play whatever. He had finished his work for the day and it was just a little family gathering. I did not think of him then as the Reverend Mr. Sunday, but just plain Billy.[82]

Mary Pickford wrote similarly of her private meeting with the evangelist: "When Mr. Sunday, hot and tired from his long talk, came up and I was introduced I did not know whether or not he had ever heard of me, but he took my hand, shook it heartily and said: 'You've done lots of good in this world, too.' Wasn't it nice of him to say that? Here is one man who is against everything sinful, evil or malicious, telling us that at least some of us are appreciated for the good we are trying to do in our small way. It is the nicest compliment I have ever been paid." [83]

The newspapers even included a story about the visit the preacher paid to "Doug Fairbanks out at the Lasky Studios practicing making love to a fair plump beauty." "You all know as well as I that he makes love far too well as it is!" Sunday was quoted as saying. "Far too well. And too far off."

When asked to give his opinion of the growing film industry, Sunday was reluctant to speak against its big business:

> Well, I'll tell you—it wouldn't do to knock the fifth largest industry in the entire world, would it—without being able to see the good of it?
>
> No. My opinion of the pictures, good pictures, is that they're fine. But I ask that the pictures keep pace morally with their pace industrially. I've got a kick coming if it's going to make money and base its standing commercially on making sin popular. You bet I have. I have never opposed the theater as an institution. I only oppose what all good people do—the evil side of it.[84]

Interestingly, all three stars, Douglas Fairbanks, Mary Pickford and Charlie Chaplin would later gravitate to Aimee after Angelus Temple was built. Los Angeles, it seemed, yearned to have its own resident evangelist, a chaplain for the stars to compliment its growing and increasingly powerful well established movie colony.

As dazzled as the stars were with the evangelist, so Sunday equally was just as smitten with Los Angeles. "I'd have been satisfied to have camped under a palm tree just to be in Los Angeles."[85] "If there is any place beneath the Stars and Stripes than can surpass this Sunkist Southwest, famed by the soft, gentle, flowers—scented breezes of the Pacific, I haven't seen it."[86]

Billy Sunday was, however, bothered by the religious diversity found in Los Angeles including Pentecostalism. It was even more troubling to him than the growing film colony. Before leaving the city he sounded a warning: "If Christianity doesn't sweep forward, the…cults and isms of your community will swamp you—then goodbye Los Angeles. The results of today (the revival) will settle your future. If Christianity is placed on the scrap heap in Los Angeles, then the tourists will stop coming from the Christian east."[87]

Sunday, leaving for a two-month campaign in Atlanta, praised the city for its cordial hospitality, and more than hinted it could very well become his future home:

> I'm going away from Los Angeles with more homesick feeling for it than I ever had for any place. Everything has been fine. I never felt better, never slept better, never worked harder, never had better results, never had better help nor more appreciative people about me, never had more friendliness shown me, never lived in so handsome a home…I'm so pleased with the old burg that I'll be durned if I don't feel that Nell and the children and I may some day turn up here for keeps…there's a lure

to the city here that is strong, and it wouldn't surprise me to find myself back here with the folks as one of you. [88]

Calling Aimee "the female Billy Sunday" then was a sign of approval and acceptance by the general public since Sunday was still for the most part fondly remembered. From her meeting in the Lyric theatre in Baltimore, December 4-21, 1919, until her disappearance on May 18, 1926, Aimee would simply tap into Sunday's pool of potential converts and make them her own. At twenty-nine years of age she represented the new and modern in American Revivalism, while Sunday at age fifty-seven had quickly become the symbol of the "old-time," "the last of his line." Once Aimee emerged as the premier American revivalist from 1921 on, Sunday would never again achieve the fame and attention he had in 1917. "Ma Kennedy" would replace "Ma Sunday" in newspaper articles as the revivalist's loyal helper.

Sunday's eclipse in American revivalism came about by his own hand as much as anything else. As late as 1929 his devoted chorister, Homer Rodeheaver, pleaded with the evangelist through private correspondence, often selecting Sunday's wife as the emissary, to change his style and tactics of revivalism in an attempt to recreate his earlier years. Rodeheaver begged Sunday to end "the constant driving and scolding about money from the beginning to the end of the meeting."[89] By 1920 Dun and Bradstreet had listed Sunday's net worth at one and a half million dollars. Millionaire Billy had also flaunted his fine clothes, fancy cars, and affluent life style. When questions had been raised about the fiscal ethics of his meetings, Sunday snapped back that it was "nobody's business."[90]

Sunday was also encouraged by Rodeheaver to become "more friendly with some of the folks in every town who would like to be friendly with you."[91] "Have you ever stopped to realize," asked Rodeheaver, "how very little opportunity there is in your party for friendly fellowship between you and the members of your party? Occasionally we have a friendly visit at the table or in your room, but more of the time there is a constant grumbling and irritation about something in connection with the work."[92] Finally, Rodeheaver argued that success in revivalism had waned for Sunday because, "You have constantly and gradually lengthened your sermons and shortened your invitation."[93]

Sunday privately confided to his wife that he wished he possessed the gift of healing to make his ministry more attractive in the 1920s. That gift never came, and Sunday refused to preach in his later years in churches he thought were affiliated with Pentecostalism. The old warrior warmed himself instead

Billy Sunday and "Ma" on his seventieth birthday in Los Angeles. Sunday declared that he was fit and ready to begin a "battle with the devil," but his death would come three years later (used by permission of the Herald Examiner Collection/Los Angeles Public Library).

by the fires of hard-core fundamentalism and received an honorary doctor of divinity degree from Bob Jones University the year of his death. Sunday died in 1935, a sad shadow of his former energetic self after having lived through years of professional eclipse and personal tragedy. William Ashley Sunday's heritage had been evangelical and mainstream. The legacy he left behind, however, was fundamentalist and marginal. Only for a few years from 1912 to 1918 did Sunday manage "uneasily to straddle the two camps."[94]

Aimee was not the last American revivalist to be compared to Billy Sunday. Thirty years after she had been labeled "the female Billy Sunday" the *Los Angeles Times* took notice of her replacement, "Tent Crusader's Drive Likened to Billy Sunday."

> A silver-tongued young evangelist tomorrow will open what has been termed the greatest evangelistic effort since the Billy Sunday campaigns thirty years ago....Known as Billy Graham, the tall blond-haired preacher will launch a 23-day campaign in a huge tent at Washington Blvd. and Hill St. The tent will seat 6000 persons.[95]

Not only would William Randolph Hearst "puff Graham," but Los Angeles would launch an evangelist who would preach in person to more people around the world than anyone who has ever lived. A year later, in 1950,

Graham would return to the Rose Bowl and speak to some fifty thousand—the largest assembled gathering in the West. Thirteen years later he would return to the Memorial Coliseum and over the course of his meetings speak close to a million people, at the time the largest campaign of his career. Los Angeles and revivalism were made for one another, a Hollywood dream factory come true. Southern California, it seemed, was just as capable of producing spiritual stars as movie stars. In time the two would practically become indistinguishable from one another. Unlike Sunday's and Aimee's career, which were only evangelical and mainstream for several years, Billy Gra-

Billy Graham, like Billy Sunday before him, arrives in Los Angeles with his wife, Ruth. In 1950, one year after being "puffed" by William Randolph Hearst, Graham returned to the Rose Bowl to preach to fifty thousand people, "the largest assembled gathering in the West" (used by permission of the Herald Examiner Collection/Los Angeles Public Library).

ham's lasting legacy was that he remained synonymous with and exemplified the best of American evangelicalism for more than half a century. His ministry may have begun as fundamentalist and marginal, but he quickly grew his role as the face and voice of popular American Christianity. What he lacked in theological depth he more than made up with his winsome personality and enormous staying power. Over the years he also remained free from the stain of scandal that plagued so many preachers. For many Americans, from the 1950s and even to the new millennium, Billy Graham was American religion.

Two months after establishing residence and a printing plant, Aimee with a "band of workers" headed north on February 25, 1919, for the mysterious city by the bay—San Francisco. On this trip the city did not evoke any special mention or commentary by her. With time the entire Bay Area

Billy Graham accepts his earthly star, the first for a clergy person, on the Hollywood Walk of Fame, October 16, 1989. Los Angeles produced spiritual stars as well as movie stars (used by permission of the Herald Examiner Collection/Los Angeles Public Library).

would take on a growing significance for her ministry. In Oakland Aimee would receive her foursquare vision and die mysteriously there in a downtown hotel twenty-five years later. In San Francisco she would pack the old wooden Coliseum at Fell and Bauer streets and receive the blessings and endorsement of some of the mainline clergy, including a city Congregational pastor and an Episcopal rector from across the bay in Berkeley. It was a city that would dazzle and charm her as it did its many tourists. "It was the city" she later observed, "of big hearts, wealth, fashion, gaiety," noted for its hospitality and art of entertaining; with its blazing lights, its hills and valleys, theaters, dance-halls, great hotels and clubs; the eddy, surge and roar of its rolling automobiles, its mixed multitudes and distinguished guests where author, artist, statesman, politician, opera-star, business magnate and tourist rub shoulders with the boot-legger, gambler, the thug and the painted women of the underworld."[96]

The five hundred-mile trip to the North in the seven-passenger "Olds Eight" was an eventful one for Aimee and passengers. The main highway between Los Angeles and San Francisco was still unpaved in places and in very poor condition. In the summer of 1919 it was closed to all traffic and finally completed. Aimee was for the first time experiencing the vastness and diverseness of the state of California.

Leaving Los Angeles at noon, via the San Fernando Valley, we passed through the citrus and olive ranches, through the Newhall Tunnel and on to Saugus with its great fields of oil wells nestling at the foot of the mountains,...From Saugus we climbed the mountain grades of the San Francisquito Canyon, skirted the edge of the great lonely Mohave Desert spread like a vast, silent emptiness far away into the blue distance. Then up and up the mighty Tejon Pass with its rocky cliffs and precipices .... From the snowy summit we dropped to plains whereon a straight road stretched before us like a long, shining ribbon.[97]

Aimee Semple McPherson
EVANGELIST

SAN FRANCISCO — April 1-23
═══ COLISEUM ═══
Situated at Entrance of Golden Gate Park   **2:30 and 7:30 P. M. Daily**

Advertisement for Aimee's 1922 meeting at the San Francisco Coliseum. The building had the largest seating capacity (fifteen thousand) of any auditorium west of the Rockies. Contrasting her arrival with that of Mary Garden the opera singer, Aimee wrote, "Mary is to sing to the rich; Aimee is to preach to the poor; Mary's seats will ... sell for between two and three dollars. Aimee's seats are free" (author's collection).

Encountering the winter rains Aimee noted, "We prayed for dry weather; soon the sky cleared, and as we crossed the bay on the ferry from Oakland to San Francisco the sun smiled down upon us from a clear blue sky, as a promise that the Lord would send down upon us the showers of blessing and the sunshine of His love whilst in this city."[98]

Aimee's meetings were held in the major center for Pentecostalism in the Bay Area. Like so many of its fledgling Pentecostal sisters, Glad Tidings Hall, 1536 Ellis Street, was midway in its evolution from "a mission" to "a temple." In 1913 Glad Tidings Mission emerged out of the old Jim Corbett Saloon at 1735 O'Farrell Street, a "damp, dark ill-smelling...old-time... saloon with the...swinging doors intact."[99] By 1916 the work was thriving and the mission moved to 1536 Ellis Street, where it was known as Glad Tidings Hall. It greatly resembled Victoria Hall in Los Angeles with the simplicity of its lodge-like atmosphere and furnishings. By 1925, two years after Aimee had dedicated Angelus Temple in Los Angeles, "Glad Tidings Temple" emerged at 1441-51 Ellis Street. Upon its stucco walls, it advertised in neon "2,000 free seats"—three thousand less than its Los Angeles counterpart.

Pentecostalism in San Francisco was more sedate and stodgy than it was in Los Angeles. "Glad Tidings" was affiliated with the General Council of the Assemblies of God and was to Northern California what Bethel Temple in Los Angeles was to Southern California. The work was co-pastored by a husband and wife team, Robert and Mary Craig, as was Bethel Temple in Los Angeles. Robert Craig was a graduate of the College of the Pacific and together with his wife shared a vision for both the inner-city and a training school for future Pentecostal ministers. In short order they formed the first Bible School of the Assemblies of God. Aimee and her "Gospel band" were the first to occupy the new school building during their stay in the Bay.

> The dear souls had prepared an entire flat of six large rooms, with bath and modern conveniences, for us in the new Bible School which they are just opening. For many years it has been my longing to attend a Bible School, and here I am in one at last, the first to occupy the new building.[100]

She also stressed her uneasiness about such accommodations both in Los Angeles and in San Francisco.

> We are asking the Lord to help us to keep very humble whilst being taken such tender care of by the California saints, that when we have to return to the humbler way of living in the tents, with only the bare ground for a floor, with sun and wind, dust and rain for constant visitors, we shall be just as happy and contented with them as in the days of yore, for we feel that God is going to let us return to our tent work next summer, by His strength and grace.[101]

Aimee's concern about returning to a "humbler way of living" was well founded for two reasons. Many women Pentecostal preachers viewed their ministry as only temporary due to the war effort. Following the war and the return of the "young men," there was also a reaction occurring in Pentecostalism itself against women ministers. Aimee intuitively sensed her ministry needed to change in order to prevent her "return to…tent work" in the summer of 1920. For their survival, both Minnie and Aimee would become more evangelical than Pentecostal (she was after all, "the female Billy Sunday"), and they would tailor their meetings more for the Protestant mainline than the Pentecostal missions. The most obvious change would come in less than three years time when Aimee attempted ordination with the Baptists, also in the Bay Area. When asked why she wished to become a Baptist, Aimee responded with, "Well, the Baptist churches form the largest segment of Protestantism in the United States."[102]

The meetings in Northern California lasted for thirty-three days and inaugurated a non-stop preaching tour taking Aimee back to Canada where she started, then across the United States eight times conducting forty large revivals between 1918 and 1923. With the San Francisco meetings it became apparent that Aimee had an unusual ability to draw crowds and attract outsiders to Pentecostalism. During her visit to the Glad Tidings Mission an extra gallery was built, "but still people were forced to stand out on the sidewalk in order to attend the closing services."[103] Due to the crowds and widespread interest, a theater in San Francisco was rented. Meetings and services were sandwiched in across the bay in Oakland under the sponsorship of Carrie Judd Montgomery at the Ebell Hall and "in the great ball room of the Hotel Oakland."[104] Aimee noted that it was her "privilege to preach the message of the latter rain outpouring of the Holy Spirit in these last days, to many of the poor, rich, and also to church members and ministers from the various churches of Oakland."[105]

The Montgomerys ran a faith home called "The Home of Peace" in the Oakland hills. Their backgrounds were interesting and diverse. For most of her adult life, Mrs. Montgomery had associated with those who practiced spiritual healing. She had personally known and worked with Dr. Cullis of Boston and Dr. A.B. Simpson of New York City. When Dr. Simpson organized the Christian Alliance, Mrs. Montgomery was appointed as the organization's first recording secretary.

George S. Montgomery had a very different background—"a very worldly life" as his wife described it.[106] A quest for health led to his conversion to Christianity. At a camp meeting near Chicago he met his future wife, and they were soon married. He had financial resources and upon his conversion generously helped to promote his faith. Both were important early leaders in the Pentecostal movement in the Bay Area and gave the movement a middle class appeal. Mr. Montgomery, having been "a man of the world," belonged to the Bohemian Club and owned Cazadero, the redwood grove where club members frolicked every summer. Following his conversion, he withdrew his membership in the club and Cazadero became the site of Christian camp meetings known as the "Union Undenomination Camp Meetings." [107] After their move to the Oakland hills and the establishment of their "faith-home," George Montgomery came into close contact with Mrs. S.L. Mills of Mills College—then Mills Seminary—becoming in time a "confidential friend" and consultant about "business matters."[108] The Montgomerys' early endorsement and sponsorship of Aimee's meetings were helpful in generating future support.

The Reverend Craig, pastor of the Glad Tidings Mission, summarized Aimee's revival meetings in San Francisco:

> It was a glad day for the kingdom of Christ in this place when the Lord directed our Sister Aimee Semple McPherson to hold a series of meetings in San Francisco.
> Literally towering mountains of prejudice against the Pentecostal movement have been swept away under the sane, candid, and forceful presentation of the claims of the full Gospel Message…Oh, how many church members, and among them many dear Scandinavians, have been swept through into their baptism…Quite a number of city ministers came to listen, wonder and view the marvelous work of God… Pity the man who goes back to his church to fight against this gracious Heaven-sent Revival. He will be writing his own epitaph.[109]

Craig's testimonial about Aimee's first meetings in San Francisco was perceptive and pointed out a number of things occurring both within the Pentecostal movement and in Aimee's revival meetings. The movement, as Craig noted, was attracting many Scandinavians. For whatever reasons, they were embracing the new religious movement along the Pacific Coast as well as the North Central states. One observer felt that Scandinavians tended to embrace the new movement because they were independent and free thinkers and were attracted to the movement's sense of democracy and simplicity.[110] Scandinavians tended to be among the least emotionally demonstrative of the early Pentecostals.

Craig also noted the growing attention paid both to the movement and Aimee by "quite a number of city ministers."[111] An eyewitness to the meetings backed up her pastor's observations: "All denominations are represented. Bro. Craig has two Methodist preachers on their knees…Back under the gallery sits an Episcopal clergyman, pastor of one of the city churches…A Baptist pastor from Colorado is down before God…A dear, old Presbyterians minister is telling God that his life seems like a failure."[112]

The "established churches" and the "mainline ministers" were beginning to discover Pentecostalism, and the majority of them, those that either supported it or at least expressed some sympathy toward it, had their initial contact through Aimee instead of the struggling Pentecostal missions. This was the period of the great fundamentalist-modernist schism in Protestantism, culminating in the Scopes Monkey Trial in 1925. Although Pentecostalism was legalistic in lifestyle, sharing the same fundamentalist cultural attitudes, its quest for an inner spiritual life based on experience and non-doctrinal dogmas helped it to transcend the fate that would soon befall hardcore American fundamentalists and their institutions. By the time of Billy Graham's era of revivalism, most Pentecostals found the new evangel-icalism as their theological home. Pentecostal scholars would teach at Fuller and not at Dallas Theological Seminary. It was not until the 1960s, however, that the truly ecumenical character of Pentecostalism emerged. When Epis-copalians, Presbyterians, and Catholics embraced the movement in large numbers, it could no longer be written off so simplistically as a return to fundamentalism. The tension between fundamentalism and Pentecostal-ism was in many ways the most draining of Aimee's energy in the course of her ministry. Fundamentalists with their moralistic attitudes and behav-ior would become her chief critics and arch enemies. Aimee's Foursquare vision and subsequent denomination was based upon spiritual experiences and not upon a reactionary return to some rationalistic doctrine. It was this tension which led to Aimee's leaving the ranks of the ordained ministry of the General Council of the Assemblies of God, the denomination she held ordination with during the San Francisco meetings.

Aimee's ministry also seemed more identified with healing in San Fran-cisco than it had been in Los Angeles. This was perhaps due to the empha-sis placed upon healing by the Pentecostal movement in the Bay Area itself. Robert Craig had become associated with Pentecostalism because of his own personal quest for healing. Immigrating to San Francisco from Canada in 1889, he eventually became the assistant pastor of the Central Methodist Church. After the 1906 earthquake, extreme demands were placed upon his time—more than four hundred of his members were burned out of their homes, and his health broke through a nervous collapse, forcing him to withdraw from the ministry. One historian has written that "the San Fran-cisco earthquake and fire of 1906 are widely considered America's worst urban disaster and one of the world's greatest urban conflagrations."[113] San Francisco's destruction paralleled the Chicago fire of 1871, Galves-ton's hurricane of 1900, New York's World Trade Center collapse of 2001, and New Orleans flooding of 2005. "Did you ever see a dog shake a rat?" asked Warren Olney. "We were like rats in a dog's mouth. Old Mother Earth appeared to be trying to shake us off her face."[114]

Robert Craig was not alone in the personal toll the earthquake took on him and his church. Across the bay in Oakland, Charles Reynolds Brown, at the First Congregational Church found himself in a similar situation:

Three hundred thousand people were turned out of their houses…in San Francisco, homeless, foodless, with no clothing save what they wore. Many of them took refuge in Golden Gate Park…but within thirty-six hours one hundred thousand of them came across the Bay to us. Oakland was then a city of less than a hundred thousand, and our population had more than doubled in a day's time.

We opened our homes, our churches, our halls…Thousands of people slept on the cushions in our church pews. All the churches were feeding the hungry without charge from six o'clock in the morning until midnight.

We went back…to the days of the early Christian church when "no one said that any of the things he possessed were his own, but we had all things in common"….But it was a time of stress and strain. The day before the earthquake, I had weighed one hundred and eighty-three pounds. In six months, I lost exactly thirty pounds without having been sick for a day. It just went![115]

During Craig's four year search for health in the wake of the earthquake, he was converted to Pentecostalism. "God led me to those despised Pentecostal people, catching me as it were by guile, but now I am one of them—Glory!"[116] After Glad Tidings Temple was built, the church's slogan, "Health-Hope-Happiness," adorned both the outside of the church and its vehicles.[117] During the temple's construction it was intended to have "healing rooms, with every necessary comfort for helpless patients brought in on stretchers, and in wheelchairs (the worst cases will be gladly welcomed)."[118] Even the First Congregational Church in San Francisco announced a sermon topic on "the Place of Mystery and Miracle in Religion" during Aimee's thirty-three day stay in the city.[119] The healing aspect of Aimee's ministry would dominate in her subsequent visits to San Francisco almost as much as it would be associated with her meetings in Denver and Balboa Park in San Diego. Aimee was quick to point out, "Throughout our meetings everywhere we have always put the ministry for the soul first, then the ministry for the body; nevertheless, miracles of healing have been wrought in almost every service."[120] A visitor to one of the San Francisco meetings wrote to *The Bridal Call* stating that he had been "a preacher, teacher, Episcopal minister and physician and …the ministry… through our Sister is unlike anything I have ever heard before. So unique is it in dynamic power."[121]

Following her San Francisco meetings, coming meetings were announced in *The Bridal Call* for the "West, Middle West and East" for the "spring and early summer of 1919." Aimee's ministry primarily affected existing centers of Pentecostalism, especially strengthening churches affiliated with the General Council of the Assemblies of God, until she received her new vision at Baltimore. Nowhere was her impact greater than the San Joaquin Valley in North Central California, where revival meetings were held in San Jose at the large Liberty Dance Hall under the sponsorship of a Reverend J.H. Sparks and his Pentecostal congregation.

The meetings were so thoroughly advertised that Aimee doubted "whether there was a family in the city but what knew of the revival meetings. Street cars bore large banners; shop windows were placarded, almost the entire city visited from house to house with verbal and written invitations."[122] Several years later in "the charming little city with its roses and palms" Aimee attempted ordination with the Baptists, scandalizing the Pentecostal movement for attempting to move her message and herself into the mainstream of American Christianity.

En route to Los Angeles, meetings were held in Turlock, where "wonder of wonders—the very church which had put out the deacon for even daring to attend our former meetings, had opened its doors and invited me to come in and preach."[123] Again, as in San Jose, this was fertile ground for Aimee and her message with the evangelist perceptively commenting, "I do not know when it has ever been my privilege to see such a hungry, earnest populace. People drove a hundred miles to attend the meetings. Twenty minutes before the service was to begin the square and streets surrounding the church were filled with automobiles and carriages. Every available inch of space was taken clear outside on the porch, and all around, the church windows were filled and doorways jammed."[124]

Upon her return home to Los Angeles and the "saints at Victoria Hall" Aimee found the mission "packed to overflowing" for a "welcome home meeting."[125] By July 1919, Aimee was able to summarize her California experience:

> We look back over the winter [of 1919]…our hearts are overflowing with praise and thanksgiving. He has raised up to us hundreds, yes, thousands of warm-hearted friends; He has given us a home for our babies where they may go to school, enabled us to get our new book *This is That* [first edition] upon the press, and has given us an abundant harvest of souls. How wonderfully He has led us from coast to coast. Surely when He leads the way, there is nothing to fear, for He doeth all things well, and sees the end from the beginning.[126]

Aimee's host pastor in San Francisco, the Reverend Robert J. Craig, accurately predicted her future when he declared that she "has before her a ministry of an unusual order."[127] And in the words of the writer John Fante, "all of California, north, south and central valley," seemingly belonged to Aimee, as well.[128] Several years later, Ma Kennedy recalled their early California campaigns:

> "California for Christ" was our motto. Everywhere throughout this glorious Golden State, churches, hearts and homes opened to us in the most miraculous way and the largest buildings, amphitheatres, coliseums and even boxing arenas were placed at our disposal.
>
> The press of every city was most kind in considering the campaigns of sufficient news value to occupy front page positions and require the services of special staff reporters throughout entire campaigns. When "the boys" were of a different faith or no faith at all, sometimes terming themselves "hard-boiled," yet they were ever ready to acknowledge instances of miraculous Divine Healing where people that they personally knew were instantly and supernaturally healed.[129]

CHAPTER NINE

Blurring Boundaries and Open Doors
The Traveling Evangelist: From Tents & Tabernacles
to Opera Houses & Municipal Auditoriums;
from Pentecostal Missions to Denominational Churches

Was there a deep-rooted tendency to mysticism in the American spirit? As the (twentieth) century advanced, the discoveries of science accelerated... But many Americans demanded a truth that was ultimate and absolute; beyond any truth attainable by science. They sought it in what William James described as an "altogether other dimension of existence."...In the larger cities, Vedanta and Baha'i prospered. Rosicrucianism, Theosophy, Yoga won adherents. There were churches of Divine Science, Religious Science, the Science of Mind, and even The Truth....There were thriving centers of New Thought and Unity. And evangelists who emphasized the supernatural and miraculous elements of Christianity effected spectacular mass conversions.

—Lloyd Morris,
"The Mysticism of the Middle Class"

I bring spiritual consolation to the middle classes, leaving those above to themselves, and those below to the Salvation Army.

—Aimee Semple McPherson

It's the Old-Time Religion, With a New Content That Makes it as Secular as it is Sacred!

—*Ladies Home Journal*

By the fall of 1919 Aimee's meetings would begin to be housed more in concrete and steel than in flapping canvas. Her fears and concerns about having to permanently return to tents and a "humbler way of living" would soon be over. The upstairs missions and street-level storefronts were also fading fast into oblivion—at least for her—although for Anglo Pentecostalism, as a whole, they would endure for another two to three more decades, largely as independent and unaffiliated missions. The Pentecostal movement, like the generation in which it was born, was young, restless, and on the move. World War I had ended. A young Army officer by the name of F. Scott Fitzgerald pledged his love to Zelda Sayre and in order to both win and maintain that love, he would chronicle the times with his "romantic readiness" and "heightened sensitivity to the promises of life" and in the words of a biographer, live out his days in "some sort of Epic Grandeur."[1]

A revolution was underway. Self-expression and self-fulfillment became key words and more often than not led to self-indulgence. The prophetic figures of the era were not the intellectuals, which is why perhaps subsequent historians in future generations would give the time period short shrift. The real apostles of the times were the emerging literary figures like Theodore Dreiser, Sinclair Lewis, H.L. Mencken, George Jean Nathan, and F. Scott Fitzgerald. They illuminated an entire era with their stories of "flaming youth," "speakeasies," "gang wars," and the "Jazz Age." Even the catchy Charleston tunes managed to convey the times as much as anything else:

> My gal's a corker!
> She's a New Yorker—
> I buy her everything
> To keep her in style.
> She's got a pair of lips
> Just like potato chips,
> Hey Boys!
> That's where my money goes.[2]

If the intellectuals had lost faith in the future because of the past, great numbers of Americans were optimistic that the promises of the past would soon become the realities of the present. Following the war, concerns shifted from the society to the individual and from the public to private-sector experience. The same people who had endured wheatless Mondays, meatless Tuesdays and porkless Thursdays and who had saved their peach pits to make gas masks were now buying indoor plumbing, electric refrigerators, and automobiles.

The extreme selfishness and self-centeredness of the era is easily illuminated by the cynicism and callousness in the writings of George Jean Nathan:

> The great problems of the world—social, political, economic, and theological—do not concern me in the slightest...If all the Armenians were to be killed tomorrow and if half of Russia were to starve to death the

day after, it would not matter to me in the least. What concerns me alone is myself, and the interests of a few close friends. For all I care the rest of the world may go to hell at today's sunset.[3]

Some have argued that preoccupation with the self was a response to the internationalism of World War I, while others have maintained that "the inner frontier" was discovered because the frontier as a place in America had largely vanished by the advent of the 1920s.[4]

World War I marked the end of an era for American Protestantism as well. By 1925 all the usual indices of institutional health and wealth were on a downward trend that would continue for at least another decade. H.L. Mencken stated the truth in his own inimitable style: "Every day, a new Catholic Church goes up; every day another Methodist or Presbyterian Church is turned into a garage. Protestantism is down with a wasting disease."[5] What Mencken lamented more than anything else was the collapse of Protestantism "in the middle."

> What remains in the middle may be likened to a torso without either brains to think with or legs to dance—in other words, something that begins to be professionally attractive to the mortician...There is no lack of life on the higher levels, where the more solvent Methodists and the like are gradually transmogrified into Episcopalians...and there is no lack of like on the lower levels, where the rural Baptist, by the route of Fundamentalism, rapidly descend to...dogmas...But in the middle there is desiccation and decay. Here is where Protestantism was once strongest.[6]

It was this void "in the middle" that Aimee would attempt to fill with her brand of Pentecostalism. Beginning in Baltimore and refined in St. Louis and Wichita, her new "middle of the road" position would be perfect for the middle class from the Middle West. This would be her greatest contribution to the making of modern Pentecostalism. Aimee, in short, took the movement out of the attics and basements of the back alleys and put it on the major boulevards—even Glendale Boulevard, just off Sunset Boulevard, on the edge of Hollywood itself. She, in essence, transformed the "savage sacred" of Pentecostalism into the "tamed sacred."

Sydney E. Ahlstrom, the masterful chronicler of America's religious life has astutely noted the era's importance:

> The decade of the twenties is the most sharply defined decade in American history. Marked off by the war at one end and the Depression at the

The traveling evangelist (author's collection).

other, it has a character of its own—ten restless years roaring from jubilation to despair amid international and domestic dislocation. It has also had a bad press, whether viewed from the right or the left...What has been lost to mind is the fact that the twenties were an exciting time of social transformation, intellectual revolution, and artistic triumph.[7]

It was also the decade in which Aimee had her most striking successes becoming a household word and as much a part of the American culture as Isadora Duncan, Sacco and Vanzetti, Amelia Earhart, and Charles Lindbergh. It was a time, as Ahlstrom notes, that "the nation found heroes cut from the new kinds of cloth [and] the newly enfranchised American woman made her brazen appearance."[8]

The heroes and heroines of the 1920s were in reality not really cut from "new kinds of cloth." The decade's creativity and tension lie in the fact that the heroes and heroines were draped with a patchwork uniform; some of it old, some of it new. America was torn between an urban industrial present and the nostalgia for an agrarian past. The symbols of the age were accorded their recognition because they, like Henry Ford and Charles Lindbergh, while utilizing products of industrialization, still retained personal ties to the past. The 1920s were indeed in Lawrence Levin's words a time of "progress and nostalgia."[9] "It is difficult," argues Levin, "to find any aspect of American culture in the twenties that did not exhibit this tension.

> Motion pictures, which came into their own as a popular art form during the decade with 100,000,000 people attending 20,000 theatres weekly by 1926, seem on the surface to have been one long celebration of the new woman, the new morality, the new youth, the new consumption patterns that marked postwar America....As uninhibited as they might have been the movies of the twenties rarely failed to conclude without a justification of the moral standards of the past. Flappers and "It" girls married at the end of the film and entered a life of middle-class respectability.

Faithless husbands and wives mended their ways and returned to patient forgiving mates. The new woman may have been depicted as tough but...their toughness was used to protect their purity, not to dispose of it. The widespread popular revulsion against the excesses of the first wave of postwar movies forced Hollywood to resort to the cliché of the happy and moral ending; a standard which never marked European movies to the same extent.

The career of Cecil B. DeMille is instructive. After attempting to make the bathroom and bedroom national shrines in his series of postwar sexual comedies, DeMille turned to the public for suggestions for new films. Impressed by the number of requests for religious themes, DeMille hit upon a new formula in his widely popular films, *The Ten Commandments* (1923) and *The King of Kings* (1927). Sex and orgies were still prominent but they were now placed within a religious framework with a moral message.

The Western heroes of the nineteen twenties...were strong, clean-living uncomplicated men....They were living embodiments of the innocence, freedom and morality which Americans identified with and longed to regain if only vicariously....The production techniques of American business in the twenties may have been new, but the images used to justify them were old and hallowed.[10]

The acceptance of Aimee Semple McPherson into America's religious life and culture reflects both the emergence of a hero cut from a semi-new kind of cloth and the appearance of the newly franchised American woman, yet one with clear personal ties to the rural past. And revivalism, which was Sister Aimee's entree into both worlds, was searching for something new in the wake of war. Revivalism has been in diverse and significant ways the pulse beat and thermometer of America's popular religious life and thought. It has also been like an enlarged X-ray machine, magnifying the inner spiritual hungers and drives of the average American without regard to the religious establishment. In fact, America's religious "establishment" has always been an elite subculture in comparison to the magnitude, power, and certitude of popular religion. And American revivalism has always been the "classic form of American religious experience."[11] America, in reality, has not been, as Sidney E. Mead claimed, "The Nation with the Soul of a Church," but rather, "The Nation with the Soul of a Camp-Meeting."[12]

Although some historians have argued that revivalism suffered a "temporary relapse" between the wars, in actuality revivalism changed like America's general religious climate and far from dying out, it became more solidly established in American life. The success of Aimee in the 1920s is due to the disaffection on many levels with the general religious climate and revivalism in particular. If Billy Sunday's career died out with World War I, and Billy Graham emerged after World War II, then Sister Aimee reflected the tastes and sensitivities of the ever-increasing middle class between the two Billys. Her influence reflected the advent of a growing worldwide international religious consciousness. It reflected a return to the private over the corporate and the triumph of the personal over the impersonal. There has never been a more noticeable shift in revivalism and in America's popular religious consciousness than the change from Billy Sunday's "muscular Christianity," which equated "salvation with decency and manliness," to Aimee's sense of spirituality and "female mystical piety."

What began in the 1920s and would fully bloom in the 1960s was a quest for personal fulfillment, a gift from urbanization and the ever-increasing amount of leisure time. Along with these came the increasing tendency toward a true feminization of American culture. (Women who engaged in non-domestic roles and activities during wartime would continue on in larger numbers during peacetime.) This increasing tendency toward the feminization of the culture in American religion seemed to manifest itself most unmistakably by the need, especially among the middle class, for strong maternal figures, especially those who offered healing through faith.

With the growing acceptance and rise of Aimee's ministry in the 1920s, it is instructive and important to remember both her image and how she was perceived by her public. She was during these years repeatedly thought to be years older than she actually was. In her starched white uniform with her bountiful hair piled high above her rather robust figure, she exuded the wholesomeness of the ideal maternal figure, especially with her own two small children in tow. Apart from "Sister," she was often referred to as "the little woman in white," being all of 5 feet 3½ inches tall. This image persisted until the middle 1920s when Aimee, more in keeping with the Jazz Age, began to discover silk fashions of both Paris and Hollywood, ultimately leading to much consternation among the "Pentecostal saints." As a writer of the era correctly noted, "It was at this period that Aimee began to respond to the compulsions and vogues of the Jazz Age. Her dowdy evangelical dress of yesteryear was suddenly replaced by new and scandalous splendor. She appeared in London with 'a coiffeur that might have been done in Bond Street,' pale yellow silk jumper, black silk gown, short skirts, and flesh-colored silk stockings—the raiment of a bride."[13]

Although often dressed in "the raiment of a bride," Aimee would still reveal her "patchwork" uniform of the 1920s by nostalgically reminding her audiences of her rural past. Aimee's remembrances of the family farm were always for her "like throwing up the window for a breath of fresh air when a room is hot and stuffy."[14]

The 1920s and post-war American religion was also a time of a strong mystical personal faith that cut across class lines and theological demarcations. This faith was seen in the lives of such individuals as Elizabeth Glendower Evans, the spiritual center of the defense of Sacco and Vanzetti. The magnitude of a mystical personal religion was far-reaching and wide-felt. It expressed itself in many forms, from the sophisticated writings of Emerson and James to the decline in mainline Protestantism to the growth and vitality of a "people's religion" such as Catholicism and Pentecostalism. The attraction some Catholics had toward Pentecostalism, especially through Aimee's ministry, also reflected the growing need for and absence of strong maternal figures within that church. Following the war, it was a time in the Catholic Church when "Sisters were pushed back behind their cloister walls and were no longer so free to respond to contemporary needs."[15]

It was during the early years of the 1920s, then, that Aimee's ministry started assuming a new magnitude, repeatedly and significantly cutting across established religious and social lines. She was entering into a period of great social transformation, one in which she would help to illuminate. In the words of *The Great Gatsby*, it was "as if [she] were related to one of those intricate machines that registers earthquakes ten thousand miles away…It was an extraordinary gift for hope, a romantic readiness."[16] In an increasingly secular age, Aimee was fast becoming not so much a religious but a spiritual symbol of transcendence. In her harsh apprenticeship she had learned, in the words of historian William McLoughlin, how to "fight fire with fire in the Jazz Age."[17] It was a battle that would mystify many but seemingly prophetically echo the Reverend Mr. Craig's statement and her mother's most innermost feelings—"That she has before her a ministry of a most unusual order."[18]

Aimee's ministry of "a most unusual order" manifested itself most clearly when she was twenty-nine years of age and culminated three years later with the founding and opening of her own church in Los Angeles. During 1919–1922 everything rapidly and significantly changed for her. Theologically and sociologically it was a time, in her words, of "open doors." Theologically, she significantly crossed the denominational barriers imposed against Pentecostalism, making the movement more acceptable to the mainstream of American Christianity, an accomplishment never to be duplicated again until the emergence of the charismatic movement in the 1960s—an accomplishment that created as much personal sorrow as joy. Sociologically, these years of "open doors" saw her permanently vacate the missions and storefronts in back alleys for downtown theaters, opera houses, and municipal auditoriums. "Churches" of canvas were replaced by concrete and steel. Again images from Hollywood come to mind. It was like an actor after years of apprenticeship on the vaudeville circuit finally coming into the big time of the glitter and glamour of Hollywood. Indeed it was a feat many actors rightly envied.

In the summer of 1919, Aimee's largest tent meeting to date was held in Los Angeles. It was reminiscent of her earlier triumph and turning point only a summer ago at the Nation-Wide Camp Meeting in Philadelphia. The style of the camp was similar, only much larger. Minnie Kennedy reported to the Pentecostal constituency that it was "the biggest meeting she ever attended in Pentecost," a tribute as much to her own managerial shrewdness as to her daughter's preaching ability, when only a summer before she was concerned about flooring for Aimee's sleeping tent and the disruption of the meetings by roving gangs of youth bent on religious persecution. The "Western State Camp Meeting" opened on Sunday, August 17, and closed a month later on September 14. It was sponsored by Warren Fisher and his brother-in-law, "Bro. Blake" of the Victoria Hall Mission, which by now had earned the reputation of "being where to go when you wanted to see the 'real thing' of Pentecost."[19] Three meetings were held daily with Aimee preaching every evening and most afternoons, being assisted at other times by a "band of the best workers, pastors and missionaries on the Western Coast."[20]

The camp meeting was a tent city with more than a hundred smaller tents billowing over nine acres of land at Washington and Orchard streets in downtown Los Angeles. Aimee's "dream tent"—the one purchased the summer before in Philadelphia—was unpacked, erected, and looked miniscule in comparison to the anticipated crowd. It was used nevertheless as an extension for a much larger rented "tabernacle tent." As at the Philadelphia meeting, the tents were laid out like an imagined utopian Pentecostal city. There was "Hallelujah Street," "Praise Avenue," "Victory Way," "Joy Boulevard," and "This is That Square" with red crosses adorning each street sign post. Again, like the Philadelphia camp, Pentecostal ecstasy knew no limits. The camp was located in the "midst of a thickly populated residential section," and a reporter for the meetings noted, "The neighbors were totally unprepared to anything like the scenes they witnessed during this meeting; they acted as though they were not sure whether to laugh or run or send for the police."[21] They did implore their more than enthusiastic neighbors to permit them some sleep, "at least between two and four a.m." [22]

Despite local streetcar strikes and "national tie-ups," the attendance increased with the length of the meeting. Even the fifty-foot pine platform was soon over crowded with visiting Pentecostal ministers, evangelists, and missionaries flocking back again to the city that was the Mecca for their movement. The most noticeable effect Aimee had upon the month-long meetings was to unify the Pentecostal movement as a whole—no easy matter especially in Los Angeles—where doctrinal differences had run deep and had threatened to destroy the infant movement. The host minister, the Reverend Warren W. Fisher reported the results to other Pentecostals:

> We are glad to see a real "coming together" of the saints, who were persuaded to take up new doctrines and almost quit the paths of Pentecost in despair…There was no wrangling over doctrine. Everyone knew the belief and stood together like giants in the battle against the common foe. Sister McPherson has won the love and respect of pastors and their confidence in her teaching cannot be shaken. Anyone can see that it is only the Lord that gives her such remarkable endurance to preach and sing and dance and then take up the long siege of prayer for saint and sinner.[23]

By the summer of 1919, Aimee had indeed "won the love and respect" of her brother and sister Pentecostals in the faith. Because of this new-found unity, it would become much easier for Aimee to attempt to move beyond denominational barriers in the next three months.

Due to the sheer dynamism of Aimee's platform presence, another aspect of her ministry was often overlooked and underappreciated. Despite her great gift of preaching, it was her writing ability that first established a solid base of financial support. Drawing large crowds in new areas of the country came as a result of her silent success as an author of Pentecostal literature. After the Los Angeles camp meeting had ended, Aimee wrote her followers about "Our Literature." Her primary concern was about the reception of her recently published first book, *This is That* (named after Acts 2: 16-18, where the Joel passage is cited by Peter on the day of Pentecost that in the "last days" God's spirit would be poured out upon all flesh "and your sons and daughters shall prophesy.") Aimee's attitude regarding the quality and construction of the book clearly revealed her feelings about what should be occurring within the larger Pentecostal movement itself.

> Almost seven hundred pages, gotten up in the best paper and binding, to be worthy of Pentecost and the message it carries to the world. It contains sixteen full-page illustrations and photos. The cost of printing

Aimee as author. Her writing ability established a solid base of financial support (author's collection).

alone for the first edition is $2.50 per copy, without freight, postage, express or wrapping. When we found that $3.00 was the least we could possibly sell the book for, my heart sank lest some of the poorer people could not afford it, and I thought of getting out a cheaper edition with poorer paper and cover, and without the illustrations. [24]

Initial sales gave Aimee extra encouragement from her book-buying public. (The book is still in print with the International Church of the Foursquare Gospel as publisher and dis-tributor.) Just like the country music artist who touches and heals other lives by songs born out of personal despair and disarray—those timeless truths of sin and redemption—Aimee too conveyed her heart-aches to her followers. "It is a plain, unvarnished account of facts as they really were in my experience," she wrote. "Lots of things which have never been related before, and which caused a pang to write, but which we believe will help many discouraged souls, are told." [25] It was her chapter about her failed second marriage that seemed to elicit the most positive response from her readers. "Many say that the chapter from Nineveh to Tarshish has been made a great blessing to them, as it relates the story of my dis-couragement." [26] Many facts were indeed omitted in regard to her personal life, but Aimee alone was unique among the classical Pentecostal clergy for possessing a sense of boldness and candor about her setbacks and discour-agements. It was her testimony as well as her personal touch that meant the most to her followers and accounted for so much of her early success.

In the fall of 1919 Aimee was gaining an international reputation due to the successful sales of *This Is That*. The publication of her life story gener-ated invitations to minister seemingly from everywhere, "urgent calls for revival meetings ranging from the tiniest mission hall to great auditoriums seating thousands; invitations from South America, from Canada, from England and Wales, from Australia, and other needy parts of the world—

letters containing wonderful words of encouragement—letters that carry many a tale of woe."[27]

Los Angeles, as it would be for the next three years, was only her part-time home. Here she would briefly return in between meetings to see her children and attend to business matters. Although it offered the security and permanence of a home base, her ministry was still very much "on the road" and away from Los Angeles. From there in the fall of 1919 Aimee and Minnie headed East again, this time by train, holding meetings in Holdrege, Nebraska; Akron, Ohio; and Baltimore, Maryland. The Nebraska "campaign" was sponsored by the growing "fellowship"—the Assemblies of God. Denominational representatives, including the chairman, the Reverend J.W Welch, were on hand and took part in the meetings. The meetings ran for fifteen days and were held in "the finest auditorium in the state—seating 3,500."[28] Aimee's meeting in Holdrege set a pattern for wherever she went in America. Arriving in a city she soon "captured the hearts of the people, pouring in the marvelous truths of Pentecost with sweetness."[29] The business interests of the city also took to Aimee—an uncommon occurrence for the reception of a new religious movement: "One of the biggest merchants offered to send out thousands of bills, circulars and sermons to his entire mailing list throughout the state. The press assured the brethren that they could have any place or space they wanted in the newspaper, and for three weeks gave them from one-third to one-half of the front page with pictures, reports, and sermons which were printed word for word."[30]

Another pattern was beginning to emerge at the conclusion of the meetings. "A new work (Pentecostal) is to be opened in Holdrege and for this purpose a Congregational Church is being secured. Brother Pope, with his band of converted opera singers, will continue to sow the seed and reap the harvest for some time."[31]

After Aimee's Akron meetings, where the local armory was transformed "into a recruiting station for King Jesus' soldiers," it was back to Los Angeles to see her children and to attend to the increasing complexities associated with the running of larger meetings. It was also a time of preparation for the forthcoming Baltimore Revival Campaign to be held at the Lyric Theatre, December 4–21, 1919. This seventeen-day meeting marked a turning point in Aimee's ministry and a major shift in the making of the larger movement. Although her theological vision of Christianity would come into focus at a later meeting in Oakland, California, it was at Baltimore where Aimee's true style of revivalism emerged and where she finally came into her own.

During the Baltimore revival, something occurred which I believe marked a turning point not only in my own ministry but in the history of the outpouring of Pentecostal Power. Yet at that time (so far as I know) not one of the dear Pentecostal people understood the vision God had given me, and severely criticized what they called a 'quenching of manifestations.'[32]

At the Baltimore meeting Aimee made her final break with the excessive, all-too-true image of "holy roller" Pentecostalism. Up to this time the energy expended in the movement was wildly excessive. Physical manifestations—shouting, dancing, loud glossolalia—had become the hallmarks of true spirituality for the movement. This excessiveness, in part, functioned as a very loud and clear protest of the equally excessive formalism that pervaded most of the mainline churches which large numbers of new Pentecostals had fled.

Everything stylistically changed for Aimee in Baltimore. The meeting was announced and advertised not as a "Pentecostal Revival Campaign," but rather as "an independent and undenominational meeting." It was sponsored by a "secular businessman" who not only came up with the required daily rental fee of three hundred dollars but also kept the entire offerings for himself—save what was collected on the last Sunday afternoon of the meeting. Even that unfair business arrangement met with Minnie Kennedy's shrewd approval:

> It has ever been our desire and intention to remain free from either financial or social obligations in order that we may speak and work as the Spirit directs. Few will ever realize what a difficult thing that is. At times even our friends would look askance at the things we did, which seemed strange to them. Many good people, God bless them, would come in and immediately set about introducing their own certain methods, allowing no room for variance as the Spirit might direct. [33]

In Baltimore Aimee finally returned to the stage of a theater—and not on the crude makeshift platform of a humble mission behind a homemade pulpit. Prior to her conversion experience it had been her greatest ambition to become an actress. And it was on a stage where she always really belonged. When the house lights went down and the spotlight and footlights were flipped on, then the real Aimee emerged and was at home. She would move that congregation/audience the way the talented play fine, delicately tuned musical instruments. The distinction between solo and unison would vanish in the worship experience, with all the participants mystically and transcendentally becoming one. That great illusive mystery of "one body of believers" has always been the ultimate Christian experience, and Aimee alone among American revivalists would repeatedly usher it in. A woman reporter for *The Baltimore Star* "wondered confusedly [about the meetings] where she had never heard of anything like it before, and mental pictures of intense moments recalled from either literature or personal experience flashed in front of her. The Storming of the Bastille—Armistice Day—a Harvard-Princeton football game."[34]

The way Aimee chose to describe her change in style to her readers was most interesting. It appears that the concept of "fishing" had long been appropriated by American revivalists. A Christian would "fish" for the "souls" of individuals and would even sing the oft-quoted chorus of becoming a "fisher of men." At the Baltimore meeting, through inspiration, Aimee decided it was time to "fish for whales instead of minnows." She was most clear in whom she perceived the "whales" to be. "Night after night—ministers, doctors of divinity, Jewish rabbis, medical doctors, and the best people of the city sat in the orchestra and boxes of this their finest theater for which we were paying over three hundred dollars a day rental in order to 'fish for whales.' "[35]

Ma Kennedy was even more precise in her description of "whales." "Did you ever see a whale in a theater box?" she asked. "Have you ever seen one attired in a conventional black suit, with high white collar, kid gloves and cane?...here-to-fore our nets had been full to overflowing, but we had only been sailing around in the shallows, close to the shore, scarcely realizing that greater 'hunting grounds' lay ahead...and God showed us that if we were deep sea fishing for whales, we could not use the same methods as we did in the shallower shore waters."[36]

Aimee's new methods of "whale catching" were more than novel attempts at improving the socio-economic status of her followers and moving away from the holiness crowd and the Pentecostal mission folk. It reflected her innermost thoughts of a Gospel based on love and compassion instead of fear and eternal punishment. The "fishing for whales" concept removed her forever from the crude and abusive styles and tactics of American fundamentalism. Further distancing her message from male counterparts in revivalism—especially Billy Sunday—Aimee reflected the growing feminization permeating American culture. In an editorial she attempted to explain her new concepts:

> Many hooks have been baited with "spiritual pride" and "holier than thou" tactics. "Now, Mrs. Fish, just look where you are, away down there

in the mire of theatre going, card parties, earthly pleasure, money getting—and just see where I am, going to prayer meetings every Wednesday night, to church three times on Sunday and….Never fish with a long,
sad face. Divine joy, contentment, hope, gladness…and a welcoming
smile are better bait and will catch more fish in a month than gloom and
long-facedness will in a life-time….Never be impatient….Never get into
an argument….Do your personal work quietly, unobtrusively. Don't try
to force your fish or drive it to the hook."[37]

The change in style of Aimee's meetings, were also reflected in her and
Minnie's accommodations. Mrs. Kennedy noted, "We were ensconced in
a splendid hotel…We had to have a good room in which to meet our
friends."[38] Minnie's frugalness, however, prevailed even while ensconced in
the Hotel Belvedere:

> When it came time to eat, those same friends would have been very
> much surprised had they seen us, slipping through the doorway into the
> alley and around the corner to the traditional "beanery" or "help your-
> self" style of restaurant, where a quarter was royally welcomed instead
> of being haughtily snubbed into hasty retreat, as would be case in the
> grandeur of the hotel dining room…to us, the nickels counted, and we
> were often glad, after the strenuous days before the public, to hide away
> to our room and there perform the little humble homey tasks.[39]

The shifts in style that Aimee underwent while at the Lyric Theatre in Baltimore were profound ones. They reflected the dissatisfaction with mainline
churches as well as her increasing disdain for the holy-roller crowd of the
Pentecostal missions and the outdated methods of American revivalism in
general.

Unknowingly for Aimee, Baltimore was also fertile ground for her new-
found vision of fishing for whales in the deeper waters of the Protestant
mainstream. Most of her mainline support on the East Coast would come
from Methodist ministers such as Charles A. Shreve, Frank C. Thompson,
Ralph S. Cushman, and the old lion of Methodism himself, Leander W.
Munhall. According to church historian William Warren Sweet, New Jersey,
Philadelphia, and Baltimore were areas where the conservative movement
within Methodism was centered. Both in 1920 and 1924 the conservatives
challenged their denomination's "course of study" program:

> They feared that reading liberal materials would cause young ministers
> to lose their faith. In 1925, they formed themselves into a Methodist
> League for Faith and Life, with a monthly periodical, *The Call to Colors*.

The league's express purpose was "to reaffirm the vital and eternal truths of Christian religion, such as the inspiration of the Scriptures, the deity of Jesus, his Virgin Birth, etc."[40]

In some ways, Aimee's "fishing for whales" in Baltimore was nothing more than a return to the roots and earlier days of Methodism.

During the Baltimore meetings, the local newspapers carried two stories that undoubtedly influenced Aimee's decision to change her methods. The two issues facing the Baltimore churches were most likely facing other urban American churches as well. One major issue facing the Baltimore churches, especially the Protestant mainline, had to do with the increasing losses in church membership since 1917 and the end of the First World War. *The Baltimore Sun* reported, "Every Protestant denomination has shown a decrease in the last year and since 1917, or at least a marked falling off in the percentage of increase…And more alarming to the church officials than the 60,000 decrease in church membership is the far larger decrease in Sunday school memberships, and in the number of Sunday schools themselves."[41]

The local clergy of Baltimore, in an attempt to change the existing conditions, identified the areas of "religious education" and "personal evangelism" as the two most significant ones to remedy the situation. Thus, evangelism, due to the dire conditions of the established churches, was becoming acceptable again among many mainline churches. The style, tactics, and methods of an older generation of revivalism, however, were no longer acceptable, and Aimee with her strong sense of intuition readily recognized that fact.

A strong, mystical personal faith was also being experienced in Baltimore as in many other parts of the country. Its expression transcended denominationalism and existing class boundaries and distinctions. Its clearest and fullest expression came in the renewed interest of spiritual and physical healing through faith and prayer and the cultivation of the spiritual life.

As early as 1899, James M. Campbell, a liberal Congregational minister in the Midwest, became interested in the doctrine of the Holy Spirit. His series of lectures on the subject given at the University of Chicago Divinity School were later published as *After Pentecost, What?* His developing interest in the inner life of the Christian led to several other books on the topic: *Paul the Mystic, The Indwelling Christ,* and *The Presence.* Campbell maintained that both "spirituality and mysticism" as well as the "redemption of the body" "…had largely been lost to orthodox Protestantism.[42]

What Campbell advocated for the churches [was] first to make the experience of God—mystically and spiritually—more central in the religious life...he urged the churches to use personal testimonials. Second...Christians could use right thoughts, along with the prayer of faith for healing."[43]

Also, like Aimee, James M. Campbell eventually moved his ministry to Los Angeles.

Pentecostalism with its best foot forward attempted to ride the crest of this new wave of mystical religious fervor and to institutionalize it. When it failed at times to do so, it retreated backwards into an archaic and demeaning fundamentalism. The movement would always be torn between "the spirit that giveth life" and "the letter that killeth."

In Baltimore, as in other major metropolitan areas, the denomination which best reflected these "new" (if anything is new in religion) theological currents by giving subsequent study and research to them and then articulating them in the most mature and refined manner, was the Episcopal Church. In the early 1920s an article appeared in *The Ladies Home Journal* (next to an F. Scott Fitzgerald short story) entitled "Are There Modern Miracles?" by Mabel Potter Dagget.

> A revival of religion as an adjunct to daily living and daily health is thrilling through the churches. Its converts are holding aloft the Bible, with its record of the practice of a Great Physician. Almost any Sunday now in your own church you may hear of divine healing....The last general convention of the Episcopal Church, the denomination that is the most established and conservative of all, indorsed the efficacy of prayer as an instrument in the cure of disease....If the new idea hasn't yet reached your town, it's as sure to as the radio that arrived a year or so ago....Catch your breath. Do you get what's going round? It's the old-time religion, with a new content that makes it as secular as it is sacred!
>
> Christ, the Redeemer of the world from sickness as well as from sin: a faith as valuable for here as for the hereafter....Christians formerly were wont to 'confess' a religious experience. But these new converts want to shout theirs...They're as enthusiastic about it as an archaeologist who might have turned up a lost art of a buried civilization....It is more than a creed that now confronts Christianity. It is a custom. The healing crusade that is sweeping over America is challenging the attention of excited throngs as watched the aeroplanes ten years ago. The religious world is divided in opinion about the manifestation.[44]

Daggett concludes her article with the following challenge to her reader: "Does Christ still heal? ... See! From the cook's cousin to the society lady and the man in the street, there's a shining in their faces, there's radiance in their whole personality. Something has happened to them."[45]

Aimee had been born for this moment. No one else would ever take "the old-time religion," add new content and unite the secular with the sacred better than she did. From Baltimore on, it became the very essence of her ministry. It also defined Pentecostalism and delineated the differences between the new American Revivalism and that of the older variety. Billy Sunday represented the old, which was "out," while Aimee represented the new, which was "in." And only Aimee had the gift of healing. It was a gift Billy Sunday envied but never acquired. Fundamentalists, for sure, had the "old-time religion." What they lacked, however, was the new content of spiritual gifts. More than anything else it was the new content of spiritual gifts (including glossolalia and healing) that prevented the merger of the two movements. For years they were parallel movements of second cousins until Pentecostalism merged with the new evangelicalism in the 1940s. No religion better suited "the Jazz Age." It was "as if something by an unknown composer, powerful and strange and strong, was about to be played for the first time….this was new and confusing, nothing one could shut off in the middle and supply the rest from an old score."[46]

No denomination would define the "new content" better than the Episcopal Church. Unlike more fundamentalist denominations, its history of openness to the new content of spiritual gifts would lead to an acceptance of Pentecostalism, under the guise of Charismatic Renewal, in the 1960s. But even by the mid-1920s they concluded that interest in the spiritual gift of healing was strong "especially among the laity… Christian Healing is an outstanding fact of contemporary religious thought and … throughout the world, Spiritual Healing is no longer the hope of a few, but the belief and practice of a large and rapidly increasing number of persons … Healing is an experience of mankind that can no longer be questioned."[47]

Although Aimee had been accepted by many in Pentecostalism, the truth is she was very much overshadowed, especially in the East, by healers in the established Protestant churches. She had been fishing for "minnows" within the narrow confines of Pentecostalism. Now it was time to fish for "whales" found in the Protestant mainline churches.

Dominating the ministry of healing in the Eastern established churches was James Moore Hickson, an Episcopal layman who began his healing ministry in America in 1919 at Trinity Chapel in New York City with the encouragement and endorsement of Bishop William T. Manning, the Episcopal churchman whom Billy Sunday admired the most. During Aimee's stay in Baltimore at the Lyric Theatre, Hickson dominated the newspaper headlines with stories of remarkable healings emerging out of his meetings at Grace and St. Peter's Episcopal Church:

> It seemed that Baltimore had become a city of broken hearts, a city of the afflicted from who all hope of being made whole except through Christ Himself, had passed. The blind, the deaf, the mute were there; and many children, who like the man of Lystra that had been "a cripple from his mother's womb." And all sought healing from Him that had promised rest to the weary and heavy laden, through the medium of a man who, outwardly, is such as one sees on the streets of any city the thousands every day.[48]

James Moore Hickson was as ordinary and common as Aimee Semple McPherson was dynamic and extraordinary. Perhaps it took Hickson's "commonplace features" and temperament to gain credibility for a ministry in "the denomination that is the most established and conservative of all," as Mabel Daggett characterized the Protestant Episcopal Church.[49] "He is," wrote a first-generation Alliance leader and theologian on healing, "a strange contradiction of what one would expect to find in one dedicated to such a work":

> Instead of a mystic, clothed in monastic garb, with pale face and deeply spiritual visage, we look upon a typical Englishman, in a conventional business suit, large in frame, stocky in appearance, with deep-set eyes, florid complexion, black hair and commonplace features. He would pass in a crowd for a commercial agent or a stockbroker. No one would deem him the man that he is.[50]

Hickson also, like Aimee, made his way to Los Angeles in early 1920 where he held healing meetings at Immanuel Presbyterian Church.

The conclusion that Aimee reached while in Baltimore, "to fish for whales," was a very natural one. It was born as much out of the times as it was her desire to bring the Pentecostal message "across the tracks" and into the mainstream of American religious life and thought. The real question Aimee was dealing with while in Baltimore was whether Pentecostalism would remain, in sociological language, within the "sect" or "cult" category or enter the Protestant mainstream as a conservative, enthusiastic but evangelical force within the Christian Church. The openness of the churches to her ministry and the endorsement by the Episcopal Church of the concept of Christian healing must have undoubtedly convinced her it was time to join the "mainstream." In four months time, by the spring of 1920, she could joyfully write to her faithful readers:

Doors—doors—doors—open doors on every hand, ever opening wider…He has opened the doors of the cities, sending thousand upon thousands…He has opened the doors of great theaters, swept the actors from the stage…He has opened the doors of the churches, and the heart of the clergy wide to the truths long untaught…The door of denominational barriers has opened… in the past three months alone dozens of urgent invitations have been extended asking two, three and four weeks' campaigns…He has opened the doors of the Associated Press, newspaper syndicates and city papers…He has opened the doors of dance halls …and in the stillness delivered the message of the King who had sent me through the open door.[51]

During 1920 doors also opened for Aimee in three Canadian cities: Winnipeg, Lethbridge, and Montreal. Winnipeg quickly became the most noted among her Canadian campaigns and it had nothing to do with conducting healing services. During her five-week stay in the city another door, a secular door, opened wide for Aimee that had previously been closed to her ministry, most likely due to Minnie. (Beginning in 1927, however, on the heels of her "kidnapping," Aimee frequently sought out these secular open doors in the many cities she visited.) Janice Dickin of the University of Calgary contends that "It was the Winnipeg revival that [was] the most important among her Canadian campaigns…because Aimee started there her practice of touring nightclubs to advertise her meetings, something for which she would become famous—and eventually infamous."[52]

The strongest barrier remaining in Aimee's path of "open doors," especially to the denominational churches, had to do with the issue of "speaking in tongues" (glossolalia) in public meetings. The history of Protestantism has been a long one of denominational rivalry and schism. And it was the "tongues issue," even more than the emphasis upon healing, that created the first Mason-Dixon Line as to how American Christians felt about Pentecostalism. It was the "tongues issue" that gave rise to the "Holy Ghoster" and "Holy Roller" stereotype of the movement, thereby helping to place it in the great catch-all category of "cult." If the healing aspect of Aimee's revivalism "opened doors," the "tongues issue" quickly and quietly closed others. If glossolalia troubled the outsiders, it gave equal consternation to many insiders. To those on the inside, its usage was not so much a matter of "right" or "wrong" as it was "when." The appropriateness of the New Testament gift became for the Pentecostal community, as it did for the early church, more a matter of etiquette. Early on a division arose among Pentecostals themselves about the public or private manifestation of the spiritual gift. Throughout her early ministry, Aimee had ecstatically and enthusiastically made glossolalia a hallmark of her meetings. Now she began to shift her stance on the subject as she began "fishing for whales" and as her meetings became larger and her "doors" opened wider.

The "speaking in tongues" issue was for Aimee the most difficult theological tight rope she had to walk in the course of her ministry. Because of her growing modification of the public manifestation of glossolalia, beginning in Baltimore, she left herself vulnerable to attack from within the movement. By 1922, the largest Pentecostal denomination, the Assemblies of God, would ask in an editorial in *The Pentecostal Evangel,* "Is Mrs. McPherson Pentecostal?"—tantamount to asking one of the movement if they were still a believer or a Christian.[53]

Despite all the attacks from Pentecostals, Aimee never turned from the course she had begun in Baltimore. By the time of the emergence of her own Pentecostal denomination, she would remind her membership that "the Foursquare Gospel teaches a sane, balanced Gospel …we want the power, but power under control…that is the difference between this Foursquare Gospel and some who may call themselves 'Pentecostal.' Do not confuse the Foursquare Gospel with Holy Rollers."[54] She would also at times muse out loud at Angelus Temple to a young secretary, who doubled at times as a temporary hairdresser, prior to the Sunday evening service that "Unless I go out there and speak in tongues—tonight—there will be some who will say, 'Sister McPherson isn't Pentecostal.' "[55]

American "majority" (insider) and "minority" (outsider) religions have always had a kind of see-saw effect upon each other. What one lacks in spirit or special doctrine, the other has in respectability and acceptability. Through time and the continual see-sawing back and forth it seems that both sides in the process learn much from each other, with both becoming affected and modified by the other until a kind of balance of neutrality— or at least a lack of hostility—is achieved. Many times in history roles are reversed. Many minority outsiders become the new majority insiders. The formal mainline is relegated to the sideline. Pentecostalism, for all its early noisy protest, much like its Methodist step-parent, has always enjoyed its upward mobility and respectability. It may have started poor, but it never took a vow of poverty. Aimee seems unique, however, among early Pentecostals in sensing the inevitability of such a drift. She alone was the doorkeeper to the future. The path that she chartered most Pentecostals would eventually follow. Like her father, James the master bridge-builder, Aimee bridged the chasm between the Pentecostal missions and the denominational churches, between evangelism and entertainment, and the perceived impossible gulf between the sacred and the secular.

The method that Aimee often chose to keep her services more orderly was to either have an usher remove the source of the disturbance, or as her first pianist recalled, attempt to drown out the outburst by having those in attendance stand and sing "something like 'Nearer my God, to Thee.'"[56] One of the first interruptions Aimee stopped occurred in the Baltimore meeting. She thought the woman who was disturbing the meeting to be "out of order" and later discovered "the woman proved to be a maniac who had been in an asylum…Yet, this was the kind of woman many of the saints would have allowed to promenade the platform and disgust the entire audience—fearing lest they quench the Spirit."[57]

When Aimee revised her first book, she made a special point of the Baltimore meetings:

> Looking backward, I can see that this meeting marked a turning point not only in my own ministry but in the history of the outpouring of Pentecostal power. Yet at the time (so far as I know) not one of the dear Pentecostal people understood the vision God had given me, and severely criticized what they called a 'quenching of manifestations.'[58]

Minnie Kennedy's remembrances of the Baltimore meetings were equally perceptive if not more so than her daughter's. She reflected on not only the churches' reaction to the three-week meetings but also how they were treated by the press:

> So intense was the interest in ministerial circles that before the campaign closed, several invitations came to return and conduct campaigns in their churches…It has never been and is not our purpose to lay any special emphasis on the matter of Divine Healing…However, the newspapers rather took the matter out of our hands at this time, and insisted upon giving great prominence to this phase of our ministry. It was also surprising to note that the paper devoting the most space to this subject was under Catholic government. We are somewhat amused and our hearts pity the new generation of evangelists who in their anxiety to attract large throngs advertise in a sensational manner a Divine Healing program… Thus it was that aristocratic Baltimore was swept by the power of God. He had sent us to "fish for whales!" We had obeyed His will and the whales had come tumbling onto the decks of the Gospel ship in an almost unbelievable manner.[59]

The churches and the secular press of Baltimore continued to debate the concept of faith healing long after Aimee Semple McPherson and James Moore Hickson had moved on to other cities. Aimee, through the power of the printed page, was emerging in the public consciousness now not so much as "a female Billy Sunday" but more as a healer. And it was the subject of healing after the Baltimore meetings that was hotly debated both from the pulpit and in the printed page. Following the Baltimore meetings, an eminent English physician and writer, Sir Arthur Newsholme, delivered a lecture at the Johns Hopkins School of Hygiene and Public Health and publicly attacked the work and efforts of both healers. "During the last week, in a city church and in a city theater in Baltimore, spectacles of attempted faith-healing of organic disease have been seen, which, unless adequately safeguarded, will be followed by (a) serious increase of physical suffering in our midst."[60]

The most articulate response to the physician's charges in *The Baltimore Sun* came from the Reverend Henry Pryor Almon Abbott, rector of Grace and St. Peter's Protestant Episcopal Church. Abbott was a central figure in the healing movement within the Episcopal Church. He served on the commission that reported to the General Convention on the subject and eventually became the second bishop of Lexington. After Hickson left his parish, Abbott ran a three-column by seven-inch church ad in the *Sun* stating that the healing mission begun in his parish by Hickson would continue on under his ministry. Other church ads also appeared, mostly Episcopal, announcing sermon subjects as "The Healing Function of the Church" and "The Revival of Healing."[61]

Abbott, in his lengthy treatment of the subject under the headline of "Christ Healing Does Not Render Physician Unnecessary," offered a history of Christian healing, arguing that it was and still is a legitimate part of the Christian tradition. He felt that there was no inherent conflict between this ministry of the church and medical science. "It is right that the sick person should visit or be visited by the physician, but it is also right that the sick person should visit God's house or be visited by God's accredited ambassadors."[62] Abbott also attacked Christian Science because of its denial of "the reality of sin and disease," saying that it has "lived through the church's neglect."[63] Abbott then looked to the more orthodox Christian reader for their sympathetic cooperation:

> May we not, then, expect the sympathy, and look for the cooperation of all orthodox and spiritually minded Christians in the effort to revive the church's healing ministry?...Here is the opportunity for the church...to be a real factor in the satisfaction of the needs, material and spiritual of our day and generation.[64]

It was this deep-seated hunger in post-World War I America for the unification of the material and spiritual, of the sacred and profane, that Aimee would uniquely fill with her ever increasing cooperative interdenominational spirit and forthcoming endorsement by various mainline churches and clergymen. After the Baltimore meetings, Aimee would mention to followers that "great interest" had occurred in the meetings, "both in worldly and spiritual circles."[65] For the next three years she would become the symbol of a growing spirituality with an emphasis upon healing and of a mounting conservative Christian unity as she barnstormed America in key cities, taking over state armories, municipal auditoriums, and city theaters for "her King." Depending on the location, crowds would range in size from between three to sixteen thousand individuals.[66]

For the next three years she would never work harder, seem happier, and enjoy so easy an acceptance and so much success in the religious world. It was not that America had run short on preachers, nor even of women ministers. [Agnes] Maude Royden, England's famous preacher, the first woman to preach in an established Anglican church, also toured the United States in the early 1920s, speaking primarily in Episcopal and Congregational churches, at such women's colleges as Mount Holyoke and Wellesley, and being entertained in New York City by the likes of Mrs. John D. Rockefeller, Jr. The Unitarian churches had a relative abundance of women ministers, many co-pastoring with their spouses (similar to what was occurring within Pentecostalism) until the advent of the Great Depression. A set of factors came together at the right place at the right time, culminating in Aimee possessing and pastoring one of the largest postwar church edifices in America. Over the next three years she was beginning to symbolize more and more the coming together of the sacred and profane in America's religious life. She was a woman preacher becoming known as well as a healer. However, she would also preach in a prizefight arena, drop Gospel tracts out of an open cockpit of an aeroplane, speak from the rear decks of crowded Pullman cars like a politician, dominate headlines like few of Hollywood could, and, in general, create an interest in a subject that had gone sour with the average American. Evangelical Protestantism, America's folk religion, through Aimee's revivalism would become popular again with the masses. It was still the "old-time religion" all right, but it was happy and joyous with a "new content." This time it would be maternal, have a hint of glamour with a twinge of Hollywood, and rival baseball and a Sunday afternoon drive in an open automobile for popular acceptance in what was fast becoming modern America.

"The sermon is a peculiarly rich art form in America, a country that is secular in its head but theological in its heart," observes the writer David M. Shribman. "The sermon was the original and maybe the finest, American theatrical form."[67] By combining the skills of both preacher and actor

Aimee would later bring together in Los Angeles entertainment and evangelicalism and create in the process a secular-spirituality.

CHAPTER TEN

Spiritual Healing in American Protestantism: Popular Religious Culture and High Church Culture

> Those who are true disciples of Jesus exercise in his name a healing ministry according to the gift which each has received from him.
>
> —Irenaeus (About AD 180)

> The ideas of Christian churches are not efficacious in the therapeutic direction to-day, whatever they may have been in earlier centuries.
>
> —William James

> Healing is *central at the depth of human consciousness*—at the depth of its human pole…Healing, along with the loss of self in sex, is the best physical act a human being can do. Of all religious acts, healing is the most innocent, the most often miraculous, the most often desired.
>
> —Edith Turner

The year 1906 was pivotal for the rise of spiritual healing within Protestant Christianity in the United States. What tends to be forgotten in its rise and evolution is that spiritual healing was not limited to the people's religion and popular culture of Pentecostalism. Spiritual healing not only made its debut among a handful of African-Americans in a tumbledown shack reminiscent of "Bethlehem's barn" in a rundown semi-industrial area of Los Angeles composed of a tombstone shop, saloons, livery stables, and railroad freight yards, but it also made an appearance on the East Coast at Emmanuel Episcopal Church in Boston's fashionable Back Bay. In 1906 spiritual healing was found not only on both coasts of the country but also on both ends of the spectrum of American Protestantism itself. It flourished within the popular culture of Pentecostalism and also within the high culture of the established Episcopal Church. The so called "Emmanuel Movement," a name coined by the press, was derived from the fact that for twenty-three years "the movement had its center at Emmanuel Episcopal Church in Boston."[1] Like its popular Pentecostal counterpart, the Emmanuel Movement also spread like wildfire from coast to coast and even to other countries. And both movements had their leaders: William J. Seymour in Los Angeles and the Reverend Dr. Elwood Worcester in Boston.

Worcester's upbringing in Rochester was a universe apart from Seymour's, who was the son of slaves and raised on a sugar-cane plantation in the deep South. Despite his affluence and education at Columbia University, General Theological Seminary, and Leipzig, Germany, Worcester was no stranger to sorrow. When not yet seventeen years old Worcester lost his "adored father" to pneumonia and with him his "world came to an end."[2] Within a year, Worces-

The Reverend Elwood Worcester, founder of the Emmanuel Movement (author's collection).

ter's mother had not only lost her husband and her eyesight, but the family fortune as well. Worcester's remaining family members, his three sisters, all "died violent deaths."[3] His sister Mary perished in the great Galveston flood. When his sister Lina learned she would lose her sight like her mother she "ended her life on earth by a pistol-shot."[4] Finally, his beloved sister Elizabeth, his "last living relative," ended her "marked fluctuations of emotional feeling" and "protracted periods of depression . . . . by leaping from a window on the fourteenth floor of a New York hotel."[5]

"Almost from my ordination," wrote Worcester, "I had been dissatisfied with the quality of a large part of the work of the church and of a minister's life."[6]

> As a student of the New Testament and of early church history, I knew that something valuable had been lost from the Christian religion, and that Christianity had not always been so unsuccessful in its appeal to human nature as it is now. What has been lost is chiefly Jesus Christ, the Gospel of a Saviour's love, and a religion of the Spirit and of Power. A sense of this loss brought me to the healing ministry of Jesus, in which we come most directly into contact with his personality, his compassion, his understanding of his mission. It is customary for rationalists... to make light of this portion of the Saviour's life, to look down upon

it with contempt from their superior height of modern medicine, to explain away these lovely, touching stories as tales…If anything is true in our life of Jesus…these acts of healing the sick in mind and body must be included as among its most certain elements….This, then was my first and greatest thought…faith in the healing ministry of Christ and the conviction that many of its saving elements could be reproduced today.[7]

"In my early days in Boston," remembered Worcester, "Emmanuel was the outstanding Episcopal church of the city."[8] And it was also everything the Azusa Street Mission in Los Angeles was not. "In the beauty of its architecture and its music…in the numbers and quality of its people, it had no equal. Trinity, after the election of Phillips Brooks to the Episcopate…was undergoing an eclipse….It was at Emmanuel that almost everything interesting happened….It was the church of the elite."[9]

Worcester was equally clear about his mission at Emmanuel. "The church that surrenders to the lure of economic and social reform and forgets that her commission is first and foremost to man as a spiritual being will eventually be found to have betrayed the cause of religion and humanity."[10] Despite his later fame as a healer of bodies, Worcester always viewed his ministry and the larger movement "primarily in spiritual terms" and as "a reintroduction of 'healing ministry of Jesus' into the church."[11]

At first Worcester confined his "healing ministry of Jesus" to tuberculosis victims in the Boston slums. Buoyant with success from his "Tuberculosis Class," he moved to undertake service "to a larger group of unhappy, unstable men and women, to persons suffering from psychical and nervous affections…and to the victims of injurious habits such as alcoholism and other drug addictions."[12] Before undertaking his new project, Worcester consulted with "a number of the foremost neurologists, psychiatrists, surgeons and other physicians in Boston, New York and Baltimore….Had their support been refused I should have gone no further, as I should not have dreamed of taking responsibility for the sick without proper medical oversight and co-operation."[13]

Worcester realized that his approach was new, radically new for spiritual healing and science to cooperate. "There was much in this project which was radically new and original, chiefly that educated men, university scholars and critical students of the Bible had been willing to undertake it, and that they had induced scientifically trained physicians to work with them. In the history of 'Spiritual Healing' that had not happened before…"[14] And in the words of one historian, "It was unquestionably this novel feature that gave the Emmanuel Movement its importance."[15] Worcester's successors not only continued his methods but also employed group treatment, being the first to use psychotherapy in the treatment of alcoholics.[16]

When Elwood Worcester wrote his autobiography, *Life's Adventure,* in 1932, he felt that the movement he founded "showed how it was possible for science and religion to co operate, that physicians and clergymen may be allies, and we helped to bring the personality and the mission of Jesus nearer to men, while to the clergy we showed a better way than committee meetings and sewing circles to minister to the spiritual needs of their congregations. When Jesus sent forth his disciples, he did not say, 'Talk, agitate questions, hold midnight meetings for infants,' but 'Heal the sick, cast out devils.' "[17]

In his autobiography Worcester admitted he was also grateful that the Emmanuel Movement was not "forced out of the Episcopal Church." Had that happened he believed that they would have "had no trouble... in gathering another large congregation in Boston [and] acquiring a dignified place of worship and work." The downside of a separatist movement for Worcester would have been in the creation of "another despicable and short-lived sect (a thing abhorrent to me) and we [would] have enhanced our own importance and fame (another vanity.)[18]

At the end of his ministry, Worcester not only felt vindicated but believed that his ministry had also been affirmed by the Episcopal Church.

> I have no claim to be a prophet but I have noticed this...fact: every new truth which touches life and human interest must live through a period when it is hated before it arrives at the period when it is loved. The world will stifle the voices of the prophets if it can, and only those prophets who refuse to be stifled, but who for years on end go on tenderly, savagely, patiently reiterating their message, at last have their way and are believed.... Without any propaganda, the idea has slowly grown and the legitimacy of 'Spiritual healing,' surrounded by the safeguards we imposed, has been definitely recognized by the Church of England and by our own Church through the action of the last General Convention.[19]

Finally, Worcester was grateful for "the great reward" that his "ministry of redemption" had brought to him, personally.

> The great reward that this ministry of redemption has brought to me has been admission to the sacred places of innumerable lives. Scattered all over this country, I have an invisible congregation consisting...of men

and women I shall never see again, but whom I know or once knew in a sense that no one else knows them. This great, shadowy group forms a very peculiar background to my thought and consciousness. I like to think of them as a cloud of unseen witnesses to the fact that, with all my limitations, faults and weaknesses, I did for them what I could.... The science of psychology will continue to develop. Many a secret of the human heart, unknown or partially known to us, will be made plain. More light on the life and thought of Jesus will continue to flow in. Other men will arrive more richly endowed, more perfectly equipped, stronger in character, higher, purer, nobler to undertake this great ministry to souls, which we, in modern times, began. But it will not be today nor tomorrow that an effort will be made which will be continued by one man so long or with such singleness of purpose as the work begun in Emmanuel Church in the autumn of 1906.[20]

Another man, seemingly "more richly endowed," did arrive as an Anglican layman—James Moore Hickson. Beginning in March 1919 in the United States and ending in New Zealand in April 1924, Hickson conducted a five-year worldwide healing crusade. During those five years Hickson personally prayed for and laid his hands on a quarter of a million people. As a contemporary of Aimee, Hickson, again as an Anglican, represented the high culture of spiritual healing while Aimee represented the popular and by now firmly entrenched middle class version of Pentecostalism.

What Elwood Worcester, James Moore Hickson, and other Episcopal healers set in motion led to the most exhaustive and sophisticated study of spiritual healing by an American denomination. At the General Convention of the Protestant Episcopal Church held in Portland, Oregon in 1922, a commission was appointed "to consider the fuller recognition of the Ministry of Healing in the church and the need of its revival under proper sanctions and safeguards."[21] The commission was headed by Bishop Boyd Vincent of Ohio and in addition to the bishops and ordained Episcopal clergymen, it included Dr. Winford H. Smith, director of Johns Hopkins University, a Dr. Cowles of New York. and a Dr. Lucas of San Francisco, both medical doctors. In 1922 the commission affirmed "that the body no less than the spirit of man was included in the work of Redemption; that the restoration of harmony of man's mind and will with the Divine Will often brings with it the restoration of the body; that the full power of the church's corporate intercession in this connection has been too little realized; and that confidence in the efficacy of prayer for restoration of health has not been sufficiently encouraged."[22]

With similar affirmations the commission with great wisdom also affirmed the advances being made by medical science:

The Church must not lose sight of the other truth that medical science is the handmaid of God…She must be thankful for all progress made in medicine, surgery, nursing, hygiene and sanitation. She must believe that all these means of healing and preventing disease and removing suffering are gifts that come from God and are to be used faithfully also for the welfare of mankind. Experience as well as reason shows that the best results are to be expected where there is a cordial cooperation of the pastor and doctor, with the patient's perfect faith in the value of ministrations of both.[23]

The value placed on medical science by the Episcopal Commission greatly separated it from the common attitude held by most Pentecostals toward the medical community. Pentecostals, more in keeping with folk religion, viewed the medical community as well as most institutions of higher learning at best with a benign indifference. Healing for the vast majority of them was theological in nature—waiting by their pools of Bethesda for an angel to trouble the water, giving rise in later years to such Pentecostal songs of protest as "The Healing Waters."

Oh, the joy of sins forgiv'n,
Oh, the bliss the blood-washed know,
Oh, the peace akin to Heav'n,
Where the healing waters flow.

Where the healing waters flow,
Where the joys celestial glow,
Oh, there's peace and rest and love,
Where the healing waters flow!

For many American Pentecostals it would take as long as the 1960s for the healing tents to fold and giving way to hospital beds and for the medical community to be fully accepted. Oral Roberts would provide the symbol with his now defunct City of Faith—a hospital where prayer and medicine "joined hands together" providing an image with the tall bronze folded hands outside the hospital like the proverbial lion and lamb lying down together in peace at long last. And that image still prevails among most Pentecostals today.

The Episcopal Commission met again at the following triennium convention held in New Orleans in 1925. Again, they re-affirmed that "Religious, mental and material means for cure must go hand in hand in ministry to the sick. It is often difficult to indicate clearly where the one leaves off and the other begins."[24] Theologically, the commission reported to the convention that the entire ministry of healing within the church was always predicated upon "Divine Will" and that the "failure to be healed in certain cases is not to be construed as an evidence of a lack of faith."[25]

The major concern the commission faced with the movement in 1925 was whether to keep the movement within the church:

> We are challenged as to whether we shall allow this essentially Christian Ministry to be sought outside the Church, or whether we are to make it a normal part of the Church's life. We must see to it that we do not afford an occasion for another separatist movement. This can best be prevented by frankly recognizing that the Healing Ministry is normal to the life of the Church. In this way we continue the ministry of Christ who revealed Himself as Healer of body and soul.[26]

The Episcopal Commission in 1925 was caught as in no other time between the proverbial rock and a hard place. They noted that "especially among the Laity, [there is] a rapidly increasing desire that the Church confirm the belief that there is therapeutic value in the Christian religion. This shows that Christian Healing is an outstanding fact of contemporary religious thought."[27]

They were faced with the double dilemma between the popularity of the faith healing concept, which threatened to take many of the laity outside the church, creating yet another denomination, or as the committee termed it "another separatist movement"—a disgrace to the ideal of Christian unity that has all too often fallen short of reality. On the other side of the coin was the fear of creating dissension among those who remained faithful to the Episcopal church and had taken an active role on the commission. This threat was realized when a committee member, Edward S. Cowles, M.D., director of the Park Avenue Hospital of New York City, issued a minority report to the convention entitled "Religion and Medicine in the Church." What Cowles argued against in his ninety-three page document was the concept of "miraculous healing" and/or "supernatural healing." His first three recommendations to the Church spelled out very clearly his fears of where he perceived his denomination was headed:

> 1. That the Protestant Episcopal Church of America renounce and denounce superstition, and remove it from her body, root, stem and branch.
> 2. That the Church recognize and openly declare that there is no such thing as miraculous healing today.
> 3. That the Canons of the Church be so revised that any bishop, priest

or layman, teaching or preaching miraculous healing in any of its guises, may be regarded and treated as one who has committed a crime against the laws of the Church, of religion, and of society.[28]

The General Convention in great wisdom decided to carry the commission on to the next triennium. Although the Episcopal church acted with much prudence and deliberation, as do most institutions having a long history, the average American desirous of a church endorsing such a concept as faith healing most likely looked elsewhere. The Episcopal church's fear of giving "an occasion for another separatist movement" in many ways became realized through the independent ministry of an Aimee Semple McPherson and her subsequent denomination, The International Church of the Foursquare Gospel, where the concept of Christ as healer was the third major tenet of the new denomination. Although much of the American religious establishment would write off Pentecostalism as the "lunatic fringe" of organized religion, the strength and power of such a movement is seen in the truth that Charles W. Ferguson so clearly stated: "It is in the babble of isms that religious life best expresses itself, for there the people have expressed their discontent with the standard forms of religion and take the reigns in their own hands."[29]

By the 1928 general convention held in Washington, D.C., the committee on healing met again, after having collected data relating to those who claimed "divine healing." The data came from many sources: local churches, the experience of missionaries on foreign fields of service, and Christian communities and societies such as the Society of the Nazarene, established in 1909 by the Reverend Henry B. Wilson, an Episcopal clergyman serving St. John's Church in Boonton, New Jersey. The commission in 1928 studying such data found "little uniformity in the outward forms that this widespread belief in Spiritual Healing takes in actual practice, but it finds that the belief itself is deep, sincere and helpful to those who hold it."[30]

The committee, again, as it did earlier, affirmed cooperation with "medical science and practice" as well as recommending "that the Theological schools (Episcopal) in their teaching give increased attention to the whole subject of 'The Cure of Souls,' emphasizing prayer as an expression of a living rather than of a formal faith."[31]

The Committee on Christian Healing gave its final report to the General Convention in 1931:

> Nine years have elapsed since the original formation of the Commission. During these years a large number of people in the Church have

manifested great and enduring interest in the subject under consideration. Many parish priests throughout the country have carried on a ministry to the sick in mind and body. Several societies have been working for years in this field and the whole Church has now the benefit of their experience…There is no doubt in the minds of your Commission about this modern health movement in the Church. It has come to stay. The ministry of healing is, as we have insisted, an inherent part of the pastoral office of the Church.[32]

The committee also attempted in 1931 to grapple theologically with the concept of divine healing—a most difficult matter:

> The whole movement must be based upon a sound, true, practical mysticism, that is, upon the truth that we can come into conscious, intimate fellowship with God, the Eternal Spirit. The fact of an ever present union with God can be lifted up into consciousness. We may actually experience God; we may have an immediate sense of the Supreme Reality; we may know that "Christ is our life." If this truth of God in Christ is kept primary, there will be no danger of going off on tangents nor of over- emphasizing the truth of spiritual healing, nor of exalting "healers," nor of adopting any peculiar methods to teach the Gospel to the sick.[33]

What the committee on healing also sought to emphasize in their report to the General Convention in 1931 was the concept of "wholeness" and "holistic" approaches to the subject, which by the late 1970s and early 1980s would become American buzzwords in both sacred and secular contexts:

> The primary stress of a constructive movement must be placed on "health," and not on "healing." The word "health" means "wholeness." It covers every part of a man's being, body, mind, and spirit, all of which are to be brought into harmonious relationship with each other. The whole man is to be made healthful.[34]

Although questions of legitimacy about the subject of spiritual healing would continue to rise within American Christianity in future decades— most notably during the 1960s—the theological debate by the Episcopal church during the 1920s undoubtedly remains one of the more definitive theological statements formulated on the subject by an American church. More importantly, the Episcopal church proved to the rest of American Protestantism, badly fragmented and divided during the 1920s, that its theological tent was inclusive and large enough to embrace such a concept in the first place. It is of little wonder then, that Aimee was attracted to the Episcopal church more than any other American denomination. Fittingly, her own future denomination would be birthed in an Episcopal parish house.

CHAPTER ELEVEN

Barnstorming America and Building a House as unto the Lord

You can't laugh Aimee McPherson off. Once you come beneath the spell of her personality you're lost.

We don't mean that you are bowled over to her exact method of expressing her religion; we don't mean that her fervent evangelism can meet the exacting taste of the intellectual or the critical; we don't mean that the modernists once having viewed Aimee, once having sat beneath the spell of her magnetic personality can accept Christianity exactly as she defines it—BUT, if you're a reasoning human being it seems to us you must accept Aimee Semple McPherson as sincere, as devout, and as burdened with the convictions of Jesus Christ as she says she is.

To begin with, Aimee is beautiful, really beautiful, and she is artistic. The very tips of her fingers are eloquent with artistry. Her uniform, spotless white with broad shining smooth collar and soft tie tipped at the ends ever so slightly with pink, the black of her flowing cape against the whiteness of her uniform, her white stocking and slippered feet, and the soft pile of her magnificent hair as radiantly marcelled as though she had just stepped from the hands of the hair dresser, her appealing eyes and the face that expresses every thought—all the studied ensemble of the artist…And the voice. Dramatic, of course. Winning, pleading, triumphant, running the entire gamut of emotion in an instant from ecstasy to woe… all the subtle artistry of the finished actress belongs to Aimee.

It is a delight to watch her. And all this, to our mind, simply goes to prove the sincerity of the woman. With her personality she could be a world renowned actress, she could earn thousands of dollars in a dozen fields of endeavor—and with half the energy, with half the agonizing strain of mind and nerve.

We can't believe that she would choose the exacting life of an evangelist but for her great sincerity.

—*Des Moines Register-Tribune*
July 13, 1920

A Catholic priest in New Jersey, Father O'Connor, wrote at least two hit songs in early modern America, "Let a Smile be Your Umbrella" and "Little Grey Home in the West." The latter is how Aimee chose to describe her residence in Los Angeles that she only visited in between meetings. "Returning to the 'little grey home in the West' between each series of campaigns, to mother my babes and care for my publishing work, I often wondered just why the Lord had set the little home down in this far off part of the country making the homing journeys each so very long."[1]

Returning to the "little grey home in the West" in the "far off part of the country," was providential for Aimee for two reasons. California—Los Angeles in particular—represented the cutting edge of Pentecostalism. Contrary to its Appalachian snake-handling, Holy Roller stereotype, Pentecostalism thrived in the country's most progressive state. In 1924, the periodical of the Assemblies of God, *The Pentecostal Evangel*, asked their readers "What State Is Most Pentecostal?" The editor furnished the following information:

> To judge from the number of *Evangels* that we send to the different states, California takes first place. It will be remembered that in the annual missionary report, California was reported as sending in most missionary money. Every week we are sending 2,317 copies of the *Evangel* to California, Texas comes second on the list,…Missouri comes third…Illinois fourth…Oklahoma fifth…It will be seen that in the 900 class there are three states—Arkansas, Pennsylvania, and New York. We appear to be weakest in Delaware, Rhode Island, South Carolina, Utah, Vermont and Wyoming.[2]

Not only were there more Pentecostals in California, like everything else in the state the movement there represented the progressive, cutting edge. It is difficult to imagine Aimee's success anywhere else—especially in places like Missouri or Kansas. "The little grey home in the West" seemed also providential for Aimee when her ministry developed an international character in the 1930s. Southern California, as Carey McWilliams noted, "seems to be looking westward across the Pacific, waiting for the future that one can somehow sense, and feel, and see."[3] Not only was Los Angeles a Mecca for the miraculous but it also had growing international connections that few American cities, apart from New York, possessed.

By the time of a "Middle West Interstate Campaign" held in Dayton, Ohio's, Memorial Hall from May 2–23, 1920, interest in Aimee's ministry as a healer was at a fever pitch. A Methodist minister declared that "hungry hearts" had come "from all over the Middle West."[4] They came by train and automobile. They came in such numbers that public appeals had to be repeatedly made from the platform of Memorial Hall for Dayton residents to rent out their rooms during the revival. They came sick, lame, palsied and paralyzed, deaf and dumb, with bandaged appendages. The strongest came on their own power or with the aid of crutches, while others were carried or wheeled in on cots, stretchers, wheelchairs, even rocking chairs. Backs of strong men bore their sick burdens; mothers, their unhealthy children, always the stronger carrying the weaker. They came as Protestants, Catholics, and Jews.

By the time of the last healing service, Aimee was clearly in awe of what was occurring and attempted to describe her final day in Dayton to her readers. As she left her hotel suite by automobile she was unprepared for the throngs and masses that engulfed the streets and over flowed sidewalks waiting to get a glimpse, hopefully a touch from their Sister as she passed by en route to the meeting. The auditorium held three thousand, and during the course of the meetings at least that number was outside anxiously awaiting a chance at the next service. Memorial Hall itself was tightly encircled by street cars, autos, ambulances, and hearses unloading the ill and the infirm. Aimee's auto approached an unobtrusive side entrance and was instantly surrounded. Clutching hands went immediately toward her as she attempted to enter the side door. "Oh, Sister, just pray for this man." "Just touch me." "We have brought this child forty miles, surely you can see that we can get in."

Six policemen clear a path to the side door. They hold back the crowd with their burly arms and husky voices. Aimee notes the beads of perspiration on their strained faces and tears in some of their eyes. Going through the carriage entrance, she observes that even the basement is full,

> 'Tis filled with people, invalids, cripples, wheelchairs and comforting relatives standing by. Oh the... pleading agony in their eyes, the outreaching hands! "Will we ever forget that sight?" Guards were posted at the basement windows. Flat faces peered back through the glass. "We had to lock them, Sister. They were passing the sick through the windows," someone exclaims.[5]

She feels "dazed, as though in a dream" as she ascends the auditorium steps and located the ladies' cloak room—a hard right, off the stage. She gathers her thoughts briefly before she is bathed by the spotlight and the hush of hope that comes from a capacity house crowd.

For a moment all is still except for the movement of Mother Kennedy's nineteen special assistants—all women—visibly cutting through the crowd with their wide sashes of crimson ribbon, cheering and comforting the sufferers, making sure that not one seat is left vacant. Everyone is in place. The most broken in health occupy the space where the altar usually is. This afternoon the body will receive the attention the soul has over the past three weeks. Finally the time has come. The pianist walks out to center stage, opens the keyboard on the grand piano, and begins to play the familiar hymn "Sweet Hour of Prayer." The choir and host ministers first kneel in prayer and then walk out onto the stage. Before she enters to offer the prayer of invocation, Aimee looks up, high into the arched dome and sees "soft rays of light streaming through the upper windows." She feels like she is on sacred ground. Memorial Hall has become a holy tabernacle. Aimee enters and hoarsely, breathlessly prays:

> O Thou Christ of God, thou compassionate Man of Calvary, Thou omnipotent Almighty King of Heaven and earth, Thou Son, who dispels all darkness, Thou Lion of Judah, who breaks every chain, Thou deliverer of the captive, Thou hope of the hopeless, and friend of the friendless...if ever we loved Thee, needed Thee, Trusted Thee, it is now. Weak, helpless, desperate, we hide, hide away in Thee.[6]

Aimee remembers "Wildly, our hearts throb up to Him in prayer. Sweetly the gentle calm of His Spirit falls o'er us like a mantle from the sky. The benediction of the Lord is resting upon our heads."[7]

She is better prepared for this hour than she realizes. The time of tents has provided for a severe but equally thorough apprenticeship. Her energy is much more focused now. No husband in the background or sidelines to worry about. No more tropical storms or fear of falling tent poles—she is safely surrounded by a structure of concrete and steel. Her mother is at her side. Even the audience/congregation is less-threatening, the great majority being just "regular Protestants," as one denominational newspaper described them. From Baltimore on, back alleys and storefronts have given way to the boulevards and municipal auditoriums. What once was considered a side show had quickly become a major event quietly flowing into the mainstream of American Christianity in the process. Undoubtedly a parade of pictures kaleidoscopically passes through her mind. One wonders if Robert Semple is among them. If so, part of the service will be rendered in his memory.

The congregation begins their participation in the service. Their hope mounts when those that can stand begin to sing the old hymn of faith, "What a friend we have in Jesus / All our sins and griefs to bear / All because we did not carry, / everything to God in prayer." They sing again another old hymn of Christo-centric faith. "Are you weary, are you heavy laden, / Tell it to Jesus, Tell it to Jesus...You have no other such a friend and brother, / Tell if to Jesus alone."

Aimee prays again and implores God to "Dry every tear, banish every pain, relieve the oppressed…As a Father pitieth his children, so Thou dost pity those that love and trust Thee. Give light in place of darkness. Give hope in place of fear. Give comfort and sweet confidence to each heart gathered in Thy presence."[8]

After a short "testimony meeting" Aimee launches into her text: "He was wounded for our transgressions. He was bruised for our iniquities; the chastisement of our peace was upon Him, and with His stripes we are healed." In a short and simple message Aimee tells her congregation that while on earth the chief business of Christ was in the forgiving of sin and in the healing of the sick. She argues that the two were not divided; but went hand in hand; a double cure. Pouring out her heart with her inimitable "vibrant contralto of the midway" she continues to preach, "None were too weak, too sinful, too sick or deformed for Jesus to love, cheer, comfort and heal…Now, Jesus is the same yesterday, today and forever! The things He loved to do when on this earth, He still loves to do today. His heart is still touched with compassion. His power is just the same."[9]

The message ends. An altar call is given and one half of the stage is cleared for the "divine healing service." Seven chairs are placed on the left side of the platform with their backs partially turned toward the audience. Before the chairs is a small table upon which rests a silver urn of anointing oil. A blackboard is also visible on the stage with seven erasable numbers. Seven sick individuals with numbers on printed cards matching those of the chalk numbers mount the platform steps in any way they can to the seven empty chairs. The cards have been distributed long before this special service in an attempt at equality. They are numbered in the order in which they were handed out. They ask the sufferer for their name, church or faith, and nature of disease. Aimee then with the assistance of the host ministers, in an attempt to duplicate New Testament Christianity, anoints the head of each with oil and prays, "In Jesus' Name" that they be made whole. "No sooner is one of the seven chairs vacated than it is filled again. On and on they come."[10]

The motion is broken only when one who is carried to one of the seats walks or dances away. The crowd goes wild as at a ball game. The choir sings "All hail the power of Jesus' name / Let angels prostrate fall. / Bring forth the royal diadem, / and crown him Lord of all." "What a scene it is," remembers Aimee. "Thousands of white handkerchiefs flutter and wave like heavenly doves on wide-spread pinions, and just to think that audience is made up of people from almost every creed and faith."[11]

The healing service continues on until Aimee has been on her feet for over six hours. "Our heads are almost swimming from the hours of constant tension, prayer, sympathy and emotions of joy and victory. We understand what the Master felt, when the Word declares, 'He was weary.'"[12] She finally, reluctantly leaves the stage at the insistence of her mother in order to change her clothes, eat, and prepare for yet another service. "Scores of sufferers" beg and plead for their Sister not to leave them, but Aimee is bodily carried out of the crowd and away from the clutching hands by her loyal band of workers. The car is not yet out of the parking lot before two men come running, approaching Aimee with an invalid in a rocker. Aimee prays, and the car lurches forward to its destination. The final healing service in Dayton, Ohio, by Aimee Semple McPherson has ended. The newspapers and those who were there will manage, however, to keep the events alive for months to come.

The denominational churches of Dayton were forced to deal with the meetings, if not during the event itself, then at least afterward. Regardless of their posture on the theological spectrum, there were results of Aimee's meetings that could not be denied or overlooked. With the Dayton meeting as with the others, the mainline clergy could not ignore that the largest auditoriums in the country could repeatedly be filled and as many as were inside were turned away from the closed doors. This was the age, they were told, in which religion would lose in competition with the movies and theaters. They were at odds among themselves to fully understand and comprehend what was occurring. It was as baffling as the original day of Pentecost. Some referred to the meetings as "a spiritual outbreak," while others referred to them as "some unusual manifestations." Most of the denominational clergymen who attended the meetings noted in retrospect the difference between Aimee's revivalism and that of the older variety. It seemed a welcomed contrast from the Billy Sunday meetings of yesterday as evidenced by the following denominational reports by two United Brethren ministers:

> There is not one-tenth the bustle of a Billy Sunday meeting, no coarse jokes—no spectacular things staged for effect—just the simple preaching of the simple gospel.
>
> I have attended, and worked in revival campaigns, conducted by some of the leading evangelists of the country, but never in my experience have I seen... meetings conducted with such sacred dignity as was demonstrated in those McPherson meetings. In most evangelistic campaigns... there is the constant appeal to the spectacular...But not so here! There was no advertising of a great chorus...no coarse jokes or spectacular display; and yet the crowds. Literally, thousands were turned away. And

what was the attraction? ...Was it the evangelist herself? She was just an unassuming little woman dressed in white....The thing peculiar to her...was the positive character of her ministry. She did not spend her time condemning preachers, nor holding up before the people the worst things of the world. She just kept on telling about Jesus...how great and abundant his love is.[13]

In late July 1920, at the conclusion of her meeting at Alton, Illinois, a battle-fatigued Aimee, well-worn from too much service for her "King" unknowingly exposes her Achilles' heel to her *Bridal Call* readers. It is her first mention of loneliness since her failed marriage to Harold—before the advent of her mother's arrival. It is but a dark shadow of things to come, for as F. Scott Fitzgerald wrote to his daughter in the last year of his life, "no Achilles' heel ever toughened by itself. It just gets more and more vulnerable."[14] Like the tragic Greek hero, Aimee is seemingly invincible except for a soft spot of vulnerability deep within. Like Achilles who dies from an arrow to the heel, Aimee endures all the harassments associated with the rise of a new religious movement and even at times significantly conquers the "enemy," but then slowly dies from within, falling victim to her ever-increasing, advancing armies of loneliness. When her final death occurs, it comes to her when she is alone in a downtown Oakland hotel room—after the successful opening night of yet another campaign for her "King." A close associate later remarked: "Her real death was from loneliness and a broken heart."[15]

That soft spot of vulnerability deep within Aimee—a gnawing, endless, aching need, which manifested itself most clearly in her deep devotion to God and others, was also Janus-faced. If it affected her ending, it equally altered her beginnings. The overwhelming response to her ministry, which by now was assuming an international dimension, was due to Aimee's ability to appeal to the "heartistic" side of her audiences and congregations. The ability to touch—even to heal—their brokenness and aching voids within was an accomplishment achieved for the most beyond the pale of organized religion.

"All one has to do," reminds Janice Dickin, of the University of Calgary, "is to look at advertisements of the era to be reminded that people lived in a world of constant pain beyond our imagining:"

Devices to hold in one's uterus, braces for cripples and jackets for hunchbacks are examples in kind. The more pervasive presence of pain also helps account for the amount of drug addiction at the time. The ranks of those addicts deemed to be "respectable" rather than "criminal" were being swollen by the injured from the war and many came to Aimee for help.....Neurotic symptoms can present symptoms of blindness or deafness or paralysis of some body part....Spiritual cure has more to offer such people than does medical treatment....The commitment of those seeking cure would have been supported by the passion of the crowd....People went to Aimee's meetings expecting to see cures....The psychologists of Aimee's heyday were focused on exactly the same thing she was: the spiritual well-being of the individual...Hers was a ministry of emotion, not intellect...it was a ministry of miracle.[16]

The Alton meetings had been very successful, not just for Aimee personally, but her audience had become more mainline Protestant as well. "Never in the history of the city," stated the *Alton Daily Times*, "has a woman attracted so much attention as Mrs. Aimee Semple McPherson, the female evangelist...The wonderful work of the woman is the talk of the town and the physicians, ministers and business men marvel at her ministry....The Jews, Gentiles, Catholics and Protestants are mingling together at these meetings...to be...cured of their diseases."[17]

The *Daily Times* reporter also noted Aimee's physical endurance following a six-hour "nerve-racking" healing effort. "How does Mrs. McPherson stand the physical strain?" asked the reporter.

> She was putting every particle of her strength into the effort...every atom of her being was working to the utmost....though she must have been tired and worn to the very brink of exhaustion, no indication was displayed. Those who scoff at her healing representations will do well to consider this. Her physical endurance is as equally remarkable as any case of healing that has yet occurred.[18]

On the editorial page of the August 1920 *Bridal Call*, Aimee revealed in utter frankness the human side to the "Miracle Woman" and "the little woman in white":

> The past three and a half months have been perhaps as busy as any we have ever known...Perhaps not one out of thousand of those who have seen the Evangelist ... smiling and singing up on the platform, have realized the loneliness and longing...Spiritually, the weeks flew like days, so much was to be done for Christ, but in the natural the days dragged leaden-footed like weeks, with longing for those wee loving arms, and the sound of childish voices—would the day ever come?[19]

The day of departure does come, coupled with a "dozen lengthy petitions signed by long rows of business men, and the city officials for the Chamber of Commerce begging us to continue the meetings just one more week…For four years the editor has never taken a month's vacation, but feels now definitely led to 'come apart and rest awhile.' "[20]

Aimee's next real vacation will come six years later at the height of her fame as pastor of America's largest "Class-A" Church. Upon her return, she would suddenly disappear the Monday after an eventful Sunday series of services. That disappearance would not only interrupt the popular nightly *Amos 'n' Andy* radio show with news bulletins but would transform "Aimee" into an American household word overshadowing "Sister" in the process and rattle Los Angeles upon its already shaky foundations like some unknown earthquake incapable of measurement.

The modern, fragmented metropolis of Los Angeles that emerged in the 1920s was something like a 367-square-mile jigsaw puzzle composed of jagged pieces of sprawling villages, parks, and places bearing names like Hancock Park, Boyle Heights, Elysian Valley, Arroyo Seco—all linked together by elaborate electric car lines, traversed over, cut through and ulti-mately surrounded by broad boulevards, avenues, and subsequent freeways. One of the jagged pieces of the puzzle, Echo Park was a thirty-one-acre municipal park situated in the hilly terrain a mile and a half northwest from the central business district. Narrowly bordering the park were Glendale Boulevard, Park Avenue, Echo Park Avenue, and Temple Street. The larger boundaries with time have become the Glendale and the Hollywood free-ways and Sunset Boulevard. The area in the 1920s was accessible by four electric railway lines.

The park itself contained an eight-acre body of water—the largest arti-ficial lake in the city—which was donated for park and reservoir purposes in 1891. In the 1870s the lake had provided water for adjacent farms and power for a woolen mill that stood at Sixth and Figueroa. By the 1920s the lake lapped at the shores of surrounding picnic grounds, provided boats for lovers and youngsters, and was home and shelter for waterfowl, Egyptian papyrus, water lilies, and lush lotus that sprang from the depths of its north-west arm every summer. The vegetation eventually destroyed the sound effect that had given the site its name. (An English landscape architect hired to lay the park out was also responsible for its name. One day, while shout-ing to his assistant, the only reply he received was an echo.)

Before the 1920s the area enjoyed an earlier period of growth from 1905 to 1918. Subdivisions occurred and houses appeared—mostly of Victo-rian style. Subdivisions increased, and single-family dwellings were created, having an average of one thousand square feet and painted for the most

"Oh, this is heaven," exclaimed mother and daughter when they found their pie slice-shaped lot in Echo Park (used by permission of the International Church of the Foursquare Gospel, Heritage Department).

part, "musk green." The "red car" trolley lines also invaded the area. With the 1920s came the area's second period of growth, chiefly of California Mission-Style homes, covered in stucco, moderate of size, and on the average, containing fifteen hundred square feet. Apartment complexes also filled in the vacant lots, constructed of brick or concrete and containing thirty to fifty unit dwellings each.[21]

As the large Silver Lake-Echo Park-Elysian Heights area grew in size in the 1920s, a colony of intellectuals—artists, writers, musicians, actors—moved in. Close proximity to existing movie studios scattered along Glendale Boulevard also drew film folk. There were at least three movie studios in the area: the Bison Company, which produced an average of one Western per day; Walt Disney's first studio, where Mickey Mouse was created; and Mack Sennett's studio, where the king of comedy, Charlie Chaplin, worked. Not only were the first movie studios found in the neighborhood but Echo Park itself "served for park and garden scenes in many of the old pictures."[22] The semi-secluded atmosphere further enhanced the area as a haven for those who refused to conform to society's standards. Old-timers remember their neighborhoods as "a very tolerant place" in which to live and still fondly recall some of their more famous neighbors such as Carey McWilliams, John Huston, Busby Berkeley, and Jake Zeitlin.[23]

At the northwest end of Echo Park, by where the lotus grows full and lush in the summer months, there remained a vacant semi-circular, pie slice-shaped lot on the corner of Glendale Boulevard and Park Avenue. Los Angeles County defined the property as "Lot fifty (50) in Block "O" of the Montana Tract." Its only inhabitant was a cow tethered to a stake grazing upon wild oats. On the third day of January 1921 the county of Los Angeles recorded that "Bernard Nussbaum and Betty Nussbaum, husband and wife, of Redlands, California, in consideration of ten dollars to them in hand paid, the receipt of which is hereby acknowledged, do hereby grant to Minnie Kennedy and Aimee Semple McPherson, both married women, as joint tenants, of Los Angeles, California, all that real property situated in the City of Los Angeles, County of Los Angeles, State of California."[24]

On that January day in 1921, both mother and daughter officially entered into the Promised Land of California by obtaining a piece of it. To Aimee as well as Minnie the transaction was nothing short of a miracle. If their first large tent was a symbol of a spiritual flight from "Egypt" then the intended wooden tabernacle they hoped to build on Lot O of the Montana Tract was a sure sign that they were now entering the Promised Land itself.

Aimee's decision to settle down and "build a house unto the Lord" came about as a result of her first attempt at a vacation. Returning to Los Angeles to "enjoy a quiet vacation," something she was quite incapable of doing, Aimee was soon back preaching at Victoria Hall, where she got her start in the city, at the First Baptist Church in Pomona, and at a Pentecostal mission in San Diego in preparation for a large forthcoming meeting there in early 1921—one destined to be one of the more significant meetings of her ministry. Since Los Angeles was the birthplace of Pentecostalism, it was the logical city for Aimee's temple.

San Francisco already had a thriving work, and Aimee gave her assurance to that church that she would never compete with it during her ministry. San Diego, a hundred and forty miles to the south, would have been the only other possibility on the West Coast. The climate was excellent, and those desirous of healing made the city the premier haven for regaining health in the country. In comparison to Los Angeles, however, it was small town and provincial. It is also possible that Aimee did not want her work confused with that of another famous California woman—Katherine Tingley, "The Purple Mother," who had dreamed of "building a White City in a Land of Gold beside a sunset Sea" which culminated in the creation of the Point Loma Theosophical Community in 1900. Tingley was continually subjected to a barrage of criticism and ridicule from both Protestant and Catholic clergy. Even Harrison Gray Otis of the *Los Angeles Times* got in on the act. Otis, a "strong supporter of the city's Anglo-Protestant culture, constantly inveighed against the Point Loma Theosophical Community and similar groups."[25]

Aimee's vision for her ministry by now was that it should be both international and interdenominational. Los Angeles, it seems, was the only place where that kind of theological vision could become a reality on a large scale. During her vacation Aimee wrote to her readership: "Our hearts long to see a large tabernacle erected in this city of Los Angeles, where the four thousand saints [Pentecostals] could meet for conventions, and special meetings for waiting on God, and united revival effort."[26]

Aimee's vision for a global ministry had emerged from a newspaper office shortly after her first visit to Los Angeles. The day before she was dubbed the "female Billy Sunday," Aimee observed a globe in a newspaper office, and noting the world as a whole, felt that she with the help of her followers could take her gospel to the entire global village before she died. It was the same kind of trusting visionary experience that led her to "say yes" to Robert and "yes to God" when she first saw a map of China.

Apart from the built-in base of four thousand Pentecostals that Aimee was hoping to capture, another factor influenced her decision to remain in Los Angeles—the tourist trade. Like the Florida beach towns she visited during her earlier revivals, Los Angeles was fast becoming a destination for the tourist. In the early 1920s approximately one million tourists visited Los Angeles annually, and the city had accommodations for housing three hundred thousand tourists at one time. Although Aimee still considered herself a Pentecostal evangelist, another dimension that accounted for a large part of her success, especially in the 1920s, was her repeated ability to reach the unchurched. Revivalism as a protest movement against ecclesiastical coldness and formality unwittingly in the process provided entertainment in the best sense of the word. Thus revivalism has never competed so much against other churches as it has against other forms of secular entertainment, such as the movie palaces of Hollywood and the dance halls of Venice Beach. The established churches, suffering from their own paranoia and declining membership rolls, were in reality never a threat or in competition with the revivalists. Revivalism was fighting fires with fire with the secular culture, a continual replay of the intense Mount Carmel experience between the prophets of God and the prophets of Baal described in the Bible's First Book of Kings. In Los Angeles as in no other place, Aimee could remain still and have the world, as Sarah Comstock would later write, beat a path to her door. Or as Aimee explained to her readership, "the Lord had shown us that this 'House unto the Lord' was to be built in the city of Los Angeles where tourists coming constantly from all parts of the earth, could receive the message, then return like homing pigeons, bearing the message in their hearts." [27]

In the December 1920 issue of *The Bridal Call* Aimee announced forth coming meetings in California. The appeal to a would-be tourist buried under a winter's avalanche of snow and ice in the Middle West or East was obvious: "All your life you have been looking forward to spending a winter in Sunny California, far from winter's ice and snow. Here is your golden opportunity; come to one of these coming campaigns or both and help win souls and visit California at the same time."[28]

Aimee's desire for permanence in the Promised Land of California overwhelmed her during her vacation. She reasoned against it on the same grounds that she had rejected her earlier call to ministry—on the grounds that she was a woman. "Whoever heard of a woman without earthly backing or any organization behind her [doing such a thing]?"

> But stronger, ever stronger, grew the … impression. Louder and clearer came the call, till one afternoon, during an interval between meetings, we [Aimee and Minnie] determined to set out and look for land. Almost irresistibly we were led to drive into a section of the city we had never before entered. And then—Echo Park came into view…our eyes fell upon the place, with its placid lake…yet surrounded by our biggest streets, Glendale Boulevard on the one side, Sunset on the other, with stores, shops, restaurants and cafeteria. "Oh, this is Heaven!" we cried simultaneously. "Right in the city, yet so restful, all the principal street cars passing constantly—this is the very spot. And yonder circular piece of property. What a wonderful place that would be for the Tabernacle!" Like a flash from heaven we visualized the whole plan. Here would be the altar, here the aisles, the galleries and prayer-rooms.[29]

Upon inquiry about the property at a real estate office she was told that it was not for sale and that many would-be buyers had already attempted and failed. Dealing directly with the owner after spotting a fresh for-sale sign, mother and daughter soon secured the land "at a reasonable figure," most likely the result of Minnie's frugalness.

On the back page of the January 1921 *Bridal Call* Aimee's intentions for permanence in Los Angeles was announced for the first time :

ECHO PARK REVIVAL TABERNACLE TO BE ERECTED
IN LOS ANGELES, CALIFORNIA

To her faithful followers she attempted to describe the plan:

> Here lay the great city of Los Angeles, affording perhaps the greatest opportunity for God of any city in the Union. Thousands of tourists are here from every State of the Union, many coming to reside; [statistics declare that two thousand are arriving daily]. Their other needs have

been provided for by the city, homes, amusements, theatres, automobile highways, and parks, but alas, few adequately large buildings where they might hear the Word of God in its blessed Pentecostal fullness. While there are several precious missions and churches…they are but 'a drop in the bucket' compared to the need.[30]

Aimee's desire to build a wooden revival tabernacle was most likely due to the model provided by the earlier revivalism of Billy Sunday and a serious underestimation of her own potential. In less than two years time Angelus Temple was opened and dedicated on the pie slice-shaped piece of property. Carey McWilliams would later describe the structure and its events as follows:

> Here she built Angelus Temple at a cost of $1,500,000. The Temple has an auditorium with 5,000 seats; a $75,000 broadcasting station; the classrooms of a university which… graduated 500 young evangelists a year; and, as Morrow Mayo pointed out, 'a brass band bigger and louder than Sousa's, an organ worthy of any movie cathedral, a female choir bigger and more beautiful than the Metropolitan Chorus, and a costume wardrobe comparable to Ziefield's.'[31]

After the "temple" instead of a "tabernacle" was dedicated, Aimee wrote to her followers:

> Little did we dream that this house should be the mighty and glorious Temple, under whose shadow I write these words. Surely it would be a wooden tabernacle, an inexpensive, temporary and very ordinary affair! Had we ever dreamed of the real plan of God for the present building, the audacity and seeming impossibility of such a gigantic undertaking, we would have been so alarmed as to forbid the very mention of it. During the brief visits in Los Angeles, my mother and myself went so far as to look at several wooden structures, saying to ourselves—"perhaps this could be built for $10,000—the other for $20,000." How little we knew the plans of God, that were to be unfolded in the immediate future.[32]

The plans of man, however, in accordance with the building codes of Los Angeles, were also responsible in transforming the intended wooden "tabernacle" into the concrete and steel "temple." Modern American cities were now requiring strict building codes, and Aimee's dream of a church seating five thousand precluded the building of a wooden structure. Her dream instead was to be constructed under "Class A" specifications, being

Aimee oversees ground-breaking for Angelus Temple. "If it weren't for Aimee, we would stil be on the wrong side of the tracks," said a Pentecostal minister at the time (used by permission of the International Church of the Foursquare Gospel, Heritage Department).

composed entirely of concrete and steel. The transition from tabernacle to temple, like the earlier one from tent to tabernacle, was a providential one for both Aimee and the Pentecostal movement. As one Pentecostal minister said, echoing the sentiments of many of his brothers and sisters: "If it weren't for Aimee, we'd still be on the wrong side of the tracks. She got Pentecost out and got them into decent churches."[33] Another Pentecostal minister stated, "She took Pentecost off the back street and put it on the boulevard—that was her whole vision."[34] That vision did not meet with unanimous approval, however, from all of the Pentecostal "saints" in Los Angeles. When some from the missions saw the elaborate structure being constructed, they prophesied that it was being "built of sand and not upon the rock" and therefore would never endure.[35] The opposite, of course, was true. Pentecostalism was taking hold in American culture, and it was the missions and tabernacles that slowly but surely began to collapse and fade away. Pentecostalism seemed continually torn in its formative stages between its enthusiastic impulse to be a part of the world and to attempt to redeem it and its holiness impulse, concerned with personal perfection and world avoidance. Aimee did much in the movement to sharpen the enthusiastic thrust of the new movement. Angelus Temple was but a symbol of its growing fervor. Defending herself against ever increasing charges that she was succumbing to "worldliness," Aimee protested that the holiness crowd was simply "giving up for God what they couldn't afford anyway."[36]

Aimee and Minnie were so overjoyed with their recently purchased property that they would often times "in the middle of the night…rise, get
in our car and drive eight miles to stand on the property, to dream and
pray…how, and where were we to begin? There were just the two little
women—my mother and myself. No great board or advisory committees
had we."[37] The first thing Aimee and Minnie did with the property was to
hire "Fresno scrapers"—eleven mules teamed with men and two-handled
scoops that removed a small hill of earth and prepared the ground for the
foundations.[38]

Mother and daughter, alone on their lot in Echo Park with their Fresno
scrapers stood in stark contrast to the vast evangelical organization of seven
hundred ministers, two hundred forty-eight churches, and twenty committees that had brought Billy Sunday to town four years earlier and had built
his sixteen thousand-seat tabernacle at Twelfth Street and Grand Avenue.

For constructing what was to become the largest Class A church in
modern America, Minnie and Aimee's method of financing the construction was novel. Since they had no board or advisory committee to guide
them, they first turned to their devoted *Bridal Call* readers. During the course
of the temple construction, its circulation doubled from fifteen thousand
subscriptions in 1921 to more than thirty thousand subscriptions by 1923.
Announcing the progress of the construction to her subscribers Aimee
wrote, "By faith, work will be pushed forward as quickly as each incoming
dollar permits, and as economically as possible. This is the opportunity of a
lifetime. Our work is undenominational and international. Every *Bridal Call*
reader in every state should have a glad share in its erection, and an opportunity to share in the eternal reward which will surely follow."[39]

Like everything else she did, Aimee dramatized and personalized the
financial contributions for the Temple Fund. Bull Durham bags, cut into
small pieces and stuffed with cotton, representing a bag of cement, were
sold for one dollar. For a donation of twenty-five dollars or more, a contributor became a "chair holder of Angelus Temple," receiving by way of
reminder a miniature chair that could be placed upon a mantle or shelf. The
large revival meetings that Aimee was conducting throughout the country
from 1921 to 1923 provided the vast majority of the funds for the temple
construction. As in her earliest meetings, very few contributed greatly, but
the many that attended gave a little. The money for the foundations would
come from one city while the walls went up with the contributions from
the next city. The offerings, like the attendance at the meetings, cut across
denominational lines, with those giving to what was being termed a "non-
sectarian and international Full Gospel Evangelism." Aimee's conception

of an international and interdenominational church seemed to strike a most responsive chord with her American audiences in the early 1920s. A conservative interdenominational movement would later re-emerge in American religion in the 1970s—especially in Southern California.

Throughout Aimee's life it would become obvious that things did not work well for her when she had an abundance of time on her hands. Whether it was peering down the forbidden family well and talking to the playmate of her reflection while Minnie was busy attending to household chores, or the recuperation from various illnesses plaguing her later life, time in lavish abundance did not befriend Aimee or serve her well. Her life simply worked best when she was going "full throttle" down the tracks toward her various destinations. That kind of dynamism and energy led Carey McWilliams to describe her as "not so much a woman as a scintillating assault."[40] The challenge of creating her own church near the rushes of Echo Park seemed to stimulate rather than overwhelm her. For two years, from January 1921 to January 1923, Aimee Semple McPherson was a "scintillating assault." Not only were her campaigns uniquely successful in American revivalism but Angelus Temple, the largest Class A church in modern America, was being built in the process. In these two years Aimee, as a sincere mother of two and an ex-Canadian farm girl, would simply share her dream with her audiences across America, down in Australia, and up in Canada. They in turn generously responded to that dream—to the young woman in white—their "Sister in the King's Glad Service." No hint of scandal accompanied her ministry, with the exception of being Pentecostal, on which grounds she was denied ordination with the Baptist Association of Northern California. Even the religious persecution, however, seemed to serve her well. It was identical to her childhood, when taunted for being a "fire and blood lassie" Aimee was able to turn the persecution into a form of play. Her acceptance in American culture can best be seen in her various meetings throughout the country while Angelus Temple was in progress. By now, Aimee was in full stride.

CHAPTER TWELVE

San Diego: The Great Jumping-Off Place
January 6 to February 6, 1921

Two colorful lives forever destined to be identified with modern America briefly came together in San Diego the first few days of 1921. John Leo McKernan, later known as Jack "Doc" Kearns, was responsible for transforming a rail riding hobo into Jack Dempsey, heavyweight champion of the world. Kearns not only originated boxing's "million-dollar gate," identified with the Golden Age of Boxing, he also may have been the first to put Pentecostalism's most famous preacher into the national spotlight. The *San Diego Union* was the first to notice this unique partnership.

> Unique in the history of revivals is the series of meetings being held at Dreamland Arena, First and A streets, by Mrs. Aimee Semple McPherson this week.
>
> The revivals…are conducted in a building usually devoted to prize fighting…The meetings are held on the first floor, while upstairs a dance usually is in progress.
>
> Another anomaly is the fact that local boxing promoter, Jack Kernan, lessee of Dreamland Arena, is doing all in his power to promote the revivals. Curious as it may be, the woman evangelist's meetings attract nightly more persons than attend the weekly boxing programs given at the arena.
>
> She is not an old woman by any means and owns to twenty-nine years. She has two children, Roberta and Rolf, who sometimes accompany her to the ring when she tackles the unbelievers for a finish fight.
>
> Instead of the bare ring, furnished only with two stools for the boxers, the space inside the ropes contains a piano, several chairs, a wicker settee and a small table with water pitcher and glasses!![1]

Aimee had responded to "a call" from a "Pentecostal band of saints" to come to the city for a seventeen-day meeting. She was convinced that the city was ideal and ready for a revival:

To this beautiful city come the tourist and traveler from every clime;

escaping the cold of winter and the heat of summer, for this is an ideal and almost unchanging climate. What a place for a Revival! How far-reaching would be its effects—like tying messages to homing pigeons and sending them abroad unto their different homes in every quarter of the globe.[2]

Her success in San Diego came from the residents more than the tourists. She unknowingly struck a responsive chord with many San Diego residents, resulting in the protraction of her meetings. For a month Aimee was seen as the answer for their quest for health. The oldest Spanish settlement in California, sixteen miles north of the Mexican border, San Diego, as Edmund Wilson once said, was "a jumping-off place—the end of the road."[3] "You seem to see [in San Diego]," wrote America's foremost cultural historian, "the last futile effervescence of the burst of the American adventure. Here our people, so long told to 'Go West' to escape from ill health and poverty…are discovering that, having come west, their problems and diseases remain, and that the ocean bars further flight."[4]

Between 1911 and 1927 San Diego had the highest rate of suicide in the country. The city also led the nation with the highest rate of sickness. Its rate of sickness in 1931 was twenty-four percent of the population, whereas for the rest of the country the rate was only six percent. As Carey McWilliams noted: "From San Diego there is no place else to go; you either jump into the Pacific or disappear into Mexico."[5] "Despondency and depression over ill health" was recorded as the motive for seventy percent of the city's suicides. Social commentators of the time noted that Southern California was especially attracting victims of so-called "ideational diseases"—diseases thought to be partly psychological in origin—and as a result their victims moved from place to place under the illusion that they were leaving their diseases behind. San Diego was the final stop on the West Coast for such a quest. If hope eluded a victim there—it was to be found nowhere else.[6]

The meetings in the city were organized by a fledgling group of Pentecostals. That connection, however, was very much downplayed as Aimee honestly explained to her followers: "Wishing this to be an undenominational meeting, upon which no certain few would 'have a corner,' the money for rent and advertising was raised by a few individuals, who sacrificed much to this end, and requested only that their names should never be mentioned."[7]

With Aimee's growing reputation, the small group of workers, mostly women, was hard put to find a building capable of holding the anticipated crowds. The roller skating rink was ruled out, and the Armory was too

Aimee preparing to fly over San Diego and scatter fifteen thousand handbills announcing her meetings (author's collection).

small. A large square corner building on First and A streets amidst taverns with three-piece bands, shooting galleries, hamburger stands, pawn shops and small hotels was the only alternative. Dreamland Arena, once a public market, was now an amusement center. The ground floor, used primarily as a boxing arena, had a seating capacity of twenty-five hundred. The upper floor was used as a public dance hall. A Methodist minister who supported the meetings echoed the sentiments of many who felt the arena out of character for a revival meeting: "The place is very undesirable for the holding of a revival meeting. The difficulty may be faintly imagined when one realizes that Sister McPherson's invitation to 'come to Jesus' is accompanied by jazz above—'Everybody's doing it, doing it, doing it.' "[8]

Aimee's concern did not seem to be so much with the jazz above as the acceptance of her preaching style in such a place. "Perhaps some pugilistic preacher or a Billy Sunday could fit in here but our message was one of appealing tenderness and love, and here the Manager, the reporters, and all who come trooping enthusiastically around seemed to expect us to deliver Satan a 'knock-out blow'... and courage failed."[9]

Jack "Doc" Kearns himself finally convinced Aimee to go ahead with scheduled meetings with the argument that "the finest people in the city are accustomed to coming here, besides thousands who seldom can be coaxed within church doors will come to the Arena, and the unchurched people will come!"[10]

Aimee's success in San Diego was based upon two primary factors: the interdenominational appeal of her message and the healing aspect of her ministry. The interdenominational character of the meetings was apparent from the outset when Aimee asked a Roman Catholic priest to offer the invocation.

> I was looking over the audience desperately for a minister to ask him to lead in prayer on one of the opening nights. Looking about, and seeing a nice looking man in a ministerial collar I had him come to the platform and lead in prayer…when he left the ring he presented me with one of his cards and I discovered that he was a Catholic priest…for a moment my head seemed to whirl, then I said 'Hallelujah! This is undenominational enough to suit anyone. Lord, bring them all in, irrespective of creed or standing.' Thereafter the city ministers flocked to our help, and from the first meetings the altars [the boxing ring] have been filled at each service.[11]

Aimee wrote to her followers that "denominational barriers are forgotten, or laid aside."[12] Personal workers for the new converts came from Methodist, Baptist, Congregational, Presbyterian, Nazarene, United Brethren, Salvation Army and Pentecostal churches. These were further assisted by military chaplains, Episcopal ministers, and workers from the Gideons and the Epworth League (a Methodist youth organization founded in 1889 to promote an "intelligent interest" in the activities of the church). The revival meetings sponsored "Church Members' Nights" where sections of the arena would be reserved for various denominations. They would sing together in unison "The Old Time Religion" adding the words:

> It makes the Methodists love the Baptists,
> It makes the Baptists love the Methodists,
> It is good for San Diego
> And it's good enough for me.[13]

The strength of the interdenominational character of the meetings was discovered by the churches that opened their doors to Aimee one night a week when the boxing matches resumed in Dreamland Arena. They represented not only the largest churches in the city but the most influential—the Normal Heights Methodist Church, the First Methodist Church, the First Baptist Church, and the First Presbyterian Church.

The quest for healing, however, is what the newspapers seemed to note most about the meetings. Aimee was very much aware of the uniqueness of San Diego. "Because of the great demand (multitudes have come to South-

Aimee (in white) in the boxing ring at Dreamland Arena, San Diego (author's collection).

ern California seeking health as in perhaps no other place) two or three divine healing services have been held each week during the revival. Faith is rising higher and higher like a great flood tide that sweeps all before it."[14]

Dreamland Arena proved inadequate in size to hold the crowds. The "continuous clamor for reserved seats" protracted the meetings for five weeks and led to two "mammoth meetings" held outdoors in Balboa Park. Through the influence of a Lieutenant M. Arthur Spotts, a chaplain with the United States Navy, the Park Commission approved the use of the Spreckels Organ Pavilion for the services. The pavilion was an open-air amphitheater having one of the world's largest outdoor organs and was located amidst the cultural and recreational center of the city. Spotts, a Presbyterian who had led something of a spiritually nomadic life, attended many "Bible Conferences, Surrendered Life and Victorious Life meetings" including one at Princeton Theological Seminary. He later assisted Aimee in Angelus Temple where he was "baptized with the Holy Spirit."[15]

The *San Diego Tribune* noted the impact of the first mass meeting upon the city:

> One of the most remarkable demonstrations ever accorded any man or woman was that given Mrs. Aimee Semple McPherson, known as the "Female Billy Sunday," yesterday at the organ pavilion in Balboa Park, when she held a special healing service.
>
> When Mrs. McPherson appeared on the platform she was accorded something of an ovation by the thousands of persons assembled for the service. Ministers of several denominations were present and assisted in getting the services underway. Hundreds of ailing persons with all sorts of afflictions and diseases were on hand to receive treatment. Many of these ailing persons came in wheel chairs and on crutches, and following the service not a few of these chairs and crutches were discarded as useless. For each one of the afflicted Mrs. McPherson said a special prayer.
>
> So great was the crowd attending the service and so many were there seeking relief from ailments and disease, that Dr. Humphrey J. Steward was compelled to postpone the usual afternoon organ recital.[16]

Aimee's healing service at the Organ Pavillion in Balboa Park. The San Diego Tribune *described it as "one of the most remarkable demonstrations ever accorded any man or woman" (author's collection).*

Special street cars were implemented to handle the crowds. The event itself was captured by panoramic and moving picture cameras with police and park officials estimating the range of the crowd from ten to thirty thousand.

In the wake of Aimee's meetings in San Diego a "Pentecostal tabernacle" was erected. However, in an interview with the *San Diego Union* shortly before her departure from the city, Aimee stressed again the ever increasing importance of the "interdenominational" character to her meetings, as well as echoes of John Wesley: "My work is undenominational and by that I mean that it is preached out under the open sky, on battleships, in airplanes—and even in dance halls, and my pulpit is the whole world."[17]

A trinity of topics shared newspaper headlines with Aimee during her sojourn in San Diego. Mary Garden in Chicago was doing for opera in modern America what Aimee was doing for religion, taking it "to the hearts of the people." Chiropractors were being persecuted by the state Medical Board for being "charlatans, fakers and impostors" while attempting passage of a proposition that would allow for them to be governed by their own board of directors. (San Diego County cast more favorable votes for the passage of such a bill than any other California county.) The final story bore a striking similarity to what the newspapers would say about Aimee in five more years, "Kidnapped Woman is Found in Shack." The stories of kidnapping in Los Angeles, complete with their subplots of revenge and ransom, would intrigue the country over the next few years, but when it was claimed to have happened with Aimee, the significance of the event would rival that of the disappearance of the Lindbergh baby.[18]

From San Diego Aimee returned to Los Angeles to edit *The Bridal Call*, supervise the ongoing construction of Angelus Temple, prepare for forthcoming meetings in the South and Middle West, and revise her autobiog-

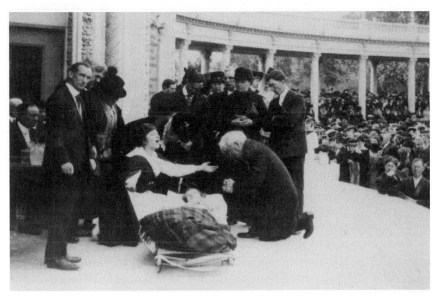

Aimee on her knees praying for an invalid at the Spreckels Organ Pavilion (used by permission of the International Church of the Foursquare Gospel, Heritage Department).

raphy, *This Is That*, for a third edition. The March issue of the monthly *Bridal Call* was a special one for Aimee "dressed in its royal purple." It was an anniversary issue marking a three-year history of production from California instead of Massachusetts. It was also produced from a brown khaki tent, formerly employed during the tent revivals and now on the site of the forthcoming tabernacle, "just out of reach of the heels of the mules" who were grading the lot.[19]

Following Aimee's return to Los Angeles, she mentioned to her faithful readers that "our telephone and doorbell are ringing almost night and day."[20] Buoyed by the response to the San Diego meetings, Aimee decided to hire Brook Hawkins, a builder and contractor with the Winter Construction Company, who was familiar with the requirements for Class A structures. Soon the earlier, more modest plans for her home base were giving way to more elaborate ones; the decision was made to add a balcony increasing the seating capacity to "either 3,500 or 5,000 which ever is considered most advisable...At any rate, the best must be secured for this great work, which will be world-wide in its effects."[21] From the offerings of the San Diego revival, $5,000 was spent to complete the excavation for the foundation. Another $2,200 purchased the architectural plans for what had earlier appeared to Aimee "like a flash from heaven."

The mortal charged with the responsibility of carrying out the "heavenly vision" was William Henry Wheeler, a prominent San Diego architect. The designer of the subsequent structure, which later appeared to a religion writer as being "half like a Roman coliseum and half like a Parisian opera house," most likely met Aimee during her stay in San Diego. The architect and the evangelist shared many of the same personality traits, for Wheeler's contemporaries remembered him as one who "dramatized everything, loved to be the center of attention and on stage; was flamboyant; and had great presence in all that he did."[22] Wheeler's clients were as diverse as his buildings. His work included the Coronado residences of John D. Spreckels and Madame Schumann-Heink; an Episcopal church, Immaculate Conception of Old Town; a Jewish temple; the San Diego Athletic Club; and most interestingly in regard to the creation of Angelus Temple, four San Diego theaters, which included the Balboa.[23] Since the San Diego revival had provided financially for "a goodly share in the foundation of the building," it was soon time for Aimee to be on the road again, holding various meetings and raising support for the intended interdenominational and international Angelus Temple.

In spring of 1921, the cities of St. Louis, Dallas, and Denver, like Aimee's ministry, were getting larger. Arriving in St. Louis, the country's sixth-largest city, for a three-week revival, Aimee discovered a city "business and pleasure-bent." "Theaters ablaze, cabarets and dance halls aglow, a beautiful city with churches aplenty, but a reputation of being immune to revivals."[24] The meetings were to be held in the "beautiful Masonic auditorium—the Moolah Temple with a seating capacity of 3,000." Aimee's only backing for the meetings was the smallest church in the city—most likely Pentecostal—with fewer than seventy members. Out of the small membership only fifteen could be mustered for a choir which was to assemble on a platform seating five hundred. At the opening afternoon service the building was half full, and the choir with their chairs spread "very far apart" sang "bravely."[25] By the middle of the first week the Moolah Temple was full, a result of "word of mouth." By the beginning of the second week, regular details of police were required to handle the assembled crowds attempting to gain admission to the twice-a-day service.

Some, especially the sick, arrived at the doors between five and seven a.m. for the noon services. By ten a.m. the streets were engulfed by the hopeful, and by a quarter past noon, when the doors were finally opened, the building was filled to capacity with a few minutes. Those inside had endured hours of alternating heat and rain while some of the thousands outside pressed hard against the building hoping to receive a cure by simply touching the sides of the building. Whenever the back of the law was turned, the healthy with an infirmed one would attempt entry into the locked auditorium by a broken window, ladders to fire escapes, and through emergency exit doors.

After two weeks time, the Reverend William H. Clagett, president of the board of trustees of the Texas Presbyterian University, negotiated the use of the one block square coliseum with a seating capacity of twelve thousand for the remainder of the meetings. The esteemed Presbyterian minister's endorsement of the meetings provided a boon for the continued revival. Clagett later commented, "I have heard all the great evangelists from Moody to those of the present day, and I have never heard the simple Gospel of Jesus Christ…more simply, more faithfully, more lovingly preached nor the unconverted more lovingly and more tenderly pleaded with than I heard from the lips of Mrs. McPherson, nor have I ever heard a stronger condemnation of the fanaticisms, extravagances and shams that are so common that are parading as a higher type of holiness."[26]

Aimee's endorsement by the leading mainline clergy of St. Louis again not only reflected a growing dissatisfaction with the older revivalism associated with Billy Sunday but demonstrated her continued appeal to the "middle of the road" theological spectrum, as evidenced by the following endorsement by the pastor of the Scruggs Memorial Methodist Church:

> Let me start out by frankly confessing that I was fearful in giving support to Mrs. McPherson and the revival. I am a "Middle of the Roader." There are two extremes in religion. One is formality and the refrigeration of faith…the other is fanaticism electrocuting and burning it out. A true "Middle of the Roader" is not a "pussyfooter" but one who does not freeze out or burn out. For years St. Louis has been the graveyard of revivals. Ecclesiastical conservatism keeps Billy Sunday out of St. Louis…While fearful of endorsing the meeting until I saw and heard for myself, I had resolved to keep an open mind and I did. I attended the opening days of the revival and saw the approval of God resting upon the ministry of Mrs. McPherson, threw aside my fears of electrocution and went on the firing line with her.[27]

Despite the growing division in the house of American Protestantism between the two polarities of fundamentalism and modernism, perhaps the vast majority of Protestants actually saw themselves like the Methodist minister— at neither end or extreme—and were more comfortable situated theologically "in the middle of the road." In 1922 a theology professor, F.L. Anderson of Newton Seminary, the oldest graduate theological institution in the United States, wrote a letter to the *Watchman-Examiner* about his fellow Baptists. Anderson identified several factions within his denomination. "The fundamentalists," he reminded his readers, "are only a fraction of the conservatives." They had mobilized, he argued, "for the purpose of capturing the machinery of the denomination." By far the largest faction of Baptists, Anderson concluded, was the "great middle-of-the road group, which both fundamentalists and radicals conspire to ignore, but which is the balance wheel of the denomination."[28]

In less than a year's time Aimee would produce a tract stating her own theological position as being "middle of the road," combating both formalism and fanaticism. It was a theological shift that led many Pentecostals to question whether or not she was still Pentecostal, but one that brought her more into the mainstream of American Christianity. Aimee's St. Louis meetings ended on a Monday afternoon in "the father of waters"—the Mississippi River—where a Methodist, Baptist, Presbyterian, Congregational, and a Pentecostal minister assisted her in a baptismal service for the new converts.

After St. Louis, Aimee and Minnie journeyed south to Dallas. The meetings were held in the State Fair Auditorium with a seating capacity of five thousand. Aimee's success in Dallas was virtually a replay of her meetings in St. Louis with a Methodist minister noting her appeal:

> I have heard all the great Evangelists from Moody down the line, but never before have I heard …Christianity presented in so clear, convincing and persuasive a manner. Pastors of our City Churches, representing all denominations—Presbyterian, Methodist, Baptists, Christian and Congregational were on the platform…Special services were held for the Mexican, Italian and the colored population. Mrs. McPherson labored earnestly for the good of all our people, without regard to Denominational, social or racial distinctions…The meeting was an epoch in the history of this city… She is anointed of God for a great work.[29]

Since the Texas authorities prevented African-Americans from attending her meetings in Dallas, Aimee practiced her own reverse discrimination at two specially arranged meetings:

> When the colored people…came and stood on the outer edge of the grounds with tears in their eyes, asking of if there would be any time for [them]…we…gave them two morning services, one in the Coliseum and one in the largest colored Baptist church. What glorious meetings they were! Seemed as though we never realized how many colored people there were in the world….No "white folks" were allowed in at the meeting and mother and I had them all to ourselves.[30]

Writing to her faithful *Bridal Call* readership, Aimee reminded them that God was "no respecter of persons." She also admitted she had adjusted her preaching style to meet the needs of her new audience. "Surprisingly soon I found myself slipping into…short phrases, with a pause between, giving them time to respond as they love to do so well.…What a delight it was to minister to them."[31] She would later recount those memorable meetings for her Bible School students. "I thrilled," recalled Aimee, "as I heard the colored people of the south sing…we cannot sing as they because we have not suffered as they have. Beatings and cruel partings! My, what a sinful dark blot on the history of America. But …out of that cauldron of suffering have originated the only folk songs we have in America."[32]

Aimee not only ministered to the marginalized and isolated in Dallas, but also found a growing acceptance in the American mainstream. Not only was she invited to speak to the students and faculty of Southern Methodist University, she was also the guest of honor at a noon luncheon by the Chamber of Commerce. Her next meeting, beginning on June 19 in Denver, would not only be unique in American revivalism but would be remembered for the extreme outpouring of love toward her during her time in the Mile-High City.

CHAPTER THIRTEEN

Denver: Awake Beyond Any City
June 19 to July 10, 1921

To make sick souls well, to bring faith and hope to an uncertain world, these are the spiritual, the psychic, the psychological functions of revivalism. By the kind of pragmatic test which Americans so dearly love, revivalism has worked, it has produced results.

—William McLoughlin

Frances Wayne was well on her way to becoming an award-winning newspaper reporter with the *Denver Post* when Aimee came to town for her regularly scheduled three weeks and four Sunday meetings. Wayne was an impressive person in modern America, the third woman to receive a university recognition medal following Madame Curie, the discoverer of radium, and Dr. Aurelia Roberts Rinehart, president of Mills College, and the first to ever receive such an honor in journalism. And Frances Wayne was clearly impressed with Aimee as a woman evangelist and introduced her to the *Post* readership:

> Does the star of Billy Sunday set as that of Mrs. Aimee Semple McPherson rises?
>
> Are the people of Denver to again witness a miracle of healing through the mediumship of faith and Aimee McPherson, as they did in the far days when Francis Schlatter, a wandering, long-haired healer, stood at the gateway of a humble house in North Denver while thousands of men, women and children passed under his outstretched hands to be healed of their maladies?
>
> Mrs. McPherson's is a warm, glowing personality. In figure, complexion, eyes, coloring and especially in her voice this woman evangel typifies health and youth at the fullness of its blooming, though she is one year past thirty…In an age designated as "woman's" the appearance of Aimee McPherson as an evangelist is significant.[1]

Denver, with the possible exception of the mainline religious establishment, more than any other American city was ready for Aimee Semple

McPherson. Before the turn of the twentieth century, Francis Schlatter had held healing meetings in Denver's railroad yards to which thousands had flocked from the Western states. Schlatter was an enigmatic individual who later died in an insane asylum. As a freelance spiritual healer, however, Schlatter had been very successful in the southwest. At Albuquerque "by laying-on-of-hands" he had "treated 60,000 persons in 60 days," all "without charge."[2] During the course of Aimee's three-week meeting, more than half a million people attended, and the crowds gave the evangelist $25,806.61 in offerings, largely through nickels and dimes in tin cans. "Denver," Aimee told the *Post*, "is awake beyond any other city I have visited."[3] A year later Aimee would confide to her followers that "our average revival meeting offering runs under two cents per head."[4]

Denver was a unique city in modern America. It was the dominant city of the interior West. It was also referred to as the "Queen City" of the Rockies and the "Magic City" because after 1870, it appeared as if it had mushroomed by magic. Eastern writers and Denver civic boosters both helped to create the myth of a special kingdom at the foot of the Rockies. Julian Ralph, writing for *Harper's* in 1893, stated, "Denver is a beautiful city—a parlor city with cabinet finish—and it is so new that it looks as if it had been made to order, and was ready for delivery."[5] A writer with *The New England Magazine* a year earlier remarked that "the chief pride of Denver is in its homes, which rank with those of the leading eastern cities, and in point of elegance and comfort are unsurpassed by those of any city of its size in America."[6] Another writer noted the daily view from Denver of "one hundred and fifty miles of mountain peaks, lying like a necklace of pearls upon the throat of the western horizon."[7] Denver's people of wealth prided themselves that their town had suddenly become "a most aristocratic city." As a result the rich had withdrawn into their insular world and lived life the way it was done in older cities, Boston and New York, to which Denver liked to compare itself.[8]

Under the veneer of the "parlor city with cabinet finish" was yet another Denver. The Queen City was also home to the "one-lunged army," the thousands afflicted with pulmonary disease. As early as 1868, Denver's Board of Trade advertised the city as having a climate "exceedingly favorable to consumptives." In Denver one was to find "instantaneous relief and rapid and permanent cure." Such claims hoping to lure new settlers to the mountain region brought thousands of sufferers (estimated as high as sixty percent of all Colorado residents) in quest of an instant panacea. Not all who arrived were well established to find balm in the new Gilead. Scores of destitute people spent their last sums of money just to reach the cure-all climate of

Colorado. An image of weak and dependent people was not one that the civic boosters of Denver enjoyed, and by the 1880s the Chamber of Commerce announced that the Queen City was in need of "manufacturers and capitalists" and not folks in need of "easy positions."[9]

There lurked other evils and ills beneath Denver's thin cabinet finish. Italians were discriminated against because few of them spoke English and the majority were practicing Roman Catholics in a predominately non-Catholic society. They were denied access to better job opportunities and instead given the most menial jobs on railroads or in factories, always subject to layoffs. The vast majority of them lived in poverty on both sides of the Platte River near the railroad yards.

The Chinese and the African-Americans fared worse than the Italians. The Chinese were threatening, not only because of their "yellow skin" but because of their strange religious traditions giving rise to the "heathen" epithet. Living in Hop Alley, the majority of the Chinese did other people's laundry, worked in restaurants, or served as janitors and servants. The fabled opium dens provided one way of dealing with an otherwise intolerable reality.

The children of Denver perhaps suffered the most abuse in the obsessive quest for growth and profits, when property rights were placed before human rights. Many children were literally indentured to individuals who were able to secure employment from them as recompense. Such a system was abusive at best, and soon the overworked children ran away from their "families" and jobs to which they were "bound out," and took to joining gangs and to thievery for survival.

Denver's ills, although highly varnished over by the patina of wealth and health, were a microcosm of what was occurring throughout the early years of the twentieth century. Aimee's enormous acceptance by Denver was due in large measure to the Progressive movement that emerged in Colorado at the turn of the century in an attempt to bring about needed social reform. The Progressive Republicans, a liberal movement within the Republican Party, gained impetus and inspiration by the precepts and work of Theodore Roosevelt and Robert M. La Follette. Prominent among what was to become the breakaway Bull Moose Party was Judge Ben B. Lindsey.

Lindsey, the chief champion of Aimee's cause in Denver, was himself a puzzle of contradictions. A life-long Democrat, he joined the Bull Moose Party and had hoped to run as vice president with Theodore Roosevelt. Often referred to as the "kid judge," Lindsey came to Colorado from Tennessee in 1880 and seven years later was admitted to the Colorado Bar Association. He was a small man, five feet, five inches tall, weighing one hundred pounds, with a bulging forehead, large black mustache, aquiline nose, expressive eyes, and a passion for justice which led to an international reputation.

In 1899 Lindsey wrote the legislation that created a juvenile court. A model of its kind, it soon attracted attention not only in the United States but throughout the world. Juvenile offenders were no longer treated as adults but as minors and were confined to separate institutions where the emphasis was upon rehabilitation rather than punishment. Social workers by the hundreds adopted Lindsey's methods of child reform.

Lindsey was more than the local "kid judge," he was deferred to by most Denver reform crusaders as their leader. In 1908, through the aid of Lincoln Steffens, Lindsey published a series of attacks in *Everybody's Magazine* against Denver's political and business leaders. Two years later the essays were published in a book entitled *The Beast*. In these essays Lindsey argued that the alliance between big corporations and politicians was responsible for the juvenile problem and that any efforts on behalf of juveniles were meaningless as long as "the Beast" remained in control.[10]

In 1905 the State Voters' League came into existence, and Lindsey was elected as its president. Its motto was "A Square Deal for Every Voter," with the contention that "The Politicians and special interests of our state are well organized. This league proposes to unite the people by pointing out to them the candidates worthy of confidence, regardless of politics."[11] By 1914, when *American Magazine* polled its readers on the question, "Who is the greatest man in the U. S.?" Judge Ben B. Lindsey placed eighth, tied with Andrew Carnegie and Billy Sunday.

Denver only mirrored what was occurring on a national level. The election of 1912 revealed how widespread the desire for radical reforms had become. It was in this election that the Socialist Party under Eugene Debs attracted almost a million voters. Discontent with the two major parties led to the creation of a prominent third-party movement. When the call for a convention to form a third party under Theodore Roosevelt's banner was issued, Judge Ben B. Lindsey was present at Chicago where the Progressive (Bull Moose) Party was organized.

The national platform of the Progressives, in essence, promised more social justice. The rule of the people was to be restored through the initiative, referendum, and recall of elected officials and the direct election of senators. An eight-hour day was promised in continuous twenty-four industries. Full and equal suffrage for women was advocated as well as a system of old-age pensions and state insurance against sickness and unemployment. Progressivism was a "fierce discontent," that sought a "middle-class paradise."[12] "Progressivism was an explosion, a burst of energy that fired in many directions across America."[13] And one of those directions most certainly helped to formulate Aimee's unique brand of middle-class Pentecostalism.

Although the Progressive party lost, its principles won, for it contributed to the Democratic victory in the national election. Lindsey's close associate, Edward P. Costigan, the Progressive gubernatorial candidate for Colorado, was appointed by Woodrow Wilson to the United States Tariff Commission in 1917 in recognition of his work within the Bull Moose Party. Lindsey himself did not fare well in Colorado. Run out of his adopted state by the Ku Klux Klan, Lindsey, like Aimee, found his final home in Los Angeles, where he passed one year before Aimee did, in 1943. His biographer concluded that Lindsey had been "an evangelist of American liberalism who [had] fought the good fight...and who [had been] in the vanguard of any movement to free the human spirit and make easier the life of man on earth."[14]

Thus Denver in the summer of 1921 was "more awake beyond any city" Aimee had visited. The old progressive, Bull Moose spirit of dissatisfaction with the status quo provided a solid basis of support for her acceptance in the Mile-High City. In a way, Aimee's later "Foursquare Gospel" was to American religion what Judge Lindsey's State Voters' League had been to politics—the attempt at a "square deal for all of the people." Noting that the old progressive spirit also carried over to religious concerns, an Episcopal clergyman visiting Denver for the first time in 1923 observed, "There seemed to be more of a love of social service than of religious dogma."[15]

Fittingly, Aimee's public meetings in Denver were sponsored by the People's Tabernacle—a nondenominational Protestant church located at Twentieth and Larimer streets. The People's Tabernacle was well known in Denver for its philanthropic activities and the charitable labors of its volunteer workers. The minister who had put it on the map had been "Parson Tom" Uzzell, a Methodist turned-Congregationalist. Uzzell had with his own modest resources opened a "Friendly Shelter" in the heart of Denver's slums. As many as four hundred men at a time who were drunk, diseased, or down on their luck were clothed and sheltered. "Parson Tom" preached a little gospel to his captive congregation but "never made conversion to Christianity, temperance, or middle-class morality a measure of worthiness or a requirement for help."[16] The tabernacle, instead of conducting fund-raising drives for a new and more impressive edifice, enlisted its own built-in army of worshipers, both black and white, to solicit money to buy tents for the homeless and clothing for the needy. Free breakfasts of coffee and pork and beans were dispensed every morning from its kitchen, and the gospel was delivered from a horse-drawn vehicle dubbed the "Gospel Wagon" that toured the streets of Denver. "Parson Tom" ran the People's Tabernacle from 1884 until his death in 1910.

> He helped establish the city's first night schools and kindergartens; he also ran a free medical dispensary and a legal aid clinic for the poor. In addition, Uzzell maintained an active employment agency, which was well respected by Denver's business community. After he was elected city supervisor and county commissioner, he distributed jobs to the needy like a ward boss. Simultaneously, however, he and the Tabernacle placed much emphasis on the conservative evangelical message. Tom Uzzell reportedly always "had one evangelist coming in the front door and another going out the back."[17]

There was also considerable distance measured more than city blocks between the People's Tabernacle and Trinity Methodist Episcopal Church, where the first ladies of the finest families attended. By the end of the three- week meeting, however, Aimee could honestly report to her faithful *Bridal Call* readership:

> Rich and poor came together, the high and low, in this revival. Never was American democracy more strikingly exemplified or manifested in a better cause...Mayor Bailey and his wife, the Governor and his wife, the Judge of the Superior Court, attorneys, lawyers, officers of high standing in the U.S. Army, business men, Congressmen and society women rubbed shoulders and mingled tears with their poorer brothers and sisters of the factory, shop, farm and gambling halls of Hop Alley and Chinatown. What a mighty leveler this great salvation is![18]

Dean A. C. Peck, then the pastor of the People's Tabernacle, was responsible for bringing Aimee to Denver. She first attracted Peck's attention through the press coverage of her San Diego meetings. Peck invited her to come to Denver "at the earliest possible day" after "inquiry and correspondence by both wire and letter established the facts of the genuineness of the work and the worker."[19] Peck was not to be disappointed with the outcome of the meetings. His final assessment of the revival was that "Denver has been swept by the fire of machine guns from Heaven...The entire city is talking about the greatest revival in the history of Colorado, and, many believe, in the history of the world since the early days of the Church."[20]

Initially only the Second Congregational Church and the Pentecostal

Mission united with the People's Tabernacle. Peck, with a loyal group of workers, made the city very much aware of the forthcoming meetings. "Denver…was sown with attractive invitations to attend the project services."[21] The city was prepared as if a political convention were coming. Banners were hung across streets at strategic intersections, street cars announced the meetings on their front sides, and business establishments pasted fliers to their storefront windows. Denver became like one large kiosk announcing Aimee Semple McPherson's arrival.

The meetings commenced the morning of June 19 at the Second Congregational Church. By the second service, the revival was relocated to the People's Tabernacle, the church with the largest seating capacity in the city—1,640. Four hundred chairs from the vestry were added to the sanctuary and "beginning with the initial service, every seat was filled and every inch of standing room occupied. The police estimated that fully as many were turned away as were assembled together, twice and thrice each day, during the first week of the meetings."[22]

Peck described the first four meetings held in the tabernacle as "purely evangelical" but also noted that "when the service for healing began, the overflow crowds increased and would remain for hours, filling the streets adjacent to the church."[23] The quest for healing in Denver made the size of the existing churches inadequate to accommodate the crowds. On Sunday, June 26, the meetings moved yet again, to the City Auditorium. Aimee explained the move to her distant readers: "So great became the pressure, so piteous the pleadings of the throng,…that special arrangements were made by Mayor Bailey, and the Auditorium, which had been engaged by a Labor Convention, was opened to us ahead of time."[24] The Denver Auditorium was the largest assembly hall in the United States when it was finished in 1908, with the exception of New York's Madison Square Garden. Its creation helped Denver fashion for itself an image as a "convention city." That image was quickly enhanced when the Democrats selected the auditorium for their national convention in 1908.

The auditorium had a seating capacity of twenty-three thousand. It was also capable of being abbreviated by an asbestos curtain, creating a smaller "theater" with a seating capacity of four thousand. For the opening Sunday service the theater was deemed appropriate to handle the crowds. This judgment proved to be a serious underestimation. The following Monday morning, Aimee wrote, "a corps of men was put to work and the change made; swinging both buildings into one. Then the real crowds began to come! The entire building became too small for the larger services, and again thousands upon thousands were turned away."[25]

The news of the meetings was carried to all of the Western states by the newspapers and telegraph wires. Such headlines brought many an invalid with the hope of health from all over the West. A newspaper reporter for the *Post,* Albert W. Stone, expressed the fear and concern the city was now beginning to experience.

> What is to become of the hundreds of cripples and sick persons left in Denver, unhealed, when Mrs. Aimee Semple McPherson, the "miracle woman" departs? This is the question that confronts the Denver author- ities and, especially, the afflicted themselves. According to Union Station officials, cripples are coming to the city in droves. Each train brings its quota, ever increasing in size...Many are coming from other states, as far away as Texas on the south and South Dakota on the north. They come from Kansas, Missouri and Nebraska. The hotels are filled with them, especially in the vicinity of the Denver Auditorium. It is feared that hundreds of these seekers after healing came to the city practically without funds.
>
> The throng hoping to be healed is now larger by far than at the begin- ning of Mrs. McPherson's meetings. Hundreds have been healed, accord- ing to their personal testimony and that of relatives and friends; but hundreds of others have been unable even to get into the Auditorium... What will the stranded ones do when the "miracle woman" departs for Los Angeles, without having had the opportunity to get a healing card or even to see the healer from an Auditorium seat?[26]

Aimee admitted that even though she worked from early in the morning until late at night, "it was impossible to touch more than the fringe of the crowd individually, some 20,000 requests for prayer cards were distributed in two services...and people were still clamoring for cards."[27] The clamor for the healing cards was so intense that the custodian of the auditorium had to organize a nightly search party to find hidden individuals who had hoped to be first in line for the cards the following morning. Repeatedly, persons would be found hidden in the attic under a network of electri- cal wires or barricaded behind heavy boxes in the ladies' restrooms. Even those outside the building hoping for an early entrance the next morning would huddle like sheep by the hundreds all night long in the alley way by the stage entrance. The custodian's assistants would collect over a hundred milk cartons from the alley way every morning.

Frances Wayne of the *Post,* perhaps better than any other newspaper reporter, was able to probe Aimee regarding the reported healings. It was the healing aspect of Aimee's ministry that clearly intrigued her the most:

STRETCHER DAY ᴀᴛ REVIVAL
MUNICIPAL AUDITORIUM
DENVER, COLORADO.

For two hours and forty minutes Aimee prayed over the afflicted on a special "Stretcher Day" at her meetings in Denver (used by permission of the International Church of the Foursquare Gospel, Heritage Department).

> If I were Aimee Semple McPherson I'd take one look at the eager people packing the Auditorium and filling the street outside and then I'd turn and run like a rabbit for cover. If I were Aimee Semple McPherson, I'd turn and run because of the awful—that's the word—responsibility hundreds of afflicted people were eager to put upon me; because of the tragedy of broken hopes and blighted faith which might follow in the wake of failure to heal the sick, the deaf, the blind, the paralytics, who, relying on a promise, seek healing.[28]

Asked by Wayne "to describe her sensations when the healing power descends upon her," Aimee gave a tolerant smile and answered the question with another one: "Can utter faith be described in words?" She did admit to the reporter that "on the days set apart to healing I fast and pray and indulge in no gossip and keep my mind on the Lord. My prayers are centered."[29] Aimee further explained her mission to the reporter as being more holistic than that of most churches:

> I find that religion and the churches are not practical enough for the needs of the people. Why shouldn't every church in the community be what it is supposed to be—a temple with open doors, through which the people might enter to pray and worship and meditate. And why should ministers lift their brows when it is suggested that healing and salvation

should go together? ...Salvation and healing should be the mission of
the church. How can people be made to love and respect and depend on
the detached God of the theologian? People are hungry for a practical
religion... [30]

Frances Wayne in her earlier columns had made some observations about
those who were "hungry for a practical religion." After attending Aimee's first
healing meeting, she also noted the gender differences in the meetings.

> Are men more anxious for salvation than women?...Mrs. McPherson...
> spoke to an audience of which more than half were men and a major-
> ity of these of hard boiled appearance. And these men, listening to the
> woman preacher...rushed to the altar when she called on converts to
> come forward...the woman evangelist ...speaks a language that children
> can understand, but with something besides; and that something is what
> moves men to become as little children.[31]

Wayne also noted the makeup of the audience: "Mostly the audience is
composed of plain folks... Tourists have a conspicuous place in the audience, judging from the license cards of automobiles parked outside."[32]

Throughout the revival meetings in Denver, response by the local clergy
had been mixed. A visiting minister writing for the *Central Christian Advocate*
clearly noted their response.

> For the most part, the Pharisees did not come. They remained away,
> in their homes or studies, for many of them (shame on them) were
> preachers. But on the platform were many ministers who had come
> from Kansas, Missouri, Colorado, Wyoming, California and else-
> where...However, some of the strongest and most influential ministers
> of Denver are in sympathy with the movement. Among them are Dr.
> Wright, a leading Congregational pastor; Dr. Lackland, pastor of Grace
> Methodist Church, and the Rector of Saint Thomas Episcopal Church.
> Many reliable laymen are giving the work their support.[33]

The *Post* throughout the meetings carried reports on how various city
clergy viewed Aimee's work, especially her ministry of healing. The Reverend W. H. Wray Boyle, pastor of the fashionable Central Presbyterian Church was quoted as saying, "I scarcely know what to say of Mrs.
McPherson...I should like to hear more of the results of the healings
before making a statement. There is, however, something indefinable about
it all...To me it is just indefinable power. Call it hypnotic if you please, but
the superhuman quality remains. One cannot attend a revival meeting and

study Mrs. McPherson without believing she is a reincarnation of super-human energy."[34]

Bishop Coadjutor Fred Ingley of the Episcopal church did not attend the meetings but was quoted by the *Post* as being "deeply interested because healing has been added to salvation as part of the Episcopal service in many churches."[35] By the end of the meetings what Aimee lacked in support by way of organized religion was more than made up for in popular support from all quarters of Denver society.

If Denver's clergy failed to unite and give Aimee their unanimous official sanction, her real source of support as always came from the people, covering all segments of the population—including the press. Noting that "denominational lines are fading," Frances Wayne pointed out the real impact of Aimee's meetings on the city: "Meantime the sick and sorrowful, the lonely and oppressed, the curious and half-believing, the poor and well-to-do are crowding…to the last inch of space and [are] hanging breathless on the words uttered by this strangely endowed woman from a Canadian farm."[36]

By the start of Aimee's second week in Denver, the *Post* reported official sanction had been bestowed upon the meetings from a far more influential quarter of the city than the clergy—the mayor's office. Aimee's support was more firmly rooted in the ethos of progressive politics and in the secular culture as a whole than it was with the Protestant religious establishment:

> Official sanction was given to the revival meetings of Aimee Semple McPherson…when Mayor Bailey…declared Mrs. McPherson to be "a wonderful woman doing good and great things that two thousand years ago would have been called miracles. She is doing a great good in helping the afflicted and spreading God's work in the community. We know that beyond any doubt she is doing a splendid work; we hope she may extend her visit, and we shall long remember her and her services when she is gone."
>
> With a word of thanks to the mayor, Mrs. McPherson called out her text from St. Luke, "Into whatsoever city or town you enter, preach the gospel and heal the sick therein."[37]

So intense was Aimee's desire to "heal all the sick" and to reach "all of the people" that she took some time off in between the meetings and visited Hop Alley in Chinatown. A journalist with the *Denver Express* recorded the event:

> Addressing the little throng as 'brothers and sisters,' she told them of

the love of Jesus for humanity…Her arms encircled the poor unfor-
tunate dope addicts, she hugged the poor, emaciated trembling bodies
and loved and kissed them…Arms that were blue and disfigured from
morphine were thrown about her neck and she soothed and rubbed
them and obtained the promise that never again would they feel the
prick of the needle…Mrs. McPherson has seen to it that they will have
reserved seats, and avoid the crowds that daily throng the Auditorium…..
There was a veritable skirmish in Hop Alley when Mrs. McPherson left.
Crowds trailed her to the automobile, tugging at her and begging her to
come again…she left behind her a night in Chinatown that will long be a
memory to its inhabitants…Jack London never painted a starker picture
in his "People of the Abyss." For here is the Abyss—the very mud sill
upon which society crushes her failures.[38]

Aimee's most unusual meeting in Denver, perhaps of her career, occurred
the forenoon of her closing Sunday. It was a healing service billed by the
press as a special "stretcher day." It was an event many in Denver had
clearly been looking forward to ever since her arrival in the city. Despite
her previous revivals in Dayton and San Diego where healings had been
prominent, the awesome responsibility of her task the morning of her last
day in Denver weighed heavily upon her. The magnitude of the need was
literally stretched before her as she entered the municipal auditorium. This
time the auditorium was far removed in appearance from either a political
convention or a revival meeting. Instead of gaily elongated banners hanging
about the large edifice there were row upon row of stretchers and cots
sustaining their victims six inches to a foot off the floor. Special railings
encircled the cots to protect them from the rush of the crowd. As many
as one hundred fifty bed-type apparatuses had passed through a special
auditorium entrance known as the "wagon door." The auditorium looked
like a hastily created trauma center erected in the wake of a war or natural
disaster. Aimee admitted, "Even though we had been expecting and planning for it, it was a shock to the writer when she entered the building to see
the great number of beds, scores and scores of them, placed row on row
in front of the platform."[39]

It took a newspaper reporter for the *Denver Post*, Albert W. Stone, to
adequately describe Aimee's final healing service in the Queen City of the
Rockies.

Reporters, as a class, are reputed to be "hard-boiled"…It took Aimee
Semple McPherson, the "miracle woman" from California, to demonstrate that even reporters' emotions can be touched….It is safe to say that

a stranger assembly of guests never was gathered together—at least, not since the time of the Man of Galilee.

They were spread out…in fan-shaped formation. Every hospital in Denver had been combed for them. Dozens of private homes had contributed their quotas. Cots, stretchers, adjustable invalid chairs, beds—every conceivable kind of furniture designed to hold and add a mite of comfort to the hard lot of a cripple or an invalid—were lined up in solid winding rows, each one with an occupant whose gaze never for an instant left the face of the woman in white up there on the platform.

On every side was the audience—12,000 strong-filling to capacity the main floor, balconies and galleries… Mrs. McPherson's eyes were wet… So were her companions at the press table, fourteen of them. One man, a journalistic political war horse who had covered every Democratic and Republican convention in Colorado in the last twenty years—many of them in the same Auditorium—touched another reporter on the shoulder. His hand was trembling and his eyes were suffused. "Never saw anything like it," he said. "Never."

The healing session was one of the most impressive of the revival services. It was literally a "revival of bodies" for many of the victims. A battery of photographers, their flashlight "pans" held in readiness, waited. As person after person rose from their cots and declared themselves healed, hands raised and faces turned heavenward, the powder flashed and the scene was recorded for other hundreds of thousands to see.

City firemen, their blue uniforms making a picturesque blotch of color against the white dresses of the feminine workers and their brass buttons gleaming, carried the cots to the stage…Stretcher bearers labored with the perspiration streaming from their faces. Mrs. Kennedy, mother of the evangelist, flitted about among the cots, stroking fevered foreheads and saying soothing things. Outside the barricaded doors the waiting thousands craned their necks and tried to see.

For two hours and forty minutes Mrs. McPherson labored. When she declared a recess every cot patient had been reached.[40]

Throughout the three-hour service Aimee stressed her belief that early Christianity could be duplicated in the twentieth century. To those upon the cots she repeatedly stressed, "None are too broken in body or soul to be healed. All things are possible to those that believe." Describing the event Aimee wrote, "One was made to realize that apart from a modern dress of the Twentieth Century, this congregation was the exact counterpart of those which Jesus drew unto Himself almost nineteen hundred years ago. Was every such an assemblage of sick, blind and lame gathered together in one place since the days of the Master, we wonder?"[41]

Crystal England was born on a farm in a small Missouri town in 1907. She began her life journey as an unwelcomed child born to a mother who had lost three children before her. Arriving prematurely, Crystal was also a sickly child with all "kinds of medical problems." When she was fourteen, her mother sold her to a much older man to be his wife. "He didn't love me either," wrote Crystal. "He treated me like a slave would be treated by a bad master." Living in Denver with her abusive husband she never forgot the day when Aimee came to town.

> I went to the auditorium to see a lady named Aimee Semple McPherson...She would be speaking and reach out her hand and people would be instantly healed. I saw cripples get up and walk. There were people who were brought there by ambulance, who got up and whatever was wrong with them would be instantly healed. The *Denver Post* sent reporters with cameras to get photographs of these miracles that were taking place there...The crowds were huge and people would come and spend the night in the streets, just so they could be sure and get in the next day...I was only fourteen, but I recognized that God was present and doing a mighty work. But it wasn't just inside that He was operating; there were people getting healed even outside the building and in the streets all around the place. That was my first exposure to a miracle experience.[42]

As meaningful as the meetings were to people like Crystal England, it was the news of healings among Denver's elite, the rich and powerful that gave Aimee a new-found identity and legitimacy, confirming her earlier decision in Baltimore to "fish for whales." Among the prominent in Denver who testified to their healing were Alma Lafferty, a former state senator; Mrs. George Dunklee, mother of a former state senator; Mrs. Dewey Bailey, wife of Denver's mayor; Horace Benson, a widely known attorney; and General Irving Hale, who had commanded Colorado's troops in the 1898 Spanish-American War. A newspaper reported that even Colorado's governor had "brought a deaf and dumb boy to the building, and he was made to hear and talk."[43] The Denver newspapers concluded that there were "more healings from deafness and blindness...than from any other ailments."[44] The editor of the *Denver Post* was so smitten by Aimee that he provided a picnic for her family on Pike's Peak. On the way up the mountain the newspaper editor confessed to the Pentecostal preacher, "I expected you to be some old lady, all dressed up stiffly in a sort of suffragette, and be very narrow and straitlaced and long-faced. I can't bear such people. But when I...saw

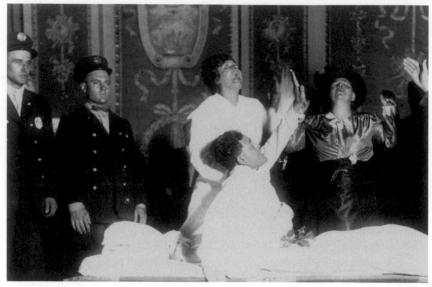

A "revival of bodies" is how one reporter described the final healing service (used by permission of the Denver Public Library).

somebody looking and acting sort of human and smiling, it just took my breath away."[45] Years later in her Bible school Aimee would recall the incident and tell her future evangelists, "So when you are angling for souls, do not try to impress upon people the fact that you live a very stringent, long-faced life. That does not necessarily mean that you are a Christian: and you will frighten more people away with your face than you will win."[46]

More than anything else, Aimee in less than a month had simply captured and conquered the Queen City of the Rockies. The police sergeant in charge of the crowds was quoted as saying, "I don't know how she does it, but this woman has captured Denver! We turn thousands away from every meeting and jam between fifteen and sixteen thousand persons into the building every meeting. One night we turned eight thousand persons away. They are coming here in carloads from almost every town in the state. She has certainly captured this town, and no man, not even a president, could fill this Auditorium two and three times a day for three weeks like she has done."[47]

Aimee's final meetings in Denver on July 10 were actually a trilogy of Sunday services: morning, afternoon, and evening. In many ways the three services were more like love feasts for the woman in white from Southern California than traditional worship services. The morning after, reporter Frances Wayne evaluated the Denver revival for her readers:

The…services, marking the last big revivals of the "Miracle Woman" here…were in the nature of love feasts. As the evangelist rose in the evening to preach her sermon, an American flag was unfurled and out of its folds dropped a shower of flowers on the head and into the outstretched hands of the Miracle Woman…Mayor and Mrs. Bailey sent a huge basket of red roses, with a message of thanksgiving for her services to Denver.[48]

With the passing of the Denver meeting it was clearly evident that Aimee was a force to be reckoned with in American religion. It was equally clear that the young woman in white had come a long way from her tent meeting days in southern Florida and Key West—even from the Pentecostal missions and tabernacles that were rapidly dotting the land. While in the Mile-High City, Aimee and Minnie stayed at the exclusive Brown Palace Hotel, usually reserved for political figures and renowned East Coast writers. In addition, a new Oldsmobile had been provided for their use. Aimee, in the words of a newspaper reporter, "captured the town…not even a president, could fill [the] auditorium two and three times a day for three weeks like she has done."[49]

The Reverend Theodore B. Tyre, pastor of Christ's Methodist Episcopal Church not only favorably summarized Aimee's meetings but was hopeful for her eminent return:

> Never before in the history of Denver has the city been stirred by such a remarkable work of Divine Grace…Were Mrs. McPherson to come back again, everybody would receive her with wide opened arms, and a tabernacle large enough to accommodate the eager, anxious crowds could be built without constant appeals for funds to make such a building venture possible. The ministry of the city, the city officials, the Jew, the Roman Catholic, and the Gentiles would unite together in welcoming those servants to our beautiful city…[50]

Judge Ben B. Lindsey not only purchased a chair in the forthcoming Angelus Temple, but added his own testimony and endorsement:

> It is a great privilege for me to bear testimony to what has been a thousand times demonstrated in Denver that the bringing of the real spirit of Christ to a community through the true Gospel in revival services conducted by Mrs. McPherson and Mrs. Kennedy is positively the most precious, the most priceless, the most wonderful thing that could happen to that community.[51]

By praying so long and hard for the sick in Denver, Aimee damaged the cartilage in both knees. Assisting her is Emma Schaeffer, her secretary, who was the last person to see Aimee before her disappearance (used by permission of the Denver Public Library).

Five months after the momentous Denver meeting had ended, the *Congregationalist*, a monthly periodical from Boston, conducted a follow-up of the revival. "Of the 10,000 converts' cards signed, not more than 150 joined the Denver churches …. It appears that without promise of healing the evangelistic results would have been very meager."[52] The Reverend E.F. Wright, the minister of the Second Congregational Church, reported that he had received sixty new members as a result of the revival. Wright characterized his new members as "substantial people, a real addition to the working force of the church."[53] He also concluded "that the spiritual condition of the church [was] much deeper and more earnest since the meetings."[54] It was the reported healings, however, that left Wright bewildered. Wright felt that none of his members "were really healed" and "that if Mrs. McPherson were to return for another series of meetings he would prefer her to leave out all attempts at healing and confine herself to wholly preaching the Gospel."[55] With time, of course, Aimee's ministry became more in keeping with the mainline minister's wish.

Ironically, it was while she was so intensely praying for others in Denver that the healer herself became physically wounded. Next to her loneliness, this was Aimee's first real "thorn in the flesh." It would not be her last. Many more were swift to follow. "By standing so long praying for the sick in Denver," admitted her long time secretary, Mae Waldron, "Sister burned out the cartilages in both knees….Doctors said she'd be in a wheel-chair in six months."[56] Aimee was not unique with ailing knees; they would become an occupational hazard for many Pentecostal healing evangelists. At the

time of his death at age fifty-
nine, A.A. Allen had secretly
left his Miracle Valley to go to
San Francisco for surgery on his
failing knees. This also explains
why Oral Roberts chose to sit
in a chair when he prayed over
the sick.

Aimee would return to
Denver in a year's time for yet
another revival. The auditorium would again be full, and
Aimee would share headlines
in the *Denver Post* with Isadora
Duncan for her marriage to a
young Russian poet and with
another evangelist in Chicago,
Paul Rader, for the firing of
"flappers" from his tabernacle choir. (He argued that no
congregation could "think of
the salvation of souls" while
viewing a choir made up of
"bobbed hair, knee skirts and
rouge."[57]) A similar battle

Kathryn Kuhlman beginning her ministry in Denver (used by permission of Flower Pentecostal Heritage Center).

would erupt in four years time within Angelus Temple over bobbed hair
and jazz "licks" on the organ. Aimee would side with the jazz and the flappers, and the first of several congregational disputes and schisms would
soon ensue.

Through ever-increasing public acceptance received in such meetings as
Denver and by developing new friendships with individuals such as Judge
Ben B. Lindsey, Aimee's life would become increasing altered, perhaps even
more than the lives of those who came to hear her. Buoyant with an ever
increasing sense of self-confidence, Aimee would slowly emerge from both
the shadow of Minnie's maternal over-protectiveness and the Pentecostal
cocoon of spiritual and religious isolation.

In fact, her Denver meetings brought to a head her ministerial standing
and relationship with the Assemblies of God. Not only did the chairman
of the Assemblies of God, the Reverend E.N. Bell, object to Aimee and
her mother holding title to the forthcoming Angelus Temple in both their

names, but the local presbytery of the Assemblies in Denver had been offended by her increasing reliance and growing cooperation with Denver's Protestant mainline churches more than the Pentecostal assemblies. They had been ignored, left out in the cold, and they resented it. The Reverend E.K. Gray, a member of the Denver presbytery, remembered how his local governing body had issued Aimee an ultimatum about working "primarily with the Assemblies of God. Mrs. McPherson emphatically rejected the demand and surrendered her credentials," said Gray.[58] The old "holiness" days were quickly coming to an end for Aimee. In Denver she appeared less straitlaced and long-faced and more human and had even learned to smile.

Denver would remain important for Aimee throughout her ministry. "[She] probably ministered more times in Denver...than in any other city except Los Angeles," claimed a future Foursquare church historian.[59] Although Aimee rejected an offer from a convert who "wanted to build her a temple there," one of her former students did, however, move to Denver in the depths of the Depression and successfully establish a Pentecostal mission in an old renovated warehouse.[60] For five years, from 1933 to 1938, Kathryn Kuhlman and her Denver Revival Tabernacle thrived in the Mile High City with two thousand members and a Sunday school that served six hundred children. Kuhlman's Denver ministry came to an abrupt end when she fell in love with a married traveling evangelist from Texas, Burroughs A. Waltrip. Kuhlman's marriage to "Mister," as she called Waltrip, ruined her ministry for the next thirty years. Like her earlier role model, she finally found fame again as "Miss Kathryn Kuhlman of Los Angeles."[61]

A month after her meetings in Denver Aimee's relationship with Harold Stewart McPherson formally ended in divorce. On August 8, 1921, the wire services picked up the story that the "female Billy Sunday" had been divorced by Harold McPherson in Providence, Rhode Island. Both parties charged desertion, with Aimee adding non-support charges for Harold's failure to provide financially for Rolf. The small news story observed that Mrs. McPherson presently lived with her mother in Los Angeles. In less than a decade's time that relationship would also rupture, to Aimee's great detriment. Aimee had replaced Harold with Minnie as her loyal and stead-fast helper. Her mother's departure, however, would leave a managerial void that Aimee could never fill. Rolf Potter McPherson, the dutiful son, would remain his mother's only non-estranged family member.

Aimee's single-focused passion for God would soon bifurcate into an equal passion and zest for life and the "world." A "new Aimee" would emerge after the completion of Angelus Temple. To future critics her new self represented a spiritual journey in reverse. Theologically, it would be her genius to create a secular form of spirituality. For such a creation she would be praised and damned. The first public detection of a theological change occurred in the spring of 1922 in the Sunflower State of Kansas, where two decades earlier the modern movement of Pentecostalism had emerged. The roots of that theological shift, however, had their origins in Northern California, where Aimee experienced denominational opposition in her attempt to become ordained as a Baptist, becoming unknowingly a casualty in the raging modernist-fundamentalist holy war.

CHAPTER FOURTEEN

Northern California: Baptists and Congregationalists

Protestantism in the New World did not have its origins in the Virginia Colony in 1607; nor in Massachusetts Bay in 1620; but, contrary to many historians, it had its origin in California. For in 1579, six years before John Cotton was born, and eleven years before the birth of William Bradford, Protestant worship was held in what is now Marin County.

—Harland E. Hogue,
The Long Arm of New England Devotion

The house was full! Why was it, you say; why this eager, anxious throng in an age of empty churches and discouraged preachers. I will tell you why. Inside is a little woman in white—a woman in the costume of a maid—a woman to whom thousands of people are listening, eager to get every word. Her personality is commanding, her attitude is fearless and her voice vibrates with depth of feeling and pulsates with emotion. Sometimes those near her can see the pearl-like tear drop in her eye and notice the intense sympathy that radiates from her countenance.

—Charles S. Price

Aimee had been greatly blessed by a benevolent providence to begin her permanent work in Los Angeles. As Harry Carr pointed out in his writings on Los Angeles, "In few other places in the world have women blossomed into such complete power."[1] With the great exception of the Reverend Robert "Fighting Bob" Pierce Shuler, the Southern Methodist fundamentalist and Aimee's chief clerical enemy in the City of the Angels, the Protestant church community of the city emerged relatively unscathed from the modernist-fundamentalist controversy that plagued the rest of the nation during the 1920s.

In the 1920s there were fundamentalist sects in Los Angeles, to be sure, but in the words of one historian, "they were on the periphery of the Protestant community, and were never a part of the voluntaristic culture."[2]

Given such a reactionary theological climate elsewhere, Aimee's original intention of building an international and interdenominational work could only have survived and prospered in a city like Los Angeles. Its Protestantism was very much unlike that of the rest of the country, a unique product of the City of Angels. Protestantism, it is to be remembered, had a slow start in Los Angeles and had to quickly accommodate to the existing culture for survival purposes. Denominational distinctions that at the turn of the century were severe had become blurred by the 1920s.

An interdenominational character emerged among many of the Protestant parishes with pulpit exchanges providing the most popular pattern. Also, as a by-product of the sprawling metropolis, church buildings and congregations by the 1920s would fast lose their neighborhood integrity. Because of sprawling urbanization, individual churches had the potential of growing into vast megachurches with membership culled from the entire city and its surrounding suburbs by means of the automobile and the electric street car lines. The crises of the churches in the East and even in the northern part of the state seemed very removed from Protestant concerns in Los Angeles, as Gregory H. Singleton has so clearly demonstrated in his *Religion in the City of Angels*:

> In the response, or rather lack of response, of Los Angeles' voluntaristic Protestants to "the fundamentalist controversy" the desire to avoid conflict and find a stable base of effective action through national agencies is most clearly seen. During the 1920s, the voluntaristic denominations all experienced national debates over the theological issues of fundamentalism and modernism…In each of the local denominational affiliates, Los Angeles Protestants demonstrated a disdain for the debate.[3]

If pleas were given to the national denominations by their affiliated Los Angeles parishes at all, it was for harmony and moderation. A prominent Presbyterian layperson in the Los Angeles presbytery when asked to vote on the "Fosdick affair" (After he preached his famous sermon, "Shall the Fundamentalists Win?" Presbyterian fundamentalists called for a heresy trial of Harry Emerson Fosdick), expressed the sentiments of many of his brother and sister Protestants in the Los Angeles basin when he stated: "this is an issue that does not really concern the work of the church. We are called to serve, not to cast aspersions on one another."[4]

The ultimate theological posture most Los Angeles Protestants finally assumed is again noted by Singleton: "There is very little in the denominational records from the 1920s to suggest a theological stance of any type. Voluntaristic Protestantism in Los Angeles had become a civic religion."[5] This emerging cooperative inter-denominationalism and civil religion in Los Angeles would have a "hot house" effect upon Aimee's ministry when she opened the doors of Angelus Temple on January 1, 1923.

"While ministers of Los Angeles are among the most progressive clergymen in America," stated the *Los Angeles Times* in the spring of 1924, "and while they do not hesitate to discuss, in their sermons, questions of political, social and scientific interest, there is a manifest desire on the part of scores of local pastors to emphasize, first of all, the deep truths of religion which lie at the foundation of the church. Instead of being a sign of narrowness or bigotry, this position of Los Angeles pastors is a token of their zealousness in the cause of true religion which makes its first appeal to the heart."[6]

No Los Angeles pastor in the 1920s exemplified "this position" better than Dr. J. Whitcomb Brougher, the senior minister of Temple Baptist Church from 1910–1926. "Many ministers," declared the *Times*, " 'make good' in Los Angeles, the best churched city in the West."[7] Brougher not only made good in Los Angeles; he also went on to make good as well on the national stage. Brougher very well might have been Los Angeles' first celebrity pastor. He not only defended "sensational methods" for attracting people to church, believing that one had to preach "the old-fashioned gospel in a way that can be understood by the man in the street," he also created sensations of his own when he secretly performed the wedding ceremony of movie stars Mary Pickford and Douglas Fairbanks at the church parsonage in 1920. Since both stars had previous marriages, there was considerable consternation in Baptist circles over the ceremony. Despite repeated calls for his ouster from his committee position in the Northern Baptist Conference, Brougher survived and later went on to lead the denomination in one of its more critical periods.

More than anything else, James Whitcomb Brougher was a peacemaker and unifier in a time when both were rare virtues. Born on January 7, 1870, in Vernon, Indiana, he received his education at the University of California and Rochester Seminary. As a Los Angeles pastor, Brougher was known for pioneering pulpit exchanges. "A notable event in local church circles," observed the *Times* in early 1920, "will be the exchange of pulpits…by Dr. J. Whitcomb Brougher, pastor of Temple Baptist Church, and Dr. Charles Edward Locke, pastor of the First Methodist Church. These two nationally known ministers, although serving different denominations, have worked side by side in Los Angeles for the last ten years, and the exchange of pulpits will be in the nature of a celebration of their long friendship."[8] Brougher's pulpit exchanges extended to his friends elsewhere, most notably to Reverend James Logan Gordon of the First Congregational Church of San Francisco.

In June 1925 the *Los Angeles Times* reported, "Hope for the organic union of Protestant evangelical churches of the United States has been strengthened in the ranks of its advocates because of the church-union movement in Canada."[9] No minister in Los Angeles picked up on this hope for church union better than James Brougher. "Will Presbyterians, Congregationalists and Methodists soon unite?" asked the *Times*. "Will Baptists ever follow Dr. Fosdick? Will church union ever be realized? If Christians follow Christ, why so many denominations? These questions will be discussed by Dr. J. Whitcomb Brougher in his speech at the Temple Baptist Church…"[10]

Ten days after Aimee went missing in 1926, Brougher made national headlines when the *New York Times* noted on the front page of its paper that, "Moderates Defeat Fundamentalists In Baptist Election."

> Dr. James Whitcomb Brougher, retiring pastor of the Temple Baptist Church, Los Angeles…whom militant Fundamentalists describe as a … "middle-of-the-roader" in the controversy over modernism, was elected today as President of the Northern Baptist Convention. With him was ushered into office the complete slate of those whom the militants have been fighting.…the new President is accredited with being the Baptist most responsible for holding the forces together. He has been termed… "the Baptist unifier." He has traveled extensively in the interest of unity, delivering an address, "Play Ball," to Baptists all over the country.[11]

Brougher was also most specific about how his fellow Baptists were to "Play Ball." "We will be ready to go," stated the newly elected president at the convention in 1926, "If every extreme modernist will resign his position and every extreme fundamentalist [will] stop his fighting and get down to business."[12]

The great "middle-of-the-roader" and "Baptist unifier" also reached out to Aimee both in Los Angeles and later in Boston. During Brougher's tenure at Temple Baptist, "The two ministers became the best of friends."[13] Aimee considered him one of the best preachers in Los Angeles. When some of his members at Temple Baptist raised their hands during songs or prayers, Brougher suggested that they transfer their membership to Angelus Temple, where they would feel more at home. And when Aimee held her famous Boston revival in 1931, "Only her old friend, J. Whitcomb Brougher, pastor of Tremont Temple, the most prestigious Baptist Church in New England, welcomed Mrs. McPherson's coming."[14]

James Whitcomb Brougher not only represented the interdenominational character of Protestantism in Los Angeles, he also as a "middle-of-the roader" displayed the theological position where Aimee felt most at home. Capable of labeling herself a "fundamentalist," especially when her orthodoxy was challenged, Aimee used the "f" word sparingly, however, usually reserving it only for shock and awe purposes.

Los Angeles Protestants with their interdenominational character were light years ahead of the rest of the country. Outside of the City of Angels, Aimee would soon begin to feel the heat of the boiling controversy. Apart from the disdain for women ministers, part of the problem grew out of the false perception of Pentecostalism as being a wing of the larger fundamentalist movement. Although Pentecostals were extremely theologically conservative and even "fundamentalistic" in lifestyle, they nevertheless were rejected by the fundamentalists early on as "a real menace in many churches and a real injury to the same testimony of fundamental Christians."[15] The bitter opposition of fundamentalism toward Pentecostalism never healed with the passing of time. With the resurgence of American fundamentalism in the early 1980s, the situation only became exacerbated. Jerry Falwell, in the grand tradition of his elder fundamentalist brother "Fighting Bob" Shuler, added the Pentecostal movement to his enemies list, a manifesto written for him by two of his Lynchburg school professors. Pentecostals did rate better than homosexuals, but the implication of failure to achieve true orthodoxy was quite clear:

> While Fundamentalists, as a group, violently reject the Pentecostal-Charismatic Movement because of its emphasis on the doctrine of tongues, it must, nevertheless, be recognized that the Pentecostal Movement is based upon an evangelical doctrinal foundation. To that foundation, however, the movement had added a stronger subjective religious experience than is accepted by most conservative Christians.[16]

At Harold Ockenga's insistence in 1943, Pentecostals finally found a theological label and home of sorts by joining the National Association of Evangelicals and subsequently providing much of the leadership in later years for that organization. "American historians and sociologists," argues Timothy L. Smith, "have been obsessed with the notion that twentieth-century Christianity was divided between pluralistic modernists and monolithic Fundamentalism." However, as Smith points out, "those who rejected modernist theologies formed a spectrum of Evangelical movements" that was both broad and varied.[17] Pentecostalism, then, was one such movement under the broader evangelical banner.

William Keeney Towner was called as pastor of the First Baptist Church of San Jose on January 1, 1920. In March and August of the following year, he invited Aimee to his church to conduct "two great revival campaigns."[18] Both the church and the pastor were impressed with the "great spiritual awakening" that occurred during and in the wake of Aimee's meetings.

No one captured Aimee's San Jose meetings better than B.J. Morris, the director of religious education at Trinity Methodist Church in Berkeley.

Originally writing for the *Pacific Christian Advocate*, Morris provided a Protestant mainline perspective on the "McPherson Meetings." "Though only a few of the churches of San Jose supported the meetings officially," Morris noted, "the city of San Jose and county of Santa Clara were stirred as never before by a public gathering of any kind, whether religious, political, industrial or educational."[19] For Morris it was also clear why both the city and county "were stirred as never before...Nine-tenths of the conversation... about the meetings concerned...bodily cures rather than...conversions....I think it indicates that the whole tendency of the meetings is to lay more stress upon bodily healing than upon forgiveness of sins."[20]

Morris was at his best when he sought to describe "the most intense moment of all"—the healing services of the McPherson meetings:

> From fifty to one hundred patients are treated at one service. As they form in line with hands lifted they are conducted to the platform while the orchestra plays soft, sweet music. It is a sight never to be forgotten to see persons with all kinds of physical ailment marching slowly with expectant faces into the presence of the one whom they believe can bring divine healing to them. The patients' faces...are radiant with hope and joyful expectation. Some of them weep and some of them laugh with joy. Some come on crutches; some are led because of blindness, while others are carried in the arms of loving friends or fond mothers and fathers. A quiet hush settles over the entire audience and Mrs. McPherson with her welcoming, winsome face, dressed in spotless white, stands before a brilliant light. The scene literally transports the audience out of the ordinary life of normal feeling into a state of ecstasy and expectancy impossible to describe or exaggerate.
>
> As the patient approaches, Mrs. McPherson takes the card and reads the written diagnosis of the ailment. This diagnosis is usually given by the patient, and is not the diagnosis of a physician. After it is read Mrs. McPherson dips her fingers into a silver vessel containing oil and anoints the patient. She then prays, using formulas as follows: "Oh Lord Jesus, in Thy name we command this paralysis, (or deafness, or blindness, or whatever it may be) to be gone. Let it fall from our brother like a mantle that is worn and old. Pour in Thy own life giving virtue and strength, in Jesus' name. Amen." After a brief prayer of this kind, Mrs. McPherson asks, "Have you faith to believe that Jesus heals you now?" Usually the patient who has passed through the long period of training answers "I have." "Then in the name of Jesus," Mrs. McPherson says, in the case of one suffering with paralysis, "lift up your arm." The patient usually tries and then Mrs. McPherson says, "Now, lift it again." This is repeated until the patient exerts his utmost to lift the arm which frequently results in some considerable degree of success.

In addition to anointing the patient with oil and repeating a prayer as stated above, Mrs. McPherson usually lays her hand on the afflicted part. The anointing of oil and laying on of hands is done, as is expressly said, to carry out the scriptural injunction concerning the healing.[21]

Despite Morris' concerns about "an excessive use of hypnotic methods in the name of faith," his conclusions about the McPherson's meetings from a mainline perspective were perceptive and instructive.

> Only a casual look at the crowds that flock to the McPherson meetings is sufficient to impress one with the tremendous soul-hunger of the great mass of people...The meetings make perfectly clear that there is on the part of the great mass of people today a hungering and thirsting after spiritual things that the churches are not satisfying. Along with the excessive use of emotional and hypnotic methods, Mrs. McPherson preaches a simple gospel of evangelism that should be heard more and more in all of our churches.[22]

Clearly the First Baptist Church of San Jose agreed with Morris' assessment. As a result of the "McPherson meetings," it showed impressive gains in membership and became one of the strongest churches within the Northern California Baptist Convention. Towner conducted his own follow-up of the meetings and was most impressed with what he found. The church had on file 3,300 cards signed by individuals who had sought healing during the course of the meetings. Towner, by sending out letters to each of those who had signed a card, noted the results for his church:

> Weeks following the meeting I sent out a card with neither return postage nor envelope, and received over 2,500 answers, thus indicating the deep and abiding interest in this branch of the services.
>
> I asked the patients to reply to the following statements, yes or no.
>
> 1. I was immediately and completely healed. (6% answered in the affirmative.)
>
> 2. I was immediately and partially healed and have continued to improve ever since. (85% replied in the affirmative.)
>
> 3. I experienced no change in my condition either for better or worse. (Less than twenty out of the 2,500 answered this in the affirmative.)
>
> 4. The ministry of anointing and prayer for healing was a great spiritual uplift to me and strengthened my faith. (Only ten out of the 2,500 failed to reply to this statement in the affirmative, thus showing that, independent of its effect upon the body, the ministry of prayer for the healing of the sick is a means of Spiritual Grace, inspiration and comfort.)[23]

So great was Aimee's influence upon the First Baptist Church of San

Jose that they soon appropriated the subtitle of Aimee's monthly magazine, becoming known as "Full Gospel," which was also becoming synonymous with the term "Pentecostal."

On March 20, 1922, Aimee by telegraphic communication was made a member of the First Baptist Church of San Jose. Six days later she was a candidate for ordination with the San Jose Baptist Association. It represented her fourth formal church affiliation and her new attempt to become a Protestant mainline minister. She originally had been ordained together with Robert Semple by Durham's Pentecostal Mission in Chicago, known as the Full Gospel Assembly, on January 2, 1909. After returning to the ministry, she was ordained as an independent Pentecostal evangelist by Nelson Magoon in Washburn, Maine, in the summer of 1917. With the recommendation and sponsorship of Robert J. Craig of San Francisco, Aimee held ordination papers with the Assemblies of God from April 7, 1919, until she returned them on January 6, 1922. She brought the opening message and healing service at the biennial general council of that denomination in September of 1919 but failed to stay with the Assemblies of God after their ultimatum in Denver and concerns over her Angelus Temple ownership, choosing not to renew her ordination papers after 1921. For a short period of time Aimee also carried clergy papers as a "licensed exhorter" with the Methodist Church.

The Reverend Hubert C. Mathews was a young recent seminary graduate and newly ordained Baptist minister serving the nearby Santa Clara church when Aimee came to San Jose in 1922. His memoirs are instructive not only as to how Aimee was perceived, but of the conflicting theological currents affecting the Protestant mainline churches of the time and how the San Jose Baptist Association responded to Aimee's request for ordination.

> Nineteen twenty-two was quite a year for me...I ... received my degree from the Berkeley Baptist Divinity School.
>
> This, too, was the year that Aimee Semple McPherson came to San Jose. She was a woman of great charm; beautiful, buxom and winsome. Her tent was lifted on the County Fair Grounds, and thousands of people flocked to hear her preach. Hundreds came in hopes of being healed; many claimed to have received healing...
>
> The First Baptist Church of San Jose accepted Mrs. McPherson and her teachings. It was not long before those in our church who had come to believe in her Pentecostal teachings drifted over to First Church. Then those who believed they should forsake our Baptist fold to turn Pentecostal began holding prayer services in their homes, drawing folks away from us.
>
> Fundamentalism and Pentecostalism had made inroads into several

churches in the Santa Clara County Baptist Association. The First Church of San Jose...became involved in Pentecostalism under the spell of Aimee Semple McPherson. In fact, Mrs. McPherson became a member of that church and asked to be ordained as a Baptist minister. The churches of the association were called in regular council, and Santa Clara sent me, their pastor.

Mrs. McPherson was beaming. Her winsome ways and her keen mind cast quite a spell over the group. Dr. Orville Coates, pastor of New Monterey Baptist Church, was the moderator. Dr. Towner, of First Baptist, presented the candidate.

After the usual amenities, the questioning of the candidate was begun.

I believe I asked the first question. "Mrs. McPherson, don't you believe you hold some theological teachings which are superior to Baptist beliefs?"

She preferred not to answer. The moderator said, "That's a fair question. You will please answer it."

"I believe my teachings in the matter of public divine healing and the speaking in tongues are necessary if we are to preach the whole gospel. Yes."

"Thank you, Mrs. McPherson. Now that you state you think you have more to offer than is found in the Baptist fold, will you kindly tell us just why you want to join up with us?"

Again she did not wish to answer. "You must answer the question," said Mr. Coates.

"Well, the Baptist churches form the largest segment of Protestantism in the United States," she replied.

"That's all I wanted to ask of you. Thank you."

There was an immediate division in the council. The Pentecostal delegates wished to go on with the questioning; those of strong Baptist leanings had heard enough. The vote to continue resulted in a tie. The council was adjourned.

Dr. Towner was not to be thwarted; he invited those who wished to see Mrs. McPherson ordained to remain.

The council can recommend, but it cannot ordain. A local church can ordain, but unless the council so recommends, such ordination cannot be recognized. It becomes purely a local action.

Mrs. McPherson was ordained as a Baptist minister by the First Baptist Church of San Jose, but since she had not been recommended for ordination by the associational council she was never recognized. Her name never appeared among the Baptist ministers of Northern California, nor nationally.

So the churches were divided even further. The two strong wedges, Fundamentalism and Pentecostalism, made the breach more evident.[24]

By May 1922 the Sunday bulletin of the First Baptist Church of San Jose listed a new minister upon its cover: "The Reverend Aimee Semple McPherson, Evangelist at Large."[25] Both the *San Jose Mercury-Herald* and the *San Francisco Chronicle* featured the denominational decision in their pages. Aimee was quoted as saying, "Some of the Baptists are not just sure what I'm going to do and are a bit afraid to take the responsibility for me, but they can't get around the fact that I am an ordained minister of the Baptist Church qualified to fill a pulpit of the church whether it be in San Jose or Bangkok, Siam."[26]

The Reverend Orville Coats, moderator of the San Jose Baptist Association, however, was most specific as to why the council failed to recommend Aimee for ordination:

> The principal points of non-acceptance were the "Pentecostal" theories of the "baptism of the Holy Spirit" and "speaking with tongues." Mrs. McPherson expressed herself as definitely out of sympathy with the extravagances and fanaticism of the so-called "tarry meeting"…The subject of the "healing ministry" was discussed in the private session of the council, which for two hours, gave careful consideration of all aspects of the case.
>
> Mrs. McPherson says her Los Angeles tabernacle represents an undenominational movement. I simply make this statement to remove any misapprehension which may have arisen in the minds of the churches and the public as to the denominational standing of Mrs. Aimee Semple McPherson.[27]

In the early 1920s the chief interpreter and defender of Baptist orthodoxy for Northern California was the Revered C.W. Brinstad, executive secretary of the Northern California Baptist Convention. In the seventy-first annual report of May 1923, Brinstad warned his brother and sister Baptists about the intrusions of both Pentecostalism and fundamentalism into the Baptist fold:

> We believe…that all denominational hyphenations should be eliminated from our vocabulary. The name "Baptist" has been good enough for our people for centuries… Baptists should not have time for "isms" of any kind, whether it be "Fundamentalism," so-called "Pentecostalism," or any other sort. As northern California Baptists have been leading the denomination for years in per capita support of our missionary enterprises, so also should they aspire to lead in defending the faith of our fathers which is based on the Word of God interpreted by sanctified Baptist common sense.[28]

Brinstad from his Market Street office in San Francisco also wrote extensively to the Oregon churches warning them of the "McPherson movement." The fact that Pentecostalism was making great inroads into the Pacific Northwest is apparent from two ministerial responses to the Brinstad letters. The correspondence also indicates the plan of action the Oregon Baptists took in dealing with the threat of the new religious movement.

> My Dear Brinstad,
> I received your letter bearing on the McPherson work and I thank you for the same.
>
> I will not use your name, but have taken the liberty to quote from it...I am desirous of heading off any similar condition in our state, if possible. The Presbyterian minister is anxious to get Dr. Price [an ex-Congregational minister converted to Pentecostalism by Mrs. McPherson] here and last evening I told the ministers that I wish that no church would do anything that would make the work more difficult than it is now by getting in some evangelist who deals in fads.
>
> I have used my influence in our meetings to prevent side-tracking our denominational program and work by the Fundamentalists getting off in a corner by themselves and organizing...If your ministers would read Cutten's *Psychological Phenomena of Christianity* and his *Two Thousand of Mental Healings* it would help them do some clear thinking...Cutten explains how men speak in "tongues" and what causes it. Like yourself, I have yet to see a single person who is really healed, but a number of our people went forward for healing. The whole thing will have its day, and pass away like similar movements of the past, but in the meantime much harm will be done, and the work greatly retarded. Great care should be taken these days in churches getting right type of men as pastors. Sorry to hear that your great work is being hindered; much patience and prayer are called for.
>
> Cordially yours,
> F.R. Leach
> Medford, Oregon[29]

> Dear Dr. Brinstad:
> I wish to thank you for your frank statement re: the McPherson Movement. Some of our pastors here are swept off their feet by it. I attended the meetings at Albany and saw some sixty of the finest cases of hypnotism I ever saw. Fellman is "healing" and his wife is babbling in glossolalia. I am seriously concerned regarding the situation. This week they have removed to our church in Corvallis. Our man in Eugene is sympathetic.

It looks as though they were going down this line. Hinson, Fillus and I seem to be pretty nearly alone in our opposition—oh, yes—let me include Leach of Medford also.

Sincerely yours,
W.T. Milliken
Salem, Oregon[30]

It would become apparent through Milliken's letter that some of the Baptist ministers who opposed the spread of "McPhersonism"—as they termed it—were also involved in attempting to persuade their general conference to adopt a statement of faith in conformity to the "Fundamentals."[31] In Oregon, then, as in California, the strongest reaction to Pentecostalism came from those who were themselves embracing fundamentalism. It is equally clear that the Baptist leadership saw them as two separate movements and both were seen as potentially dangerous to their denominational standards of orthodoxy.

Not all of the Protestant mainline churches in northern California responded to Aimee and to Pentecostalism in similar fashion as did the Baptists. Many Congregationalists gave Aimee much needed support, such as James Logan Gordon and Charles S. Price, while others of the denomination at least maintained a stance of benevolent neutrality.

The Reverend James Logan Gordon was pastor of the First Congregational Church of San Francisco when Aimee met her opposition from the Baptists in San Jose. He was known as the only churchman who could interest the ordinary person in reading the church advertisements in the Saturday newspapers. He was the most well-known churchman in San Francisco if not on the West Coast. He had held pastorates throughout the country, including one in the national capital, and during his tenure in that city easily became the most popular preacher. It was said of Gordon that he combined "the evangelism of Charles Haddon Spurgeon," "the oratorical gifts of Henry Ward Beecher" with "the fine phrasing of Philips Brooks." A "catholicity of spirit" characterized his theological approach. As a result, the First Congregational Church in San Francisco under Gordon appealed to men and women of every race and religion. His congregations included Jews and Christian Scientists, Roman Catholics, and Protestants of every shade and belief. "He breathed the atmosphere of human brotherhood and manifested in word and deed the spirit of brotherly love."[32] First Congregational summarized Gordon's ministry as a time of "Spiritual Awakening Under Dynamic Leadership."

Although Gordon was not ordained to the Congregational ministry until the age of forty, he was revolutionary and a free thinker. In 1927 he gave up his successful pastorate in San Francisco to journey south to Los Angeles to hold independent religious services at the Ambassador Auditorium. Although Gordon "owed much to the Congregational Church and denomination" he decided to become independent because he wanted to preach to the masses behind a pulpit "unhampered by the machinery of modern ecclesiasticism." He was further convinced he should try "to span by a sympathetic approach to every angle of truth" the gap between an "intensely spiritual fundamentalism" and "an intelligent but cold, and almost bitter modernism." Gordon's dream was to establish a "Metropolitan Church… avoiding those things concerning which, most of us differ and emphasizing the vital things concerning which most folks agree." "My real object," stated Gordon upon his resignation, "is to secure the wholesome effect of a great evangelical service devoid of the clap-trap of modern evangelism and without assuming the burden and responsibility of official ecclesiasticism." Gordon was also convinced that "unusual developments may be looked for in the spiritual life and religious growth of our Western States…if America is to produce a world religion," he claimed, "the creed of such a religion will…be written on this side of the Rocky Montains."[33]

It was no doubt Gordon's interdenominational spirit and independent thinking that attracted him to Aimee when she held meetings in the San Francisco Coliseum on April 1–23, 1922. He not only endorsed and introduced Aimee to the Bay Area on the opening day of her campaign; he also had some words for the Baptists who had recently failed to ordain her:

> Mrs. McPherson fifteen years ago was a plain country girl. Today she is preaching to thousands. Aside from the gift of healing, which she is reputed to possess, she is a natural born preacher. For presence, dignity, magnetism, language, and unction of appeal, Aimee Semple McPherson is the equal of Charles H. Spurgeon or Dwight L. Moody. I am informed that certain of the ecclesiastical brethren in this part of the State have hesitated about ordaining this young woman to the ministry; but Aimee McPherson can PREACH, and that is something which some of the ordained class cannot do.[34]

Even *The Pacific*, the West's oldest periodical and the official organ of the California Congregational Conference, treated Aimee with respect. In its July 1922 issue a question addressed to the "Question Drawer" column asked, "Is Mrs. McPherson performing miracles?" The "official" denominational answer was as follows:

Mrs. McPherson is an extraordinary woman, and through her instrumentality people are being healed. She makes no claim for herself.

The power, she declares, is the power of God. By her preaching, the weight of her personal appeal, her presence, her prayers, she gets people into a right attitude towards God. The healing follows. This is exactly what the surgeon does: he removes impediments, sets the broken bone, puts on the bandages, then the miracle of healing begins. No doctor, no surgeon, no faith healer, can heal. When it is possible they remove the cause of disease, every impediment to health, physical, mental, moral, then healing takes place. Yes, Mrs. McPherson is performing miracles.[35]

It also appears that the Congregationalists from Northern California were much more supportive of Aimee's revivalism than their Southern California counterparts. A history of Southern California Congregationalism notes "that Moody was one of the few evangelists who were acceptable."[36] In 1905 J. Wilbur Chapman also conducted "interdenominational campaigns" in the southern part of the state. "In those the Congregationalists cooperated, but not without some criticism....ideas such as, personal work by the local pastors and Christian nurture dominated the evangelism of the [Southern California] Congregationalists from 1905 to this day."[37]

It is doubtful that Aimee's influence over a mainline minister was ever as great as it was upon the life of the Reverend Charles Sydney Price, a Congregational minister from Lodi, California, the center of the Tokay grape industry. Price was a rare man—refined, intelligent and, above all else, extremely gifted. Like Aimee, in many ways, he belonged as much on stage as he did behind a pulpit. A gifted orator, Price had been appointed a "four-minute man" selling war bonds during World War I and had spoken from every theater stage in some of the cities in which he lived. He had also been under contract with the Ellison-White system as a Chautauqua lecturer. Born in England and educated at Wesley College with the intention of becoming a lawyer, Price immigrated to Canada as a young man. If his oratorical abilities characterized much of his life, he would equally be known for the spiritual fits and starts and religious transformations that also appeared throughout his life. Beginning his career in the United States as a candy maker producing "huge caldrons of caramels of every kind and shape," Price soon became a minister by pastoring small, struggling Free Methodist Churches in the Pacific Northwest. Soon his presiding elder took him to task for his "modernistic utterances." Price then severed his Methodist ties for the "broader field" that the Congregational church offered him. Serving the Congregational church in Valdez, Alaska, Price became in rapid

Charles S. Price, a Congregational minister, gifted orator, and Aimee's most famous convert (used by permission of the Flower Pentecostal Heritage Center).

succession the superinten-dent of the Congregational Missions, a member of the United States Alaskan Float-ing Court, and a chaplain in fraternal orders. Acquiring a dog team, the energetic Price also became a wild game hunter, providing himself with enough harrowing expe-riences to later thrill the most jaded of the Chautauqua cir-cuit's audiences. Slowly Price began climbing the rungs on the ladder of ministerial as well as civic success. Accept-ing a "call" to the First Con-gregational Church of Santa Rosa, California, he attempted to run the best "institutional church" in the city and during his stay in the town became well acquainted with Luther Burbank, the renowned botanist.[38]

"With the calling of Charles S. Price an era of many attractions began," noted the church historian at Santa Rosa. "Mr. Price was a talented man, an orator, a musician, a man of varied experiences, young, full of energy and brilliant plans."[39] After noting Price's many gifts, the historian observed the changes in the church affected by Price's ministry.

> The Sunday school took on new life and the ladies redoubled their efforts. Mr. Price gave illustrated lectures on Alaska which helped out....Since coming to Santa Rosa, Mr. Price has preached consistently to greatly interest congregations, his Sunday morning sermons being especially enjoyed by an audience that is steadily growing.[40]

In 1918, after three years in Santa Rosa, Price resigned his pastorate "wishing to enter Chaplain war work." "The lowest ebb" in the life of the First Congregational Church, claimed their historian "was the year following Price's departure."[41] After the war, Price accepted another call to a Congregational church in Oakland, where he became even more active in civic events and where he could be "on the stage during the week and in the pulpit on Sunday."[42]

At Oakland, Price sought to create a thoroughly modern church in touch with the 1920s. A "white maple dance floor with the capacity of 1,500 and smoking lounges" were installed. "I used to love to rise in my pulpit," recalled Price, "and tell the folks of the theatres I had attended the past week, just to show how broad I was...I belonged to almost every lodge and club that I could join."[43] And for a short time it seemed that the theatre instead of the church was Price's true calling. Leaving his church in Oakland for the crowds at Camp Curry in Yosemite Valley, Price was a comedic entertainer by summer and a lecturer by winter.

When the pulpit committee of the First Congregational Church of Lodi was formed to fill their ministerial vacancy, they soon discovered Price. They noted he was "interesting, alert, inspirational, able and consecrated! He is just the man. A most efficient wife, a delightful and wide-awake quartet of children whom you will be proud to have in the parsonage."[44]

The history of the Lodi church likewise noted Price's early ministerial efforts. "In just a few weeks the Sunday church attendance increased to a full house. People came early to get a seat. Mr. Price possessed a wonderful memory and had a graphic way of portraying scenes and events. Soon the townspeople, especially the businessmen, were regular attendants."[45] But despite his success, all was not well internally with Charles Price. Years later after his religious transformation under Aimee's ministry, Price would become known for his famous sermon "The Lonely Cabin on the Forty-Mile." The sermon was simply the story of the downfall of a mainline minister through modernism, which led to alcoholism and the loss of his family. The wayward minister is reclaimed only after the whiskey barrel runs out and he is snow-bound in an Alaskan cabin—a lonely cabin on the "forty-mile." He is reunited with his family and subsequently becomes a Pentecostal minister. In some ways the story parallels the life of Charles Price. Price in his autobiography tells the reader:

> Two roads were opened before me and I took the wrong one. I foolishly turned my back on the cross and started along the trail that led to the labyrinth of modernism...The conflict within my own breast was the age-old battle of reason against faith. How grieved and sorry I am today to have to record that reason won. I very soon got to the point where I could explain every religious emotion from the standpoint of psychology...I preached what I believed and believed what I preached,

but just the same I was spiritually blind, leading many people into the ditch…Then something happened. I come now to the part of the story that I love to tell the most…[46]

What Charles Price loved to tell the most was a conversion experience, or, "a new ideological orientation," as Erik Erikson would have termed it, which he had under the ministry of Aimee at San Jose. Price originally went to the meetings as a critic. Aimee's reputation had spread to Lodi, and Price went to the San Jose meetings with a "bitter antagonism."

They told me of a great campaign where…thousands were being healed. I answered with my explanation of "mob psychology" and "mental and physical reactions."

Inserting an advertisement in the paper that I would preach the following Sunday on "Divine Healing Bubble Explodes," I made my way down to San Jose, armed with pen and paper to take notes. I intended to return the following Sunday and blow the whole thing to pieces. That was my frame of mind. My automobile rolled over the hundred miles that separated my home town from San Jose and as I neared the city a peculiar feeling came over my heart. Across the street was a huge sign in startling, flashing letters, "Aimee Semple McPherson; auspices William Keeny Towner."

I could hardly believe my eyes. Dr. Towner had been pastor of the First Baptist Church in Oakland during the time that I was pastor at Calvary Church. We had been friends and more than once I had seen him laughing at me as I was on the theater stage and on more than one occasion we had gone into the theater together. He was a splendid man, noble and kind, but I knew he was not the type of preacher to back an old-fashioned Holy Ghost revival meeting. I thought that he must be getting something out of it or that he had done it to carry out some policy.

When we were all alone I said to him, "Come on, now, be honest with me, tell me all about it. What are you getting out of it and what is all this 'Hallelujah' business about?"

Looking into my eyes with a serious expression, he said, "Charlie, this is real. This little woman is right. This is the real Gospel. I have been baptized with the Holy Ghost. It is genuine, I tell you. It is what you need."

In amazement I gazed at him. Then I said, "Do you mean to tell me that you, one of the leading Baptist preachers in the West—William Keeny Towner—have actually swallowed this stuff?"

His eyes twinkled. "Charles," he said, "I have swallowed the pole, line, reel, hook, bait and sinker – and yet I am so hungry, I am looking around for some more."[47]

Struggling with the meetings in San Jose, Price recalled, "Deep down in my heart, something told me in recent years I had been wrong—not insincere, but wrong...The next night a masterful message came from the lips of the evangelist and my modernistic theology was punctured until it leaked like a sieve... I did not have to pray. Something burst within my breast. An ocean of love divine rolled across my heart. This was out of the range of psychology and actions and reactions. This was real."[48]

Price returned to his Congregational Church in Lodi a changed man, almost like the hero of his story of "The Lonely Cabin on the Forty-Mile." The church records of the First Congregational Church carefully documented what occurred next to their pastor and ultimately to their church:

> The fall work was barely underway, when our pastor asked for a leave of absence that he might go east... Permission was granted. The purpose of his visit was to study the methods of Mrs. Aimee Semple McPherson, then conducting revival and healing meetings in the east. After being away six weeks, the church wired that they would expect him back in two more weeks. He came home filled with enthusiasm for this new phase of religion.
>
> So filled was our minister with what he had seen in the east and so anxious was he that Lodi hear Mrs. McPherson that permission was given him to wire her an invitation to speak in our church at her earliest convenience. She came December 28. The church was thronged. After this appearance in Lodi, our pastor with some of our members and others from other churches, deeming a series of meetings here with Mrs. McPherson would be beneficial to all the churches of the town and the town, itself, arranged for and built what was known as "The Tabernacle" on North Sacramento Street. Here, in January, the meetings largely sponsored by the Congregational and Methodist Churches, opened. The McPherson program consisted of tarry meetings held during the day or evening. In addition to her preaching, augmented by a large chorus choir, there was held after the preaching, healing meetings.
>
> With the coming of the change in Reverend Price and his preaching, the businessmen ceased to attend services, the men's club languished, and a new group of church attendants was to be seen...In the church meeting of August 1, Mr. Price stated he had a call to the associate pastorship of the Echo Park Tabernacle in Los Angeles besides a number of calls to conduct evangelistic campaigns...so he proposed to submit his resignation as pastor at the regular monthly meeting August 8... Before the fall months passed, a new church organization composed of those who embraced the "foursquare" gospel of Mrs. McPherson was formed and many left our church to attend it, some taking their letters

then. Others asked for and were granted letters as time went on. From
our Sunday school went ten teachers some of them taking whole classes
with them.[49]

The senior deacon of the First Congregational Church summarized with
pathos not only what occurred with their church and minister, but what
could be said equally well of the other Protestant mainline churches, especially in the West, as a result of Aimee's revivalism:

 This has been an eventful year for our Church. We have enjoyed a
 spiritual uplift and then had the shadow of sorrow cast over us, as many
 of our ardent and beloved members with other fellow worshipers have
 withdrawn to worship by themselves. Our hearts are grieved and follow
 them in love, as children are followed, when they leave the old home
 where they were born and nurtured, to start a new one with all its untried
 possibilities.[50]

CHAPTER FIFTEEN

Rochester: "The Most Antagonistic City" and The Burned-Over District Revisited
November 2–25, 1921

Few areas of the United States have seen the flowering of as many diverse enthusiasms and social and moral reforms as blossomed along the old Mohawk Trail and the early Erie Canal in New York State in the nineteenth century. As settlers poured into what had been the traditional lands of the Iroquois Nation, experiments of all kinds of a religious and of a social nature found a haven in these new lands. At one religious extreme were the celibate Shakers...At the other end of the ...scale was the creation of the Perfectionist Oneida Community.... In between these extremes, the religious effervescences gave the name of the "Burned Over District" to western New York. Just as a forest fire can sweep all before it, the religious and reforming urges swept their way across the Ontario Plain between Albany and Lake Erie, changing the religious and social approaches to life....Out of this experimental milieu were to come reforms in religion, new religious sects, the development of the anti-slavery and temperance forces, and the beginning of the Women's Rights movement. Western New York was to become a cauldron of new ideas and attitudes between the 1790s and the century which followed.

—John H. Martin
Saints, Sinners and Reformers:
The Burned-Over District Re-Visited

The site of Rochester," wrote Blake McKelvey, the city's historian, "has, from the beginning, been linked with the future rather than with the past."[1] Before Aimee's campaign in November 1921, the future-oriented city and "cauldron of new ideas and attitudes" had evolved at least four times into something newer and better. Inventions and industry played their part but so too did the religious and reforming urges that continuously bubbled up in the larger, yeasty cauldron of western New York, the legendary "Burned-over District" itself.

In the summer of 1811 Colonel Nathaniel Rochester surveyed his hundred-acre tract on the Genesse River near its mouth on Lake Ontario. On May 1, 1812, the village's first permanent settlers arrived. After the War of 1812 and the return of peace in 1815, the small village at the site of the Genesee falls had three hundred thirty-one residents and a Presbyterian church. Envisioning nothing more than a mere "rustic village," Colonel Rochester himself soon purchased a house overlooking the river for his family. "He hastily set out a pear orchard back of the house, but before the young seedlings could blossom, they had to be uprooted to make way for a canal basin."[2]

When the route of the Erie Canal, "DeWitt Clinton's ditch," was finally determined in 1817, the "rustic village" of Rochester was quickly transformed to a "bustling market town," and by the 1820s Rochester had become "America's first boom town," increasing ten-fold faster than any town had ever grown before.[3] One of the last major settlements in western New York, its growth occurred not without a heated debate between those "who wished to plan for the future city and those who preferred to cling to the old village traditions."[4] In the end, the future won out and a "Booming Canal Town: 1822–1834" was born.

The "Young Lion of the West" is how the booming canal town described itself in the first village *Directory* published in 1827. It quickly became a cosmopolitan "young lion of the West" as well. Newcomers streamed in from the East: French Canadians, Irish and German immigrants, "and some 200 Negroes."[5] With visitors and travelers arriving on five stage lines and on the "canal packets" or lake boats, as they were called, the "young lion of the West" was lustily roaring. With travelers and boatmen alike overflowing the taverns, "reckless elements in nightly revels...taxed the patience of the village."[6] In 1830 a tall, handsome charismatic preacher with striking blue eyes and a dramatic voice arrived in Rochester by boat and soon the "young lion of the West" was tamed and roaring no more. The canal boom town quickly returned to normalcy.

It was Charles Grandison Finney who gave the larger region its name, referring to it as a "burnt district" because so many revivals had occurred in western New York during America's Second Great Awakening. Finney, declared the historian Richard Hofstader, "must be reckoned among our great men."[7] Finney's greatness was not simply discovered on the "scoreboard for Jesus." Rather, "Finney's work and the way he understood the gospel 'released a mighty impulse toward social reform' that shook the nation and helped destroy slavery."[8]

Born in 1792, Finney was raised in central New York. He was starting a career as a lawyer when on October 10, 1821, he witnessed a bright light in his law office and underwent a profound spiritual conversion at the age of twenty-nine. Prior to his conversion he had been studying the Bible "to better understand law-book references to Mosaic legislation."[9] He had also been the subject of his fiancée's prayers and religious entreaties. The morning after his spiritual experience he announced to a startled client: "Deacon, I have a retainer from the Lord Jesus Christ to plead his cause and I cannot plead yours."[10]

Like any good lawyer turned evangelist, Finney was controversial for his introduction of "new measures" into revivalism. Rejecting traditional Calvinist theology and Unitarianism, Finney "became a founder of New School Presbyterianism that emphasized an evangelistic style of religion."

> His preaching style was popular and colloquial, though forceful and laced with the logic of the lawyer. He popularized the "protracted meeting" that continued for several days or weeks and employed the anxious bench, "a row of seats in the front of the church for those under 'conviction' " of sin. Perhaps the most controversial of his "new measures" was encouraging women to pray and speak in "promiscuous" or mixed assemblies.[11]

Both Finney and Rochester were changed by the revival of 1830. "Thousands flocked to hear him, until the fame of the Rochester Revival spread throughout the country and brought listeners from distant cities."[12] "No more impressive revival has occurred in American history," wrote Whitney R. Cross. "Sectarianism was forgotten and all churches gathered in their multitudes."[13] Part of the success in Rochester came from the evangelist's own personal appeal and natural abilities:

> Graceful in motion, skilled in vocal music, with a voice of extraordinary clarity, tone, and ranges of power and pitch, he spoke without mannerisms in concise, familiar figures. Having been not only a lawyer but also an accomplished horseman, marksman, and sailor, he could utilize parables meaningful to common folk.[14]

After Rochester, Finney was preaching to large crowds in Philadelphia, Boston, and New York. "Calls for the evangelist's services flooded in from all sides as the news spread, and for four years he answered the most pressing of them."[15] In 1835 he published his lectures on *Revivals of Religion* and became a professor of theology at the newly founded Oberlin College. "Except for frequent revival trips to New York, England, and elsewhere, Finney spent the rest of his life in Oberlin, becoming president of the college in 1850."[16]

Oberlin College was not only the first coeducational college in the world but one of the few places that actually encouraged women to get an education. Oberlin's first president, Asa Mahan, was so proud of this fact that he suggested his tombstone epitaph read, "The first man, in the history of the race who conducted women, in connection with members of the opposite sex, through a full course of liberal education and conferred upon her the high degrees which had hitherto been the exclusive prerogatives of men."[17] In 1850 Oberlin "even granted a theological degree to a woman, Antoinette Brown, who after many difficulties was ordained three years later."[18]

Elizabeth Cady Stanton was one of Finney's more famous converts. After her conversion at one of his revivals, Stanton helped guide *The Woman's Bible* into production. An immediate best-seller, *The Woman's Bible* was "an attempt to purge the Christian scriptures of anti-female interpretations."[19] (Eventually becoming a Unitarian, in the end Stanton became "a skeptic."[20])

"It is significant," wrote Rochester's historian, that "Finney's influence was greatest among the more intelligent elements of the community whom other evangelists found hard to move."[21] Some of this was intentional on Finney's part. He was less concerned with "the dramatic conversion of profligate sinners," and his message instead was "directed primarily to church people or 'professors of religion' not living up to the fullness of Christian existence."[22]

"On his first incursion," concluded the city historian, "the results had been truly remarkable.....from that time forward nearly every succeeding year until 1842 saw some sort of religious outpouring, while no less than thirteen new churches were founded in Rochester between 1834 and 1844."[23] In addition to the creation of new churches, the established churches were also strengthened. "Six hundred and thirty-five persons joined the three Presbyterian churches in the city; 203 were added to the First Baptist church; and the Methodists were so uplifted that they felt justified in building a church capable of seating 2,000 people."[24] When Finney left Rochester in the spring of 1831 after six months of daily preaching, "it was a changed community, animated by a new spirit of self-conscious restraint. The days of the boom town were over."[25]

A much sobered Rochester evolved as "The Flour City: 1834–1854." The excellent wheat of the surrounding Genesee lands, coupled with the latest milling devices, secured Rochester's reputation for flour for the next two decades. Constructing two large mills, "the largest in the world," the city produced upwards of five hundred thousand barrels of fine flour annually. In addition to the two largest mills in the world, "substantial brick and stone churches, topped by lofty spires" also began to dominate Rochester's skyline. The spires were symbols not only of New England but of a "transplanted heritage" from the South as well as Irish and German Catholic parishes and other Old World communities.[26] With a population of 43,877 in 1850, Rochester's fifty churches won it "the title of banner city in the New York Sunday School movement."[27] Bible, tract, and missionary societies also quickly established regional headquarters in the city during this time. Prior to Finney's return to Rochester in 1842, other revivals stirred the city in 1833. One of the revivalists was Glezen Fillmore, pastor of the Methodist Church and brother of Millard Fillmore, a future President of the United States.[28]

Finney's second Rochester revival in 1842 "was only slightly less enthusiastic."[29] Unlike the earlier revival, this one "was especially famous for its wholesale conversion of the lawyers of the city."[30] With the ex-law student himself applying "all the logical and proven methods" of the courtroom to the cause of Christ, many lawyers converted. One of the converted presented Finney "with a legal deed complete in every detail 'in which he quitclaimed to the Lord Jesus Christ all ownership of himself and of everything he possessed.' "[31]

Finney's revivalism left Rochester with two lasting results: "a rigorous orthodoxy amongst Protestant Christians" and a "spirit of moral reform."[32] This was, of course, the enduring legacy of Charles Grandison Finney himself, who stressed that revival and reform went hand in hand. In his *Lectures on Revivals of Religion,* Finney wrote that "revivals are hindered when ministers and churches take wrong ground in regard to any question involving human rights."[33] "If the church fails to speak out against such an issue as slavery," continued Finney, "she is perjured, and the Spirit of God departs from her."[34] "One of the reasons for the low state of religion at the present time," he continued, "is that many churches have taken the wrong side on the subject of slavery, have suffered prejudice to prevail over principle, and have feared to call this abomination by its true name."[35]

With an increasing concern with the growing ills of society, a united, reform-minded Protestantism went to work in Rochester "filled with glowing hope for the future…that all things might with good spirit, be made whole."[36] On the reform agenda were temperance, education, and the abolition movement. Sectarian rivalries prevented the Presbyterians from establishing a college at Rochester in 1846. Two years later the Baptists took up the initiative, rallying widespread support, and in November 1850 both the new University of Rochester and the Rochester Theological Seminary opened their doors in the old United States Hotel. Reform in Rochester was found with individuals as well as institutions. And the city had produced at least three of them by mid-century.

Susan B. Anthony was undoubtedly Rochester's most famous resident. Born in Massachusetts, she moved to Rochester as a young woman of twenty-five with her parents in 1845. Teaching school in Canajoharie, Anthony missed the first Woman's Rights Convention, the 1848 Seneca Falls Convention, "held in the heart of Finneyite territory and convened by Elizabeth Cady Stanton."[37] By 1852 Anthony became a leader in the cause that would become her life's work.

In 1872, after reasoned arguments on behalf of women's right to vote proved ineffective, Anthony decided to test her right before the courts. Along with thirteen other women from Rochester, she appeared at the polls in November demanding the right to register and vote in the national election. "The ballots they attempted to cast were challenged, and Miss Anthony was arrested and brought to trial on a charge of illegal voting."[38] Although a judge found her guilty and levied a $100 fine against her, Anthony had the last word on the issue as woman suffrage finally triumphed a half-century later.

Helpful to Anthony's cause was her friend and colleague, Francis E. Willard. A Methodist crusader and head of the Women's Christian Temperance Union, "it was…Frances Willard…who made suffrage palatable to the masses by tying the issue into 'temperance' and 'home protection.' "[39] Temperance became both a great Protestant and Progressive crusade and on January 16, 1920, the Eighteenth Amendment came into effect. Later, in the same year, the Nineteenth Amendment was passed, establishing the right of women to vote.

Anthony did not live to see her life's work become legislation. She passed quietly fourteen years earlier on March 13, 1906. "For the first time in Rochester's history, the flags fluttered at half mast and the Court House bell tolled the passing of a woman. Ten thousand people plodded through a deep snow to do her honor during the funeral held in the spacious Central Presbyterian Church."[40]

No Rochesterian achieved wider fame in the 1850s than Frederick Douglass. At the time he was considered "the leading Negro statesman in the country."[41] Editor of the *North Star* (later renamed *Frederick Douglass' Paper*), Douglass was not only in demand as a popular speaker, but he traveled widely "across the land advocating the abolition of slavery."[42] Douglass had also been at the Seneca Falls Conference in 1848 "to discuss the social, civil, and religious condition and rights of women."[43] More importantly, however, he, unlike Mrs. Stanton's husband and several close friends, supported Stanton's ninth resolution that stressed the value of the ballot for women. "The first word of encouragement" the convention received came from Douglass' *North Star* on July 28, 1848.[44] The battle for the ballot was a cause Douglass was engaged in for himself as well as his race. Douglass was also a frequent visitor in Susan B. Anthony's Rochester home.[45]

When the Civil War broke out in 1861, Douglass persuaded the North to enroll African-Americans as full-fledged soldiers. When several black Union soldiers were captured and executed by Confederate troops, Douglass requested an interview with President Lincoln. "The first Negro to enter the White House, other than as a servant, he had a respectful hearing from the President, who promised to do all that was humanely proper to assure the equal treatment of all soldiers and all captives whether white or black."[46]

Zebulon Brockway came to Rochester in 1854 to become the first superintendent of the newly opened penitentiary out on South Avenue. Two years later, after attending another revival conducted by Finney, Brockway "came away determined to reform his men."[47] At first, Brockway organized a Sunday school at the penitentiary, only to discover "that the men who sang and prayed the loudest, were the first to come back after their discharge."[48] Next he came up with the idea of "an indeterminate sentence," holding men until they were "reformed." Not being able to implement his new plan at Rochester, Brockway went to the new state reformatory at Elmira in 1877 "where he developed modern penal techniques and became the father of prison reform."[49]

"The characteristic of Rochesterians" of this era, noted the city historian, "was faith in their country, in their city, and in themselves." It was an "age of optimism, of ready adaptation to circumstances, of willingness to press forward gallantly toward the unknown future."[50]

It was the "ready adaptation to circumstances" that also help prepare Rochester for its third transformation into "The Flower City: 1854–1890." "Riding high on the swelling tide of western wheat," St. Louis by mid-century replaced Rochester as the nation's "preeminent flour milling center."[51] Meanwhile, in 1840 on the city's outskirts, George Ellwanger from Germany and Patrick Barry from Ireland established a nursery.

By the mid-1850s their Mt. Hope Nurseries "had become the largest in the nation…and the reputation of their products, sold far and wide throughout the expanding West…helping to win Rochester the title of Flower City"[52] The change in the city's title from "Flour—to flower city" was "symbolic of the shift of emphasis from the older rustic virtues of the Yankee period to the more exotic values of the cosmopolitan community which emerged during the second half of the nineteenth century."[53]

It was during this new era in the Flower City's growth and development that Rochester began turning its back on the water resources "that had been the pride and glory of its first half-century."[54] The city began to rely increasingly on railroads instead, especially the expanding monopoly of the New York Central. Local ties to regional cites were quickly becoming less important to Rochester than its contacts with larger cities and "with more distant cultures, with new ideas and techniques."[55]

The Civil War, with its demand for ready-made supplies, had also given Rochester an added impetus for "new ideas and techniques." Soon shoes and clothing were leaving Rochester in railcars. By the mid-1880s "Rochester stood fourth among the clothing manufacturing cities of America and third among those making shoes."[56] The first application of the sewing machine to shoes in Rochester (possibly in the world) occurred in 1852. Thirty years later the shoe factories employed some five thousand workers. The sewing machine also found its way into the clothing factories, and soon Rochester was "developing a name for quality in men's suits."[57] The myth of progress was, however, taking a heavy toll and exacting much more than a fair price. "The sweatshops of the subcontractors, where perhaps twenty-or-so recent immigrants of all ages labored in crowded houses, characterized this industry."[58]

The influx of thousands of newcomers from abroad presented a challenge to the older, more established Protestant churches. Many immigrants brought staunch religious ties with them, and the growth of various Catholic and Lutheran churches as well as Jewish synagogues reflected their presence. Both the Baptists and Methodists helped fellow believers from abroad establish chapels and churches in their own languages. The Rochester Theological Seminary even created a German Baptist Department under Dr. August Rauschenbusch. But it would be the German Baptist professor's son, Walter, born in Rochester in 1861, who not only would speak most eloquently to the growing ills of the city, but to the nation as well.

The "prophet of the social gospel" in some ways simply "brought the early evangelical zeal of Charles G. Finney up to date." His call, likewise, was not for sinners to repent, "but for good and righteous citizens to re-examine their responsibilities to society."[59] Walter Rauschenbusch died at age fifty-six, shortly after publishing his third and final book, *Theology for the Social Gospel*. His "writings and influence" will live on, noted Rochester's historian, especially "in theological schools and pulpits all over the land." And as a reminder to the citizens of Rochester, the historian concluded, "He should not be without honor here, too."[60] In many ways Rauschenbusch was the proverbial lonely prophet without honor in his own hometown. As will be noted below, his liberal record of reform also left a legacy of racial exclusion in the city of his birth. Additionally, as a leading proponent of Social Christianity, Rauschenbusch also failed to breach the denominational barriers which separated the churches where he lived and taught.

The Parliament of Religions at the World's Fair in Chicago in 1893 had stimulated several movements for religious unity across the country. One such organization, the Brotherhood of Christian Unity, formed a local chapter in Rochester in 1895. It drew primarily on the support of liberal ministers such as the well-known Unitarian William Gannett and Rabbi Max Landsberg. Some residents "rallied to the cause, but little was accomplished."[61] In 1901, Rochester's federation of churches was created, with Professor Rauschenbusch serving on the committee that drafted its charter. The "E" word that had figured so prominently in Robert Baird's *Religion in America*, published in 1842, also plagued Professor Rauschenbush's committee. "The committee's decision to omit the word, 'evangelical,' in order to bring in the Unitarians and the Jews, produced a revolt on the right led by the Methodists who refused to join such a body."[62] Even though Gannett and Landsberg offered to withdraw from the federation, Rauschenbusch was unable to breach the city's denominational divide. "Tempers had risen to such a point that nothing could be accomplished. Ultimately a Ministerial Association was formed in 1903, admitting only those who met the evangelical test."[63]

Aimee herself purposely and resourcefully utilized "evangelical" whenever she could. From Baltimore on it replaced "Pentecostal" in her theological vocabulary. By refusing to drop her ministry of "Divine Healing," however, more often than not she too would fail to meet the ever-constricting standards of evangelical orthodoxy. Her best chances for winning over Protestant establishment support would come from evangelicals liberal enough to embrace spiritual healing, and from Methodists who still remembered their own revivalistic past. She would find such ministerial support in Rochester, but their numbers would be meager, and they would be in the clear minority.

Aimee entered a far different city than Finney had a century before her. From 1890–1940, Rochester experienced its golden age. No longer the "young lion of the West," Rochester had grown and matured into a city of many industries. "Rochester-made means quality" was far more than a successful advertising slogan. It was also the very essence of what the city aspired to be. "Not only did Rochester specialize in quality products…to win a rich market….it strove for the best schools, the best parks, the best water system, the best medical care....the best government....the best in every field where that goal could possibly be achieved."[64] And in Rochester that also included religion. "The churches enjoyed wide support and...the theological seminary was richly endowed by Rockefeller."[65]

Doubling its population between 1900 and 1930, Rochester had also become, despite its diversity of industries, "Kodak City." "Just as Detroit grew with the demand for automobiles...Rochester grew with the expanding markets for photographic apparatus and supplies."[66] George Eastman's original company of 1880 required only a few rooms on the third floor of a music store. Within a decade, his small box camera, the Kodak, had opened the hobby to amateurs. "All one had to do was aim the camera and press the button, and after taking 100 pictures, mail it back to the Eastman Company for development and reloading."[67] The Eastman Kodak Company quickly became one of the most extraordinary success stories in modern America. Kodak Park, the company's main manufacturing facility, grew from fifty-four acres in 1910 to two hundred thirty-five in 1920, and four hundred eight in 1930. "By 1934 Kodak employed 23,000 Rochesterians." In the early 1920s, when Aimee came to hold a revival, most people would have been in agreement with George Eastman's assessment that Rochester had come of age and "is well started on its way toward being the finest city in the world to live in and bring up families."[68]

Ninety-one years after Charles Grandison Finney arrived in the "young lion of the West" by a packet canal boat, a Methodist minister wrote that "a spiritual aeroplane flew over Rochester and dropped [Aimee Semple McPherson] as it were, from the clouds."[69] The Methodist minister making this assessment was no ordinary Methodist minister either. Dr. Frank Charles Thompson, prior to coming to Asbury Methodist Church in 1912 as its associate minister, had completed thirty-two years of independent ministry and "was the author of two books: a children's classic and the *Chain-Reference Bible*."[70]

In 1890 Thompson began work on a project that not only would outlive him but remains in print today. The *Thompson Chain-Reference Study System* offers "a complete study library in one volume," while the companion *Thompson Chain-Reference Bible*, originally published in 1908, has sold more than four million copies. When the reader completed "thought suggestions" opposite the Biblical verses, these became the "chain-links" of the Thompson system. Seeing their pastor's Bible with its marginal references, some of the men in Thompson's church had encouraged him to have his work published. In 1908 the first edition of the *Thompson Chain-Reference Bible* was printed by the Methodists Book Concern of Dobbs Ferry, New

York. "The following year saw the publication of C.I. Scofield's *The Scofield Reference Bible.* Thompson provided the model of a study system that was doctrinally objective, while Scofield presented a specific system of interpretation in his notes. Most modern study Bibles fall into one or the other category, established by these pioneering works."[71] Not only has Thompson's study Bible stood the test of time, but it has always been identified as being mainstream Protestant, unlike Scofield's work.

"My father's home," wrote Thompson in 1921, "was in Rochester and I have kept in close touch with the city during a ministry of forty-one years and I can testify that nothing like [the McPherson] meetings has ever occurred here before."[72] Before listing the distinctive traits of the revival itself, Thompson admitted its rather bleak beginnings:

> She came in as quietly as Paul entered Rome…A few friends with audacious faith had secured the largest auditorium in the city….Looked at from a purely human standpoint, such an enterprise was bound to fail. The average evangelist that had come to our city in late years, even when backed by several churches, had counted himself happy if he had three or four hundred people out to hear him on week nights.
>
> But here comes a woman with absolutely no local organization behind her, who within a few days…has filled our largest hall to overflowing and soon thousand are being turned away.[73]

In the style of completing objective "thought suggestions" for his chain-reference Bible, Thompson thoughtfully and carefully observed and noted what made Aimee's preaching and the services in Rochester so "phenomenal."

> The messages of Sister McPherson were beautiful…unlike many modern evangelists, there was no bitterness in her messages, nor underhanded flings at the church nor criticisms of ministers….the audience was swayed as the waves of the sea and with tears in their eyes moved to the altar in crowds….the keynote of every service was Jesus Christ, the same yesterday, today and forever, not the great "I was" but the real "I am."
>
> The most startling and pathetic feature in the campaign was the faith healing services.
>
> Never before had I fully realized what the passages in the Gospels meant when they said the multitudes pressed upon Christ and thronged Him, seeking healing.
>
> In many services large portions of the hall were filled with those seeking physical relief…
>
> The meetings closed with vast numbers beating at the doors trying to get in.[74]

Despite packing out the city's Convention Hall with "vast numbers beating at the doors trying to get in," the meetings at Rochester were far more controversial than those in either San Diego or Denver. With the exception of the Asbury Methodist Church, there was little to no mainline religious support. Shortly before leaving the city, Aimee told a reporter for the *Herald* that "Rochester is the most antagonistic city in which she has ever held a revival."[75] Under headlines that read, "Woman 'Healer" Cuts Rochester Stay Short, Admitting That Local Folk Are Most Antagonistic She Had Met With," the reporter suggested in his story that Rochester's lack of response to the evangelist was directed not at her preaching "but her healing." Aimee countered back with, "God does not limit us to pray for our souls. He says we may also pray for our bodies."[76] But in Rochester, the reporter was right. Aimee's healing was by far the most controversial aspect of her revival. Few newspapers provided daily coverage of the meetings. Most were hit-or-miss. Even the most extensive coverage provided by the *Democrat and Chronicle* appeared on the back pages. And it is not that Rochester wasn't concerned with health and healing—it was.

On the day Aimee opened her meetings in Convention Hall, headlines in the *Democrat and Chronicle* read, "In Health Rochester in Time Will Rank Second to No Other Place in World, Belief of George Eastman."

> Rochester will be a medical center of the first importance when plans being formulated for the School of Medicine of the University of Rochester have become effective, according to George Eastman. Mr. Eastman said yesterday that the time is near when it will be possible for the poorest family in Rochester to have the benefits of all that modern medicine and surgery afford in the treatment of cases of sickness and in preservation of health.[77]

Nowhere else in all of Aimee's revivals was there such a sharp contrast between "modern medicine" and "divine healing." And the mainline Protestant religious clergy of Rochester left no doubt where they stood on the subject. The day after Aimee left the city, the Federation of Churches made reference to the recent "'divine healing' meetings conducted in Convention Hall by Mrs. Aimee Semple McPherson."[78] The federation issued a statement in its semi-monthly publication:

> Whatever be our attitude on the matter of "divine healing," as carried on at Convention Hall, we will probably all agree that the number and thoroughness of the "cures" have slight effect on the volume of human ills....the real miracles of healing...are on the operating tables in the hospitals.[79]

The federation did note, however, that the McPherson meetings "may be looked upon as a protest and evidence that something is lacking in the life of the church today."[80]

Ironically, despite early press reports hailing her "as the greatest evangelist of the age and known to thousands of her converts as 'The Woman in White' because of her practice of wearing a simple white gown when preaching and healing," Aimee sought at the outset of her revival to downplay the healing aspect of her ministry. On November 2, 1921, the *Democrat and Chronicle* noted,

> Healing meetings will be held two or three times a week during the course of her stay here…in the opinion of Mrs. McPherson they are not the most important part of the services since, according to her view, "the body does not last very long anyway; it is the work that is done for the soul that counts." . . . ."These miracles only show the power of prayer" . . . ."I am not a wonderful person endowed with superhuman ability but a firm believer in the power of prayer … There are many who are not healed, but they are in the minority and I should say that at least 85 percent of the persons who come to us for healing are made well. It is necessary, however, that a person come to us with faith and attend at least four or five of our meetings."[81]

Aimee had arrived in Rochester with her own "extraordinary gift for hope" and "romantic readiness," and she also came well armed with Charles Price for a spiritual showdown with the city's established churches. And when Price's credentials failed to garner more mainline support in what Aimee called "this dear old conservative city," she quickly brought in even more theological artillery with yet another Congregational and Methodist minister. Price was on leave of absence from his Congregational Church in Lodi, California so that "he might become better acquainted for the work before him" and "to study the methods of Mrs. Aimee Semple McPherson…conducting revival and healing meetings in the east."[82] Rochester would provide his proving and training ground. In addition to conducting the services and leading the singing, Price would give his personal testimony several times during the Rochester revival. The story Price often told was that "he was a minister of an aristocratic Congregational Church in California" who had been converted "to Mrs. McPherson's faith."[83] He explained that "he did not hold a doctor of divinity degree, but a doctor of philosophy degree, obtained from a college in Sheffield, England."[84] Due to his education, he had given "sermons on philosophy, psychology, sociology and pathology to his congregations, but never had an altar call or preached the gospel directly."[85] That had all changed, Price said, after his hundred-mile journey to visit the McPherson meetings in San Jose. After witnessing first hand "the work performed by Mrs. McPherson" he "consecrated himself...received the born-again blessing and...felt a tingling and a warm sensation from head to toes, his chest heaved and he spoke through no force of his own."[86] He had received "the faith."

On Saturday, October 29, 1921, a large maternal-seeming picture of Aimee, taken by the Gerhard Sisters of St. Louis, appeared in the church section of *The Rochester Herald*. Above the picture, the headline read: "Woman Evangelist Here Tomorrow." The caption below the picture noted her uniqueness in American revivalism:

In the 1920s Time magazine described Aimee as having "high-piled, unshorn dark hair, full wide lips a little irregular, unusually white teeth, a generous nose, eager long-lashed eyes" (author's collection).

MRS. AIMEE SEMPLE M'PHERSON, noted woman evangelist, will speak here to-morrow at Calvary Baptist Church...and at Asbury Methodist Church...She will begin evangelistic campaign meetings at Convention Hall here next Wednesday...Mrs. McPherson's work is undenominational and her belief is based on the Bible alone. Her faith healing powers have attracted countrywide notice. Her visit to Rochester is expected to result in a great spiritual uplift to the community.[87]

Aimee's two Sunday services at a Baptist and Methodist Church were due to the fact that the city's Convention Hall had been booked for a return visit by Mary Garden, the famous opera star. Despite their differences, the opera star and the evangelist would be similarly described by the newspapers as being "colorful, magnetic and dramatic."[88] During her stay in Rochester Aimee would also share headlines with several other famous visitors to the city.

Two days after Aimee's meetings began in Convention Hall, "William Jennings Bryan, standard bearer of the Democratic party in three presidential elections, whose silver tongue has spoken in trumpet tones on great political and moral issues that have engaged the attention of the nation and the world…visited Rochester not as Bryan, the politician, but as Bryan, the Christian."[89] The *Rochester Democrat and Chronicle*, while observing that there was not "the 'silver' in his voice that he had in younger years," still concluded that his lengthy time of forty-one years on the national stage had "not robbed him of his splendid vigor, infectious enthusiasm…masterly diction, and…spell over his hearers."[90] Indeed, Bryan's "splendid vigor" enabled him to speak three times on November 4, 1921, "in defense of the principles of Christianity."[91] "I am trying to bring some of the honesty of politics into the church," Bryan said.[92] Characterized as "worse than ward politics" were the nation's theological seminaries, who were "instructing students not to let churches know what they think until they have been in them a year or two."[93] After fighting "boss control" for forty years as a politician, Bryan said he was now ready for his new line of work "to take the church out of the hands of the bosses and put it into the hands of the worshippers."[94] Despite the fact that this was exactly what Aimee was doing in her ministry, there is no indication that Aimee and the "great commoner" met during their time together in Rochester. Less than two years later, on September 30, 1923, William Jennings Bryan was one of Aimee's first invited guests to speak in the pulpit of Angelus Temple. It is quite possible that their initial mutual attraction in Los Angeles was more rooted in Progressive politics than theology. Bryan's life was an amazing contradiction: he was politically progressive yet theologically reactionary. Martin Marty, in his *Modern American Religion*, reminds his readers:

> Bryan was a political progressive, a supporter of liberal causes like Woman Suffrage, a federal income tax, the rights of organized labor, full disclosure of their finances by political campaigns, the League of Nations, Prohibition, and more democratic ways of electing the president. All these Bryan neglected when he led the Fundamentalist ranks in public issues in the twenties. In church politics Bryan thus sided with people who would have opposed most of his old political program.[95]

Precisely because Aimee's vision of the church was in "the hands of the worshippers," both her and Charles Price's initial attempts to gain ministerial support from the "bosses"—the mainline ministers of the city— were quickly thwarted and derailed. An unexpected audience showed up at the Convention Hall opening day, practically guaranteeing that Rochester's finest religious establishment would close their doors to any future endorsement. The *Rochester Democrat* and *Chronicle* noted that despite the first snow of the season mixed with heavy rain, on opening day, both "afternoon and evening evangelistic meetings conducted…by Aimee Semple McPherson filled Convention Hall almost to capacity."[96] The article's headlines, however, told the real story of the revival's opening: "GYPSIES TRAVEL LONG DISTANCES TO SEE HEALER."[97]

"The meeting in Convention Hall was no sooner opened than a wonderful thing happened," wrote Aimee to her followers back home.

> A band of Gypsies, headed by their chief, came to attend the revival services. The chief had been in communication with others by letter and telegram for some time as… the tribes…were stirred to the depths through the healing of one of their number from a terrible tumor during the revival in Denver….the news had spread like wildfire. It resulted in…their quaint heart touching pleading that we tell them the story… about Jesus who maketh happy and healthy.[98]

More than anything else the gypsies also transformed Charles Price's experience from his "aristocratic Congregational Church in California" into a real "people's religion" in Rochester, New York. Even his normal eloquence seem to fail him when it was his turn to tell the story.

> Because it is my custom to go a little early and see that everything is orderly and ready for Sister McPherson…I make my way to the Hall, and am greeted by a riot of color… in the front seats. If it were not for the more soberly dressed American people in the other seats you could almost imagine yourself translated to some Oriental country.
>
> Imagine these gorgeously dressed, dark skinned Romany wanderers, doing obeisance to their monarch….yards and yards of almost priceless silks made up their dresses. White shawls from the looms of Persia were wrapped around heads and draped around shoulders…around the necks of all women are hanging string after string of gold coins gathered from all countries of the globe, in such quantities that it seems they must be too heavy to wear.
>
> Sister McPherson walks toward the edge of the platform and her eyes are immediately riveted on the gorgeous array of color in the front seats….That is as far as she got….As I look into Sister McPherson's face I see she is crying and laughing at the same time. Then unable to stand it any longer she holds out her hands and says, "Oh, I just love you and Jesus loves you too."
>
> That is all they need. Out of their seats they come. They kneel and make the sign of the cross, they kiss her hand…they kissed her feet and the hem of her dress, and cried out their petition: "Tell us 'bout Jesus, lady." "Heal my baby, he is so sick, lady. Please, lady, we come long, long way."
>
> Back of me the choir is sobbing…I look at the audience. Is there a dry

eye anywhere? Did Convention Hall ever see such a scene before?[99]

Most likely Rochester's Convention Hall had never witnessed such a scene before, and the Protestant establishment was quickly making plans that it would never happen again. Instead of directly attacking the McPherson meetings at Convention Hall, the publicity machine for the Federation of Churches began an early campaign for a forthcoming five-day evangelistic meeting at the end of the month "to be led by Rev. Dr. John Timothy Stone, pastor of Fourth Presbyterian Church, Chicago."[100] Stone was everything Aimee was not, and the federation was more than happy to draw the contrast between the two. In the words of William Jennings Bryan, Stone derived his support from the "hands of the bosses," while Aimee drew hers directly from "the hands of the worshippers."

The Federation of Churches also saw the two meetings as a battle between the churched and the unchurched. And they left little doubt as to whose side they were on. "The Committee of One Hundred promoting the John Timothy Stone meetings to be held…November 28 to December 2," noted the newspaper is "an effort…to interest the leading laymen and women of all the Protestant churches in the Rochester district. Letters have been sent to the ministers requesting lists of persons to whom invitations should be directed."[101] Still another newspaper noted that the upcoming evangelistic committee had been organized by "a large group of prominent men."[102] The executive secretary of the Federation of Churches noted that the purpose of the forthcoming meetings was "not so much to reach the unchurched as to inspire and fit the churches themselves."[103]

The secretary also did his best to contrast the future meetings with the current meetings at Convention Hall. "The evangelism which Dr. John Timothy Stone represents," he stated, "[is] that which appeals to the modern man. It is not a faddist evangelism, nor is it sensational…The world is full today of religious enthusiasts who think that a strong emotionalism is religion, or that a program of future events is Christianity, or that health of body obtained by prayer or philosophy is the highest good which the church can bring us."[104]

And then, as if the contrast between Stone and Aimee was not enough, the secretary added that Dr. Stone's messages were both "sane" and "virile."[105] Manliness, it seemed, was equated with sanity while insanity accompanied femininity. "Our churches," concluded the secretary, "received their bent in the early day from the evangelism of Charles Finney, who gripped the intellectual leaders of the community."[106] Finally, to leave no doubt as to what type of Rochestarian would be supporting the meetings, it was finally noted that "Harold P. Brewster, president of the Rochester Savings Bank ... would be host to Dr. Stone during the five days that the clergyman will be in Rochester. Mr. Brewster and Dr. Stone are friends. Dr. Stone will be the guest of Mr. Brewster at the banker's home."[107]

Faith healing, then, was viewed by many in the Protestant mainline establishment as not only leading to fanaticism but also to a feminine form of Christianity itself. On the West Coast another Presbyterian minister warned "that divine healing could seriously harm churches and Christianity." The Reverend E.S. Chapman, pastor of a Presbyterian church in Oakland and "a liberal advocate of muscular Christianity, was convinced that faith healing produced a form of Christian fanaticism and a 'weak and effeminate type of Christian character,' not a 'rugged, heroic, pain-enduring, battle-fighting, victory-winning' type."[108]

Aimee's assessment of Rochester as "this dear old conservative city" was not only accurate but a vast understatement. "The political history of Rochester," wrote the historian Mary Young, "reveals an underlying dynamic of strong radical movements countered by a bed-rock of conservatism."[109] According to Young, Rochester's countering bedrock of conservatism showed up most clearly in its treatment of persons of color. "Despite its reputation as a seat of abolition and progressive reform movements, Rochester placed social, economic, and political limitations upon the lives of its African American citizens."[110] And the churches of Rochester, it seems, were as guilty of these limitations as the corporations. The prophet and architect of the Social Gospel, Walter Rauschenbusch himself wrote about the exclusion of African Americans in his home town.

> The most important part of a city is not the houses or the stores, but the people; their race and national descent, their physical and intellectual vigor, their skill in work, their moral soundness....Fortunately, we are hardly touched by the race question. With the exception of 601 persons of African blood and thirteen of the yellow race, we are all white men.[111]

"The discrepancy between Rauschenbusch's response to immigrants and his response to African Americans is instructive," concluded Young. "This strongly suggests that Rauschenbusch...assumed that assimilation was an appropriate goal for European immigrants but not African-Americans. Rochester's liberal record of reform left a legacy of racial exclusion."[112]

Blacks in Rochester were confined primarily to the service sector: domestic servants, red-caps, porters, and messengers. The first African-American to attend the University of Rochester did not do so until 1926. "When he did not finish, the University 'claimed blacks incapable of college studies and did not admit others for some time.' "[113] When Beatrice Amaza Howard graduated from the University of Rochester in 1931, the first African-American woman to do so, her graduation came "with the explicit stipulation that she not look for a job in Rochester."[114] Racial exclusion continued to operate in Kodak City "during the teens, twenties, and thirties."[115] "For African Americans there were few if any jobs available...Neither Bausch and Lomb, nor Eastman Kodak, the major recruiters, hired African-Americans, even if qualified."[116]

Rochester's religious "bosses" would have just as easily rejected Aimee's "colorful congregation" as they did her faith healing. In addition to the imported "dark skinned Romany wanderers," some of Rochester's own African-American community were in attendance at the city's Convention Hall. *The Rochester Times-Union* noted the healing of a local "young colored woman" but emphasized she was also of a "refined, intelligent appearance."[117]

The last thing conservative Rochester wanted was an influx of imported, colorful, sick folk left behind in the wake of Aimee's revivalism. What the church federation failed to do to the meetings, the city's health officer accomplished. "All forms of faith healing are 'plain unvarnished treachery' declared George W. Goler, health officer of the city," reported *The Rochester Times Union* on November 7, 1921.

> I have no sympathy for any individual who goes to such a meeting with the belief that his ill may be cured. They not only harm themselves, but the community as well. We will admit the fact that, in certain cases, the sufferer may feel better temporarily, but after a time, when the spell of the healer wears off, they are as bad as ever. It is the psychology of the thing that brings about the apparent improvement or cure.
>
> A man, woman or child who becomes sick in any city, unless financially independent, ultimately becomes dependent on the community.... The so called faith healer keeps people, away from medical benefits... and makes them a burden of the municipality.[118]

Goler was one of Rochester's most well-known yet controversial and colorful public servants. Serving as the city's chief health officer from 1896 until 1932, his mission was to usher in the modern scientific age when it came to sickness and health care. He began his career by heroically battling successive epidemics of smallpox, rabies, and scarlet and typhoid fever. He won national attention for his creation of public milk stations, where mothers from poor neighborhoods received pure milk as well as helpful advice for their infants. He brought modern sanitary standards to garbage collection crews, meat markets, and food vendors. He replaced the old "pest house" on the river flats with an up-to-date municipal hospital. He was the first to experiment with the use of iodine in drinking water to prevent an outbreak of goiters. He even took on the most powerful person in town, George Eastman, by opposing his proposed model-tenement plan. Goler waged war "against rats, house flies, slums, and venereal diseases, aroused criticism and created many enemies, but his unrelenting defense of public health won… more friends….Always alert to new medical advances, he made Rochester one of the healthiest cities in the country."[119] George Goler was more than his own man. He was also, in the words of the mayor, "the biggest crank and the best health officer in the United States."[120] And as "the best health officer in the United States, "Goler wanted to put an end to "all forms of faith healing" forever.

Although the newspapers noted that at least "eleven states and Canada" were represented among the visitors to the meetings and that "the out-of-town crowds seem to increase daily," Aimee was able to answer decisively the charge about keeping "people away from medical benefits."[121] Several days after Goler made his attack in the press, the newspapers also made it known "that one of the members of the McPherson entourage had been taken to a local hospital, where he was operated on for appendicitis and where he is being treated."[122] Speaking through statements issued by her mother, Aimee said she had encouraged Mr. Balf, who assisted in the singing, "to undergo an operation for appendicitis [at her earlier meeting] at Canton [Ohio]."[123] She further stated that Mr. Balf "was almost unknown to them" and that she always "advises people seeking to be healed at the services to take their physicians into their confidence."[124]

On Saturday, November 5, 1921, Aimee shared headlines with another famous woman minister, the Rev. Antoinette Louisa Brown Blackwell. After Blackwell's passing at the age of ninety-six, the newspapers noted that she was "believed to have been the first woman ordained to the ministry in this country and a pioneer with Susan B. Anthony."[125] Sixty-eight years separated Blackwell's ordination date with Aimee's Rochester revival. And, like Aimee, Blackwell had also left the denomination of her ordination for another one offering more freedom.

At Saturday night's meeting "the 'Standing Room Only' sign again was hung out at Convention Hall."[126] "From the moment she began to speak," a newspaper reported, "there was complete silence and before she had finished there was scarcely a dry eye in the auditorium. Men and women wept freely as she talked."[127]

"The power of healing did not stop with the death of the disciples," Aimee assured her audience. "It has gone on and on for hundreds of years down through the days of John Wesley, who in his journal recites of his healing those with cancer, tumor and palsey. Jesus is still the Great Physician and can still heal."[128] The momentum of the meetings would continue to build until one week later two thousand would be turned away while another five hundred persons stood at her feet. [129]

Buoyed by the headlines that read, "HALL NOT LARGE ENOUGH TO HOLD GREAT AUDIENCE," Aimee added a morning service to the two previously scheduled for Sunday. The newspapers described it as "A special love feast, communion, prayer and healing service."[130] In all three Sunday services Aimee launched a two-pronged offensive, hoping to stem the growing tide of controversy of her healing ministry in Rochester.

Her first offensive was to attack the local press—something she had not done before. She asked how many in her audience had read the reports of the meetings in the morning papers. When a few hands went up, she responded by asking her audience not to read them anymore because "they were of a highly critical, slurring nature."[131] She continued on with a plan of her own to set the record straight. "The reporters set out to knock the revival, calling it sensational and morbid. All of you who oppose such criticism enter a protest with your editors either by telephone or letter, for unless something favorable can be said of a meeting such as this, nothing should be said."[132] As far as Aimee was concerned, the press corps of Rochester were not only unfair, but unique. "We have never met with criticism in any of the other cities we have visited."[133]

When asked by the press why the McPherson party "had come to Rochester without any credentials introducing them to the ministerial leaders," Charles Price replied that he had suggested that to Mrs. McPherson, but that she had said, "I will go in the name of the Lord."[134] Unlike Price, who saw value in credentials, Aimee placed her hope and confidence in her calling and in the lives of the people she touched. On Sunday morning she had something of a change of heart. She would not only attack the press, but she would also attempt to woo the mainline ministers—those "bosses" who controlled the churches. *The Post Express* noted both approaches in Monday morning's headlines: "EVANGELIST ASKS CO-OPERATION OF CITY MINISTERS"—"Press Must Be Favorable or Remain Silent—Claims Never to Have Met Criticism in Other Cities."[135] "Mrs. McPherson," stated *The Post Express*, "has asked for the co-operation of the ministers of the city who seem to be preoccupied with their own parish work though at least two have been on the platform and several more have attended meetings as spectators."[136]

Only one Rochester minister answered Aimee's call: Dr. Ralph S. Cushman, senior minister of Asbury Methodist Church. He had not only been one of the two ministers on the platform of Aimee's meetings—his associate Dr. Frank C. Thompson was the other minister—but he had also been very preoccupied with his own parish work. On Monday morning Cushman made his own headlines in the papers. "Time Christians Revolted, Says Asbury Minister." Based upon his Sunday-morning message, Cushman had urged his congregation to adopt a resolution in favor of disarmament and sent it to President Harding. In his sermon Cushman declared, "The time has come when the Christian conscience in America is so well educated about the un-Christian character of war that the followers of Christ will unite in a great passive resistance movement, ready to suffer imprisonment and seizure of their goods rather than pay one-third of their taxes to the Federal Government for the purpose of preparing for future wars, while at the same time more than 60 per cent of taxes are going to pay for the wars of the past."[137]

At first glance, Ralph Spaulding Cushman was an unlikely champion and spokesman for Aimee Semple McPherson. Only eleven years her senior, he was relatively new to Rochester, arriving in 1920 to become the senior minister of Asbury Methodist Church. Like Aimee, Cushman had been born on a farm. Also, like Aimee, ministers ran in the family, and a young Ralph Cushman once vowed to be neither—"a farmer or a minister."[138]

Educated at Wesleyan University, Cushman was president of his class, captain of the football team, and president of the YMCA. He later attended the University of Edinburgh and the American Seminary in London. From 1903 to 1914 Cushman held pastorates in Methodist churches in Massachusetts and Connecticut. In 1914 he was transferred to the Central New York Conference as the minister of the First Methodist Church in Geneva. Asbury in Rochester was something of a reward for having completed "a brilliant term" at Geneva "freeing it from an $80,000 debt."[139]

Arriving in Rochester in his early forties, Cushman was later remembered as "a vigorous minister with interest in young people and in athletics. He instituted a hundred thousand dollar building program that included a gymnasium and a new organ."[140] During his last two years at Asbury, Cushman served as president of the Federation of Churches—Aimee's nemesis during her meetings.

Rochester could not contain this vigorous minister, and in 1932 Cushman was appointed the Methodist bishop of Denver. In 1939 he became the presiding bishop of the St. Paul-Minneapolis area, where he retired in 1952.

Before his death in 1960, Cushman had a remarkable career in the Methodist church. Twice a bishop, he was also secretary of the Methodist Centennial Movement, president of the anti-saloon league, and the author of many books and poems. His *Hilltop Verses and Prayers* contain his most well-known work, "The Secret." Another book, *Dear Bob: Letters of a Preacher to his Son,* was written for his son, Robert Earl Cushman, who not only followed in his father's footsteps, but served as dean of Duke University's divinity school from 1958–1971.

After urging disarmament in his Sunday morning message, Cushman heeded Aimee's call in the Sunday-evening service by launching a series of messages on "religious fanatics." John Wesley, General Booth, Martin Luther, John Knox, Paul, and Jesus served as examples for his six-week study of fanaticism in religion. It could just as well have been a six-week sermon on why he, as senior minister of Asbury Methodist Church, was the only mainline minister in town supporting Aimee Semple McPherson.

After Aimee's first week in Rochester, the newspapers noted that the "Rev. Ralph S. Cushman…placed the stamp of his approval on the work of the faith healer…at Convention Hall."[141] "We in Rochester need just this thing," Cushman was quoted as saying. "Great church leaders," he claimed, "have won their place through seas of criticism by persons who should know better. Those seeking to harm these meetings are opposing God's work. I thank God for these meetings."[142] Cushman then took on the city's health officer, who had called faith healing "plain, unvarnished treachery." Cushman defended Aimee against Goler's attacks by claiming "a little live fire is better than a lot of dead wood."[143] Aimee's fire of faith healing, however, did not remain little for long.

Perhaps because Aimee was now holding services in the backyard of a major Baptist seminary, Rochester Theological Seminary, two Baptist ministers from the West contacted the Rochester Federation of Churches with their concerns about Aimee's faith healing. The first communication came, noted the newspapers, "from the minister of an influential Baptist church in Denver."[144] He not only felt that Aimee was "self-deceived" but also "after careful investigation" he was unable "to find one case of a genuine cure in Denver." "I do not think," he concluded, "she will do your city any lasting good."[145]

Two days later, another Baptist minister's assessment from San Diego was made public in the Rochester papers. The Rev. Frank O. Belden of the First Baptist Church of San Diego, who also had had Aimee speak twice in his church, noted that during the time of her meetings in the city, "she received…little criticism" and he gave her "great credit for the effectiveness of her evangelical appeal."[146] Belden concluded that although "Some felt they were helped at the time...later their condition was apparently no better. This has been true especially of deafness and with some people who have been unable to walk."[147] And even though there appeared to be "some very remarkable cures...very many were not helped."[148]

Aimee responded to the criticisms made by the Baptist ministers by reading supportive telegrams to her audience that had been sent by what she considered to be far more authoritative and impressive sources than the Protestant religious establishment. "Many permanent cures had been made" and her campaigns had yielded "lasting benefit," claimed the telegrams wired by Judge Ben B. Lindsey and the editors of both the *Denver Post* and the Kansas City *Post*.[149] She read a letter sent from Canton, Ohio, that claimed that "85 per cent of the...persons who had been prayed for... by her had shown cures"—even those who had "organic diseases."[150] She emphasized to her Rochester audience that "she had no quarrel with physicians" and that she believed in using all the "means for health which God had placed in the world."[151] "But you all know," continued Aimee, "that there are often cases in which the physician will say, 'I have done everything I can. If you are to be cured, it must be by a higher power than mine.' It is that higher power to which I want to lead you."[152] And then, again, as she often did in her meetings around the country she reminded her audience that healing was not the most important part of her work. "I came," concluded Aimee, "to conduct a revival, to turn...minds back to Christ and to...Christian belief and life."[153]

But just conducting a revival in Rochester itself Aimee found was a difficult task. Signs of opposition, noted the newspapers, were not lacking even during the meetings. Once, while the audience was praying, one protestor attempted to "engage some of the workers in an argument."[154] Another protestor, "a Methodist minister from a nearby town, attracted considerable attention" when he made his way to the edge of the platform and loudly proclaimed his unbelief in healing. "He left the hall," observed a newspaper reporter, "declaring that he would like to see a 'scientific investigation' made of the cures."[155]

"Having heard that there was...opposition to the meeting in Rochester," the newspapers also reported that ministers who had supported Aimee elsewhere soon arrived in town to lend support and provide testimony. Once again, it seemed that the more liberal the minister, the more open they were to Aimee's gift of healing. Dr. William Longsworth of the First Congregational Church in Canton, Ohio, was the first to speak. "I am a graduate from Yale and a Congregational minister, so I am no freak," proclaimed the preacher.[156] Longsworth went on to testify "that Mrs. McPherson is a wonder and has accomplished great things."[157] He predicted that before the Rochester revival was over, "you will see some healings that will open your eyes. Some in Canton thought she hypnotized her audience but they saw differently before she was through."[158]

The next speaker was of special interest, noted the newspapers, since two years had elapsed since he had participated in a McPherson meeting. Dr. Charles A. Shreve, pastor of the McKendree Methodist Church in Washington, D.C., testified "that not only had wonderful cures been made during Mrs. McPherson's campaign, but that the cures had continued to occur at meetings which he had held since and that the spiritual state of the church had been improved as a result of the meetings."[159]

One week later, near the end of her meetings, Aimee won an endorsement far more important than either visiting mainline ministers or the local church federation could give her. Dr. R. W. Kimball, a local Rochester physician, made headlines in the newspapers when he declared "that two of his patients…had been cured at the meetings."[160] Kimball, it was noted, "was glad to give his support to the movement as he had become convinced of the possibility of healing through prayer."[161] Perhaps as a result of Kimball's endorsement, the newspapers also noted that "a number of ministers are showing interest in the…services. Yesterday afternoon ministers from Presbyterian, Baptist, Methodist and Evangelical churches were on the platform and assisted in praying with the hundreds of converts…at the close of the service."[162] And as if to further prove her orthodoxy to the local clergy, Aimee "denounced the doctrines of the spiritualists and Christian Scientists."[163]

Aimee's Rochester revival officially ended with a trio of Sunday services in Convention Hall on November 19, 1921. "Convention Hall," claimed the *Democrat* and *Chronicle*, was "packed to overflowing" with "people standing along the walls" and "with a tussling, pushing mob outside that prevented any access whatever to the building."[164] "The crowd," summarized the reporter, "was tremendous in size and overwhelming in enthusiasm."[165] When Aimee related how Jesus' apostles were thrown into prison for healing the sick, she told her audience "that she was glad that there were no ministers of this kind in Rochester."[166] That statement, noted the reporter, "was met with deafening applause."[167]

As Aimee was conducting her final healing service in Convention Hall, two city ministers, the newspapers noted, also delivered "an entire sermon to the subject" during their Sunday-evening service.[168] The Reverend Clinton Wunder, pastor of the Baptist Temple, "speaking to an exceedingly large audience partly made up of doctors and nurses to whom invitations had been given," preached on the topic, "How God Heals."[169] Wunder concluded there were four ways in which God "heals today: prayer, proper care of the body, preventive health measures, and by physicians and nurses."[170]

Dr. C. Waldo Cherry of the Central Presbyterian Church was far less optimistic in his sermon on "The Healing of the Seamless Robe." Claiming that "pain and suffering have a great part in the education of the soul," Cherry further argued that in all "the various cults of faith healing" none of them could show "an authenticated case of healing...organic disease."[171] "The disappointment of those...who thought they were healed and then found they were not," concluded Cherry, "constitutes one of the great problems of the religious leaders in this community."[172]

Historian of religion Catherine L. Albanese rightly views "American religions and religious people...as ...eminently practical."[173] The spiritual landscape of the United States, for Albanese, is ever-changing and dynamic due to the "choreographies of contact and combination" that exists among all American traditions. "We need to think about religions in America...more as 'additive,' " suggests Albanese, "they let go and add on; they lose; they gain; they exchange."[174]

At high noon on Monday, November 21, 1921, at the Seneca Hotel, just several blocks away from Convention Hall, there was a great "gift exchange" between Aimee and three hundred of her most loyal and faithful Rochester supporters. It would prove to be one of the most important days in her ministerial career. Not only did Aimee "add on" something significant to her ministry, her Rochester recipients too received a far lasting gift that would also shape modern America.

The luncheon at the Seneca Hotel had originally been scheduled for "chairholders"—those who had paid twenty-five dollars apiece for seats in the tabernacle being constructed in Echo Park. Attempting to limit the luncheon to no more than two hundred, Aimee was happily surprised when "more than three hundred persons" turned out for the event. Aimee proceeded to paint an overly optimistic progress report on her newly created Echo Park Evangelistic Association. "The tabernacle," she emphatically stated, would be "undenominational....Representatives from nearly every church and creed are [already] in the association."[175]

Ground had been broken in March 1920 for a tabernacle which would seat five thousand. Although Aimee had originally expected to have "the building completed within one year from the month in which it was begun," it was obviously taking much longer to complete.[176] In fact, at the time of the Rochester revival, she had raised less than a third of the projected total cost of $150,000. "Money from her meetings in San Diego," reported Aimee, "provided for the plans and excavations, …money from St. Louis…for the foundation,…[and] money from the Denver campaign for the walls" which were already thirty feet in height.[177] Three prominent guests then followed Aimee's report with a "brief talk" of their own.

The first speaker was Dr. R.W. Kimball, the Rochester physician who testified that several of his patients had been cured and who had helped to stem the tide of criticism regarding faith healing. Despite their pastor's previous night's attack on Aimee and all the other "various cults of faith healing," the next two speakers were influential and powerful men, not only as lay leaders at Central Presbyterian Church but also as civic and business leaders in Rochester. Aimee and Minnie's decision "to fish for whales" in Baltimore less than two years earlier was about to pay off just as handsomely in Rochester at it recently had in Denver. Rochester's "whales," like Denver's, also seemed rooted in the Progressive spirit and ethos.

Judge Willis K. Gillette, the son of a Presbyterian minister and "a prominent and respected leader in Rochester," was the second speaker at Monday's luncheon.[178] Growing up in Rochester, Gillette had graduated from the Rochester Free Academy and later from the University of Michigan Law School. In 1909 he became sheriff of Monroe County. Due to his investigations of a string of suspicious fires, legislation was passed that ended questionable insurance practices. In some ways, he was the Progressive equivalent of Denver's Lindsey. In 1918 Gillette became a county judge, and ten years later he was appointed to the State Supreme Court.

What the city ministers and the Rochester Federation of Churches failed to do, was more than made up for by Gillette as both a prominent Christian layman and civic leader.

I am a layman, but I believe that we laymen should do more in…testifying to our faith…I want to commend the ministry of this noble woman who has been ministering to you for the past few weeks, one who is following closer in the footsteps of that Holiest One than anyone I know of.

The redemption of souls…is far more important than any physical healing. Mrs. McPherson…believes also that healing is merely an incident in the redemption of souls.

Some of us have chosen…public service…but…all our combined efforts pale into insignificance compared to the supreme service this sister…has been rendering not only in this community but in other communities she has visited.

I want to congratulate her again upon the good she has done to this beautiful city…And I hope that some co-operative movement shall be made after her departure that will see these souls garnered in the churches, placed amid religious surroundings where the temptation to backslide will not be great.[179]

Malcom E. Gray was the luncheon's final speaker. Not only was Gray, like Gillette, a member in good standing at the Central Presbyterian Church, but Gray was also a newly minted member in the recently formed Rochester branch of the Echo Park Evangelistic Association. And Gray also had the distinction of being the largest "chairholder" in the local branch with his check of one thousand dollars for forty chairs. Like Aimee, Gray had been born in Ontario, Canada. At the age of thirty-one Gray moved to Rochester, and in 1908 he established the Rochester Can Company. Despite the "Kodak City" nickname, metalworking in the 1920s was still among the five largest industries in Rochester. And it was metalworking in Rochester where Gray's inventive genius flowered.

> He designed and manufactured more than 100 different metal products under the Iron Horse brand name. No company in the world made more metal flower vases than Rochester Can. His catalogue of metalware included…more than 500…garbage can[s]. In World War I, the company tripled its size to 600 employees in order to fill U.S. Army needs for helmets and canteens.[180]

By 1921 the Rochester Can Company was enormously successful, with several hundred employees and annual sales of more than a million dollars. Malcolm Gray was more than an inventor and business success; he also cared about his workers both physically and religiously. Rochester's own church historian especially noted the ever widening gap between Protestant churches and the working man. "The working-classes," observed Winthrop Hudson, "tended to be impervious to the message and ministry of the churches. It was not that the churches had 'lost' these people; they never had most of them."[181]

Among other reasons for the churches not having "these people" was due to the workers' schedule and work week itself. If you were an office or factory worker in early twentieth-century Rochester, you started work at 7 a.m. and went home at 6 p.m. Six days a week you were summoned to work by the blasts from the factory horn on top of the Kimball Tobacco Company smokestack along the Genesee River. "The blasts were so loud they could be heard throughout…Rochester…your time clock was the Kimball horn."[182] Mercifully, at 6 p.m. its loud blast also "dismissed you for the day….Only Sunday, the Christian Sabbath, was a day of rest for most workers. The term, weekend, wasn't in anyone's vocabulary, including dictionaries."[183]

Both Gray and his wife had been smitten by the ministry of Aimee Semple McPherson. Not only was Gray Rochester's largest chairholder in the Echo Park Evangelistic Association, but his wife was the secretary-treasurer of the local branch. (Rev. Frank C. Thompson was president and Judge Gillette the vice-president). Following the luncheon at the Seneca Hotel, Gray invited Aimee that afternoon to speak "to the men of the Rochester Can Company…on the need of Christ in their lives [so] that they might become better citizens, have better homes and do better business."[184]

A hundred years earlier in Rochester, Charles Grandison Finney demonstrated that revivalism and social reform were not mutually exclusive. A century later Aimee Semple McPherson obtained the same result with her brand of revivalism, perhaps accomplishing more social reform in three weeks time than the hometown's own social prophet, Walter Rauschenbusch, did in a lifetime.

Because his heart had been touched and strangely warmed by Aimee's ministry, a month later, as Gray sat down with his family for Christmas dinner,

> [He] announced that he wanted to do something really special for his valued workers. His decision was to give them a five-day work week, which he did, starting January 2, 1922.
>
> Gray's dramatic step did not go unnoticed in the industrial world. It received national attention, especially…the fact that productivity increased…Henry Ford…visited Gray and the Rochester Can Company…He was so….impressed that he applied the same idea at Ford Motor Company.
>
> Soon, the five-day work week swept industrial America and became the employment standard. Most Americans…have never known any other situation in their working lifetime.[185]

During Aimee's meetings the various railroads, in particular the Santa Fe, ran ads for train travel to California. "You dread the cold of winter," read the ads. "Run away from winter. Go to winterless California." Close to midnight on November 22, 1921, Aimee and Minnie boarded a late train for their return trip to "winterless California."[186] Aimee was going home a changed person, as she would after all her major meetings. There had been "contact and combination" at Convention Hall but, especially at Asbury Methodist Church, something new and different had also been "added" to

her ministry. She had given much to gypsies and railroad porters, chairholders and can company workers, visiting mainline ministers and lay Rochesterians, but, she too, had also received.

Aimee's last meeting had been held, fittingly, not in Convention Hall but
in Asbury Methodist Church the evening of her eventful chairholders' luncheon. Both ministers of Asbury had been enormously supportive of her, so
much so that Frank C. Thompson would later go to work for Aimee in Los
Angeles. Her final message was to offer instruction and spiritual guidance
for the recently converted, estimated at forty-two hundred. Taking inspiration from one of Asbury's stained glass windows, she became enthralled
with its beauty and workmanship. She discovered after the meeting that the
window was the work of a local artist, George W. Haskins, who had created
windows for fifty-one Rochester churches and more than two thousand
others across the country. The largest work order Haskins ever received,
however, came from Aimee for eight double-story stained-glass windows at
the cost of fifteen thousand dollars. Aimee may have been the first preacher
to put the "cost into Pentecost," as she was accused of doing, but she was
equally the first to believe that "Rochester-made means quality" belonged
as much in Pentecostalism as it did Methodism. Asbury Methodist Church
was her new guiding symbol and vision, which would soon manifest itself
in the splendor of a more permanent structure, a temple and not the more
temporary Billy Sunday-style tabernacle.

Rochester continued to demonstrate its skepticism and antagonism to
Aimee's faith healing claim even in her absence. The morning after her
midnight departure from New York's Central Station, where she had used
an overturned ash can as an improvised platform to say good-bye to the
two hundred persons that had gathered to bid her farewell, headlines again
fanned the flames of the faith-healing controversy.[187] "Startling Revelations
of Work of Woman 'Healer' Printed By Colorado Medical Publication"
promised the headlines of the *Rochester Herald* the morning of November
23. "That faith healing has not universal approval," read the article, "may
be seen from a pamphlet and booklet that reached Rochester…on the eve
of the departure of Mrs. Aimee Semple McPherson from the city."[188]

The pamphlet that reached Rochester on the heels of Aimee's departure was in actuality a journal article that had recently been published. The
article, "Faith Healers: With Special Reference to Aimee Semple McPherson," had been authored by a C.S. Bluemel, M.D., of Denver and published in the July, 1921 issue of *Colorado Medicine*. Bluemel was blunt and
to the point. "I am fortunate," he wrote, "in having personal knowledge
of a number of 'cures' wrought by the evangelist" in her recent meetings

in Denver. Bluemel stated that none of the "cures" lasted and that in fact "one young man suffering from tuberculosis…died…thirteen days after the miracle of healing."[189] Bluemel, sought in his article to give a historical review of not just Aimee's meetings in Denver but other faith healers as well and how all their "cures" were accomplished:

> Faith healers have been rampant in Europe and America during the past two years….The sick applying for healing [in Denver] …[were] carefully sorted over by the evangelist's mother, and if they…[appeared] to be good risks, they…[were] given cards which entitle[d] them to the evangelist's healing prayer….there are many cases of hysterical lameness, deafness, blindness…which yield to the stimulus of intense emotion….Such cures are the only positive cures that an evangelist can achieve. They are not miracles, but they are extraordinary spectacular. The occasional occurrence of such cures is the foundation of faith healing.[190]

"Faith healing in its last analysis," concluded Bluemel, "seems to consist in curing an hysterical or imaginary disease or in imagining a cure of a real infirmity."[191] The passing of time confirmed some of Bluemel's insights, especially the role that Minnie Kennedy continued to play in determining who would be prayed for by her daughter. One year later California newspapers reported that Minnie was still determining who was qualified to receive Aimee's prayers. Worse yet, they observed, that some sufferers who had previously been rejected by Ma Kennedy as unsuitable candidates for healing suddenly became eligible after purchasing a twenty-five-dollar tabernacle chair.

Returning to "winterless California, the Santa Fe way," that catered "to highest class travel," Aimee was ever the optimist. While looking out upon the mountains and plains of New Mexico from the window of her speeding railway car, she began writing down her thoughts to share with her *Bridal Call* readers. Left unmentioned by Aimee was Rochester's antagonism and skepticism of her divine healing services. "Enthusiasm," recalled Aimee for her readers, "ran high in this dear old conservative city…it was a glorious revival for soul winning."[192] She also told a reporter that her Rochester audience had not only been "enthusiastic" but her most "intelligent."[193] And it was very likely that her "intelligent" audiences in Rochester had convinced her to tell a reporter covering the opening of Angelus Temple not to think "that praying for people is the dominant note of our religion. Just about one day a week will be set aside for praying for the sick. The real mission is to save souls."[194]

The fact that Aimee's healings "were more successful in the West than in the East," claims Janice Dickin, "adds credibility to the suggestion that social change was a key factor…The cities of the West were new creations, struggling for a sense of identity, open to change…In these instant communities, instant cures…seemed all the more possible and were all the more desirable."[195]

CHAPTER SIXTEEN

Wichita: The Middle Road
May 7–21, 1922

An advertisement appeared in the Wichita newspapers the morning of May 7, 1922, announcing Aimee's standard three-weeks meeting to be held at the Forum. Following the headlines of "Aimee Semple McPherson, Today Forum, A Message for Soul and Body" was a brief paragraph noting the sponsorship of her meetings: "Mrs. McPherson has a local advisory committee, composed of members from the leading denominations. In prayer and faith they give you this invitation to share in the good news."[1] It was Aimee's first visit to the Sunflower State —a place where intolerance in both religion and politics had often flared into violence, the future setting for Truman Capote's brilliant *In Cold Blood*, where under "the big sky, the whisper of wind voices in the windbent wheat."[2] Two decades earlier, the modern movement of Pentecostalism had been birthed in the state and also experienced its most violent opposition. Prophetic figures flourished for a time, like wheat under the big Kansas sky and many, like grain at harvest time, were just as quickly cut down. Somehow the struggles and significance, the tensions and triumphs of Aimee's early ministry are seen with the greatest of clarity during her three-week stay in Wichita. It was as if she became prismatic under the hot Kansas sun, refracting for all to see a visible spectrum of previously held inner thoughts. Nowhere else is her place in American religious history so easily revealed in so short a period of time.

Unlike many of their earlier campaigns where Aimee and Minnie were both evangelist and host committee, Aimee was able to write to her faithful followers, "Back of the [Wichita] campaign, staunch as the rock of Gibraltar, capable as a fleet of dreadnoughts, stood the most wonderful Interdenominational Laymen's Committee with whom it has ever been our privilege to work. This committee [is] composed of some of the most well-known and influential men and women in business, political and church circles of the city."[3]

Indeed they were. Their congregational affiliations and occupational identities covered the spectrum of Methodist, Congregational, Episcopal, Baptist, and Friends; and they included the president of the Universal Motor Car Company, an oil man, a dentist, and an attorney. Conspicuously absent on "the most wonderful Interdenominational Laymen's Committee" were two groups—Pentecostals and the Protestant mainline ministers of Wichita. By the end of the meetings, Aimee would meet her Waterloo with organized Pentecostalism, and relations would be strained with the Assemblies of God. From her time in Wichita, Aimee would formulate a new theological perspective called "The Narrow Line" and "The Middle Road." This theological persuasion was born out of Aimee's dissatisfaction with both Pentecostalism and the Protestant mainstream. It was a desire to stake out new theological territory between the existing boundaries of the "fanaticism" of Pentecostalism and the "formalism" of the denominational churches. "It is the narrow gauge line between 'fanatical flesh masquerading as the Spirit' on the one side, and 'cold, backslidden, worldly formality' on the other."[4]

> Everything human in one usually longs to be in favor with either the one side or the other. Most everyone wants to play safe with at least one faction. Many follow the line of the least resistance…Live or die, sink or swim, whether we walk with the crowd or walk alone, by God's grace we will be true to that vision.[5]

Actually, Aimee found it quite easy to follow her new found vision of "middle ground," explaining to followers:

> And yet it is not so difficult to keep one's balance. For on the one hand your friends (?) hit you a whack and hurl their favorite epithet for those who do not see eye-to-eye with themselves in all things; "You're NOT Pentecostal." And on the other side your friends (?) hit you another whack and say "you ARE Pentecostal." And thus it goes whack—"You ARE"—Whack—"You are NOT."… "Whack—whack!" and between the two they keep one pretty well balanced on the middle of the line.[6]

In Wichita Aimee easily managed to maintain her "middle of the line" theological perspective by taking equal "whacks" from both sides. Many Pentecostals, especially those affiliated with the Assemblies of God, were upset after reading a reporter's interview published in the *Wichita Eagle*. The reporter's second question to Aimee was, "It is charged that you are a member of a sect similar to the Holy Rollers and that you put converts into trances, sometimes holding them for hours." Aimee's response was simply that "this question is too foolish to answer. Of course I do not." Still the reporter pressed Aimee about her denominational affiliation, asking, "Is it true that you are a member of the Pentecostal Church, Assembly of God, and that 'The Evangel,' published by the Gospel Publishing Company, Springfield, Mo., is the organ that attracts members from over the country to your meetings?" "No, I am not a member of that sect," Aimee was quoted as saying and further elaborated:

> I know some of the Assembly of God people and they are fine people. I know some of the people of all faiths and they also are fine, but I am not one of the cult and have nothing whatever to do with publishing *The Evangel.* I publish *The Bridal Call,* an undenominational magazine. I have done everything in my power to curb the apparent wildness of the Pentecostal believers.[7]

Such a published response touched off a stream of protest reaching all the way to the chairman himself of the General Council of the Assemblies of God. The response by the Assemblies to Aimee's published interview was swift, both formally and informally. Privately, the chairman of the denomination, the Reverend E. N. Bell, wrote to the Assembly of God minister who had brought the interview to his attention. It is apparent from the chairman's letter to his fellow minister in the faith that Aimee had indeed "sold out" to the denominational churches and had "backslid" with Pentecostalism.

> At the time our minutes were published Mrs. McPherson was a minister of the Assemblies of God. But since that time, of her own accord, she has sent in her Fellowship Certificate. She did not say that she was joining some denomination at that time, but since then papers have been sent us from California showing that she is now an ordained Baptist minister. We do not desire to be put in the light of fighting Mrs. McPherson, but now since she has come out into the open and publicly said that she does not belong to us it might be well for us to pass on her own information as a guide to all our people. There is no question but what under great pressure Sister McPherson has been for nearly two years gradually shrinking from the reproach of Pentecost, and trying to tone it down to suit the denominations, and that this effort has much hurt her usefulness, and some claim to a large extent has already cut the fire and power out of her messages. I wish everybody would pray for her that she may not totally backslide under her persecution, and that God may use them simply to drive her back to the full Pentecostal message. I have not lost hopes that the Lord may yet recover her in His mercy to all the Pentecostal power which she once had.[8]

Formally, in *The Pentecostal Evangel*, the General Council of the Assemblies of God responded to the *Wichita Eagle* interview with an editorial asking the question, "Is Mrs. McPherson Pentecostal?" In their editorial the Assemblies of God not only published portions of the newspaper interview but further stated the facts regarding Aimee's attempted Baptist ordination. Finally, for all of their subscribers they gave out the following admonition to their one-time credentialed Sister:

> We desire to see Mrs. McPherson reclaimed to the full Pentecostal faith which it would seem that she is fast losing and also to the full Pentecostal power, which is reported to us to be greatly decreasing in her meetings. If Sister McPherson can get to the place where she can joyfully bear reproach for the sake of the Master, and where she is fully determined to go through with God in spite of criticism, and where she does not compromise in any way the full Gospel, she can certainly be a mighty power for God. Let us pray to this end.[9]

Aimee was not above responding to all of this by delivering a few "whacks" back of her own. Responding to the editorial in *The Pentecostal Evangel*, she wrote her followers:

> The heads of this paper [the General Council Office of the Assemblies of God] had no more discernment than to quote this unreliable man, and ask the favorite question of all that do not conform exactly to their mould—"Is Mrs. McPherson Pentecostal"—and publish such a thing "as news" with terms and statements we had never used. All this without even the common courtesy, brotherly love, or Bible-taught justice of writing us direct, for truth, preferring to rush into print with untruths and admitting they were based only on reports. Such hasty and unproved evidence one would not have expected of a magazine— especially one "from Missouri." It is almost inconceivable that people calling themselves the "General Council of Pentecost" would condescend to such a silly and unjust position. How pitiful! …Well are you Pentecostal you ask? That depends altogether on what you mean by the term. Pentecost really means 50 and I'm only 31. This seems to be an unscriptural term never used by the early Church as far as we can learn, no more used because they received the baptism of the Holy Spirit on the day of Pentecost, than, we would say, "I'm Christmas" if we were born again on Christmas day.[10]

The debate whether or not Aimee was still "Pentecostal" even had its lighter moments. An Assemblies of God minister from Denver wrote to the General Council office complaining because Aimee had compared Pentecostals to 1914 back-firing Fords.

She used illustrations against the Pentecostal people that I never heard any preacher use that has opposed us. She likened us to 1914 back-firing Fords hitting on two and three cylinders, making so much noise going up the street, and when they stopped you had to get out and crank and crank to get them started again, and when you did it was the same old popping and sputtering, trying to attract the attention of the people. She likened the modern way of getting the baptism to a nice new twin six Packard, all you had to do was step on the starter and off up the street you went without any noise at all.

But she seemed to forget that the new up-to-date Fords have a starter also, and there was a time when you had to get out and crank a Packard, too. Her description of a Ford was an injustice to the car, much more her reference to us as Pentecostal people, but I have noticed this one thing that a Ford will go where any other car has gone before, and sometimes it will go where those fancy ones can't or won't...Well hallelujah, bless God for Fords, even though they do backfire once in awhile. I don't see hardly how the world could get along without them.[11]

The truth was Aimee had, indeed, discovered the luxury version of Pentecostalism. Her "new twin six Packard" version would cruise the boulevards, while the majority of Pentecostals remained in the back alleys "popping and sputtering, trying to attract the attention of the people." In the end, at least in America, Aimee's luxury model won out. By the turn of the twenty-first century more Lincoln Town Cars were parked in Pentecostal parking lots than Ford Pintos. Aimee had only been ahead of the curve. Prosperity preachers abounded in Pentecostalism while few if any were calling for poverty.

Years later, while teaching a course in homiletics to future Foursquare ministers, Aimee recalled how difficult it was to maintain her "middle-of-the road" theological stance:

The Pentecostal mission started out to girdle the globe, but, in many instances, fanaticism stepped in, and they wound up in basement[s] and attic[s]; and today, the cities at large do not know the Pentecostal mission exists. It is "us four and no more."

When I took that stand, [in Wichita] I kicked up a veritable hornet's nest. It was as though I were walking on a wire and keeping in balance, with opposition on either side. But I took that MIDDLE-OF-THE-ROAD stand, while from one side I heard, "Don't have anything to do with her. She is too Pentecostal," and, on the other hand, I heard them say, "She quenches the Spirit. She does not allow the Holy Spirit demonstration[s]." I kept on walking down the middle of the road, keeping my balance and going right on.[12]

"WE ARE NOT HOLY ROLLERS," Aimee reminded yet another class of LIFE Bible College students.

> I drive a Packard car, but it is not a "Packard roller'"—it is a Packard automobile, designed for service. The Foursquare Gospel teaches a sane, balanced Gospel, and may I emphasize again, we want the power, but power under control…That is the difference between this Foursquare Gospel and some who may call themselves "Pentecostal." DO NOT CONFUSE THE FOURSQUARE GOSPEL WITH HOLY ROLLERS….FOURSQUAREDOM TAKES THE MIDDLE OF THE ROAD—Formality and ice-bergs to the left of us—Fanaticism and wild-fire to the right of us …. Foursquaredom is supported on the left hand by the orthodox teachings upon which denominations, now grown cold, were founded in their infancy; and on the right hand by the power and glory of Pentecostal fullness of the old-time religion of those early disciples. Foursquaredom advocates moderation and especially no wildfire, but POWER UNDER CONTROL. The SALVATION OF SOULS is the main consideration. Fousquaredom is a balanced Gospel, leaning not to the right nor to the left, dropping a plumb-line right down the middle of the road.[13]

"Whacks" from the other side came from Wichita's mainline religious establishment, primarily from the clergy. Although they were on the whole more sophisticated and subtle in their attacks than the Pentecostals, the attacks were real nevertheless. Responding in the *Wichita Beacon* to charges that the mainline ministers were boycotting the meetings, the Reverend Ross W. Sanderson, executive secretary of the Wichita Federation of Churches, attempted to persuade Kansans that "failure to approve, endorse or cooperate does not amount to a boycott." The Wichita Federation of Churches had, however, earlier passed the following resolution: "In view of the fact that Aimee Semple McPherson's campaign has been advertised as an inter-denominational meeting it is only fair that the general public should know that the campaign has not been endorsed by the Ministerial Association of Churches."[14] (The clergy obviously felt they could speak for the laity.) A week after Aimee's campaign opened the city's ministerial association still chose silence as the best way of dealing with the revival. The *Wichita Beacon* carried the news in its headlines:

> Gypsies throng Forum to hear Mrs. McPherson, Many of the Wanderers Claim to Have Been Healed Thru Evangelist, Ministers Silent. The Wichita Ministerial Association held its regular weekly meeting today. The session was marked by absolute lack of reference to service being conducted by Aimee Semple McPherson at the Forum.[15]

A graphic depiction of Aimee's calling to walk "the middle road" between cold formality and wild fire. "Pentecostal worship," claims Harvey Cox, "lured anarchy into the sacred circle and tamed it" (used by permission of the International Church of the Foursquare Gospel, Heritage Department).

Not all of the mainline ministers remained silent. A young member of a Methodist Church who was to become the pastor of one of the largest future Foursquare Churches recalled that his minister had more than a few words to say about Aimee Semple McPherson during his Sunday morning message. He informed his congregation that Aimee was in town, that she prayed for the sick, and that healings were claimed, but that she was a fake. He remembered his minister graphically comparing Aimee to a "freight train with empty box cars, rattling through the country-side and little calves that were hungry would take out after it and find there was nothing there but empty box cars." "In fact," stated the Methodist minister, "this Aimee Semple McPherson is a modern Jezebel, that's the kind of woman she is."[16] Such statements, of course, only helped to create more interest in the meetings and the Forum was soon packed.

Midway through the revival the *Beacon* reported on one of Aimee's messages. A text taken from the thirty-fourth chapter of Ezekiel formed the basis of her sermon: "I will feed my flock, and I will cause them to lie down, saith the Lord God. I will seek that which was lost, and bring again that which was driven away, and will bind up that which was broken, and will strengthen that which was sick."[17] From that Old Testament passage Aimee launched into her sermon declaring that "skinny sheep" suffering from spiritual malnutrition were to be found in many churches across America. She implored her audience to return to a "full Gospel" by giving up their churches' "canned goods" in exchange for a "full spiritual dinner menu." With wit she mocked the mainline ministers for their lack of endorsement by exhorting the crowd: "Stay in your own pasture—you don't know that woman, little lambkin, that is telling you that the clover is good. I have not endorsed her. Stay away." Then Aimee continued on in her own inimitable style with her "vibrant contralto of the midway" growing stronger with each new word:

> But the little sheep take a nibble through the bars, and it is so good, so good. And even now the skinny sheep here in the Forum are taking nibbles through the bars, and they are finding it so good, also....Oh little sheep; my little lambkins; come home, come home, come home. Jump the fence, my lambkins, jump the fence and eat of the clover of Christ.[18]

Again in Wichita Aimee's real strength was with the people. Writing to her constituency about the meeting, she relayed the following information: "Singers and musicians came from the various churches and in every sense of the word this was a Laymen's Revival. It would seem as though laymen all over the world are reaching up and demanding a return to the old time religion and an old time revival and as though they are oft times outstripping the clergy in their efforts and success."[19] This is what Charles F. Parham had also argued when he organized the first group of Pentecostals in Kansas, his Apostolic Band. His conviction was that "the people" wanted "the old time religion." [20]

Like many previous American revivals, however, it was a combination of both the preaching and music that attracted the laity. One Methodist layperson recalled, "We had never heard preaching before like that, also, we had never heard music like that. Singing those gospel songs was especially intriguing to us as young people."[21] An astute reporter for the *Wichita Eagle* also readily noticed the difference between Aimee's revivalism and that of the older variety:

> She is a woman of charming personality and not the Billy Sunday type of evangelist. There is in the light of her eyes and countenance depicted

an unmistakable earnestness that at once becomes contagious. One local minister has declared that she will "out-Sunday Billy Sunday" before she closes the series. Certain it is that she possesses a magnetism that is unusual and has the same posture to reach the hearts of her hearers that is claimed for the celebrated Sunday.[22]

In Wichita, as it would be throughout America until the day she died, Aimee's most important message to the people was her autobiographical sermon, "The Story of My Life," based on the words of the Old Testament prophet Jeremiah: "Before I formed thee, I knew thee; before thou camest, I ordained thee a prophet unto the nations...whatsoever I command thee thou shalt speak...Behold I have put words in thy mouth." Aimee recounted for her audience her earlier struggles in the ministry. When she came to the part in the story she loved most to tell—the vignette about her tall, handsome Irish husband, Robert Semple—a newspaper reporter noted, "The big building was noiseless except for her voice. At the close her head dropped, her voice choking. Tears shone in the eyes of practically every person in the building. Several sobbed softly."[23] From the illustration of Robert's death, Aimee would complete her sermonic story by admonishing those in attendance that God can be "the husband to the widow" and "the father to the fatherless." Preaching the story of her life, Aimee used the medium of radio, which in future years would alone make her ministry famous. Reports came back to the broadcasting station from a thousand miles away noting that the sermon had been heard "very clearly."

What Aimee lost by way of Protestant mainline ministerial support in Wichita she more than made up in the secular press. Increasingly it was the newspapers that fanned the flames of Aimee's growing successes. Inevitably she was compared with Billy Sunday, and invariably she came out the winner. The baseball evangelist had only been a preacher. Aimee was a healer. Respected hard-boiled journalists of many years became Aimee's greatest promoters and advertisers. The silence of the mainline clergy was answered by the roar of the reporter's typewriters. They "sainted" her. They attributed divinity to her. For them she was the "miracle woman." Often lengthy columns appeared in the papers describing the services and increasingly the healings in the greatest of detail. Names, addresses and towns of the "healed" were all made public.

W.R. Waggoner, a *Wichita Eagle* staff reporter and a journalist for thirty-five years, attempted to summarize Aimee's stay in the city.

Mrs. McPherson is beginning to be recognized as a revivalist without a parallel in the country. Comparing her with Billy Sunday, whose famous

339

saw dust trail was trodden by many Wichitans, those who have heard them both say the woman's power over a congregation far surpasses those of the baseball evangelist.

Eighteen thousand persons heard the evangelist at the three Sunday services, while more than this number were turned away…At each, the doors were locked prior to the hour set for the beginnings and at night, the Forum was jammed before 6 o'clock.

As to the healing of the sick and afflicted, I have seen with my own eyes some of the most amazing and unbelievable sights of my 35 years' career in journalism….I have seen the lame discard crutches and walk; the epileptic and palsied grow calm, the totally blind receive their vision, the deaf restored to hearing; children afflicted with infantile paralysis, grow stronger.

I have, in the capacity of a newspaper man, "done" many revivals and have witnessed many religious demonstrations, but am here to attest that I have never seen any revivalist expounder of the gospel who comes as nearly approaching the divinity, as does this unselfish, praying, marvelous woman of God, whose heart is overflowing with compassion for the world of afflicted, and who never has an unkind word for those who attempt to malign her. I make these statements as a man who does not affiliate with any church and attends the meetings only as a reporter, seeking to print the truth.[24]

Waggoner concluded, "The biggest news break that ever happened in Wichita was the McPherson meetings."[25] He also observed that during the meetings the city of Wichita had served as the host for visitors from "twenty-five different states…besides some foreign countries" and almost "three hundred thousand dollars" had been spent by them.[26]

Lying sixty-one miles southeast of Wichita and just four miles north of the Oklahoma border was the Kansas town of Arkansas City. On Monday, May 15, 1922, the local newspaper, the *Arkansas City Traveler*, bore the following front page headline: "Aimee Semple McPherson: Still in Wichita Healing." The ensuing article reported that a local resident, Mrs. W. E. Miller, residing at 207 North C Street, had been an invalid for seven years. While attending the McPherson meetings at the Wichita Forum the paper noted that Mrs. Miller "got up from her wheel chair at the forum yesterday morning…She walked unaided across the platform. She came back and pushed the chair along in front of her. The vast audience sat in breathless silence. Another miracle had been wrought by the woman whose performances in Wichita have been nothing short of a sensation."[27]

There were more miracles and more witnesses from Arkansas City, the *Traveler* reported: Mr. and Mrs. Walter Probst, Guy Hadley, and Mrs. Rose

Vedder of 111 West Walnut Avenue. The newspaper then captured the entire town's attention by stating that one of their very own reporters, "little Joe Moore, a crippled boy, who writes the sport and high school notes for the *Traveler,*" had left for Wichita leaving a note behind. "I am going to Wichita to see Mrs. McPherson," read Moore's note. "I thought that maybe she might make me throw away my crutches. I will be back on the job Tuesday morning." "All the force at the *Traveler,*" concluded the newspaper, "is trying its best to have faith that Joe will be cured by the wonder woman. If he is cured, the *Traveler* will feel like taking off a day to offer up Thanksgiving."[28]

When little Joe Moore arrived at the Forum and expressed a desire to be prayed for by Mrs. McPherson, one of Minnie Kennedy's helpers handed him a prayer card to be filled out. The healing prayer card asked for the following information: "Give your name and address. Are you a Christian? Are you a church member? What church? What disease? How long afflicted? Are you in medical care? Have you faith that Jesus will heal you now, and will your life and healing be for the glory of God?"[29]

Joe Moore experienced despair and disappointment his first Monday morning at the services:

> I sat in the large forum and watched this wonderful woman perform her miracles. I went there to see if she could make me throw away my crutches; but on account of the jam, I was unable to have her treat me. I shall go back Wednesday and try to see her. I found out that the healing services that were to be held Monday morning would be for Gypsies only.[30]

Yet on Friday morning, May 19, 1922, the *Arkansas City Traveler* broke the unbelievable news to the town in front-page headlines that read, "Joe Moore Casts Crutches Aside. Prayers of Women of A.C. Play Big Part in the Healing of Youth." The newspaper's "telephone rang all morning with inquiries about Joe. Many people came to the office to see him walk without his crutches. Friends swarmed about him on the street." Inside the morning newspaper, "little Joe Moore," whom everybody in town knew, told the story of his healing:

> I don't know hardly how to tell it. My heart is so full of joy and my whole being so overflowing with gratitude that I feel like I am living in a new world since I cast aside my crutches at Wichita yesterday.
> I have been forced to walk with crutches since nine years ago when I suffered an accident that rendered one leg shorter than the other. My short

leg has not had the strength to help support me when I am walking.

Today I can walk as well as anyone. It happened this way:

I went to Wichita yesterday to have Mrs. McPherson pray for me. The healing services began at 10:30 a.m. There were close to 1,000 afflicted persons holding cards to see Mrs. McPherson.

Through the influence of Mrs. William Gardner and Mrs. John LeUnes, of this city, I was allowed to pass under the rope and was the third person for whom Mrs. McPherson offered a healing prayer. She placed one hand on my shoulder and her other hand on the shoulder of a woman next to me, and prayed for us both at the same time. This was a disappointment to me for I wanted her to pray for me alone. I was so depressed over the incident that I cried, and after she walked away, I sobbed until I thought my heart would break.

Mrs. Gardner and Mrs. LeUnes came to me. They knelt beside me and prayed. I prayed with them. Mrs. Kennedy, mother of Mrs. McPherson joined us in prayer. A strange feeling came over me. I know my face must have worn a beatific expression. I felt like a man born again. My whole being surged with confidence.

Mrs. Gardner said to me: "Now, Joe, you can get up and walk. Don't pay any attention to your crutches. They are just unbelief." I looked over where I had left my crutches and they were gone. It seemed like they had been spirited away because I wouldn't need them anymore. I rose to my feet and was astonished when I found that I could stand so well without my crutches. My short leg seemed as strong as my other leg. I started out to walk and it was just as easy as if I had been walking that way all my life. I started up the aisle. I walked the length of the forum with that vast crowd watching me. I did not know that the hump on my back had been reduced until I reached the seat where Mrs. Collinson and Mrs. Parks were seated. I noticed they were looking at my back instead of at my leg.

Then they told me that my back was straighter than before, and that my coat, which generally fit me tight, was wrinkled and looser. I was not aware of this transformation because I was overjoyed at being able to walk unaided by crutches.

I sat down but I couldn't keep still. I got up and strutted all around. I wanted everyone to see what had happened to me. At this time, there were hundreds of afflicted persons crushing forward to receive the healing prayers of Mrs. McPherson. Many were healed and some were not. Mrs. McPherson said she could not do anything for a person who did not have the love of God in his heart and faith in his healing power. The meeting did not end until 2 o'clock in the afternoon and she still did not get to pray for all who had cards. I walked uptown for dinner and returned for the next service without my crutches. Scores of people, white and colored, shook my hand and rejoiced with me.

The last time I saw my crutches, Anthony Carlton was going up the street carrying them and I was walking along behind him. When I got out of bed this morning, it was the natural thing for me to look over at the stand table for my crutches, but they were not there. They were in Wichita and I was in Arkansas City. So I started out on another day without them. Although I limp some I will get better as time goes by, and some day I will be as well as anyone. I am going to have my shoe on my short leg built up so that I can walk with more ease. I can testify to the healing power of God if any afflicted persons in Arkansas City will only have faith in his teachings and practice them.[31]

The Arkansas City Ministerial Association by a majority vote passed a motion inviting Aimee and her mother to a Monday night meeting to be held in Wilson Park on May 29. Dr. Wentworth of the Methodist Church "voted against the motion, saying that he was opposed to such things."[32] The Reverend W. M. Gardner of the Presbyterian Church and the Reverend J. E. Tedford of the Congregational Church officially represented the Arkansas City Ministerial Alliance and—most likely over the protests of Minnie Kennedy—persuaded Aimee to include the one-night meeting before returning to her busy schedule. Due to the story of "little Joe Moore" and all the excitement it had created, even ever-protective Minnie Kennedy could not say no.

On Monday, May 29, 1922, the day of the meeting, the *Traveler* reported, no doubt due to the insistence of Minnie Kennedy, that "Mrs. McPherson …is giving souvenir seats to those who buy a seat in the Echo Park Revival tabernacle now being built at Los Angeles, California. The seats average $25.00 apiece. The name of the purchaser is placed on the seat and will remain there as long as the tabernacle stands."[33]

The article also included the following pledge about the "tabernacle" that reflected Aimee's more-than-generous spirit. Minnie's frugalness most likely prevented it from happening. "[The tabernacle]…is being built as a community house according to Mrs. McPherson's representatives, and after her death will go back to the city of Los Angeles."[34]

At 11:00 a.m. on Monday morning "Tex" Jones, "prominent oil man and one of Mrs. McPherson's staunch disciples" rolled up to Aimee's Wichita hotel in his "big Winton six" to drive her to Arkansas City. Accompanying Aimee were her mother; a personal assistant, Mrs. J. E. Foulston; and W. R. Waggoner, the reporter for the *Wichita Eagle*. The party drove to August, where they had lunch and then "visited the big oil fields of Butler County" before arriving at the Osage Hotel in Arkansas City, where Aimee ate dinner, rested, and dressed prior to the evening meeting.

More than five thousand people were waiting for her at Wilson Park. "The first two rows…were filled with those who had bodily ills."[35] Before the outdoor service could begin, the vast crowd was startled by a crash of thunder. Soon they were drenched to the skin by a torrential rain. The town's First Presbyterian Church was on standby in case of rain, but so many people had come from outlying areas that it was too small. Aimee, more recently the "Miracle Woman," then stepped to the platform. All the ministers of Arkansas City were there except for Dr. Charles Wentworth, the Methodist minister, who had voted against her coming. Aimee opened the meeting, herself, with a prayer:

> Oh, Lord, stay this rain and this storm. You can hold it in the hollow of your hand, Lord. These people have come from miles around to hear your message tonight. We don't mind going home in the rain, dear Lord, but if it is thy will, stay it and if the land hath need of it, let it fall after the message has been delivered to these hungry souls.[36]

After Aimee's prayer, the *Traveler* noted, "In less than five minutes a deluge of rain lapsed into a drizzle and in ten minutes, the stars were shining… Expectant persons marveled when there was an instantaneous cessation of the downpour and the sky cleared."[37] The newspaper commented that "Mrs. McPherson is 31 years old" and that she was dressed "in a plain, attractive white ankle length dress." "Standing in the midst of a bank of flowers with her face alight with divine love and inspiration, she seemed like an angel from heaven to speak the word of God."[38]

"Speaking the word of God like an angel from heaven," on the flower banked stage in Wilson Park was hard for Aimee. She had had little rest, and her voice was harsh and hoarse. It only slowly began to warm and grow in volume as she read her text from the Gospel of Luke: "The Spirit of the Lord is upon me, because he has anointed me to bring good news to the poor. He has sent me to proclaim release to the captives and recovery of sight to the blind, to let the oppressed go free, to proclaim the year of the Lord's favor." "Tenderly and lovingly she smiled at the audience. What we need," she declared, "is the old time religion."

> Jesus is the same today and tomorrow as he has always been. The world is hungry for the old fashioned religion. Let's put more fire into the pulpit instead of in the stove in the basement to cook oysters….I feel that the Spirit of the Lord is upon me tonight. I feel that the Lord is among us tonight, and that his power is with us as it was with the poor people to whom he preached. One of the first things that the church did

was to lose that mighty power of preaching of Jesus. A great reformation is beginning....We need the old time religion so that every minister and every evangelist could say 'I feel the spirit of the Lord is upon me.' We need a return of the old power of the gospel in the church and the mighty faith that the people once had in the Lord to cure their bodily ills and their sins.[39]

The newspaper also took note of Aimee's congregation: "The minds of the people were enthralled with her sincere and earnest talk. Their eyes were enraptured with the shining beauty of her face. An understanding shone from her eyes that God does and can heal today as he did yesterday and will do tomorrow. The sick waited for the moment when she would pray for them alone."[40]

Aimee instead asked for a show of hands for those who wanted to be Christians. Five hundred people raised their hands, and Aimee "turned to go away." Sensing that they would not have any "personal word" or "attention" from the "Miracle Woman," the sick sat stunned in disbelief and slowly began to sob for their Sister's return. "Over the faces of the sick unfolded an expression that would have aroused the sympathy of a stone hearted person."[41] But Aimee had given her all—there was nothing more to give.

The sick stayed in their seats and remained upon their cots, refusing to leave. Their hope picked up momentarily when an evangelist, H. W. Lewis of Springfield, Illinois, not formally associated with Aimee, began praying over them. Soon there was a reported healing of a small stammering boy. The sick in desperation began surrounding the evangelist. Minnie Kennedy, taking it all in, decided to stop the impromptu healing service and ordered the caretaker of the park to "put out the lights," stating, "Mrs. McPherson doesn't want to go until the lights are extinguished."[42] The caretaker informed Minnie that she was in a public park, and the lights stayed on until the last person left. "Tex" Jones, the rich oil man who had driven Aimee to Arkansas City, attempted to intervene next by asking the independent evangelist "why he didn't hire his own hall." "Mr. Lewis made no retort. The crowd stood by without comment, but the sick continued to sob."[43] Minnie Kennedy ended the discussion and the evening on a less-than-positive note. She informed the evangelist that she did not object to his "using divine healing power." But she did not consider it fair to operate in an audience that had gathered to hear her daughter, because "if the sick were disappointed over not being helped...the blame usually rested upon Mrs. McPherson."[44] Mr. Lewis later informed the *Traveler* that he had "assisted

Mrs. McPherson at her meeting in Wichita and she did not complain of my help…. I do think, however," he concluded, "that her mother…does not have the vision of her daughter nor the sympathy and compassion for the sick."[45]

Despite her exhaustion, Aimee's refusal to pray over the sick in Arkansas City reflected a growing tension mounting in her ministry. The healing aspect of her ministry had alone made her famous. Increasingly, however, it was the one part of her ministry she found least attractive. It was a spiritual gift that increasingly mystified and baffled her as well as wore her out—a gift she could not quite comprehend or understand. It was thrilling, yet an uncomfortable gift and burden. Always some were healed, but many were not. With the passing of time she would be known more as a preacher than a healer. For Aimee, in the end, "soul-winning" rather than healing was "the one big business of the church."[46] By the close of her meetings in Wichita, her reputation as a "miracle woman" was well established. And as much as Aimee personally wanted the approval of the Protestant mainline ministers, her real endorsement, as always, came from the people and increasingly from the secular press. Summarizing the recent meetings for the *Wichita Eagle*, W. R. Waggoner could have been describing every one of Aimee's major meetings in America when he observed that "few of the local ministers have endorsed her to the extent of lending their presence [but] many of the leading laymen have joined the throng of religious workers that grow larger with each succeeding day."[47]

On May 31, 1922, the *Arkansas City Traveler* reported that the final Sunday offering for Aimee had been "approximately $1,850."[48] Minnie Kennedy was quoted as saying that the Sunday offering was "about an average" and was "all that we expected."[49] She reminded the reporter that the two women had come to Wichita in the first place "without a guarantee and upon their own expenses."[50] In addition to Sunday's plate offering, the newspaper noted that another $1,850 had been raised by seventy-five persons subscribing twenty-five dollars each for chairs in the forthcoming tabernacle in Los Angeles. When questioned about how they preferred their income, Minnie the business manager was quoted as saying, "Many persons have asked us whether we would rather have subscriptions to chairs, or donations to Mrs. McPherson. We invariably tell them that we would rather have donations toward completion of the tabernacle, because that is the goal to which we aim. Whatever money we collect, after expenses are paid, invariably goes to the tabernacle fund, so we prefer that the donations be made directly."[51]

It was not the first nor would it be the last time that Aimee's mother's actions would reflect badly on her. The next morning a lone headline in the

Traveler told the town the story, "Five Healed at Park Last Night."[52]

Finally, in the Wichita campaign there was new evidence that Aimee's vision of Christianity was also broadening beyond healing and moving messages. It took the form, as it would during the Depression years in Los Angeles, of what Aimee called "remembering the poor." In between her services she visited Wichita's "Squatter Town" and noted to her followers that "the poverty stricken live in frail shacks made out of canvas and tin cans which they had opened and nailed flat, and where people dwelt under wagon tops, which had been placed upon the ground."[53] Finding "sick and dying people living without the bare necessities of life, empty cupboards, filth, squalor and half-naked people living among the city dumps covered with flies and dirt," Aimee returned to the Forum and laid out the immediate needs before her audience. As a result, "food, clothing, great baskets full of groceries, mosquito netting, toys, etc., were taken thither in trucks and automobiles and distributed by the Committee instead of being handled by the Associated Charities."[54]

This every-increasing non-sectarian vision of her ministry was adequately summarized by a *Wichita Eagle* reporter before Aimee left town:

> She preaches non-sectarianism...she speaks of the hills and valleys encountered since her evangelistic career began and in her descensions, has met her Gethsemane and Golgothas. But the masses that have heard her in Wichita cannot picture her in the lonely stretch between the peaks. Rather she appears as one on the mountain top...she goes apart with the Saviour, casts conventionalism to the winds and takes a broad view of humanity as she meets its various units. She knows not one creed, one color, one nationality.[55]

Before leaving Wichita Aimee told those in attendance at the Forum, "I have preached under all kinds of conditions, some of them heartbreaking. In some places I am somewhat alone. But whether the band plays with me or I am alone, with cooperation or without it, by the grace of God, I am going to preach the gospel, praise the Lord!"[56] Two months later in Oakland, California, Aimee would receive the greatest mainline religious cooperation of her entire evangelistic career. "The band would play with her," this time, in the city where, ironically, she would die alone in twenty-two years later.

CHAPTER SEVENTEEN

Oakland: The Interdenominational Foursquare Gospel July 15–30, 1922

Father Abraham, whom have you in heaven? Any Episcopalians? No. Any Presbyterians? No! Any Independents (Baptists & Others) or Methodists? No, no, no! Whom have you there?....We don't know those names here. All who are here are Christians....Oh, is this the case? Then God help us to forget party names and to become Christians in deed and truth.

—George Whitfield
Preaching from the courthouse balcony, Philadelphia, 1740

Divisions into sects have been called "the sin of schism," "the luxury of denominationalism." It is the wasteful extravagance and folly of self-will. Against the reproach of such waste and wrong no good defense is possible.

—Alfred Williams Anthony,
"The New Interdenominationalism,"
American Journal of Theology, 1916

Well, the denominations have the right to fight
They ought go on and treat each other right
And that's all, I tell you that's all
'Cause you better have Jesus
I tell you that's all
It's right to stand together, wrong to stand apart.

—Ry Cooder
"Denomination Blues"

As I spoke, God revealed to the assembled multitude...the four-fold ministry of the Lord Jesus Christ....A perfect gospel! A complete gospel for body, for soul, for spirit, and for eternity! A gospel that faces squarely in every direction! "Why—why, it's the F- O- U- R –S- Q- U- A- R- E Gospel" burst from the white heat of my heart.

—Aimee Semple McPherson

Writing to her followers in the early summer months of 1922, Aimee announced a forthcoming meeting in the East Bay of San Francisco. "What could be more delightful," she asked, "than a Revival Campaign in a big tent just across the sparkling bay from San Francisco in [the] heart of [a] back bay metropolis?"[1]

Despite her recent failure in the spring to win full support for her attempted Baptist ordination in San Jose, the San Francisco Bay Area was becoming an ever increasing center of strong support. The Bay Area and later Portland, Oregon, would rival Los Angeles as strong centers of Aimee's support on the West Coast. Local church records were also beginning to indicate the results of her recent meetings. One such church was the Howard Presbyterian Church in San Francisco. The session minutes documented the church's hesitation at first to endorse "the McPherson meetings." By the end of Aimee's San Francisco Revival, however, the story was quite different. On April 26, 1922, the church session dutifully recorded that "after a very interesting and instructive talk by the pastor of the work of the McPherson meetings and the meetings in Howard Church, and the great good that has been accomplished, it was moved and carried that we continue the Ministry of Healing and Prayer every Wednesday evening."[2]

At the close of 1922, the Howard Presbyterian Church continued to note in their session minutes the lasting effects of "the McPherson meetings."

> Our people (were prepared) for an earnest and active participation in the larger evangelistic services conducted in the nearby Coliseum building by Mrs. Aimee Semple McPherson. From the converts at the McPherson meetings a number of members were received into the Church. Spiritually, the congregation had manifested, by the grace of the Holy Spirit unmistakably abiding in its midst, quickened conscientiousness, deepened love for God, and increased knowledge and joyous acceptance of the comfort and peace afforded by the blessed Gospel promises....The increased attendance at the mid-week meetings is a source of rejoicing. Prayer for the sick has been a feature of the meetings during the year, and many instances of the efficacy of united appeal to the Divine Physician and of confident faith in His compassion, might be cited.[3]

What Aimee symbolized in American religion was also occurring quite independently in other Bay Area churches. The most prominent of these was the old Grace Episcopal Church perched atop Nob Hill—later transformed in the 1920s to Grace Cathedral—the former home of the "bonanza kings" from the Gold Rush days. The Reverend James Wilmer Gresham, the rector in charge of creating the cathedral, was remembered by his bishop for being "a mystic."[4] Dean Gresham, under the influence of James Moore Hickson, opened the Grace Cathedral Mission of Healing in the Diocesan House in the early 1920s. Regular office hours were established for the mission every Tuesday and Thursday from 11 a.m. until 2 p.m. Healing Services with the motto "thy touch hath still its ancient power" were conducted in the cathedral for an hour by Dean Gresham every Thursday evening from 8 to 9 p.m. Additionally, Gresham published a weekly tract on the subject titled "The Healing Messenger," and numerous editions of his book *Wings of Healing* were published.[5]

With strong interest in healing in the Bay Area it is of little wonder that Aimee was invited to attend a luncheon in her honor on Nob Hill at the conclusion of her earlier spring meetings. She informed her followers, "A luncheon for the chairholder members of the Echo Park Evangelistic Association was held in the Fairmont Hotel to talk over the cause of Evangelism so near and dear to all of our hearts. About two hundred were present... as we broke bread together."[6]

Although the mid-July Oakland meeting was Aimee's sixth campaign in Northern California in less than a year, again attesting to her growing strength in the Bay Area, she was overwhelmed at the solidarity of that support. "Never," wrote Aimee, "during our fourteen years of ministry from coast to coast have we ever met a more kindly, enthusiastic people. Never have we been treated with more consideration, confidence and tender solicitation."[7]

By 1922, Oakland was a rapidly maturing metropolis on the eastern shore of San Francisco Bay. The city was the West Coast terminus for three transcontinental rail lines, where goods from the rural hinterland were shipped in and processed. In addition to the railroads, Oakland had also experienced a manufacturing boom in both shipbuilding and automobile production. Migration to Oakland by refugees from the 1906 San Francisco earthquake and the annexation of outlying areas east of the city had raised the city's population from 66,960 in 1900 to 216,216 by 1920. In 1890 Oakland had led the nation with "the highest statistical score for religious diversity."[8] By the early 1920s, Oakland was ninety-five percent white and in essence was becoming much like Los Angeles to the south, the growing home for the "native white Protestant middle class."[9]

Aimee was amazed to find such a large reception with more than a thousand individuals awaiting her arrival at the train depot. For a moment she felt mistaken and quietly wondered if those who were pushing and crowding around her coach and spilling out onto the tracks were not welcoming a theatrical troupe or a baseball team. Even the "movie-men" were there silently recording the event, while their less sophisticated counterparts, the newspaper photographers, scrambled about hoping to find perches offering the most panoramic views. All apprehension left her when the smiling sea of people, many bearing silver musical instruments sparkling brightly in the summer sun, began to sing the familiar refrains of "Revive Us Again" and "The Old Time Religion." Aimee felt very much at home in the place where "the sunset sea kisses the foot-hills and the beaches of the great Pacific Coast."

A newspaper reporter for the *Oakland Tribune* described Aimee's standard demeanor and perceived image among the crowds accompanying her early meeting.

> The eagerly watching crowd at the depot failed, at first, to recognize the quiet, motherly-appearing lady of between 30 and 35 [She was 31.] who stepped from the train. Then some of those who had met her on previous occasions recognized her and she was fairly overwhelmed with greetings and well wishes.[10]

Aimee and Minnie were quickly put in an open car draped in green and white bunting symbolizing fragrant green pastures and purity. The open car was the lead vehicle in a parade of fifty automobiles through downtown Oakland announcing the meetings while en route to her room at the Oakland Hotel. Another open car—a new "Chummy" roadster—was made available for her two-week stay. An air of expectancy prevailed under the big-top of the billowy "tabernacle-tent" hovering over eight thousand vacant seats on Twenty-sixth Street between Broadway and Telegraph Avenue. The tent itself was the largest ever used in Aimee's meetings, and a newspaper reporter noted that it was virtually "a city within itself." An interdenominational committee composed of six hundred members had not overlooked a single detail—a far cry from the early days when the committee in charge was Harold Stewart McPherson.

Again in Oakland, as it had been in Denver, Wichita, and elsewhere, Aimee's real source of support was derived from the laity. The chairperson of the Oakland committee was an active Christian layperson as well as a medical doctor. It was his first experience with American revivalism and almost became his last. He remembered his initial phone call to the president of the Oakland Ministerial Association relating the news that Aimee Semple McPherson was coming to town:

> With great glee…I called up the President of the Ministerial Association, and with my head swollen almost the size of a bass drum, and with

the enthusiasm of a boy with a new top, I told him the glad news. At once the phone began to freeze—words would meet on the way, freeze, and inside of five minutes, the wire was one chain of glittering icicles, many of them two feet long.[11]

Whether or not the Bay Area clergymen followed their parishioners to Aimee's meetings, Dr. Sherman noted their later involvement:

> We had no active ministers with us until almost the last…when the rostrum was made, we planned for a few ministers but when the meetings opened we were all but swamped with them. Oh what a glorious sight to see as high as thirty-five of God's trained workers, of all the denominations and missions of more types than I have yet been able to find out, sitting on the platform with their arms around each other, none of them there for over four services before they were shouting "Hallelujah!"[12]

At Oakland, one of the biggest ministerial surprises of Aimee's evangelistic career occurred when the dean of Yale Divinity School and pastor of Yale University Church, the Reverend Charles Reynolds Brown, offered the invocation at one of the meetings. Brown, formerly the minister of the First Congregational Church of Oakland and moderator of the National Council of Congregational Churches, had also lectured at Stanford, Harvard, and Columbia and was noted for his eloquence and power of pulpit utterance. It was Brown's role as an author, however, that interested him most in the McPherson meetings. One of his published works included a book on the subject of *Faith and Health*, a life-long interest.[13]

Charles Reynolds Brown's support of Aimee more than anything else demolished the socio-economic deprivation model for explaining away the Pentecostal movement—at least Aimee's brand of it. Not only was Brown's former church, the First Congregational, the largest in the city, it also had the largest membership in the county. And First Congregational of Oakland not only possessed the costliest church edifice in the city but also again, in all of Alameda County, valued at four hundred thousand dollars in 1918.

The newspaper coverage of the meetings was extensive, due to the size of the opening crowd, and for the most part was written by the religion editor of the *Oakland Tribune*. The editor noted that fully half of those in attendance during the opening meetings were from San Francisco. "Hundreds had come from San Jose and large groups from other outlying cities. About fifty of the visitors were from outside of the state, representing eighteen different states, some coming from as far as New York, and some from Alberta, Canada."[14]

The bulk of Aimee's meetings across America had developed common patterns and themes—an informal liturgy of sorts. There were the "gospel songs," followed by the short and simple "gospel message." There would be "testimonies" by way of response from the audience/congregation of conversions and healings. Local churches, including both the Protestant mainline and Pentecostal, would grow stronger as a result of the revival. No future meeting would ever define Aimee so succinctly in American religion as one night under the "Oakland big top—'just across the sparkling bay from San Francisco.' " Through a personal vision experienced in an intense moment while preaching, Aimee envisioned a four-fold symbol, which not only gave expression to her basic theological tenets but would in time become the basis of a new American denomination, contrary to her original interdenominational intentions. On that night all eight thousand folding chairs were full of occupants, while hundreds more encircled the tabernacle-tent when its canvas side walls were rolled up high. An air of expectancy much like the sea breeze itself prevailed over the place. Aimee sensed that even the "people leaned forward in expectancy, as God poured the message forth from out of my innermost being."[15]

The sermon was based upon the Old Testament prophet Ezekiel's vision of the four cherubim with four faces. True to her Pentecostal interpretation of scripture, which borrowed heavily upon the typological or allegorical method of exegesis, the number four figured prominently for Aimee and seemed to clarify everything she believed, preached and taught:

> As I spoke, God revealed to the assembled multitude that the four faces typified the four-fold ministry of the Lord Jesus Christ.
>
> In the face of the LION we beheld that of the mighty Baptizer with the Holy Ghost and with fire. Jesus is the "lion of the tribe of Judah." As a lion denotes strength and power, it is a fitting symbol for Christ as the Giver of the Holy Spirit.
>
> In the face of the MAN we beheld the "man of sorrows and acquainted with grief"—the Savior of the world!
>
> In the face of the OX we beheld the Great Burden-Bearer, who "himself took our infirmities and bore our sicknesses." Jesus is the Great Physician and the Healer of our bodies.
>
> In the face of the EAGLE we saw reflected a vision of the coming King of Kings, whose pinions would soon cleave the shining heavens as he returns to catch his waiting bride away!
>
> A perfect gospel! A complete gospel for body, for soul, for spirit, and for eternity!

A gospel that faces squarely in every direction!

As the wonder—the power—the majesty of it cascaded o'er the battlements of glory, filling, flooding, enveloping my very being, the whole tent seemed enveloped as well—aquiver with the praises of God!

I stood there still and listened, gripping the pulpit, shaking with the wonder and the joy of it, then—

"Why—why, it's the F-O-U-R-S-Q-U-A-R-E Gospel!" burst from the white heat of my heart.

Instantly the Spirit bore witness! Waves, billows, oceans of praises rocked the audience.[16]

In time Aimee would expand upon her topology with scriptural references adding recognizable color coordination to the four tenets, even creating her own multi-colored Foursquare flag.

In studying the Word of God I have discovered that the word, "Foursquare," is entirely scriptural, and that it is woven throughout every phrase of the Old and New Testaments. As revelation follows revelation, it seems as though life itself would be too short in which to express the fullness of it all!

Four colors were revealed through a study of the scriptures which I applied to the four phases of Christ's ministry: Red, typifying the precious blood which he shed on the cross for dying humanity, for the first phase—Salvation. Gold, symbolic of the fire which fell from heaven on the day of Pentecost, for the second phase—Baptism of the Holy Spirit. Blue, the color of heaven itself from whence cometh the third phrase—Divine Healing. And Purple, the color of royalty, for the fourth phase—the Second Coming of Christ as King.[17]

The newly created "Foursquare Gospel" was not some new form of religion, as William McLoughlin has argued, any more than Theodore Roosevelt's "Square Deal" was a new form of government.[18] Since beginning her ministry Aimee seemed uncertain as to the exact name or label by which it should be known. For example, *The Bridal Call* was subtitled "a Pentecostal Monthly." When the term "Pentecostal" began to be used in a pejorative manner, Aimee substituted "Full Gospel Evangelism." She had been quite clear from the start, however, that her ministry had fourfold content to it.[19]

Thus the essential tenets were well-established and long in place before the Oakland meeting. Compounding the problem, of course, was the multiplicity of names by which the larger Pentecostal movement itself was known. In some very concrete and creative ways, Aimee gave the entire

Aimee and the cornerstone of Angelus Temple, dedicated to an interdenominational and international gospel (used by permission of the International Church of the Foursquare Gospel, Heritage Department).

Pentecostal movement its fullest and most streamlined theological definition with the "Foursquare" designation.

The concept of a "Foursquare Gospel" took root early on during the Oakland campaign. It readily became a byword and theme for the entire revival. In an afternoon service on July 17, Aimee implored every minister and Sunday school teacher present to return to their churches to "teach the Foursquare Gospel." "This world" she insisted, "is in need of positive preaching; someone to tell us what to do, instead of what not to do." She declared that "denominational questions are to be forgotten during this revival. We haven't time for them."[20] The following day, a solo was sung by professor W. B. Kramer entitled "The Four Square Gospel." Aimee declared to her audience:

> We may dress a little different, we may talk a little different, we may have a few additional inventions, but at heart we are the same as the people were twenty centuries ago....we don't want psychology or politics in our pulpits. What we want and need is the unadulterated word of God.[21]

The concept of a "Foursquare Gospel" so captured the imagination of those in attendance that an announcement was made on July 17, 1922—just two days after the revival opened—that during the following week "special meetings will be held in the morning for ministers and church workers... who are interested in carrying on the work of the revival campaign after the close of the present meetings."[22]

On July 25 a three day ministers' and evangelists' conference "to further the evangelistic work" commenced at the Parish House at Oakland's Trinity Episcopal Church. Trinity was not an insignificant Episcopal church either. Of the ten Episcopal churches in Oakland, Trinity had the largest membership. In fact it was also the largest Episcopal church in all of Alameda County. Given Aimee's theological vision it was altogether fitting and proper that the "Foursquare Gospel" should emerge out of an Episcopal church rather than a Pentecostal mission on the "wrong side of the tracks." It was an Episcopal church, St. Stephen's of Providence, Rhode Island, where Aimee had found solace during her near-death experiences, her reaffirmation of her theological calling, and her decision to leave Harold Stewart McPherson. It was the one denomination Aimee felt was "the most beautiful church in the world." Her love of the Episcopal Church would explain her later attachment to clerical vestments. It was also the church in which healing was officially sanctioned.[23]

The Episcopal ministers who supported Aimee during the Oakland Revival were most likely of the "Low Church" style. A national organization of Episcopal clergymen was organized in the 1920s as "the Liberal Evangelicals." After a few years of existence it was thought wiser to emphasize the "evangelical" rather than the "liberal" aspect of their mission, "since its most important function was to throw emphasis upon what is commonly called the evangelical aspect of the church's mission."[24] Most likely, those Episcopalians who supported Aimee would have been part of the larger

"Liberal Evangelical" movement. In fact most of the Protestant mainline ministers in general who supported Aimee during the early 1920s, including Chaplain Spotts in San Diego, Dean Peck in Denver, James Logan Gordon of San Francisco, Dean Brown of Yale Divinity School, and W. K. Towner from San Jose were most likely theological representatives of "evangelical liberalism." As John Corrigan and Winthrop Hudson point out,

> The striking feature of the liberal movement in Protestantism that began to take shape during the 1870s was its conservative intent. Leaders of the movement were evangelicals, standing firmly within the church, cherishing their Christian experience, and uncompromising in their loyalty to Christ....The goal of the New Theology, as William Adams Brown was to point out in 1898 in his inaugural address as professor of systematic theology in Union Theological Seminary, was no more than the "old cry, 'back to Christ.' Let no theology call itself Christian which has not its center and source in him."
>
> Although these evangelical liberals clung tenaciously to the bible... they viewed it as...a record not of a theology but of an experience that was to be reproduced "in our own times and in our own souls."....The great advantage...of a revived evangelicalism was that proponents were enabled to maintain what to them was the heart of the inherited faith without coming into conflict with the intellectual climate of the modern world.[25]

Perhaps the Church of England gave the best definition of "Liberal Evangelical" when they noted in the early 1920s the growing movement within their own ranks:

> The title of Liberal Evangelical...suggests that the "heredity" of their movement is rooted in the great Evangelical Revival, and that the 'environment' in which they are at home is the modern world with its historical method, its philosophy of personality, and its scientific view of the universe....[A Liberal Evangelical celebrates] the glorious freedom of the Gospel, the elasticity of the Spirit's working, the superiority of the inward to the outward ...and the progressive character of God's revelation in Christ.[26]

"Progressive Orthodoxy," was how the faculty of Andover Seminary described its mission as Evangelical Liberals in 1884.[27]

The *Oakland Tribune* on July 28, 1922, took careful notice of a new religious organization that emerged out of the parish house of Trinity Episcopal Church:

With Dr. W. K. Towner of the 1ˢᵗ Baptist Church of San Jose acting as temporary Chairman of the conference of laymen and ministers yesterday morning, an organization was formed which is to be known as the Pacific Coast Foursquare Gospel Association.

It has been organized for the purpose of spreading the Foursquare Gospel, as it is interpreted by Mrs. McPherson and for promoting fellowship and cooperation between members of evangelical churches who believe in, subscribe to and practice the Foursquare Gospel as outlined in the constitution of the association as follows, with emphasis on:

Jesus Christ, the Son of God, our only Savior; Jesus Christ the great Physician, present with his church throughout this age to confirm His word with signs and wonders and miraculous gifts of the Spirit; Jesus Christ, the Risen, ascended and glorified Lord, the Baptizer of His people with the Holy Spirit, personal and imminent.

The organization is to be interdenominational and any individuals interested in the furtherance of evangelism as preached by Mrs. McPherson are to be permitted to join. More than 1,000 joined the organization yesterday. Officers are to be elected today and future plans arranged.[28]

Geography played an important role in the establishment of the "Pacific Coast Foursquare Gospel Association." The newly created organization represented what the Reverend James Logan Gordon of the First Congregational Church of San Francisco thought would sooner or later be an inevitable product of the West:

Unusual developments…may be looked for in the spiritual life and religious growth of our Western states. The light of prophecy rests upon the Pacific coast. Visions and dreams possess those who reside on the edge of "the last sea of history." If America is to produce a world religion, the creed of such a religion will probably be written on this side of the Rocky Mountains.[29]

On July 29, 1922, one day before the close of the revival, the *Oakland Tribune* reported that the organization known as the Pacific Coast Foursquare Gospel Association had elected its first officers. Perhaps the most interesting feature of the following list of names is that all of the officers had mainline church connections.

Announcement as to the completion of the organization to be known as the Pacific Coast Foursquare Gospel Association was made at the opening of last night's service and the following officers were unanimously elected: Mrs. Aimee McPherson, president; Dr. W. K. Towner, pastor of the First Baptist Church of San Jose, first vice-president; Dr.

Charles S. Price, pastor of the First Congregational Church of Lodi, second vice-president; Fred Hart of Salinas, recording secretary; Claude Stutsman of San Jose, field secretary and Rev. H. D. Harkins of the Methodist Episcopal Church at Portola, treasurer.[30]

The growing impact of the new organization in the Bay Area could readily be seen by a casual reading of the church newspaper advertisements the following Saturday. Many mainline churches ran ads soliciting the new "McPherson converts."[31] One denominational church went so far as to proclaim: "We preach the Foursquare Gospel."[32]

Pentecostalism, especially as preached and practiced by Aimee—the old time religion of experience—struck much more of a responsive chord among evangelical liberals than it ever did among the fundamentalists. Pentecostalism at its best represented new territory, a growing middle ground between the coming fundamentalist-modernist controversy. It would take another seventy years for a truly successful evangelical interdenominational church organization to be realized in America. What Aimee attempted to create in 1922 with her Pacific Coast Foursquare Gospel Association, Bill Hybels achieved in 1992 with the creation of his Willow Creek Association. Founded by the desire "to link like-minded, action-oriented churches with each other and with strategic vision, training, and resources," the WCA, like Aimee's Foursquare vision, is also both truly interdenominational and international. "The WCA is a ...ministry, with more than 12,000 Member Churches from 90 denominations and 45 countries. These churches...represent a wide variety of sizes, denominations, and backgrounds, and are ministering in literally every corner of the world."[33]

Four factors enabled Aimee to launch her fledging Foursquare organization as an interdenominational association. American revivalism itself has not only brought denominations together but it was also responsible for integrating races, at least for worship. But it was the winning combination of the laity and the revivalists that promoted and produced interdenominational harmony, as Timothy L. Smith points out in *Revivalism and Social Reform*:

> A soul-winning laity understandably cared less than ministers about dogmatic distinctions between the sects....Revivalists were likewise foremost among those clergymen who abandoned feuding among themselves in favor of a united front against the devil....They joined laymen of a similar outlook in promoting the Bible, tract, and home mission societies. Inevitably...such men emphasized the saving simplicities of the gospel, stressed compassion over creeds, and regretted more and more the weakness which internal dissension brought to Christianity.[34]

In city after city Aimee always concluded that her campaigns were the result of "the most wonderful Interdenominational Laymen's Committee."[35]

A second factor responsible for promoting interdenominational harmony was the Progressive Pietists. In recent years the "Progressive Era" has been stretched and redefined to include the early 1920s. The one item on the Progressive agenda that both conservatives and liberals found common ground on which to unite forces was Prohibition. "The prohibition movement during this period," notes the historian Ferenc Szasz, "extended beyond the desire to regulate the consumption of alcohol by the individual to include a view of the ideal social order. The advocates of prohibition saw it as the chief cure for poverty, crime, and prostitution. To destroy alcohol would in large measure destroy the others."[36] Unfortunately this church unity was short-lived and all but extinguished by the mid-1920s. "Never again," concluded Szasz, "would the social question have the undivided church support of the years before World War I. In large measure it declined when liberal and conservative pastors began to see each other as more dangerous enemies than the social evils around them."[37]

A third factor in the rise of the interdenominational tide in the early 1920s was, of course, the first World War. "Americans found World War I," argues John F. Piper, "a glorious, shameful, wonderful, catastrophic, magnificent, appalling war.....[It] was an important turning point in American religious history."[38] Not only did the Great War introduce American churches to the modern world, it also "gave some men a vision of what that world would be like religiously. They saw that above all else the new day that was coming would recognize the plurality of religion in America and would demand that religious...groups raise a voice that was more than an echo of the culture."[39]

One of the boldest ecumenical moves toward true interdenominationalism that came out of the Great War was the creation of "Liberty Churches" established on seven ordnance reservations. In 1919 the Federal Council of Churches noted their uniqueness in American religious history.

> These Liberty Churches were required by the conditions prevailing in the reservations which made it impossible to establish denominational Churches and which brought about the order of the War Department that there should be only one Protestant, one Catholic and one Hebrew church [sic] in each reservation. The Liberty Churches are religious societies, representing American Protestantism....These Liberty Churches represent a striking achievement in cooperation. They will continue as Liberty Churches during the period of reconstruction or until the communities are turned back to civil control.[40]

Not all of American Protestantism, however, viewed the creation of Liberty Churches as "a striking achievement in cooperation." The Southern Baptists especially viewed them suspiciously as a bastardization of Christianity itself. The majority of Southern Baptists rejected the rise and acceptance of interdenominationalism, claiming that "a denominationalized Christianity...is yet the strongest expression of Christianity,"[41] James Gambrell, president of the Southern Baptist Convention, even took on the War Department, claiming that "the whole trend and...desire of the [war] department is in the interest of breaking down rather than emphasizing denominational distinctions."[42] In an emotional sermon emulating William Jennings Bryan, a Southern Baptist preacher asked, "Shall we go with the federated throngs of the day by compromising our spiritual message and adopting a half materialistic philosophy, or shall we stand alone in the sustaining truth that Christ is fulfilling his promise, 'Lo I am with you always.'" Answering his own question, the preacher concluded, "I choose the latter alternative and hereby declare that the world shall not crucify our convictions upon a cross of unionism nor will we sell our principles for thirty pieces of popular praise."[43]

The fourth and final factor that led to the creation of an interdenominational Foursquare movement also highlights another difference between the Pentecostals and the fundamentalists. If the fundamentalists were denominational separatists like the Southern Baptists, many Pentecostals opposed denominationalism all together and rejected it outright. They viewed themselves instead as "undenominational."

An article appearing in the February 26, 1916, issue of *The Weekly Evangel*, written Florence L. Burpee, a future Assemblies of God minister herself, asked the question, "What Denomination Are You?"

> This is a question we are all familiar with, some of us more than we wish. Wherever I go this is almost the first question asked. When I go to a strange place and tell the people... I am a missionary, the questions comes at once, "What denomination are you?" And when I reply, "I am undenominational," the query arises, "To what church do you belong, are you Methodist, Baptist, etc? What denomination?"
>
> When I try to rent a church, hall, school-house or private dwelling to hold services in, these words are sure to greet me, first of all. "What denomination are you?"
>
> I am refused admittance many times to places where I might do good, because someone does not like the ring of the undenominational note...A brother or sister, when they attend services of any kind, should have enough Christian courtesy, to say nothing about love, to

remain silent on doctrinal points wherein they may differ from the ones who are conducting the services.

If we attend a church, Roman Catholic or any other, we should have respect enough for God and love for our brother, to sit still and listen… When will God's people learn, like Mary, to keep some things to themselves and ponder them in their hearts? I confess I am heartily tired of the question, "What denomination are you?"

If St. Peter stands at heaven's door, as some believe he will, I am glad he will think of other words to use to the anxious seeker for an entrance…Reader, He will never ask us the question, "What denomination are you?"[44]

Aimee created her Foursquare movement by intuitively tapping into this new spirit of interdenominational Protestantism created in part by revivalism, Progressivism, World War I, and the non-denominational character of Pentecostalism itself.

Two other interesting events occurred during the Oakland Revival. Aimee was requested by the station management of the Oakland *Tribune's* radio station KLX to speak to their listeners on the subject of divine healing an hour before "charming Bessie Barriscale, popular moving picture star known to millions on the screen." This was the second time that Aimee was broadcast over radio in California. In just a few short years, Aimee's magnetic voice "to the great unseen audience" along the Pacific Coast would become as familiar on the radio as any motion picture star's face upon the silver screen. While declaring that "it was almost unbelievable" to be talking to fifty thousand or more listeners, Aimee told her hearers that the radio was in reality not that new. "The Lord, Himself, in heaven upon His great throne," she declared, "has been sending radio messages to the earth for these past 6,000 years."[45] However she defined it, Aimee was, remembered her daughter Roberta, "quick to make use of anything new."[46]

The sociologist David Martin rightly sees Pentecostalism as bringing "together the most ancient and the most modern."[47] What separated Pentecostals from the mainline liberal evangelicals, who supported them in the early 1920s, were their differing embraces and views of modernity. While Pentecostals embraced modernity sociologically, the mainline embraced it theologically. Liberal Evangelicals were at home "with the intellectual climate of the modern world," especially its "historical method…and scientific view of the universe."[48] In Martin Marty's words, "Modernism adapted, using theological naturalism, but Pentecostalists were raging supernaturalists."[49] Chris Armstrong, a professor of church history at Bethel Seminary, refers to theological modernism as " '*Star Trek* theology': the faith that through natural and social sciences, we can all live longer, solve world hunger, and make war obsolete."[50] Yet while Pentecostals stubbornly remained pre-modern theologically, the mainline rejected modernity culturally and the sea of social change it created. Charles Reynolds Brown, a former dean of Yale Divinity School, for instance, rejected much of modernity's "Changes" in his autobiography, *My Own Yesterdays*:

> The automobile, the moving picture, and the radio are interesting and useful inventions.....They certainly have a place in this modern world. But to multitudes of people they are like new toys—the children do not know yet quite what to do with them. Their minds have not gained a true perspective or a just sense of relative values. They have not learned to put the first things first.[51]

While Aimee took to preaching over the airwaves, the former Congregational pastor denounced such modern advances in "public worship."

> The general feeling among ministers is that the radio is not an asset but a liability. It teaches millions of people to accept a feeble, unworthy substitute for the real thing....it is often an encouragement to spiritual laziness.
>
> Here is a robust man who sits down at home on Sunday in dressing-gown and slippers, with a good cigar, and listens in for fifteen or twenty minutes to Dr. Cadman or Dr. Fosdick, and thinks he has been to church....He has not been to church. He has not cast his vote for spiritual values by going through the streets of his hometown to the church of his choice. He has not organized and socialized his worship with that of his fellows in a way to make it spiritually effective for the higher life of the community. He has not even paid his fare. The salaries of Cadman and Fosdick are paid by people who go to church.
>
> And the poor chap does not get much! The difference between going to church and listening in somewhere (at a safe distance from the collection plate and all other forms of responsibility) is like the difference between spending the evening with a charming young woman and telephoning to her.[52]

The other event occurring for Aimee a second time in her ministry was her "kidnapping" by the Ku Klux Klan and her invitation to preach "a sermon of salvation" to the double formation of white-robed men who sat before her. Aimee's acceptance of a hundred dollar bill (for four chairs in Angelus Temple) from the sacred Klavern meeting represented more her political naiveté than any alliance with such an extremist group. Just two months prior to her Oakland campaign on May 5, 1922, fifteen hundred men in white robes and masks had gathered in the still of the night in a valley in the hills above Oakland. In the course of the evening five hundred more men had "marched four abreast toward the altar, to take their oaths and be initiated into the order of the Knights of the Ku Klux Klan."[53] With the decline of immigration in World War I and the rise of Oakland's white Protestant middle class, the city became a center of Klan activity in California. By 1924 the Oakland Klan had grown to more than two thousand members. Late in the decade the city's Klan enjoyed political success, winning elections for county sheriff in 1926 and for city commissioner in 1927. The Klan's power in Oakland "was finally broken in a celebrated graft trial prosecuted by Alameda County District Attorney (and later United States Supreme Court Chief Justice) Earl Warren, and the scandal led directly to a major reform of the Oakland city charter."[54] Oakland was by no means unique for Klan activity among California cities. Throughout the 1920s, the Klan thrived in both San Diego and Los Angeles. In 1928 used-automobile-parts dealer and Klan leader John Porter was elected mayor of Los Angeles. Between 1920 and 1924, the Klan grew nationally from five thousand members to an estimated five million.

The Klan had made earlier overtures to Aimee in Denver. And again, one evening in 1924 "a group of white knights in full regalia entered...Angelus Temple." Aimee, never at a loss for words quickly extemporized, "You men who pride yourselves on patriotism, you men who have pledged yourselves to make America free for white Christianity, listen to me. Ask yourselves how it is possible to pretend to worship one of the greatest Jews who ever lived, Jesus Christ, and then to despise all living Jews? I say unto you as our Master said, 'Judge not, that ye not be judged.' "[55] One by one the Klansmen got up from their seats and left. "According to reports, white hoods and robes were left in several trash cans around the temple."[56]

Aimee's invitation to speak over the *Oakland Tribune's* airwaves and her endorsement by the KKK reflected her unusual ability in Oakland, as elsewhere, to be accepted by extremely diverse groups. It was this acceptability factor that most impressed the *Tribune's* religion editor at her concluding meeting.

> The thing that impressed me most was the lack of any emotionalism at the meetings, in spite of the fact that the huge audiences were made up of people from both extremes...The sermons delivered by Mrs. McPherson struck me as being straight to the point that she was driving at, without any back-biting or radical censure which seems to be so

prevalent in many of the pulpits of today, when one extreme is trying to down the other with sharp rebukes while if they were both to strike a happy medium in their own particular belief, they would find themselves riding on the same trains.[57]

An eyewitness of many of Aimee's Northern California campaigns during 1922 readily recalled both her appeal and congregational audience makeup adding validity to the above impressions.

> She was a very gracious woman, a very gracious person She preached a beautiful message. She had an indomitable wholesome spirit of faith about her, nothing got her down, if something went wrong, nothing bothered her…I thought her preaching was excellent.
>
> She cut across many theological lines. It wasn't generally speaking, a Pentecostal bunch. They came among them but were very definitely a minority. They helped a lot during the "tarrying meetings."[58]

Aimee said goodbye to Oakland after her thirty-one "round robin revivals" in just two weeks. The religion editor for the *Oakland Tribune* reported the drama of the fond farewell:

> Tears and sighs battled with smiles and laughter last night when more than twelve thousand congregated at the tent tabernacle…to bid farewell and hear the final evangelistic sermon of Aimee Semple McPherson, who during the last two weeks has addressed more than 150,000 people at thirty-one revival meetings.
>
> Milady and the hikers and tourists who were there…side by side with the frocked clergyman and the laymen, from Oakland and vicinity, and from outside the state, vied with each other when they waved their handkerchiefs in a "Chautauqua salute," forming a sea of billowy white, covering more than an acre, while they sang hymn after hymn. The singing was followed by the custom established at the beginning of the meetings, that of each person turning around and shaking hands with three others and saying "God bless you." Thirty-six thousand handshakes and words of cheer were exchanged in less than a minute.[59]

At the end of the meeting an exuberant Aimee bid farewell, too, to the twelve thousand or so enveloping the tent tabernacle. She had successfully completed her sixth revival in Northern California in less than a year's time and launched a new religious organization, the Pacific Coast Foursquare Gospel Association. "There is nothing Oakland has forgotten," she exclaimed. "I have been through many campaigns in the past fourteen years, but I don't believe that any are going to linger in my memory with as many sweet recollections as this one just coming to a close. It has been one of the happiest meetings of my life and I don't believe that I have ever enjoyed my ministry more sincerely. We haven't shed a tear nor had a single sigh or heartache or feeling of regret since we came here…I have been treated so wonderfully here that I almost wish my tabernacle was being built here instead of at Los Angeles."[60]

CHAPTER EIGHTEEN

Angelus Temple: Multitudes and Miracles

Temple—a building, usually of imposing size...serving the public or an organization in some special way.

—Webster's New World Dictionary

I am Angelus Temple. Within my portals, one name is lifted up, Jesus, the living Christ. The same yesterday, today and forever. Because he is here, I am a sanctuary for life's journeying pilgrims who worship at my altars. In me, human hearts find salvation and peace. Within my sheltering walls, broken bodies find the balm of his healing touch...I am the church of the understanding heart and the helping hand. My doors are always open in welcome to whosoever will come and share the blessing I offer in the name of Jesus.

—Aimee Semple McPherson

This tour, through the northwestern part of Los Angeles, pauses at Angelus Temple and the former site of Walt Disney Studios, and it passes such less publicized points as the city's first oil field, and Griffith Park, the largest municipal park in the United States. Angelus Temple...1100 Glendale Blvd., an immense, circular, buff-colored concrete building with a setback and a low-domed roof, is identified by numerous banners and posters, and by electric signs on its façade and upon the broadcasting towers on the roof; on the top of the dome is a revolving cross outlined with neon lights at night, showing red on one side and blue on the other. This is the mother church of the Foursquare Gospel, founded by Aimee Semple McPherson.

Within the auditorium, aisles soft with blood-red carpets lead to an altar under a great proscenium arch. The ceiling of the huge unsupported dome is sky-blue behind fleecy clouds, and light enters through tall stained-glass windows. The temple has four robed choirs, several orchestras, bands, and smaller musical organizations, an expensive costume wardrobe, a vast amount of stage scenery and properties, and a 5,300- glass communion set.

—Los Angeles, A Guide to the City and Its Environs, 1941

There is a steady drift, back and forth, between denominations and from church to church....the chief motive which leads the average American from one church to another is the desire to find a congenial social environment rather than to satisfy or express a profound theological revolution in thought. The next five decades will witness a tendency to migrate from fold to fold.

—The Reverend James Logan Gordon
Minister, First Congregational Church of San Francisco, 1926

I went for a walk through the streets. My God, here I was again, roaming the town. I looked at the faces around me, and I knew mine was like theirs. Faces with the blood drained away, tight faces, worried, lost. Faces like flowers torn from their roots and stuffed into a pretty vase, the colors draining fast. I had to get away from that town.

—John Fante
Ask the Dust

He felt an alien, a stranger in a foreign city whose language was mysteriously his own. Never could it seem home. Surely some kind of fate would snatch him hence. San Diego, Santa Barbara, San Jose, San Francisco, any saint would serve if only he might shake the dust of Los Angeles from his feet.

—Mark Lee Luther
The Boosters

This is a lonesome town. I don't know the name of the people who have lived across the street from me for ten years. Outdoor life tends to destroy neighborliness. No one stays home. People live, die, suffer, sorrow, have good luck and bad, and the neighbors do not know or care. Los Angeles is like a boarding-house. No one really knows anybody else.

—Harry Carr,
Los Angeles, City of Dreams, 1935

During the summer of 1922, a temple and not a tabernacle was in the process of being built in Los Angeles. Incorporating two hundred tons of steel and twenty thousand bags of cement, the imposing edifice was assuming its intended form on its wedge-shaped lot opposite the rushes of Echo Park. By the conclusion of the Oakland campaign, the temple had almost been completed. The building contractor reported to the new Pacific Coast Foursquare Gospel Association that as of July 31, 1922, the walls were up and the gallery and balcony were both in place. "Now only remains the completing of the enormous dome which surmounts the whole structure."[1] Since the building was required by the city of Los Angeles to meet

Angelus Temple at night with its revolving cross and twin radio towers. An Episcopal minister wrote that it "shone out like a great marble hall, white and clean and durable in appearance, with a style of architecture half like a Roman coliseum, half like a Parisian opera house" (used by permission of the International Church of the Foursquare Gospel, Heritage Department).

the requirements of Class A construction, no wood was permitted in any part of the building with the exception of the doors and window frames. The required fireproof form of construction also resulted in the structure's name change. "About the middle of 1922, the tentative name 'Echo Park Revival Tabernacle' was dropped in favor of the enduring name 'Angelus Temple.' Certainly the term 'tabernacle' was not adequate to describe the building as re-structured to Class A specifications."[2] Pentecostalism as an entire movement was gaining permanence during the decade of the 1920s, and true to its Old Testament vision of finding a "Promised Land," many "temples" of concrete and steel were fast replacing the oblong wooden box "tabernacles" of an earlier era. Aimee gave the structure its new name with the principal thought in mind that the building would be like an "Angel's Temple." That intention was never lost upon an audience once inside the doors of the building. Attempting to appeal to the "eye-gate" of her congregation as well as their "ear-gate," she saw to it that parishioners were surrounded by the imagery of bells and angels. Unlike the megachurches of today, devoid of symbolism—including the cross—Angelus Temple was rich, churchy, sacred, and secular. A very feminine frieze work of bells adorned the front of the gallery and upper balcony, while fourteen large

369

angels loomed from the top of the grey and rose-colored walls, standing wing-to-wing. Symbolically, bells of good news were to peel forth while guardian angels hovered overhead welcoming the weary home. Church, for Aimee, was always to be a joyous experience, somewhere in between childhood memories of her father's Methodism and her mother's experiences with the Salvation Army.

In 1997, Donald E. Miller, a sociologist of religion at the University of Southern California, wrote a book about the changing religious landscape in Southern California. In his *Reinventing American Protestantism: Christianity in the New Millennium,* Miller argued that the United States was "witnessing a second reformation that is transforming the way Christianity will be experienced in the new millennium."[3] The new reformation, Miller stated, would be led by "new paradigm churches" who are "challenging not doctrine but the medium through which the message of Christianity is articulated."[4] What is most interesting, and what Miller neglects to identify, is that the three movements he uses as examples of his "new paradigm" either directly or indirectly emerged out of Aimee Semple McPherson's ministry. Miller is most perceptive, however, in describing their setting:

> The typical new paradigm church meets in a converted warehouse, a rented school auditorium, or a leased space in a shopping mall. These meeting places boast no religious symbols, no stained glass, and no religious statuary....The clergy are indistinguishable from the audience by dress.[5]

What Miller is describing at the end of the twentieth century was a lot like the classical Pentecostalism that was born at the beginning of the century. Both classical Pentecostalism and Miller's new paradigm churches are utterly devoid of religious symbolism.

A French writer with an interest in the occult, Jules-Bois, in his attempt to explain "The Holy Rollers" as one of "The New Religions of America" in the early twentieth century, noticed that the parishioners and their places of worship were rich in faith and nothing more.

> Poverty saturates the atmosphere, but no sadness; these parishioners are rich with faith....it is faith, abundant faith, which prostrates them in these halls, bare of adornment, without altars, without beauty, without even the atmosphere of piety, in front of a wooden rail or a nondescript platform—Faith! It exists, it overflows[6]

Aimee's ministry, therefore, was unique among early Pentecostals for

Angelus Temple and the larger Echo Park area (used by permission of the International Church of the Foursquare Gospel, Heritage Department).

its rich symbolism. Her embrace and use of religious imagery, it could be argued, led to the movement's middle-class acceptance and permanence. Angelus Temple was very much a church with its revolving neon cross, towering two-story stained glass windows, carved mahogany pulpit, and communion table, pipe organ and river Jordan baptistery. And there was no mistaking Sister Aimee for one of the parishioners when she made her appearance in flowing robes and gowns, holding aloft a white Moroccan leather Bible and bouquet of red roses. But unlike other Protestant mainline churches of the era, the rich symbolism of the temple never declined into a stone cold, dead formalism. When Aimee was present, everything came alive. In addition to being a spiritual feast for the eyes, the temple was always "the church of the understanding heart and the helping hand." Religious symbolism was simply an added bonus to Aimee's bodily and emotional dimension of religion. John Henry Newman once observed that the essence of American Protestantism is the search for a "fabulous, primitive simplicity."[7] Aimee's genius was to take the "fabulous, primitive simplicity" of early Pentecostalism and combine it with a variety of color and texture. She was not satisfied with just the "full gospel" or even her own brand of the foursquare gospel. She also wanted a Technicolor gospel, a theatre and a church, something secular, as well as sacred. Without Aimee's rich addition of both symbolism and ritual, classical Pentecostalism may well have languished and remained in its sectarian phase, never making the necessary transition to either a church or denomination. Unlike the megachurches of today, more shopping mall than cathedral, Angelus Temple—when Aimee was present—was always very much a church, perhaps even more Roman Catholic in appearance than mainline Protestant.

The interior of Angelus Temple (author's collection).

The completion of Angelus Temple was much in Aimee's mind as she set sail on August 4, 1922, for Australia with her mother and children. Leaving San Francisco aboard the *S.S. Maunganui*, while more than a thousand well-wishers crowded the pier, Aimee was overwhelmed with the demanding attention to details the temple required as it neared its completion. Moreover, she had simply lived at too high a speed and tension to just relax and enjoy a month at sea. The exterior of the temple had to be designed and sketches sent back to the States, including the drawings for eight two-story stained-glass windows, which when completed would each measure 7 x 23 feet. The new Pacific Coast Foursquare Gospel Association also had its organizational demands, and future editions of *The Bridal Call* had to be written in advance. Aimee would later recall the "eventful years in California—the years when we laid the foundation and reared the physical structures and organizations of Angelus Temple" as years of "multitudes and miracles."[8]

Aimee's personal style had not really changed much since her early days of tent ministry in Florida beach towns with Harold McPherson. She neglected for the most part in 1922, as in 1917, to tell her followers about the personal setbacks she endured while en route to her goal. Left unmentioned and unwritten were the criticisms and attacks she received for attempting such a project in the first place and which came, interestingly enough, from the Pentecostal movement itself. The independent Pentecostal missions scattered throughout Los Angeles saw the building of the temple as a succumbing to worldliness and a place that would no longer honor the "manifestations of the Spirit." Humble surroundings as well as freedom to do almost anything during a Pentecostal service (often termed "wild-fire" or "gully-washers") seemed to be equated with true spirituality for many of the mission folk. Pentecostals of the time, living in the shadow of the Second Coming, were only comfortable with makeshift, temporary, worship spaces. "I remember," wrote Aimee, "when I came to Los Angeles, I went to a lovely church called Bethel Temple…[Assemblies of God] and when I was going to build this structure with steel, they said, 'You are preaching the second coming and people will not believe you what you preach about his coming soon.' "[9]

The weightier criticisms for building Angelus Temple also came from the office of the General Council of the Assemblies of God. Through written correspondence between the two parties, it was evident that the Assemblies of God opposed the creation of the proposed tabernacle for two reasons—both of which involved the temporal concern of finances. The large Pentecostal denomination launched its criticism of the project by the "suggestion that the Pentecostal missionaries were suffering" due to Aimee's fundraising endeavors for her proposed tabernacle.

Aimee never knew that letters had been written to the headquarters of the Assemblies of God in the wake of her Denver meetings six months earlier. One of them, in particular, quoted her as having preached against the Pentecostal missionaries: "They are a lazy lot, they are no good for anything, they could not pray a soul through, but just sit around to get a collection, and go off with it."[10]

On January 5, 1922, Aimee had responded to the chairman of the Assemblies of God, the Reverend E.N. Bell, by returning her "Fellowship Certificate" and informing "the brethren at Springfield" about the real source of her support. It was estimated at the time that approximately 90 percent of the funds for the construction of Angelus Temple came from outside California:

> Dear Brother Bell…Am sorry that you should have thought… that the building of the Tabernacle as a base for the Evangelistic work which God has so graciously put in many hands, to be taking money from missionaries which you might be helping on the field, for this is not the case. With very few exceptions the money for the erection of the Tabernacle is not coming from and is not being donated from the dear Pentecostal people in the various places of holding our revival meetings among the various Churches and in our city-wide meetings which have been attended at times by as many as from 18,000 to 20,000 persons at one service. Out of this number not one out of a hundred are members of Pentecostal Churches as you would realize with a moment's thought. The money is often given by sinners who have been converted, sick who

have been healed, etc., people who never before had heard of Pentecost and would have spent their offerings in gum, candy, theater tickets, dancing slippers, or spent it over the card tables or for doctor's bills... Not large sums from anyone but offerings coming from every State in which the meetings have been held—the Congregational and Presbyterian Churches of Denver, Colorado, having given the biggest boost toward the same, are urging us to come back and let them put the balance over the top and wipe out the remaining amount needed.....Our Pentecostal brothers alone seem to be fearful lest some missionary be robbed or personal funds be swelled but these fears, however, are ungrounded as this international, interdenominational Evangelistic Association Tabernacle is being erected almost entirely by ones who had never heard of Pentecost before and therefore could not have given toward the same.

Glory to Jesus, Bro. Bell, we have wonderful news to report which will gladden your dear heart...The Latter Rain is falling in copious showers in northern California, drenching all the...Churches that open the door to the Spirit's incoming. As you know, Dr. Towner and practically his whole Church have been filled with the Spirit in truly apostolic fashion, then went out to preach in several Churches, Methodist, Baptist and Presbyterian. They too have received the fullness of the Spirit from pulpit to the door. The other night when I preached in the First Baptist Church of San Jose it was my happy privilege to meet the members of the Presbyterian Church, scores of which have received the baptism; and also at the tarrying meeting of this said service, to witness the baptism with power of the precious Presbyterian pastor, in the old fashioned style, hallelujah! Dr. Price received the Spirit during the San Jose meetings, as you will perhaps remember, and with his wife attended us during our Eastern campaigns. We went down and held a meeting in his Church the other Sunday and, praise the Lord, on the following Fri. night seventy five of his number receiving the outpouring of the Holy Spirit, Acts 2:4. Oh, is it not truly wonderful what the Lord hath done! Truly He meant what He said, 'In the last days, saith God, I will pour out My Spirit upon all flesh.'

> Hoping to hear from you soon I beg to remain
> Your sister in love and sincerity,
> Aimee Semple McPherson[11]

Eudorus Neander Bell was far more than the first and fourth chairman (general superintendent) of the Assemblies of God. He was perhaps the most influential founder of the young fellowship and the most educated. As a Baptist minister with a bachelor of divinity degree from the University of Chicago, Bell took a year's leave of absence in 1907 from his pastorate in Fort Worth, Texas. Making his way back to Chicago, Bell

The "brethren" of Springfield, Missouri—some of the General Presbytery at the General Council meeting of the Assemblies of God in Chicago, 1919. The chairman, E.N. Bell, is in the front row at far left (used by permission of Flower Pentecostal Heritage Center).

sought out a new kind of religious mentor, William H. Durham, at the humble North Avenue Mission. On July 18, 1908 Bell was "baptized in the Spirit." When he returned to Fort Worth with resignation in hand, his church refused to accept it. Most likely his church did not want to lose their beloved pastor, because in addition to his newfound Pentecostalism, he was also "big-hearted" and the "sweetest, safest and sanest" man in the movement. Durham described his prodigy as a sharp-looking "big fellow."

Eventually leaving his church in Fort Worth, Bell soon took on big tasks. In addition to his two tenures as chairman, Bell also was the first editor of two important Pentecostal periodicals—*Word and Witness* and the *Weekly Evangel*, precursors to the *Pentecostal Evangel*. His influence was widely felt in the fledgling movement especially via his question-and-answer column in the *Evangel*. In addition to recommending Springfield, Missouri, for the national headquarters, Bell—no doubt because of his Baptist background—championed congregational church polity and the authority and autonomy of the local church. Sadly, in the last year of his life, the "sweet" and "sane" man had to cross swords with his little sister in the faith. On February 2, 1922, a month after receiving Aimee's credentials, the chairman of the Assemblies of God more than made clear what he felt about a proposed tabernacle being legally held by private individuals:

Dear Sister McPherson:

If the tabernacle for which you are collecting funds, as you say largely from the denominations, which we believe truly to be the case, is held or to be held in your name, or in the names of private individuals, and not in the name of bona-fide trustees perpetually for the service of the Lord, then we are just as much opposed on moral grounds to such methods as we would be if the money were collected from Pentecostal people alone. We do not question your honesty or purpose to use it solely for the glory of God. We do not question your sincere interest for the salvation of souls. Many others who have done such things have been just as sincere as they could be, but the results have always been bad in the end. We hope sincerely that you are not holding this tabernacle in your own name, or in that of yourself and one of two other private individuals. We have never said that you were doing so, and trust that you are not. But we cannot see how you take exception to what we wrote unless you are doing so, and if you are doing so, we are first, last and all the time and totally and forever opposed to such unwise principles which usually end in a great religious graft to the shame and dishonor of God and His cause.

But if you are collecting these large sums of money from anybody, even though they be sinners, and holding the same as a private and personal possession forever completely under your own individual control, then the principles involved so violate all common sense and wisdom and good ethics that we cannot put our stamp of approval upon such bad principles in anybody, high or low. If you are so holding this property, then we not only gratefully accept your Fellowship Certificate, but most earnestly demand that you also immediately return your Credentials from the General Council of the Assemblies of God. We do not propose to approve of any minister in our fellowship collecting public moneys to build institutions to be held as an individual and private possession.

We leave the matter entirely up to you as to which is the case and what course you should pursue. You should either inform us just exactly how the property is to be held so as to clear up the question which you have raised by applying our answer to yourself, and let us send back to you the Fellowship Certificate which you have sent in, or if you are violating the principles to which we are opposed you should immediately also send in your Credentials. The credentials and Fellowship Certificate should either both stay with you or should both come back to us.

Be assured of our personal love for you as a child of God, and our prayers for you as a soul winner. We trust that you will not allow any lack of faith in others to cause you to violate great moral principles. Be assured if you do not do so that our confidence will continue unabated in you. If you are doing so, and will not cease then our confidence is already destroyed. With prayers and best wishes for the glory of God, and your own best usefulness in the Master's kingdom, we are

Your little brothers in Christ Jesus,

E.N. Bell, Chairman

In behalf of the Credential Committee[12]

Bell also stressed in his letter to Aimee "that we have no objection to your running an interdenominational evangelistic association, or in your being the leader, or chief officer of such association. All of our ministers are absolutely free to engage in any work to which God calls them. So there is nothing on that line which we are objecting to any way."[13]

If Aimee had been tempted to cave into the demands made by the Assemblies, she was restrained by Minnie, who controlled the purse strings. As far as Minnie was concerned, a gender war had now broken out in Pentecostalism. Ever-protective ever-vigilant Minnie was ready for battle. Her daughter had been "taken" by men many times before. Minnie Kennedy would later go on record defending her decision to hold title to Angelus Temple in her and her daughter's names.

> When we purchased the property, and it was just from the love offerings and from what we had saved for…and from the people who believed in us, and the only thing that many of the people in our campaigns who gave us money asked me to see was that while Mrs. McPherson lived, I see that she never let any bunch of men get in their hands, that she was to preach the Four Square Gospel, and I have stood by that.[14]

In both mother and daughter's eyes the General Council of the Assemblies of God represented nothing more than a "bunch of men" attempting to get their hands on their hard-won assets.

On March 28, 1922, Aimee wrote a final letter to her "little brothers in Christ Jesus" at Springfield, Missouri. She stated her ambiguity about having joined the Assemblies in the first place, how she helped build up the denomination and finally how she had misplaced and lost their precious ordination certificate:

> You will recall that when the matter of our accepting credentials with the Assemblies was first mentioned we were not clear about it. However, we have been glad to have been of service to the Assemblies from coast to coast. A few follow us still with letters of gratitude and love…Assemblies have been built up and your work established more than I believe you realize. All this adding not only numerically and spiritually but financially for the work at home and foreign fields.

Regarding the ordination certificate I would explain that soon after receiving this and the first fellowship paper a letter came requesting that these be returned for renewal, not being familiar with your methods both were enclosed and the certificate has not since been received by us to our knowledge. We wrote you of this at the time. It runs in my mind that you will find the correspondence to show a statement that this had not been located in your office. We have never troubled about it, have never used either the certificate of the fellowship paper. We have had a careful search made thinking this might have come without our knowledge but have not found it. Should we do so it will be forwarded immediately. This does not lessen our love for you, however, or our fellowship in the Gospel's service. We pray that God will add His blessing and will fill every heart to overflowing with you till we meet at Jesus' feet,

Your little Sister in His service,
Aimee Semple McPherson[15]

Again, sadly, the "little Sister" had told the truth. She, indeed, had "built up" and "established" their assemblies, more than they realized.

As Aimee sailed to New Zealand and Australia, she did not realize her forthcoming meetings would further erode the Assemblies of God's confidence in her endeavors. Not only did correspondence from the largely independent Pentecostal churches in Australia arrive at the Assemblies of God headquarters soon after Aimee's arrival, but the same letters remain on file with that denomination today—some sixty-five years after her demise. The letters alleged in essence that Aimee was not truly Pentecostal and had during the meetings in Australia sold the Pentecostal churches down the river. "Had they (Aimee and Minnie) elected to be Pentecostal," wrote the secretary to the Pentecostal missions, "they would have swept many ministers and probably whole congregations into a great forward movement for Pentecost; but their actions in refusing to pray for the sick and attempting to crucify the Pentecostal friends who brought them here for the sake of gaining favour with a few anti-Pentecostal lights in the religious world, have alienated the sympathy of the best amongst those ministers who are interested in the movement."[16]

Some of the Australian Pentecostal ministers would protest by publicly walking off the platform of her meetings, while others through letters expressed their hope that she would "return to spiritual gifts" instead of relying upon her "natural ability and drama."[17] It is of little wonder with the passing of time that one of Aimee's favorite songs, the first one to be found inside her *Foursquare Favorites* paperback songbook declared,

> You can talk about me just as much as you please,
> I'll talk about you down on my knees;
> You can talk about me just as much as you please,
> I'll talk about you down on my knees;
> I ain't gonna grieve my Lord anymore.[18]

The fact of the matter is that Aimee's visit to New Zealand and Australia did much to revive the ministry of healing in the churches Down Under, and she would be fondly remembered by them for that contribution, as would James Moore Hickson and Charles S. Price.

After a month at sea, Aimee and her mother spent the weekend in Wellington, New Zealand, holding services in both a Methodist church and in the town hall. Aimee was warmly received by her overflow audiences as a "healthy happy looking woman in white."[19] The press in New Zealand covered the meeting, and as with their American counterparts their appraisal was positive:

> What is appealing about Mrs. McPherson is her extremely pleasant and agreeable presence and the plain homely way in which she sheds light on the teachings of the Bible. It was not for her to go into the intricacies of psychology, mental analysis and the higher criticism of theological wranglers. She has a message for the world and is so filled with her mission that she simply pours out her message but never is she unclear or blurred. Her strong Canadian accent may puzzle the New Zealand ear here and there but there is no hesitancy as to the formation of her phrases...Mrs. McPherson believes that dry rot has got into many of the Churches and its leaders and the whole world is crying out for grand old revival of religion in the simple form of our forefathers....the speaker spoke...to her large audience and such was her winning power and frankness that she gained a big response to her every appeal.[20]

Upon her arrival in Australia, Aimee discovered that the sponsoring churches, a fledgling band of Pentecostals, "were ostracized and feared by the most earnest ministers and Christian workers who believed them to be unsound in doctrines and methods."[21] The Australian Pentecostal leaders' theological position was that she had been a "fool" for once having been a Methodist and that that affiliation had caused her to take "the first step toward carnality."[22] "Instead of bands, choirs, ministerial cooperation and confidence," Aimee "faced a stone wall of resistance which must be broken down, a mountain of prejudice which must be removed...a shattered confidence which must be restored, a quagmire of doubt and misgiving about your own doctrinal views."[23]

Aimee's Australian visit, apart from her brief excursions into Canada, represented a first attempt at making her ministry international as well as interdenominational. As she rightly perceived it, future international success depended heavily upon the strength of the Australian meetings. The Australian Pentecostals, in disarray much like their Los Angeles counterparts, were in a sense sold down the river by Aimee when she successfully sought to broaden the appeal of their meetings. Similar to what she had been doing the last two years in America, Aimee was able to blur the Australian denominational distinctions during their three weeks of meetings. A testimonial attesting to the fact was signed by the leading clergymen of Australia. Conspicuously absent were the names affiliated with the Pentecostal missions. More importantly, for Aimee, was the assertion in the testimonial by the clergymen, "Mrs. McPherson's preaching…has been strictly orthodox and that her methods were extremely wise and effective. She possesses great natural ability, but the outstanding feature is spiritual power and her intense love for souls."[24]

Aimee's Australian mission was cut short when she discovered that an earlier ship was available to return to America. Australian Pentecostals, still smarting and upset, viewed it as beating a hasty retreat home. Every day her excitement mounted at the prospect of opening Angelus Temple on the first day of the New Year. For Aimee it was like a birth, with her mother as the attending midwife. There had been years of careful and cautious incubation. The most critical time of the temple gestation had been the eleven months between August 1921 and July 1922. She found it hard to fathom that "from the cocoon of that little white tent" (her first preaching tent) would soon be born the "beautiful shrine" of Angelus Temple. Ragged tents, dance halls, theatres, and coliseums would once and for all be replaced by this more permanent structure. As Aimee left Australia, the attending crowds at the wharf sang for her, Minnie, and the children the "Old Songs of Zion" and pressed souvenirs and flowers into their hands while urging them to commit to a return visit. As the steamer puffed out to sea the saints on the dock remained connected to their Sister by rolls of ribbons which rhythmically unwound with the passing of the waves. The slender threads at long last ran out and vanished forever into the sea. It was a fitting tribute for one coming into the height of power and the ability to significantly touch other lives and bridge so many differences. Aimee was her father's bridge-building daughter.

The fall of 1922 was Minnie's finest shining hour in the life of her daughter. Her organizational genius and business acumen had transformed their nickels and dimes in tin cans into concrete and steel. Roberta remembered that her mother's average donation during her barnstorming years was a mere three cents. The offering plates rarely contained dollar bills, but "a lot of buttons and an occasional diamond ring."[25] However, more than one hundred thousand dollars had been raised in 1922 by the gifts of more than four thousand Angelus Temple "chairholders" at twenty-five dollars each. The creation of Angelus Temple not only reflected Aimee's success in American religion but the strength and bonds of the love of a very strong-willed and equally determined mother. On stage or behind a pulpit, Aimee was uniquely and magnetically herself. Away from the crowd, she was still very much her mother's daughter, a non-person when it came to having her own private adult life. What little opportunity there was for such an existence was quickly subjugated by the needs of her children or the demands placed upon her by Minnie. It was a sacrifice Aimee willingly seemed to accept in order that her dreams would come true. Their mother-daughter relationship was unique even among female leadership in American religious history. The support role to a successful woman religious leader was one most often filled by a husband.

This unique mother-daughter relationship was not lost upon Alma Whitaker, a columnist for the *Los Angeles Times*. Not only was Whitaker one of the first journalists in Los Angeles to secure a private interview with Aimee, she also was one of the first to compare Minnie Kennedy's role with that of a successful stage mother.

> Mrs. Kennedy is still with her daughter and, somewhat as Mrs. Charlotte Pickford has fostered and protected the career of Mary (and spared her much of the business and mundane exactions of that career) so has Mrs. Kennedy served her almost equally famous evangelist-daughter. This point is important, for it explains why Aimee Semple McPherson can keep her sweet smile, why she is free to lead, free to preach, free to heal, to console, to inspire, to enthuse. For every preacher will concede that the financial, the publicity, the business side of an immense religious organization…is very exacting.[26]

Upon returning to San Francisco aboard the *S.S. Ventura* on November 8, 1922, Aimee, Minnie, and the children were met and welcomed by various committee members from the momentous Oakland campaign. The Pacific Coast Foursquare Gospel Association formed in the summer months continued to thrive amidst Aimee's absence. Special trains had been arranged in order to accommodate those in the Bay Area desirous of attending the opening of the temple. Similar delegations were also being formed throughout the country. Thus Angelus Temple, apart from its physical structure, had not really been built in Los Angeles. Rather, it had come together much like Aimee's "love offerings" in bits and pieces throughout America. In some ways, the creation of Angelus Temple was more a monument to "everybody's Sister in the King's Glad Service," honoring fourteen years of ministry than it was the building of a local church congregation.

Despite the fact that most of the money for the building of Angelus Temple had come from outside Los Angeles, its creation was not atypical of other city projects being conceived and carried out during the same time. It was clearly part of the developing Los Angeles pattern. Many other city buildings and institutions including the Biltmore Hotel, the Los Angeles Coliseum, and the Automobile Club of Southern California were started or conceived like Angelus Temple in 1921 and officially opened in 1923. A reliable account of the growth of Los Angeles correctly observed that the city "did not really get her post-war stride until the year 1921. Then, indeed, the Old Pueblo stepped out on the 'Big Time' circuit, and definitely took her place among America's metropolitan cities."[27]

The year 1923 was the apex of the Los Angeles building boom, with more buildings started or completed during its twelve months than ever before or in a single year. "The value of the building permits rapidly rose from $28 million in 1919 to $200 million in 1923, placing Los Angeles third in the nation behind New York and Chicago. Within a ten-mile radius from the heart of the city, nearly 1,400 new tracts were opened, comprising 143,000 lots and covering nearly 29,000 acres between 1922 and 1923."[28]

In 1920 Los Angeles had a population of 580,000. A decade later the population numbered 1.2 million. "Put another way, seven new people joined the local population every hour of every day for ten years. County residents numbered more than two million by decade's end."[29] The move to Southern California in the 1920s represented the largest internal migration in the history of the American people.

The building boom of Los Angeles and the opening of "Aimee's Temple" also symbolized events occurring in the Jazz Age. The era's leading literary prophet, F. Scott Fitzgerald, was on target when he once remarked that the Jazz Age actually peaked as early as 1922. *The Smart Set*, the major literary voice of the age, responsible for publishing many first works of the decade's most promising writers, closely paralleled Aimee's evangelistic career. It too exerted its maximum influence from 1918 to 1923. Not only were many Jazz Age institutions born in the early years of the 1920s, but many swiftly reached their peak and merely coasted on their enormous reserves of energy until their enforced closure by the Great Depression. This would indeed make the 1920s, in the words of Loren Baritz, "a kind of parenthesis in historical time."[30]

Despite the building boom and bustle, Los Angeles throughout the decade was still an "cnormous village," or in a less-charitable description by the journalist H. L. Mencken, "Double-Dubuque." Carey McWilliams captured well the unfinished state of the "enormous village" in the early 1920s. "Westwood was yet to be; in the spring after the rains, the area between La Brea and Beverly Hills would be ablaze with wild mustard growing in what were then open fields. Hollywood was still a village and San Fernando Valley largely undeveloped." According to McWilliams, Aimee Semple McPherson was also to become one of the enormous village's best-known residents with the opening of her temple in early 1923.[31]

Aimee's growing reputation in Los Angeles in late 1922 came not so much from newspaper headlines about her meetings elsewhere as it did by word of mouth in the large village that "one woman was building so large a church" and that "she could never expect to fill it."[32] Total seating capacities for Angelus Temple would be set at 5,300. The main floor would accommodate 2,300, the first balcony 1,700, and the top balcony 1,300.

On September 27, 1922, the *Los Angeles Times* took notice of Aimee Semple McPherson. It was the first occasion that the *Times* acknowledged her presence in the city. It was a presence they could no longer ignore. On page one of part two in the newspaper the headline read:

LONE WOMAN FULFILLS MISSION .... VAST TEMPLE,
Aimee Semple McPherson, Noted Evangelist,
Soon to Give Los Angeles Unique Edifice.

"On January 1, 1923," noted the *Times,* "will be dedicated one of the largest church edifices in the city of Los Angeles. It will be known as the Angelus Temple...and will have for its pastor, Aimee Semple McPherson, its founder and builder."[33] Pictures of a maternal-like Aimee and of the ongoing construction of the temple accompanied the article. Events in the life of the evangelist and her career not noted in the *Times'* feature were as significant as those that were. The Azusa Street Mission, Victoria Hall, and Pentecostalism did not appear in the article. Rather, Aimee, the paper noted, had begun "active work as an independent undenominational preacher."[34] The story of her arrival in Los Angeles no longer included the Pentecostal upper room mission of Victoria Hall. "Shortly after Mrs. McPherson arrived in Los Angeles she began a revival campaign housed in a large tent on West Washington Street. That was her start in California."[35] The new temple being built, according to the *Times*, would not be a Mecca for the miraculous in Pentecostalism but rather would provide "a place of worship for thousands of nonsectarian devotees as well as those from any denomination who wish to attend."[36]

Even more revealing than the *Los Angeles Times'* first article on Aimee, was how she herself chose to advertise in the *Times'* church section. Never once did her advertisement mention Pentecostalism. The ads did include, however, a quickly designed four-square logo that read: "Health," "Happiness," "Heaven," and "Holiness."[37] The early ads for Angelus Temple always included the line "The Latchstring is out to you—whosoever you may be" and were for the most part always placed under the "Undenominational" section of the church page.[38] In essence, Aimee believed that her church and its message belonged more under the banners of "evangelical" and "undenominational" than "Pentecostal." It was another stroke of genius on her part in terms of growth for American Pentecostalism. Initially damning her new self-definition of the movement, most American Pentecostals over the next half century would slowly but surely follow her lead and likewise prefer for themselves the "evangelical" label rather than the older "Pentecostal" designation and the stigma that so often accompanied it. Aimee's brand of Pentecostalism would essentially be evangelicalism with a middle-class appeal. (*The Bridal Call* clearly demonstrates how Aimee saw her ministry evolving over time. In January 1921, "Full Gospel Evangelism" replaced the sub-title of "Pentecostal." By November 1923 "The Four-Square Gospel" replaced "Full Gospel Evangelism.")

Close to a century later the word Pentecostal would still conjure up negative connotations in American culture. In the fall of 2008, when the media began exploring the religious background of Republican presidential candidate John McCain's dark-horse running mate Sarah Palin, she took great pains to disavow and distance herself from her Pentecostal past. Even though she had been raised in the Assemblies of God and had been an active adult member of that denomination for years, Palin attempted to appeal to mainstream voters by claiming she was really an evangelical and a nondenominational Christian. Evangelicalism, America's folk religion, was a much safer spiritual port in the high seas and turbulent storms of a presidential campaign and election. A hundred years after its birth, the label of Pentecostalism was worn with greater pride outside the country of its origin, seemingly more at home south of the border or globally than nationally. Perhaps white Americans especially and Protestants in general still stumbled over its African-American past or sought to categorize it as a less than orthodox "ism" or worse yet, as a cult.

The clearest example of the evangelicalization of American Pentecostalism can be found with the movement's various denominational colleges and universities. Begun in the 1920s and 1930s as three-year Bible institutes, they had graduated to four-year Bible colleges by the 1940s and 1950s. By the 1960s and 1970s they had morphed yet again into private church-related liberal arts and sciences colleges and universities. The Bible, so central to their founding, had been relegated to the Department of Religion and Philosophy. Such departments downplayed Pentecostal distinctiveness by emphasizing instead the broader evangelical movement. One such university affiliated with the Assemblies of God required its religion majors to "be familiar with the main themes of Evangelical Theology" and to "be able to present an evangelical Christian apologetic."[39] Apparently a Pentecostal apologetic was unnecessary. Such majors, the catalogue declared, "should be well prepared for advanced study in seminary or graduate school."[40] And as to leave no doubt that this particular school had become a mainstream, real university it was pointed out with great pride that its sixth president had advanced degrees, not from some fundamentalist school or even an Assemblies of God graduate program, but from Princeton Theological Seminary and Columbia University.

Not everyone, however, celebrated the arrival of the Evangelical Secular City in American Pentecostal churches, colleges, and universities. Recently at least one ordained Assemblies of God minister and university professor sounded a warning about the arrival of the great "American Evangelical pot of goo." Pentecostal distinctions, he argued, have been replaced by "contemporary conservative American Protestant features such as an emphasis on the nuclear family in sermons, the destiny of the United States as God's favored nation, a form of corporate worship that turns the focus from the Triune God to the individual Christian, and alarming measures of therapeutic sermonizing that borrow variously from pop-psychology, positive-thinking schools of thought, and success-for-living business strategizing that are all routinely passed off as serious pastoral counsel….By 'pot of goo' I mean…the vapid, indistinct, and prophetically fainthearted amalgam that is, unfortunately, only too characteristic of…Evangelical… churches.[41]"

On December 15, 1922, an information bureau opened at the main entrance of Angelus Temple on Park Avenue. At the bureau, musicians, ushers and "other helpers" were recruited, registered and enlisted for service. Aimee, through her monthly *Bridal Call*, continued to admonish those coming from various cities and towns:

The interdenominational spirit of this Evangelistic Association will be truly exemplified at the opening… people of all evangelical orthodox churches working as one and for one God and Saviour of us all…efforts will not be toward the building up of one particular denomination but the bringing of the greatest blessing to all, and the working on an equal footing the one with the other.[42]

As 1922 came to an end, Aimee shared her innermost thoughts with her faithful subscribers in the editorial pages of *The Bridal Call*:

The dawning of this year is as an epoch in our lives. It is as though we had been steadily climbing, climbing, toiling up a high steep hill; too busy pressing on and finding hand and foot-holds to look back before, and now having reached the hilltop we stopped to wipe our brow, and panting still from the climb, turned on the summit of the great divide to gaze back across the fields and distant reaches of the yesterday.[43]

The opening of Angelus Temple was indeed "the summit of the great divide" in Aimee's ministry. For Aimee, as she said many times in many places, it was "the crowning glory of fourteen years of ministry." If Aimee was tempted in the final hours of 1922 to linger on "the summit of the great divide," Minnie was just as apt to be found in battle against the swift onrush of the coming year. A curious onlooker who gained entrance into the temple in late December of 1922 noted, "The first person we recognized was little Mother Kennedy, down on the main floor of the great auditorium, giving instructions to the contractors and builders. It surely looked as though it would be impossible to ever clear out the scaffolding… in time for the dedication, which was only 48 hours away. Decorators, carpenters, plumbers, electricians were busy all over the place inside and outside. Seats were being installed—fire escapes completed—great windows installed."[44] Again enjoying her finest hour in the life of her daughter, Minnie appeared to those around her "as calm, self-possessed and quietly confident as ever, seeming rather rested and refreshed and outwardly undisturbed by all the confusion about her."[45]

The first service at Angelus Temple was held on New Year's Eve 1922, as a "watchnight service" and was led appropriately by a layperson. Although it was Sunday, some two hundred workmen continued to rivet the theatre-style seats to the floor and either hang the enormous two-story stained glass windows or replace their gaping holes with a canvas-like fabric. A full moon lit up the Southern California sky, and balmy breezes blew through the Los Angeles basin. For those in attendance that New Year's Eve, paradise or something akin to it seemed within tomorrow's reach. The sentiment of that watchnight service could have been easily expressed by the Spanish proverb *Mañana es la flor de sus ayeres* — Tomorrow is the flower of its yesterdays.

On Monday, January 1, 1923, at 2:15 p.m., the religious aspirations and deepest spiritual yearnings of thousands were fulfilled when a thirty-two year old woman stood in front of the glass doors to her temple opposite the rushes of Echo Park Lake. On a makeshift wooden platform, Aimee Semple McPherson stood alone, flanked by the two center columns of her temple while thousands below sang the familiar refrain of "All Hail the Power of Jesus' Name." A large American flag draped the front of the temporary platform, a gift to the evangelist from the women's auxillary of the Grand Army of the Republic, an organization of Civil War veterans. Deep within the temple, Mother Kennedy was giving her final commands. Brooms were doing their touch-up sweeping while the last of the carpet was being laid and a piano was being brought in a back door.

Then, appropriately, Aimee read with "a choke in our voice and a catch at our heart" the Old Testament story of the long-awaited dedication of the glorious temple by Solomon. Like the early Israelites, American Pentecostals had been something of a nomadic flock in search of sacred pastures. And like Abraham who had to first go down into Egypt, the symbol of material wealth and wisdom, before the spiritual heritage could be found, so Pentecostalism, it seemed, had to also build its most permanent habitation of the sacred amidst that which was most popularly perceived to be profane. Earlier Protestants had, in fact, likened their futile efforts in 1865 to penetrate the City of the Angels as being trapped in Egypt. Said one, "The abomination of desolation seemed to have possession...I confess it looked dark—dark as Egypt."[46] And like Solomon's temple, Angelus Temple was without a doubt the most glorious structure of Pentecostalism—the long-awaited symbol of permanence—no longer subject to forced evictions, the raising of rent, or falling tent poles in tropical storms. Aimee concluded the reading of the biblical story by reciting Solomon's dedicatory prayer, "O Lord who hast chosen to dwell in thick darkness, here have I built thee a lofty house, a habitation for thee to occupy forever." After another song and prayer Aimee was assisted from the platform to the pavement. With a trowel and mortar in hand she completed the laying of the two granite dedicatory plaques on the Temple's two center columns. The simple inscriptions were unveiled and stated for all to see the double purpose and mission of the Temple. "Angelus Temple, Church of the Foursquare Gospel, Aimee Semple McPherson, Founder" and "Dedicated unto the cause of Interdenominational and World-wide Evangelism January First in the year of our

Lord Nineteen Hundred and Twenty-Three."

In many ways an episode in America's Protestant sect-church developmental cycle ended with the 1920s. The "new religious movements" of the 1960s that attracted enormous media coverage, much more than their meager numbers called for, were for the most part an abysmal failure in terms of creating lasting social and religious institutions. Their quest for personal transformations, although couched in traditional American revivalistic and apocalyptic jargon, failed in the final analyses of leaving behind many permanent structures on the American landscape. (Calvary Chapel, the Vineyard Fellowship, and the Metropolitan Community Churches are the exceptions) America's turn inward during the late 1960s and early 1970s left few outward manifestations.

Men continued to play major roles in Aimee's life, especially during her times of transition. Although a great number of women would later serve under Aimee in important leadership roles within the emergent hierarchy of Angelus Temple, the consensus always remained that no woman "was ever next or close to Sister."[47] Even for future female Foursquare ministers it would always be "all business" with Aimee Semple McPherson. Minnie would be the accessible one for the women. And Minnie would defend her daughter's privacy by simply stating to the inquisitive that Aimee "was not someone you can ask questions."[48]

Apart from a trio of men, however, the majority of the men who entered Aimee's life were like the oddly shaped pieces of a jigsaw puzzle always placed on the periphery. Few of them, if any, were ever able to match the major center parts and pieces of Aimee's life. She, it seems, gave more meaning and shape to their lives than they did to hers. There was James who had given Aimee a kind of grandfatherly love; Robert—mentor, brother and husband; and in later years there would be Rolf, the dutiful son and loyal keeper and steward of his mother's flame.

With the opening of the temple on that Monday afternoon in early January, men again were needed in Aimee's life, even if they could only form the peripheral pieces. As she marched down the right ramp (which had been inspired by a visit to the Pantages Theatre early on in the construction of the temple), Aimee was surrounded by men at her every side. Their presence again bore silent witness to her ability to blur denominational boundaries. The men surrounding Aimee that day were all Protestant mainline ministers—Methodist, Baptist, and Congregational. Like Charles S. Price, the Congregational minister from Lodi, California, they had all experienced spiritual transformations under Aimee's revivalism and had for the most part given up their own churches to pursue a more evangelistic and/or healing ministry.

Minnie was not at her daughter's side the opening day of the temple. Instead she took her reserved seat as she always did high up in the first balcony four rows back of the railing and directly across from the door her daughter opened when she made her descent down the ramp toward the pulpit. It was a place where "Bonnie," as the developing, loyal temple membership would affectionately call her, could "have her eye on everything that went on [and where] she never missed anything."[49]

But even the male ministers, as gifted as some of them were, seemed to pale during Aimee's public remembrances of Robert Semple. During the early days and years of Angelus Temple the Robert Semple remembrances were frequent. They came to an audience through what Aimee termed the "eye-gate" as well as the "ear-gate." Near the altar was a large stained-glass window dedicated to Robert's memory and appropriated titled "Gethsemane." The majority of the other eight windows conveyed standard Biblical themes such as the nativity, the crucifixion, and the ascension. Other windows, although depicting similar biblical themes, more clearly revealed Aimee as a person. Their imprint upon the audience's eye-gate were most likely seen in the "women's window"—the depiction of Christ forgiving the adulterous woman; the "healing window"—the depiction of Christ's earthly healing ministry; and in "Robert's window"—the depiction of Christ at Gethsemane. They spoke specifically to the prevalence of universal suffering, sorrow, and loss. Robert's memory would be cyclical in its effect upon Aimee in Angelus Temple. With the passing of the years, Aimee's mentioning of his name would wane, only to rebound stronger during the last few years of her life, when she would call out his name and state for everyone to hear that she was "on her way to meet him" even though the path had at times been strewn with difficulty.

But on Monday, the first day of January, 1923, it was a bright and glorious day for Aimee. Even the sun was straining to get through the Gethsemane window and around the cracks of the canvas adorning the other soon-to-be completed windows. It was "the summit of the great divide" of Aimee's ministry.

Brook Hawkins, builder of the temple, announced before the capacity crowd that the structure was "the greatest and largest auditorium in the City of the Angels," and with a touch of civic boosterism declared "that it is the most unique building in America, and probably in the world."[50] More accurate was a description given by Aimee herself six months later when she stated matter-of-factly to her *Bridal Call* readers: "The Temple decorations both inside and out are most suited to the message herein preached—strong, simple lines."[51] The dedication ceremonies momentarily halted when Aimee discovered her theatrical-style architect attempting to make his way into the crowded temple. Leaving the platform, Aimee met William Wheeler midway down the center aisle and informally introduced him to the congregation with a hug and a kiss—a moment in Wheeler's life he never forgot.

For her first message in the temple, Aimee again chose another Old Testament theme, this time from the Book of Ezra about the rejoicing of the people when the foundation for the house of the Lord was laid. From that text, Aimee related how the people of God had attempted throughout biblical history, in spite of repeated hardships, to build altars, synagogues, and temples for their Lord God Jehovah. And like her other inimitable sermons she made it personal by relating her own struggles with tents and tabernacles to likewise build a more permanent habitation as unto the Lord. Fittingly a thousand voice choir sang Fanny Crosby's "Open the Gates of the Temple." Especially appropriate for the occasion were the words of the old hymn:

> Open your hearts, O ye people, that Jesus may enter today.
> Hark! from the sick and the dying, forgetting their couches of pain.[52]

The afternoon dedication service ended when a Baptist minister pronounced the benediction. Charles S. Price, the Congregational minister, captured the sentiment of the day when he declared, "The gates of the temple have been opened and the King of Glory has come in."[53]

The only misfortune to occur with the opening of the temple was that Aimee had in the process created something much larger than herself and Minnie, for that matter. The afternoon service ended only for an evening service to soon begin, thus setting in motion an inhumane and completely impossible schedule to maintain. It was rather like being a screen actress who so charmed her audiences that for the next twenty-one years the camera would continue unmercifully to roll and the crowds continue their clamor for a finished product. Although Aimee's barnstorming days had been a burden, there was still another city ahead and the respite of a day of rest, even if on a train or the backseat of a car. With the opening of Angelus Temple, however, days would blur indistinguishably into each other like the Southern California seasons and soon Aimee would pastor one of the largest churches in modern America—complete with its attendant problems.

When Aimee "dared to settle down," in the words of the Episcopal writer James Sheerin, she seemingly violated the general pattern exhibited by most American revivalists. Undeniably, it was a calculated professional risk, most likely self destructive in most American cities during the 1920s. Dwight Lyman Moody (1837-1899), for example, obtained his fame in American revivalism in precisely the opposite manner: the leaving of a city pastorate for the broader fields of evangelistic endeavors. In similar fashion to Aimee, Moody carved out his own independent and non-denominational church—the Illinois Street Church—with Chicago's "odds and ends" of life—street urchins and city drifters. Moody's fame and rise in American revivalism, however, was not as meteoric as Aimee's. It took Moody an additional twelve years to become something of a Chicago civic fixture—a feat accomplished by Aimee in Los Angeles in three years. Only after many successful years in the pastorate did Moody, with the assistance of his talented chorister Ira David Sankey, enter the ranks of professional evangelism. Perhaps the closest parallel in the Christian church to Aimee's ministry as a pastor of a large urban church (apart from the ministry of healing), would have been found in London at the Metropolitan Tabernacle under the leadership of Charles Haddon Spurgeon.

Even Aimee's detractors noted the risk she took when she "dared to settle down." And once again the inevitable comparison was made with Billy Sunday.

> It has been noted that the Rev. Billy Sunday, skillful soul-saver that he is, seldom cares to stay in one place. This practice accords with the best traditions of evangelism, which dictate a short campaign and a quick clean-up. The moment interest begins to lag... Sunday...closes the show and decamps, thus preserving his reputation for keeping the mourner's bench always filled. But out in Los Angeles is an evangelist who has conducted a continuous salvation-mill...with never a let-down and still is equaling Sunday at his very best....She is Aimee Semple McPherson...twice married, twice a mother, once widowed, once divorced, still young...Not Billy Sunday, nor Pastor Russell, nor Mary Baker G. Eddy, nor Alexander Dowie had such swift rise to notoriety and affluence.[54]

Writing to her faithful readers back home who had contributed much to make the opening of Angelus Temple, a reality, Aimee mentioned the beginning of a vicious cycle that was about to overtake her. "But now the first meeting is dismissed. It is only a little while till it will be time for the night meeting...And so day follows day, meeting follows meeting in such quick succession that one might well call them all-the sun each day and continue long after the setting thereof."[55]

Her spirits were still buoyant, however, in the early days of January because at long last she had completed her dream, and the dream had come true in the new Eden and Promised Land of Southern California.

> Oh, it is so wonderful to have a building we do not need to give up on Monday night for a boxing tournament, or Thursday night right in the midst of a revival for a grand ball or Saturday night for some prima donna, as we have had to do in many city auditoriums. And to think that this shall be a steady and permanent work…Those who were unable to come for the opening come as soon as you can…remember that out here where the sun is shining in January like a balmy summer day, where the palms are waving and the roses nodding to their reflection in the placid Echo Lake, a hearty welcome and a multitude of loving hands await yours across the Rockies in sunny California.[56]

Aimee and Angelus Temple would supply many needs to the 1920s newcomers upon their arrival in the bewildering City of the Angels or "the enormous village." In some ways the most overlooked function of the Angelus Temple, as well as one of its most important ones, was identified when Los Angeles columnist and author Harry Carr noted that Aimee "runs the best Lonesome Club on earth."[57] The incredible lure and pull of the promise of Los Angeles as the fabled city of dreams had its shadow side that too often was overlooked by the civic boosters, future historians, and Aimee herself. The dark side of the city was described for the most part in novel form by a handful of gifted authors. "Los Angeles," wrote Carey McWilliams, "was a very strange community," a kind of mushroom civilization where "the surface was bright and pleasing, but the nether side was often dark and ugly."[58] Lonesomeness and aloneness were the dominant themes in these brave novels exploring the inner thoughts of the inhabitants of the city of dreams by the sea. Mike, the central character in Frank Fenton's *A Place in the Sun,* in many ways was the archetype of migrant to California in the 1920s and a prime candidate for membership in Angelus Temple. His life had been in a rut in the Middle West and had been going nowhere in California.

> He was going to begin a new life. His leaf was going to turn out there. In a couple of days he would be there, and that arrival would mark the turning point in his destiny. He was going to accomplish something. He was almost 26 now and it was time. As his mother would have said, it was "high time." "Well, it's high time," she always said.[59]

Mike thought much about his deceased mother back in Ohio as he journeyed westward when California came into view.

> He wished that his mother had lived to come, because she would have loved this vast bed of flowers that was California; she would have gasped at such sights and shut her eyes and breathed in the perfume and been wonderfully happy. It was not like spring coming, as it comes in Ohio, breaking out through muddy melding earth, bursting from cold bare trees and rushing down flooded creeks. Here it had always been.
>
> It all seemed new. It was filled with signs of new work. The trees were short and looked young. The houses were flat and flimsy with air blowing through them. Nothing seemed old in the lush youth of this country.[60]

Mike soon found himself in a housing subdivision sparsely dotted by white and yellow bungalows in the southern tip of the San Fernando Valley—only seventeen miles from downtown Los Angeles. For twenty dollars a month and for the first time in his young life he became the master of his own private stucco and wood kingdom. He would sit back at night as thousands of new Angelenos did in their new easy chairs to revel in their newfound kingdoms. The euphoria was always short-lived with the passing of day and the darkness of night. Suddenly, Mike, like so many other newcomers to Los Angeles, felt inexplicably so all alone.

> The evening light fell on the green walls and it was cool. He looked around and smiled. It was the first house he had ever lived in where he was sole master...Here he was. The sun went down like a lost and bloody cause beyond the hills...the hills like castles in the blue haze, the sea beyond, the open windows, curtains blowing, and the golden days; there was an olive tree; there was a lemon tree near the ash can...
>
> The house grew ugly in the gloom as night came. The blue flames from the gas jet swirled in the darkness. He did not feel like eating. He did not want to go out on the porch and look at those hills. He felt sick inside him and lonely, never before in his life so lonely.[61]

Aimee and Angelus Temple would appeal directly to that rampant loneliness in the enormous village of Los Angeles, the city compared to a boarding house in the early literature. In giving "interesting facts about Angelus Temple" during the early months of 1923, Aimee asked her readership,

> Do you know that if you are hungry, sick and in trouble, friendless or alone, you need not remain so another moment, but you are surrounded with the most warm-hearted, enthusiastic, friendly folk that could be found this side and that no one ever leaves this Temple without three

big, hearty handshakes, smiles, and "God bless you's" and that if you
are without a church, home or a pastor, you are welcome to enjoy the
privileges and blessings, so lavishly given here.[62]

In John Fante's superb novel of Los Angeles, *Ask the Dust*, with its underlying theme of loneliness and aloneness, only two churches are mentioned;
a Catholic church and "Aimee's Temple."[63] Once newcomers were inside
the glass doors of Angelus Temple, both Aimee and Minnie employed a
technique that further reduced any feeling of loneliness: they simply put
people to work. A motto of Aimee's often heard around the Temple was
"saved to serve."[64]

The secular press, of course, helped to sustain interest in both Aimee and
Angelus Temple. No film actress or religious organization ever enjoyed the
sustained interest of the Los Angeles press more than did Aimee Semple
McPherson and the affairs of Angelus Temple. Even the short walkway
from the parsonage to the temple soon became known as "Reporter's Row."
The *Los Angeles Times* noted the opening of the temple with a story about it
in its second section, while other Los Angeles dailies, such as the *Los Angeles
Record*, gave a more detailed account of the event, placing the story on page
one. The *Times* interest was not so much in Aimee herself as it was with
her followers. What especially caught their attention was the fact that so
many gypsies were present at the opening of the temple. A woman reporter
for the *Times* spent a week camping with the "Romany tribes" and wrote
a feature article on the event that overshadowed the significance of the
temple opening. "Few persons are aware," wrote the reporter, "that there
are hundreds of gypsies, belonging to a dozen different tribes, camping just
outside the city. They have come here to help Aimee Semple McPherson
open the temple of the Foursquare Gospel near Sunset Boulevard. Delegates from every tribe in this country packed their women and children into
some kind of an automobile and made the long trip across the desert."[65]

Several tribes of Serbian gypsies had a love affair with Aimee. Over two
hundred of them had purchased Temple chairs at twenty-five dollars each
as well as contributing money for a stained-glass window and had provided
the throne-like pulpit chairs, the highly carved pulpit itself, the hand-carved
inscription that hung above the pulpit declaring "Jesus Christ; the same Yesterday, Today and Forever," the communion table, and the heavy burgundy
velour curtain that served as a backdrop for the platform. On the dedication day, they were in force, "some five hundred of them," in their gaily
decorated costumes while their Stutzes and Packards, equally bedecked with
ribbons and lace, lined Park Avenue. As they left the dedication service they

swamped the entire platform floor of the temple with their "love offerings" of colored baskets of flowers for "their Sister."

It was a reporter for the *Los Angeles Record*, an independent Scripps-Canfield paper, that came the closest in capturing the significance of both Aimee and the opening of Angelus Temple. Reporter Don Ryan, with some amount of reverence, noted the enormous physical appeal of Aimee and the almost secular appeal of the temple itself:

> If Aimee Semple McPherson had not chosen to be a revivalist, she could have been a queen of musical comedy. She has magnetism such as few women since Cleopatra have possessed.... It would be indiscreet to speculate on her age. If you look closely you can see a gray hair or two. But to all intents and purposes the evangelist is 25. [She was 32.] Full-bosomed, Junoesque in mold, she seems to have paused at the age when womanhood is fully ripened…
>
> "Don't think that praying for the people is the dominant note of our religion," warned Sister McPherson. "Just about one day a week will be set aside for praying for the sick. The real mission is to save souls."
>
> Her large brown eyes were liquid as she spoke of her dreams for a great interdenominational, international religious brotherhood. She explained how the Echo Park Evangelistic Association has 4500 members stretching across the continent…[This] "is the culmination of my dream" she said. "For 15 years I have been in the work and every year was a step toward the opening of this temple. I chose Los Angeles for the site because I think this is the city to which everybody is coming."
>
> "The work is a binding together of the people who are interested in the cause of evangelism. The money for building that temple—it cost a quarter of a million—came from Canada, Australia, England, Denmark, Sweden and from all over the United States. I put my little all in the project. The cause is interdenominational in spirit, evangelical in message, and international in project."
>
> Standing beneath the dome the revivalist explained her inspiration for the temple. "I wanted it like God's own outdoors," she said. "So the gypsies and people of that sort would feel more at home. The churches seem to have lost the intimacy we get in theaters. I tried to get that intimacy here."
>
> The cheerful intimacy of the theater had been achieved. The building is much like a theater. It has numerous foyers. The seats are opera chairs. The only churchly touch is in the windows.
>
> While I was picturing the scene when 5000 persons would sit in the auditorium under the spell of sister McPherson's eloquence, she plucked my arm and led me into a section opening off of the social foyer. It was an elaborate nursery where each baby has a private room, pink, white,

blue or ivory—as he may choose. A nurse is always in attendance.

And I could imagine [psychoanalyst] Andre Tridon nodding his head sagely and muttering: "thwarted sex complex. Strong maternal instinct. Often takes the form of religious expression."

The thing the white sister brings us is the old-time religion—the religion of Billy Sunday and the revivalists who preceded him. But it isn't every day that we can see it expounded by a personality like Sister McPherson's.[66]

Indeed, personality itself was something of a modern term and creation. Life was now lived in a mass society. How did one stand out in the crowd? In his book *Culture as History, The Transformation of American Society in the Twentieth Century,* Warren I. Susman convincingly argues that early in the twentieth century personality replaced character as the essential ingredient for success in the culture:

> From the beginning the adjectives most frequently associated with per-sonality suggest a very different concept from that of character: *fascinat-ing, stunning, attractive, magnetic, glowing, masterful, creative, dominant, forceful.* These words would seldom if ever be used to modify the word *charac-ter*....character...is either good or bad; personality, famous or infamous. "Personality is the quality of being Somebody."[67]

Until her dying day Aimee Semple McPherson was always "Somebody" and in equal measure famous and infamous. If Billy Sunday represented manly character in American revivalism, than Sister Aimee was the symbol par excellence of feminine personality. Fundamentalism would continue to embrace the older virtue of character while Pentecostalism more often than not aligned itself with the cult of personality.

Other religious presses and periodicals would also manage to catch up with the "white sister" and Angelus Temple. In general they lagged behind their secular counterparts in terms of timeliness and seemed more inter-ested in the phenomenon of religion in the West as a whole rather than in individual personalities. The most interesting narrative on West Coast reli-gion written from a mainstream Protestant point of view was by an Episco-pal clergyman, the Reverend James Sheerin, who in time managed to catch up with the "white sister." Sheerin was inspired for his series of articles on West Coast religion by a travel book written by Richard Harding Davis, entitled the *West from a Car Window.* In a series of articles entitled "A Little Journey in the West," published in the *Southern Churchman* throughout 1923, Sheerin perceptively commented on religion in the West and how it differed

on the Pacific slope from the Atlantic seaboard. More than any other com-
mentator of the 1920s, either social or religious, Sheerin factually laid to rest
many common and equally false assumptions about "religion out west." At
first he shared his sense of disappointment with the reader because of the
lack of church buildings upon the Western landscape:

> There are clubs and hotels unsurpassed in any metropolis; and there are
> schools, art galleries and university buildings that outshine the best in
> Eastern cities…but churches are not so evident…in the Western half
> of the United States as they are in its Eastern section. They are certainly
> not prominent in Los Angeles.[68]

The discovery of religion on the West Coast despite a dearth of architecture was rewarding theologically, however:

> When one has crossed the great plains and mountains of the far West,
> and comes down into the broad, fruitful valleys near the Pacific Ocean,
> not only does the atmosphere become warmer and clearer, but men's
> minds seem able to think in larger ways. There is, therefore, less funda-
> mentalism apparent on the Pacific coast than there is among the corn
> fields of Illinois and Iowa, big as they are!
> It may be too fanciful to attribute broadening theologic influences to
> oceans, but it does seem to be a fact that the great cities on either coast
> have a freer intellectual atmosphere than is usual in interior places.[69]

In visiting Denver Sheerin observed that the city had been influenced "by
an unusually cultured element coming there in search of health," concluding that the city had "always been more religious, artistic and educational in
its ideals than most other Western cities." Sheerin was disturbed by the city's
"aggressive element of excessive Churchmanship" and "a tendency to run
after healing and other evanescent cults." He could overlook that aspect of
religion in Denver, however, because the city also demonstrated "more of
a love of social service than of religious dogma. This better atmosphere
seemed to increase as one approached the Pacific Ocean."[70]

In San Francisco Sheerin observed "some fine church buildings" but
noted that "neither of them had a congregation exceeding twenty-five."
Grace Cathedral, he observed, "has a wonderful location at the top of one
of San Francisco's finest residence hills, within a block of its greatest hotel
and close to the fashionable clubs. But it is as yet only as basement….The
voice of Religion in San Francisco is less in evidence than that of commerce or amusement since its great fire."[71]

In journeying to Southern California, Sheerin soon discovered what he termed "the three most prominent places of worship" in the state. Interestingly, all three religious structures were referred to as "temples" and all three had been founded directly or indirectly by women. "We have, then, in Southern California forms of the three most permanent qualities of religion— the occult, (the semi-Hindu temple at Point Loma—Katherine Tingley) the mystic-healing (the Christian Science Temple—Mary Baker Eddy) and the evangelic-healing (Angelus Temple—Aimee McPherson.)"[72]

He quickly concluded from his mainline religious point of view which "temple" was the most "useful in bringing on the Kingdom of God.... [One was quickly brought] to a belief in the superiority of the type found in the Angelus Temple...which proclaims itself as the headquarters of 'the Foursquare Gospel,' in which conversion and healing are mingled."[73] Sheerin first heard of Aimee during his visit to Denver and in meeting an Episcopal clergyman who proclaimed himself "an out and out Catholic in the ritualistic sense."

> He mentioned that a woman revivalist named McPherson, had been there...and had made much of healing as a vital part of her evangelistic work...But the added feature, that the lady in question had been a sort of female Billy Sunday, led me to think that this was something new in modern evangelism, and worth looking into.[74]

Sheerin was writing his "Little Journeys in the West" for the Episcopal Church periodical *Southern Churchman*, which two months earlier featured an article titled "Evangelism—The Churchman's Need." That article concluded,

> It is our responsibility to attempt to bring the man on the street into the Church and the method must be through an organized city-wide Mission, addressed to the outsider, and held in a public hall or theatre... We are trying to prove that it is possible for this Episcopal Church to be not only a Church for the cultured, a post-graduate course in religion, but that it is also possible for us to be an evangelistic Church, expressing our real interest in the outsider or non-churched, by going to him and striving to bring him to a point of decision for God and His Church, not only by an appeal to the emotions, the conscience and the will.[75]

This kind of theological openness toward evangelism and the working class would have undoubtedly contributed to Sheerin's interest in observing the "female Billy Sunday." He immediately, like so many others did in the early

Angelus Temple, home of a secular spirituality—a theatre and a church (author's collection)

1920s, contrasted Aimee Semple McPherson with Billy Sunday:

> When…I arrived in Los Angeles and heard that Mrs. McPherson had an enormous temple which she filled every night, and that Billy Sunday, who had a beautiful mansion on a hill overlooking Hollywood, had no permanent temple or church anywhere, I could see that there was a considerable difference. All modern revivalists seem to have made fortunes…But here was an evangelist who dared to settle down in a great city and build a permanent structure to house, so far as she could, her religious ideas.[76]

In finding Angelus Temple by the rushes of Echo Park, Sheerin had anticipated "a homely, flimsy tabernacle…akin to the more temporary Billy Sunday type. But, as seen across Echo Park, Angelus Temple shone out like a great marble hall, white and clean and durable in appearance, with a style of architecture half like a Roman coliseum, half like a Parisian opera house."[77] Aimee was also physically appealing. Admitting that he was "partly prejudicial against the fact of a woman preaching," he nevertheless found Aimee in person to be a "handsome, rather fashionable looking woman in white, with a great and glorious crown of black hair." Aimee's style of delivery also suited him: "The little offenses in religious peculiarities, the impractical other worldliness of some evangelists seemed either fewer or entirely absent in her exhortations. There was humor and zeal in every paragraph."[78] Sheerin concluded that Aimee alone out of the "three most prominent places of worship in the West was eclectically orthodox."

The essence of her message was as old as that of St. Peter on the Day of Pentecost, it was the gospel of St. Francis, it was the teaching of John Wesley and of Moody…There is in her that strange, almost fanatical, faith in her mission that all the prophets must have had, and that every true priest truly professes.[79]

After a personal meeting with Aimee before Sheerin returned East, he commented,

> She expressed great admiration for the great background of historic belief in the Episcopal Church, intimating that it seemed to her the most perfect in the world. An item in this admiring belief seemed to be that the Episcopal Church was also the most alive to the need of Divine healing. She even went so far as to say, "Maybe the Episcopal Church should take me and send me on as its herald in the blessed work!" There was humor in her manner, for both of us were conscious of how hostile an element we have to women preaching in the Churches.[80]

Sheerin then surprised his mainline readership by asking the following series of questions: "But why is it not a possibility? We have tried other ways through manifold types of men and failed. Why not try a woman whose Gospel seems peculiarly sane, whose sole 'madness' seems to be that apostolic belief that she is possessed of the Holy Ghost and must work as and when He directs?"[81] From gypsy tribes to mainline religious writers, Angelus Temple from its earliest days of 1923 fast became a social and religious melting pot. This would of course give rise in subsequent fact and fable that religion "out West" was indeed something new and different.

A future Foursquare minister and denominational official remembered how he had first heard about Angelus Temple's "lady preacher" and what occurred at his first visit:

> I was born and raised on the plains of eastern Colorado and our families gradually came to California. A tobacco chewin', cussing', spittin' uncle of mine as tough and as hard as the prairies of those eastern plains went to the Angelus Temple and there converted. He came to our house and our non-religious family was dumb-founded! He said he did not "chew no more, cuss no more" and that he was going to church three to four times a week to hear a lady preacher in Echo Park at the Angelus Temple in Los Angeles, California. My father and mother agreed to go with him. Finally they suggested that I come along. I was instantly galvanized by the pretty woman in white with the beautiful smile and face and for the first time in my life I heard the plan of salvation. I was first at the altar along with my mother and father and from that day,… have endeavored

to serve Him—with all of my heart.[82]

The vast majority of those who found their way to "Aimee's Temple" in the early months of 1923, however, were for the most part like those who had discovered Aimee in many an American city—"regular Protestants." In Los Angeles "regular Protestants" usually meant "the middle-aged from the middle class from the Middle West." While Carey McWilliams, Aimee's neighbor, later contended that "80% of Aimee's followers were city residents, mostly lower-middle class people,"[83] it could have just as easily been argued that it was also the middle class on the rise. Those in regular attendance at the temple equally maintained that Aimee "absolutely reached people from all walks of life."[84] At least half of the temple membership owned their own homes, and Angelus Temple probably had more babies in its pink, blue, white, and ivory layettes than any other church in modern America. Its membership had clearly not been culled from either the Pentecostal missions or from those who had come to spend their final days out under the Southern California sun. Temple membership would have simply been the same cross-section of the country found either at a county fair or a sporting event. The spirit of inter-denominationalism alone attracted many mainline church members who participated in the affairs of Angelus Temple through an "associate members" status—while retaining their original membership in various individual mainline denominational churches. "Our converts range from the highest class of society to the most humble and lowly," Ma Kennedy told the *Los Angeles Times* in 1926. "Here in Los Angeles one can scarcely turn the corner without seeing someone who has been brought into a better life because of Aimee Semple McPherson."[85]

Less than two years after the temple opened, the old lion of Methodism, L.W. Munhall, paid a tribute in his sermon to both Aimee and Angelus Temple. What he discovered in his visit reminded him of the Methodism of his youth. "I have been at home here," declared Munhall. "The very things you stand for, and the very things you believe, and the very way you do it…I was brought up on, for the old Methodists forty, fifty, sixty years ago did all that, only they are a little bit noisier than you are."[86]

Aimee had been raised, as she often said, with "literally one foot in the Salvation Army and the other in the Methodist Church." And that creative tension from her background remained with her throughout her ministry. To the "odds and ends" of life, as Dorothy Day termed them, Aimee offered love to the lonely, hope for the defeated, healing for the broken, while to the middle class she was a very real symbol of much sought-after success in the often illusionary world of Southern California country.

But it was really among the "flowers torn from their roots and stuffed into a pretty vase"—their colors draining fast—the "odds and ends" of life—that Aimee had her greatest ministry. She always remained, much to her mother's dismay, the little girl of make-believe who lived among and cared for the wilted jonquils and faded pink lilies of the maple sugar bush; the youngster who had a natural tendency to be around sick folk and believed that she could help them; the daughter who fantasized while sitting high atop the family barn that it was she who was holding up her father while he shingled down the sides of the roof. She was forever the little girl who, like her childhood heroine, dreamed about becoming a light-house keeper and with her father save people from the treacherous seas that threatened their stricken ships. It was such naïve optimism coupled with equal amounts of gullibility and vulnerability that led to her later difficulties, yet always remained her saving grace.

During a class session for her future Foursquare men and women ministers she once exclaimed,

> Some of the wildest jackasses I have ever seen sit in that top balcony and talk and whisper. Wild? If I were wanting to preach to…wild people…I would start right out in that top balcony. Why there is a group that meet me at the gate, and among them a boy and a girl who mean no good. Even the Park Commissioner complains about them. They say, "Hello, Aimee!" I am Sister McPherson to you—always have been and always will be. Wild? Yes, but instead of showing them the door or giving them the boot, get them in and get them thoroughly saved and they will go right on with God…Jesus Christ came to seek and to save the lost.[87]

And that was why people—"all of the people"—came to her Temple to see and hear the Junoesque "white sister" who seemed "to have paused at the age when womanhood is fully ripened." The woman with "the religion of Billy Sunday" who worked like a man and who even had in the early days of Los Angeles the dirt under her fingernails to prove it, yet a minister with a "strong maternal instinct" who preached a gospel based upon love. A woman considered too "fanatical" for mainline religious ordination and too "sane" for the Pentecostal missions and upper rooms.

The people came in early January of 1923 as they had done elsewhere, and they kept on coming. They came as flappers in their flivvers, or for a nickel each on the red cars and seven cents apiece on the yellow ones they rode on a small portion of the 1,163-mile street railway system, attired in their best Midwestern Sunday dress. Angelus Temple was in close proximity to the subway terminal, main street station, and the Southern Pacific

Station. Four red car lines of the nation's largest electric streetcar system—the Edendale, Glendale, Burbank and the Hollywood lines—went past the doors of the Temple, while the yellow cars made their stop at Temple Street at the entrance of Echo Park. They came as church members, the unchurched, and as tourists. They came from multi-family rented apartments and from single family mortgaged bungalows. They came from within the city limits and from the newly created sprawling suburbs surrounding Los Angeles in all directions.

Aimee attempted to summarize the joyous happenings to *Bridal Call* readers calling the meetings "a continuous revival."

> Rich and poor sit side by side. The padded limousine and the dilapidated Ford, rub fenders in the street....Special street-railway service was provided by the city...Even then, many hundreds must stand for a long time, awaiting transportation... Our message...is bringing members of all denominations, sects and creeds into one common meeting place—as a great cauldron...[88]

An evangelical writer from Oakland also noted the "great cauldron." "Many Jews, Catholics and Christian Scientists" he wrote, "are being saved at these altars."[89]

"If any symbol captures the religious West," wrote D. Michael Quinn, "it's the symbol of a giant aquarium—God's aquarium. Throughout the wide spaces in God's western aquarium, there are schools of familiar (but easily startled) denominational species, there are slow-moving crustaceans, there are religious exotics from the depths...and unchurched plankton are floating everywhere."[90] More often than not it was the free-floating "unchurched plankton" of Los Angeles that attached themselves to Angelus Temple during its early years. Continually fishing for new prospective members, Aimee admonished the readers of her church ads appearing in the *Los Angeles Times* that "the Latchstring is out to you—whoever you may be."[91] A latchstring was simply a cord attached to a latch passed through a hole in the door, allowing the lifting of the latch from the outside. Aimee was first and foremost concerned with those left outside of organized religion. And in the giant aquarium of Los Angeles there were many "unchurched plankton" afloat. Much of Western religious experience, observes Quinn, "has, in fact, been private, distant from clergy and churches."[92] Aimee, more actress than clergyperson, and Angelus Temple, more theatre than church, obviously appealed to the free-floating hidden spirituality found in the vast theological aquarium of Los Angeles.

"Everywhere in southern California," wrote Marcus Bach in his report to mainline Protestants, "I encountered Christians in flight, holding common stock in a corporation called The Church, but no longer interested in even watching the market."

> They were homeless, churchless Protestants whose names were fading on the dusty ledger of some congregational roll. They were spiritual windfalls and they were being garnered in by a most efficient crew of high-powered cultists [whose] advertisements were slanted toward the market of Protestant migrants streaming out of the Bible Belt and the great Midwest....They did not represent religion as I knew it. But they offered the religion some people wanted—people who had become dissatisfied with a traditional faith and with their churches and ministers back home.[93]

"How Religious is the City of Los Angeles?" asked the *Los Angeles Times* in the "first survey ever made" of the city's church-going population in 1926. The article by George Burlingame began by noting the city's recent Protestant growth:

> During the first twenty years of its history as an American city, Los Angeles was for most of the time destitute of Protestant worship.... Protestant Christianity was in a highly precarious condition.
>
> Today there are upward of 500+ Protestant churches in Los Angeles. Every Protestant denomination in America is represented here and within recent years the numerical and financial strength of Protestant Christianity has manifested itself in the creation of church edifices and other institutions which are among the finest and most splendid in America.[94]

Burlingame went on to note that Roman Catholicism was also strong and that "Judaism is virile and active." Yet the "remarkable fact" remained for the author that out of an estimated population of 1,350,000 there could still only be found in the city 142,625 Protestants, 131,000 Catholics and 17,000 Jews.

> This statement and analysis involve conclusions which are indeed startling, and which, if accurate, are serious even unto tragedy:
>
> (1.) Only one person in fifteen is a member of any Protestant church in Los Angeles;
>
> (2.) Only one person in eight is a member of any religious organization in Los Angeles;
>
> (3.) Eleven hundred thousand residents of the city...have no definite affiliation with any religious organization here....and if there be more than 1,000,000 persons in Los Angeles who are in the way of

becoming pagans, the outlook from the Christian point of view is quite appalling.[95]

Writing from an obvious Protestant perspective, Burlingame took time to reprimand his fellow believers for keeping their membership in "the dear old church back home." Calling them "backsliders" and "tightwads," Burlingame concluded "of this inarticulate and intangible type of Christians Los Angeles has a disproportionately large number."[96]

The survey revealed that the six leading Protestant denominations of Los Angeles in 1926 were as follows: Northern Methodist, 67 churches, 24,387 members; Baptists, 67 churches, 20,469 members; Presbyterians, 47 churches, 20,184 members; Disciples of Christ, 43 churches, 11,307 members; Episcopalians, 32 churches, 8,989 members; and the Congregationalists with 39 churches and 8,690 members. These six denominations made up two-thirds of the entire membership of all non-Catholic Christian churches in greater Los Angeles for a total of 295 churches and 94,026 members. "Independent evangelical churches," which would be identified with the later megachurch phenomenon, numbered 81 churches and had a membership of 21,522.[97]

Burlingame finally took notice of the "religious exotics" that were also found in the "giant aquarium" of Los Angeles. He quoted John S. McGroarty:

> It would be quite impossible to name any religion or creed or philosophy or school of thought under the sun that is without representation in Los Angeles. More than that, we find ourselves able to say that very many religions…are found in Los Angeles and nowhere else. Maybe it is the climate, and maybe it is something else, but whatever it is, the fact remains that Los Angeles is the most celebrated of all incubators of new creeds…and no day passes without the birth of something of this nature never before heard of. Indeed Los Angeles has acquired a fame of freak religions.[98]

Angelus Temple in three years had become so large that the survey placed it eighth in size when comparing the various Protestant denominations. Despite the fact that the Congregationalists had thirty-eight more churches, Angelus Temple alone had only 1,690 fewer members than all of them combined. Angelus Temple's membership exceeded all of the city's Lutheran churches and the twelve wards of the Latter-day Saints. Outside of the six major Protestant denominations previously mentioned, only Christian Science surpassed Angelus Temple in membership. Combined together, however, both Angelus Temple and Christian Science would have placed fourth in membership following the Methodists, Baptists, and Presbyterians. Not only were Angelus Temple and Christian Science founded by women, but health and healing were part of their major tenets. The only other large "independent" Protestant church, the fundamentalist church of the Open Door, home to The Bible Institute of Los Angeles (BIOLA), significantly trailed Angelus Temple with 5,600 fewer members. Even the Southern Methodists with six churches and represented for the most part by "fighting Bob" Shuler had nearly three thousand fewer members. By 1926 Angelus Temple had clearly become the largest church in the city, capturing close to five percent of all church-going Protestants.

A young American Indian boy born in Los Angeles distinctly recalled attending both the Church of the Open Door and Angelus Temple and remembering the differences between the two. When the Indian wars ended in 1890, the Bureau of Indian Affairs used nonmilitary methods to extinguish American Indian identity. One of the "model programs" for Indian assimilation was the "Outing Program" created by Captain Richard H. Pratt, superintendent of the Indian Boarding School at Carlisle, Pennsylvania. Most of the Outing Program participants from the 1920s until 1938, when the program came to a temporary halt due to the Depression, were Southwesterners from Arizona and New Mexico.

Born into a Pima Indian family relocated to Los Angeles, Clinton Pedro remembered his early days in California before returning to the reservation in Arizona. As a young boy growing up in a multi-racial apartment complex in downtown Los Angeles, Pedro first attended the Church of the Open Door with his mother, due to the close proximity of the church to where they lived. One day, he recalled, his mother "took an interest in the ministry of Aimee Semple McPherson," and soon they were attending Sunday evening services at the temple. And things at the temple were vastly different from his days at the Church of the Open Door. His first impression was of the enormous "crowd of people attempting to get into the service. And not everybody got in. A lot of them couldn't get in." His second impression of hearing his first woman minister was even stronger:

> She made a strong impression with her body language. She was so animated. Her style of speaking was unique. She was talking to a great number of people, but also, to you as an individual. And as she talked, people leaned forward in their seats. There was an energy, an expectancy. Her arms would fly out. Her body would twist and turn, but it was a guided motion. Everything she did drew attention to her.[99]

Pedro's final lasting impression of the two Los Angeles landmark churches came from the parishioners themselves. Those who attended the Church of the Open Door appeared to him "as if they had just come in from off the street. They were not dressed up."[100] But at Angelus Temple, "everybody dressed nicely, they were very well dressed."[101] He especially remembered how the men "wore shiny black shoes, starched white shirts, and stick pins in their ties."[102] "There may have been a few Hispanics, but they were generally white."[103] (Actually there were Hispanics, since Sunday School at Angelus Temple was taught in Spanish, Armenian, Japanese and English.) And the parishioners, like their minister, were also "expressive in their body language. There was a freedom of spirit."[104]

More than any other Protestant church in Los Angeles, Angelus Temple, especially in its Sunday School, reflected the demographic shifts that were occurring in the 1920s:

> [Although] the population remained overwhelmingly Caucasian and Protestant...the decade...witnessed the beginnings of two "great migrations": of Mexicans uprooted by the Mexican Revolution and of African Americans leaving the South. Combined with a growing Japanese population, they gave Los Angeles the second-highest percentage of nonwhites of any major city in the nation (after Baltimore). Substantial communities of Jews, Slavs, Italians, Russians, and Armenians had also taken shape.[105]

Aimee's own "star of hope," her daughter Roberta, perhaps had the best perspective on Angelus Temple and how it differed from the rest of its Christian competitors. "Established religion," remembered Roberta, "built a fence around the church with its forms and ceremony."

> What people wanted was an outward expression of their religious fervor. This could not be found in the formal churches. It was like being in love with a beautiful girl and you couldn't kiss her. [Pentecostalism] was a positive, active religious experience. Religion wasn't practical. It wasn't down to earth. It was too educated with its Greek and Hebrew. My mother would have probably been that way, too, had she gone to seminary. All she had was drama lessons in High School. So she read the Bible as an actress. She put back the drama that was already there. She retranslated the Bible into common, everyday language for the people. She put the punctuation in, putting back what the cold churches had taken out. The people could understand her and they responded.[106]

"Mother," concluded Roberta, "had a keen sense of audience awareness.

The Echo Park Evangelistic and Missionary Training Institute opened on February 6, 1923. It was built next to the parsonage (author's collection).

She could always get their attention back. She would make a wide gesture and then snap them back by making her point again. She also had a vitality and energy. She was strong and healthy with a country girl glow. Her sense of drama made the sermons live and breathe. She met her audience's needs."[107]

A time had finally come for Aimee where all she had to do was remain in one place and have the world, as Sarah Comstock would soon observe, "beat a path to her door." Speaking of her continually changing congregations, Aimee wrote, "It is a great painting in kaleidoscopic colorings, ever changing—picture melting into picture—a slate, filled with beautiful pictures and carefully molded figures, which is immediately wiped clean and filled with other pictures of still more gorgeous colorings."[108] By the end of the first six months, the "great painting in kaleidoscopic colorings, ever changing" had some quantitative dimensions to it: eight thousand reported conversions and fifteen hundred recorded baptisms. In addition, *The Bridal Call* was being sent to thirty thousand households. Aimee's original intention of spending half of each year at the temple and the remainder of the time in various American cities never materialized during the early years of Angelus Temple. It would take another decade before that wish would be fulfilled. A former secretary observed Minnie Kennedy to be like a careful and calculating stage mother who "kept Aimee walking that straight little narrow path from Manse to Temple back to Manse."[109]

The "Continuous Revival" was not as chaotic as Aimee's early ministry had been. There soon emerged a natural ebb and flow to the weekly activities and a very clear and discernible schedule—a far cry from Aimee's first meetings in Los Angeles held at Victoria Hall. "With rare ingenuity," wrote Carey McWilliams, "Aimee kept the Ferris wheels and merry-go-rounds of religion going night and day. Her showmanship was superb; her timing matchless; her dramatic instinct uncanny."[110]

Adding permanence to the "continuous revival" or the "factory of faith," as some of the more irreverent journalists referred to the affairs of Angelus Temple, were two more swift creations of Aimee's from the opening months of the temple. Three short phrases used in much of its literature attempted to capture the intents and purposes of the continuous revival—"evangelical in message," "interdenominational in spirit," and "international in project." The "international in project" intent of "the continuous revival" resulted in the opening of the Echo Park Evangelistic and Missionary Training Institute on February 6, 1923. The following month the name was changed to Angelus Temple Evangelistic and Missionary Training School and on December 13, 1937, the final name change occurred when LIFE Bible College—Lighthouse of International Foursquare Evangelism—was granted power by the state of California to confer degrees.[111] Like so many other Pentecostal and fundamentalist Bible Schools in contrast to the mainline theological seminaries, the emphasis of the burgeoning institutes was upon evangelism and missionary activity—concerns no longer paramount at the time with other major Protestant groups. These twin concerns of missions and evangelism provided most of the impetus for the "continuous revival" at Angelus Temple and became the reason for the larger Pentecostal movement itself. The early curriculum at LIFE Bible College was the standard fare found at most other similar institutions across America. Aimee's indelible stamp to everything she did added another difference, the practical dimension. Like her father, James, the master bridge-builder, Aimee had the practical originality of thought in meeting human need. To her *Bridal Call* audience she explained the purposes of the newly formed school she envisioned.

> Those wishing to enter the Training School…to be fitted for the evangelistic or missionary field should write immediately for their application

blanks…there will be a practical training in the Holy Ghost Revival now being conducted.

A thorough course in fishing, altar work, singing, music, street-meetings, hospital visitation, prison work and preaching of the gospel will be given….the young student, so desirous of becoming a minister and soul-winning evangelist needs a practical training. Book-learning and theory taught in colleges, seminaries, university…when located miles from the nearest Holy Ghost revival…must of necessity lack that one great essential—practical training.[112]

When Aimee preached, she covered many topics, with their texts ranging from Genesis to Revelation. She clearly had some favorite books and texts—the books of Ruth and Esther were favorites—the Song of Solomon the most favorite. Sermons on healing, the Holy Spirit, and the Foursquare Gospel were often heard within the temple walls. A sermon that most epitomized Aimee's message was one entitled "Practical Christianity." It not only reflected her desire that her students receive a "practical training" but that her entire work be built upon "practical Christianity."

The teachings of the Lord Jesus were not mere flights of oratorical and flowery eloquence, neither were they great swelling, well-rounded, fancy tickling words. His was the Gospel that went straight down into the hearts and homes of the people. A ministry that found the burden and lifted it; located the trouble and banished it; touched the festering sore spot and healed it; entered the desecrated temple and cleansed it; found the hungry multitudes and fed them; walked the storm swept sea and calmed it; met the devil squarely and drove him out of the hearts of the oppressed….Practical Christianity means visiting the prisons, preaching in the shops and factories, visiting the hospitals and the country farm. It teaches us not to be afraid to sew for the poor, scrub the floor for a sick person, usher in the church, and stand on our feet all day with nothing to eat but a cold sandwich.[113]

"Practical Christianity" according to Aimee, was not a panacea, either. As in most of her sermons, an autobiographical part always surfaced. "This does not mean" she wrote, "that your heart will never ache, that you will never stagger, falter, nor have to cry out to God in the way, but it does mean that underneath you shall be the everlasting arms and that He will hold you fast."[114] The practical aspect of Aimee's training school for future evangelists and missionaries, later functioning more as a seminary for her own forthcoming Foursquare ministers, can be noted by its opening on a Tuesday. Mondays in the "enormous village" of Los Angeles were "sales day" and an enterprising student could find all day work on both Mondays and Saturdays at such places as the Old Famous Department Store on Main Street.

Almost a year after Aimee's written invitation for students to "write immediately for the application blanks," she was able to give something of a progress report to her *Bridal Call* readers

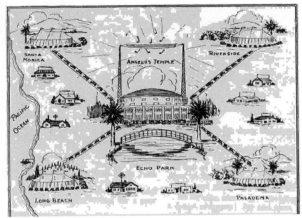

Khaki tents radiate from Angelus Temple to the surrounding suburbs, forming future Foursquare churches (author's collection).

as well as request funds for the building of a permanent structure. (The school was started in what became the temple parsonage. Due to ever-increasing numbers in enrollment it moved twice—to a choir room and to a larger room called the 500 Room.) Aimee reminded her invisible network of 30,000 friends and financial supporters:

> The Temple...was not built by one or two, nor even a hundred rich folk; it was built by thousands of devoted and humble children of the Lord and by years of actual evangelistic service....And so, perhaps, will the Institute itself be erected...when Uncle Sam needed soldiers for the field, he could throw up his building and training barracks almost overnight. King Jesus now needs soldiers and officers, trained, skilled and ready for marching orders...Are we able to do it? Alone, no! Together, yes![115]

The school had become in a year's time a built-in base of support for the "continuous revival." "The school," wrote Aimee, "has indeed proved a blessing, a benediction. The students form the backbone of the choir, the orchestra, the altar workers, the street, shop and prison work. What would we do without them? ...already they are holding some fifty meetings a week outside of Temple services in shops, factories, foundries, jails and on street corners."[116]

Unknowingly, Aimee's request for students to "write immediately for their application blanks" to receive training in "Practical Christianity" resulted early on in the unforeseen genesis of yet another Pentecostal denomination.

An early graduation class of LIFE Bible College. The women outnumber the men and appear as clones of their foundress (author's collection).

The seeds for a new church were planted in the summer of 1924 when the student body was divided into four sections and given "brand new, eighteen ounce, mildew-proof Foursquare Gospel tents." With Angelus Temple as a hub, khaki tents soon radiated to the surrounding suburbs of the "enormous village" of Los Angeles—Santa Monica, Long Beach, Riverside and Pasadena. As Aimee's earlier tents had incubated into a famed temple, so too, her students' summer tents pitched in the nearby surrounding suburbs formed the cocoon for future emerging Foursquare churches.

Apart from their highly distinguishable dress (the women imitated Aimee down to their white stockings and shoes, worn with a starched white cotton uniform adorned only by a dark tie) the students additionally stood out by most accounts because they were "a rather joyous lot." Somehow they seemed to capture their founder's indefatigable sense of optimism and ready humor. Their happy faces were on Los Angeles street cars, and their many silver musical instruments scattered the sparkling rays of the Southern California sun. "Everybody happy?—say 'Amen.'" They said "Amen" a lot. Aimee, conducting a tour of the temple, once confided to a state senator that the school classrooms had to be "locked up at night" due to a recurring epidemic of "spooning among her students." Many of her students did fall in love, and Sister subsequently not only married many of the students but ordained the newlyweds as "co-pastors" for future Foursquare churches. When her students assembled for their first class portrait in June of 1923, it was apparent that a large number of women had enrolled in the "Angelus Temple Evangelistic and Missionary Training Institute." Clearly Aimee had become a role model for future women ministers within the Pentecostal tradition, because there were only two men in the first graduating class. Women would later provide much of the leadership not only within the school but as well within the emerging structure of the Four-square denomination.

A professor who taught at both LIFE Bible College and Southern California Bible College (Vanguard University), affiliated with the Assemblies of God, remembered the marked differences between the two student bodies. "LIFE students," he recalled, "were more alive, warm and friendlier, reflecting their leader. The excitement, aliveness, and vitality of the students reflected their charismatic leader."[117]

Most likely Aimee and Minnie's idea of branch churches had originated with J.F. Sartori, president of Security Bank in Los Angeles. Until Sartori arrived on the scene, "the idea of a big city bank having branches in the suburbs was unheard of in Los Angeles."[118] In 1919 Sartori "expanded slowly, one branch at a time, and…only in communities close to the heart of the city. It was not long before other banks established branches and the system became general."[119] Once again, a "secular" model for future church growth provided more inspiration for mother and daughter than more traditional "sacred" ones.

Aimee's second creation during the opening months of the temple also added permanence to her ministry and the "continuous revival," although in a less tangible, visible way than the Bible school. In a sermon on "Practical Christianity" Aimee admonished her listeners:

> Like some fantastic dream! Like a visionary tale from the Arabian Nights! Like an imaginary fairy tale is the story of the radio. Swifter than the six-league boots of a giant; miraculous in so much as to be almost beyond comprehension:
>
> A beautiful priceless gift from the Loving Father God; Almost unheard of opportunity for converting the world, and of reaching the largest possible number of people in the shortest possible time…Now, the crowning blessing, the most golden opportunity, the most miraculous conveyance for the Message has come—the radio.[120]

Like Aimee, the radio was something of an immigrant. Also, like Aimee, nothing really symbolized America better during the 1920s than the radio. Aimee's place was not to be found upon the silver screen but over the air waves, with her arresting "vibrant contralto of the midway." Unlike the automobile and the airplane, which had been invented some time before, the radio was an authentic product of the 1920s. Although not as important as the automobile, the radio still became one of the great forces—along with its own subsidiary industries—of sustaining the decade's boom years. The radio "transformed American society during the 1920s, like the Internet has impacted contemporary America…the radio replaced magazines

413

"Like some fantastic dream." Aimee discoveres radio, "a beautiful, priceless gift from the Loving Father God"(author's collection).

and catalogs as the lifeline to the world, especially in the West, where distance worked against a sense of community."[121]

The radio was not an American invention; rather, it evolved through international research and various experiments. A German, Heinrich Hertz, was the first to detect the presence of radio waves (Hertzian waves) in the air; Alexander Popov, a Russian, created the first antenna for radio transmission; Guglielmo Marconi, an Italian, perfected the means of transmitting and receiving radio waves; Reginald Ressenden, a Canadian-American physicist, created "radio" in that he modulated the radio waves to reproduce speech and music; and Lee De Forest, an American, amplified weak radio signals by using a vacuum tube, the precursor to modern radio tubes.

Commercial radio broadcasting began on November 2, 1920, when an East Pittsburgh station, KDKA, began its regular schedule with the results of the Harding-Cox presidential election. Sales of radio equipment reached $60 million in 1922 and by 1929, $842 million. Before the end of 1921, the country had thirty-two stations and by 1928, 677 had been established. Radio quickly became another large American business enterprise. In 1926 the National Broadcasting Company (NBC) was formed, and the Columbia Broadcasting System (CBS) came into existence the following year. The new invention also raised new questions about the relationship of public and private interests, so in 1927 Congress created the Federal Radio Commission (reorganized as the Federal Communications Commission in 1934) "to oversee licensing and regulate broadcast traffic."[122]

Within a few years after its introduction radio became an indispensable part of American life:

> Radio had the effect of promoting national feeling and homogeneity. Products, heroes, entertainers and preachers became known nationally; people in different regions learned about important events simultaneously; big city values and attitudes filtered across the air waves into town and country. The radio connected Americans in hundreds of ways although regional differences, loyalties and dialects continued to survive.[123]

The enormous popularity of radio in American culture rested firmly on the fact that programming was tailored to the "average" American listener in anticipation of reaching the widest possible audience. Special-events broadcasts were popular, such as the Demsey-Carpenter fight, the Rose Bowl games, and baseball broadcasts. Thriller detective and adventure stories soon emerged, such as *The Lone Ranger, The Shadow, The Adventures of Sam Spade*, and *Sergeant Preston of the Yukon*. And, of course, *Amos 'n' Andy*. (It was estimated that seventy-five percent of American radios tuned in to its daily comedy team of Freeman Gosden and Charles Correll.)

"American radio is the product of American business," stated J. Harold Ryan, President of the National Association of Broadcasters in 1925. "If the legend still persists that a radio station is some kind of art center, a technical museum, or a little piece of Hollywood transplanted strangely to your hometown, then the first official act of the second quarter century should be to list it along with the local dairies, banks, bakeries, and filling stations."[124]

If a "little piece of Hollywood could be transplanted strangely" to one's hometown, then so could Angelus Temple, reasoned Aimee. She had been the first woman ever to preach over the radio in many an American city: Wichita, San Francisco, Oakland, and Harry Chandler's station in Los Angeles, KHJ, whose station identification was made by singing canaries. A month after making her request known for her own station, Aimee reported to her followers:

> Since the first notice of the proposed Radio Broadcasting Station was announced in the last issue of *The Bridal Call*, letters and telegrams have been showering in from our faithful friends and helpers throughout the nation.
>
> Truly whatever we have taken in hand to do…loving friends have been quick to respond with their encouragement and means…And now that it has been proposed that a radio be installed to help carry the message to hundreds of thousands who would not otherwise be able to hear it, *The Bridal Call* readers are again surging to the front.[125]

Like everything else Aimee set out to accomplish, she wanted the most modern and the best. She originally asked for $25,000 from her followers to install a "powerful 500-watt Class A Broadcasting Station" complete with twin 125-foot steel towers that would be perched on opposite sides of the temple's dome. The broadcasting equipment itself had to be built in New York, while the steel towers came from San Francisco by ship. By October 1923 Aimee was able to write, "So prompt and unanimous has been the

Aimee preaching over the radio, "the visionary tale from the Arabian Nights (author's collection)

response that the funds for [the] actual mechanism and the great steel towers…are well in hand."[126]

On February 6, 1924, KFSG (Kall Four Square Gospel) entered the airwaves on the wavelength of 278 meters. In so doing, it became one of the earliest radio stations in the enormous village of Los Angeles, following behind KNX, KJS, KHJ AND KFI. Until its demise in 2003, KFSG "was the oldest operating religious station in the nation. Its total years on the air on AM and FM had made it the 5th oldest radio station in Los Angeles."[127] It was "a powerful 500-watt station"—a Western Electric—and capable of roaming 4,000 miles in any direction….dedicated to God and the people of the United States, Canada, Alaska, Mexico, Panama, Hawaii, and the South Sea Islands."[128] With its dedication Aimee became "the first woman to own and operate a Christian radio station."[129]

If Los Angeles city officials had been reluctant to take Aimee seriously when she opened the doors of her temple, her adoption of radio undoubtedly changed their opinions. Her accomplishments were different from those of other mainline ministers. She was clearly more of the age in which they lived. A kind of secular-spirituality was forming at Angelus Temple. Steel radio towers took the place of steeples on the structure that looked "half like a Roman coliseum, half like a Parisian opera house."[130] Electric signs on the sides of the structure lit up the Southern California night like an amusement park, while directly overhead in the center of the dome a cross, visible from Catalina Island twenty-six miles across the sea, revolved in red and blue neon. With Aimee, church indeed was different. They wished her well that February evening in 1924, inaugurating in the process a trend many Los Angeles politicians sought to maintain over the years—being seen on the platform of Angelus Temple.

Uncle John Daggett—the master of the *Los Angeles Times'* KHJ spoke first. "Good evening, friends of radioland! We have knocked at your doors and bid you open to the friendship of a remarkable woman, Aimee Semple McPherson, your new guest in Radioland. This wonderful Angelus Temple of Los Angeles, through K.F.S.G. is going out into a new Channel with a new message. We ask you to give it your thought and study."[131]

Boyle Workman, president of the Los Angeles City Council and acting mayor, declared, "We are very proud of our city and invite you all to come here. When you come we want you all to visit this wonderful Temple which is doing so much good in the world."[132] Finally a benediction of blessing was heard from the powerful publisher Harry Chandler himself:

Thoroughly appreciative of the noble work that Mrs. McPherson has done through the instrumentality of the God-given powers with which she is endowed, it gives me great pleasure to know that, through the medium of a modern, highest type radio equipment that she will be able to greatly expand and multiply the results of her efforts.

Where she had heretofore been able to speak directly to only a few thousand, through the instrumentality of the radio she will be able... to address more than 1,000,000 auditors in more than a quarter of a million homes.[133]

Aimee admonished her faithful friends who had so generously provided in so short a time the "powerful 500-watt radio station":

Draw up your chair, attach your loud speaker and listen in. Three times daily...you may hear Angelus Temple and the great Revival in sermon, for the shut-ins. May God grant that the radio prove a mighty blessing to old and young, rich and poor, to sick and well, to one and all.[134]

Aimee also quickly figured out a way for the temple members to "sponsor" the day-to-day expenses of the radio station. Weekdays cost twenty-five dollars, while the full Sunday service was double the amount. "People donated a day," remembered Roberta, "to celebrate their mother's birthday, a wedding anniversary, or the day they joined Angelus Temple. And each day the KFSG announcer told the listeners, 'Today's broadcast is sponsored by...' and gave the name of the donor."[135]

During the first few months of KFSG "the great revival" was indeed heard by "one and all"—sometimes listeners had no choice. Roaming all over the airwaves, Aimee's vibrant contralto of the midway trampled other stations' programming. A young Secretary of Commerce, Herbert Hoover, part of whose duty for Congress was to regulate radio in its infancy, came to the rescue. In his memoirs he recalled what happened:

> A vivid experience in the early days of radio was the Evangelist Aimee Semple McPherson of Los Angeles. One of the earliest to appreciate the possibilities in radio, she had established a small broadcasting station in her Temple. This station, however, roamed all over the wave band, causing interference and arousing bitter complaints from the other stations. She was repeatedly warned to stick to her assigned wave length. As warnings did no good, our inspector sealed up her station and stopped it. The next day I received from her a telegram in these words: "Please order your minions of Satan to leave my station alone. You cannot expect the Almighty to abide by your wavelength nonsense. When I offer my prayers to Him I must fit into His wave reception. Open this station at once." [signed] Aimee Semple McPherson.
>   Finally our tactful inspector persuaded her to employ a radio manager…who kept her upon her wave lenth.[136]

In early 1924 a twenty-eight-year-old radio engineer with quiet good looks and a noticeable limp went to work for KFSG to keep the station, among other things, on its assigned 278-meter wavelength. Kenneth Gladstone Ormiston—a name that in two years time would be sensationally linked with that of Aimee Semple McPherson—was an early radio pioneer and a Southern California native. He continued to make history in his field after he left Angelus Temple. Ormiston, with the assistance of Gilbert Lee, successfully transmited the first television image from New York to Los Angeles in 1928. He was chief engineer for radio station KNX from 1932 until his untimely death in 1937 of complications from an appendectomy. Kenneth Ormiston was never a member of Angelus Temple but nonetheless authored a monthly column in *The Bridal Call* called "Listening In" and "Radio Answers." His columns displayed both professionalism and handy hints on how to get the most out of one's receivers. Ormiston's technical savvy rendered much success to Aimee's early radio days. The advent of radio seemed to open new doors for Aimee. She seemed more than ever to have, in the Great Gatsby's words, "Some heightened sensitivity to the promises of life, as if [she] were related to one of those intricate machines that register earthquakes ten thousand miles away…an extraordinary gift for hope, a romantic readiness…never found in any other person."[137]

Mark Goodman of Mississippi State University has argued that the Radio Act of 1927 was in reality "a product of progressivism….What Congress sought for the new medium was a voice that would articulate middle class ideology."[138] Once again, Aimee's timing was perfect. Perhaps the radio, more than any other modern device at her disposal, gave her message a solid middle-class appeal, especially since "Congress did not want the voices of the Socialist…the Bolsheviks, the evolutionists or the obscene heard on the radio."[139]

The year 1924 opened other new doors as well. The format of the ever-faithful *Bridal Call* was changed. Gone from the cover was the apocalyptic imagery of Christ coming in the clouds. The words *Bridal Call* in the masthead became smaller, overshadowed by the larger name *Foursquare*. The format

The Bridal Call's *new dress. The bridal mysticism and the apocalyptic imagery of Christ coming in the clouds has disappeared (author's collection).*

grew both in size and professionalism, rivaling any secular monthly magazine with outstanding photographs and beautiful art work. Aimee explained,

> In keeping with the magnificent Angelus Temple and the Evangelistic School, we have given *The Bridal Call* a new dress. We hope you will like the change. It is indicative of our growth and development. With our new magazine and the Angelus Temple radio we hope to reach everyone by either the written or spoken words.[140]

Innocence had ended—a secular spirituality based on middle-class values was forming and Aimee, much like the radio, had come of age. Unknowingly she had two remaining years left to bring together and unite in her ministry "the most ancient" with "the most modern."

Even the Assemblies of God seemed to have a change of heart about Aimee a year after Angelus Temple opened. In the January 5, 1924, issue of *The Pentecostal Evangel* the following report was included:

> One who has recently returned from Los Angeles brings a splendid

419

report of the work done by Sister McPherson in the Angelus Temple. This temple has been opened nearly a year and during every week in the year there has been a baptismal service at which forty to eighty, mostly converts, have been baptized in water....There was a time, when Sister McPherson turned in her Council credentials and was ordained as a Baptist pastor, that we feared that she was going back on our Pentecostal testimony....There are many who are in these days greatly depreciating the ministry of women, believing that such is unscriptural....when our God is using the sisters to the salvation of souls, to the healing of the sick, and to the baptizing of believers, who are we that we should withstand God?[141]

CHAPTER NINETEEN

New Protestant Boundaries:
Salvaging Methodism and Saving the Mainline by Purging
Pentecostalism and Pushing it to the Periphery

On October 11, 1918, the Reverend Charles A. Shreve wrote a letter to his new parish, McKendrce Methodist Church, 921 Massachusetts Avenue, N.W., Washington, D.C. Among other things, Shreve sought to explain his absence to his new congregation:

> On account of sickness, I have not been able as yet to meet the members of the church either in public services or in their homes, so I am taking this means of introducing myself to you until such time as I can see you face to face. I trust that you and yours are being kept safe from the prevailing disease which has overtaken so many of us...in the troublous times... [1]

"The prevailing disease" that prevented Shreve from assuming pastoral duties at his new parish in Washington, D.C. was the influenza epidemic of 1918, which also accounted for one of the Nation's more "troublous times." Prior to coming to McKendree, Shreve had played an important role in the other major event of 1918—the war effort. Serving as field secretary of the War Work Department on the Board of Home Missions, Shreve had been commended by his bishop for "doing better work...in... Washington...than any other denominational representative."[2] Early on in his ministry at McKendree, his church observed that "His messages...were scriptural and captivating [and] they graciously appealed to the spiritually minded."[3]

Perhaps because of his own recent brush with death, Shreve asked Aimee in March 1920 to assist him in special meetings at McKendree. The church's historian recorded the outcome:

> Crowds attended...her ministry...it was impossible...to get into the church. The audience chamber and lecture room could not accommodate them. The people would assemble in the avenue in front of the church long before the time for the services awaiting opportunity to

enter when the door was opened. The Holy Spirit's power was wonderfully in evidence in the meetings in conversions and Divine helps and healings.[4]

When Shreve himself received "'the coveted blessing' of the baptism of the Holy Spirit .... Our church," the historian concluded, "was taken back... to the historic times when enthusiastic Methodist ministers preached the Word. Brother Shreve...kept the fires of evangelism continuously burning... emphasizing the baptism of the Holy Spirit, the healing of diseases and the second coming of our Lord, insisting that Jesus Christ is the 'same, yesterday, today and forever.' Yes, preaching with power.[5]"

At the end of 1921 a report on the "McKendree Charge" appeared in the denominational periodical, *The Methodist.*

> The Heavenly breezes are still blowing on this charge. For more than a year the work of the Lord has been going forward with revival power. In twelve months there have been about 500 conversions, and many have been baptized with the Holy Spirit. Over 150 members have been added to the church since ...1920....Numbers of people have been healed of their diseases and testimonies from these are very helpful to the faith of others in the meetings. Some have been healed instantly, while others have improved gradually.[6]

In addition to the numbers associated with conversions, healings, and membership, the report mentioned other numbers. "Finances have gone far beyond anything known before...and a spirit of optimism prevails among the people....One hundred and eighty-eight have signed tither's cards.... Reverend Shreve received the highest salary ever paid up to his time by the church."[7]

Not only did the church experience growth and change due to its acceptance of Pentecostalism, Shreve's ministry also greatly expanded. "His ministrations," wrote the historian, "were in demand from practically every part of the country. He was continually flooded with letters from the north, south, east and west, urging him to...help...[with] the speeding of the world's evangelism."[8]

Five and a half years after Shreve's arrival at McKendree, there were nine hundred conversions, four hundred fifty new members, and a debt of $2,600 was retired. Shreve refused to take any credit for McKendree's success, simply stating, "The Lord had done the work."[9] It was also stressed that the church's success was not the result of "spectacular" or "sensational" methods. "The Gospel just as it appears in the Bible has been preached and the people have believed in the fact that Jesus Christ is 'the same yesterday and today and forever.' "[10]

McKendree's Pentecostalism had also expanded Shreve's social vision. "Besides... [the] specialty of revival work," Shreve shared the following as vision for his congregation:

> A Vocational Training Institute...
> An Emergency Hospital for those unable to get into other hospitals from financial or other reasons...
> An Emergency Home for Old People...
> An Emergency Temporary Home for homeless...
> An Industrial Department in touch... with employers...[11]

The truth was that after five and a half years of ministry at McKendree, Shreve's Pentecostal inspired vision had expanded not only beyond the boundaries of his church but also his denomination. "Brother Shreve," declared the church historian, "has lifted McKendree Church out of the ranks of obscurity, and into national prominence so that today the church of the 'lighted cross' is known and loved across the continent...Brother Shreve will leave behind him a heart-broken congregation." It was also recorded by McKendree's historian that in the spring of 1925 "Brother Shreve...withdrew from the ministry of the Methodist Episcopal Church and entered evangelistic work."[12] As Martin Marty noted in his *Modern American Religion*, "The mid-twenties...produced a permanent schism between Protestantisms and within the culture at large."[13] By the mid-1920s, mainline Protestant boundaries were no longer expansive or elastic enough to embrace Pentecostalism. Although Aimee had blurred the boundaries in the early 1920s and had introduced the movement to the Protestant mainstream, a reaction quickly ensued, and McKendree Methodist Church was representative of that story as well.

On April 13, 1924, the Reverend S. Carroll Coale preached on "The Spirit-Filled Life," his first sermon as the new pastor-in-charge of McKendree Methodist Church. Coale's take on "The Spirit-Filled Life" was not what his congregation was used to or expected from their new minister. Aware that his predecessor had withdrawn "from the Baltimore Conference of the Methodist Episcopal Church to engage in evangelistic work in the Pentecostal faith," Coale knew he had a hard road ahead. "I will never forget that moment," Coale wrote, "when Bishop W.F. McDowell read these words, 'McKendree, S. Carroll Coale.' My heart seemed almost to cease its beating. But soon it was stirred again by the challenge of that glorious old hymn

which the Conference had just sung—
> A charge to keep I have;
> A God to glorify;
> O may it all my powers engage
> To do my Master's will."[14]

It would be a difficult charge for Coale to keep, made even more difficult by performing not his Master's will, but his district superintendent's. Upon adjournment of the conference, recalled Coale, "my brother ministers gathered about me to wish me 'well,' but their remarks were rather disquieting....My District Superintendent said, 'I want you to go to McKendree and salvage what you can for Methodism.' "[15] If Methodism by the end of the twentieth Century was tempted to claim parentage of Pentecostalism, it is equally clear that by the mid-1920s it viewed the movement worse than a bastard child.

Slowly at first Coale, with the blessings of his bishop, began to dismantle all that Shreve had worked so hard to put in place. "I found the church," claimed Coale, "hopelessly divided over certain religious practices which we have come to accept as thoroughly unmethodistic. McKendree had become a sort of headquarters for the Pentecostals."[16]

> Let me name several perplexing problems which I faced as I began my pastorate.
>
> One question which caused strife and contention was the use of unknown tongues....Fortunately this was discontinued at the very beginning of my pastorate, but the trouble which had begun could not be readily healed.
>
> A second difficulty arose out of the practice of anointing with oil. In the first service which I conducted some of the officials made the request that I anoint a woman with oil....When I declined to do this, I was severely and openly criticized.
>
> A third problem was caused by the kind of emphasis which a large group placed upon divine healing.
>
> Still another problem was the clash between the fundamentalists and modernists. How these two groups loved each other!
>
> I need not tell my readers how hopeless it seemed to bring about a reconciliation.
>
> I will go no further with this...story except to say that many letters of transfer had to be issued for the sake of harmony, and many changes had to be made in the personnel of committees and boards in the interest of efficiency and cooperation.[17]

The hundreds who left McKendree more for the sake of hegemony than harmony were lost to the Methodists for good. They faced few options. Purchasing the former North Capitol Methodist Church on K Street, they quickly transformed it into the Full Gospel Tabernacle. By 1935 it was noted that the tabernacle had "a large congregation and Sunday School."[18] In 1934 the congregation called Ben Mahan as their pastor. Mahan was regarded "as one of four well-known pioneer preachers in the Assemblies of God" and as "a man with rugged convictions, a preacher of solid Bible messages."[19] Not only did Mahan bring the Full Gospel Tabernacle into the General Council of the Assemblies of God less than three months after his arrival, he was also able three years later to purchase McKendree Methodist Church itself. After the church was purchased, it was extensively remodeled and enlarged for the growing congregation. Mahan was especially well suited for his role as a Pentecostal pastor in the nation's capital. "He looked a lot like Franklin D. Roosevelt...and he wore dark pants and a dark, silk-looking coat in the pulpit which was very becoming."[20] And as at Angelus Temple "an orchestra played on Sunday evenings."[21] Under Mahan's leadership "several government employees" also began attending the church.[22] And despite the Reverend Coale's claim that "the use of unknown tongues" had been "discontinued at the very beginning of my pastorate," they were soon back at McKendree under Mahan. "Ben...maintained good scriptural order in the services and was sensitive and open to the moving of the spirit, including the operation of tongues and interpretation."[23]

McKendree Methodist Church in many ways served as a microcosm for what was occurring in American Pentecostalism as a whole. Not only was Aimee able to win many mainline converts for the movement, she was also both directly and indirectly responsible for adding many Full Gospel Tabernacles and churches to the ranks of the Assemblies of God.

For the Reverend S. Carroll Coale and the many ministers just like him, one thing was certain: salvaging Methodism and saving the mainline meant purging Pentecostalism and pushing it to the periphery. Aimee had served as a bridge in the early 1920s, bringing Pentecostalism into mainstream Protestantism. She had been able to do so partly because of her unique personality, which was so well suited to the rise of modern America. She was also able to tap into what was still left of the once united front of the Progressive Era and in the process receive the much-needed support that some of the liberal evangelical pastors extended to her. But the times were quickly changing, and her days of fishing for whales in the deep waters of mainstream Protestantism would soon end. The coming of the fundamentalist-modernist controversy "produced a fatal crack in the prevailing Protestant ethos," as Ferenc M. Szasz notes in his *The Divided Mind of Protestant America, 1880-1930*. "From the united front of the Progressive Era, which was characterized by a unified attack against injustice, the Protestants of the 1920s turned against each other, splitting into separate factions."[24]

Nowhere was the theological split among mainline Protestantism as noticeable as the one that played out on the stage of Princeton Theological Seminary. Lefferts A. Loetscher, a 1923 graduate and future professor of the seminary, has written, "The unfolding events had finally made mutually incompatible two tendencies which had existed side by side in the Princeton Theology from the beginning—a broad and warm evangelicalism on the one hand and a highly rational orthodoxy and extreme literalism on the other."[25]

Prior to the Protestant fracture and even after it, "a broad and warm evangelicalism" had been Pentecostalism's best theological friend, while "a highly rational orthodoxy" proved to be its worst enemy.

Not only did the coming controversy push Pentecostalism to the periphery, forcing it from the mainline to the sideline, the movement itself was forced to take a theological stance and position. Dogma was rapidly replacing dance in Pentecostal self-definition. Again, as Szasz astutely points out, "The Seventh-Day Adventists, Pentecostals, Holiness groups, Church of the Nazarene...sided with the Fundamentalists. They all shared a common conservative interpretation of Scripture."[26] As early as 1919, E.N. Bell, a former Baptist minister, graduate of the University of Chicago Divinity School, and the first general chairman of the Assemblies of God, sought to theologically identify and define the churches he had been elected to serve.

> These assemblies are opposed to all radical Higher Criticism of the Bible and against all modernism and infidelity in the Church, against people unsaved and full of sin and worldliness belonging to the Church. They believe in all the real Bible truths held by all real Evangelical churches.[27]

The creation of new Protestant boundaries in the mid-1920s had a far greater impact on mainline Protestantism, however, than it ever did upon Pentecostalism. That movement did just fine sitting on the sideline. Pentecostalism, much like the African-American religious experience from which it was derived, "rendered the margin a site of power and creativity, an activity that necessarily alters the character of the center."[28] By becoming hardline and losing its elasticity and expansiveness, the center of mainline Protestantism collapsed. Between 1916 and 1926 the mainline churches (The Presbyterian Church in the U.S.A., the Congregationalists, the Disciples, and the Methodist Episcopal Church) lost 5,631 congregations, while those on the sideline (the Southern Baptists, the Assemblies of God, Church of God, Christian and Missionary Alliance, Church of the Nazarene, Churches of Christ, Free Will Baptists, the Pentecostal Holiness Church, and the Salvation Army) grew a staggering ten thousand new churches during the same decade.[29]

Over the next half century, evangelicalism, America's folk religion, would replace the Protestant mainline as the country's new big tent of Christianity. By 1981, Cullen Murphy could rightly argue in *The Wilson Quarterly* that American evangelicalism had become a veritable "12-ring show" made up from a dozen various groups ranging from "peace-church conservatives" to "lively black Pentecostals." More importantly, argued Murphy, was that anyone who peered into the vast tent of evangelical faith would "find a lively 12-ring show in progress, with true fundamentalists holding the attention of only part of the crowd."[30] "Fundamentalism," concluded Murphy, "was merely a subculture within 'mainstream' evangelicalism, a relatively young and extreme movement within an older, moderate one."[31] And David R. Swartz's recent Notre Dame Ph.D. dissertation under George Marsden brilliantly chronicles a more up-to-date version of American evangelical diversity by examining the origins and rise of "the evangelical left" from 1965–1988.[32]

With a divided mind, mainline Protestantism quickly lost its own soul. By 1933, Alfred North Whitehead was able to observe, "Its dogmas no longer dominate; its divisions no longer interest; its institutions no longer direct the patterns of life."[33] By failing to erect the big tent of inclusiveness, ironically, Protestantism itself was pushed to the periphery, a sideshow of its former self, no longer the major American altar where the vast majority congregated and worshipped. The once proud and prosperous Protestant mainline was reduced to an alternative altar as one more religious option among the many. "In the 1880s, the nation's culture," concludes Szasz, "was largely dominated by organized Protestantism...By 1930 no one could make that claim....Protestantism had been pushed from the center of national life to the periphery."[34] And it was also, in Sydney Ahlstrom's words, "the critical epoch...when the mainstream denominations grew increasingly out of touch with the classic Protestant witness."[35] "In the long run," observed the cultural historian Richard Wightman Fox, "the much more significant cross-denominational evangelicalism...displaced liberal Protestantism from its position of cultural dominance."[36]

Historian of religion Catherine L. Albanese broadens the discussion beyond the theological categories of fundamentalism and modernism by arguing that there are "two kinds of religion" and that "Protestantism, more than any other religious movement, tried to make a clear distinction between the two."[37] Using Albanese's model and typology mainline Protestantism was "ordinary religion":

> The religion that is more or less synonymous with culture. Ordinary religion shows people how to live well within boundaries. [It] tends to be at home with the way things are....Because it is about living well within boundaries, it values the social distinctions that define life in the community and respects the social roles that people play.[38]

Pentecostalism, on the other hand, fits Albanese's definition of "extraordinary religion":

> The religion that helps people to transcend, or move beyond, their everyday culture and concerns. Extraordinary religion grows at the borders of life as we know it and seeks to cross over. [It] encourages a special language that also distinguishes it...The special language...maps a landscape that people have not clearly seen. It gives people names for the unknown and then provides access to a world beyond....Here, then, are forms of "spirituality" that unlike the spirituality of ordinary religion, challenge believers to pass into unknown territory. Mystics and prophets are the heroes and heroines of extraordinary religion.[39]

Since Pentecostalism thrives in parts of the world untouched by the fundamentalist-modernist controversy, the distinction Albanese makes between ordinary and extraordinary religion is far more useful in delineating the historical differences between mainline American Protestantism and Pentecostalism. The question that American Pentecostals face presently is why has their once extraordinary religion of new wine become trapped today in the old skins of ordinary religion? And when did the movement's heroes and heroines, those colorful and controversial mystics and prophets, become mere mortals, now forgotten and replaced by bureaucrats and priests?

CHAPTER TWENTY

May 18, 1926

An Evangelist Drowns

Through green-white breakers swift I leap,
Sun-sparkled seas by body keep;
Bearer of Gospel-Glory I
With singing angels in my sky,
And earthly chorus at command,
The trumpets of my silver band!
The cripples to my temple crowd,
I heal them, and they shout aloud.
A thousand miles my raptures go
Upon my magic radio.
Time, space and flesh I rise above,
I turn them into singing love...
What's this? A terror-spasm grips
My heart-strings, and my reason slips.
Oh, God, it cannot be that I,
The bearer of Thy Word, should die!
My letters waiting in the tent!
The loving messenger I sent!
My daughter's voice, my mother's kiss!
My pulpit-notes on Genesis!
Oh, count the souls I saved for Thee,
My Savior-wilt Thou not save me?
Ten thousand to my aid would run,
Bring me my magic microphone!
Send me an angel, or a boat...
The senseless waters fill her throat.
Ten million tons of waters hide
A woman's form, her Faith deride;
While thousands weep upon the shore,
And searchlights seek...and breakers roar...
Oh, gallant souls that grope for light
Through matter's blind and lonely night!
Oh, pity our minds that seek to know
That which is so—
And piteously have forgot
That which is not!

—Upton Sinclair,
New Republic, June 30, 1926

Louis Adamic, who Carey McWilliams called the "prophet, sociologist and historian" of Los Angeles, wrote after visiting Angelus Temple that "Mother Kennedy is the engineer who keeps the machine in good shape, sees that the wheels are well greased and the nuts screwed tight."[1] Minnie was also the engineer who "kept Aimee walking that straight little narrow path from Manse to Temple back to Manse."[2] Minnie was even more direct and to the point in describing their working relationship. Years later after she had left the temple for good, she mused to an inquiring reporter that "There was a day when I was needed at the Temple to keep Sister Aimee in the harness—to rein her back when she was inclined to scamper."[3] But in the process of her treadmill and tightrope existence, Aimee Elizabeth Kennedy had become far more than just her mother's daughter—more than the extension of maternal dreams and fantasies. Aimee had become for her followers during "the continuous revival" what Emile Durkheim the French sociologist of religion called a "collective representation."[4] Durkheim believed that human communities tended to project their deepest feelings about their own collectivity on some person or emblem, because at an intuitive level they knew that their own lives depended on the survival of the group. The group itself, however, is too large and shapeless to become the object of such throbbing, surging energies, so they are focused instead on the collective representation.[5] By early 1924 Aimee Semple McPherson clearly fit the concept of a collective representation. The "throbbing, surging energies" were most present on Sundays when Aimee's treadmill existence began its weekly cycle. Those who knew her claimed they "never knew

"Sheep without a shepherd," Angelus Temple members watch the surf being dragged in a search for Aimee's body. The temple paid three hundred dollars for airplanes and forty dollars per day for drivers to search for her (used by permission of the Herald-Examiner Collection/Los Angeles Public Library).

The parsonage in the shadow of Angelus Temple. Minne kept "Aimee walking that straight little narrow path from Manse to Temple back to Manse" (author's collection).

anyone who worked so hard, so tirelessly and kept such long hours."[6]

Sunday, especially, was the "electricity" day. The most common expressions to describe the services on Sunday were ones having to do with electricity: "The people were electrified," "there was expectancy and something electric in the air," "the service, itself, would be electrified." "Even over the radio her voice had an electrical vibrancy," recalled Harry Carr, the *Los Angeles Times* columnist. "It was a trumpet call to battle."[7] A trio of electric-like "trumpet call to battle" Sunday services started early. At 8:30 a.m. the three-hundred-foot frontage of doors—all seventeen of them—opened. When the temple doors open, the streets are temporarily closed—flooded with people exiting either from parked cars or from the overflowing red street cars stacked up like Western cattle cars en route to market. An hour later some 2,500 children have gone to their 106 classes to receive instruction from 153 officers and teachers—including lessons in Spanish, Armenian, and Japanese. At 10:20 the seventy-five male ushers under their captains and the sixty "lady orderlies" under the direction of Mother Kennedy spring into quiet, efficient action. Crowds of thousands are quickly and quietly moved from the streets into the 5,300 theatre-style seats spread out on the main floor and the two galleries. The dome a hundred feet overhead shines brightly from its six hundred concealed light bulbs. At 10:30 the mighty Kimball organ peals forth, and down the ramps marches the choir—robed like their Sister in white. Soon, Sister herself opens the upper door on the right side of the first balcony—directly across from where her mother is stationed. The red tint of her abundant auburn hair catches the far corner of the spotlight, and the feeling of electricity begins. Quickly down the right ramp she walks. She fills out her cotton uniform, and her black wool cape lifts off from behind like an airplane going down a runway. (With increased prosperity, crepe and satin will replace the cotton and wool.) Her movement toward the pulpit is only interrupted when on occasion she briefly pauses to greet a happy "sister" always waiting—joyfully waiting to see her. That sister is always there at all three services, come rain or shine, sitting in the curve where the right rampart connects to the platform. She is the black face in the sea of smiling otherwise white ones, always decked out, always wearing her high black boots with hook and eye buttons and always waiting for her "sister."

Aimee pauses temporarily in her throne-like pulpit chair while the organ produces the effect of chimes ringing in the distance. Stepping up to the pulpit, she begins the service by pressing a button on a small black signal box that tells Kenneth Ormiston in the radio control room to disengage the organ microphone and activate the loudspeaker. With the opening hymn, the first service at Angelus Temple is underway, and Aimee is on the radio with "over a million listeners composing the cathedral of the air."

The Sunday morning service was always a standard evangelical worship service. The songs and special music would all fit around the theme of Aimee's message. The sermon itself would be highly inspirational, with background material coming from her two favorite sources of information: *Matthew Henry's Commentary* and various works by Charles Spurgeon. If it was the first Sunday of the month, communion would be served. In what was undoubtedly the largest partaking of the sacrament, sixteen quarts of grape juice and four pounds of unleavened bread were consumed at every service. The event moved with precision in less than twenty minutes, with the assistance of ninety-eight deacons, eight deaconesses, and four elders. On the second Sunday of the month the equivalent of child baptism— child dedication—was observed. The service would end promptly by 12:30 so that the next service could begin on schedule—two hours later.

The afternoon service at 2:30—again always full when most Southern Californians were either at the beach, mountains, or amusement parks— was highly eclectic and seemed to be something of an afternoon holdover from Aimee's camp meeting days. In the temple's "program of services" it was simply listed as an "interdenom-inational-dispensa-tional address." More accurately, however, was a description by one of Aimee's future Foursquare ministers: "[There is] a sermon to Christians on the deeper life and consecration, and an old-fashioned altar service where battles are fought and victo-

An early illustrated sermon (author's collection).

ries won, backsliders reclaimed and sinners converted."[8] It was obviously a time Aimee immensely enjoyed, for between forty to sixty new members were taken into fellowship with Angelus Temple every Sunday afternoon. (Of the 12,023 reported conversions of 1924, 5,304 claimed they had never before been connected with any church.) This Sunday matinee of sorts would end by 5:30 when all seventeen doors would again be locked. In preparation for the final trilogy of services, a janitorial squad swarmed over the three floors while large fans concealed behind the organ grill circulated the auditorium air. Meanwhile the streets were congested again with many waiting an hour to an hour and a half in hopes of getting a seat. Once the doors opened, the temple would fill to its capacity in five to ten minutes time.

Coupled with the Wednesday afternoon healing service, Sunday evening's "evangelistic message" (often times "illustrated") was the heart and soul of both Aimee and Angelus Temple. It was for Aimee that magic transcendent moment when the treadmill was broken and she was back preaching her heart out to throngs of strangers and tourists—back to being an evangelist. Also, with the illustrated sermons, Aimee in some ways fulfilled her childhood wish of becoming an actress. On Sunday evenings the sacred and the profane came together harmoniously.

A feature of the Sunday evening service was the "musicale hour." For an hour the temple band dispensed such familiar secular and quasi-religious selections as Sousa's "Washington Post March," Sullivan's "Lost Chord," a waltz-time arrangement of "Mighty Lak' a Rose," and "Radiant Morn

433

March."[9]

At five minutes to seven the familiar figure in white makes her final Sunday appearance at the first balcony door. Aimee, although fatigued, looks beautiful clutching her three dozen roses while standing alone in the darkness of the Temple, about to be bathed by the brilliance of the spot-light. Soon she is down the ramp, the button on the small black signal box has been pressed, and Aimee joyfully, triumphantly with vibrant voice and waving arms is leading the standing congregation in two stanzas of "Stand Up, Stand Up for Jesus." Other favorites follow in swift succession while the audience is allowed to sit temporarily. A stereopticon aids the tourists and visitors in their attempt to join in on the singing by flashing the catchy words on a large bare spot on the left-hand wall. A secular journalist from the 1920s astutely observed that on Sunday evenings, "It is her service, let no man forget that. Not for one moment does she drop the reins."[10]

If Aimee was preaching an "evangelistic message," then the house lights were dimmed and a spotlight from a booth in the first balcony illuminated her. She as always would cut a striking figure in the light, holding aloft her Moroccan white leather Bible in her right hand with sermon notes safely concealed inside. Sunday evenings were "soul-winning" nights and by the time Aimee reached her famous line, "Ushers, jump to it! Turn on the lights and clear the one-way street for Jesus!" the altar would be engulfed with penitents.[11] For churchgoers who witnessed and experienced those "elec-tric" Sundays, Aimee's success was simple to describe. "She made Christ so real in those early years, recalled one loyal member, "because she was so in love with him, herself." Aimee as the bride of Christ "gave meaning to lives in their search for God."[12] The highly carved pulpit Aimee preached from bore two inscriptions. The one the audience saw declared that it was "not by might, nor by power, but by My Spirit, saith the Lord." The inscription only Aimee saw simply stated "We Would See Jesus." For Aimee the actress it was her basic script, one she never deviated from nor failed to deliver. Her competition had, argued Aimee, "dethroned the experience of the heart and lifted to pre-eminence the experience of the head."[13]

"Right at the outset," Aimee later wrote, "there was borne in ...me the realization that the methods...used to impart religion were too archaic, too sedate, and too lifeless ever to capture the interest of the throngs."[14] Capturing the interest of the throngs as she did in Los Angeles, Aimee replaced the archaic, sedate, and lifeless methods with modern messages that were less characterized as sermons and more as "a series of stories within one big story that spoke to the heart."[15] As a storyteller Aimee used "short, chopped sentences...grouped in [a] series and made the discourse

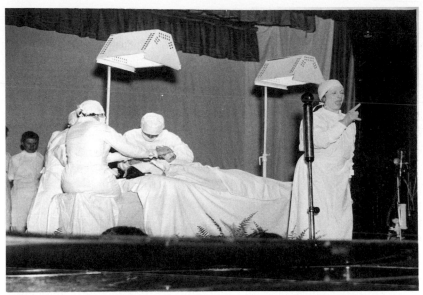

A later, more sophisticated version of an illustrated sermon (author's collection).

move at a rapid pace."[16] Following only an outline neatly tucked inside her Bible, such stories were told extemporaneously by using one and two syllable words. Much like Mark's Gospel, the simplest of the Synoptics, Aimee's stories were both simple and full of impetuous activity. "Such words created clear-cut imagery, keeping interest at a high pitch....They [also] added to the action and excitement created by the situation in the story."[17] More often than not, humorous illustrations followed each short narrative in an attempt to show the audience how such a story paralleled their own lives. Interestingly, one researcher found that only 2.5 percent of Aimee's messages were quotations from scripture.[18]

Monday was something of a day of rest for Aimee and the temple, although not entirely. By high noon, Thompson Eade, her close associate in charge of producing the illustrated sermons, would make his way over to the parsonage. Aimee would then inform Eade of her sermon topic the following Sunday evening and offer her ideas for scenes and props to illustrate the message. Eade, with the help of his two paid assistants and the "construction gang" of artists, electricians, and carpenters, would then turn by week's end the rough sketch into finished form. Beginning rather modestly as "chalk talks" based upon simple Bible stories, with time the "illustrated sermons" became rather elaborate productions complete with lighting, Max Factor makeup, and costumes from the Western Costume Company of Los Angeles. The illustrated sermons were much like television in its infancy in the fact that anything could happen. Since there were no rehearsals, it was very much "live" and things did in fact happen. Aimee would at times lose her petticoat and manage to either kick it into the pulpit or behind the proscenium arch curtains while other "actors" temporarily forgot where they were and accidentally fell into the full baptismal tank.[19]

The previously mentioned 1926 religious survey of Los Angeles disclosed that "74.3 per cent of the total adult population were not members of any religious group, Protestant, Catholic, or Jewish."[20] Of the 290,625 church members, not quite half, 142,625, were Protestants.[21] Religious disaffiliation was not unusual or unique to Los Angeles. The city simply was part of the larger "Unchurched Belt" of the Pacific West.[22] Despite the lack of church members, the survey also took note of the fact that moving picture theaters in Los Angeles were selling "approximately a million tickets per week."[23] Less than ten years later the University of Southern California published Carl Douglas Wells' *The Changing City Church*. In chapter two of his study, "The Motion Picture Versus the Church," Wells argued that "the urban Protestant church and the motion picture theater furnish an interesting comparison; and such a comparison is enlightening as a study of why certain institutions in city life are more popular than others."[24] A casual glance of Wells' chart of comparisons between "The Church" and "The Movie" clearly shows that Aimee's messages especially on Sunday evenings had much more in common with the movies than they did the church. A theater marquee later attached to the exterior of Angelus Temple itself only aided the comparison. Aimee's religious genius was in the creation of a "secular-spirituality," combining the most ancient with the most modern. It was a theology of the vernacular. "She marched," said Jerry Sheppard, "to an older drummer in the history of the Christian church, to…a jazz drummer in the history of divisive enthusiasm."[25] Like the movies, Aimee's Sunday evening services had "efficiency and swift movement." They appealed "directly to strong human desires" and "to the fundamental wish for new experience." Even the mechanics were the same; "the story, drama, artistically chosen and rendered music" with "colorful lighting effects."

Carey McWilliams not only captured the essence of Los Angeles in the early 1920s but his neighbor's Sunday evening services:

> Los Angeles…was beginning to experience a major boom. The postwar period…had already given birth to the Jazz Age….It was a time…for movie "palaces" and automobiles. Los Angeles itself was just emerging from a long period of a glacial fundamentalism, its ice age of Protestant orthodoxy. In near-by Hollywood, the movie colony was in its "purple

period" full of scandal and commotion. All America was stepping out on an emotional binge, and Aimee was determined to lead the parade on a grand detour to Heaven....Here Aimee proceeded to entertain "the folks" with pageants, picture slides of the Holy Land, music, dramatized sermons...She reveled in love and happiness. She invited the folks to feel at home, to relax, to have a good time. She released their minds from frightful visions of eternal damnation. Instead, she gave them "flowers, music, golden trumpets, red robes, angels, incense, nonsense, and sex appeal."[26]

Again, as he did with radio, Charles Reynolds Brown helped to illustrate the "ice age of Protestant orthodoxy" when it also came to modernity and the movies:

Forty years ago there were no movies...now they are everywhere. They have wrought a...change in the mental habits of multitudes of people. They offer a cheap, easy kind of diversion which cannot by any stretch of the imagination be called a form of art. When real actors and actresses do their work on the stage, they are engaged with real people. They have the sense of response from an audience.

But when one goes to the movies, all he sees is a lot of people having their pictures taken in a social vacuum out at Hollywood....it is pathetic.

But those films are carried...to every street corner in the cities and to every crossroads in the country. The number of people who go almost passes belief—sixteen millions a day....when a whole generation of people has been fed profusely upon that sort of gruel, it is not easy to interest them in a square meal of the bread of life.[27]

For churches to grow in modern America it seemed it was more important to embrace modernity socially and culturally rather than theologically, especially in Los Angeles, the new "national and international symbol of urban frontier modernity."[28] Los Angeles was also the capital of the entertainment industry. From 1920 to 1940, movie production was the city's largest industry, followed by real estate, oil, and oranges. While Pentecostalism remained pre modern theologically, it increasingly bought into the popular culture associated with rise of Southern California. The declining mainline Protestant establishment, on the other hand, while accepting modernity theologically, simply could not adapt to or accept modernity's changes "in the attitude of multitudes of people." California gave the impression, wrote one mainline religious historian, "of a religious circus in the tents of secularity."[29]

Aimee's brand of Pentecostalism quickly adapted to mid-dle-class values, becoming the newest version of American civil religion (author's collection).

Marcus Bach in his *Report to Protestants: A Personal Investigation of the Weakness, Need, Vision, and Great Potential of Protestants Today* reminded his mainline readers that there was great variety within Pentecostalism. There was the Pentecostalism of the Assemblies of God and of Aimee Semple McPherson:

[Aimee's] was Pentecost, Hollywood style. This was Pentecost with the last and greatest of the women evangelists. Visitors to southern California used to say, "What shall we do tonight—go to a show or go to hear Aimee?" This was Pentecost with…a prayer tower to keep in touch with the heavenly powerhouse, a training school to turn out leaders…a radio station…to give the Devil some competition on the airways, commercial bookshops, and free commissaries to attract both the rich and the poor. [30]

Terry Lindvall reminds us in *Sanctuary Cinema* that during the Progressive Era, the mainline Protestant church "sought to maintain its authority as the arbiter of morality and taste" by creating its very own "Sanctuary Cinema that would …enhance its mission to a public slipping away into a mass culture of silent dreams."[31] By the early 1920s, however, when several scandals erupted in Hollywood, spokespersons for the Protestant establishment such as Charles Reynolds Brown, "began to look more askance at the place of movies within its holy boundaries."[32] Lindvall rightly concludes, "The church's ambivalent relation to the moving picture reflected the uncertain and schizophrenic connection the church had to modernity itself [especially since] the spirit of modernity reigned over the realms of the motion picture industry."[33] Aimee's Hollywood-style brand of Pentecostalism had no such problems with the spirit of modernity. And it was her style, her imprint that would shape the movement's megachurch future. If Pentecostalism began as a lower-class protest movement preaching "A Christ Against Culture," it was quickly transformed by Aimee into a more middle-class accommodating movement offering the more acceptable "Christ of Culture" instead, becoming in the process the latest and newest version of American civil religion. By relaxing its tension, especially with the surrounding Southern California culture, American Pentecostalism was quickly able to complete its sect-church cycle by the start of the Second World War. Aimee herself could have just as easily penned Amos Wilder's famous phrase, "If we are to have any transcendence today, even Christian, it must be in and through the secular."[34]

"People with practical Christianity," preached Aimee, "are not slow pokes. They are wide-awake folk. When there is a new invention such as the radio, they seize upon it and use it for the glory of God."[35] And seemingly there were no modern weapons in the secular arsenal either that were off-limits for Aimee's "practical Christianity." In May 1923 *The Bridal Call* announced yet another "secular" first for Sister. "Sister McPherson...made the first eight-minute record ever known...she is putting her whole heart into it and the records are going to be a great success."[36]

"Remember you have competition," Aimee told her students in her class on homiletics. "There are the movies and the boxing-galleries and the bowling alleys. Students, beat the old devil at his game and come prayed through, with the power of God upon you and [use] every means you can at your disposal to get the message over."[37]

Beating "the old devil at his game" supports the thesis advanced by the anthropologist Richard T. Antoun that Aimee in actuality was practicing "selective modernization" and "controlled acculturation":

> Selective modernization is the process by which certain technological and social organizational innovations are accepted at the same time that other innovations are rejected....Controlled acculturation is the process by which an individual of one culture accepts a practice or belief from another but integrates that practice or belief within his or her own value system. One particularly appealing and effective version of controlled acculturation...is antagonistic acculturation, the process by which an individual of one culture accepts new means from another without adopting the corresponding relevant goals; on the contrary, the new means are utilized to oppose the goals of the other culture, to undermine them and to realize one's own goals.[38]

"Pentecostalism," notes Walter J. Hollenweger, "has a certain down-to-earth this-worldliness secularity, and that makes it attractive."[39] And nobody ever made the movement's secularity spiritually more attractive than Aimee. She was its founder and greatest practitioner. By the early 1960s the president of Princeton Theological Seminary, John A. Mackay, saw that "the true hope of ecumenism" was charismatic renewal because "uncouth life [was] better than aesthetic death."[40]

At noon on Mondays and most every day, the students and workers with their musical instruments held "shop meetings" at fourteen local factories such as the Ford assembly plant or the Southern Pacific shops. The radio station KFSG remained silent on Mondays, when the incoming mail was especially heavy. In the afternoon at l: 30 the famed Five Hundred Room—the very heart and soul of Angelus Temple—opened for its daily services, with the exception of Sundays. This was the modern pool of Bethesda, or as the deaconess in charge put it, "This might well be called the melting pot of Angelus Temple, for it is here that the rich and poor, sick and well, Christian and sinner, mingle together seeking a common level for brotherhood in Christ."[41]

Under the guidance of a deaconess, between five and six hundred persons attended the daily meetings and were taught the Scriptural basis for divine healing. They also registered to be prayed for by Aimee on either Wednesday afternoon or Saturday evening. Each candidate for healing was required to fill out a questionnaire in advance during the daily meetings. Either a verification slip or a doctor's certificate was required, documenting that the candidate was in fact ill. A complete record of each case prayed for by Mrs. McPherson was then kept in the office files. The deaconess in charge of the "Five Hundred Room" reported that 96,259 ailing souls attended in 1924 alone.

> How heart-rending has been this throng! Coming on crutches, in wheel chairs, and on stretchers; coming blind, deaf, halt and maimed; suffering with cancers, tumors, rheumatism epilepsy, this great procession has come day after day, throughout the year. Patient they have been for the most part; each in honor preferring the other ahead of themselves.[42]

Mondays at Angelus Temple concluded with music department rehearsals and Sunday school staff conferences. Aimee would often accompany her students on Monday evenings, preaching again either in tent meetings or various halls of the sprouting branch churches. At 10:30 Tuesday morning and for the next consecutive four mornings Aimee was on Radio KFSG with *The Sunshine Hour* "for the sole benefit of those who are lying on beds of pain, cripples in their chairs, mothers in the home and all who need a bit of sunshine in their hearts." With *The Sunshine Hour* Aimee attempted to dispel the loneliness, darkness, and silence out in the vastness of her "great unseen audience." On Tuesdays, the day after the downtown merchants' sales day, the Bible School was back in full operation, including both morning and evening classes. After giving an afternoon address on "The Holy Spirit" Aimee would give an "evangelistic address" in the evening either at the temple or in the other fledgling Foursquare churches in the surrounding suburbs.

Next to Sundays, Wednesday was obviously a favorite day for Aimee. It was a day in which her other concern—health and healing—held sway, and in the evening service a very down-to-earth Aimee would emerge. Perhaps wanting to avoid the reputation as a "faith healer," she permitted only two weekly services in which she prayed for the sick. The first of these occurred on Wednesday afternoons at 2:30. It was held in the main auditorium, and there was an average of three thousand five hundred people in attendance from all classes of society. After the usual song service and devotional, there was a "healing testimony service"—a cause for hope among the sufferers.

Early in the spring of 1923 a reporter for the *Los Angeles Times* attempted to describe the type of person that came to an afternoon healing service.

> They came in haughty limousines, dusty flivvers, wheelchairs, stretchers, by street car and on foot. Drawn from all of the various strata of life, most of them were members of the middle class—and most of them were women. The ratio was about six women to one man, but since it was an afternoon session, the average may not be a just one.[43]

The surplus of women to men in the Wednesday afternoon healing service was atypical for the rest of the services. It simply reflected a time when most men were at work. (The 1936 federal census of religious bodies showed a high ratio of 65.5 men per 100 women for the International Church of the Foursquare Gospel.)[44]

The success of the Wednesday afternoon "Divine Healing Service" led to two more Angelus Temple creations: the Bethesda Service Society and the Miracle Room. The former, according to an early directory of the temple, was "possibly...the most unique society of the entire Angelus Temple organization. Its membership is entirely composed of those who have been definitely healed in answer to prayer."[45] With their motto 'healed to serve,' not only do they pray for the sick and afflicted, but they render actual physical aid to those in distress."[46]

The Miracle Room was a trophy room from the Wednesday and Saturday Divine Healing Services. "Here are displayed," read a brochure about the room, "crutches, braces, hypodermic needles, x-rays of injuries or broken bones and other evidences of past illnesses and suffering left by those who have been healed, as a testimony to the world that Jesus is indeed the Great Physician and is able and willing to heal."[47]

An article appearing in *The Bridal Call* in late 1924 about the weekly activities of Angelus Temple stated,

> At 7:30 p.m. the weekly church prayer meeting is conducted by Mrs. McPherson, who usually gives a series of doctrinal sermons....This service is largely attended by members of Angelus Temple. A rousing testimony meeting always precedes the sermon...One thing about this service that will impress the stranger is that members do not have to be urged to testify. Fifty or seventy-five people will be standing awaiting their turn, and the meeting sometimes almost runs away from the pastor's hands.[48]

And it was in this mid-week meeting, largely attended by members of Angelus Temple, that Aimee was less an evangelist and pastor "of the world's largest Class A church" and more "Beth," a very real and at times bewildered person. It was on such occasions that she would unknowingly among her perceived friends expose her Achilles' heel. America's most personal playwright, Tennessee Williams, suffered from the same affliction—"the affliction of loneliness," which became the major theme of his writings. Williams in his memoir wrote, "This greatest affliction followed me like a shadow, a very ponderous shadow too heavy to drag after me all of my days and nights."[49] Aimee's "great affliction," which came from deep within, was more like an overflowing well than a ponderous shadow, which politely waited for family and friends before it would spill over. But spill over it did, usually among her Bible School students or in her mid-week teaching messages, always through an autobiographical illustration or sermon. The Wednesday evening services undoubtedly provided the only opportunity for the Angelus Temple membership to truly know their "Sister."

Thursday afternoons were set aside as "deeper teachings for Christians," while the evenings were reserved for the "water baptismal service." Every Thursday evening, with Sister conducting and Brother Arthur assisting, at least forty and not more than one hundred fifty converts were immersed in the temple baptistery. A former Methodist minister, Arthur was the temple's mainstay, "perhaps the most beloved and respected staff member Angelus Temple ever had, serving from the opening of the church until his death in 1935."[50] A *Bridal Call* article on the subject for those who couldn't attend captured the spirit of the weekly event:

> The Baptismal service each Thursday night is a very impressive scene. The lights are turned out by the electrician, the big Kimball organ is

humming in soft tone, the curtain slowly rolls back and you see a beautiful picture of the winding river Jordan, with beautiful mountains and fertile valley. At the edge of the picture are seen artistically arranged cobblestones with water cascading down. A powerful, bright light is thrown upon the picture, which gives it a very realistic effect. The converts are gracefully immersed.[51]

Fridays and Saturdays were more or less given over to young people and children. On Friday evenings the "Crusaders" met—some fifteen hundred of them for their own service. Then on Saturday afternoons anywhere from eight hundred to twelve hundred children gathered and conducted their own weekly church service. Their supervisor noted, "In this service the children do all the work, from the ushering, and leading in singing and prayer, to the preaching and giving of the altar call."[5] Saturday evenings concluded the weekly activities with the second "divine healing service." The average weekly attendance at the temple was between forty and fifty thousand. KFSG would average thirty two hours of air time a week, with Aimee preaching anywhere from six to twenty-one hours in any given week.

Charles S. Price, the Congregational minister converted under Aimee, wrote of the opening of Angelus Temple for *The Bridal Call* that he related the events in fairy-tale fashion. "Once upon a time—I suppose I had better begin that way, for this story sounds like a fairy story, and all such stories do begin with—once upon a time."[53] The opening months of Angelus Temple did in fact read like a fairy tale—however, in such tales lurk villains in the crooks of the road, and the fairy tale of Aimee was of no exception.

The chief villain in the crook of the road of the fairy story of Aimee Semple McPherson was a Southern Methodist clergyman and a fundamentalist—the Reverend Robert Pierce "Fighting Bob" Shuler. Edmund Wilson, writing about religion in Los Angeles, observed that the Reverend Shuler's only charm came from the "whiff of the cow manure from his heels."[54] *The Christian Century* concluded that Shuler "was a blatant and obnoxious personality."[55] The *Los Angeles Times* summarized its hometown minister as a "mischievous and trouble-making gossip" who "threatens the good name of the city of Los Angeles and the safety of its citizens."[56]

"Fighting Bob" had been born rural poor, and when he came to Los Angeles in the early 1920s, he insisted on at least remaining the former. He spoke, as Edmund Wilson noted, with "the cracker box vernacular of the backwoods," and he lived out at El Monte like a farmer, raising his own stock and vegetables on a ten-acre farm. El Monte was the ideal suburb for Reverend Bob—it had a reputation for being rough and tough. An early

Porter Barington, pastor of Hollywood First Baptist Church, left, with Billy Graham, center, and "Fighting Bob" Shuler, in 1948 (used by permission of the Herald Examiner Collection/ Los Angeles Public Library).

description of the community summarized it as follows:

> The settlers, generally referred to as the "Monte Boys," were South-
> ern Democrats of the fire-eating type, excellent farmers and stockmen,
> quick on the trigger, hard drinkers, devout Protestants, and so true to
> the Texas tradition that the citizens of Los Angeles invariably turned to
> them for help when the lawless elements in the city's decidedly mixed
> population threatened to get beyond control.[57]

"Fighting Bob" rode into Los Angeles one day in the early 1920s fresh
from a Texas town and rapidly became convinced that he could preserve the
"enormous village" of Los Angeles as an "ideal Protestant town," saving
it from becoming "Tinsel Town"—a place of picturesque characters or a
haven for exotic cults. In his championship of true Protestant orthodoxy,
Aimee would become one of the first of his many intended victims.

Shuler, who had "no trace of theatricality or sophistication," received a
thorough ministerial apprenticeship before coming to Los Angeles. Born
in a log cabin in the Blue Ridge, he was preaching the Methodist gospel by

age seventeen in small coal mining towns of Virginia and Tennessee. Early on, he was transferred to Texas by his bishop, where for a dollar a day he rode a small circuit of churches. In Texas Shuler soon became "Fighting Bob," at times employing his fists in the Lord's work against the saloons and liquor interests. But it was as pastor of the Trinity Methodist Church in Los Angeles that he both tasted success and really began to fight. Earning ten thousand dollars a year in 1925, while his fulltime associate was paid only three thousand dollars, "Fighting Bob" had graduated to other causes beyond saloons and liquor. Armed with the free services of a private detective, Shuler set up his own private police force to rid Los Angeles of perceived corruption. Soon the exposés were coming with rapidity from both his pulpit and pen—the crusade against high school girls who posed in the nude for a friend, the exposé of a couple (both school teachers) who trysted in public until a streetcar hit and killed the man, and who's who of the latest Hollywood scandal. He was given his own radio station in 1926, KGEF, by the wealthy widow Lizzie Glide of San Francisco. His station, as *Time* magazine noted, "fairly screamed against Roman Catholicism, religious and social liberalism, pacifism. [Shuler] succeeded in discrediting a district attorney, a city prosecutor, two chiefs of police. He was sued for libel by the Knights of Columbus…and by one time mayor George Edward Cryer whom he accused of graft. Twice found guilty of contempt of court, he was jailed once…By vilifying a whole field of candidates, he helped elect Los Angeles Mayor John Clinton Porter (an ex-auto parts dealer and Klansman)."[58]

When Angelus Temple was dedicated in January of 1923, "Fighting Bob" was dominating the local Los Angeles headlines for his attempt at running the comic actor Fatty Arbuckle out of Hollywood after the actor was tried and acquitted on a charge of manslaughter in the death of an aspiring actress. Shuler insinuated that Will Hays, first president of the Motion Picture Producers and Distributors of America, had reinstated Arbuckle "because he was bought off by Jewish money." Shuler vehemently argued that Arbuckle should never go back to motion pictures "because his appearance on the screen would contaminate the youth of America."[59]

In a year's time, Shuler, perhaps out of jealousy as well as "doctrine" (his pastoral reports reveal a constant striving for more money), aimed his guns across town at Aimee. Shuler's attacks on other faiths were not new. Catholicism to Shuler was "Romanism," which was "un-American." "It is foreign in its sympathies and activities…Its pathway is one of human illiteracy, the pauperizing of its willing slaves, and the degradation of the highest and best in man."[60] However, it is doubtful that Shuler unleashed any more of

445

his poisonous venom than he did on what he termed "McPhersonism—a study of healing cults and modern day 'tongues' movements."

The attacks began as Sunday evening sermons—a month of Sundays—starting January 6, 1924. The series became so popular that Shuler turned the sermons into pamphlets, publishing several editions with the latest one offering more sensational revelations regarding Aimee's personal life. Shuler also ran a condensed version of his "McPhersonism" sermon in his booklet, *Series of Sermons on Doctrine*. Choosing the Biblical text John 4:l, "Beloved, believe not every spirit but try the spirits whether they are of God: because many false prophets are gone out into the world," Shuler attempted to save the orthodox from the following: "Christian Science," "Paganism of Romanism," "McPhersonism and Kindred Cults," and "Spiritualism and Salvation by Psychology." Shuler was hoping to keep Los Angeles the ideal Protestant town—as pure as could be found out on the West Texas prairie. Aware of the growing pluralism of the "enormous village," Shuler hoped that the advancing evils, including Aimee and Pentecostalism, could be purged by a return to fundamentalism:

> Los Angeles is perhaps sheltering today more isms and schisms, more conflicting notions, more new and so-called advanced ideas, more alluring systems and enticing programs than any city in the whole world. Everybody has come here. Everything has been brought along. All gods and no God have their forums in this beautiful city. Therefore, I as a pastor of a Methodist Church, feel that the hour has come to make a very clear and certain statement...upon some of these theories...that deny what our fathers have taught from the beginning...[61]

Shuler's personal attacks on Aimee are best seen in a small sample of "Some Interesting Facts" published in the pamphlet, *McPhersonism*:

> Mrs. McPherson has posed for more photographs than any other woman in America, outside of the show business.
>
> Mrs. McPherson's early ministry was directly connected with what is known as the "Holy Roller movement."
>
> Today, Mrs. McPherson confines all "tongues" demonstrations to a "sound-proof," padded room within her Temple.
>
> Mrs. McPherson's attitude to her husband and home, if sanctioned by Christianity, would strike a death blow at the marriage relation.
>
> An astonishing percentage of insanity has also followed Mrs. McPherson's campaigns, the wife of one of her leading Disciples having been among the victims.
>
> The most startling and serious moral delinquencies are reported in

connection with the work at Angelus Temple certain prominent workers having been among those thus offending.[62]

At the conclusion of the pamphlet Shuler published an interesting letter written by a former member of Angelus Temple. The member defected to Shuler's fold due to the increasing worldliness of Aimee. Evidence of worldliness was cited as follows:

> Your apparent mania for making yourself the cynosure in so many pictures, and scattering photos of yourself…over the world, is shocking… Entrenching yourself behind the "big business" of Los Angeles; joining its Chamber of Commerce, and repeatedly telling your audiences that you are a member of same—I ask you, what do you do with our instruction: "Be ye not unequally yoked" together with unbelievers…And have you never read where it says: "Thus saith the Lord: Cursed is the man that trusteth in man (including L.A. press)…for several months past I have been hoping for better things, but my heart has been deeply pained to see a still stronger worldly trend."[63]

The "worldly trend" continued, however, with Aimee's growing unification of the secular and spiritual. When Los Angeles failed to become the ideal Protestant town and became Tinsel Town instead, Aimee would be ready. "Fighting Bob" by January 1924 had clearly put Aimee on his enemies list, documenting again the fact that the infant movement's chief enemies were the fundamentalists.

Not all of the villains lurking in the crooks of the road in the fairy tale of Aimee and Angelus Temple came from the outside. Increasingly, "the engineer who keeps the machine in good shape, sees that the wheels are well greased and the nuts screwed tight," Ma Kennedy herself, was being perceived as a possible villain. On August 24, 1923, only seven months after the temple opened, a group of one hundred "loyal supporters of the work at Angelus Temple" signed a petition addressed to Aimee. In seven statements "the committee" elaborated their discontent—most of it having to do with Mrs. Kennedy's style of running the temple. "The committee" then proposed a four-fold remedy:

> 1. That a church organization be effected with the regular and legally constituted officials.
> 2. That Mrs. McPherson be relieved of all obligations and responsibilities, by such officials, save that of her ministry to the congregation.
> 3. That the property be secured to the organization.
> 4. That Mrs. Kennedy be immediately relieved of all connection with

Angelus Temple and paid the sum of $25,000 as remuneration for her services in building up the financial affairs of the Temple.[64]

Aimee attempted to smooth over the rift, even as other cracks of a much larger magnitude began appearing in the temple walls—all having to do with the engineering of Ma Kennedy. Sharing headlines with stories about the attempted kidnapping of actress Mary Pickford and how silent-film star Rudolph Valentino's second wife deserted the "idol of the flappers" were stories about the Santa Ana branch church of the Foursquare Gospel. Suing their leader in the Orange County Superior Court, the branch church alleged misrepresentation on the part of Aimee and Minnie, the "reputed power behind the throne." The suit charged that their "flapper evangelist," Miss Bessie Mae Randall, had been taken away from them, that there had never been an accounting of the money sent to the temple by the branch church, that local members had been discharged by the temple, that fifty chairs and a communion set had been taken by the temple, and that two branch members had been excommunicated by Angelus Temple leadership.

At the heart of the lawsuit was the issue of church polity. The members of the Santa Ana branch believed that once their building loan, advanced by Angelus Temple, had been paid off, they would receive a deed to their property as well as a voice in governing their affairs. By her drastic actions taken against them, Ma Kennedy made it abundantly clear that it would never happen on her watch as the temple's business manager. Rather her daughter, "Aimee Semple McPherson [was] to have full control and authority and dictatorial power over [their] religious organization." Furthermore unless everyone "would promise and agree to follow Aimee Semple McPherson now and forever, they could no longer be members of the Four Square Church of Santa Ana."[65]

When the news about the Santa Ana branch church lawsuit reached "Fighting Bob's" ears across town, he felt vindicated and predicted the fate of his church competitor: "The dupes are suddenly awakening and our modern day prophetess of Angelus Temple is in for it."[66] Although Aimee was on a collision course with her mother, she attempted to remain the dutiful daughter. Minnie's dictatorial policies extended even to Aimee, who was paid only twenty-five dollars a week by her mother, while the temple was rife with stories about Minnie hoarding money in various receptacles around the building. By 1925, however, Aimee—to use her mother's colorful language from the farm—had clearly grown tired of too many years spent in her harness. And she was no longer willing to be reined in by her mother anymore. She was getting ready, in Minnie's words, to "scamper."

A former secretary to Aimee, who later became a therapist, remembered both mother and daughter as "two strong women." But once "Aimee tasted freedom she wasn't willing to go back under her mother's strong domination." Because Aimee acted "out of her tremendous energy and spontaneity, never logically thinking things through," Minnie had "kept her in line." Despite her "lack of judgment due to her impulsiveness" Aimee, however, by her mid thirties had simply "too much drive and energy to stay repressed."[67]

On August 26, 1925, less than a year's time before when she would mysteriously disappear, Aimee unknowingly shared some most personal thoughts with her followers. It was a mid-week Wednesday evening service composed mainly of Angelus Temple members and a time when the real Aimee or "Beth" was present. She was teaching her favorite Biblical book the one she called "the jewel box"—the Song of Solomon. She knew of "no other book" that she would rather preach. She had just finished talking about "trials and valley experiences" when she impulsively, inexplicably stated the following:

> I do want to so fix the eyes of Angelus Temple on Jesus Christ that if anything happened that I should be called home to Glory, or go to England or Scotland or Wales; if I should say "Folks, I have to go," I would feel the church would go on and not go to pieces. I like to feel that we have people here who would go on with the work just as though I were here. Then if your leader makes a mistake or your leader dies or backslides, it would not shake you, you would not stumble over her, because your eyes are on Jesus.[68]

In a very similar tone was the final sermon that she preached in 1925. It was given just before her vacation to the Holy Land—her first vacation in fifteen years and first absence from the strenuous temple activities. It was entitled "Carry On." "Last works of famous people have ever been of great interest," declared Aimee in the sermon. Starting with the story of Abraham, Aimee related how the vision of God was passed to each successive generation. As always she made the message personal:

> Ne'er forgotten shall be that precious day when my mother put in my hand the lighted word and said: "Carry on, Aimee! Carry on."
>
> Now I reach over to my little girl and say "Roberta, go out and go on with the work! Carry on, dear heart! Carry on!"
>
> Had anyone told me fifteen years ago that I would occupy this pulpit,

Paul Rader saying goodbye to Aimee and Roberta. Rader was the only evangelist who could fill the temple in Aimee's absence (used by permission of the International Church of the Foursquare Gospel, Heritage Department).

and become the pastor of the largest fireproof Church in America, have this powerful radio, be the editor of this Foursquare magazine which is translated into other languages and goes around the world; I would have said, "Never! Never! I am but a farmer's daughter in the Canadian countryside. I am only little Aimee Kennedy."

Brother! Sister! Will you help me? May not every one of us become a mighty evangel of the Gospel of Jesus Christ?

The Old Testament prophets carried on! The disciples carried on! Our fathers carried on! It is now for us, of 1925, to carry on![69]

"I detect a far-away look in her eye," wrote H.L. Mencken about Aimee in the 1920s, "and I detect a heavy heart....I suspect that she is by no means as happy as she tries to look."[70] On January 11, 1926, Aimee left the temple with her mother and Chicago's Paul Rader to "carry on." Aimee and Minnie earlier agreed on separate vacations—Minnie's was to commence after Aimee's return. Toward the end of her three and one half years of strenuous activities, tell-tale signs of fatigue were showing—mostly the dark circles under Aimee's eyes. She seemed momentarily revived that January day, when in a trim blue tailored suit holding a bundle of American Beauty roses in her arms, she said goodbye to "nearly 10,000" of her followers congregated at the train station.[71] Paul Rader, the only evangelist who could sustain the crowds at the temple in Aimee's absence, used the observation-car platform as a pulpit and offered a final prayer. Minnie wept as the train pulled out of the station.

Rader, the most overlooked figure in modern American evangelicalism, was far more than Angelus Temple's supply pastor for Aimee's first real vacation. The author of the famous healing song, "Only Believe," pastor of the famed Moody Church (1915-1921) and his own Chicago Gospel Tabernacle (1922-1933), Paul Rader in many ways had provided the template for Aimee's ministry in Los Angeles. Not only did Aimee carefully copy Rader's entrepreneurial skills as a successful evangelist-pastor and denominational administrator, she also altered his long coat tails when it came to her subsequent use of radio, publicity, church music and programs, and even the role of divine healing in her ministry. And when she reached her lowest ministerial ebb in 1932, the only person she secretly consulted about purchasing her religious empire was Rader.

Suffering from the long shadow cast by Billy Sunday, Paul Rader was far more than one of the many, dime-a-dozen, Sunday fundamentalist clones sprouting up in the 1920s. In tone and style, Rader and Aimee had been cut from the same modern ministerial cloth. Unlike their predecessors, they represented the future, not the past. Only eleven years her senior, Rader displayed a preaching style and tone more in keeping with Aimee's than either Sunday's or his faithful followers such as "Fighting" Bob Shuler and J. Frank Norris. "Rader," notes Larry Eskridge "could not be categorized as a 'fire and brimstone' preacher.[His] sermons accentuated the love of God...He was a preacher of the gospel of grace that aimed to motivate the hearer to Christ out of love, rather than out of fear. Often weeping during his sermons, many were impressed by what they felt was Rader's sincere love of God and sense of joy in his faith."[72] A former associate of Rader's always remembered the time a large African-American woman jumped to her feet and urged the preacher on with "Preach on, you beautiful angel! Preach on!"[73] "His style," recalled his daughter, Pauline, "was not Billy Sunday's although they were good friends."[74] "He had a gift of story telling...unequal to anybody I've ever heard," remembered the wife of one of Rader's musicians and youth leader. "Words just flew out...poured out of his mouth. And people sat there and could sit there for hours and listen to him. Every time a sermon...came to the end, they wished that he would keep on longer....He had a wonderful personality....People laughed. They were happy. They loved to come."[75]

If Rader and Aimee shifted gears theologically, they also made the transition to modernity, unlike many of their conservative contemporaries. Many fundamentalists simply saw radio as the Satan described in Ephesians 2:2, the "prince of the power of the air."[76] Some of the leading lights of fundamentalism viewed radio as "a worldly medium unsuitable for the purpose of spreading the Gospel." The 1920s, as far as they were concerned, were not a time for experimentation but a time to stick "to the tried and true methods of revivalism." For many a fundamentalist, radio was simply a "helpmeet of the movie, the lust of the ear… the serpent's mate that had crawled from the window of the theater on main street and [had] coiled herself right in the parlor."[77] Rader, like Aimee, viewed the new medium of modernity as blessed and heaven sent, even as a fulfillment of biblical prophecy itself.

Rader was not only a bridge to modernity but also to the megachurch future. A quick learner when it came to church polity, especially after the loss of his Moody Church pulpit, Rader rebounded a year later with the creation of his own Chicago Gospel Tabernacle. Not only was the tabernacle pastor-led, but it was also "without membership, church board, or denominational hierarchy to restrain him."[78] Paul Rader reclaimed all the necessary power and control to make his theological vision a reality. Never forgetting a boyhood spent in a Methodist parsonage where he had witnessed first-hand "the dirtiest politics," Rader "believed that cumbersome organizations, multiplicity of boards and committees, and inflexible denominational hierarchies created conflict and stifled the love and enthusiasm of the Church's rank and file."[79] Aimee was never as successful a pastor as Rader was in his monopoly of church polity. Ever dependent upon her mother and business managers, her ministry suffered many schisms and setbacks as a result. Church polity, or who really has the power and control, has always been the megachurches' best kept secret.

Finally, Rader was remarkably at the time a theological bridge between conservative evangelicals and Pentecostals. After the creation of his own Chicago Gospel Tabernacle, Rader emphasized healing in his ministry "in a way that he had not been able to do at the more staid Moody Church."[80] Heavily influenced by the healing ministry of A.B. Simpson, Rader offered prayer for the sick at his tabernacle's Wednesday-afternoon prayer services. It was a theological model Aimee quickly and quietly employed at Angelus Temple. Such services, whether in Chicago or Los Angeles "bore little resemblance to the chaos and hysteria …of many Pentecostal faith healers."[81] In addition to his alignment with Aimee, Rader also associated with such early Pentecostal healing evangelists as Raymond T. Richey and F.F. Bosworth. "Rader's associations with these types," as Larry Eskridge astutely notes, "automatically earned him a place in the theological dog house of many fundamentalists."[82] Perhaps Rader's greatest influence on Aimee came from his limited use of healing as "a secondary role" in his ministry. His earlier example simply confirmed Aimee's spiritual intuition as to the priority and place her gift should receive.

Paul Rader not only filled in for Aimee during her Holy Land absence but provided a theological blueprint for Angelus Temple. Additionally, Rader served as a theological bridge to the future of American evangelicalism itself. One of Paul Rader's many converts, Charles E. Fuller, would help to usher in the new evangelical, post-fundamentalist era that his spiritual mentor had earlier envisioned.

Aimee's first real vacation was a personal as well as professional triumph for her. Roberta accompanied her mother on much of the trip, visiting for the first time her father's parents in their village home near Belfast in Northern Ireland. Aimee had also longed for years to travel the same streets and villages as her beloved husband. Personally, she was beginning to feel renewed away from the grueling schedule of the temple and Minnie's omnipresent watchful eye. Professionally the trip added more headlines to her career. She preached several times by invitation in England and on Easter Sunday filled the Royal Albert Hall, the largest auditorium in the British Isles, which seated twelve thousand people. From London Aimee journeyed back to Belfast, where she held yet another meeting in the Coliseum. The Lord Mayor of the city not only attended the meeting but sat on the platform, posed for pictures with the evangelist, and gave her a personal tour of City Hall.

Through the pages of *The Bridal Call* she kept faithful followers informed as to how she was feeling and what she was doing. Her first letter reflected some homesickness for the temple and the desire for more rest.

> We have not found any place like Los Angeles or Angelus Temple any-where and you may be sure that we pray for it every day…I am having a lovely time and praising God for His goodness in providing this wonder-ful vacation, but I am looking forward to the day when I will once more be back in Angelus Temple, refreshed and ready for another three years Holy Ghost Revival …[83]

In a second letter Aimee indicated more purpose to her ministry than ever:

> The vision of worldwide evangelism is clearer to me today than ever before. My heart is stricken when I think of the hundreds of churches and schools whose purposes and aims are bound by their own city…

Aimee returning to New York from France in the spring of 1926 after her first vacation. Her style of dress had begun to change and her followers said, "This is not the Sister who went away" (author's collection).

Their own doctrine and even their own walls…Wherever I have gone in my journey, I find that *The Bridal Call* has paved the way. Friends in Sweden, Norway, England, Ireland, Wales and other parts of the continent tell of the inspiration to "press on'" that has come through this messenger.[84]

On Saturday, April 24, 1926, after four months of absence, Aimee returned home to her city and people. As always her flock didn't fail her. Twelve thousand strong welcomed her back at the railroad tracks while another five thousand waited patiently at Echo Park. The city's acting mayor extended an official welcome home, a far cry from when Aimee first drove into the slumbering village with "Where will you spend eternity?" on the side of her Oldsmobile. That very evening Aimee was back in full swing of the temple schedule, conducting the weekly Saturday night healing service.

But the Aimee who had come back was different than the Aimee who had gone away. Minnie, of course, was the first to observe the change as well as the temple's faithful. "When she returned," Minnie wrote, "hundreds of people said, "That is not the Sister who went away.""

> No it wasn't. She was different. There was something almost ethereal about her when she stood on the platform. We could not persuade her to talk about business. Just a few days ago I tried to interest her in the improvement of the foyer which she always loved to have beautiful; but she just smiled and said nothing. I tried to interest her in the lights for the new school. She looked at them and smiled and said they were very pretty; but she never entered into any business of any kind…only the other day in the Bible school she said, 'Would you all carry on if the Lord took me home?'[85]

The temple schedule was more demanding upon Aimee's return than it was before she left. The crowds clamored to hear and see more of their Sister than ever before. Sister's absence had in fact made the temple's heart grow

fonder. On Sunday evening, May 16, 1926, Aimee, owing to the continuous crowds repeated her sermon, "The Scarlet Thread" three times and
declared to the capacity crowds:

> We of the world are children lost in the mighty mountain passes of life.
> The shadows are deep and dark. We have tried to find our way home
> by many paths but we have failed and become tangled and lost. Thank
> God! There is a Scarlet Thread which is attached to the throne of God
> in the Homeland far aways.[86]

Aimee's return had also rekindled the wrath of her chief enemy, "Fighting Bob" Shuler. Shuler even attempted to crash her homecoming party by
announcing from his pulpit on the same Sunday, May 16, that "The skids
are being put under Angelus Temple."[87]

Ordinarily Aimee did not speak at the temple on either Monday or
Tuesday evenings. However, the crowds continued their clamor for Sister
to present an illustrated travelogue of her Holy Land trip. The response,
like the previous evening's, was so overwhelming that Aimee repeated the
service at 9:30. The streets emptied again, and the temple had yet another
capacity crowd. Even the second service failed to completely empty the
streets, so Aimee promised a repeat performance the following evening.

Tuesday morning, May 18, 1926, Aimee bounded down the parsonage stairs "happy as a little child for a morning romp," remembered her
personal secretary and member of the family, Emma Schaeffer. She also
remembered that Aimee "greeted each one in the house with love and
kisses which was her usual custom." After "a delightful breakfast," Aimee
announced she would drive her Kissel car out on Wilshire Boulevard and
do some "shopping for her children." Around ten o'clock Aimee left the
parsonage and arrived a few minutes later at the original Bullock's department store. After purchasing a dress for Roberta, she looked for an outfit
for herself. Finding a black-and-white dress that she was somewhat unsure
about, she asked the saleswoman to hold it and telephoned Emma Schaeffer for another opinion. She made another stop at a small shop near Bullock's and returned back to the parsonage by 11 a.m. She then consulted
with Harriet Jordan, dean of the Bible School.

Desiring some rest from her ever-increasing schedule, Aimee decided
to return to her retreat—Ocean Park at Venice Beach. Venice was sixteen
miles out of Los Angeles—a residential community, oil-producing town,
and beach resort. It had been founded in 1904 by Abbott Kinney, who
not only named it but attempted to lay it out after Venice, Italy. Build-

Aimee presenting an illustrated travelogue of her Holy Land trip (author's collection).

ings were designed with Italian motifs, and artificial waterways served as streets, complete with gondolas poled by singing boatmen. Kinney sought to have his American Venice a place of culture with improving lectures, Chautauqua meetings, and art exhibits. The many tourists and area visitors, however, preferred the beach to culture, so in 1906 Kinney converted his dream city into an imitation Coney Island. The sixteen miles of canal were filled in, and dance halls, pleasure zones, imported freaks, and side shows replaced the art exhibits and public lectures. At the Ocean View Hotel at the corner of Ocean Front and Rose Avenue, Aimee had found a friend. Frank Langan, the manager of the hotel, insisted that whenever Aimee went to the beach that she use his rooms for changing instead of the public bath house.

At noon on Tuesday, Minnie was busy, Roberta in school, and Rolf was on a ranch in Northern California, so Aimee asked Emma Schaeffer to accompany her to Venice Beach. Her bathing suit was still in the car from the previous Friday's excursion. Aimee took her Bible, concordance, and some papers, intending to work on the next Sunday evening's sermon. It took a little longer than usual to reach Ocean Park, as Aimee got detoured on Pico Boulevard, which was torn up at the time.

Emma Schaeffer remembered that on the way to the beach Aimee "spoke often of her happiness…she loved even those who persecuted her and she mentioned how, if necessary, she would lay down her life for them…Oh, darling, you don't know how happy I am! Why shouldn't I be happy? I have never asked for a thing but that it has been given me!"[88] Aimee also talked about her mother's forthcoming vacation, scheduled for the following week.

Aimee parked her Kissel in front of the Ocean View Hotel and without seeing or conversing with anyone except the manager, changed into her bathing suit. After a glass of water and a waffle, Aimee and Emma walked to the beach. Upon renting an umbrella tent, Aimee began to outline her next Sunday's evening message, "Darkness and Light." She grew restless and went swimming, giving Emma an assignment to look up references—"the finishing touches for that sermon." Aimee gave Emma some additional assignments—to place a call to her mother and to return with some orange juice and candy. Emma recalled:

Brother Arthur, the temple's mainstay, preaching over the radio (used by permission of the Herald Examiner Collection/ Los Angeles Public Library).

We both left the tent together; she entered the water and I went on the errand. I was gone but a few minutes when I came back with the orange juice and candy which I held aloft. She was just in the edge of the surf and she called just as she often did, 'Bring it out—the water's fine!' I replied as usual, 'Oh, I can't.' She knew that I didn't swim, and did that just to tease. Lots of times she would call us just for fun to hear us answer back that we couldn't swim.

Opening the Bible I busied myself searching for promises, looking up every few moments to see her enjoying herself in the breakers.

Perhaps my eyes were down for ten minutes…when I looked up I could not locate her…I arose but still could not see her. Shading my eyes from the sun and scanning the waters anxiously, I failed to find any sight of her. After that I walked toward the Pier, but Sister was not anywhere to be found.[89]

The sad news was relayed back to the temple. As Emma Schaeffer sobbed out her story over the phone, "Brother Arthur," the temple's mainstay, quietly listened and took notes. Hanging up the phone, Brother Arthur hurriedly walked to the parsonage in search of Minnie Kennedy. "God bless you," Arthur stammered out when Minnie came to the door. "I don't know how to tell you, but Sister went swimming this afternoon at twenty minutes

Roberta Semple, Aimee's heir apparent, preaching at Angelus Temple (author's collection).

to three and she hasn't come back yet."[90] Minnie Kennedy turned back from the door to glance at the parsonage clock. It was after five p.m. Her daughter's Holy Land travelogue was scheduled to begin in less than two hours.

"Drowned. She is drowned." Mrs. Kennedy exclaimed to the bewildered Brother Arthur. It was a strange conclusion for a mother to draw so quickly about a daughter who was such a strong swimmer. It was even stranger, since Aimee had rescued Minnie from the strong undertow on the "same stretch of beach the previous year."[91] That night, while a score of temple workers set up a hastily erected headquarters at the beach to look for their leader's body, Minnie Kennedy stayed put in the parsonage. It wasn't until a week later that Minnie went to Ocean Beach, joining the thousands of temple searchers for her daughter. Less than two hours after Arthur delivered his message, the scheduled Tuesday evening service oddly went on as planned. Minnie Kennedy, "dry-eyed and in robes of spotless white," stood in her daughter's pulpit and announced Aimee's "home going." She then introduced her fifteen-year-old granddaughter, Roberta, to the capacity crowd, saying "This is Roberta…She will carry on the work of her mother for God."[92] Scared as never before in her life, young Roberta slowly and carefully began to speak, "It is my ambition to take up Mother's work just where she left off and if possible to do as much in the service of God as she did."[93] After she solicited prayers for her strength and guidance, the service mercifully ended.

In an ever increasing age of child evangelists who rivaled their contemporary Hollywood child actors in popularity, Roberta really was now more than ever a symbol of her missing mother. As the only heir apparent of Robert and Aimee, Roberta was simply too young and inexperienced to succeed her mother. Ma Kennedy realized she had to give in to convention and call on a famous male evangelist to rescue the temple's pulpit. Paul Rader, premier star evangelist, was immediately sent for. But Rader, who had just completed his tour of temple duty during Aimee's Holy Land vacation had previous commitments that prevented his encore return. During that eventful first week it seemed that everything mother and daughter had worked so hard to achieve was about to come crashing down. At the May 22 Saturday night service a church member from the Pasadena branch jumped to his feet and ran down the aisle toward the platform. Standing behind the pulpit while waving his arms and shouting at the top of his lungs, he attempted to convince the temple that he was, in fact, "ordained by God to take Mrs. McPherson's place."[94]

What may have worked in Victoria Hall or countless other Pentecostal storefronts and upper room missions no longer played in Angelus Temple. By now it was far more evangelical in style and substance than Pentecostal. Corralled by Mother Kennedy's efficient band of workers and ushers, Aimee's would-be successor was led outside while still shouting "Hallelujah." Fifteen minutes later he returned with a similar revelation. This was what Minnie had feared the most in her daughter's ministry. It could never again be allowed to get out of control. The incident also reminded her of her earlier decision to dictate to her daughter to no longer fish for the Pentecostal minnows but to go after the Protestant mainline whales. As if to reaffirm that earlier decision made in Baltimore, their good friend Dr. Charles Shreve from the McKendree Methodist Church in Washington, D.C. agreed to fill the pulpit. Shreve had also come to Aimee's rescue in Rochester, five years earlier.

For several days the Los Angeles newspapers mourned the loss of the "enormous village's" Good Samaritan. A feature story also appeared the next day about a temple member who claimed Sister's last words to her were "that when the time came for her to go to the arms of Jesus she prayed she might go by the way of the sea."[95] Such revelations, however, did little to console the grief-stricken temple. An old Irish ballad especially summarized the feeling of those in the "Five Hundred Room," the modern pool of Bethesda when it declared,

Sheep without a Shepherd;
When the snow shuts out the sky—
Oh, why did you leave us…
Why did you die? [96]

A Los Angeles columnist wrote to the missing evangelist:

> Your greatest miracle was turning our eyes to the long ago….Did you
> ever wonder why men and women with serene faces and hair as white as
> the frost in the meadows were moved to tempestuous tears?
>
> Not for their sins or their blunders….They wept because their
> Memory Bells were ringing when you pulled the silver cord that binds
> yesterday and today together….Again they were little children.
>
> And this, Aimee Semple McPherson, was the greatest miracle you
> wrought in your gentle, blameless life.[97]

The Assemblies of God, Aimee's former denomination and nemesis, also
mourned her loss in their periodical *The Pentecostal Evangel*:

> Aimee Semple McPherson was a gift from God…Many thousands in
> every part of the world have reason to thank the Lord for his gift of
> Aimee Semple McPherson, for she was the means through her evan-
> gelistic ministry of their being brought from death unto life….The
> news has come to us as a shock. Sister McPherson will surely be greatly
> missed. She has fought the good fight. She is one that has turned many
> to righteousness and we know that she will shine as the stars forever
> and ever.[98]

It was another Pentecostal periodical, however, *The Latter Rain Evangel*, that
best summarized the uniqueness of Aimee's ministry and even mentioned
the premonition of her passing:

> The whole Pentecostal world is shocked at the untimely death of Mrs.
> Aimee Semple, who was drowned in the Pacific Ocean…Mrs. McPher-
> son was a daring swimmer. She was daring in everything she undertook
> and had a fearlessness in her ministry which has rarely been equaled….
> Few evangelists have had the success which has followed Mrs. McPher-
> son's ministry. She preached the full Gospel with great simplicity….
> Before building Angelus Temple and confining herself to Los Angeles
> she had a remarkable ministry among the churches, carrying the full
> Gospel into a number of denominations and causing a number of min-
> isters and their congregations to seek the baptism of the Holy Spirit

and step out along the line of Divine Healing….A few days before her death she told the students of the Bible School to carry on the work should she pass away….There have been many reports concerning her mysterious death.[99]

Indeed, there were many reports concerning her mysterious death. Drowning. Suicide. Soon all the reports and "rumors began boiling over."[100] A manager of the Burns Detective Agency, J.W. Buchanan, was quickly retained by Minnie Kennedy. Buchanan, speaking simultaneously to the church and its vast radio audience exclaimed, "The air is full of wild rumors and that is all there is to it."[101] "Several thousand rumors surfaced in the first six days," reported the newspapers.

In addition to the wild rumors and reports, there were more sane speculations and theories to what might have happened to the missing evangelist. "Beyond doubt she wore herself out in the struggle to be the dynamo for so many thousand hopeless…despairing souls," wrote Harry Carr in his *Los Angeles Times* column three days after Aimee's disappearance. "There is nothing in the world so wearing—so devastating to the nerve force as to pull discouraged people out of their mental and spiritual mire."[102] None however seemed as specific as the one offered by Aimee's personal physician, Dr. Gustave Haas, who had attended to Aimee's physical needs in the past two years. Haas offered his own personal theory to reporters:

> Mrs. McPherson had a splendid physique but was undoubtedly working too hard. She was doing the work of three women in addition to being almost constantly under the emotional and psychological strain of her type of work. We frequently find in the cases of religious enthusiasts… that their zeal carries them actually past the point of physical endurance and for a time makes it possible for them to go on. But when that force snaps as it is quite likely to do, there is no reserve strength. Merely as a theory, I should say it would have been possible for Mrs. McPherson to have gone…and perhaps found refuge in some cabin.[103]

CHAPTER TWENTY-ONE

Resurrection in Arizona

Well.....she ended up here after she supposedly was kidnapped out in
Santa Monica, California...She dove into the ocean, into the waves, and
ended up ten miles east of Douglas on the Mexican side of the border
—Jean Lusk, a Douglas, Arizona, resident for eighty-seven years

RESURRECTED FROM 'DEAD' AIMEE SAFE
—*Arizona Daily Star*, June 24, 1926

There are no second acts in American lives.
—F. Scott Fitzgerald

Shortly after midnight on June 23, 1926, the custodian of the quaran-
tine slaughter house that sat on the international border between Agua
Prieta, Mexico, and Douglas, Arizona, heard a call for help from a stranger.
It was none other than Aimee Semple McPherson. Local newspapers, the
Douglas Daily Dispatch and *The Bisbee Daily Review*, had provided front-page
coverage of the evangelist's disappearance for five weeks. Their headlines
announced that she drowned while swimming at Venice Beach. The *Dispatch* on June 19, 1926, printed a story about the Los Angeles coroner
denying a request from Aimee's mother for a death certificate. On Sunday,
June 20, 1926, a memorial service for Aimee was held by her mother at
Angelus Temple. An estimated seventeen thousand persons paid their final
respects through a trio of services, while millions followed the three services by radio.[1]

For the official farewell for her daughter, Minnie had crafted a makeshift message on "Light and Darkness," taken from Aimee's sermon notes
that she had left strewn behind on the beach. The faithful temple devotees
sobbed aloud in the safety of their sanctuary as a soloist sang the anthem
"Asleep in the Deep." Back at the beach "an airplane dropped red and
white roses over the sea where Sister had last been seen."[2] Mustering all
her Salvation Army training for this time of trial, Minnie did her best, but
she too was rapidly failing. Her personal attendant who was a registered
nurse recalled,

Mother was down among the audience shaking hands with the people, not seeming to know just what she was doing, and the tears were streaming down her face....she seemed dazed and she sighed deep sighs as she walked....Her face was gray and she showed her lack of sleep and food. She appeared to have lost at least ten pounds and her breath was foul as a person's always is when suffering from sickness or deep sorrow and not eating properly.[3]

Despite her weakened condition, Minnie's persistence still prevailed both in the affairs of the temple and in the details of her daughter's perceived death. Meeting in secret session, the Los Angeles City Council listened to the pleas of Minnie Kennedy, presented on her behalf by Judge Carlos S. Hardy for permission "to bury Sister in a marble crypt beneath her favorite stained glass window."[4] Aimee's favorite window was fittingly the "healing window" next to Robert's "Gethsemane window."

Aimee, remembered her mother, "was always taken up by the windows, especially the one portraying Jesus healing the woman. She said she would like to rest under that window."[5] Despite a sympathetic city council, no amending of the ordinances governing the city's cemeteries could be made without a death certificate, which Coroner Frank Nance would not issue without a body. Finally, wearily, at the evening service Minnie suggested that Aimee's empty throne-like pulpit chair "would remain permanently empty," a silent symbol of Sister's absence.[6]

Four days later on June 24, 1926 the *Arizona Daily Star* read like a page in the New Testament when it proclaimed: "RESURRECTED FROM 'DEAD' AIMEE SAFE." Aimee Semple McPherson's "resurrection" in Arizona had severe consequences for her ministry and the remaining eighteen years of her life. If Southern California had defined Sister Aimee as a successful evangelist and revivalist, the event at the border town of Douglas, Arizona, quickly served to redefine her life and ministry. For the rest of her life Aimee Semple McPherson was no longer the spiritual "Sister," she quickly became "Aimee," someone perceived in a far more secular way.

The Protestant mainline churches would begin to withhold their support and approval because of the events that unfolded six hundred miles away in the Sonoran desert. One year later, in 1927, Aimee changed her "interdenominational" and "international" ministry into a separate denomination—The International Church of the Foursquare Gospel—one of few ever founded by a woman. The decision to create a new separate denomination was necessitated by survival reasons that began with the bordertown saga.

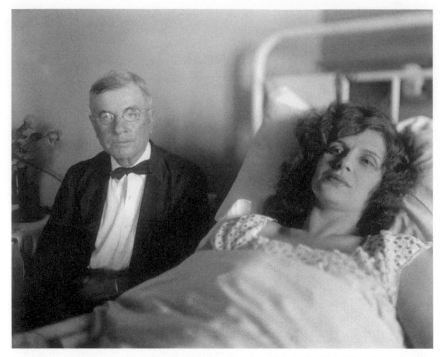

Arthur E. Hinton, mayor of Douglas, Arizona, at Aimee's bedside. "I feel," said Aimee, "like one almost resurrected from the dead" (used by permission of the Douglas Historical Society).

When the town of Douglas woke up to the news on the morning of June 23, 1916, that the famous missing evangelist Aimee Semple McPherson had been "resurrected" across the border in Agua Prieta and was now safe in their very own Calumet and Arizona Hospital, it seemed too good to be true. Her "resurrection" would be "their resurrection." From the mid to late 1920s things were looking good for the smelter city. The town's population, 14,000, was the third largest in Arizona. Even the municipal airport, begun during the war, had recently expanded into Mexican territory, earning the right to be called an "international" air terminal. Douglas was on a roll, hoping to become the "second Denver." Sister Aimee had provided a miracle. The world would beat a path to their door and soon the world itself would know all about the "Wonder City of the West." It was even declared a holiday by Douglas mayor Arthur E. Hinton.

On Thursday morning, June 24, 1926, the *Douglas Daily Dispatch,* which every day reminded its readers that "Douglas Is the Second Largest City on the Southern United States Border and the Gateway to Sonora, the Treasure House of Mexico," printed its most important edition in twenty-three years, with two-inch-high letters announcing,

"AIMEE SEMPLE M'PHERSON FOUND HERE
MOTHER AND CHILDREN ARRIVE 7 A.M."

The newspaper broke to the world a story surpassing Pancho Villa's raid on Agua Prieta in 1915.[7] The front-page news story especially noted, "CASE ATTRACTS WIDE ATTENTION TO THIS CITY."[8] On the same day headlines from the *Arizona Daily Star* in Tucson more dramatically proclaimed, "Nation Wide Search for Aimee Semple McPherson Ends in Arizona Border City."

> RESURRECTED
> FROM 'DEAD'
> Kidnapped from Beach
> Evangelist Held
> For Ransom
> STAGGERS TO BORDER
> Relates Lurid Story of
> Adventure and Cruelty. [9]

The following day the *Star* ran an editorial appropriately titled "Aimee Semple McPherson."

> There are many angles to the story of the return of Aimee Semple McPherson, Los Angeles evangelist, which have not appeared outspokenly in the news report.
> First of all, an advertising plum fell in the lap of the city of Douglas when Mrs. McPherson crossed the line and entered the Calumet and Arizona hospital. Douglas, being a wide-awake western town, was quick to recognize the return of the woman evangelist was the biggest news story that ever "broke" within its city limits. Douglas became the cynosure of western eyes. Telephone and telegraph wires buzzed; automobiles and airplanes raced to the Smelter City; photographers were pressed into extraordinary service; police guards were formed; searching parties organized; curious crowds gathered and speculated as to the how, where, when and wherefore. Douglas was virtually the news center of the west.[10]

Douglas had, indeed, become "the news center of the west." Over a hundred thousand words of copy were filed by reporters from Douglas in a single day."[11] One Arizona newspaper called it "A Strange Case," saying it was "the most bewildering in the history of the Southwest.[12] Still another Arizona paper declared it "The Perfect News Story." "A lonely trail through

cactus and mesquite...A good looking
and well known woman...A hinted love
affair...A tale of kidnapping...An international boundary...Even the subject
of sermons in the churches."[13]

Talbot T. Smith, a newspaper reporter
writing from Douglas, was perhaps the
most astute of all when he wrote, "There
is only one Aimee, but there are at least
five cameras and by actual count 22
newspapermen and women who must
have columns...about the 'resurrection'
of Aimee...All in all, it is the biggest
thing that ever happened to Douglas. As
a press agent, Aimee has made good, but
the question is whether she or Douglas
is getting the more benefit and the odds
seem to favor Douglas."[14]

*Percey Bowden, colorful Southwest lawman
and chief of police of Douglas, Arizona
(used by permission of the Herald Examiner Collection/Los Angeles Public
Library).*

His words proved prophetic. In the
end, Douglas seemed to benefit the
most from Aimee's "resurrection," but
in the beginning the odds were clearly
on Aimee. Four factions in Douglas unwittingly conspired to make her the
odds-on favorite. The first of these was the *Douglas Daily Dispatch*. One of
the first individuals to positively identify Aimee in her hospital room was
the newspaper's editor, William McCafferty. McCafferty had met Aimee
earlier at her revival in Denver in 1921—one of the most important in her
career. In her hospital room, McCafferty "recognized Sister McPherson
and she claimed to have remembered him."[15] Obviously a fan of Aimee's,
McCafferty printed her "lurid tale" of kidnapping word for word in the first
few issues of the *Dispatch*. Among Aimee's first words to McCafferty upon
his second visit to her bedside were, "I feel like one almost 'resurrected
from the dead.' "As other reporters came in, the evangelist announced,
"Douglas people are wonderful." She heaped praise upon the local newspaper. "I want to commend the veracity, the rapidity with which the *Douglas
Dispatch* got out their first extra. The story was absolutely correct."[16]

As Aimee was preparing to leave Douglas on the evening of June 25 she
once again singled out the *Dispatch* and its editor for special thanks:

> The *Douglas Dispatch* has been so splendid in its handling of the news
> for people here and the entire country. It was the *Douglas Dispatch* that

informed my mother that I was alive. I will never forget…Mr. William Fraley McCafferty's unfailing and splendidly efficient and brilliant service has brightened hours so dark.[17]

The second faction that portrayed a favorable image of Aimee in Douglas was the police department. When the former chief of police of Douglas, Percy Bowden, was eighty years old and in poor health, he decided to tell his story (and Aimee's) to writer Ervin Bond.

I went to my home at 648 Eleventh Street to get a bite to eat…the telephone rang. It was my night desk man, telling me in a shaken voice that Aimee McPherson had escaped from her captors, shown up in Agua Prieta, and was on her way to Douglas….I climbed into my car and rushed down to the police station.

I asked her to tell me how it all happened. She started telling me how she had been swimming off the coast of California at Los Angeles…. "two men grabbed me and put a blanket over my head…They kept me this way until dark. By then I am sure we…were headed to Mexico…Finally, we arrived beside an old adobe shack which I was informed would be our home until a large sum of money was paid for my release…After looking around, I saw a rusty tin can…I soon had the ropes cut, and out the window I went…As soon as darkness arrived, I could see the lights from the two smelters in Douglas and made straight for them."

All this time I had been looking her over, and at this point I told her that I could not believe her—that this whole thing was a hoax. At this I thought she was going to faint…I told her…if she had been kept in an old adobe shack for a month…her clothes as well as she would be filthy dirty…and if she had walked so far through the desert on a hot day like this one, that her clothes and shoes would be in shreds. I…told her… she had planned her story very poorly…she pulled a fainting spell and requested to be sent to a hospital…This request we granted.

After Aimee had been in the hospital…I got a call…from one of the doctors who was extremely angry. He asked me what I could do with the preacher-woman; the commotion was too great for the sick people… newsmen were taking over the whole place; groups were gathering on the porch praying; some people were climbing poles in order to get a look at her; and one would think that her mother owned the place…he said she might be a little tired but never had she had even one degree of temperature since she arrived…I told him…to…get her a room at The Gadsen Hotel.

I told her [Aimee's mother] that I would keep my story to myself and would send all news seekers of any kind to her, and this pleased her very much. I cautioned her that I still did not believe the story and would always stick to that.

No other incident ever happened in this small border town that gave it so much wide publicity as did Aimee's showing up here. She surely did have a staff writer on our local paper on her side.[18]

Bowden's observations were also shared by others. Sheriff James F. McDonald of Cochise County reached a similar conclusion when he too examined Aimee's clothing. After inspecting them for himself, he quickly locked them up in the vault of the First National Bank.[19]

The daughter of the night nurse who attended to Aimee in the early morning hours of June 23 "at the old Douglas Hospital" recalled what her mother had told her at the time:

> She told us they had a celebrity in the hospital. She told us all about Aimee. She said she had been in the desert and she had walked for miles and miles and finally found her way into Douglas....She could not have walked. Her clothes were too clean and her shoes weren't dusty. She herself didn't look like she walked any distance....gee whiz; she just looked like she just got out of the bathtub. She didn't look like she had walked ten miles across the desert. You don't come across that way without getting a little bit dirty.[20]

One reason Percy Bowden, Douglas' veteran police chief of fifty years, "covered for Aimee" was revealed in a May 1951 interview. When Bowden accompanied Herman Cline, chief of detectives for the Los Angeles Police Department, and Joseph Ryan, Cline's son-in law who was an assistant district attorney for Los Angeles County, in their search for a desert shack in Mexico, Bowden could see that "they [Cline and Ryan] were itching to explode Mrs. McPherson's story by getting her to identify some shack as the one from which she escaped. They never succeeded....and, although Bowden frankly admits he personally doubted her story, he was unwilling to see Aimee 'jobbed' by the Los Angeles city detectives."[21]

A woman in Douglas who also remembered Aimee's "resurrection" had a very different kind of memory. "She [Aimee] sure had all the men in town on the run, all she had to do was look at the men and they all fell down. One woman became so angry at her preacher husband she beat him up and left Douglas, which for a couple of days was in the national spotlight."[22]

The clergy (all male) provided the third faction that gave Aimee a favorable image in Douglas. While the Rev. Julian C. McPheeters of the University Methodist Church in Tucson delivered a negative, nasty sermon on Aimee Semple McPherson, not one lone voice of ministerial dissent

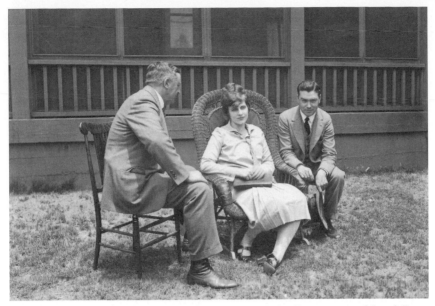

Herman Cline, chief of detectives for the Los Angeles Police Department and Joseph Ryan, Cline's son-in-law, assistant district attorney for Los Angeles County, interrogating Aimee in Douglas about the kidnapping (used by permission of the Douglas Historical Society).

existed in Douglas.[23] "Douglas people," said Aimee, "are just a little bit more warm-hearted than one ordinarily meets. Perhaps this may be due to the wonderful climate and the warm sunshine. Positively, I was particularly pleased with the prayers of the ministers…I want to print them every one in my own magazine."[24]

The ministers of Douglas did not disappoint her. Before her departure on Friday evening June 25, the clergy of Douglas organized a city-wide religious service with Aimee as their guest preacher. It is doubtful that Aimee ever again received such widespread ministerial support as she did at the Tenth Street Park. It was most certainly the last time in her career she was endorsed by so many Protestant mainline clergy at one time. But on that day in Douglas, they were all there—marginal and mainline, Baptist, Presbyterian, Methodist, Episcopal, Christian Church, Assembly of God, Salvation Army, African Methodist Episcopal church and even the Church of Jesus Christ of Latter-day Saints.[25] The Catholic church was the only one absent. Civic, social, educational and religious groups were all represented.[26] The band from Camp Harry J. Jones played military selections as well as "two famous hymns, 'Faith of Our Fathers' and 'Onward Christian soldiers.'"[27] Hundreds of cars lined the curbs surrounding the park, while thousands of eager listeners crowded about the bandstand to hear the "resurrected" evangelist preach. "Neither the heavy wind nor the rain which at periods fell rather heavily detracted from the gathering. The crowd was curious and the crowd was enthusiastic."[28] Aimee was short and to the point, using Psalm 107 as her text.

> O Give thanks to the Lord, for he is good…some wandered in desert wastes, finding no way to an inhabited town; hungry and thirsty, their soul fainted within them. Then they cried to the Lord in their trouble, and he delivered them from their distress; he led them by a straight way, until they reached an inhabited town.[29]

There was no mistake that Douglas, Arizona, was that "inhabited town." And everybody there also heard Aimee say that "every word I have uttered about my kidnapping and escape is true."[30] *The Bisbee Daily Review* noted how the service concluded. "Tears streamed down her face as she closed her short talk with 'God Bless you all.' Others in the crowd were crying openly as they pressed forward to touch her dress."[31] The crowd was estimated at five thousand and was "without doubt" the largest gathering ever held in Douglas.[32] Despite the all-male clergy present, that day a little girl from Douglas heard her first female preacher at the Tenth Street Park. It left such a memorable impression that years later when she moved away, she became an ordained Methodist minister.[33]

One of the civic groups that joined together with the clergy in honor of Aimee Semple McPherson at the Tenth Street Park was the Borderland Climate Club. This fourth and final faction conspiring to make Aimee look good was also the one segment, more than the rest, that expected "Douglas to reap as much or more benefit than Aimee, herself." Joseph W. Tardy, president of the Borderland Climate Club admonished Douglas residents to take full advantage of the city's latest bonanza and to quickly get on board the Aimee-Douglas bandwagon. Tardy claimed under the following headline:

AIMEE SEMPLE M'PHERSON OPENS WAY FOR DOUGLAS TO ADVERTISE CITY'S WONDERS TO THE WORLD

> Henceforth and forever those two names, Aimee and Douglas, will be linked together in the minds of the people of this country. From now on the inhabitants of the United States will know that there are more than two cities in Arizona; namely, Tucson and Phoenix…but that will be different from now on. Douglas will be remembered….We must advertise this city to the world. Mrs. McPherson has made our task much easier.

One of the many shacks discovered by the search parties. Despite the offer of reward money, no shack was ever found matching Aimee's description. Left to right: Harold Henry, reporter for the Douglas Dispatch; *Omar A. Ash, law enforcement officer; Deputy United States Marshal Tom Simms; Sergeant Leslie Gatiff, Douglas Police Department (used by permission of the Douglas Historical Association).*

> We all gave Mrs. McPherson the benefit of the doubt and in so doing endeared ourselves and our city to her and those who came here by reason of her....Why? First, because this town is made up of hospitable people. Second, it was for the welfare of Douglas...ALL ABOARD THE AIMEE McPHERSON-DOUGLAS SPECIAL.[34]

Within a month's time, Douglas was swamped with requests for information. "Since her reappearance came at the beginning of summer, many families put the place of the evangelist's 'resurrection' on their vacation schedule." [35] Tourists continued to pour into Douglas through 1927, with many of their automobile windshields proudly bearing an "Aimee Slept Here" sticker.[36] Aimee remained for the next two years and perhaps forever the biggest "wonder" in the "Wonder City of the West."

Prior to her departure to Los Angeles on June 25 aboard The Southern Pacific's Golden State Limited, she had been asked about briefly stopping in Tucson. "Yes," she replied. "I expect to say a few words in Tucson on my way back to Los Angeles…I at least must wave my hand to the people of Tucson, for Arizona has been very good to me."[37]

The *Arizona Daily Star* ran an editorial after Aimee was safely home in Los Angeles.

> Arizona is breathing more easily as it begins a new week. Aimee Semple McPherson, "resurrected" from the desert sands of the Mexican border and welcomed home over a path of roses, is safe within the boundaries of her beloved city, Los Angeles…. The train that carried Mrs. McPherson to the coast carried a great portion of this excitement to Los Angeles. Now it is California's turn to feature Aimee Semple McPherson…Mrs. McPherson had a remarkable experience. So has Douglas and Arizona. Now its California's turn.[38]

Aimee's homecoming over a path of roses. More than one hundred thousand persons surrounded the train station and lined the track for nine miles out of the city—giving her the largest ovation in the history of Los Angeles (author's collection).

Aimee had been right about Arizona. The state and especially the people of Douglas had been good to her, indeed very good to her. Arizona authorities not only waited until Aimee was home "safe within the boundaries of her beloved city" but then let the Mexican officials tell the world that her "lurid tale" of kidnapping was doubtful. It was Ernesto Boubion, the mayor of the Mexican border town of Agua Prieta, who on July 2, 1926, told the press that "in reality [Aimee had] been driven by automobile from Douglas to a shack four miles east of Agua Prieta, then brought even closer to town from which point she staggered into the border community."[39] Aimee refused to comment on Boubion's findings but Minnie quickly struck back with "an uncomplimentary gesture and three words, 'That's Mexico, Mexico.'"[40] Less than two days later, however, Aimee quickly joined forces with her mother in demonizing Boubion in her Sunday evening messages:

> She attacked…Boubion and his "lies," and stated that…things had been turned upside down for people were paying more attention to the word

Ernesto Boubion, mayor of Agua Prieta, Sonora, Mexico. His finding on July 2, 1926, contradicted Aimee's story. Minnie's response was, "That's Mexico, Mexico" (used by permission of the Herald Examiner Collection/Los Angeles Public Library).

of "one Mexican" than she had ever known them to do before. She paced back and forth on the platform ranting and raving about "that Mexican" [41]

When it was "California's turn to feature Aimee Semple McPherson," Aimee wished, perhaps more than anything else, to be back with the "dear people" in the "marvelous city of Douglas." Despite her welcome home "over a path of roses" with "more than 100,000 persons" surrounding the train station and lining "the railroad tracks for nine miles out of the city"—"the largest ovation" in the history of Los Angeles—life for her would never be the same.[42] Her life forever would be fractured, literally torn in two. One month later when it was "California's turn," Los Angeles District Attorney Asa Keyes requested an investigation into the alleged "kidnapping" by a grand jury. On September 16, 1926, Aimee, her mother, and alleged lover were charged with "corruption of morals and obstruction of justice."[43] Aimee's preliminary hearing from September 27-November 3, 1926 was the longest in California history. Even one of the Los Angeles newspapers grew tired of the scandal, editorializing on the front page:

> Let's forget it. At the worst, Mrs. McPherson is accused by rumor of a moral lapse, and of lying about it afterwards like a gentleman.... It is about time that all of us—the newspapers included—find something more worthwhile to discuss than whether or not a well-known Los Angeles woman, 34 or 35 years of age, of previously unblemished reputation, committed a quite human indiscretion in Carmel, Salinas or Timbuctoo.[44]

Finally, on January 19, 1927 all charges were dropped, but not before Asa Keyes made a final statement, intended as much for the public as the court room:

> The fact that this defendant fabricated a kidnapping story, or that she

473

Aimee being carried back to Angelus Temple after her return from Arizona (author's collection).

spent a time at Carmel, are not, in themselves, offenses of which this court can entertain jurisdiction. Reputable witnesses have testified sufficiently concerning both the Carmel incident and the return of Mrs. McPherson from her so-call kidnapping adventure to enable her to be judged in the only court of her jurisdiction—the court of public opinion.[45]

Ultimately Aimee Semple McPherson was judged in "the court of public opinion." Unlike Douglas, Arizona, its verdict was swift and not favorable. Within a year's time the Los Angeles press no longer referred to her as "Sister Aimee" or even "Mrs. McPherson." She had simply become "Aimee." On June 24, 1926, Aimee's name appeared for the first time on the front page of the *New York Times*. It was not a cause for celebration. The Protestant mainline so important for Aimee's acceptance into the wider culture of the early 1920s quickly withdrew their valuable support, no longer wishing to have any contact with a scandalous evangelist. Aimee, contrary to her original interdenominational intentions, created her own separate Pentecostal denomination, the International Church of the Foursquare Gospel on August 15, 1927. It was a denomination created for her survival as much as anything else.

Perhaps the greatest Pentecostal beneficiary of Aimee's "kidnapping"

Back in Los Angeles, Aimee kneels in gratitude for "her people" (author's collection).

was none other than the Assemblies of God. Data on church growth for the denomination was recorded in two-year increments. From 1923 to 1925 the denomination grew by 118 churches. From 1927 to 1929, 259 new churches were added. But from 1925 to 1927, an impressive 444 new churches joined the Assemblies. It is very possible that many of these were born in the wake of Aimee's revivalism and were started as independent Full Gospel Tabernacles. It is also very likely that in the sensational aftermath of Aimee's court trial these churches sought to identify with the largest, most stable, and respected Anglo Pentecostal denomination, the General Council of the Assemblies of God.

The Protestant mainline did not remain silent for long, either. If Pentecostals voted with their feet by moving from independent tabernacles to the Assemblies of God, the Protestant mainline sought both to marginalize and isolate Aimee to that curious city of "irreligious paganism"—Los Angeles. As early as August 12, 1926, their skeptical and doubting voice was heard in an editorial in *The Christian Century*:

> Every reader of the newspapers has by this time formed some opinion on the relation of Aimee Semple McPherson to the recent Los Angeles kidnapping episode. With the exception of the thousands who are devoted members of her church, the majority seem to suspect that she perpetrated some hoax on her followers....Perhaps her case will forever remain a mystery....Mrs. McPherson is undoubtedly the most prominent preacher

Katheryn Kuhlman, who took Pentecostalism into the Protestant mainline in the 1960s, just as her role model had done in the 1920s (used by permission of the Flower Pentecostal Heritage Center and Doug Grandstaff Photography).

in Los Angeles, that curious city where irreligious paganism and religious bigotry and charlatanism contend with one another to such a degree that they almost obscure the honest efforts of its real Christians. Mrs. McPherson's eminence has been achieved by a combination of personal magnetism, religious obscurantism, healing occultism and consummate showmanship. Whether this combination is informed by sincere purpose or corrupted by more or less conscious ulterior motives has been an open question in Los Angeles. The debate is now bound to be renewed with added vigor.[46]

Aimee would engage herself for the remaining years of her life with the "added vigor" of that "debate." "From this time on a telltale repetitive pattern can be discerned in her life," observed her astute Los Angeles neighbor and historian, Carey McWilliams.

> A pattern that must have reflected a mounting sense of insecurity, exhaustion, and despair. The new sequence of events had a rhythm of its own: flight, new beginning, fiascoes, quarrels, new efforts, defeat—regularly interspersed with periods of "breakdowns" and "nervous exhaustion."[47]

Aimee did manage, however, to prove the secular prophet of the era, F. Scott Fitzgerald, wrong in his pronouncement of "no second acts in American lives." Act one had indeed ended. Her time in the Protestant mainline churches was over, her bridges burned. Charles S. Price, her former associate pastor, would carry on that ministry in the Northwest and into Canada. And Kathryn Kuhlman, a former student at LIFE Bible College who had so intently watched Aimee preach from the first balcony in Angelus Temple, would help carry Pentecostalism back into the denominational churches in the 1960s much like her role model had done in the early 1920s. Astute as ever, Aimee remarked, "Well, to the world, I might be Aimee, but to my own dear people I am Sister."[48] When she was no longer welcome in mainline churches and dismissed by secular skeptics, her "own dear people" sustained her for the remaining eighteen years of her life. In the end it was her "own dear people" of Pentecostalism who forgave her fleshly foibles and granted her many more "second acts." By doing so, they proved they were neither hard-core fundamentalists nor cold, calculating modernists. Sister's sense of spirituality had kindled warm fires in their hearts. Such hearts, strangely warmed, proved to be both truly liberal and evangelical, the sign and promise of a future, global, progressive Pentecostalism and perhaps of Christianity itself.

EPILOGUE

Testimony, People's Religion, and the Search for Spirituality

It is in the babble of isms that religious life best expresses itself, here the people have expressed their discontent with standard forms of religion and taken the reigns in their own hands....We shall not know America until we know the religions that America made and embraced.

—Charles W. Ferguson

Outside the orthodox ranks there are thousands, even millions groping toward God....Out of these struggles have arisen the many new religions of America. Often the butt of the ridicule of the orthodox and skeptical, these religions have, nevertheless, grown and prospered.....in America they number thousands and millions!...a dim electric sign cried faintly the legend "Mission." In this shabby building we detected at last a church of the Holy Rollers...."The Holy Rollers," though famous, are in reality almost unknown. To tell the truth this denomination is still without a name.

—Jules Bois
The New Religions of America

Whenever Christianity has become the religion of the fortunate and cultured and has grown philosophical, abstract, formal and ethically harmless in the process, the lower strata of society find themselves religiously expatriated by a faith which neither meets their psychological needs nor sets forth an appealing ethical ideal. In such a situation the right leader finds little difficulty in launching a new movement which will, as a rule, give rise to a new denomination.

—H. Richard Niebuhr

The really creative, church forming, religious movements are the work of the lower strata.

—Ernst Troeltsch

If religion were a thing money could buy, the rich would live and the poor would die.

—Peter, Paul and Mary

R Laurence Moore, esteemed cultural historian, recently made a rather startling confession: "If I were starting my career over," wrote the Howard A. Newman Professor of American Studies/History at Cornell University, "I would turn to the subject of Pentecostalism and for a lot

GREETINGS FROM

MR. AND MRS. H. M. BARFOOT
and CHARLES HOWARD

PASTORS OF THE

WEST SIDE ASSEMBLY OF GOD

701 SOUTH THIRD AVENUE

YAKIMA, WASHINGTON

of reasons. Pentecostalism, as what is surely the fastest growing segment of Christian faith, forces our attention on cross-cultural study.... Everywhere it defeats our expectation about neat class categories, not to mention racial, gender, and ethnic categories. It almost seems to demand starting from scratch."[1] Beautiful, well-chosen words from the pen of a writer who argues that religion "is always about something else." "Pentecostalism," Moore concluded, "is about the formation of popular culture."[2] I think it is safe to assume that Professor Moore did not always share this sentiment nor have this critical insight about the world of Pentecostalism, a world that now numbers roughly six hundred million souls worldwide. His earlier works, in fact, betray his latest thinking.[3] Perhaps more than anything else, at its most elemental level, the field of religious studies is all about conversion, how minds and lives are continually changed and remade. In her Harvard Divinity School Ingersoll Lecture for 2005–06 Karen Armstrong argued that "religion is about transformation," how "we become fundamentally different."[4]

I for one am convinced that religious conversions can and should occur throughout the "three-score and ten" of life. My first "religious" conversion occurred when I was four going on five. Although both my parents were Pentecostal preachers, my earliest recollections of church included the memory of having to "sit up straight" on harsh, unforgiving, cushionless metal folding chairs while watching my mother lead the singing as my father accompanied her on his silver trombone. Sunday church was a rented Teamsters' Hall that came furnished with the leftover incense of stale beer and cigarette butts. Pews, pianos and organs, professional male song leaders and "real" churches came later with upward mobility. During the first four years of my life I had only been nurtured in my parents' faith. I had yet to make it mine. Conversion was expected and as their only child I did not want to disappoint them.

During eight years of a childless marriage, Nora Lager Barfoot had heard more than her fair share of the many versions of the often-repeated tale of the rebellious, prodigal preacher's son. She resolved that by God's grace and with the "rod of correction" thrown in for extra measure, her son would break the mold and would be unlike all other boys. I discovered early on the existence of life in two different worlds. There was the world of my parents and church and then the world of everyday and playmates. Compared to my non-church friends, however, it seemed to me that despite the lack of television (called "hellavision" by some Pentecostals) and movies, I lived in a far richer, more multi-dimensional, Technicolor world. My friends' worlds seemed flat and mono-chromatic in contrast and comparison with mine. My spiritual world— where I lived most of the time—had a split-level floor plan and was always exciting. Never once in childhood did I feel deprived. To the contrary, everyday was eventful and colorful. Participating in two different worlds left little room for boredom.

My mother, more than anyone else, prepared me for life in my split-level universe. Every night at bedtime I was read a Bible story. For whatever reason both our favorite stories came from the Old Testament. The cast of characters was always larger than life, but the model for earthly, "worldly" success, it seemed, was found with the story of Moses. Somehow when my mother told me the story of Moses, it was no longer a mere Bible story from long ago. Literally we were there. It was a story for the two of us, mother and son, our scriptural secret. It included no one else—no room existed for a husband or a father. Like Moses' mother, Jochebed, my mother hid me for "many months," even years. And like Moses I too would be placed one day in a papyrus basket plastered not with bitumen and pitch, but woven with love and faith and then taken to the banks of the mighty river of life to be swept down stream to enter a strange new world. Like Moses, the Hebrew growing up in Egypt, I too was being prepared for life as "an alien residing in a foreign land." More than anything else, my mother like Jochebed wanted her son to grow up in "Pharaoh's court" and to receive the finest education "Egypt" had to offer. But never for one moment did she ever want me to lose my identity as a "Hebrew"—a Pentecostal. It was only by going to the land of Egypt, I was taught, that I too would see "the misery of my people," "hear their cry," and "know their sufferings." And finally my mission, my purpose in life, again like Moses, was to help bring "my people" "up out of that land to a good and broad land, a land flowing with milk and honey" even to the Promised Land of Canaan, to suburbia itself. Fortified with such stories of spiritual nurture, I was ready for my first conversion—at least a year before I encountered and entered the first of my many "Egyptian" schools—the first grade at Nob Hill Elementary in Yakima, Washington.

For some strange reason my mother was not with me the night of my conversion. Looking back, it was a sure sign of things to come. Due to a devastating, debilitating disease, the mother I once knew would soon cease to exist. From the age of ten on, I knew all too well what it was like to be a motherless child. "When you lose your mother at a young age," wrote Sandra Scofield, "you lose a part of who you are; you spend years navigating what amounts to chaos without any sort of reliable compass…The past is a site of great injustice…the place where you see, nonetheless, the only possibility for connection."[5] Scofield's words not only ring true for me, but Harvey Cox was perceptive enough to tell my mother before she died that the "Aimee project" was also my way of reconnecting with her.

My father that particular night—and as it would be for the majority of my life—took me by the hand, little cold hand in big, warm hand, and the two of us took off for church in our new V-eight two-tone, maroon-and-white 1954 Dodge—very similar to the Pace Car of that year's Indy 500. That night was one of the first times in my life that I had entered the double doors of a "real" church, which is undoubtedly why its memory is so powerful and so well-preserved. No dark, dirty, dank Teamsters' Hall basement that night. No pungent smell of a bar there. Not even a single folding chair in sight. No cops either, rapping on the windows with their nightsticks telling us to be "quiet down there." Instead this church—one of my first real ones—was light and bright. I had crossed the threshold into a beautiful new religious world, one I never wished to leave. Everything was larger than life to a boy of four going on five. There were large stained-glass windows on all sides. Presented in glass was the largest Jesus I had even seen—at least twenty feet tall, carrying safely home upon his neck the little lost lamb. There was a band—really an orchestra— not just one trombone but several more, and saxophones too, and the largest piano I had ever seen—a Steinway grand—and an organ—a Hammond organ. Two things caught my wide-open astonished eyes next: the platform and the balcony. The platform, as my Dad called it, was semi-circular and elevated, not like the homemade pulpit on the ground floor back at the basement of the Teamsters' Hall. And the balcony close to the chandeliers, even closer to heaven itself, was wrapped three-quarters of the way around the church. It looked long and comfortable—plenty of space for a boy to stretch out and sleep, especially high up in the balcony. I was too wound up, however, too excited for sleep that night. From the outside looks had been deceiving. The church was downtown, and we had passed by it, it seems, hundreds of times en route to eat dinner at the Chinook Hotel. It looked old and dirty, built of grey square stone, and that is why, I guess, everybody called it the "old stone church." I knew according to my parents that "they were one of us." I know now that the "old stone church" had once been an imposing downtown Methodist or Baptist church built long before the flight of the 1950s to the suburbs or to places like Nob Hill where we lived. Cold and foreboding on the outside, inside it was warm and inviting. I felt safe and secure in the old stone church—it was my new found "Rock of Ages."

Dad was not preaching that night; even so we quickly parted company. He made his way to the platform while I climbed the stairs to the balcony. This was new. Going to church before had meant going "down" stairs. Tonight I was going "up" stairs. I was not alone. I had been entrusted to the care of a teenager—Daniel—a deacon's son, who Dad was sure one day would enter the ministry, which he later did. I had been warned that once in the balcony I was not to leave until my father picked me up. No bathroom breaks or drinks of water from the fountain were permitted.

We were there that night for a city-wide "full gospel meeting," which meant there were a lot of Pentecostal congregations attending from all over the Yakima Valley. Yakima in the 1950s was the undisputed fruit capital of Washington State. We lived rent free in the Nob Hill house courtesy of one of the Marley Brothers of the Marley Brothers Orchards' fame. Usually every year around Christmas a new Dodge car would be parked in our driveway, again courtesy of Marley Brothers Orchards. Grover Marley, our benefactor, was a huge fan of the *Lawrence Welk Show*, and Dodge was a proud sponsor.

Yakima undoubtedly also bore much spiritual fruit, at least as far as Pentecostals were concerned. They seemed everywhere, especially swarming to the fairgrounds in summertime where the latest and newest visiting evangelists pitched their tents. Even "God's Man of Faith and Power," A. A. Allen himself, then an ordained Assemblies of God minister, began his tent ministry in Yakima. Just months before he died, alone and alcoholic, at age fifty-nine in San Francisco's Jack Tar Hotel, Allen wrote about his first tent revival in Yakima.

> On July 4, 1951, a day of celebration for the nation and a day of special celebration for me, the A. A. Allen Revival Tent went up for the first time, an eagle with outstretched wings against the good, clean, cotton-white clouds of Yakima, Washington.
>
> The people came; at some meetings it seemed almost as if all 25,000 residents of the city were trying to get into the tent.
>
> My freshman revival under my first tent was a rip-roaring victory for Jesus. People streamed down the aisles for the altar calls, responding to

Him as they had responded to no other experience in their lives....

It was a turning point, my maiden voyage with Christ under my own canvas.[6]

Likewise for me, for whatever reason or spiritual coincidence, "my turning point," "my maiden voyage with Christ" also occurred in Yakima on some unrecorded date and night in the late winter of 1954, three years after "God's Man of Faith and Power" had come to town.

High up in the balcony with Brother Daniel, I sat mesmerized throughout the entire service, even more so during the sermon. The Pentecostal congregations of the Yakima Valley (my father was the president of their association) had united to bring Betty Baxter, a promising evangelist, to town. Other than my mother, she was one of the last Pentecostal women evangelists I would ever hear in person. (Hattie Hammond and Kathryn Kuhlman were the final two.) All I can remember was the incredible love and compassion that seemed to pour forth from her very being, especially when her arms were outstretched. With her arms open wide she seemed to embrace us all as her entire brood—main floor and balcony, sinner and saint together. The preaching, although "anointed," was different, far different from all the men's, even to my young ears. There were no points. No one, two three—only stories richly tied together forever tugging at our hearts.

Little did I know that three years before my conversion, Oral Roberts had introduced this unique woman evangelist to the world. Writing the foreword to *The Betty Baxter Story*, Roberts told the reader,

> Jesus appeared to Betty Baxter, talked with her, laid his nail-scarred hands on her twisted, matted spine and in a moment's time straightened her bent body and made her whole....For several months she has been appearing one night in my healing campaigns to give her story. Each time we cannot seat the great crowds numbering up to 14,000 for a single service, who come to hear her. From 300 to 500 people have been converted each time she has spoken in my campaigns. That alone is a miracle....Jesus of Nazareth, who healed Betty Baxter will do something for you....You won't be the same person anymore.[7]

And neither was I. When Betty Baxter gave her altar call, I told Brother Daniel that I wanted to "go forward," providing for him his first case of pastoral discernment. He knew that he risked my father's displeasure for leaving our assigned bench in the balcony, but he also was experiencing my insistence, which eventually won out. Down the stairs and up the center aisle he carried me—just like the larger-than-life depiction in the stained-glass window looking down upon us. I felt very much that night like the hundredth little lost lamb, "Oh Lamb of God, I come, I come," coming to be reunited with the remaining "ninety and nine that safely lay in the shelter of the fold."

Looking back, I suppose I wanted to be near this mesmerizing woman on the platform, to make the magic of the moment endure, as much as I wanted to come to Jesus. But whatever the reason everything changed that bright winter night in the old stone church in Yakima, Washington. Nurture had given way to conversion. On that night "I met the Holy" and became "one of them." And as if to prove the point, it wasn't long after that my dad and I, both dressed alike in white pants and shirts with matching black bow ties, stood together in the baptismal tank of our new church on a hot summer Sunday evening. A grainy three-minute eight-millimeter movie still bears silent witness of the event. Before I was baptized—really baptized, butch wax and all—my father required me to "testify." I am sure that I said I was happy to be "one of them" and how I too "wanted to go all the way with Jesus." And then my father's large hand, holding a hidden white handkerchief, went over my nose and down, down, and down I went. This was the real thing, no "little dab will do you." Once completely submerged, I was "dead to trespasses and sin." I rapidly reappeared, rising from my watery grave. In the words of Woody Guthrie, folk poet and songwriter, "I was born again, my past…dead and gone. This great eternal moment [was now] my great eternal dawn."[8]

Growing up Pentecostal my religious boyhood heroes were the tent-toting, globe-trotting, faith-healing evangelists of the 1950s. Since "Brother Allen" had fallen from grace (at least in the eyes of the Assemblies of God), defrocked for a drunk-driving arrest in Knoxville, Tennessee in 1955, Oral Roberts quickly became the Billy Graham of the Pentecostal world. As soon as I could read, my mother placed in my hands *My Life Story* by Brother Oral Roberts from Tulsa, Oklahoma. It was a book that I read from cover to cover and over again. "Brother Roberts" had become my new spiritual mentor. It was not just enough now to be a preacher like my parents. To really be like Brother Roberts meant I also needed the "spiritual gift of healing." In my ministerial daydreams the last thing in the world I wanted to do was to settle down with a pastorate like my parents. As a boy I possessed what Merle Haggard called "rambling fever." I knew that I would get bored too long in one place. I had also become increasingly streetwise to all the petty feuds and intramural skirmishes that accompanied many Pentecostal deacon-possessed churches. While sitting with my mother behind the protective plate glass window of the sanctuary's "cry room," the nursery, I witnessed my father voted out of one such church in Anacortes, Washington—a church born, like so many other Assemblies of God churches, from a healing received at an Aimee Semple McPherson revival in the 1920s. (By the time the church began compiling its history, however, Aimee's name was omitted from their origin myth and narrative.)

The votes were tallied live that Wednesday night and carried over the nursery loudspeaker for our benefit. We were witnesses to my father's ministerial execution, carried out in exacting detail by a well-organized squad of "clergy killers."[9] "No, no, no, no" came back the votes with an occasional "yes." "Voted out," that's what they said. No pulpit, no parsonage. No job, no house, no finishing of school. Get gone. How could this be? In the midnight hour of a recent Sunday evening prior to the congregational vote, I had completed my teenage pilgrimage and spiritual rite of passage. Down at the altar with the saints, mostly women, who had been hoisting my arms high toward heaven, I had at long last begun to babble. "He's getting it," I heard them say. "Stammering lips," said another. Still another shouted in my ear, "Don't give up now, Brother Charles, it's coming, you're almost there." The freedom came, my tongue rolled. My long-awaited climax occurred when my spiritual midwives birthed me, utterly exhausted, into the euphoria and ecstasy of "speaking in other tongues." Worn and weary, I had finally achieved by their standards "the baptism of the Holy Ghost." I had passed my prescribed tribal rite of passage with flying colors. I was no longer a boy. I was a young, fit, spiritual warrior, no mere Christian, either, for I had joined the elite ranks of the "Spirit-filled." So the loss of my family of faith on that cold winter Wednesday night, usually reserved for Bible study and prayer, was devastating, leaving me spiritually shattered and heartbroken for years. If it could happen to my dad, I reasoned, it could surely happen to me. And it would.

As a young Pentecostal spiritual warrior, I wanted my freedom—especially after the Anacortes experience. I never wanted to be beholden to some church board telling me what to do, how to do it, and where to live. Maybe I would even leave the Assemblies of God and go "independent" just like Brother Allen—and what my dad often threatened to do. After all, I was a spiritual Westerner. "Just turn me loose… Underneath the western skies,…let me wander over yonder till I see the mountains rise…Oh, give me land, lots of land under starry skies, Don't fence me in."[10] What I really wanted was those intense spiritual one-night stands that tent evangelism afforded, those instant confrontations between good and evil while the smell of sawdust burned strong in my nostrils. And if I ever made it "big,"

I wanted my very own tent, larger than a football field, complete with television cameras, again just like Oral Roberts and A.A. Allen. No church, not even a large one, could ever compete with a canvas cathedral. They were mobile megachurches. The overhead rings of lights, the gassy generators, the "church tramps" in their endless search for spiritual and physical satisfaction and relief, the prayer lines and ramps were all part of the drama of a successful tent ministry. In Willie Nelson's words, it would soon be time to be "on the road again"—summer in the Northwest, winter in the Southwest. Always the bright lights of a new town, a bigger city would continually beckon. Bigger tents, larger fairgrounds, "all things were possible." A Berkeley colleague once sent me remembrances of her family's "church tramping days." It, too, represented a search for physical as well as spiritual health. Her baby brother had entered the world early arriving with brain damage and cerebral palsy. Her first religious memories were similar to my own.

> Fragments of the past running forward
>   to meet and shape the present.
> Trying to understand the years of wandering,
>   the long and rootless search
> to know the truth,
> to be accepted,
> to be set free,
> we were Caleb and Joshua spying out the land;
> could we find the promised land?
>
> Each different church a different God
> Divine creation or human inflation?
> Curiously we roamed
>   from church to church
>   mission to mission
>   faith healer to faith healer
> Seeking our thrills
> at some of the "Greatest Shows on Earth."
>
> We encountered extremes of the nineteenth kind
> with trancing and dancing, and ecstatic frenzies
> while other were holy and pious, and ever so stately.
> The chasm too vast to express
> And yet I was there experiencing it all.[11]

"Only believe," we sang, and believe I did. But something strange and sad started occurring in Pentecostalism about the time I began preaching at age sixteen. Slowly, imperceptibly at first, then later in rapid succession like falling dominoes, the healing evangelists began folding their tents one after another. And like the old soldiers they were, they just as quickly faded away. The younger ones among them, who attempted to continue on, simply traded in their tents for the safer and saner hardtops of convention halls and Holiday Inns. A.A. Allen's death in 1970 signaled the passing of the last great colorful Pentecostal convertible in American religious life. Before he died, Allen's tents, like Detroit's Buick, had become "bigger and better" with the passing of every year. An era ended in American Pentecostalism with Allen's death.

Despite increasingly tougher city permits and zoning ordinances, in the end the tents came down for good due to the Pentecostals themselves. The movement as a whole was experiencing a massive, convulsive conversion. Beginning in the early 1950s and concluding by the mid-1960s, education for most Pentecostals had replaced evangelism. This is another reason why if R. Laurence Moore was starting his career over, he would turn to the subject of Pentecostalism. "Pentecostalism," observes Moore, "attracts a mass audience, provides a fascinating subject of inquiry not simply because of what it looks like during an initial period of flourishing but because of what it looks like ten or fifty years later. Niebuhr was right in thinking that exuberant religions settle down and send their faithful partisans to get degrees....A change in class location changes behavior."[12]

The two prominent healing evangelists of the 1960s, Oral Roberts and A. A. Allen, will forever serve as symbols of what occurred in American Pentecostalism during my teenage years. Roberts, representing the majority, traded in his healing tent for a major new university. "Dr. Roberts" the educator replaced Oral Granville Roberts the evangelist. Shortly before his death, he reflected back on a lifetime of accomplishments and said he was "most proud of ORU."[13] It was not healing revivalism, nor tent evangelism, but education. Even more symbolically Roberts left his little Pentecostal denomination behind, joining the ranks of the much larger Methodist Church. Dr. Oral Roberts had gone "mainline."

Not so, however, with the "James Cagney of the Sawdust Trail"—Asa Alonso Allen—who represented the minority of Anglo Pentecostalism. Less than a year before he died, *Look* magazine astutely summarized his newly found place in America's religious life:

> Now that Oral Roberts has dropped out and turned Methodist and Billy Graham has become Richard Nixon's guru-in-waiting—A.A. Allen, 58

is the nation's topmost tent-toting, old-fashioned evangelical roarer. …
Allen is at least a practical zealot with a sense of style that sets him
well apart from that frowzy netherworld of mystical crackpot charlatans,
snake handlers, wandering bush-league Bible thumpers, street-corner
messiahs and questionable colleagues….In the God business of today,
A.A. Allen is a mogul.[14]

Even more telling in *Look*'s article was the writer's perception of the tent
settings and Allen's congregation/crowd/audience:

The tent stands in a clearing between the roller-coaster tracks and a
fenced-in grandstand and circular dirt track…used for…stock-car
races….always a real crowd-pleaser in this lower-working-class part of
town, second only to tent revivals. From a nearby hill outside the park,
low-rent public-housing units gape down at the tent and those who feel
drawn to it…..Dancing blacks and whites crash to the ground in indis-
criminate rapture while the attendants scurry from body to body, among
the fallen women, covering any parts exposed.[15]

The crowds at Allen's tent, the writer concluded, "are a cacophony of smells
and a scramble of ages and shapes and races and bottomless frustrations….
They come in quest of soothing balm."[16]

Several months earlier in 1969, *Time* magazine had also taken note of
Allen, featuring him in its Religion section. *Time*'s assessment of Allen was
remarkably similar to *Look*'s:

Now that Oklahoma's Oral Roberts has joined the Methodist ministry and de-emphasized the curative aspects of his high-decibel revivals,
Allen is probably the best-known faith healer in the nation. Although
ignored by mainstream Protestant churchmen, he has a large and enthusiastic following among…Christians in the South and Southwest.[17]

By the late 1960s, A.A. Allen's tent meetings were remarkably similar to
the Azusa Street revival, which had given birth to the worldwide movement
some sixty years earlier in a rundown, semi-industrial area of Los Angeles.
One of the many unique experiences of Azusa Street was found in the
words of a participant who exclaimed, "The color line was washed away in
the blood."[18] More than anything else, A.A. Allen's tent meetings restored
the old Azusa Street of multiracial and ethnic harmony. Recent research
also indicated that Allen's ministry far exceeded and lasted longer than the
multiracial character of the fabled mission, itself. Sadly, the death of "God's
Man of Faith and Power" signaled the end, at least among American Pen-

tecostals, of "a cacophony of smells and a scramble of ages and shapes and races."[19]

Skipping my senior year in high school at age seventeen, literally two roads, two tracks, or two paths in Pentecostalism lay before me. "And sorry I could not travel both and be one traveler; long I stood and looked down one as far as I could."[20] Again, Roberts and Allen provided the competing symbols and models. Roberts had created a brand new, modern, Disneyesque, fully accredited major university in Tulsa, Oklahoma, while Allen stubbornly, tenaciously held on to the idea of the old-fashioned Pentecostal Bible school in rural southeastern Arizona. "Miracle Revival Training Center," read an early brochure, "does not offer a complete theological course, or philosophical and theological degree... Its courses are courses NOT offered in the seminaries."[21] Indeed they were not. Many of the courses in Allen's school contained the word "Miracle" in their title: "Miracles in the Church Age," "Miracles in the 20th Century," "Miracles in the Bible."[22]

The dilemma for my parents of competing models of education for their only child—Bible college or an accredited college or university—was quickly resolved. An Assemblies of God Bible college, hastily transformed and converted from a former World War II Army airbase situated on 128 acres of prime agricultural land lying among the bean fields in between Santa Ana and Costa Mesa, had recently become accredited as a private liberal arts college. Educationally, I was able to pursue the path of Pentecostalism "more traveled by" simply by driving south on the Santa Ana freeway. A true "Bible school" education, at least in the Assemblies of God, would have required a major move to Northern California, or worse yet, a pilgrimage to the Mecca of Anglo Pentecostalism and the place my parents met, Springfield, Missouri. My spiritual roots may have come from Pentecostalism, but culturally, as a child of Southern California, I was reluctant to give up that secular identity. To a large extent geography also determined theology in the Assemblies of God. Southern California was the undisputed Disneyland of progressive Pentecostalism.

Southern California College, now Vanguard University, did have an outstanding faculty in both religion and education and had the distinction of becoming Orange County's first private college as well as "the world's first Pentecostal four-year degree granting college."[23] Teaching today in the largest public university in the United States with more than sixty-five thousand students, I find it unfathomable to conceive of a college with fewer than five hundred students. Such, however, was my college experience. It was a bittersweet decision for my parents. Until the day they died, they must have wondered if they made the right decision. President Woodrow Wilson, a Presbyterian minister's son and the former president of Princeton University, once remarked that the purpose of a college education was to make the "son as different as possible from the father." At the end of four years during the height of the turbulent 1960s, no doubts remained in my parents' mind that their son indeed was different. I had undergone and experienced yet another conversion. My role models and heroes changed. Educators and professors like Russ Spittler and Gordon Fee replaced evangelists and ministers like Oral Roberts and A.A. Allen. And like Oral Roberts, I too switched my church affiliation and went "mainline." I let my ministerial license with the Southern California District of the Assemblies of God lapse (I was too young to be ordained) and joined the fourth largest Presbyterian church (USA) in the country. St. Andrew's Presbyterian Church in Newport Beach, with Charles H. Dierenfield's encouragement, gave me their endorsement for both seminary and ordination. I was about to leave, I thought, my Pentecostal past behind once and for all. I had even arranged for a pre-famous Robert H. Schuller to speak in the campus chapel. Remembering my mother's story of Moses, I realized I no longer felt like "an alien residing in a foreign land." I was beginning to feel at home. Unlike Moses, I was now no longer willing "to share ill-treatment with the people of God." I was choosing instead "to be called a son of Pharaoh's daughter." I was trading in my Pentecostal "abuse" for the "treasures of Egypt."[24]

Before I divorced my religious past and remarried Presbyterianism I remember Kathryn Kuhlman paying a visit to my church-affiliated college. By this time my mother was confined to a wheelchair and weighed all of sixty-eight pounds. But for several years in her life a ray of hope dawned once a month when Kathryn Kuhlman came to the Old Shrine Auditorium in Los Angeles. Often I went with my mother in the hopes of her healing. More often than not when those many doors finally opened after several hours of waiting on those long, hot, Sunday afternoons, we would literally be swept into that large auditorium by the rush and surge of the crowd.

There was an atmosphere of expectancy—there was electricity. "He Touched Me," written by Bill Gaither in 1963, was Kathryn Kuhlman's signature song, her hymn of faith. And as a sea of diverse worshippers from every conceivable background and denomination and no tradition, we would stand on the tiptoe of hope and sing again, again, and yet again:

> Shackled by a heavy burden,
> 'neath a load of guilt and shame;

Then the hand of Jesus touched me,
And now—I am no longer—the same.
He touched me, O, He touched me, and,
O, the joy that floods my soul!
Something happened,
and now I know,
He touched me."[25]

And who can forget Kuhlman's signature radio greeting—"Well, Hel—lo the—re and have you—u b—e—e—n wa—i—t—ing for m—eee?"

Having a second home in neighboring Newport Beach, it was only logical that Kuhlman would pay a visit to our small college. It was the last time I would ever hear a woman Pentecostal preacher. At the college she seemed sadly, oddly out of place, a relic from the past, a left over from the 1950s. I never did get the falling down part—"slain in the spirit." That was new for me, having never witnessed it before in any of my dad's churches. "If it really was God's power," I reasoned, "why didn't it make people stand up instead of fall over?" Stand up from their wheelchairs and bed cots! If it had happened that way, I guess I could have been more of a true believer. And no, my mother was never healed, never made well again. But those experiences and the questions they raised would undoubtedly sneak back into my later academic work and life. It was James Cone of Union Theological Seminary in New York City who opened my eyes to the wellspring and source material of my later academic and theological reflection.

> More often than not, it is a theologian's personal history, in a particular...setting, that serves as the most important factor in shaping the methodology and content of his or her theological perspective. Thus theologians ought to be a little more honest, and let the reader know something about those non-intellectual factors that are so important for the opinions they advance.[26]

On July 3, 1970, after four years of a carefully supervised and scripted courtship by our small church-affiliated school, I married my college sweetheart. A month or so later we said goodbye to family and friends in California and headed east in our Volkswagen for Princeton, New Jersey. I had been accepted finally at Princeton Theological Seminary. The first time that I applied, I had been rejected. I was devastated. What went wrong, I wondered? I had been class president, president of the college honor society, and religious activities director. My grades could have been better, but they were above average and respectable, given before grade inflation occurred.

I quickly began developing conspiracy theories. Had my Pentecostalism, I wondered, caused me to flunk the psychological and personality tests Princeton required? Over the telephone I received the terrible truth. "We have a quota on people like you," said Dean Arthur Adams. "I shouldn't tell you this," he confided, "but if you reapply as a Presbyterian there will be no problem at all." I, of course, quickly, officially, became a Presbyterian and vowed to myself that if I ever got to Princeton, I would tell no one, absolutely no one, about my Pentecostal past.

Looking back on my theological education, it is obvious to me now that Union Theological Seminary in New York City would have been a far better fit for one with my religious background. Although founded like Princeton by Presbyterians, Union's Presbyterians were "ecumenical Presbyterians" that sought "intellectual and ecclesiastical diversity."[27] Even the seminary's charter required that "equal privileges of admission and instruction [would] be allowed to students of every denomination of Christians."[28] More importantly, Union, unlike Princeton, placed an "emphasis on religious experience, on religion as lived."[29] Perfect for one with a Pentecostal past. Union would go on to develop an "inclusive liberalism" while Princeton maintained a well-entrenched "exclusive conservatism."[30] (Unfortunately I never attended Union but I have always been proud of the fact that I was accepted into their Ph.D. program in 1977.)

Like so many other ex-Pentecostals (if one can ever be an "ex" anything) in the quest for upward mobility and social acceptance, I learned to conveniently and quickly change the subject when someone unintentionally asked that potentially exposing, embarrassing question, "And what is your religious background and tradition?" If I told the truth, I knew I would be penalized just like my earlier rejection from Princeton. To admit to being Pentecostal or to even having been raised Pentecostal was forever to be instantly labeled, catalogued, and placed on the sectarian shelf. I knew the labels all too well, and I wasn't going to be identified with any of them, any more, even if it meant denying my past. "Holy Roller." "Snake Handler." "White Trash." I became "mainline"—Presbyterian—more for social and cultural reasons than religious ones. My Pentecostalism was quickly stashed behind the closet door at Princeton. I now know, of course, that I was not alone. There were many others going through the same type of religious journey and spiritual pilgrimage as I made in the 1970s. Walter Hollenweger has recently commented on the Pentecostal switching phenomenon. "The transfer of Pentecostals to Catholic, Orthodox and Protestant churches is considerable. One finds nowadays in all churches...former Pentecostal pastors in leading positions. Ex-Pentecostals would be a fruitful field of research."[31]

In the fall of 1970, I had the good fortune to find a young professor fresh out of Harvard University with a Ph.D. in sociology. Although Dean R. Hoge held a divinity degree, also from Harvard, he was far more sociologist than minister or theologian. Over the next three years as my advisor he introduced me to all the classics: Max Weber, Ernest Troeltsch, and H. Richard Niebuhr. I slowly began to "out" myself to my advisor. I not only revealed my religious past to Hoge, I wrote papers about it for his classes. I was beginning to understand and come to terms with my past. Soon I would be experiencing yet another conversion.

During my second year in seminary, in a theology course taught by a young Daniel L. Migliore, now the Charles Hodge Professor of Systematic Theology, I was exposed to the writings of Harvey Cox—Harvard's most famous theologian. Harvey Cox by then had even eclipsed his former mentor Paul Tillich. I not only resonated with what I read but I was soon quoting Cox in sermons that I gave in Miller Chapel and in various American Baptist, United Presbyterian, United Methodist, and Reformed churches in New Jersey, New York, and Pennsylvania. Never was I more honored than when my Preaching professor, Donald McLeod, announced before my classmates one day that "Mr. Barfoot belongs in a university chapel." I was thrilled. I thought to myself Professor McLeod could have said a "tent" or a "mission." Instead he used the word "chapel"—a university chapel. I had fooled him! My Pentecostal past had not shown or seeped through.

So taken was I with Harvey Cox that I applied my senior year of seminary to Harvard Divinity School for further graduate study. Shortly before graduating from Princeton in the spring of 1973, my Preaching professor, seeing me in the library, asked what parish I would be serving. I informed him I was staying in school, going on for more work. "Where" he asked? When I said the word Harvard, he showed immediate concern and disappointment. "You need to be careful," he cautioned, "you could lose your faith there." Quietly I chuckled to myself, remembering that was what all the Pentecostals had said when I made the long trip from Southern California to Princeton.

A funny thing happened at Harvard Divinity School. Instead of losing my faith, I came away with a greater understanding and appreciation for my religious past than I ever had at Princeton. And, unlike the Princeton application, I was no longer willing to hide and bury my religious roots. On my Harvard application I included my Pentecostal history. Wasn't Harvard all about inclusiveness anyway? Yes and no. Thirty years later, John Dillenberger more than anyone else helped me sort out the Harvard experience. In 1957 Dillenberger was appointed Parkman Professor of Divinity at Harvard, the second oldest chair in the United States. In 1977, as the head of the Graduate Theological Union in Berkeley he sent a welcoming letter informing me of my acceptance in the GTU doctoral program. In 2004 Dillenberger reflected on his illustrious theological past. His memory of his time at Harvard is instructive.

> The existing faculty and students at the time of my arrival were largely in the liberal Unitarian tradition or conservative, if not fundamentalist. From both angles, the main theological traditions could be ignored…. Hence, one could enter Harvard, do the necessary work, and leave without having been confronted by other positions. The left leaning liberals and the ultra-conservatives respected each other, but rejected positions in between.[32]

Reflecting back, I can see through my own experience what Dillenberger meant. Compared to Harvard, Princeton was much more concerned with "the main theological traditions." One was confronted there "by theological questions." And as a theological school and seminary, Princeton was vastly superior to Harvard in all most every way. The truth is that with my background it may have been at the time much harder to get into Princeton than Harvard.

My real reason in going to Harvard Divinity School—to work with Harvey Cox—was frustrated and thwarted for the next two years. During my first year, he was on a sabbatical. All was not lost, however. Oscar Handlin, in Harvard Yard, increased my love for American cities, and Sister Marie Augusta Neal deepened my work in the sociology of religion at the Divinity School. The next year was spent on staff in my new-found church home on the West Coast. Away from school, my eyes were opened to the destructive reality of church politics. It took less than a year's internship for me to quickly conclude that a church is a church is a church, be it Presbyterian or Pentecostal, mega, large, or small.

On Thursdays, during the year I was living in Southern California, if my dad wasn't golfing with his brother, he would drive down the coast to spend some time with his son. I will never forget his words of warning one afternoon as we walked along the beach together while the sun sank fast into the ocean. "Just remember, Charles," he said, "If you make one mistake, these people [Presbyterians], will be much harder on you than either your father or a Pentecostal church. They will be merciless." How right my dad was with his Bible school education, and how blind I was as a Harvard seminarian! My dad's words of wisdom, derived from years in the real world and common "horse sense," as he called it, never left me. I often replayed his advice mentally when I wondered who the true liberals were when it came to the Christian virtues of compassion and forgiveness. I was slowly beginning to understand why my Pentecostal ancestors referred to the mainline churches as "cold, dead, formalism." If they tended to be "heartless," I also discovered that fateful year in Newport Beach that fundamentalism was alive and well in the Presbyterian Church. Far from dying out, its surviving strain was far more virulent than anything that I had ever been exposed to in the Assemblies of God. In the game of fundamentalism, Pentecostals were softball minor-leaguers at best. Presbyterians, I quickly discovered, were the true heavy hitters, hardball major-leaguers. It was Presbyterianism, after all, not Pentecostalism, that had given birth to the fundamentalist movement in the first place.

By the fall of 1975, I couldn't wait to finally meet my mentor after a two-year delay and detour. Up the creaking winding staircase I climbed until I reached the third and final floor. My anticipation in climbing the stairs was not unlike my experience twenty years earlier in the discovery of a balcony in the old stone church in Yakima, Washington. This too I knew was going to be exciting, new, and different. It was not difficult finding the right office. A "Hello my name is…" sticker lovingly colored in crayon by Harvey's daughter Sara was stuck to the door. It simply stated, "Mr. Cox [in large letters] by Sara [in small letters.]" I knocked at the door, a warm voice responded, and soon I was sitting in what one writer described as a "small study nestled under the gables on the top floor of Harvard Divinity School." In reality, Harvey's cramped office with a door for a desk, overlooking a parking lot, had recently been converted from a dorm room. Another Harvard myth was quickly shattered. I glanced around the small study, quickly realizing that no diplomas adorned the walls as they did the professors' offices of my small church-affiliated college. Nothing to show for all those years spent at Penn, Yale, and Harvard. No framed accolades from the past. Here was a professor very much in touch with the present. Beside the books, two things caught my eye—a brightly colored woven cross called an *ojo de dios,* made from yarn and sticks by native peoples of Mexico and Harvey's draft card blown up into poster size perched on top a metal file cabinet. The draft card informed me that he was born in May 1929—twenty years and a month before me. More than anything else, however, my mentor made me feel at home while sitting in his comfortable worn, green vinyl chair. From that day on he never was Mr. Cox, Dr. Cox, or even Professor Cox, just Harvey Cox. Each time I climbed the stairs to see him my heart would pound with anticipation. In the academic world,

Harvey Cox, was for me, the real thing.

On an autumn afternoon in 1975 I was unprepared to discover my academic calling. Harvey simply returned me to my theological and religious roots. As much as I thought Harvard was exciting, new, and different, Harvey thought Pentecostalism was exciting, new and different. Harvey had not only rejected so many of the prevailing myths surrounding the movement, he had also rightly separated Pentecostalism from fundamentalism. I began to see my past with new found eyes of appreciation and understanding.

My academic journey backward was not an early exercise in Pentecostal chic either. In his first family memoir, *All Over But The Shoutin'*, Rick Bragg reminds his readers that "dreaming backwards can carry a man through some dark rooms."[33] Pentecostalism, at least my version of it, had plenty of dark, non-supernatural rooms, ones I had no desire to re-enter or revisit. Yet I also came to see that the one-time Harvard graduate student and Jewish poet of alienation, Delmore Schwartz, had it right when he penned that "every kind of experience is limited and ignorant."[34] And yes, that even included the Harvard experience itself. Pentecostalism never did own the exclusive rights to ignorance. Ironically, a more sophisticated form of fundamentalism was also alive and well in the divinity school, especially in the Department of Church History. A reductionist fundamentalism of the left was still fundamentalism. My new academic task required focusing on the fountains of my tradition's holy water instead of the ever-popularized dark rooms of its hogwash. The thin patina of spiritual stereotypes often prevents a person from finding the deeper layers of a religious movement's meaning.

Although on that autumn day in the mid-1970s I never returned home "nevermore to roam," I for the first time began to face the fact that I had not fully, completely left home either. The saints had left the porch light on for their prodigal, and I was still very much emotionally connected to my tribal past. If my head had journeyed on ahead to the far country of the academy, my heart was still safely at home in my father's house. In his book about rites of passage in a man's life, Ronald L. Grimes reminds the reader that a religious past is not some sort of excess baggage easily discarded.

> Upbringing and culture are more skinlike than baggagelike. We cannot just decide to put the stuff down and walk off from it. We remain whatever we are….Though we convert, we remain the same. It is easy to exaggerate the degree of transformation…experienced in converting from one tradition to another.[35]

"Humanity," echoed C.S. Lewis, "does not pass through phases as a train passes through stations: being alive, it has the privilege of always moving yet never leaving anything behind. Whatever we have been, in some sort we are still."[36]

Unlike my new-found Presbyterian and Congregational traditions, "dance" had literally preceded "dogma" in my religious roots. I had discovered "the holy" experientially, not intellectually. And despite Protestant mainline scoffers at my "primitive" religion, "religion as experience" has always been the primary approach, according to many early theorists of religion. The successor to Sir James Frazer's chair of social anthropology at Oxford, R.R. Marett, maintained that religion was "not so much thought out as danced out."[37] Friedrich Schleiermacher argued that the essence of religion "is neither thinking nor acting, but intuition and feeling."[38] And America's most influential philosopher of his day, William James, wrote that "feeling is the deeper source of religion...philosophic and theological formulas are secondary products, like translations of a text into another tongue."[39] "If you wish to grasp her [religion's] essence," concluded James, "you must look to the feelings."[40]

The famous British Pentecostal pioneer Donald Gee wrote,

> When we "came out for Pentecost," we came out not merely for a theory, or a doctrine; we came out for a burning, living, mighty EXPERIENCE that revolutionized our lives. The Baptism in the Spirit which we sought and received was a REALITY, even though we probably understood little of the doctrines involved at the time. How different, then, from the purely doctrinal and theoretical issues involved in this matter.[41]

Because dance did precede dogma, old time Pentecostals would often affirm their belief in experience instead of doctrine by repeatedly singing over and over a favorite chorus that declared: "Oh, it's real! It's real! I know it's real, this Pentecostal message, I know, I know it's real!"[42]

Discovering country music during this time (I was really getting in touch with my roots and feelings) I realized that my religious journey and spiritual history read at least to an outsider like a sad country song about a love gone wrong, yet managed to still hold on. Despite our religious breakup and spiritual separation, it had always been a lover's quarrel for the two of us. Like a divorced distant lover, I saw with time, the good, for the most part, outweighed the bad, that the rooms of my religion, flooded with spiritual sunshine, had indeed been much lighter than darker. As a child, a new week and my Sunday morning ritual began by listening over the radio to Charles Fuller's *Old Fashioned Revival Hour*. Who could ever forget the opening signature song of that thirty-eight year broadcast? "Heavenly Sunshine," sang the great unseen church choir for those of us in radio land, "Heavenly Sunshine, Flooding my soul with Glory Divine, Heavenly Sunshine, Heavenly Sunshine, Hallelujah, Jesus is Mine." Like any old flame my religious past was always hauntingly there, just around the bend, in the next memory, or in the sound of an old familiar hymn. And more times than not, it was the music not the preaching that managed for a few minutes at least to sing me "back home." Perhaps Alan Jackson says and sings it best in a country song, "I don't know what brought us together, what strange forces of nature conspired to construct the present from the past, but, I'll go on loving you."[43] Jackson especially manages to sing me back home whenever I listen to his *Precious Memories* album. All the great "classics" (and not one mindless praise song) I grew up with are there; "Softly and Tenderly," "I Love To Tell the Story," "In the Garden," and "What A Friend We Have In Jesus."[44] My soul has been dreaming backwards now, for more than thirty years, attempting to understand and make some sense of my religious roots and past, to discover in James Cone's words, "what all the shouting was about."[45] "On ne doit pas ecrire que de ce qu'on aimee—One should write only about what one loves," declared Renan, the biographer and historian. Needless to say, I have taken Renan's advice to heart.

Over the years the word syncretism has fallen on hard times. Hopefully, Anita Leopold's and Jeppe Jensen's *Syncretism in Religion* will help to rehabilitate the concept once again in religious studies. This controversial category is also well suited for the study of Pentecostalism. As Anita Leopold notes, "We construct meaningful borders such as those of religious...traditions...and...by way of the myth of belonging to a particular history. Syncretism confronts our certainty of belonging."[46] Nowhere does syncretism confront the certainty of belonging better than Pentecostalism. More than anything else Pentecostalism dissolves and destroys boundaries, the boundaries of ageism, sexism, racism, even nationalism. The promise of the spirit, after all, was that it would be poured out "upon all flesh."

Pentecostalism, an orphan daughter of American religion, had many a stepparent, even more grandparents and aunts and uncles, and plenty of second cousins to go around. It is impossible to accurately trace its lineage. Pure blood lines do not exist. Because the movement was made from thousands of "testimonies," no one master story can be found. Pentecostalism came in all shapes and sizes and included—in the language of the King James Bible—all sorts of "divers doctrines." Like Crayolas it too came in assorted colors. Because of its diverse parentage, it is only possible to trace the lineage of Pentecostalism with very broad genetic markers. Instead of speaking of the origins of the movement, I think it is better to mention the movement's markers and characteristics. I will now attempt to do so using the following categories.

I. Radical: A Left-Wing Heir of the Reformation

Arriving at Princeton Theological Seminary in the fall of 1970 I was unprepared for all the men I met. They were seemingly everywhere. My only memory about the first worship service in Miller Chapel was how I had never heard so many men singing in one place before. All that testosterone and all those powerful male voices seemed literally capable of raising the chapel's rafters. Coming from Pentecostalism, where the women had vastly outnumbered the men and were always requesting prayer for their "unsaved husbands," it took me a while to adjust to all the men in the mainline. Even in my entering class of a hundred or so students, there was only a modest handful of women. Where the men really outnumbered the women, of course, was the faculty. Not only were there many men, but the majority of them, it seemed, were older men on the cusp of retirement. The "grand old men" of Princeton Seminary is how I remember them today. Always dressed in their Sunday best of white, starched shirts and three-piece suits, they were the epitome of the vanishing breed of the gentleman scholar. By the time of my arrival, their days at Princeton Seminary were numbered as surely as the women preachers I had heard as a child in Pentecostalism.

In addition to my classes with Bruce M. Metzger, Norman Victor Hope, and Dean Adams, I also had Lefferts A. Loetscher in Church History. Among all the gentlemen scholars, Loetscher seemed to me to be the most Presbyterian and personal. Our small seminar met one night a week in a former carriage house across the street from the main campus. At the end of one of the class sessions, the distinguished Dr. Loetscher asked me if I would accompany him home and assist him in carrying a load of extra books back to his home study on campus. Somehow, as we were walking and talking along the path to his house, the dreaded background question came up. Perhaps he had heard through the grapevine that one of his students was a former Pentecostal and about to graduate. "So, Charles, what is your religious background?" "Well, I was raised in the Assemblies of God," I slowly stammered out, but then quickly added what I thought was a new redemptive sentence. "But I'm a Presbyterian now, a Presbyterian in good standing at the fourth-largest church in the country." "Splendid," replied Dr. Loetscher. At first I thought the "splendid" response was reserved for the Presbyterian part of who I was, but I soon discovered it was meant for my religious past. "Splendid, Charles, you come from the left wing of the church." Unfortunately, I didn't have a clue as to what the good professor was attempting to tell me. I wasn't aware at the time of the church having sides or wings, but if I had, I would have guessed that my religious past placed me on the right side, the conservative side. And I would have been wrong.

Later I would learn that despite the popular conception and notion of the Protestant Reformation beginning with Martin Luther, both Luther and Calvin came late in its development simply "riding to triumph on the crest of a tide that had been rising for centuries."[47] The tide of the Protestant Reformation itself had come from the left side or wing of the church, created by a radical lower-class movement drawn from four sectarian groups: the Cathars, Waldenses, Lollards, and Hussites. These four radical Christian sectarian groups had revolted from the eleventh to the fifteenth century when Catholicism was at the peak of its power. What made Luther so popular was the wayward monk's identification with the lower social classes and his embrace of sectarian Christianity.

> The son of a peasant, Luther always claimed to be proud of his lowly origin. Its traces were evident in his healthy animality and in his coarse manners, his fondness for ribaldry, his tempestous fits of anger, his impassioned language, often vulgar and violent, but at its best rich with the tang of earth and all growing things. He was a creature of imagination and emotion rather than reason, a mystic without the ascetic tendency that usually accompanies mysticisim.[48]

Roland H. Bainton, a specialist in Reformation history and Titus Street Professor of Ecclesiastical History at Yale for forty-two years, published an article in 1941 pointing out five characteristics of "The Left Wing of the Reformation." The first concern and characteristic among the Reformation radicals was an ethical one. "The primary defect in the…Reformation according to the radicals was moral. The Reformation had not produced an adequate transformation of life. The Lutheran was not distinguishable from the Catholic at the point of conduct."[49] Much of the ethical concerns for the radicals had to do with the church's practice of infant baptism. Their detractors soon had a new name for them, Anabaptists, because of their insistence on adult baptism. (*Ana*, Greek for "again.") Conversion, inner conviction, and moral fruits constituted real faith. One was no longer simply born into it.

The second characteristic of the left wing was Christian primitivism. According to Bainton, "The restoration of primitive Christianity and the spiritual new birth were practically synonymous for the Anabaptists. The gift of the spirit which they craved had a twofold function: to produce, on the one hand, moral transformation and, on the other, to give religious knowledge." [50] The pursuit of religious knowledge led to two additional spiritual byproducts. Whereas Christian liturgical services had been performed before quiet worshippers, the Anabaptists quickly became the original "holy rollers." Preaching was energetic and worship services were emotional, interactive, new and revolutionary. The pursuit of religious knowledge by the radicals also led to mysticism. "The disciples of the inner word...turned to mysticism and...to communications of the spirit in dreams and vision." [51]

Ernest Sutherland Bates in his discussion of "The Left Wing of the Reformation" argues that it was mysticism that struck a new note in Protestantism and would later move beyond the bounds of religion into every walk of life.

> With the intellectual climate what it was, the most promising approach... was through mysticism....Here at last a new note was struck in Protestantism, and one destined to vibrate ever more loudly in the coming years, as the inner logic of Protestantism would slowly force an acceptance of this appeal to direct experience as the central core of philosophic meaning in the new religion—an appeal that would in time be carried far beyond the bounds of religion into art, science, politics, and every walk of life. [52]

The third characteristic of the churches' left wing was a heightened sense of eschatology. "All the Reformers," claimed Bainton, "were steeped in the Scriptures and all were affected by a sense of the imminence of the end." [53] This "sense of the imminence of the end" also led to the creation of anti-intellectualism among the radicals. "A favorite figure among the anti-intellectuals was the penitent thief who was saved without any knowledge of the substance and persons of the Godhead, paedo-baptism, consubstantiation, transubstantiation, predestination, election, reprobation, etc." [54]

Perhaps the most radical characteristic of the Anabaptists was "its demand for the separation of church and state. Government was ruled out of the sphere of religion." [55] The radicals' rejection of politics and failure to serve in the military brought swift punishment and severe persecution. Thousands were baptized a third and final time   drowned—while others were either tortured or burned at the stake. Martyrdom only served to reinforce their belief that they had discovered a true, pure unadulterated Christianity. It is not without irony that centuries later their theological heirs in

America would seek to unite church and state by forming the religious right. No act could have been more blasphemous to the radical reformers than the unity of church and state.

Finally, the fifth characteristic of the left wing of the Reformation was that although it was thoroughly suppressed in Europe, "the spiritual descendants of the left wing gained a permanent foot-hold and did even more than the established church to fashion the temper of England and America."[56]

II. Theological: "Pietistic Spirituality"

Pentecostalism may be best understood theologically as Pietistic spirituality. With roots in the German and English Protestant movements of the seventeenth and eighteenth centuries, Pietistic spirituality is concerned with a direct, inner experience with the Divine that transcends dogma or institutional religion. "It is a 'heart religion' reacting against the 'corpse cold orthodoxy' of scholastic institutionalism."[57] In many ways Pietism was simply the second phase of the Protestant Reformation. "It was the extension of the reform principle to the Christian life, a principle which the earlier reformers applied chiefly…to the areas of doctrine and polity."[58]

Pietism also explains Harvey Cox's long abiding interest in Pentecostalism. Admitting "an inclination that started in my boyhood," Harvey has always "felt personally drawn to those religions which major in the 'affections' rather than in doctrines."[59]

> I have never forgotten…that it was through a personal experience of Christ that I first came into the presence of the Divine Spirit. Given this pattern of life trajectories, it was probably inevitable that one day I would develop a strong interest in Pentecostalism, the experiential branch of Christianity par excellence.[60]

"Pietism," concluded Sydney E. Ahlstrom in his monumental work, *A Religious History of the American People*, "was…a movement of revival, aimed at making man's relation to God experientially and morally meaningful as well as socially relevant. It stressed the feelings of the heart. It emphasized the royal priesthood and sought to revive the laity. It called always for a return to the Bible."[61]

F. Ernest Stoeffler has identified four theological characteristics also found in Pentecostalism: the experiential, perfectionistic, biblical, and oppositive. "Experiential" suggests that Christianity was discovered only by a personal experience with God. Theological speculation and liturgical formalism were only secondary concerns. Both the Pietists and the medieval mystics were also closely related in emphasizing the primacy of the inward response to God. "Bridal mysticism" flourished in formative Pentecostalism and in Aimee Semple McPherson's early ministry.

Pietism as "perfectionistic" promoted a type of religious idealism, a life of wholeness and complete devotion. One was never "almost a Christian" or "becoming a Christian." The silver-tongued Henry Smith made clear the distinction in his sermons: "Almost a son is a bastard; almost sweet is unsavory, almost hot is lukewarm, which God spueth out of his mouth (Rev. 3:16). So, almost a Christian is not a Christian."[62] This religious idealism was also manifested in evangelistic and missionary outreach. It was the Pietist "who felt upon himself the compulsion of taking the gospel to the whole world."[63]

Since Pietistic spirituality was grounded in scripture, it was often characterized by an intense "biblicism." The Bible in essence became the guide book for daily life. Pietists, by their appeal to the Bible, permitted lay people to testify, exhort, and even to preach. This led in turn to the rise of women preachers. As early as the 1520s, women preachers were common among the Anabaptists in Germany. "It was this implicit, somewhat naïve, trust in the Word, rather than in man's words about the Word, which is...responsible for the fact that the Pietists really trusted the religious opinions of theologically untrained laymen."[64] This intense biblicism led to legalism and later to fundamentalism itself. Stoeffler argues that "legalism quickly became and always remained the greatest temptation of Pietists."[65]

Finally, Pietism was an "oppositive" response to prevailing doctrinal and liturgical issues. It was a spiritual reaction to failures in the established religion of the day.

The sociologist David Martin also makes a very important point about the connection between Pietism and Pentecostalism. "The lineage running from Pietism to Pentecostalism is linked positively to modernity....And since Pietism is prone to be understood as culturally narrow and socially passive, it is well to remember that its roots were not only in a deepening of inner life but in the founding of schools, orphanages and missions."[66]

III. Mystical: Ernst Troeltsch's Long-Forgotten Third Type of Christianity

Mysticism is simply the insistence upon a direct inward and present religious experience....It expresses itself in ecstasy and frenzy, in visions and hallucinations, in subjective religious experience and 'inwardness,' in concentration upon the purely interior and emotional side of religious experience.

Above all, eroticism…plays a leading part, since [it] is also used to
stimulate religious enthusiasm…The imagery of Love…and certain
Christian interpretations of the Song of Songs, harp upon the same string
in the spiritual life….It is to this mysticism that the so-called 'Enthusiasm' of the Primitive Christian Church, a large part of the 'spiritual
gifts', the 'speaking with tongues', the power of exorcism, the whole of
its spiritual activity, belongs; this phenomenon recurs again and again…
bringing home with great power the redemptive energy of the Gospel
to the individual soul…Mysticism…sees itself as the real universal heart
of all religion, of which the various myth-forms are merely the outer
garment. It regards itself as the means of restoring an immediate union
with God; it feels independent of all institutional religion, and possesses
an entire inward certainty…This is mystical 'spiritual religion'…a life in
the spirit which rises above and conquers the world.

—Ernst Troeltsch
The Social Teaching of the Christian Churches

In 1929 H. Richard Niebuhr published a soon-to-be American classic,
The Social Sources of Denominationalism. He drew heavily upon the writings
of Ernst Troeltsch, the German theologian and social theorist, introducing to the American public the "sect-church" dichotomy. Niebuhr adopted
Troeltsch's "church-type" and "sect-type" but ignored and neglected Troeltsch's third and final type of mysticism. Since Troeltsch's *The Social Teaching of the Christian Churches* was not translated into English for another two
years, Troltsch's mysticism received short shrift in attention and influence,
at least in the American church. And yet no typology of Troeltsch's fits
Pentecostalism better than mysticism.

Theodore M. Steeman notes especially how mysticism is lived and
played out in a community of faith. Mysticism is characterized "by a profound individualism, the emphasis being only on 'the relations between the
soul and God.' As a consequence," observes Steeman, "social organization is weak…Mysticism leads to forms of organization that are 'loose and
provisional'…There is little emphasis on doctrine or on formal liturgy, on
priestly functions or on organizational structure….What counts is the fellowship of like-minded souls."[67]

Troeltsch's typology is most helpful when looking at the formative
years of modern American Pentecostalism. Not only were early twentieth-century Pentecostals short on doctrine, unlike their spiritual second
cousins, the fundamentalists, but they vehemently denied that they were
creating denominations or even a new sect. What the largest Anglo body
of Pentecostals, the Assemblies of God, sought to create in the place of a

denomination came right out of Troeltsch's third typology, a "fellowship of like-minded souls."

Not even adopting "a statement of faith," the Pentecostal saints gathered at the Opera House at Hot Springs, Arkansas, in the spring of 1914 and affirmed only that they were creating a "cooperative fellowship." Two years later, one of their leaders sought to reassure both clergy and laity alike that the fledging Assemblies of God movement had not morphed into another new denomination or worse yet succumbed to sectarianism. "Please be sure," wrote W.F. Carothers in the fellowship's major periodical, "that we are as firm as ever against 'organization' as it has been practiced in the modern church movements."[68] Less than ten years later, however, the general secretary of the "cooperative fellowship" conceded defeat. "[The constitution] declared we were not a sect and not an organization, and then we turned right around and organized."[69] The 1927 General Council (church business meeting) was a watershed between the old ideal of a cooperative fellowship of ministers and the new reality of an emerging denomination. One of the ministers in attendance sadly concluded that their actions at the council were "going to make the saints laugh in their sleeve" and it would prove to them "that we are growing sectarian."[70] What had started as a mystical experience with the baptism of the spirit, with little emphasis placed on either doctrine or organization had slowly become sectarian with priestly functions usurping prophetic roles. The major problem Pentecostals have faced everywhere is how to organize, not a doctrine or dogma, but the dance of experience.

Harvey Cox, astute as ever at eighty years of age, recently stated that he thinks of Pentecostals as "mainstream mystics." "Pentecostalism brings to awareness," claims Cox, "central aspects of the Christian mystical tradition and the fact various traditions of secular liberalism and mainline Christianity have been unsatisfying for a wide range of people." [71]

In addition to his role as a late nineteenth and early twentieth-century German Protestant theologian, Troeltsch may have been something of a prophetic visionary of future Christianity when he wrote that "Gradually in the modern world...the third type [mysticism] has come to predominate."[72]

IV. Sociological: "A Folk Religion"

The sacred and profane mingle harmoniously within classical Pentecostalism the way that they do in American country music. Detractors argue that both are mindless and simplistic. What their critics fail to understand is the profundity expressed in the simplicity. Timeless truths, the roots of one's raisings, and the treasures of oral tradition are preserved and expressed in shorthand form so that the least learned may understand. Country music, argues George O. Carney "deals with universal themes…subjects that other forms of music would not touch. The simplicity and commonality of this expression…appeal to make it understandable to the average person."[73] Similarly, some of the most profound truths of the gospels are to be found in the parables of Jesus. The recognition of such truths is achieved by resonating with the life experiences of those for whom the truths are conveyed. The highest compliment that the Pentecostal preacher or country artist, through their largely autobiographical sermon or song, can receive is simply, "He or she understands." "He preached my life." "She sang my story." Merle Haggard notes this relationship between listener and song by simply stating that "no one could really know [country music] unless they've been there."[74]

To continue the analogy, one can say that Pentecostalism is to religion what "country" is to music. They both sociologically fit in the folk tradition—religion and music "of the people." Country music, originally the folk music of the working class, has also been identified as being "America's only native musical art form."[75] (Jazz, it seems, would be the only exception.) Both movements are alarmingly prophetical. Prophecy results as a product of social failure when secular alternatives and answers break down. Both movements share the protest by the people of the current state of affairs while at the same time either sing or preach about the promise and possibilities of the future.

Like Pentecostalism and Christianity itself, country music was also syncretistic in its origins. Charles F. Gritzner writes that country music's folk character is the "…outgrowth of a blending of styles representing a cross-section of American music."

> A Saturday night *Grand Ole Opry* show might include samples of Appalachian, bluegrass, Louisiana 'Cajun' music, East Texas honky-tonk, Mexican border melodies, mountain spirituals, western swing, African-American rock 'n roll, and alas, a touch of pop….References may be made in lyrics to whites, blacks, Chicanos, or native Americans; indeed, the stage performers themselves, may represent each of these groups.
>
> A well-tuned musical ear may catch a note of the blues, a fleeting jazz beat, or the high-pitched nasal rubato of a true Anglo-Celtic folk tradition. Musical punctuation may take the form of a Swiss yodel, a Cajun "AAA-HYEE," or a fervent fundamentalist backwoods stomp-and-holler. Accompaniment will most certainly include hot-licks guitar picking introduced by blacks, the African banjo, the harmonica (introduced to

the Opry by Deford Bailey, a black) or the haunting wail of the Hawaiian-introduced steel guitar. Top it off with a gaudy spangled suit adopted from Mexican Mariachis and a cowboy hat, and one begins to get the notion that there is a degree of eclectic purity, albeit somewhat homogenized, to the stage performance.[76]

Recently Miriam Longino argued that even African-Americans can "hear ourselves in country music."

> Like much of the blended culture of the South...country music has a rich legacy of multiracial influences. Before there was...even an Opry, African-American musicians were on the scene, playing banjos in string bands, writing some of the earliest country fiddle tunes, and blowing harmonicas in dance halls and juke joints....The sainted father of modern country music, Hank Williams Jr., learned his guitar licks and phrasing from an old black bluesman, Rufe Tee-Tot Payne. Blues artists, such as Leadbelly, relied heavily on country storytelling in their recordings.[77]

And just as denominationalism segregated Pentecostalism along racial lines, so too, was country music segregated from the 1920s onward by modern marketing and the recording industry. Not until the 1960s did black artists such as Ray Charles begin to blur the boundaries again with a return to country. Likewise in the 1960s Pentecostalism blurred the boundaries once again between mainstream and minority religion, between religious insiders and outsiders. From the 1920s onward, both country music and Pentecostalism were products of a modernizing world. The overall influence of Pentecostalism on Southern music is also worth mentioning. Among the artists who were shaped by a Pentecostal experience are James Blackwood, Johnny Cash, Jessi Colter, George Jones, Larry Gatlin, Mickey Gilley, Jerry Lee Lewis, Dolly Parton, Carl Perkins, Elvis Presley, and Tammy Wynette.

Today, of course, lines continue to cross and boundaries blur. No longer do Pentecostals come from cultural and economic ghettos, or country or folk music fans from the farm. Pentecostalism thrives and is as much at home in Greenwich, Connecticut, as it is in Harlem or the barrios of Los Angeles. Country music likewise has finally arrived uptown in American culture and is as much at home in Manhattan's Upper East Side as it is in East Texas honky-tonks. The themes in country music of broken dreams and unhappy lives are given a much wider interpretation as they transcend social and economic barriers and speak, instead, to the common plight. The lyrics of Merle Haggard, Emmy Lou Harris, Dwight Yoakam, and Alan Jackson speak as much to those in cities as those down home on the farm. Most Americans regardless of their socio-economic status can resonate with the despair in songs such as Keith Whitley's, "Lord, I wish hard livin' didn't come so easy for me" or Alan Jackson's, "Monday Morning Church."

> You left my heart as empty as a Monday morning church.
> It used to be so full of faith and now it only hurts.
> And I can hear the devil whisper, "Things are only getting worse."
> You left my heart as empty as a Monday morning church.[78]

The feeling of transcendence can also be felt, however, when Willie Nelson sings,

> I looked to the stars, tried all of the bars
> and I've nearly gone up in smoke.
> Now my hands on the wheel of something that's real
> and I feel like I'm goin' home.[79]

Likewise, the healing of Pentecostal spirituality is no respecter of social class when it touches emotional brokenness. Sociologically, then, country music, like Pentecostalism, is a unified world of the common person—sin and salvation, transgression and redemption, human suffering and compassion, emotional brokenness and spiritual healing. The secret of a Pentecostal preacher's success, like that of a country music artist, is the ability to accurately articulate these dual emotions.

Folk religion often has been difficult to discover because it has eluded the reach and grasp of scholars. "How does one 'study' people's religion?" asks Harvey Cox.

> During my long formal training as a theologian I was taught, and taught very well, how to interpret the meanings of sacred scriptures and religious texts, some of them in their original languages. But no one ever taught me how to interpret *living* religion, especially the actions of ordinary people. I regret this lapse in my training, because in the final analysis it is always just such people who are the real bearer of religion.[80]

In his opening Gifford Lecture in 1901 at the University of Edinburgh, William James remarked that "It seems the natural thing for us [Americans] to listen whilst the Europeans talk. The contrary habit, of talking whilst the Europeans listen, we have not yet acquired."[81] Perhaps it has taken close to a century for American scholars to reverse James' observation. Pentecostalism may have lacked scholarly interest for years, because its birth lacked a foreign mystique and intrigue. Pentecostalism, part of the folk religion of America, is as homegrown and American as Coca-Cola, Elvis Presley, Harley-Davidson, and Chevrolet. Catherine L. Albanese has rightly placed Pentecostalism as part of the larger evangelical movement in its revivalist context as representing the "classic form of American religious experience."[82] And perhaps because this "classic form of American religious experience" is now transnational and global, American scholars can no longer dismiss it or simply wish it away.

V. Historical: "The New Methodists?"

For a quarter of a century, from 1953–1978, the Reverend C.M. (Charles Morse) Ward was the voice of the Assemblies of God. Ward was the radio evangelist for *Revivaltime*, the weekly broadcast of the Assemblies of God, heard by millions around the world on the ABC network. Born in Toronto in 1909, Ward graduated from Central Bible Institute, Springfield, Missouri, in 1929. After graduation and marriage Ward returned to Eastern Canada, beginning an evangelistic ministry. While he was holding a meeting in Owen Sound, Ontario, a young hockey player on the farm team of the Toronto Maple Leafs was converted. Howard M. Barfoot, my father, had been raised in the United Church of Canada but rarely attended and lived only to play hockey. My father and his younger brother not only converted to Pentecostalism under C.M. Ward but were soon barnstorming together both in Canada and the United States as the Barfoot Brothers Evangelistic Team. C.M. Ward was their mentor. Ward was larger than life—perhaps the Assemblies of God's first living legend. At the twenty-sixth General Council held in San Antonio in 1959, where Thomas F. Zimmerman was elected general superintendent, Ward was one of the featured preachers. After the service ended, my father took me to Ward's suite at the Menger Hotel to meet his favorite preacher—and the one I listened to every Sunday morning before going to church from a radio the size of forthcoming television sets. I remember sitting on the edge of the bed facing the larger-than-life preacher, who was positioned in a chair and who had his big, black shiny shoes propped up on the bed where we were sitting. I felt uncomfortable as Ward studied me from head to toe. I wondered, does he think I have what it takes to become a future preacher? It seemed to me he had some kind of spiritual X-ray vision that was capable of probing my inner being, even knowing my thoughts. It was what Ward said, however, that I never forgot. Turning to Dad, he said, "Howard, if Jesus is nothing but a myth, I'll still bank on him." And then he said, "I don't know why we Pentecostals are so controversial. There's nothing controversial about us. We simply do what the earlier Methodists did. We are the new Methodists." It was not some idle boast or Pentecostal braggadocio. Ward knew first hand what he was talking about since his father, the Reverend A.G. Ward, had been a circuit-riding Methodist preacher in Western Canada before converting to Pentecostalism.

Scholars today from Nathan Hatch to David Martin prove that Ward's words in the mid-1950s were both prophetic and accurate. As early as 1980 a British scholar noted the similarities between the two movements in an aptly titled lecture, "The Mantle of Elijah: Nineteenth-century Primitive Methodism and Twentieth-century Pentecostalism."[83] In his presidential address to the American Society of Church History in 1994, Nathan Hatch concluded, "The Methodists are the fountainhead of mainline denominations…and, indirectly, of twentieth century Pentecostalism—a movement as stunning in its growth both here and abroad as Methodism was in the early Republic.[84]

Likewise, David Martin in his book *Pentecostalism: The World Their Parish* notes that by 1900 Methodism had become America's largest and wealthiest Protestant denomination. "The time was ripe for Pentecostalism to pick up Methodism's 'unfinished task.' "

> In almost every respect Pentecostalism replicated Methodism: in its entrepreneurship and adaptability, lay participation and enthusiasm and in its splintering and fractiousness. It did so also in the place it offered to blacks and women…Where the two movements differed was in the "third blessing" of Holy Spirit baptism, in the intensity of millennial expectation, and in a shift to a Christ of power rather than the Man of Sorrows….Yet such differences may not be all that great.[85]

He concludes, "Most of the features of Pentecostalism tell tales of Methodist paternity, but fatherhood is only rarely acknowledged."[86] So important has Pentecostalism become in recent years that some scholars refer to this modern American religious movement "as a third wave" following Puritanism and Methodism in its influence. All three movements were also Pietistic—religions of the heart.

In 1866 the Reverend C.C. Goss wrote a book in celebration of the "first century of American Methodism." One of the first things Goss observed about the uniqueness of Methodism was its mode of preaching. "As a rule, a Methodist addresses himself directly to the heart, while many others appeal to the intellect….Methodist preachers never converted the pulpit into a professor's chair."[87] As late as the mid 1920s Gilbert T. Rowe was affirming in his book *The Meaning of Methodism* that "Methodism keeps constantly in view the spread of pure, personal religion and subordinates the form of organization to the object to be attained. From the beginning it has appealed to experience."[88]

Donald Matthews in his apt description of early Methodism's creativity could have been describing Pentecostalism as well:

> The movement provided a process through which ordinary people found their own voices. They spoke. Others listened; and then they too spoke. Others joined them. They sang and wept and felt renewed—in the love of Christ. The language of origins was dynamic and evocative; its testimonies in the vernaculars of the people was the dynamic creativity of the movement.[89]

Again, Pentecostalism carried on this Pietistic tradition. Russell Paul Spittler, a Harvard Ph.D. and an ordained Assemblies of God minister, was my first academic advisor and mentor. I remember him frequently saying that an education served a Pentecostal preacher "like a mill-stone hung around his neck." Early Methodism had also disparaged a theological education for its ministry much the same way its unruly and noisy theological offspring later did. In 1784 a course of self-directed study was recommended to Methodist ministers, but it came with a disclaimer: "Gaining knowledge is a good Thing, but saving Souls is...better....If you can do but one, let your Studies alone."[90] Methodism had gone on to win a major market share of nineteenth-century American Protestantism "by speaking the language of the people, winning those people to a heart-felt religion, and creating a system of circuit riders and local lay leaders and exhorters to establish societies of Methodists across the frontier."[91] A frontier saying summed up the role of the Methodist parson in short eloquence: "There is nothing out today but crows and Methodist preachers."[92]

In 1834, when a plan was presented to establish a theological school, the proposal touched off a stream of protest that included the claim that the creation of a seminary was "a dangerous and ruinous innovation" that would eventually "sap the foundations of the ecclesiastical structure."[93] Education, it seemed, would only hamper and hinder the growing movement's remarkable success. Twenty years later, when the debate was renewed, James Sewell of Philadelphia sought to remind his fellow Methodists that "the great body of our people prefer heat to light, and strong spiritual common sense to all the literary refinements that were ever concocted in all the theological seminaries in the universe.[94] As late as 1872, after the new Methodist university of Vanderbilt had been established, a Southern bishop sought to remind his denomination of its unique heritage: "Methodism was born when the world was piled full of other churches, filled to the rafters with dead forms and shadows of religious experience. Methodism came and brought to the world a live experience."[95] But a growing religion, especially one based on "experience," continually evolves and never remains stagnant. Methodists soon reaped huge dividends and high rewards from their strict, demanding faith — rewards that were tangible and secular, not just spiritual. By joining the ranks of the upwardly mobile, urban middle-class, the marriage between an uneducated preacher in the pulpit and a educated laity in the pew would soon end in dissolution and divorce. Not only would Pentecostalism pick up where Methodism left off with its "unfinished task" among the urban poor, but it would also replicate half a century later its spiritual stepparents' same doubts and struggles about the value of an educated ministry. In the end, Pentecostalism too succumbed to the siren song of the academy, "hurrying toward Zion," in Conrad Cherry's memorable phrase, in their own creation of "an exemplary city formed of the materials of religion and education."[96]

Methodism and Pentecostalism not only created new educational Zions, they also in their infancy sang the same old "songs of Zion." Hymnology provides another important link between the two movements. A Methodist minister's wife remembered the hymns from Aimee Semple McPherson's turning point tent meetings in Philadelphia the summer of 1918:

> The beautiful singing…from the Pentecostal tent came floating over to us and I said to my husband, "They are singing the same hymns as we sing in the Methodist church." There seemed to be such a lovely spirit in it and I said, "What beautiful singing," and he said, "Let us go over and investigate." I have always loved music and this seemed to go through me.[97]

And, even more than their hymnology, Methodists in Philadelphia resonated with Aimee's message.

> Mrs. McPherson's evening address held her audience spellbound. She grips her hearers from start to finish; preaches the Gospel, the real thing, no fads, no sensationalism. The fundamental doctrines of Methodism are emphasized….Mrs. McPherson emphasizes the Methodist doctrines, [and] quotes frequently from John Wesley.[98]

So great was Aimee's acceptance by the Methodists in Philadelphia in the early 1920s that she felt the need to explain her success to the "brethren in

Springfield"—the Assemblies of God. On January 8, 1921, *The Pentecostal Evangel* printed their "little sister's" story under the headline "Methodism and Pentecost."

"We wanted you [the Assemblies of God]," wrote Aimee, "to be the first to know...lest any enemy tongue or pen should endeavor to place a misconstruction upon this matter. The fact is we preached Pentecost more emphatically and laid much more stress upon 'tongues' than in other campaigns."[99] Aimee also reminded her fellow Pentecostals of her family's Methodist roots. "Since the earliest days of Methodism and John Wesley, our families on both sides were true Methodists (some being preachers and teachers), and our early associations...were wrapped up in Methodism, Sunday school, choir and church."[100] "Is it not perfectly wonderful?" she concluded, "What a change God hath wrought! How many of our beloved Pentecostal brethren have suffered expulsion and loss of church fellowship because their experience had not been understood or welcomed."[101] Aimee saw Pentecostalism as a return to "real Methodism" instead of a newer, competing, religious movement.

Methodism, however, "was never able to sweep large cities in the way that it once did in rural communities and smaller towns."[102] Pentecostalism, instead, took hold in major American cities and from there spread out around the globe. David Hempton perceptively notes this transition.

> As it turned out, it was not Methodism that was poised to sweep the world but its Holiness offspring, Pentecostalism. Here was another movement giving voice to ordinary people, thriving on mobility, depending on women, privileging personal transformation over public reform, and vigorously organizing dislocated people into noisy cells of perfectionist excitement. Above all, Pentecostalism is an enormously successful continuation of Methodism's energy and mobility, which transformed the religious landscape of the North Atlantic region...The next Christendom, already under construction in the global south, would not look the same if Methodism had never existed.[103]

VI. Liturgical: Song, Story and Strange Tongues

Harvey Cox was one of the first theologians to remind his readers that "a religion of the poor is not a poor religion."[104] "Those who support justice for the poor cannot spit on their devotions because a people's religion is one way it saves its soul."[105]

Walter Hollenweger explains that Pentecostals, much like the first Christians, have an "oral liturgy." And an oral liturgy is not a "poor" liturgy, either:

513

> Oral people are not necessarily people who do not read and write…they
> are people whose main medium of expression is the oral form—story,
> proverb, parable, joke, dance, song…in short, all the forms…which (as
> form-criticism has shown us)…framed the elementary, original source
> material of the Bible. [That] people from middle-class backgrounds and
> highly trained intellectuals find the "oral order" more satisfying than the
> written one is demonstrated by the great attracting power of the charis-
> matic movement within the mainline churches.[106]

The oral nature of Pentecostalism, again, points to its Methodist parentage. "Methodism," claims David Hempton, "was largely an oral movement….the Methodist message was inexorably bound up with the medium
of oral culture. Itinerants preached, exhorters exhorted, class members
confessed, hymns were sung, prayers were spoken, testimonies were delivered, and revival meetings throbbed with exclamatory noise."[107]

Theologian Morton Kelsey has argued that ultimate meaning is expressed
in two ways: by means of thoughts, ideas and concepts, and through symbols
and images.[108] The myth of progress and upward mobility dictate that one
must leave one for the other. The symbolic, always the most creative, is
usually left behind for the more rational, conceptual framework of thought.
What smacks of being "primitive" and "elementary" is readily discarded for
the more advanced, complex and sophisticated.

Song and story, the primitive and elementary, have always been the
primary art forms of religious life. Together they evoke spontaneity and
energy of religious feeling as opposed to conformity to an abstract, codified
creed. They affect the hearer's heart; they convict and convert the emotions.
Both were the primary and basic modes of discourse of early Christianity.
Long before they found their way into the Bible, the hymns and stories of
both the Old and New Testaments were passed on through time to successive generations by oral tradition. Christianity with its stories and songs
began as a "people's religion." This "new religious movement" found favor
with the people as it addressed itself to the poor in the land; fishermen and
peasants, publicans and outcasts. In Corinth and in Galilee, not many "wise
after the flesh, not many mighty, not many noble were called"—a condition which existed into the third century. Origin and Tertullian as well as
the critics of Christianity noted the fact that "the uneducated are always in
a majority with us."[109]

That astute observer of the Christian church H. Richard Niebuhr noted
the change when Christianity moved too far away from its original roots.
"When the new faith became the religion of the cultured, of the rulers,

of the sophisticated; it lost its spontaneous energy amid the quibbling of abstract theologies; it sacrificed its ethical rigorousness in compromise with the policies of governments and nobilities; it abandoned its apocalyptic hopes as irrelevant to the well-being of a successful church."[110] What so often in church history has been branded as heresy has been the attempt of various people's religions to capture again the simplicity of the original Gospel through their various songs and stories. Niebuhr again accurately observed, "Montanism, the Franciscan movement, Lollardy, Waldensianism, and many similar tendencies are intelligible only as the efforts of the religiously disinherited to discover again the sources of effective faith."[111]

Western Christianity largely became a religion of the book. Its ultimate meaning was expressed by thoughts, ideas, and concepts. Its theologies have grown abstract and complex. Classical Pentecostalism, like African-American religion, early Methodism, and religion in the Global South, rejects the myth of progress, the creed and the code, for the song and the story. Hollenweger observes, "In these…cultures the medium of communication is just as in Biblical times—not the definition but the description, not the statement but the story, not the doctrine but the testimony, not the book but the parable, not the summa theologica but the song, not the treatise but the TV programme."[112] Rejecting symbolic expressions based on ideas and concepts, Pentecostal spirituality seeks symbols that bypass the head and reach the heart. Richard A. Baer has suggested that Quaker silence, Catholic liturgy, and Pentecostal glossolalia are similar:

> [They are] indicative of the means by which the spiritual life may be cultivated through three different liturgical tools. In each case the "analytical mind," objective, cautious and calculating, is allowed to rest while the "spirit," that searching, struggling element within the individual, seeks a deeper spiritual perspective. Glossolalia, silence and liturgy becomes forms whereby the person transcends the immediate rational event to a "new level" of spiritual encounter.[113]

Glossolalia for Pentecostals, argues Hollenweger, "is a linguistic symbol of the sacred…Glossolalia says, 'God is here; just as a gothic cathedral says, 'Behold God is majestic.'"

> Here are people without a gothic cathedral…Their symbol of the sacred, their liturgical space, their scenarios is not set in stones and architectural design but in a design of another kind of language. The nearest parallel for us is probably the space which is created by music.[114]

VII. Ecumenical: "The Old Time Religion Makes the Methodists love the Baptists"

"Most Pentecostal churches," claims Walter Hollenweger, "started as ecumenical renewal movements."[115] When Hollenweger began his doctoral research at the University of Zurich that would later lead to his ten-volume *Handbuch der Pfingstvewegung,* he quickly discovered that Pentecostalism was "a bewildering pluralistic worldwide ecumenical movement."[116] Thomas Ball Barratt, who founded the Pentecostal movement in Norway and became its apostle in northern Europe early on, recognized Pentecostalism as a movement made up of various Christian traditions and not a new denomination. "As regards salvation, by justification;" declared Barratt, "we are Lutherans. In baptismal formula, we are Baptists. As regards sanctification, we are Methodists. In aggressive evangelism, we are as the Salvation Army. But as regards the Baptism in the Holy Spirit, we are Pentecostal."[117]

In 1958 the Scandinavian scholar Nils Bloch-Hoell published *The Pentecostal Movement* in his native Norwegian. The manuscript was later translated and published in English in 1964. In Bloch-Hoell's first chapter, "Historical Background of the Movement in the USA," he includes something that most American scholars and observers leave out.

> From our point of view the establishment of the Evangelical Alliance in London in 1846 and in America in 1867 is of special significance… The Alliance adopted interdenominationalsim as a programme, the idea of which had been an element in American revivalism from the beginning of the eighteenth century. In fact, interdenominationalism is deeply anchored in the dynamic and subjective Christianity of America.
>
> The Pentecostal Movement came into existence in the milieu of interconfessional revivals and holiness movements. This background made possible the crossing of confessional borders and expansion within different denominations.[118]

Bloch-Hoell was accurate in his assessment that "interdenominationalism" was "deeply anchored in the dynamic and subjective Christianity of America." Robert Baird, America's first church historian, took great pains in 1845 to convince his largely European audience that religion in America was both "evangelical" and "revivalistic." In chapter eight of *Religion in America*, "Supplemental Remarks on Revivals of Religion," Baird documents by first-hand knowledge that revivals have been experienced "in the evangelical churches of all denominations throughout the United States. I have been myself a witness to these blessed movements in almost every one of those States, at one time or another and have even found their effects to be, in all essential respects, the same."[119] Baird also noted America's inter-denominationalism in his section about "How Churches are Built in the New Settlements."

> Someone proposes that they should build a good large schoolhouse, which may serve also for holding religious meetings, and this is scarcely sooner proposed than accomplished....Being intended for the meetings of all denominations of Christians, and open to all preachers who may be passing, word is sent to the nearest in the neighbourhood. Ere long some Baptist preacher, in passing, preaches in the evening, and is followed by a Presbyterian and a Methodist....And at last the house, which was a joint-stock affair at first, falls into the hands of some of the denominations and is abandoned by the others, who have mostly provided each one for itself....Such is the process continually going on in the West, and indeed, something of a like kind is taking place every year, in hundreds of instances, throughout all the states.[120]

Finally, Baird points almost prophetically to a coming unifying revival and "a great outpouring" of the Holy Spirit in the latter days. "The true source" of all church success, argued Baird, was the help of the Holy Spirit.

> "It is not by might, nor by power, but my Spirit," saith the Lord. Here is all our hope; ...there is, in all evangelical and truly converted Christians among us, some sense of their dependence upon the Spirit for success... There is... much earnest prayer for the outpouring of the Spirit ....It has been the great dominant idea... which has pervaded and influenced the Church of Christ in America during the last hundred years....Surely God has led his people to expect a great outpouring of his Spirit in the latter days.[121]

In attempting to define and describe the Azusa Street Revival in 1906, its leaders crafted something of a mission statement. "The Pacific Apostolic Faith Movement stands for the restoration of the faith once delivered unto the saints—the old time religion, camp meetings, revivals, missions, street and prison work and Christian unity everywhere."[122] The leaders concluded by carefully pointing out, "We are not fighting men or churches, but seeking to displace dead forms and creeds or wild fanaticisms with living, practical Christianity. 'Love, Faith, Unity' is our watchword."[123] At the end of 1906, after eight months of operation, the mission leaders stated, "We recognize every man that honors the blood of Jesus Christ to be our brother, regardless of denomination, creed or doctrine."[124]

When Aimee Semple McPherson began her Pentecostal ministry, not only did she preach that it was "the great outpouring of the Spirit in the latter days," but she clearly felt that her message was also interdenominational and international in its scope. Most of the money raised for the construction of her temple came from the Protestant mainline denominations, especially Presbyterian and Congregational churches. Aimee's vision of a truly ecumenical Pentecostalism would not come into full flower until the 1960s with the birthing of the charismatic movement. And again, Pietism, one of Pentecostalism's theological parents, knew no denominational boundaries.

VIII. Supernatural: "Divine Healing for the Body"

Next to glossolalia or "speaking in tongues," divine healing was a distinctive hallmark of classical Pentecostalism. The best treatment to date on the subject is Jonathan R. Baer's excellent Yale University dissertation, "Perfectly Empowered Bodies: Divine Healing in Modernizing America." Two of Pentecostalism's previously mentioned spiritual parents, Pietism and Methodism, also emphasized supernatural or "divine healing." Baer claims that Continental Pietism, "particularly its Germanic expressions, influenced the development of divine healing in America."

> Pietism's general openness to modern miracles and its stress on overcoming sin and its effects fostered healing ministries…By the 1850s, several notable figures had established healing centers… in Germany and… in Switzerland….Charles Cullis' tour of Europe after the Civil War bridged the parallel developments of Pietist healing and American holiness healing.[125]

Baer equally points to the contributions made to the movement by John Wesley and Methodism:

> From their founding, Methodists practiced ministries of healing….Like many eighteenth-century clergymen, John Wesley diagnosed patients and prescribed medicines—especially for the poor who could not afford physicians—in the regular course of his ministry….Wesley recorded several cases of healing by prayer in his journals and letters, including his own healing and, most famously, that of his ailing horse. Further, he endorsed divine healing claims made by Methodists and others, including cases of demon possession.[126]

After the American Civil War, a National Camp Meeting Association for the promotion of Christian Holiness was formed. The organization was created for "brothers and sisters of the various denominations" pursuing both holiness and health.[127] Although the Methodists were early leaders in the organization, "the movement," as Gaustad and Schmidt point out, "had too much vitality and lively spirit to be contained within a single ecclesiastical institution."[128] By the 1880s many new denominations and organizations were created and dedicated to the twin causes of holiness and healing. None of these were more influential upon Aimee Semple McPherson than the Christian and Missionary Alliance created by the former Presbyterian minister A.B. Simpson in 1887. Simpson's "fourfold gospel" and "interdenominational evangelicalism" provided the foundation and template for Aimee's ministry. By substituting the "baptism of the Holy Spirit" for "sanctification," Aimee's later "foursquare gospel" was nothing more than the Pentecostal version of the Christian and Missionary Alliance's "fourfold gospel."

In the 1880s and 1920s "holiness and Pentecostal healing resonated as a central concern across American Protestantism."[129] Although Aimee undoubtedly had women holiness healers such as Carrie Judd Montgomery and Maria Woodworth-Etter as her early role models in ministry, her real source of support for the larger healing campaigns of her career came from an unexpected quarter, liberal Protestant male ministers. Pentecostalism, for years confused with fundamentalism, was in reality violently rejected by the vast majority of the fundamentalists. G. Campbell Morgan, one of the contributors to *The Fundamentals*, referred to Pentecostalism as "the last vomit of Satan."[130] Fundamentalists rejected just about everything Pentecostalism had to offer, often labeling it a "counterfeit" movement. Especially objectionable to the rationalism of fundamentalist thought were women ministers, glossolalia—the "tongues movement"—and divine healing. Fundamentalism rejected Pentecostal healing because as Baer points out "healing was central to Christian Science and the various New Thought bodies it influenced" and also because "liberal Protestants developed a strong interest in the connections between religion and health."[131] By 1919 Protestant fundamentalists left little doubt how they felt about the fledging movement of Pentecostalism when the World's Christian Fundamentals Association resolved,

> Whereas the present wave of Modern Pentecostalism, often referred to as the "tongues movement," and the present wave of fanatical and unscriptural healing which is sweeping over the country today, has become a menace in many churches and a real injury to sane testimony of Fundamental Christians.

519

> Be it resolved, that this convention go on record as unreservedly
> opposed to Modern Pentecostalism, including the speaking in unknown
> tongues, and the fanatical healing known as general healing in the atone-
> ment, and the perpetuation of the miraculous sign-healing of Jesus and
> His apostles, wherein they claim the only reason the church cannot
> perform these miracles is because of unbelief.[132]

No one better exemplified liberal Protestant interest in the connection
between religion and health at the turn of the twentieth century better than
Charles Reynolds Brown. And Brown as dean of Yale Divinity School—a
bastion of liberal Protestant thought—not only endorsed Aimee's ministry
but offered an invocation at one of her momentous meetings in Oakland,
California, during the summer of 1922. In 1910 Charles Reynolds Brown
published *Faith and Health*:

> It is indeed impossible for the church to close its eyes to the example
> of its Founder who not only preached His matchless Sermon on the
> Mount, but opened the eyes of the blind and caused the lame to walk. It
> is impossible for the church to disregard that portion of its great com-
> mission which says "Heal the sick" as well as "Preach the Gospel"....
> the help of the ever-present Christ who thus healed men of old is still
> available for health....Make your alliance with the Unseen and Eternal
> an immediate and an available alliance! Strive, if you will, to make it an
> alliance helpful on the physical as well as on the moral levels of your
> personal life.[133]

Brown's *Faith and Health* was no mere tract of the times. It represented a
lifelong search on the part of the author. Not only had Brown been a sickly
youth, but twenty-three years earlier in February, 1887, he set out to study
Christian Science in earnest.

> I did not get up my knowledge of Christian Science overnight or cram
> up on it hastily in a week for some Sunday evening sermon....I went to
> the fountain head for my instruction. At that time Mrs. Eddy herself was
> lecturing in Boston and it was my great privilege to attend her lectures...
> I have in my home, signed, sealed and delivered by a regularly chartered
> school, a diploma certifying that I have completed the prescribed courses
> of study and am entitled to practice as a Christian Science healer. If I
> chose to hang out my sign as a healer at my home in Oakland, California,
> tomorrow morning no one could say me nay.[134]

Despite his diploma and years of study, Brown concluded, "Taken as a system, I believe Christian Science to be a colossal humbug and for certain reasons…in many instances, a cruel and a wicked humbug."[135] Brown did not end his quest for "faith and health" with Mary Baker Eddy and Christian Science. He also traveled to visit Dr. Cullis of Boston, Dr. A.B. Simpson of Brooklyn, and Dr. Dowie in Zion, Illinois. Impressed by what he witnessed under these three healers Brown reached a far different conclusion than he had with Christian Science:

> I have been present in meetings led by Dr. Cullis, by Dr. Simpson, and by Dr. Dowie, where each of these men called up certain people from the audience to testify as to their having been healed from certain diseases through their faith in God.
>
> Now what shall intelligent, discriminating people say to all this? We cannot sweep it all aside with a wave of the hand and a curl of the lip, calling it mere ignorant superstition, or deception and fraud. Take into consideration, as you must, all the failures—and they form a pathetic array when you inquire closely….But taking all these failures into consideration, there still remains a nucleus of success to be considered.[136]

Charles Reynolds Brown was no lonely prophet preaching in the wilderness. Despite his Methodist background and seminary degree from Boston University, Brown spent twenty-two years in the Congregational Church serving churches in Cincinnati, Boston, and Oakland. Later as dean of the divinity school at Yale, he preached and gave religious addresses in "one hundred and eighty-eight different colleges and universities, in eighty-two preparatory schools and in over three hundred and fifty churches, North, South, East and West."[137] Brown, with his orientation toward practical theology and the Social Gospel, also had a strong abiding interest in psychology, "particularly in William James and pragmatism… [and] Brown believed… that Christianity ought to turn inward, to strengthen the inner life."[138]

The connection of faith and health was very much then a central concern among American Protestants. Liberal male Protestant clergymen such as Charles Reynolds Brown were invaluable for Aimee's acceptance into the mainline churches in the early 1920s. Ironically, it was not the conservative but the liberal wing of American Protestantism that accepted as authentic the divine healing aspect of Pentecostalism.

The "supernatural" aspect of Pentecostalism, "Divine Healing for the Body" is still very much a hallmark of the movement especially in Latin America, noted today with increasing interest:

> A spiritual revolution is transforming the socio-religious landscape of Latin America from the *ciudades perdidas* (shanty towns) of Tijuana to the

favelas [slums] of Rio de Janeiro,...Pentecostalism, has replaced Catholicism as the leading form of popular religion...In...Rio de Janeiro... the great majority...(91 percent) are Pentecostal, [and] have founded an average of one church per workday since the beginning of the decade [the 1990s].[139]

Not only has Pentecostalism had an impact on Catholicism, it has also transformed the mainline Protestant churches of Latin America as well.

Many members of the mainline Protestant have seceded from their parent denominations to establish "reformed" (*renovada*) or Pentecostal congregations. These churches preserve much of their denominational heritage while integrating the Pentecostal gifts of the Spirit.[140]

What accounts for Pentecostalism's explosive growth in Latin America? Why has the religious landscape in Latin America been so radically altered and transformed by the movement? R. Andrew Chestnut spent a year in the city of Belem, "the cradle of Brazilian Pentecostalism," producing an ethnography of believers.[141] After conducting ninety life-history interviews, which included members of the Four-Square Gospel Church, the denomination founded by Aimee Semple McPherson, Chestnut concluded that Brazilian Pentecostals "are not escaping rampaging armies or suffering anomie."

Rather, they seek immediate solutions to their health problems stemming from poverty. Illness is one of the most common and life-threatening manifestations of poverty in Latin America...Pentecostalism... offers the powerful remedy of faith healing. The great majority ... in Belem converted to Pentecostalism during or shortly after a serious illness.... Pentecostalism's message of healing power reverberates among the popular classes, particularly women, whose already precarious household economics are further debilitated by alcoholism, unemployment, and domestic strife.[142]

If anything, the "supernatural" aspect of Pentecostalism has increased over the years, especially outside the United States, helping to define Pentecostalism in the process as a truly global religion.

IX. Geographical: "A Religion Made to Travel; The World Their Parish"

As a theological outsider looking in, Harvey Cox makes many insightful observations about Pentecostalism in *Fire from Heaven: The Rise of Pentecostal Spirituality and the Reshaping of Religion in the Twenty-first Century*. He is especially observant about the power of this people's religion being unleashed worldwide:

> At Azusa Street, (the birthplace of modern Pentecostalism) a kind of primal spirituality that had been all but suffocated by centuries of western Christian moralism and rationality reemerged with explosive power....Not only did missionaries travel all over the globe (thirty-eight left from Azusa Street within six months of the mission's origin), but wherever they went, the people who heard them seemed to make the message their own and fan out again. Almost instantly Pentecostalism became Russian in Russia, Chilean in Chile, African in Africa. Within two years the movement had planted itself in fifty countries. It was a religion made to travel, and it seemed to lose nothing in the translation.[143]

"What is global," writes the anthropologist Karla Poewe, "are traditions that reach across national boundaries, take on local color, and move again."[144] And unlike its parental contributors of Pietism, Puritanism, and Methodism, Poewe again rightly observes "Pentecostalism and charismatic Christianity are still growing."[145]

But why is Pentecostalism still traveling, still growing, still encircling the globe? Rejecting theology, doctrine, even aggressive evangelism as the most important reason, Walter Hollenweger, argues, "The most important reason is that...[Pentecostalism] is an oral religion. It is not defined by the abstract language that characterizes...Presbyterians or Catholics. Pentecostalism is communicated in stories, testimonies, and songs. Oral language is a much more global language than that of universities or church declarations. Oral tradition is flexible and can adapt itself to a variety of circumstances."[146]

Perhaps one reason for Pentecostalism's rivaling Catholicism, its nearest competitor for souls in the marketplace of global Christianity, is its stubborn refusal to buy into the myth of progress, forever breaking free of what Max Weber saw as society's "iron cage," and its essence being in Karl Marx's words, "the sigh of the oppressed creature, the heart of a heartless world," and "the spirit of a spiritless situation."[147] David Martin suggests that the secret to Pentecostalism's undying and universal appeal owes its strength to spiritual encounters "which do not lie under the guillotine of progress but are intrinsic to the human condition."[148]

X. Conflictual: Growth by Division and Subtraction

On the eve of the centennial celebration of the birth of Pentecostalism at the fabled Azusa Street Mission in downtown Los Angeles, the major periodical of mainline Protestant thought published an article on "Pentecostalism's Dark Side." *The Christian Century*, certainly no fan of the movement over the years, seemingly waited for the hundred-year birthday bash to remind its readers once again of Pentecostalism's other side. The article's author, Roger E. Olson, was an ex-Pentecostal raised in a breakaway church from Aimee's Foursquare denomination and is presently a Baylor University professor of theology. Olson aimed his theological guns at Harvey Cox and Philip Jenkins in particular and began firing away at the two scholars for succumbing to and helping to spread what he termed "Pentecostal chic."

> In this centennial year of American Pentecostalism's founding…I feel compelled to register some concerns about its enduring immaturity as a movement. Some non-Pentecostal religious scholars, such as Harvey Cox (*Fire From Heaven*) and Philip Jenkins (*The Next Christendom*), have succumbed to "Pentecostal chic"—a kind of romantic view of Pentecostalism as a much-needed spiritual movement of the poor and oppressed that fills the western world's "ecstasy deficit." Missing in some of these accounts is an awareness of the movement's dark side.[149]

Like any ex-Pentecostal preacher-boy's experience, mine included, Olson's account, of course, rang true. It was all there—the anti-intellectualism, the cult of personality, and the "rampant sexual and financial scandals" that also began a hundred years ago and are still with us. What Olson misses, however, in his wholesale condemnation and dismissal of "Pentecostal-chic" is that for the past one hundred years all outsiders ever heard about was Pentecostalism's "dark side." Despite the movement's many failures and a century's worth of immaturity and immorality, Pentecostals can take some comfort in knowing they come very close in description to their Corinthian cousins.

> Consider your own call, brothers and sisters: not many of you were wise by human standards, not many were powerful, not many were of noble birth. But God chose what is foolish in the world to shame the wise; God chose what is weak in the world to shame the strong; God chose what is low and despised in the world, things that are not, to reduce to nothing things that are, so that no one might boast in the presence of God.[150]

Perhaps God, ever the trickster, is still today confounding the wise, even the once proud and mighty Protestant mainline, with "Pentecostalism's dark side."

The greatest problem facing Pentecostalism in both its hundred-year history and present hour has less to do with sex, money, and anti-intellectualism and more to do with conflict. Addressing the Asian Pentecostal Society in the Philippines, Lap Yan Kung noted the real fault and failure of the movement:

> No Christian theology can avoid paying attention to the significance of Pentecostalism. Apart from the growing numbers of Pentecostals, Pentecostalism retrieves the forgotten person of the Trinity, namely, the Holy Spirit, in Christian doctrine and living. Nevertheless, the Pentecostal movement not only brings the churches to renewal, but also to schism. This ambiguity is a basic fact that we have to take seriously.... schism gives Pentecostalism a bad name, because schism is exactly a sign that the Spirit is not at work.[151]

Contrary to Olson's argument that "sexual promiscuity and financial misconduct" constitute the movement's "dirty little secret," schism is the real culprit. *The Encyclopedia of Religion and Society* defines Pentecostalism as "a group of independent sects formed by schism."[152] In 1929 H. Richard Niebuhr revealed the real "dirty little secret" of the entire church when he observed that "The division of the churches closely follows the division of men into the castes of national, racial, and economic groups. It draws the color line in the church of God;...it seats the rich and poor apart of the table of the Lord, where the fortunate may enjoy the bounty they have provided while the others feed upon the crusts their poverty affords."[153]

Everyday en route to my Tempe office at Arizona State University I pass by the Center For the Study of Religion and Conflict. Living in a post-9/11 world, one is very much aware of religious conflict today. For Pentecostalism to continue to thrive in its second century of existence it needs to rediscover its ancient Book of Acts playbook of growth by daily addition and multiplication and set aside its long-standing practice of subtraction and division by schism. Entering a new century, Hollenweger also concludes that "Pentecostalism must confront its tendency to segregate and separate into countless denominations. It's happening all the time, and it really is a scandal."[154]

XI. Biographical: "Friedrich Max Muller, Friedrich Schleiermacher, William James, and Max Weber Reconsidered"

In 1979 the dean of church historians, Robert T. Handy of Union Theological Seminary, New York City, noted the return of a once-familiar approach to American religious history. "The biographical approach to religious history," wrote Handy, "has recently regained some of the favor it once had."[155] Although I have argued at the outset that Pentecostalism had many a parent and that the movement was made from thousands of "testimonies" and that no one master story can be found, the movement still had its leaders. And according to many of the early theorists of religion one looked to the individual leaders and not to the churches or even to its theology and followers to best understand the movement in its most pure form and representation. Friedrich Max Muller, the father of *religionswissenschaft*, the "science of religion," was very much concerned in his writings with a religion's "founder" and "fountainhead."

> No religion can continue to be what it was during the lifetime of its founder...What they desired to found upon earth... offer often a strange contrast to the practice of those who profess to be their disciples.
>
> Whenever we trace back a religion to its first beginnings, we find it free from many of the blemishes that offend us in its later phases....As soon as a religion is established...the foreign and worldly elements encroach more and more on the original foundation, and human interests mar the simplicity and purity of the plan which the founder had conceived in his own heart, and matured in his communings with his God.[156]

"Except for a few chosen ones," wrote Friedrich Schleiermacher, "every person surely needs a mediator, a leader who awakens his sense for religion from its first slumber and gives him an initial direction."[157]

> In religion there is, of course, a mastership and discipleship. There are individuals, to whom thousands attach themselves, but this attachment is no blind imitation and they are not disciples because their master has made them into this; he is rather their master because they have chosen him as that.[158]

The amazing thing about William James' *The Varieties of Religious Experience* is its timelessness. It is hard to believe that *Varieties* was the Gifford Lectures on Natural Religion delivered in 1901 and 1902 at the University of Edinburgh. There is freshness to James' findings and insights despite a century's passage. James accomplished at least two things in his classic text he called a "descriptive survey." First, James attacks what he calls the "survival theory" of religious interpretation.

> There is a notion in the air…that religion is probably only an anachronism, a case of "survival," an atavistic relapse into a mode of thought which humanity in its more enlightened examples has outgrown…I unhesitatingly repudiate the survival-theory of religion as being founded on an egregious mistake.[159]

Religion for James was far from dying out or becoming an anachronism. Rather, religion, provided "zest," "meaning," "the enchantment of life," "a force that re-infuses the positive willingness to live."[160] "Religion" he argued, "must necessarily play an eternal part in human history."[161]

The second thing that James accomplished in *Varieties* was his novel proposal "to ignore the institutional branch [of religion], to say nothing of the ecclesiastical organization, to consider as little as possible…theology and… ideas…and to confine myself…to personal religion pure and simple."[162] In his selection of the "personal" over the "institutional" James aligned himself with the tradition of Schleiermacher as opposed to Durkheim. "Religion…shall mean for us the feelings, acts, and experiences of individual men in their solitude; so far as they apprehend themselves to stand in relation to whatever they may consider the divine."[163] James' preoccupation with the "personal" and "individual" as opposed to the "ecclesiastical" and "corporate" most likely was the result of his godfather Ralph Waldo Emerson's influence. Emerson defined transcendentalism as the realization of a higher consciousness within the individual personality and in 1838 admonished Harvard Divinity students to replace dogma in their lives with experience.

The real strength of James' "personal" approach to religion, however, lies in his recognition of religious leadership—"geniuses," as he calls them.

> I speak not now of your ordinary religious believer, who follows the conventional observances….It would profit us little to study this second-hand religious life. We must search rather for the original experiences which were the pattern-setters…These experiences we can only find in individuals for whom religion exists not as a dull habit, but as an acute fever…such religious geniuses have often…fallen into trances, heard voices, seen visions….Often…these pathological features…have helped to give them their religious authority and influence.[164]

James, like Friedrich Max Muller before him, was also concerned with the "fountain-head" of religion. Like Muller, James sees the "original" as "best" and free from latter contamination and corruption.

Religious geniuses attract disciples...When these groups get strong enough to "organize" themselves, they become ecclesiastical institutions with corporate ambitions of their own. The spirit of politics and the lust of dogmatic rule are then apt to enter and to contaminate the originally innocent thing....First-hand individual experience...has always appeared as a heretical sort of innovation to those who witnessed its birth...when a religion has become an orthodoxy, its day of inwardness is over: the spring is dry, the faithful live at second hand exclusively and stone the prophets in their turn.[165]

Finally, Max Weber, one of the fathers of the sociology of religion, was also concerned with religious leadership and change. Weber was especially concerned with how this leadership provided stability for society ("priests") and how it also led to breakthroughs and cultural change ("prophets.") In addition to describing two types of religious leadership, the charismatic vs. the legal-rational or bureaucratic, Weber was one of the first of the theorists to note the role of women leaders in what he termed "Religion of Non-Privileged Classes." The religion "of the disprivileged classes," he observed, "is characterized by a tendency to allot equality to women."[166] Weber went on to note, however, that this leadership equality extended to women rarely lasts in a religious movement's evolution.

Only in very rare cases does this practice continue beyond the first stage of a religious community's formation...as routinization and regimentation of community relationships set in, a reaction takes place against pneumatic manifestations among women, which come to be regarded as dishonorable.[167]

Modern American Pentecostalism was characterized by an abundance of charismatic leaders. Early theorists of religion would remind us that to truly know and understand the movement and its evolution over time, we must make a historic pilgrimage and return back to its founders and fountainheads. These "religious geniuses," as James called them, really were "the pattern-setters." Religion existed for them, "not as a dull habit, but as an acute fever."[168] Far from perfect and not without their problems, these prophetic figures nevertheless blazed the trail and set their followers' hearts on fire. As Martin E. Marty reminds us, "There are tens of thousands of religions in the world, and millions of faith communities." Yet, "every one of them has been shaped by founders and interpreters, agents of change and prophets of...promise."[169] And as an equally colorful and controversial new religious movement, Pentecostalism was of no exception.

A final thought about Pentecostalism in particular and religion in general. Often overlooked in theological and theoretical discussions alike, Pentecostalism is thriving today, and religion is still with us, because for many people, it simply works. Americans especially like things that work. They are pragmatic. And if things don't work they are quickly discarded by their owners for products that perform according to their expectations. There were several instances in this biography where Pentecostals compared their faith to their cars. Their homespun analogies serve to remind the professionals that for many practitioners of faith there is first and foremost a very pragmatic element. If religion didn't work, it would no longer be practiced. The great black, blind bluesman, the Reverend Gary Davis, who peacefully coexisted in the secular world as well as a religious one, said it best in a song:

Things I used to would do I don't do no more,
It's been a great change since I was born

Lies I used to would tell I don't tell no more,
It's been a great change since I was born

People I used to would hate I don't hate no more,
It's been a great change since I was born

Roads I used to walk I don't walk no more,
It's been a great change since I was born

A new song been sung since I been born.
Been a great change since I been born.[170]

Notes

Because some interviewees requested anonymity, their interviews are simply numbered with Roman numerals, e.g., "Interview 25, October 24, 1981, San Francisco." All such interviews were conducted by the author.

Preface

1. Robert Leckie, *The Wars of America* (New York: Harper & Row, 1981), 537.

2. T.S. Eliot, "Little Gidding," *Four Quartets* (New York: Harcourt, Brace and Company, 1943)

3. Merle Haggard and Tommy Collins, "The Roots of My Raising," Delta Records, 1994.

4. Thomas Wolfe, *Look Homeward Angel* (New York: Charles Scribner's Sons, 1929).

5. Daniel W. Conway and K.E. Gover, *Soren Kierkegaard: Critical Assessments of Leading Philosophers* (London: Taylor & Francis, 2002), 21.

6. *U.S. Religious Landscape Survey, Religious Affiliation: Diverse and Dynamic*, The Pew Forum on Religion & Public Life, February 2008, Washington, D.C.

7. Sandra Scofield, *Occasions of Sin: A Memoir* (New York: W.W. Norton & Company, 2004), 19.

8. Winthrop S. Hudson, *Religion in America, An Historical Account of the Development of American Religious Life* (New York: Charles Scribner's Sons, 1973), 280.

9. Oral Roberts, *The Fourth Man* (Garden City, N.Y.: Country Life Press, 1951).

10. Bernie Taupin, "Candle in the Wind," *Goodbye Yellow Brick Road*, MCA Records.

11. William G. McLoughlin, "Aimee Semple McPherson: 'Your Sister in the King's Glad Service,'" *Journal of Popular Culture* 3, no. 3 (1967): 193.

12. Ross Douthat, "The 100 Most Influential Americans of All Time," *The Atlantic*, December 2006, 63.

13. Ferenc Morton Szasz, *Religion in the Modern American West* (Tucson: University of Arizona Press, 2000), 111.

14. Douthat, "The 100 Most Influential Americans," 62.

15. Ibid.

16. Ibid.

17. Warren I. Susman, *Culture As History: The Transformation of American Society in the Twentieth Century* (New York: Pantheon Books, 1984), 277.

18. John Updike, "Famous Aimee, The Life of Aimee Semple McPherson," *New Yorker*, April 30, 2007.

19. Matthew Avery Sutton, *Aimee Semple McPherson and the Resurrection of Christian America* (Cambridge, Mass.,: Harvard University Press, 2007).

20. Taupin, "Candle in the Wind."

21. Alfonso A. Narvaez "Guido Orlando, 80, Press Agent Who Devised Outlandish Stunts," *New York Times*, May 28, 1988.

22. Guido Orlando, "Trouble Shooter in Paradise," unpublished manuscript in author's possession, 1.

23. Ibid., 285-286.

24. Ibid., 289.

25. Ibid., 293.

26. Ibid., 300-301.

27. McLoughlin, "Aimee Semple McPherson," 194-195.

28. Ibid., 195.

29. *Spirit And Power, A 10-Country Survey of Pentecostals, The Pew Forum on Religion & Public Life*, October 2006, Washington, D.C.

Ibid., 1.

Charles H. Barfoot and Gerald T. Sheppard, "Prophetic vs. Priestly

Religion: The Changing Role of Women Clergy in Classical Pentecostal Churches," *Review of Religious Research*, 22, no.1 (1980): 14.

32. Grant Wacker, "Travail of a Broken Family: Evangelical Responses to Pentecostalism in America, 1906-1916, *Journal of Ecclesiastical History*, 47, no. 3 (July 1996): 528.

33. Peter L. Berger, *The Sacred Canopy, Elements of a Sociological Theory of Religion* (New York: Doubleday, 1967), 41.

34. Robert N. Bellah, et all, *Habits of the Heart, Individualism and Commitment in American Life* (Berkeley: University of California Press, 1985), 153.

35. Timothy L. Smith, *Called Unto Holiness; The Story of the Nazarenes* (Kansas City: Nazarene Publishing House, 1962), 351.

36. Allison Silver, "Writing the Good Life," *New York Times*, November 8, 1981.

37. David Martin, "Rescripting Spiritual Autobiography," *Exchange*, 35, no. 1 (2006): 92.

38. Robert A. Orsi, "Is the Study of Lived Religion Irrelevant to the World We Live In?" *Journal for the Scientific Study of Religion* 42, no. 2 (2003): 174.

39. Walter J. Hollenweger, *Pentecostalism: Origins and Developments Worldwide* (Peabody, Mass.: Hendrickson Publishers, Inc., 1997), 5.

40. Henry F. May, *Ideas, Faiths, and Feelings, Essays on American Intellectual and Religious History, 1952-1982* (New York: Oxford University Press, 1983), x.

41. John Bunyan, *The Pilgrim's Progress From This World to That Which is to Come* (London: J. Mawman, 1816), xxvi.

Acknowledgments

1. Bruce Jay Friedman, "One for the Books," Review of Al Silverman, *The Time of Their Lives, The Golden Age of Great American Publishers, Their Editors and Authors*, *New York Times*, September 14, 2008.

2. Michael O'Neill, *Poems of W.B. Yeats: A Sourcebook* (New York: Routledge 2004, 180.

3. Daniel Dorchester, *Christianity in the United States, From the First Settlement Down to the Present Time* (New York: Phillips & Hunt, 1888), 3.

4. O'Neill, *Poems of W.B. Yeats: A Sourcebook*, 180.

5. Stanislaw Baranczak and Clare Cavanagh, *Polish Poetry of the Last Two Decades of Communist Rule* (Evanston, Ill.: Northwestern University Press, 1

Chapter One

1. Isabel Leighton, ed., *The Aspirin Age, 1919-1941* (New York: Simon and Schuster, 1949), xi.

2. F. Scott Fitzgerald, "Echoes of the Jazz Age," *Scribner's Magazine*, November 1931, 459-65.

3. Flora Rarsson, *My Best Men Are Women* (London: Hodder and Stoughton, 1974), 33.

4. Roberta Semple Salter, "James Kennedy, Father of Aimee Semple McPherson," New York, 1979, author's files.

5. Ibid., 4.

6. *Foursquare Crusader*, January 22, 1936.

7. Salter, "James Kennedy," 2, 3.

8. Aimee Semple McPherson, *This Is That* (Los Angeles: Bridal Call Publishing House, 1919), 11.

9. Ibid., 14.

10. I Samuel l: 1-28.

11. Margaret Morgan Lawrence, "Creativity and the Family," *Gender & Psychoanalysis* 4 (1999): 399.

12. Aimee Semple McPherson, "Reminiscences," dictated "ASM/mf, December 7, 1926 for Mr. Jordan of the *Examiner,* Los Angeles, author's files.

13. *The Latter Rain Evangel*, June 1926.

14. McPherson, "Reminiscences," 7.

15. Ibid., 4.

16. Ibid., 6.

17. *Foursquare Crusader*, February 5, 1936.

18. Ibid., 7.

19. McPherson, "Reminiscences," 12.

20. Aimee Semple McPherson, "Class Notes on Homiletics," LIFE Bible College, Los Angeles, 8.

21. *The New York Times*, 25 February 1986. See also Vera John-Steiner, *Notebooks of the Mind: Explorations of Thinking* (Albuquerque: University of New Mexico Press, 1985).

22. Ibid.

23. Carolyn G. Heilbrun, *Writing a Woman's Life* (New York: W.W. Norton, 1988), 27.

24. George Routledge, *Routledge's Manual of Etiquette*, http://www.djmcadam.com/first-steps.html.

25. McPherson, *This Is That*, 25.

26. Aimee Semple McPherson, "Rebekah at the Well," Sermon (Los Angeles: Foursquare Gospel Publications, no date), 6.

27. McPherson, *This Is That*, 27.

28. Newspaper article on old Ingersoll Collegiate Institute, International Church of the Foursquare Gospel Archives, Los Angeles.

29. McPherson, *This Is That*, 29-30.

30. McPherson, "Reminiscences," 20.

31. Aimee Semple McPherson, "A Short Autobiography of Aimee Semple McPherson's Life, Publicity," International Church of the Foursquare Gospel Archives, Los Angeles, 1-2.

32 McPherson, *This Is That*, 28.

33. Ibid., 29.

34. McPherson, "Reminiscences," 15.

35. Ibid., 14.

36. Ibid., 16.

37. Ibid., 17.

38. McPherson, *This Is That*, 31.

39. McPherson, "Reminiscences," 20.

40. McPherson, "*This Is That*, 34.

41. Ibid., 35.

42. McPherson, "Reminiscences," 20.

43. *Foursquare Crusader*, May 20, 1936.

44. McPherson, *This Is That*, 38.

45. Ibid., 37.

46. *Bridal Call*, January 1924.

47. Aimee Semple McPherson, "*Life Story*," unpublished manuscript, International Church of the Foursquare Gospel Archives, Los Angeles, no date, 18.

48. Ibid., 18.

49. McPherson, *This Is That*, 40.

50. Ibid., 40.

51. Ibid, 41.

52. Ibid, 42.

53. McPherson, "A Short Autobiography," 6.

Chapter Two

1. Aimee Semple McPherson, *This Is That* (Los Angeles: Bridal Call Publishing House, 1919), 49-50.

2. Aimee Semple McPherson, *Life Story*, International Church of the Foursquare Gospel Archives, Los Angeles, no date, 27.

3. Aimee Semple McPherson, *In the Service of the King* (New York: Boni and Liv-

eright, 1927), 14.

4. Charles H. Barfoot and Gerald T. Sheppard, "Prophetic versus Priestly Religion: The Changing Role of Clergy in Classical PentecostalChurches," *Review of Religious Research* 22, no. 1 (1980): 2-17.

5. Ibid.

6. Aimee Semple McPherson, *Life Story*, 25.

7. Aimee Semple McPherson, *This Is That*, 52.

8. Ibid., 53.

9. Ibid., 55.

10. Ibid., 60.

11. Ibid., 62.

12. Aimee Semple McPherson, *Life Story,* 16.

13. Ibid., 35.

14. *Foursquare Crusader*, July 15, 1936.

15. Notes from newspaper article, International Church of the Foursquare Gospel.

16. Ibid.

17. Ibid.

18. Ibid.

19. *Bridal Call*, January 1925.

20. Ibid.

21. Aimee Semple McPherson, *This Is That*, 68.

22. *Assemblies of God Heritage*, Winter 1991-92.

23. Douglas J. Nelson, "For Such a Time as This: The Story of Bishop W.J. Seymour and the Azusa Street Revival" (PhD. diss., University of Birmingham, United Kingdom, 1981), 247.

24. A.C. Valdez, Sr., with James F. Scheer, *Fire on Azusa Street, An Eyewitness Account* (Costa Mesa, Calif.: Gift Publications), 41.

25. McPherson, *This Is That*, 68.

26. Ibid.

27. Ibid.

28. Nelson diss., 248.

29. Louis De Caro, *Our Heritage, The Christian Church of North America* (Sharon, Pa.: Christian Church,1977), 31-36.

30. McPherson, *This Is That*, 73.

31. Ibid., 74.

32. Emily Volpe, interview by Charles H. Barfoot, March 6, 1981.

33. McPherson, *This Is That*, 77.

34. *Word and Work*, December 1909.

35. McPherson, *This Is That*, 77-78.

36. *Foursquare Crusader*, September 30, 1936.

37. Ibid.

38. Ibid.

39. Ibid.

40. McPherson, *This Is That*, 79.

41. Aimee Semple McPherson, *Give Me My Own God* (New York: H.C. Kinsey, 1936), 49.

42. Ibid.

43. Ibid.

44. Interview 25, October 24, 1981, San Francisco.

45. Ibid.

46. McPherson, *Give Me My Own God*, 50-51.

47. Ibid.

48. McPherson, *This Is That*, 84.

49. Ibid., 83. For an update of Christianity in China today see David Aikman, *Jesus in Beijing, How Christianity is Transforming China and Changing the Global Balance of Power.* (Washington, D.C.: Regnery, 2003)

50. McPherson, *Give Me My Own God*, 53.

51. Ibid., 56-57.

52. McPherson, *This Is That*, 86.

53. Ibid.

54. McPherson, *Life Story*, 28.

55. Ibid.

Chapter Three

1. Aimee Semple McPherson, *This Is That* (Los Angeles: Bridal Call Publishing House, 1919), 93.

2. Aimee Semple McPherson, *Life Story* (unpublished manuscript) International Church of the Foursquare Gospel, Archives, Los Angeles, 79.

3. *Bridal Call*, January 1925.

4. Ibid.

5. Ibid.

6. Ibid.

7. Interview 25 , October 24, 1981, San Francisco.

8. Roberta Star Semple Salter, "Harold Stewart McPherson," New York, November, 1979, author's files.

9. Harold Stewart McPherson, "How Harold Met Aimee Semple McPherson," unpublished manuscript, author's files.

10. Ibid.

11. Ibid.

12. Salter, "Harold Stewart McPherson," 6.

13. Ibid.

14. Harold Stewart McPherson, "How Harold Met Aimee," 1, 2.

15. Ibid.

16. Salter, "McPherson," 7.

17. McPherson, *This Is That*, 94-95.

18. Aimee Semple McPherson, "Life Story," International Church of the Four-

square Gospel, Los Angeles, 29.

19. Ibid.

20. McPherson, *This Is That*, 95.

21. Salter, "McPherson," 8.

22. John Fante, *Ask the Dust* (Santa Barbara: Black Sparrow Press, 1980), 160-161.

23. Harold McPherson, Letter to Roberta Semple Salter, 1.

24. Salter, "McPherson," 9.

25. Ibid.

26. Ibid.

27. Sarah Comstock, "Aimee Semple McPherson, Primadona of Revivalism," *Harpers Monthly Magazine*, December 1927, 13.

28. McPherson, *Life Story*, 29-30.

29. Salter, "McPherson," 10.

30. Ibid.

31. Ibid., 11.

32. McPherson, *This Is That*, 96.

33. Ibid., 96, 97.

34. *Foursquare Crusader*, December 16, 1936.

35. William G. McLoughlin, "Aimee Semple McPherson, 'Your Sister in the King's Glad Service,' " *Journal of Popular Culture* 1, no. 3 (1967): 199

36. Ibid.

37. McPherson, *This Is That*, 97.

38. *Foursquare Crusader*, January 20, 1937.

39. McPherson, *This Is That*, 98.

40. *Southern Churchman*, December 15, 1923, 23.

41. McPherson, *This Is That* (Los Angeles: Echo Park Evangelistic Association, 1923), 78.

42. Ibid., 79.

43. Charles H. Barfoot and Gerald T. Sheppard, "Prophetic versus Priestly Religion: The Changing Role of Clergy in Classical Pentecostal Churches," *Review of Religious Research* 22, no. 1 (1980): 7.

44. *Weekly Evangel*, March 18, 1916.

45. McPherson, *This Is That*, 1923, 79.

Chapter Four

1. Roberta Star Semple Salter, "Harold Stewart McPherson," New York, November 1979, author's files, 13.

2. Ibid, 13.

3. Aimee Semple McPherson, *Life Story* (unpublished manuscript), International Church of the Foursquare Archives, Los Angeles, 71.

4. Ibid., 74.

5. Ibid., 79.

6. Salter, "Harold Stewart McPherson," 13.

7. Ibid.

8. McPherson, *Life Story*, 74.

9. Aimee Semple McPherson, *This is That*, 1923 ed., 85.

10. McPherson, *Life Story,* 79-80.

11. Ibid.

12. Ibid., 80-81.

13. Ibid., 81.

14. Ibid.

15. Salter, "Harold Stewart McPherson," 14.

16. Ibid.

17. McPherson, *This Is That*, 88.

18. Salter, "Harold Stewart McPherson," 14.

19. McPherson, *This Is That*, 89.

20 McPherson, *Life Story*, 85

21. McPherson, *This Is That*, 90.

22. Ibid.

23. McPherson, *Life Story*, 92.

24. McPherson, *This is That*, 91.

25. Ibid.

26. Ibid.

27. McPherson, *Life Story*, 97.

28. Ibid.

29. Ibid., 103.

30. Ibid.

31. Ibid., 105

32. Ibid.

33. Salter, "Harold Stewart McPherson," 15. *The Southern Churchman*, February 10, 1923.

34. Roberta Star Semple Salter, interview, by Charles H. Barfoot, November 4, 1978.

35. Ibid.

36. Harry S. Stout, *The Divine Dramatist: George Whitefield and the Rise of Modern Evangelism* (Grand Rapids: W.B. Eerdmans, 1991), 160.

37. *Bridal Call*, October 1917.

38. *Foursquare Crusader*, December 30, 1936.

40. Ibid.

41. *Bridal Call*, October 1917.

42. McPherson, *This Is That*, 98.

43. Ibid., 101.

44. *Bridal Call*, June 1917.

45. Ibid.

46. Ibid.

47. Daniel N. Maltz, "The Bride of Christ Filled with His Spirit," in *Women*

in Ritual and Symbolic Roles, ed. Judith Hoch-Smith and Anita Spring (New York: Plenum Press, 1978), 32.

48. Phyllis Mack, "Women as Prophets during the English Civil War," *Feminist Studies*, 8, no. 1 (1982): 21.

49. *Bridal Call*, October 1917.

50. Ibid.

51. Ibid.

52. *Bridal Call*, September 1917.

53. Ibid.

54. Ibid.

55. Winthrop S. Hudson, *Religion in America*, (New York: Charles Scribners Sons, 1973), 140-41.

56. Ibid.

57. *The Word and Work*, April 1915.

58. McPherson, *Life Story*, 84.

59. McPherson, *This Is That*, 111.

60. *Bridal Call*, October 1917.

61. Salter, "Harold Stewart McPherson," 18.

62. McPherson, *This Is That*, 115-116.

63. Ibid., 116.

64. Ibid., 118-119.

65. *Bridal Call*, November 1917.

66. *Bridal Call*, March 1918.

67. Interview 14, July 17, 1981, Los Angeles.

68. Salter, "Harold Stewart McPherson," 18.

69. Ibid., 18-19.

70. Ibid., 19.

71. *Bridal Call*, September 1925.

72. Roberta Star Semple Salter, "The Story of My Mother's Life," illustrated sermon, August 7, 1932, International Church of the Foursquare Gospel Archives, Los Angeles.

73. Traditional, "Camping in Canann's Happy Land."

Chapter Five

1. *Bridal Call*, January 1926, 23.

2. Roberta Star Semple Salter, interview by Charles H. Barfoot, November 4, 1978.

3. *Bridal Call*, December 1925, 30.

4. *Bridal Call*, October 1925.

5. *Bridal Call*, December 1925.

6. *Bridal Call*, May 1918.

7. Ibid.

8. *Bridal Call*, January 1926.

9. Ibid.

10. Ibid.

11. Aimee Semple McPherson, *This Is That*, (Los Angeles: Echo Park Evangelistic Association, 1923), 132.

12. Ibid.

13. *Bridal Call*, December 1925.

14. *Bridal Call*, January 1926.

15. *Bridal Call*, September 1918.

16. Ibid.

17. *Bridal Call*, January 1926.

18. Traditional, "Victory Song."

19. *Bridal Call*, September 1918.

20. Ibid.

21. Ibid.

22. *Philadelphia Ledger*, August 16, 1918.

23. Ibid.

24. Ibid.

25. Ibid.

26. John Henry Hepp IV, *The Middle-Class City: Transforming Space and Time in Philadelphia, 1876-1926* (Philadelphia: University of Pennsylvania Press, 2003), 168.

27. Roberta Star Semple Salter, "Harold Stewart McPherson," New York, November 1979, Author's files, 20.

28. Ibid.

29. Ibid.

30. Ibid.

31. Ibid., 20, 21.

32. *Bridal Call*, January 1926

33. Nancy Barr Mavity, *Sister Aimee* (Garden City: Doubleday, Doran & Co., 1931), 3-25.

34. Salter, "Harold Stewart McPherson," 21.

35. Ibid.

36. Ibid., 23.

37. *Bridal Call*, February 1926.

38. Ibid.

39. Ibid.

40. *Bridal Call*, January 1926.

41. Interview 5, January 28, 1981, Santa Ana, California.

42. *Bridal Call*, February 1926.

43. Ibid.

44. Ibid.

45. Ibid.

46. Interview 4, January 28, 1981, Los Angeles.

47. *Los Angeles Times*, September 9, 1918.

48. Aimee Semple McPherson, *A Short Autobiography of Aimee Semple McPherson's*

Life, International Church of the Foursquare Gospel, Los Angeles, 3.

49. *Bridal Call*, September 1918.

50. *Bridal Call*, October 1918.

51. Ibid

52. Ibid.

53. *Word and Work*, October 1918.

54. *Bridal Call*, November 1918.

55. Ibid.

56. McPherson, *This Is That*, 1923, 40.

57. Ibid., 141.

58. "The Influenza Pandemic of 1918." http://virus.stanford.edu/uda/6/10/2007.

59. Ibid.

60. *The Latter Rain Evangel*, July 1919.

61. McPherson, *This is That*, 1923, 142.

62. Ibid.

61. Ibid., 144.

62. Ibid.

63. *Bridal Call*, June 1926.

64. McPherson, *This is That*, 1923, 149-150.

65. Rolf K. McPherson, interview by Charles H. Barfoot, February 5, 1981,

66. McPherson, *This Is That,* 150.

67. *Bridal Call*, December 1918.

68. *The News* (Framingham-Natick, Mass.), May 30, 1970.

69. McPherson, *This Is That*, 1923, 146.

70. *Bridal Call*, December 1918.

71. Ibid.

72. Ibid.

73. Ibid.

74. Ibid.

75. Laurance L. Hill, *La Reina, Los Angeles in Three Centuries* (Los Angeles: Security Trust & Savings Bank, 1929), 61.

76. Ibid., 161-162.

77. Workers of the Writer's Program of the Work Projects Administration in Southern California, *Los Angeles, A Guide to the City and Its Environs* (New York: Hastings House, 1941), 56.

78. Carey McWilliams, "Sunlight in My Soul," in *The Aspirin Age 1919-1941*, ed. Isabel Leighton (New York: Simon & Shuster, 1949), 60.

79. McPherson, *This Is That*, 1923, 156.

80. Ibid.

81. Rolf K. McPherson, interview.

82. *Bridal Call*, April 1926.

83. *Bridal Call*, March 1929.

Chapter Six

1 . Publicity Department, Equitable Branch, Security Trust & Savings Bank, *El Pueblo, Los Angeles Before the Railroads* (Los Angeles: The Equitable Branch of the Security Trust and Savings Bank, 1928), 8.

2. John and Laree Caughey, *Los Angeles, Biography of a City* (Berkeley: University of California Press, 1976), 9.

3. Herbert D. Austin, "New Light on the Name of California," *TheQuarterly Historical Society of Southern California*, 12:3 (1923), 29; and Alice Kesone Melcon, *California in Fiction* (Berkeley: California Library Association, 1961), 980.

4. George P. Hammond, "The Search for the Fabulous in the Settlement of the Southwest" in *New Spains Far Northern Frontier, Essays on Spain in the American West, 1540-1821*, ed. David J. Weber (Albuquerque: University of New Mexico Press, 1979), 17-33.

5. John D. Weaver, *El Pueblo Grande, A Non-Fiction Book About Los Angeles* (Los Angeles: Ward Ritchie Press, 1973), 12.

6. Harry Carr, *Los Angeles, City of Dreams* (New York: Grosset & Dunlap, 1935), 23.

7. Ibid.

8. Ibid.

9. Caughey, *Biography of a City*, 50.

10. Ibid., 67.

11. Security Trust & Savings, *El Pueblo*, 12.

12. Ibid., 15.

13. Ibid., 16.

14. Weaver, *El Pueblo Grande*, 18.

15. Ibid., 16.

16. The Federal Writers' Project of the Works Progress Administration for the State of California, *A Guide to the Golden State* (New York: Hastings House Publishers, 1939), 211.

17. Weaver, *El Pueblo Grande*, 20.

18. Ibid., 21.

19. Federal Writers' Project, *Guide to the Golden State*, 21.

20. Security Trust & Savings, *El Pueblo*, 58.

21. Lindley Bynum, "Los Angeles in 1854-5, The Diary of Rev. James Woods," *The Quarterly Historical Society of Southern California* 23 (1941): 70.

22. Ibid., 70, 72, 77.

23. George G. Smith, "Parson's Progress to California," *The Quarterly Historical Society of Southern California* 21 (1939): 74-75.

24. Caughey, *Biography of a City*, 153-154.

25. Federal Writers' Project, *Guide to the Golden State*, 211.

26. Security Savings & Trust, *El Pueblo*, 60.

27. Federal Writers' Project, *Guide to the Golden State*, 211.

28. Leonard Pitt, *The Decline of the Californios, A Social History of the Spanish-*

Speaking Californians, 1846-1890 (Berkeley: University of California Press, 1966), 249-50, 274-75.

29. Federal Writers' Project, *Guide to the Golden State*, 212.

30. Ibid., 211-12.

31. Ibid., 42.

32. John E. Baur, *The Health Seekers of Southern California, 1870-1900* (San Marino: Huntington Library, 1959), 137.

33. Caughcy, *Biography of a City*, 185.

34. Ibid., 185.

35. Baur, *The Health Seekers*, 32.

36. Caughey, *Biography of a City*, 186.

37. David L. Clark, "Miracles for a Dime—from Chautauqua Tent from Radio Station with Sister Aimee," *California History*,47, no. 4 (Winter, 1978-79): 361.

38. Will Irwin, *The City That Was* (New York: B.W. Huebsch, 1906), 27.

39. Baur, *The Health Seekers*, 75.

40. Ibid., 92.

41. Ibid.

42. F. Weber Benton, *Semitropic California, The Garden of the World* (Los Angeles: Benton & Company, 1914), 54.

43. Carey McWilliams, *Southern California Country* (New York: Duell Sloan and Pearce, 1946), 165.

44. Ibid.

45. Gregory H. Singleton, *Religion in the City of Angels: American Protestant Culture and Urbanization, Los Angeles, 1850-1930* (Ann Arbor: UMI Research Press, 1979), 54.

46. McWilliams, *Southern California Country*, 113, 135.

47. Ibid., 136.

48. Workers of the Writers' Program of the Works Projects Administration in Southern California, *Los Angeles, A Guide To the City and Its Environs* (New York: Hastings House, 1941), 70.

49. Singleton, *Religion in the City of Angels*, 18.

50. Workers of the Writers' Program, *Los Angeles*, 4.

51. Michael E. Engh, S.J., "Practically Every Religion Being Represented," in *Metropolis in the Making, Los Angeles in the 1920s*, ed. Tom Sitton and William Deverell (Berkeley: University of California Press, 2001), 201.

52. Ibid.

53. Clark, "Miracles for a Dime," 360.

54. Workers of the Writers' Program, *Los Angeles*, 71.

55. Robert E. Lang, Andrea Sarzynski, Mark Muro, "Mountain Megas: America's Newest Metropolitan Places and a Federal Partnership to Help Them Prosper," The Brookings Institution, July 20, 2008, http://www.brookings.edu/reports/2008/0720-mountainmegas-sarzynski.aspx 8/11/2008.

56. Leslie Wilson, "The Rise of the Golden City, Los Angeles in the Twentieth Century," *Journal of Urban History*, January 2004, 275.

57. F. Scott Fitzgerald, *The Last Tycoon* (New York: Charles Scribner's Sons, 1941), 101.

Chapter Seven

1. D. Michael Quinn, "Religion in the American West," in *Under An Open Sky: Rethinking America's Western Past*, eds. William Cronan, George Miles, and Jay Gitlin, (New York: W.W. Norton, 1992), 161.

2. *Los Angeles Times*, April 18, 1906.

3. Cecil M. Robeck, Jr., *The Azusa Street Mission and Revival* (Nashville: Thomas Nelson, Inc., 2006), 1.

4. Robeck, *Azusa Street*, 9.

5. William Deverell, *Whitewashed Adobe, The Rise of Los Angeles and the Remaking of Its Mexican Past* (Berkeley: University of California Press, 2004), 7.

6. Publicity Department, Equitable Branch, Security Trust & Savings Bank, *El Pueblo, Los Angeles Before the Railroads* (Los Angeles: The Equitable Branch of the Security Trust and Savings Bank, 1928), 61.

7. Douglas Flamming, *Bound For Freedom: Black Los Angeles in Jim Crow America* (Berkeley: University of California Press, 2005), 23-24.

8. Ibid.

9. Rufus Gene William Sanders, "The Life of William Joseph Seymour: Black Father of the Twentieth Century Pentecostal Movement" (PhD. diss., Bowling Green State University, 2000), 119.

10. Flaming, *Bound For Freedom*, 112-113.

11. Timothy E. Fulop, "The Future Golden Day of the Race: Millennialism and Black Americans in the Nadir, 1877-1901," in *African-American Religion: Interpretive Essays in History and Culture*, ed. Timothy E. Fulop and Albert J. Raboteau (New York: Routledge, 1997), 230.

12. W.E.B. DuBois, "Of the Faith of the Fathers," in *African American Religious History" A Documentary Witness*, ed. Milton C. Sernett (Durham: Duke University Press, 1999), 335.

13. Albert J. Raboteau, " 'Ethiopa Shall Soon Stretch Forth Her Hands,' Black Destiny in Nineteenth-Century America," in *African American Religious Thought*, ed. Cornell West and Eddie S. Glaude, Jr., (Louisville: Westminister John Knox Press, 2003), 399.

14. Ibid.

15. Ibid.

16. Ibid.

17. Ibid., 398.

18. Ibid.

19. Ibid.

20. Douglas J. Nelson, "For Such a Time as This: The Story of Bishop W.J. Seymour and the Azusa Street Revival," (PhD. diss., University of Birmingham, United Kingdom, 1981), 150.

21. Ibid., 141.

22. Ibid., 157.

23. Ibid.

24. Albert J. Raboteau, *Slave Religion: The "Invisible Institution" in the Antebellum South* (New York: Oxford University Press, 2004), 5.

25. Ibid., ix.

26. Nelson, "For Such a Time as This," 158.

27. Ibid., 159

28. Ibid., 161.

29. Ibid., 162.

30. Ibid., 163.

31. Ibid., 164.

32. Ibid., 165.

33. Ibid.

34. Ibid.

35. Ibid.

36. Ibid., 166.

37. Ibid.

38. Ibid.

39. Sanders, "Seymour," 77.

40. Nelson, "For Such a Time as This," 167.

41. Ibid., 168.

42. Robert Mapes Anderson, *Vision of the Disinherited: The Making of American Pentecostalism* (New York: Oxford University Press, 1979), 1.

43. Interview, 21 January 16, 1982, Tustin, California.

44. *Apostolic Faith*, September 1906.

45. *Apostolic Faith*, December 1906.

46. Robeck, *Azusa Street*, 6.

47. Flamming, *Bound For Freedom*, 50.

48. Nelson, "For Such a Time as This," 183

49. Lawrence B. DeGraaf, "The City of Black Angels: The Emergence of the Los Angeles Ghetto, 1890-1930," *The Pacific Historical Review*, 39, no. 3 (August 1970): 324.

50. Flamming, *Bound For Freedom*, 55.

51. Ibid.

52. Ibid., 197.

53. Ian MacRobert, *The Black Roots and White Racism of Early Pentecostalism in the USA* (London: MacMillian Press, 1988), 51.

54. J. Max Bond, "The Negro in Los Angeles," (PhD. diss., University of Southern California, 1936), 26.

55. Nelson, "For Such a Time as This," 192.

56. Ibid.

57. Cecil M. Robeck, Jr., "The Earliest Pentecostal Mission of Los Angeles," *Assemblies of God Heritage* 3, no. 3, (1983): 3.

58. Ibid.

59. Nelson, "For Such a Time as This," 192.

60. Flamming, *Bound For Freedom*, 50.

61. Ibid., 51.

62. Ibid.

63. Ibid.

64. Nelson, "For Such a Time as This," 56.

65. Ibid., 188.

66. Ibid.

67. Robeck, *Azusa Street*, 5.

68. Grant Wacker, "Searching for Eden With a Satellite Dish" in *Religion and American Culture,* ed. David G. Hackett (New York: Routledge, 1995), 415.

69. Vivian Eilythia Deno, "Holy Ghost Nation: Race, Gender and Working-class Pentecostalism, 1906-1926, (PhD. diss, University of California, Irvine, 2002), 20.

70. Nelson, "For Such a Time as This," 56.

71. Ibid., 57.

72. Ibid., 192, 202.

73. Acts 2:17-18, 20.

74. Nelson, "For Such a Time as This," 13.

75. Ibid., 58

76. Ibid., 194.

77. Frank Bartleman, *Witness to Pentecost: The Life of Frank Bartleman*, ed. Donald W. Dayton (New York: Garland Publishing, Inc., 1985), 53.

78. Earl R. Babbie, *Science and Morality in Medicine: A Survey of Medical Educators* (Berkeley: University of California Press, 1970), 191.

79. Rick Bragg, *The Prince of Frogtown* (New York: Alfred A. Knopf, 2008), 93.

80. Ibid., 93-95.

81 David Martin, *Pentecostalism: The World Their Parish* (Malden, Mass.: Blackwell Publishers, 2002), 8.

82. Troy Messenger, *Holy Leisure, Recreation and Religion in God's Square Mile* (Minneapolis: University of Minnesota Press, 1999), 65.

83. Bartleman, *Witness to Pentecost*, 53.

84. Howard Nelson Kenyon, "An Analysis of Racial Separation Within the Early Pentecostal Movement" (M.A. thesis, Baylor University, 1978) 31.

85. Ibid.

86. Ibid.

87. *The Apostolic Faith*, September 1906.

88. Mel Robeck, "The Azusa Street Revival and Its Legacy," paper presented at Spirit in the World, An International Symposium Hosted by the USC Center for Religion and Civic Culture, October 6, 2006, Los Angeles .

89. *The New York Times,* June 8, 1908.

90. Nelson, "For Such a Time as This," 60.

91. Rick Bragg, *The Prince of Frogtown,* 93-95.

92. James R. Goff, Jr., *Fields White Unto Harvest: Charles F. Parham and the Missionary Origins of Pentecostalism* (Fayetteville: University of Arkansas Press, 1988), 118-119.

93. Ibid.

94. Nelson, "For Such a Time as This," 60.

95. *The Apostolic Faith*, September 1906.

96. Ibid.

97. *The Apostolic Faith*, October 1906.

98. Deno, "Holy Ghost Nation," 52.

99. A.C. Valdez, *Fire on Azusa Street* (Costa Mesa: Gift Publications, 1980), 15.

100. Interview 21.

101. Robeck, *Azusa Street*, 14.

102. Nelson, "For Such a Time as This," 208.

103. Ibid.

104. Ibid., 209-10.

105. Glenn A. Cook, "The Azusa Street Meeting: Some High Lights of this Outpouring," (Los Angeles: published by the author, no date)

106. Ibid.

107. Charles F. Parham, *The Sermons of Charles F. Parham* (New York: Garland Publishing, 1985), 106-107.

108. Goff, *Fields White Unto Harvest*, 132.

109. Parham, *Sermons*, 70-73.

110. William E. Connelley, *History of Kansas State and People* (Chicago: American Historical Society, 1928), 1,342.

111. Ibid.

112. Ibid., 1,343.

113. Ibid.

114. Ibid.

115. Ibid., 1,342

116. Goff, *Fields White Unto Harvest*, 159.

117. Ibid.

118. Nelson, "For Such a Time as This," 213.

119. *Apostolic Faith*, November, 1906.

120. Ibid.

117. Ibid.

118. Ibid.

119. Ibid.

120. Ibid.

121. Ibid.

122. Ibid.

123. Ibid.

124. *Apostolic Faith*, December 1906.

125. Nelson, "For Such a Time as This," 255.

126. Ibid., 216.

127. Ibid., 217.

128. Randall K. Burkett, *Garveyism as a Religious Movement: The Institutionalization of a Black Civil Religon* (Metuchen, N.J.:Scarecrow Press, Inc. / American Theological Library Association, 1978), xix.

129. Albert J. Raboteau, *A Fire in the Bones* (Boston: Beacon Press, 1996), 42, 54-56.

130. Marcus Garvey, "Garvey Tells His Own Story," in *African American Religious History, A Documentary Witness*, Milton C. Sernett, ed. (Durham: Duke University Press, 1999), 461.

131. Nelson, "For Such a Time as This," 217.

132. Ibid.

133. Edith L. Blumhofer, *Pentecost in My Soul: Explorations in the Meaning of Pentecostal Experience in the Early Assemblies of God* (Springfield, Missouri: Gospel Publishing House, 1989), 86.

134. Ibid., 90.

135. Ernest S. Williams, interview by Charles H. Barfoot, December 30, 1976, Springfield, Missouri.

136. Ibid.

137. Estrelda Y. Alexander, *Limited Liberty: The Legacy of Four Pentecostal Women Pioneers* (Cleveland: Pilgrim Press, 2008), 32-33.

138. Ibid., 34.

139. Deno, "Holy Ghost Nation," 67.

140. Ibid., 68.

141. Ibid.

142. Ibid., 69.

143. Ibid.

144. Ibid., 70.

145. Williams, interview.

146. Alexander, *Limited Liberty*, 38.

147. Robeck, *Azusa Street*, 301.

148. Ibid.

149. Sanders, "Seymour," 138, 140.

150. Robeck, *Azusa Street*, 310.

151. Williams, interview.

152. *Time,* August 19, 1935.

153. Nelson, "For Such a Time as This," 217.

154. Ibid., 218.

155. Ibid.

156. Valdez, *Fire on Azusa Street*, 48-49.

157. *Los Angeles Times*, September 9, 1910.

158. Martin E. Marty, *Modern American Religion, Vol. 1, The Irony of It All, 1893-1919* (Chicago: University of Chicago Press, 1986), 247.

159. Ibid, 245.

160. Harvey Cox, "Into the Age of Miracles," *World Policy Journal* 14, no. 1,

http://sas/epnet/com.ezproxyl.lib.asu.edu2/6/2006, 5

161. Ibid., 6.

162. Ibid.

163. Walter J. Hollenweger, "An Introduction to Pentecostalisms," *Journal of Beliefs and Values* 25, no. 2 (August 2004): 128.

164. Valdez, *Fire on Azusa Street*, 91-92.

165. Hollenweger, "Introduction to Pentecostalisms," 133.

166. Valdez, *Fire on Azusa Street*, 26.

167. Ibid.

168. Ibid.

169. Ibid., 26-27.

170. Ibid., 27.

171. Edith Blumhofer, "The Finished Work of Calvary: William H. Durham and a Doctrinal Controversy," *Assemblies of God Heritage* 3, no. 2 (Fall 1983): 19-11.

172. Melvin Harter, president of Miracle Valley Bible School, e-mail to author, February 13, 2009.

173. Robeck, *Azusa Street*, 1.

174. *The Apostolic Faith*, May 1907.

175. Ibid.

176. Wayne Warner, "The 1913 Worldwide Camp Meeting," *Assemblies of God Heritage*, 3, no. 1 (Spring 1983): 1.

177. Robeck, *Azusa Street*, 98.

178. Ibid.

179. *Apostolic Faith*, May 1907.

180. Messenger, *Holy Leisure*, 44-45.

181. *Los Angeles Times*, July 18, 1907.

182. Ibid.

183. Ibid.

184. Ibid.

185. Ibid.

186. Ibid.

187. *Los Angeles Times*, August 14, 1907.

188. Robeck, *Azusa Street*, 299.

189. *Los Angeles Times*, August 14, 1907.

190. Robeck, *Azusa Street*, 300.

191. *Los Angeles Times*, August 14, 1907.

192 Parham, *Sermons*, 73.

193. Robeck, *Azusa Street*, 329.

194. *Los Angeles Times*, August 14, 1907.

195. Ibid.

196. Valdez, *Fire on Azusa Street*, 42.

197. David Arthur Reed, "Origins and Development of the Theology of Oneness Pentecostalism in the United States" (Ph.D. diss., Boston University,1978), 97.

198. Ibid.

199. Ibid., 1.

200. Ethel Goss, *The Winds of God* (New York: Comet Books, 1958), 155.

201. Ibid., 107.

202.. Ibid.

203. Allen L. Clayton, "Another Side of Oneness Controversy," Letters From Our Readers, *Assemblies of God Heritage*, Spring 1985-1986, 15.

204. Deno, "Holy Ghost Nation," 159.

205. Edith Waldvogel Blumhofer, *The Assemblies of God: A Popular History* (Springfield, Mo.: Radiant Books, 1985), 37.

206. Deno, "Holy Ghost Nation," 168.

207. H. Richard Niebuhr, *The Social Sources of Denominationalism* (Cleveland: World Publishing Company, 1970), 6.

208. Marty, *Modern American Religion*, 245.

209. Deno, "Holy Ghost Nation," 169.

210. Nelson, "For Such a Time as This," 130.

211. Ibid., 132.

212. Roebeck, *Azusa Street*, 320.

213. Ibid.

214. Ibid.

215. Ibid.

216. Nelson, "For Such a Time as This," 273.

217. James S. Tinney, "William J. Seymour: Father of Modern-Day Pentecostalism," *Journal of the Interdenominational Theological Center*, Fall 1976, 44.

218. Valdez, *Fire on Azusa Street*, 75.

219. *Bridal Call*, January 1919.

220. Nelson, "For Such a Time as This," 289-290.

221. Ibid., 267.

222. Ibid.

223. Ibid., 270.

224. Acts 2:12.

225. Harvey Cox, *Fire From Heaven: The Rise of Pentecostal Spirituality and the Reshaping of Religion in the Twenty-First Century* (Reading, Mass.: Addison-Wesley, 1995), 101.

226. Ibid., 120.

227. Martin, *Pentecostalism*, 5.

228. Amanda Porterfield, *Healing in the History of Christianity* (New York: Oxford University Press, 2005), 174.

229. Ibid.

230. Linda H. Connor and Geoffrey Samule, eds., *Healing Powers and Modernity: Traditional Medicine, Shamanism, and Science in Asian Societies* (Westport, Conn.: Bergin & Garvey, 2000), 37.

231. Stewart E. Guthrie, Review of Michael Winkelman, *Shamanism,: The Neural Ecology of Consciousness and Healing, Journal of Ritual Studies* 18 (1) 2004, 97.

Chapter Eight

1. Interview 4, January 28, 1981, Los Angeles.

2. Ibid.

3. Interview 9, February 4, 1981, Los Angeles.

4. A.C. Valdez, *Fire On Azusa Street: An Eyewitness Account* (Costa Mesa: Gift Publications, 1980), 76.

5. William R. Swigart, *Biography of Spring Street in Los Angeles* (Los Angeles: published by the author, 1945), 9.

6. Ibid.

7. Roberta Star Salter, interview by Charles H. Barfoot, November 4, 1978, New York.

8. *Los Angeles Times*, January 19, 1919.

9. Ibid.

10. Ibid.

11. Interview 4.

12. Douglas J. Nelson, "For Such a Time as This: The Story of Bishop W.J. Seymour and the Azusa Street Revival" (PhD. diss., University of Birmingham, United Kingdom, 1981), 222.

13. Ibid., 185.

14. Interview 4.

15. *Bridal Call*, January 1919.

16. Ibid.

17. Interview 9.

18. Traditional, "The Ark is Coming Up the Road," c. 1919.

19. Margaret J. Harris, "I've Pitched My Tent in Beulah, " 1908.

20. Taped Interview number 9.

21. Ibid.

22. Taped Interview number 4.

23. *Bridal Call*, January 1919.

24. *Christian Evangel*, January 25, 1919.

25. Aimee Semple McPherson, *This Is That* (Los Angeles: Echo Park Evangelistic Association, November 28, 1923), 158.

26. Glenn A. Cook, "The Azusa Street Meeting: Some High Lights of this Ourpouring," (Los Angeles: published by the author, no date), 239.

27. *Bridal Call*, February 1919.

28. *Word and Work*, February 1919.

29. Salter, interview.

30. McPherson, *This Is That*, 232.

31. Robert Mapes Anderson, *Vision of the Disinherited: the Making of American Pentecostalism* (New York: Oxford University Press, 1979), 70.

32. *Bridal Call*, March 1919.

33. Ibid.

34. Daniel P. Fuller, *Give The Winds A Mighty Voice: The Story of Charles E. Fuller*

(Waco: Word Books, 1972), 36.

35. Ibid.

36. Carol Dunlap, *California People* (Salt Lake City: Gibbs M. Smith, 1982), 142.

37. Interview 30, November 4, 1978.

38. Ibid.

39. *Bridal Call*, March 1919.

40. McPherson, *This Is That*, 159.

41. Ibid., 159-160.

42. Ibid., 160.

43. *Bridal Call*, March 1919.

44. Ibid.

45. *Word and Work*, June 1919.

46. *Bridal Call*, May 1919.

47. Ibid.

48. Ibid.

49. Winthrop S. Hudson, *Religion in America*, (New York: Charles Scribner's Sons, 1973), 294-295.

50. Joseph Wilson Cochran, "The Church and the Working Man," *The Annals of the American Academy of Political and Social Science* 30, no. 3, (November, 1907): 445.

51. Sydney E. Ahlstrom, *A Religious History of the American People* (New Haven: Yale University Press, 1972), 738.

52. H. Francis Perry, "The Workingman's Alienation From the Church," *American Journal of Sociology* 4, no. 5 (March, 1899): 626.

53. James C. Deming and Michael S. Hamilton, "Methodist Revivalism in France, Canada, and the United States," in *Amazing Grace, Evangelicalism in Australia, Britain, Canada, and the United States*, ed. George A. Rawlyk and Mark A. Noll (Montreal: McGill-Queen's University Press, 1994), 132.

54. B.F. Lawrence, "Apostolic Faith Restored: A History of the Present Latter Rain Outpouring of the Holy Spirit Known as the Apostolic or Pentecostal Movement," *Weekly Evangel*, March 18, 1916.

55. *Bridal Call*, May 1919.

56. Ibid.

57. Ibid.

58. Ibid.

59. William G. McLoughlin, *Billy Sunday Was His Real Name!* (Chicago: University of Chicago Press, 1955), 287.

60. *Bridal Call*, May 1926.

61. *Los Angeles Times*, March 23, 1919.

62. Interview 23, October 10, 1981, Hemet, California.

63. Jonathan M. Butler, *Softly and Tenderly Jesus is Calling: Heaven and Hell in American Revivalism, 1870-1920* (Brooklyn: Carlson Publishing, 1991), 3.

64. Lawrence Lealand Lacour, "A Study of the Revival Method in America, 1920-1955, with Special Reference to Billy Sunday, Aimee Semple McPherson and Billy Graham." (Ph.D. diss., Northwestern University, 1956), 218.

65. Roberta Star Salter, interview by Charles H. Barfoot, November 4, 1978, New York City.

66. David L. Clark, "Sister Aimee," *California History* 47, no. 4 (Winter 1978-1979): 357.

67. Roy E. Bell, *LIFE Bible College Notes*, Vol. 4, "Homiletics." Los Angeles.

68. "Woman Preacher," *Atlanta Constitution*, July 19, 1919.

69. William L. O'Neill, *Echoes of Revolt: The Masses, 1911-1917* (Chicago: Quadrangle Books, 1966), 224-25.

70. *Bridal Call*, July 1922.

71. Lacour, "A Study of the Revival Method in America," 219.

72. Ibid.

73. Homer Rodeheaver, *Twenty Years With Billy Sunday* (Winona Lake: Rodeheaver Hall-Mack Co., 1936), 141.

74. *Los Angeles Herald*, September 22, 1917.

75. Rodeheaver, *Twenty Years*, 109.

76. Ibid., 74-75.

77. *Los Angeles Times*, October 29, 1917.

78. *Los Angeles Times*, September 21, 1917.

79. Ibid.

80. *Los Angeles Times*, September 7, 1917.

81. Robert Shuster, ed., *The Papers of William and Helen Sunday, 1882-1974*, the microfilm edition, Wheaton College, Billy Graham Center, Section 7, Scrapbooks, reel 25.

82. *Los Angeles Herald*, September 10, 1917.

83. *Los Angeles Herald*, September 6, 1917.

84. *Los Angeles Herald*, September 22, 1917.

85. *Los Angeles Times*, September 3, 1917.

86. *Los Angeles Herald,* October 26, 1917.

87. *Los Angeles Herald*, September 22, 1917.

88. Shuster, *The Papers of William and Helen Sunday*, reel 25.

89. Shuster, *The Papers of William and Helen Sunday*, Section l, Number 38, Homer Rodeheaver Letter to William Sunday, October 20, 1929.

90. Charles H. Lippy, ed., *Twentieth-Century Shapers of American Popular Religion* (Westport: Greenwood, 1989), 413.

91. Shuster, *The Papers of William and Helen Sunday*, Homer Rodeheaver Letter.

92. Ibid.

93. Ibid.

94. Lippy, *Twentieth-Century Shapers*, 415.

95. *Los Angeles Times*, September 24, 1949.

96. McPherson, *This Is That*, 391.

97. Ibid., 161.

98. Ibid., 162.

99. Everett A. Wilson, "Robert J. Craig's Glad Tidings and the Realization of a Vision for 100,000 Souls," *Assemblies of God Heritage* 8, no. 2 (Summer 1988), 9.

100. *Bridal Call*, April 1919.

101. Ibid.

102. Hubert C. Mathews, *Hubert: Here, There, and Yonder* (Springfield, Mo.: published by the author, 1976), 46-49.

103. *Bridal Call*, May 1919.

104. McPherson, *This Is That*, 247.

105. Ibid.

106. *Triumphs of Faith*, January 1919.

107. Ibid.

108. Ibid.

109. McPherson, *This Is That*, 275-276.

110. Interview 16, July 11, 1981, San Francisco, California.

111. McPherson, *This Is That*, 276.

112. *Pentecostal Evangel*, October 1, 1921.

113. Philip L. Fradkin, *The Great Earthquake and Firestorms of 1906: How San Francisco Nearly Destroyed Itself* (Berkeley: University of California Press, 2005), 3.

114. Ibid.

115. Charles Reynolds Brown, *My Own Yesterdays* (New York: Century Company, 1931), 102-103.

116. Wilson, "Robert J. Craig's Glad Tidings," 9.

117. *Glad Tidings* 3 (1922): 1.

118. Ibid.

119. *San Francisco Examiner*, March 23, 1919.

120. McPherson, *This Is That*, 162.

121. *Word and Work*, April 1919.

122. *Bridal Call*, July 1919.

123. Ibid.

124. Ibid.

125. Ibid.

126. Ibid.

127. The Assemblies of God Northern California and Nevada District Council, Inc., *Chronicle of the Past Fifty Years* (San Jose: Prunetree Graphics, 1971), 16.

128. John Fante, *Ask The Dust* (Santa Barbara: Black Sparrow Press, 1980), 160.

129. *Bridal Call*, May 1926.

Chapter Nine

1. Matthew J. Bruccoli, *Some Sort of Epic Grandeur: The Life of F. Scott Fitzgerald* (New York: Harcourt Brace Jovanovich, 1981).

2. Unification Theological Seminary, *Toward Our Third Century,* (Barrytown, N.Y.: Unification Theological Seminary, 1976), 57.

3. Winthrop S. Hudson, *Religion in America*, (New York: Charles Scribners Sons, 1973), 362.

4. Richard W. Etulain, "The American Literary West and Its Interpreters: The Rise of a New Historiography," *Pacific Historical Review* 45, no. 3 (August 1976): 383, 323.

5. Sidney E. Ahlstrom, *A Religious History of the America* (New Haven: Yale University Press, 1973), 915.

6. H.L. Mencken, ed., *A Mencken Chrestomathy* (New York: A.A. Knopf, 1949), 76.

7. Ahlstrom, *A Religious History*, 895.

8. Ibid., 896.

9. Lawrence W. Levine, "Progress and Nostalgia: The Self Image of the Nineteen Twenties," in *The American Novel and the Nineteen Twenties,* ed. Malcolm Bradbury and David Palmer (London: Edward Arnold Publishers, Ltd., 1971), 37-56.

10. Ibid., 50-53, 56.

11. Catherine L. Albanese, ed., *American Spiritualities, A Reader* (Bloomington: Indiana University Press, 2001), 179.

12. Sidney E. Mead, *The Nation with the Soul of a Church* (New York: Harper Forum Books, 1975).

13. Carey McWilliams, "Aimee Semple McPherson: Sunlight in My Soul," in *The Aspirin Age, 1919 to 1941*, ed. Isabel Leighton (New York: Simon and Schuster, 1949), 62.

14. Aimee Semple McPherson, *Life Story,* International Church of the Foursquare Gospel archives, Los Angeles, 7.

15. Mary Ewens, "Removing the Veil: The Liberated American Nun," in *Women of Spirit, Female Leadership in the Jewish and Christian Traditions* , ed. Rosemary Ruether and Eleanor McLaughlin (New York: Simon and Schuster, 1979), 273.

16. F. Scott Fitzgerald, *The Great Gatsby* (New York: Charles Scribners Sons, 1925), 8.

17. William C. McLoughlin, "Aimee Semple McPherson: Your Sister in the King's Glad Service," *Journal of Popular Culture* 1 (1967): 215.

18. *Bridal Call*, November 1919.

19. Interview 4, January 28, 1981, Los Angeles.

20. *Bridal Call*, September 1919.

21. *Bridal Call*, October 1919.

22. Aimee Semple McPherson, *This Is That* (Los Angeles: Bridal Call Publishing House, 1923), 167.

23. *Bridal Call*, October 1919.

24. *Bridal Call*, January 1919.

25. Ibid.

26. Ibid.

27. Ibid.

28. *Bridal Call*, December 1919.

29. Ibid.

30. Ibid.

31. Ibid.

32. *Bridal Call,* June 1916.

33. Ibid.

34. *Bridal Call,* January 1920.

35. McPherson, *This Is That,* 170.

36. *Bridal Call,* June 1926.

37. *Bridal Call,* January 1920.

38. *Bridal Call,* June 1926.

39. Ibid.

40. Ferenc Morton Szasz, *The Divided Mind of Protestant America,* 1880-1930 (Birmingham: University of Alabama Press, 1982), 102.

41. *Baltimore Sun,* 9 December 1919.

42. Sandra Tamar Frankiel, *California's Spiritual Frontiers: Religious Alternatives to Anglo-Protestantism, 1850-1910* (Berkeley: University of California Press, 1988), 87.

43. Ibid., 90.

44. Mabel Potter Daggett, "Are There Modern Miracles?" *Ladies Home Journal,* June 1923.

45. Ibid.

46. F. Scott Fitzgerald, *The Last Tycoon, An Unfinished Novel* (New York. Charles Scribners Sons, 1941), 113-114.

47. *Journal of the General Convention of the Protestant Episcopal Church in the United States of America,* New Orleans, 1925, 649 and *Journal of the General Convention of the Protestant Episcopal Church in the United States of America,* 1928, 466.

48. *Baltimore Sun,* 9 December 1919.

49. Daggett, "Are There Modern Miracles?"

50. Kenneth MacKenzie, *Our Physical Heritage in Christ* (New York: Fleming H. Revell Company, 1923), 60.

51. *Bridal Call,* April 1920.

52. Janice Dickin, " 'Take Up Thy Bed and Walk': Aimee Semple McPherson and Faith-Healing," *Canadian Bulletin of Medical History* 17 (2000): 141.

53. *Pentecostal Evangel,* June 10, 1922.

54. McPherson, Life Story, 25.

55. Interview 26, October 25, 1981, Palo Alto, California.

56. Interview 9, February 4, 1981, Los Angeles.

57. McPherson, *This Is That,* 174.

58. Ibid., 175.

59. *Bridal Call,* June 1926.

60. *Baltimore Sun,* 13 December 1919.

61. Ibid.

62. *Baltimore Sun,* 20 December 1919.

63. Ibid.

64. Ibid.

65. *Bridal Call,* January 1920.

66. Aimee Semple McPherson, *The Personal Testimony of Aimee Semple McPherson* (Los Angeles: Foursquare Publications, Inc., 1928), 36.

67. David M. Shribman, review of *American Sermons: The Pilgrims to Martin Luther King, Jr., Wall Street Journal*, April 23, 1999.

Chapter 10

1. Raymond J. Cunningham, "The Emmanuel Movement: A Variety of American Religious Experience," *American Quarterly* 14, no. 1 (Spring, 1961): 50.

2. Elwood Worcester, *Life's Adventure, The Story of a Varied Career* (New York: Charles Scribner's Sons, 1932), 38.

3. Ibid., 30.

4. Ibid., 32.

5. Ibid., 33.

6. Ibid., 275.

7. Ibid., 276-277.

8. Ibid., 220.

9. Ibid.

10. Cunningham, "The Emmanuel Movement," 52.

11. Ibid., 53.

12. Worcester, *Life's Adventure*, 354.

13. Ibid., 355.

14. Ibid.

15. Cunningham, "The Emmanuel Movement," 52.

16. See Sanford Gifford, *The Emmanuel Movement (Boston 1904–1929): The Origins of Group Treatment and the Assault on Lay Psychotherapy* (Cambridge, Mass.: Harvard University Press, 1998).

17. Worcester, *Life's Adventure*, 298.

18. Ibid., 297.

19. Ibid., 350, 356.

20. Ibid., 312-313.

21. *Journal of the General Convention of the Protestant Episcopal Church in the United States of America*, 1922, 718.

22. Ibid.

23. Ibid., 718-719.

24. *Journal of the General Convention of the Protestant Episcopal Church in the United States of America*, 1925, 649.

25. Ibid., 650.

26. Ibid., 649.

27. Ibid.

28. Edward S. Cowles, MD, *Religion and Medicine in the Church*, (New York: Macmillan, 1925), 92.

29. Charles W. Ferguson, *The Confusion of Tongues: A Review of Modern ISMS* (New York: Doubleday, 1928).

30. *Journal of the General Convention of the Protestant Episcopal Church in the United States of America*, 1928, 465-466.

31. Ibid., 466.

32. *Journal of the General Convention of the Protestant Episcopal Church in the United States of America*, 1931,556, 560.

33. Ibid., 556.

34. Ibid., 557.

Chapter Eleven

1. Aimee Semple McPherson, *The Personal Testimony of Aimee Semple McPherson* (Los Angeles: Foursquare Publications, Inc., 1928), 37.

2. *Pentecostal Evangel*, January 5, 1924.

3. Carey McWilliams, *Southern California Country* (New York: Duell, Sloan & Pearce, 1946), 377.

4. *Bridal Call*, July 1920.

5. Ibid.

6. Ibid.

7. Ibid.

8. Ibid.

9. Ibid.

10. Ibid.

11. Ibid.

12. Ibid.

13. *Religious Telescope*, May 29, 1920, 8.

14. F. Scott Fitzgerald, *Letters to His Daughter*, ed. Andrew Turnbull (New York: Charles Scribners Sons, 1965), 128.

15. Interview 14, July 17, 1981, Los Angeles.

16. Janice Dickin, " 'Take Up Thy Bed and Walk': Aimee Semple McPherson and Faith-Healing," *Canadian Bulletin of Medical History* 17 (2000): 147.

17. Aimee Semple McPherson, *This is That* (Los Angeles: Bridal Call Publishing House, 1921), 249.

18. *Pentecostal Evangel*, June 24, 1920.

19. *Bridal Call*, August 1920.

20. Ibid.

21. James E. Thomas, *A Look at Los Angeles in the 20ᵗʰ Century* (Sacramento: Johnson Publishing Co., 1963), 4l, 43.

22. Margaret Romer, "The Story of Los Angeles," *Journal of the West* 3, no. l, (January 1964): 30.

23. *Los Angeles Times*, November 2, 1983.

24. *Los Angeles County Book of Records*, Book 5l, 250.

25. Sandra Tamar Frankel, *California Spiritual Frontiers: Religious Alternatives to Anglo-Protestantism, 1850-1910* (Berkeley: University of California Press, 1988), 79.

26. *Bridal Call*, December 1920.

27. McPherson, *This Is That* (Los Angeles: Echo Park Evangelistic Association, 1923), 508.

28. *Bridal Call*, December 1920.

29. *Bridal Call*, August 1921.

30. *Bridal Call*, January 1921.

31. McWilliams, *Southern California Country*, 260.

32. McPherson, *This Is That*, 1923, 5-9.

33. Interview 14, July 17, 1981, Los Angeles.

34. Interview 5, January 28, 1981, Santa Ana.

35. Interview number 14.

36. Roberta Star Semple Salter, interview by Charles H. Barfoot, November 4, 1978, New York.

37. *Bridal Call*, April 1921.

38. Interview 14,.

39. *Bridal Call*, April 1921.

40. McWilliams, *Southern California Country*, 259.

Chapter Twelve

1. *San Diego Union*, January 1, 1921.

2. Aimee Semple McPherson, *This Is That* (Los Angeles: Echo Park Evangelistic Association, 1923), 242.

3. Carey McWilliams, *Southern California Country* (New York: Duell Sloan & Pearce, 1946), 259.

4. Richard Rodriquez, "Paradise Lost: California Has Always Been the Last Chance for Eden on the American Continent," *Los Angeles Times*, March 30, 1997.

5. McWilliams, *Southern California Country*, 259.

6. Ibid.

7. *Bridal Call*, February 1921.

8. *Bridal Call*, April 1921.

9. *Bridal Call*, February 1921.

10. Ibid.

11. Ibid.

12. Ibid.

13. Ibid.

14. *Bridal Call*, March 1921.

15. *Bridal Call*, November 1923.

16. *San Diego Tribune*, February 3, 1921.

17. *San Diego Tribune*, February 9, 1921.

18. Ibid.

19. *Bridal Call*, April 1921.

20. Ibid.

21. Ibid.

22. Notes from Richard George Wheeler, son of William Henry Wheeler, author's collection.

23. Ibid.

24. McPherson, *This Is That*, 1923, 303.

25. Ibid.

26. *Bridal Call*, June 1921.

27. Ibid.

28. Martin E. Marty, *Modern American Religion, Vol. 2, The Noise of Conflict, 1919-1941* (Chicago: University of Chicago Press, 1997), 170-71.

29. *Bridal Call*, July 1921.

30. Ibid.

31. Ibid.

32. Roy E. Bell, *LIFE Bible College Notes*, Vol. 4, "Homiletics." Los Angeles.

Chapter Thirteen

1. *Denver Post*, June 19, 1921.

2. Walter W. Dwyer, *The Churches' Handbook for Spiritual Healing* (New York: Ascension Press, 1965), 3.

3. *Denver Post*, June 19, 1921.

4. *Bridal Call*, May 1922.

5. Lyle W. Dorsett, *The Queen City, A History of Denver* (Boulder, Colo.: Pruett Publishing, 1977), 87.

6. Ibid., 282.

7. Ibid., 87

8. Ibid., 90, 97.

9. Ibid., 152, 154.

10. Edward P. Costigan, *Papers of Edward P. Costigan Relating to the Progressive Movement in Colorado, 1902-1917* (Boulder: University of Colorado Press, 1941), 13-14.

11. *Southern Churchman*, December 8, 1923.

12. Michael McGerr, *A Fierce Discontent: The Rise and Fall of the Progressive Movement in America, 1870-1920.* (New York: Free Press, 2003), xiii, xv.

13. Ibid., xv.

14. Charles Larsen, *The Good Fight: The Life and Times of Ben B. Lindsey* (Chicago: Quadrangle Books, 1971), 267.

15. Dorsett, *The Queen City*, 115.

16. Ferenc M. Szasz, *Religion in the Modern American West* (Tucson: University of Arizona Press, 2000), 61.

17. Ibid.

18. *Bridal Call*, August 1921.

19. Aimee Semple McPherson, *This Is That* (Los Angeles: Echo Park Evangelistic Association, 1923), 351.

20. Ibid.

21. Ibid., 352.

22. Ibid.

23. Ibid.

25. Ibid., 326.

26. Ibid.

27. *Denver Post*, July 10, 1921.

26. *Bridal Call*, August 1921.

28. *Denver Post*, June 28, 1921.

29. *Denver Post*, June 19, 1921.

30. Ibid.

31. *Denver Post*, June 21, 1921.

32. Ibid.

33. *Bridal Call*, September 1921.

34. *Denver Post*, July 1, 1921.

35. Ibid.

36. *Denver Post*, June 21, 1921.

37. *Denver Post*, July 3, 1921.

38. McPherson, *This Is That*, 1923, 348–50.

39. Ibid., 343.

40. *Denver Post*, July 11, 1921.

41. *Bridal Call*, August 1921.

42. *The Testimony, Christian Chronicle*, May-June 2004, 8, http://www.the testimony.cc/May-June04?page8.htm.

43. Raymond L. Cox, "Revival in Denver," http://www/geocities/ruinum/denver.htm? 2/21/2006

44. Ibid.

45. Ibid.

46. Ibid.

47. B.J. Morris, "The Revivals of Aimee Semple McPherson," *Pacific Christian Advocate*, 1923, 4.

48. *Denver Post*, July 11, 1921.

49. *Bridal Call*, August 1921.

50. *Bridal Call*, September 1921, 10.

51. McPherson, *This Is That*, 1923, 358.

52. Morris, "The Revivals of Aimee," 36.

53. Ibid., 35.

54. Ibid.

55. Ibid., 36.

56. Cox, "Denver."

57. *Denver Post*, June 7, 1922 and June 15, 1922.

58. Cox, "Denver."

59. Ibid.

60. Marcus Bach, *They Have Found A Faith* (New York: Bobbs-Merrill, 1946), 85.

61. Barbara Brown Zikmund, "Kathryn Kuhlman: The Woman Behind the Miracles," *Christian Century*, August 2, 1995.

Chapter Fourteen

1. Harry Carr, *Los Angeles, City of Dreams* (New York: Grosset & Dunlap, 1935), 6.

2. Gregory H. Singleton, *Religion in the City of Angels: American Protestant Culture and Urbanization, Los Angeles, 1850-1930* (Ann Arbor: UMI Research Press, 1979), 154.

3. Ibid., 152.

4. Ibid., 153.

5. Ibid., 155.

6. *Los Angeles Times*, March 1, 1924.

7. *Los Angeles Times*, October 22, 1927.

8. *Los Angeles Times*, February 14, 1920.

9. *Los Angeles Times*, June 20, 1925.

10. Ibid.

11. *New York Times*, May 29, 1926.

12. Martin E. Marty, *Modern American Religion, Vol. 2, The Noise of Conflict, 1919-1941* (Chicago: University of Chicago Press, 1986), 173.

13. Raymond L. Cox, "The Greatest Nine Days, Revival in Boston," http://www.geocities.com/ruinum/boston.htm.

14. Ibid.

15. Karla Poewe, ed., *Charismatic Christianity as a Global Culture* (Columbia: University of South Carolina Press, 1994), 110.

16. Jerry Falwell, ed., *The Fundamentalist Phenomenon, The Resurgence of Conservative Christianity* (Garden City: Doubleday, 1981), 7.

17. Mark Noll, *The Old Religion in a New World* (Grand Rapids: William B. Eerdmans, 2001), 155.

18. First Baptist Church, San Jose, *Diamond Jubilee History* (San Jose: 1925), 14.

19. B. J. Morris, "The Revivals of Aimee Semple McPherson," *Pacific Christian Advocate*, 1923), 5.

20. Ibid., 23

21. Ibid., 16-18.

22. Ibid., 28.

23. W. K. Towner, *Church Notes, 1921*, International Church of the Foursquare Archives, Los Angeles.

24. Hubert C. Mathews, *Hubert: Here, There, and Yonder* (Springfield, Mo.: published by the author, 1976), 46-49.

25. First Baptist Church, San Jose, "First Church Advocate," May 14, 1922, 1.

26. *The San Francisco Chronicle*, April 2, 1922.

27. Ibid.; see also *San Jose Mercury*, April 1, 1922.

28. Seventy-First Annual Session, C.W. Brinstad, executive secretary, 17.

29. Leach Letter, December 12, 1922, American Baptist Seminary of the West Library Archives, Berkeley, California.

30. Milliken Letter, December 12, 1922, American Baptist Seminary of the West

Library Archives, Berkeley, California.

31. Singleton, *Religion in the City of Angels*, 153.

32. First Congregational Church, San Francisco, "Reverend James Logan Gordon: An Appraisal and Appreciation," October 14, 1930, First Congregational Church Archives.

33. Ibid.

34. First Baptist Church, San Jose, "First Church Advocate," May 14, 1922, 1.

35. *The Pacific,* July 1922, 8.

36. George William Haskell, "Formative Factors in the Life and Thought of Southern California Congregationalism, 1850-1908" (PhD. diss., University of Southern California, 1947), 61.

37. Ibid., 62-63.

38. Charles S. Price, … *And Signs Followed: The Life Story of Charles S. Price* (Plainfield, N.Y.: Logos International, 1972).

39. *Annals of the First Congregational Church of Santa Rosa, California,* 1915, 17.

40. Ibid.

41. Ibid., 18.

42. Price, … *And Signs Followed,* 33.

43. Tim Enloe, "Dr. Charles S. Price," *Assemblies of God Heritage,* 2008, 8.

44. First Congregational Church of Lodi, California, *Seventy-Five Years in Lodi, A History of the First Congregational Congregational Church of Lodi, California, 1872-1947* (Lodi, Calif.: by the author, March 1947), 69.

45 Ibid.

46 Price, … *And Signs Followed,* 28, 29, 34.

47 Ibid.

48 Ibid., 40-43.

49 First Congregational Church of Lodi, *Seventy-Five Years,* 70, 71, 72, 74.

50 Ibid., 76.

Chapter Fifteen

1. Blake McKelvey, "Rochester in Retrospect and Prospect," *Rochester History* 23, no. 3 (July, 1961): 1.

2. Ibid., 5.

3. Blake McKelvey, "Economic Stages in the Growth of Rochester," *Rochester History* 3, no. 4 (October, 1941): 1.

4. Ibid.

5. McKelvey, "Rochester in Retrospect," 6.

6. Blake McKelvey, "A Panoramic Review of Rochester's History," *Rochester History* 11, no. 2, (April, 1949): 5.

7. Donald Dayton, *Discovering An Evangelical Heritage* (New York: Harper & Row, 1976), 15.

8. Ibid.

9. Ibid., 16.

10. Ibid.

11. Ibid.

12. Dexter Perkins, "Rochester One Hundred Years Ago," *Rochester History* 1 no. 3 (July, 1939): 15.

13. Whitney R. Cross, *The Burned-Over District: The Social and Intellectual History of Enthusiastic Religion in Western New York* (New York: Harper & Row, 1965), 155.

14. Ibid., 152.

15. Ibid., 154.

16. Dayton, *Evangelical Heritage*, 16.

17. Ibid., 88.

18. Sydney E. Ahlstrom, *A Religious History of the American People* (New Haven: Yale University Press, 1972), 643.

19. John Corrigan and Winthrop S. Hudson, *Religion in America* (Upper Saddle River, New Jersey: Prentice-Hall, 2004), 308.

20. Ibid.

21. Perkins, "One Hundred Years Ago," 15.

22. Dayton, *Evangelical Heritage*, 17.

23. Perkins, "One Hundred Years Ago," 14-15.

24. Ibid., 15.

25. McKelvey, A Panoramic Review," 6.

26. Ibid.

27. Ibid.

28. Perkins, "One Hundred Years Ago," 15.

29. Ibid.

30. Ibid.

31. Ibid.

32. Ibid., 16.

33. Dayton, *Evangelical Heritage*, 18.

34. Ibid.

35. Ibid., 18-19.

36. Perkins, "One Hundred Years Ago," 16.

37. Corrigan and Hudson, *Religion in America*, 215.

38. McKelvey, "A Sesquicentennial Review of Rochester's History," *Rochester History* 24, no. 3 (July, 1962): 20.

39. Dayton, *Evangelical Heritage*, 95.

40. McKelvey, "Susan B. Anthony," *Rochester History* 7, no. 2 (April, 1945): 24.

41. McKelvey, "A Sesquicentennial Review, 16.

42. Ibid.

43. Blake McKelvey, "Woman's Rights in Rochester, A Century of Progress," *Rochester History* 10, nos. 2-3 (July, 1948): 4.

44. Ibid.

45. McKelvey, "Susan B. Anthony," 5.

46. Ibid.

47. Ibid., 19.

48. Ibid.

49. Ibid.

50. Perkins, "One Hundred Years Ago," 23.

51. McKelvey, "Economic Stages," 11.

52. Ibid.

53. McKelvey, "A Panoramic Review," 10.

54. Ibid.

55. Ibid.

56. McKelvy, "Economic Stages," 14.

57. Ibid., 13.

58. Ibid.

59. McKelvey, A Sesquicentennial review," 28-29.

60. Blake McKelvey, "Walter Rauschenbusch's Rochester," *Rochester History* 14, no. 4 (October 1952): 27.

61. Ibid., 7.

62. Ibid.

63. Ibid., 8.

64. McKelvey, "A Panoramic Review," 16.

65. Ibid., 20.

66. Joseph W. Barnes, "The City's Golden Age," *Rochester History* 35, no. 2 (April 1973): 5.

67. McKelvey, "A Sesquicentennial Review," 24.

68. Barnes, "Golden Age," 22.

69. Aimee Semple McPherson, *This Is That* (Los Angeles: Echo Park Evangelistic Association, 1923), 431.

70. Richard Henn, *The History of Asbury First United Methodist Church*, fifth ed. (Rochester: Asbury First United Methodist Church, 2001) 65.

71. John R. Kohlenberger, III, *All About Bibles* (New York: Oxford University Press, 2000) 2.

72. McPherson, *This Is That,* 2nd ed., 431.

73. Ibid.

74. Ibid., 432-434.

75. *Rochester Herald*, November 11, 1921.

76. Ibid.

77. *Rochester Democrat And Chronicle*, November 2, 1921.

78. *Rochester Herald*, November 25, 1921.

79. Ibid.

80. Ibid.

81. *Rochester Democrat and Chronicle*, November 2, 1921.

82. First Congregational Church of Lodi, California, *Seventy-five Years in Lodi, A History of the First Congregational Church of Lodi, California, 1872-1947.* (Lodi, California: First Congregational Church, 1947), 40.

83. *Rochester Democrat and Chronicle*, November 13, 1921.

84. Ibid.

85. Ibid.

86. Ibid.

87. Ibid.

88. *Rochester Herald*, October 29, 1921.

89. Ibid., October 30, 1921.

90. *Rochester Democrat and Chronicle*, November 5, 1921.

91. Ibid.

92. Ibid.

93. Ibid.

94. Ibid.

95. Martin E. Marty, *Modern American Religion, Vol. 2, The Noise of Conflict, 1919-1941* (Chicago: University of Chicago Press, 1986), 186

96. *Rochester Democrat and Chronicle*, November 3, 1921.

97. Ibid.

98. McPherson, *This Is That*, 2nd ed., 417.

99. Ibid., 423-425.

100. *Rochester Post Express*, November 2, 1921.

101. Ibid.

102. *Rochester Times-Union*, November 2, 1921.

103. Ibid., November 22, 1921.

104. Ibid.

105. Ibid.

106. Ibid.

107. Ibid.

108. Robert C. Reinders, "Training for A Prophet: The West Coast Missions of John Alexander Dowie, 1888-1890," *The Pacific Historian*, 30:1 (Spring, 1986), 8.

109. Ingrid Overacker, "And the Work was Accomplished: The African American Church Community in Rochester, New York" (PhD. diss., University of Rochester, 1995), 254.

110. Ibid., vi.

111. Ibid., 66.

112. Ibid., 67.

113. Ibid.

114. Ibid., 155.

115. Ibid., 77.

116. Ibid., 153.

117. *Rochester Times-Union*, November 10, 1921.

118. Ibid., November 7, 1921.

119. Blake McKelvey, "Civic Medals Awarded Posthumously," *Rochester History*, 22:2, (April 1960), 21.

120. McKelvey, A Sesquicentennial Review, 25.

121. *Rochester Democrat and Chronicle*, November 5, 1921.

122. *Rochester Times-Union*, November 10, 1921.

123. Ibid.

124. Ibid.

125. *Rochester Post Express*, November 5, 1921.

126. *Rochester Democrat and Chronicle*, November 6, 1921.

127. Ibid.

128. Ibid.

129. *Rochester Democrat and Chronicle*, November 13, 1921.

130. Ibid., November 7, 1921.

131. Ibid.

132. Ibid.

133. *Rochester Post Express*, November 7, 1921.

134. Ibid., November 10, 1921.

135. Ibid., November 7, 1921.

136. Ibid.

137. *Rochester Democrat and Chronicle*, November 7, 1921.

138. Henn, "Asbury first United Methodist," 175.

139. Asbury First United Methodist Church, "History of Asbury First," http://www.asburyfirst.org/content/view/56/.

140. Ibid.

141. *Rochester Herald*, November 9, 1921.

142. Ibid.

143. Ibid.

144. *Rochester Times-Union*, November 8, 1921.

145. Ibid.

146. *The Rochester Herald*, November 10, 1921.

147. Ibid.

148. Ibid.

149. *Rochester Times-Union*, November 9, 1921.

150. Ibid.

151. Ibid.

152. Ibid.

153. Ibid.

154. *Rochester Times-Union*, November 10, 1921.

155. Ibid.

156. *Rochester Democrat and Chronicle*, November 10, 1921.

157. Ibid.

158. Ibid.

159. *Rochester Times-Union*, November 10, 1921.

160. Ibid., November 17, 1921.

161. Ibid.

162. Ibid.

163. Ibid.

164. *Rochester Democrat and Chronicle*, November 20, 1921.

165. Ibid.

166. Ibid.

167. Ibid.

168. *Rochester Post Express*, November 21, 1921.

169. Ibid.

170. *Rochester Times-Union*, November 21, 1921.

171. Ibid. and *Rochester Post Express*, November 21, 1921.

172. *Rochester Times-Union*, November 21, 1921.

173. Catherine L. Albanese, "Exchanging Selves, Exchanging Souls: Contact, Combination, and American Religious History," in *Retelling U.S. Religious History*, ed. Thomas A. Tweed (Berkeley: University of California Press, 1997), 225.

174. Ibid., 224-225.

175. *Rochester Democrat and Chronicle*, November 22, 1921.

176. Ibid.

177. Ibid.

178. Brittany Soper, "The Gillette Family," (Rochester: Speaking Stones, 2006), 6.

179. McPherson, *This Is That*, 2nd ed., 434-436.

180. Richard O. Reisem, "The Man Who Invented The Five-Day Work Week, *Epitaph Newsletter*, 17:1, 7. (http:///www.lib.rochester.edu/index.cfm?PAGE+3093

181. Corrigan and Hudson, *Religion in America*, 313.

182. Reisem, "Five-Day Work Week," 6.

183. Ibid.

184. *Rochester Democrat and Chronicle*, November 22, 1921.

185. Reisem, "Five-Day Work Week," 7.

186. *Rochester Democrat and Chronicle*, November 18, 1921.

187. Ibid., November 23, 1921.

188. *Rochester Herald*, November 23, 1921.

189. C.S. Bluemel, "Faith Healers: With Special Reference to Aimee Semple McPherson," *Colorado Medicine*, July 1921, 145.

190. Ibid., 143-145.

191. Ibid., 146

192. McPherson, *This Is That*, 2nd ed., 420.

193. *Rochester Democrat and Chronicle*, November 23, 1921.

The Los Angeles Record, January 2, 1923.

195. Janice Dickin, " 'Take Up Thy Bed and Walk': Aimee Semple McPherson and Faith Healing." *Canadian Bulletin of Medical History*, Vol. 17 (2000): 146-147.

Chapter Sixteen

1. *Wichita Beacon*, May 7, 1922.

2. Truman Capote, *In Cold Blood* (New York: Random House, 1965), 343.

3. *Bridal Call*, June 1922.

4. Aimee Semple McPherson, "The Narrow Line or Is Mrs. McPherson Pentecostal?" (Los Angeles: Echo Park Evangelical Association, Inc., no date), 1.

5. Ibid., 6-7.

6. Ibid., 8-9.

7. *Wichita Eagle*, May 16, 1922.

8. E.N. Bell Letter to Paul H. Ralstin, May 23, 1922, Assemblies of God Archives, Springfield, Missouri.

9. *Pentecostal Evangel*, June 10, 1922.

10. McPherson, "The Narrow Line", 6, 9.

11. W. H. Boyles Letter to E.N. Bell, August 24, 1922, Assemblies of God Archives, Springfield, Missouri.

12. Aimee Semple McPherson, "Class Notes on Homiletics," no date, LIFE Bible College, Los Angeles, 9.

13. Aimee Semple McPherson, "Class Notes on *The Book of Acts*," no date, LIFE Bible College, Los Angeles, 19, 16.

14. *Wichita Beacon*, May 12, 1922.

15. Ibid.

16. Interview number 5, January 28, 1981, Santa Ana, California.

17. *Wichita Beacon*, May 12, 1922.

18. Ibid.

19. *Bridal Call*, June 1922.

20. William E. Connelley, *History of Kansas State and People* (Chicago: American Historical Society, Inc., 1928), 1343.

21. Interview number 5.

22. *Wichita Eagle*, June 10, 1977.

23. *Wichita Beacon*, May 15, 1922.

24. W.R. Waggoner, "Admit Miracles are Performed by M'Pherson," *Arkansas City Traveler*, May 16, 1922.

25. Ibid.

26. Ibid.

27. *Arkansas City Traveler*, May 15, 1922.

28. Ibid.

29. Ibid., May 16, 1922.

30. Ibid.

31. Ibid., May 19, 1922.

32. Ibid., May 17, 1922.

33. Ibid., May 29, 1922.

34. Ibid.

35. Ibid., May 30, 1922

36. Ibid.

37. Ibid.

38. Ibid.

39. Ibid.

40. Ibid.

41. Ibid.
42. Ibid.
43. Ibid.
44. Ibid.
45. Ibid.
46. *Bridal Call*, December 1927.
47. *Wichita Eagle,* May 16, 1922.
48. *Arkansas City Traveler,* May 31, 1922.
49. Ibid.
50. Ibid.
51. Ibid.
52. Ibid., May 30, 1922.
53. *Wichita Beacon*, May 15, 1922.
54. Aimee Semple McPherson, *This Is That* (1923 edition), 385.
55. *Wichita Eagle*, May 15, 1922.
56. *Wichita Beacon*, May 16, 1922.

Chapter Seventeen

1. *Bridal Call*, June 1922, 19.

2. Howard Presbyterian Church, Session Minutes, San Francisco, California, April 26, 1922, San Francisco Theological Seminary Archives.

3. Howard Presbyterian Church, Session Minutes, San Francisco, California, December 13, 1922, San Francisco Theological Seminary Archives.

4. Bishop Edward L. Parsons, "Bishop Parsons Recalls Memories of Dean James Wilmer Gresham," *Pacific Churchman* 2 (May 1951) 13.

5. Ibid., 13.

6. *Bridal Call*, May 1922.

7. Aimee Semple McPherson, *This Is That* (Los Angeles: Echo Park Evangelistic Association, Inc., 1923), 463.

8. D. Michael Quinn, "Religion in the American West," in,*Under an Open Sky, Rethinking America's Western Past,* William Cronon, et al., eds. (New York: W.W. Norton, 1992), 161.

9. Chris Rhomberg, "White Nativism and Urban Politics: The 1920s Ku Klux Klan in Oakland, California," *Journal of American Ethnic History*, 17:2 (Winter 1998), 40.

10. *Oakland Tribune,* July 16, 1922.

11. *Bridal Call*, September 1922.

12. Ibid.

13. "Charles R. Brown, Remembered," (Oakland: First Congregational Church of Oakland, n.d.), 1., First Congregational Church of Oakland Archives.

14. *Oakland Tribune*, July 17, 1922.

15. Raymond L. Cox, "Aimee Semple McPherson" (unpublished manuscript, International Church of the Foursquare Gospel Archives, Los Angeles), 250.

16. Ibid., 251.

17. Ibid., 252.

18. William G. McLoughlin, "Aimee Semple McPherson: Your Sister in the King's Glad Service," *Journal of Popular Culture* (Winter 1967), 207.

19. Very similar, of course, to A.B. Simpson's "Four-Fold Gospel." "Healing" replaces "Sanctification" as the second tenet.

20. *The Oakland Tribune*, July 18, 1922.

21. Ibid., July 19, 1922.

22. Ibid., July 18, 1922.

23. Especially notable in this area was Dean James Wilmer Gresham.

24. Edward Lambe Parsons, *A Quarter Century, 1915-1940, Diocese of California* (Austin, Texas: Episcopal Church Historical Society, 1958), 137.

25. John Corrigan and Winthrop S. Hudson, *Religion in America*, 7th ed. (Upper Saddle River, New Jersey: Prentice Hall, 2004), 283-285.

26. The Church of England, *Liberal Evangelicalism, An Interpretation*, Fourth Edition (London: Hodder and Stoughton, 1924), v, viii.

27. Sydney E. Ahlstrom, *A Religious History of the American People* (New Haven: Yale University Press, 1972), 782.

28. *The Oakland Tribune*, July 28, 1922.

29. "Reverend James Logan Gordon, An Appraisal and Appreciation," (San Francisco: First Congregational Church of San Francisco, October 14, 1930, 3, First Congregational Church of San Francisco Archives.

30. *The Oakland Tribune*, July 29, 1922.

31. Ibid., July 22, 1922.

32. Cox, "Aimee Semple McPherson," 252.

33. Willow Creek Association, "About Us," http://www.willowcreek.com/about/

34. Timothy L. Smith, *Revivalism and Social Reform; American Protestantism on the Eve of the Civil War* (New York: Harper & Row, 1957), 83.

35. *Bridal Call*, June 1922.

36. Ferenc Morton Szasz, *The Divided Mind of Protestant America, 1880-1930* (Birmingham: University of Alabama Press, 1982), 64-65.

37. Ibid., 67.

38. John F. Piper, Jr. "The American Churches in World War I," *Journal of the American Academy of Religion*, 38, no. 2 (June 1970): 147.

39. Ibid., 155.

40. *Annual Report of the Federal Council of the Churches of Christ in America, 1918* (New York: Missionary Education Movement of the United States and Canada, 1918), 97-98.

41. James J. Thompson, *Tried As By Fire: Southern Baptists and the Religious Controversies of the 1920s* (Macon, Ga.,: Mercer University Press, 1982), 153.

42. Ibid., 21-11.

43. Ibid., 23

44. *Weekly Evangel*, Febuary 26, 1916.

45. *San Francisco Call*, April 3, 1922.

46. Roberta Star Salter interview, November 4, 1978, New York City.

47. David Martin, *Pentecostalism: The World Their Parish* (Malden, Mass.: Blackwell Publishers, 2002), 5.

48. Church of England, *Liberal Evangelicalism*, v.

49. Martin E. Marty, *Modern American Religion, Vol. I, The Irony of It All, 1893-1919* (Chicago: The University of Chicago Press, 1986), 239.

50. Chris Armstrong, "Embrace Your Inner Pentecostal," *Christianity Today* 50:9 (September 2006) http://www.christianitytoday.com/ct/article_print.html.

51. Charles Reynolds Brown, *My Own Yesterdays* (New York: Century 1931), 314.

52. Ibid., 312-313.

53. Rhomberg, "White Nativism and Urban Politics," 39.

54. Ibid.

55. Katherine G. Aiken, "Sister Aimee Semple McPherson and the Interwar West, 1920-1940," in *Western Lives: A Biographical History of the American West* , ed. Richard W. Etulain (Albuquerque: University of New Mexico Press, 2004), 312.

56. Ibid.

57. *Oakland Tribune*, July 2, 1922

58. Interview 16, July 11, 1981, San Francisco.

59. *Oakland Tribune*, July 20, 1922

60. Ibid., July 20, 1922; July 31, 1922.

Chapter Eighteen

1. *Bridal Call*, August 1922.

2. Raymond L. Cox, "Aimee Semple McPherson," (Unpublished manuscript, International Church of the Foursquare Gospel Archives, Los Angeles), 383.

3. Donald E. Miller, *Reinventing American Protestantism, Christianity in the New Millennium* (Berkeley: University of California Press, 1997), 11.

4. Ibid.

5. Ibid., 13

6. Jules-Bois, "The New Religions of America," *The Forum*, March 1927, 421.

7. John Henry Newman, *An Essay on the Development of Christian Doctrine*, 9th ed. (London: Longman, Green and Company, 1894), 382.

8. *Bridal Call*, April 1927.

9. "Angelus Temple Business Meeting Notes," June 25, 1943, 15.

10. Letter to E.N. Bell, chairman of the Assemblies of God, August 21, 1922, author's collection.

11. Aimee Semple McPherson, letter to E.N. Bell, January 5, 1922, author's collection.

12. E.N. Bell, letter to Aimee Semple McPherson, February 2, 1922, author's collection.

13. Ibid.

14. *Los Angeles Times*, October 2, 1926.

15. Aimee Semple McPherson, Letter to E.N. Bell, March 28, 1922, author's possession.

16. Phone conversation with the Reverend Wayne Warner, Archivist, The Assemblies of God Archives, Springfield, Missouri, August 10, 1983.

17. Ibid.

18. *Foursquare Favorites* (Los Angeles: Echo Park Evangelistic Association, 1927), 1.

19. J.E. Worsfold, *A History of the Charismatic Movements in New Zealand* (Julian Literature Tract, 1974), 136.

20. Ibid., 136-137.

21. McPherson, *This Is That*, 2nd ed., 480-481.

22. Ibid., 481.

23. Ibid.

24. Ibid., 485.

25. Roberta Star Salter, interview, November 4, 1978, New York City.

26. *Los Angeles Times*, March 23, 1924.

27. Laurance L. Hill, *La Reina, Los Angeles in Three Centuries* (Los Angeles: Security Trust and Savings Bank, 1929), 160.

28. Ibid., 161-164; 170-171.

29. Douglas Flamming, *Bound For Freedom: Black Los Angeles in Jim Crow America* (Berkeley: University of California Press, 2005), 197.

30. Carey McWilliams, *The Education of Carey McWilliams* (New York: Simon and Schuster, 1978), 39, 41, 52.

31. Ibid., 45.

32. Interview 29, January 7, 1982, Los Angeles.

33. *Los Angeles Times*, September 27, 1922.

34. Ibid.

35. Ibid.

36. Ibid.

37. *Los Angeles Times*, September 19, 1925.

38. *Los Angeles Times*, June 14, 1924.

39. Northwest University, Undergraduate Programs Religion and Philosophy. http://www.northwestu.edu/programs/majors/philosophy.php.

40. Ibid.

41. Edmund J. Rybarczyk, "American Pentecostalim: Challenges and Temptations," in Eric Patterson and Edmund Rybarczyk, eds., *The Future of Pentecostalism in the United States* (Lanham: Lexington Books, 2007), 7. Most likely major Pentecostal universities will follow their predessor's well worn path away from denominational influence. For further reading see James Tunstead Burtchaell, *The Dying of the Light, The Disengagement of Colleges and Universities From Their Christian Churches* (Grand Rapids: Eerdmans, 1998); George M. Marsden, *The Soul of the American University* (New York: Oxford University Press, 1994); Douglas Sloan, *Faith and Knowledge: Mainline Protestantism and American Higher Education* (Louisville: Westmin-

ister John Knox, 1994).

42. *Bridal Call*, November 1922, 1.

43. Ibid.

44. *Bridal Call*, April 1923, 5.

45. *Bridal Call*, January 1923, 9.

46. George W. Haskell, *The Southern California of Congregationalism* (San Bernardino: published by the author, no date), 11.

47. Interview 21, January 1, 1982, Tustin, California.

48. Ibid.

49. Interview 23, October 10, 1981, Hemet, California.

50. *Bridal Call*, January 1923.

51. *Bridal Call*, June 1923.

52. Ibid.

53. *Bridal Call*, January 1923.

53. Edward Campbell, "Aimee at Work Saving Souls," *Haldeman-Julius Monthly*, February 1926, 15-16.

54. Ibid.

55. *Bridal Call*, January 1923.

56. Ibid., 14-15.

57. Harry Carr, *Los Angeles, City of Dreams* (New York: Grosset & Dunlap, 1935), 336.

58. Tom Sitton and William Deverell, eds., *Metropolis in the Making: Los Angeles in the 1920s* (Berkeley: University of California Press, 2001), 1.

59. Frank Fenton, *A Place In the Sun* (New York: Random House, 1942), 62.

60. Ibid., 65.

61. Ibid., 68, 80.

62. *Bridal Call*, March 1923.

63. John Fante, *Ask the Dust* (Santa Barbara: Black Sparrow Press, 1980).

64. Interview 30, November 4, 1978, New York.

65. *Los Angeles Times*, January 14, 1923.

66. *Los Angeles Record*, January 2, 1923.

67. Warren I. Susman, *Culture as History: The Transformation of American Society in the Twentieth Century* (New York: Pantheon Books, 1984), 277.

68. *Southern Churchman*, December 8, 1923, and December 15, 1923.

69. Ibid.

70. Ibid.

71. Ibid.

72. Ibid.

73. Ibid., December 15, 1923.

74. Ibid.

75. Ibid., October 10, 1923.

76. Ibid., December 15, 1923.

77. Ibid.

78. Ibid.

79. Ibid.

80. Ibid.

81. Ibid.

82. Sidney Correll, letter to author, May 1, 1981.

83. Carey McWilliams, *Southern California Country* (New York: Duell, Sloan & Pearce, 1946), 262.

84. Interview 14, July 17, 1981, Los Angeles.

85. *Los Angeles Times*, Septembr 18, 1926.

86. L. W. Munhall, "A Tribute to Angelus Temple and Aimee Semple McPherson," October 12, 1924, 5.

87. Aimee Semple McPherson, "Class Notes on Homiletics" (Los Angeles: LIFE Bible College, no date.)

88. *Bridal Call*, April 1923.

89. Ibid, 14.

90. D. Michael Quinn, "Religion in the America West," in *Under An Open Sky: Rethinking America's Western Past,* ed. William Cronan et al. (New York: W.W. Norton, 1992), 164.

91. *Los Angeles Times*, September 19, 1925.

92. Quinn, "Religion in the American West," 165.

93. Marcus Bach, *Report to Protestants: A Personal Investigation of the Weakness, Need, Vision And Great Potential of Protestants Today* (Indianapolis: Bobbs-Merrill, 1948), 156.

94. George Burlingame, "How Religious is the City of Los Angeles?" *Los Angeles Times*, August 28, 1927.

95. Ibid.

96. Ibid.

97. Ibid.

98. Ibid.

99. Clinton Pedro interview, October 15, 2006, Sacaton, Arizona.

100. Ibid.

101. Ibid.

102. Ibid.

103. Ibid.

104. Ibid.

105. Jules Tygiel, "Introduction," in *Metropolis in the Making, Los Angeles in the 1920s*, ed. Tom Sitton and William Deverell (Berkeley: University of California Press, 2002), 2.

106. Roberta Star Semple Salter interview, November 4, 1978, New York City.

107. Ibid.

108. *Bridal Call*, April 1923.

109. Interview 26, October 25, 1981, Palo Alto, California.

110. Carey McWilliams, "Aimee Semple McPherson: 'Sunlight in My Soul,'" in *The Aspirin Age, 1919-1941*, ed. Isabel Leighton (New York: Simon and Shuster, 1949), 59.

111. LIFE Bible College Brochure, April 1980.

112. *Bridal Call,* February 1923 and March 1923.

113. Aimee Semple McPherson, "Practical Christianity," sermon, International Church of the Foursquare Gospel Archives, Los Angeles.

114. Ibid.

115. *Bridal Call,* December 1923.

116. Ibid., 28.

117. Helen Bridges, interview, September 18, 1981.

118. Margaret Romer, "The Story of Los Angeles," *Journal of the West* 3, no. 2 (April, 1964): 209.

119. Ibid.

120. McPherson, "Practical Christianity."

121. Katherine G. Aiken, "Sister Aimee Semple McPherson and the Interwar West, *1920-1940*," in *Western Lives: A Biographical History of the American West,* ed. Richard W. Etulain(Albuquerque: University of New Mexico Press, 2004), 313.

122. Stephen Mark Halpern, *Looking Back: Modern America In Historical Perspective* (Chicago: Rand, McNally, 1975), 37.

123. Ibid., 38.

124. Ibid., 272-273.

125. *Bridal Call,* August 1923.

126. *Bridal Call,* October 1923.

127. Jim Hilliker, "History of KFSG, Pioneer L.A. Christian Station Stops Broadcasting After 79 Years." http://members.aol.com/jeff560/kfsg.html.

128. Ibid.

129. Ibid.

130. *Southern Churchman,* December 15, 1923.

131. *Bridal Call,* April 1924.

132. Ibid.

133. Ibid.

134. Ibid..

135. Roberta Star Salter, interview, November 4, 1978, New York City.

136 Herbert Hoover, *The Memoirs of Herbert Hoover: The Cabinent and the Presidency, 1920-1933* (New York: MacMillian, 1952), 142-143.

137. F. Scott Fitzgerald, *The Great Gatsby* (New York: Charles Scribners Sons, 1925), 8.

138. Mark Goodman, "The Radio Act of 1927 as a Product of Progressivism." http://www.scripps.ohiou.edu/mediahistory/mhmjour2-2.htm.

139. Ibid.

140. *Bridal Call,* January 1924.

141. *Pentecostal Evangel,* January 5, 1924.

Chapter Nineteen

1. A.O. Latham, *History of the McKendree Methodist Episcopal Church of Washington,*

D.C., 1845-1935 (1935), 97.

2. Ibid., 98.

3. Ibid.

4. Ibid., 99.

5. Ibid., 100.

6. Ibid.

7. Ibid., 101, 104.

8. Ibid., 106.

9. Ibid., 107.

10. Ibid.

11, Ibid., 108.

12. Ibid., 110-111.

13. Martin E. Marty, *Modern American Religion, Volume 2: The Noise of Conflict, 1919-1941* (Chicago: University of Chicago Press, 1986), 193.

14. Latham, "McKendree Methodist," 119.

15. Ibid.

16. Ibid., 120.

17. Ibid., 120-121.

18. Ibid., 123.

19. Glenn Gohr, "The Ministry of Ben Mahan: A Man of Prayer and Conviction," *Assemblies of God Heritage*, 14, no. 4 (Winter 1994-95): 7.

20. Ibid., 34.

21. Ibid.

22. Ibid.

23. Ibid.

24. Ferenc Morton Szasz, *The Divided Mind of Protestant America, 1880-1930* (Birmingham: University of Alabama Press, 1982), 137.

25. William K. Selden, *Princeton Theological Seminary: A Narrative History, 1812-1992* (Princeton: Princeton University Press, 1992), 95.

26. Szasz, *Divided Mind*, 101.

27. Gary B. McGee, "The Pentecostal Movement and Assemblies of God Theology," *Assemblies of God Heritage*, 14, no. 1 (Spring 1994): 24.

28. Judith Weisenfeld, "On Jordan's Stormy Banks, Margins, Center, and Bridges in African American Religious History" in *New Directions in American Religious History*, ed. Harry S. Stout and D.G. Hart (New York: Oxford University Press, 1997), 433.

29. Roger Finke and Rodney Stark, *The Churching of America, 1776-2005, Winners and Losers in Our Religious Economy* (New Brunswick, N.J.: Rutgers University Press, 2005), 206.

Cullen Murphy, "Protestantism and the Evangelicals," *Wilson Quarterly*, 5, no. 4 (Autumn 1981): 108.

31. Ibid., 106.

32. David R. Swartz, "Left Behind: The Evangelical Left and the Limits of Evangelical Politics, 1965-1988" (PhD. diss., University of Notre Dame, 2008).

33. Szasz, *The Divided Mind*, 137.

34. Ibid., 138.

35. Sydney E. Ahlstrom, *A Religious History of the American People* (New Haven: Yale University Press, 1977), 899.

36. Richard Wightman Fox, "The Culture of Liberal Protestant Progressivism, 1875-1925," *Journal of Interdisciplinary History* 23:3 (Winter 1993), 640.

37. Catherine L. Albanese, *America Religions and Religion* (Belmont, California: Wadsworth Publishing Company, 1981), 6-7.

38. Ibid., 6.

39. Ibid., 6-7.

Chapter Twenty

1. Louis Adamic, "Aimee McPherson's Great Faith Factory," in E. Haldeman-Julius, *The Truth About Aimee Semple McPherson*, Big Blue Book Numer B-28 (Girard, Kansas: Haldeman-Julius Company, no date), 9.

2. Interview 26, January 25, 1981, Palo Alto, California.

3. *Los Angeles Times*, May 6, 1936.

4. *Harvard Divinity School Bulletin*, October-November 1979, 15.

5. Ibid.

6. Interview 5, January 28, 1981, Santa Ana, California.

7. Harry Carr, "The Lancer," *Los Angeles Times*, May 21, 1926.

8. *Bridal Call*, September 1924.

9. George Sullivan, *Unknown God* (Los Angeles: published by the author, 1928), 166.

10. Ibid., 167

11. Carey McWilliams, "Aimee Semple McPherson: 'Sunlight in My Soul,'" in *The Aspirin Age, 1919-1941*, ed. Isabel Leighton (New York: Simon and Schuster, 1949), 59.

12. Interview 26, January 25, 1981, Palo Alto, California.

13. Aimee Semple McPherson, "What's the Matter With the Churches? The Preacher, The Pew, The Seminary, The Old-Time Religion" (Los Angeles, Echo Park Evangelistic Association, 1928), 30.

14. Harry Ebeling, "Aimee S. McPherson: Evangelist of the City," *Western Speech* 21:3, (Summer 1957), 153.

15. Ibid., 156.

16. Ibid., 157.

17. Ibid., 156.

18. Ibid.

19. Interview 2l, January 16, 1982, Tustin, California.

19. George Burlingame, "How Religious is the City of Los Angeles?" *Los Angeles Times*, August 28, 1927.

21. Ibid.

22. D. Michael Quinn, "Religion in the American West," *Under An Open Sky:*

Rethinking America's Western Past, ed. William Cronon, et al. (New York: W.W. Norton, 1992), 158.

23. Carl Douglas Wells, *The Changing City Church*, (Los Angeles: University of Southern California Press, 1934), 12.

24. Ibid., 8.

25. Gerald T. Sheppard, Letter to the author, March 30, 1978.

26. McWilliams, "Aimee Semple McPherson," 59-60.

27. Charles Reynolds Brown, *My Own Yesterdays* (New York: Century Company, 1931), 310-311.

28. Eldon Ernst, "The Emergence of California in American Religious Historiography," *Religion and American Culture*, 28: 1 (Winter, 2001), 41.

29. Ibid., 26.

30. Marcus Bach, *Report to Protestants: A Personal Investigation of the Weakness, Need, Visiion and Great Potential of Protestants Today* (Indianapolis: Bobbs-Merrill, 1948), 155.

31. Terry Lindvall, *Sanctuary Cinema: Origins of the Christian Film Industry* (New York: New York University Press, 2007), 14.

32. Ibid., 14.

33. Ibid., 204

34. Harvey G. Cox, "Why Christianity Must Be Secularized," *The Great Ideas Today* (Encyclopedia Britannica, 1967), 19.

35. Aimee Semple McPhersonm "Practical Christianity," sermon (Los Angeles, n.d.).

36. *Bridal Call*, May 1923.

37. Aimee Semple McPherson, "Class Notes on Homelitics," October 4, 1938, LIFE Bible College, Los Angeles.

38. Richard T. Antoun, *Understanding Fundamentalism: Understanting Christian, Islamic, and Jewish Movements*, 2nd edition (Lanham, Md.: Rowman & Littlefield: 2008), 118.

39. Walter J. Hollenweger, "The Black Roots of Pentecostalism," in *Pentecostals After a Century*, ed. Allan V. Anderson and Walter J. Hollenweger (Sheffield: Sheffield Academic Press, 1999), 35.

40. John A. MacKay, *Ecumenics: The Science of the Church Universal* (Englewood Cliffs, N.J.: Prentice-Hall, 1964), 198.

41. *Bridal Call*, January 1925.

42. Ibid.

43. *Los Angeles Times*, April 1, 1923.

44. Nils Bloch-Hoell, *The Pentecostal Movement: Its Origin, Development, and Distinctive Character* (Oslo: Universitetsforlaget, 1964), 58.

45. *Angelus Temple Directory*, International Church of the Foursquare Gospel Archives, Los Angeles, 31.

46. Ibid.

47. *Angelus Temple Pictorial Review*, International Church of the Foursquare Gospel Archives, Los Angeles.

48. *Bridal Call*, December 1924.

49. Tennessee Williams, *Tennessee Williams Memoirs* (Garden City, N.Y. : Doubleday, 1975), 183.

50. Raymond L. Cox, "Guilty Until Proven Innocent," unpublished manuscript, International Church of the Foursquare Gospel Archives, Los Angeles, 16.

51. *Bridal Call*, December 1924.

52. *Bridal Call*, January 1925.

53. Ibid.

54. *Los Angeles Magazine*, December 1977.

55. *Time Magazine*, February 8, 1932.

56. *Los Angeles Magazine*, December 1977.

57. George W. Haskell, *The Southern California of Congregationalism* (San Bernardino: published by the author, no date), 7.

58. *Time Magazine*, February 8, 1932.

59. *The Los Angeles Record*, January 4, 1923.

60. R.P. (Bob) Shuler, *McPhersonism, A Study of Healing Cults and Modern Day Tongues Movements*, 2nd ed. (Los Angeles: J.R. Spencer, 62. Ibid., 67-68.

63. Ibid., 69 70.

64. Mark Sumner Still, "'Fighting Bob' Shuler, Fundamentalist and Reformer" (Ph.D. diss., Claremont Graduate School, 1988,) 213.

65. W.H. Dixon, et. Al. vs. Aimee Semple McPherson, et.al. Superior Court, County of Orange, State of California, October 16, 1925.

66. Still, "Fighting Bob," 213.

67. Interview 26.

68. Aimee Semple McPherson, "Teaching Message, Songs of Solomon l:1-3," sermon, August 26, 1925, Angelus Temple, Los Angeles.

69. *Bridal Call*, December 1925.

70. H.L. Mencken, "Two Enterprising Ladies," *American Mercury*, 13, no. 49 (January 1928), 507.

71. *Los Angeles Times*, January 12, 1926.

72. Larry K. Eskridge, "Only Believe: Paul Rader and the Chicago Gospel Tabernacle, 1922-1933" (MA thesis, University of Maryland, 1985), 37.

73. Ibid., 86.

74. Wheaton College, Billy Graham Center, *Jazz Age Evangelism,* "Interview with Virginia Latham," http://www.wheaton.edu/bgc/archives/exhibits/cgt/rader04xtra14.html

75. Eskridge, "Only Believe, " 37.

76. Ibid., 115.

77. Ibid.

78. Ibid., 69.

79. Ibid., 68

80. Ibid., 81.

81. Ibid.

82. Ibid., 84.

83. *Bridal Call*, March 1926.

84. *Bridal Call*, June 1926.

85. "Aimee Semple McPherson Memorial Bulletin," Angelus Temple, Los Angeles, May 23, 1926.

86. *Bridal Call*, July 1926.

87. Still, "Fighting Bob," 24.

88. *Bridal Call*, July 1926.

89. *Los Angeles Examiner*, May 19, 1926.

90. Raymond L. Cox, "Guilty Until Proved Innocent," unpublished manuscript,
International Church of the Foursquare Archives, Los Angeles.

91. Ibid.

92. *Los Angeles Examiner*, May 19, 1926.

93. Cox, "Guillty," 19.

94. Ibid., 20.

95. *Los Angeles Examiner*, May 19, 1926.

96. Benjamin C. Bradley, *Conversations With Kennedy* (New York: W.W. Norton 1975), 163.

97. Jennie Van Allen, "Her Greatest Miracle," *Los Angles Times*, June 16, 1926.

98. *Pentecostal Evangel*, June 5, 1926.

99. *Latter Rain Evangel*, June 1926.

100. Cox, "Guilty," 22.

101. Ibid.

102. Carr, "Lancer," *Los Angeles Times*, May 21, 1926.

103. Cox, "Guilty," 22-23.

Chapter Twenty-One

1. Lately Thomas, *The Vanishing Evangelist: The Aimee Semple McPherson Kidnapping Affair* (New York: Viking, 1959), 50.

2. Gordon Hall, *The Sawdust Trail; The Story of American Evangelism* (Philadelphia: Macrae Smith, 1964), 188.

3. Raymond L. Cox, "Guilty Until Proved Innocent," unpublished manuscript, 46-47, author's possession.

4. Hall, *The Sawdust Trail*, 188.

5. Ibid.

6. Ibid., 189.

7. *Douglas Daily Dispatch*, June 24, 1926.

8. Ibid.

9. *Arizona Daily Star*, June 24, 1926.

10. *Arizona Daily Star*, June 25, 1926.

11. Carey McWilliams, "Aimee Semple McPherson: Sunlight in My Soul" in *The Aspirin Age, 1919-1941,* ed., Isabel Leighton (New York: Simon and Schuster, 1949), 67.

12. *Bisbee Daily Review*, September 15, 1926.

13. *Arizona Daily Star*, July 12, 1926.

14. *Arizona Daily Star*, June 25, 1926.

15. Larry D. Christiansen, "Henceforth and Forever Aimee and Douglas," *Cochise Quarterly*, 8-9, no. 3-4, (1977, 1978), 7.

16. Ibid., 10-11.

17. *Douglas Daily Dispatch*, June 26, 1926.

18. Ervin Bond, *Percy Bowden: Born To Be A Frontier Lawman* (Douglas, Ariz.: Ervin Bond, 1976), 48, 49, 51, 53, 57.

19. Larry D. Christiansen, "Henceforth and Forever," 13.

20. Rachel H. Stephens, Oral History Interview, 13 May 1971, AV0206 (Tucson: Arizona Historical Society).

21. Robert S. Jeffrey, "The History of Douglas, Arizona" (MA thesis, University of Arizona, 1951), 104.

22. Burke Johnson, "The Reappearance of Aimee Semple McPherson: How It Was, From the People Who Were There," *Arizona,* June 22, 1969, 10 11.

23. *Arizona Daily Star*, June 26, 1926.

24. *Douglas Daily Dispatch*, June 26, 1926.

25. Ibid.

26. Ibid.

27. Ibid.

28. Ibid.

29. PS.107:4-7. (New Revised Standard Version).

30. *Bisbee Daily Review*, June 26, 1926.

31. Ibid.

32. Christiansen, "Henceforth and Forever," 36.

33. Jean Lusk, interview, October 28, 2004, Douglas, Arizona.

34. *Douglas Daily Dispatch*, July 1, 1926.

35. Christiansen, "Henceforth and Forever," 60.

36. Ibid.

37. *Arizona Daily Star*, June 24, 1926.

38. *Arizona Daily Star*, June 29, 1926.

39. *Douglas Daily Dispatch*, July 3, 1926.

40. Christiansen, "Henceforth and Forever," 46.

41. Ibid., 47.

42. *Arizona Daily Star*, June 29, 1926.

43. Thomas, *The Vanishing Evangelist*, 225.

44. Ferenc Morton Szasz, *Religion in the Modern American West* (Tucson: University of Arizona Press, 2000), 114.

45. Thomas, *The Vanishing Evangelist*, 320.

46. "Mrs. McPherson Is A Type," editorial, *Christian Century*, 43, no. 32 (1926): 1004.

47. McWilliams, "Aimee Semple McPherson," 72-73.

48. Roy E. Bell, "Life Bible College Notes," Vol. 4, *Homiletics*, Los Angeles.

Epilogue

1. "Forum: American Religion and Class with contributions by David G. Hackett, Laurie F. Maffly-Kipp, R. Laurence Moore, Leslie Woodcock Tentler," *Religion and American Culture* 15, no. 1 (Winter 2005): 22.

2. Ibid.

3. See especially R. Laurence Moore, *Religious Outsiders and the Making of Americans* (New York: Oxford University Press, 1986). Moore follows the well-worn (and worn-out) path of the Deprivation model in his treatment of Pentecostals. Pentecostalism is presented in its stereotypical fashion.

4. Karen Armstrong, "Is Immortality Important?" *Harvard Divinity Bulletin* 34, no. 1 (Winter 2006): 22.

5. Sandra Scofield, *Occasions of Sin* (New York: W.W. Norton , 2004), 19-20.

6. A.A. Allen with Walter Wagner, *Born to Lose, Bound to Win* (Garden City, N.Y.:Doubleday, 1970), 133.

7. Betty Baxter, *The Betty Baxter Story* (Tulsa: Rev. Don Heidt, Publisher, 1951), 1-2.

8. Woody Guthrie, "This Morning I Am Born Again" (New York: Woody Guthrie Publications, Inc., 2001).

9. For this under-reported behavior in the church see: G. Lloyd Rediger, *Clergy Killers* (Louisville, Kentucky: Westminister John Knox Press, 1997) and Kenneth C. Haugk, *Antagonists in the Church* (Minneapolis, Minnesota: Augsburg Fortress Publishers, 1988).

10. Robert Fletcher and Cole Porter, "Don't Fence Me In," *Adios, Argentina*, 20th Century Fox, 1934.

11. Carol Davies, "Goin' To Church, A Story of Religious Consciousness" *The Nature of Religious Experience*, Spring 1978, 2.

12. "Forum: American Religion and Class," 23.

13. Chad Bonham, "Oral Roberts Praises ORU Leaders*,"* *Charisma*, April 2009, 23.

14. William Hedgepeth, "Brother A.A. Allen on the Gospel Trail: He Feels, He Heals & He Turns You on With God" *Look*, October 7, 1969, 24-25.

15. Ibid., 28.

16. Ibid.

17. "Faith Healers, Getting Back Double From God" *Time*, March 7, 1969.

18. Donald W. Dayton, ed., *Witness to Pentecost: The Life of Frank Bartleman* (New York: Garland, 1985), 54.

19. Hedgepeth, "Brother A.A. Allen," 28.

20. Robert Frost, "The Road Not Taken" *Mountain Interval* (New York: Henry Holt, 1916), 9.

21. *Miracle Magazine* (June 1958), 13.

22. Ibid.

23. Lewis Wilson, "An Early Pioneer in Pentecostal Education," *Vanguard Magazine*, Winter 2006, 23.

24. Hebrews 11:24-26.

25. William J. Gaither, "He Touched Me," 1963.

26. James H. Cone, *God of The Oppressed* (New York: The Seabury Press, 1975), vi.

27. William J. Weston, "Princeton and Union: The Dialogue of Pluralism," *Union Seminary Quarterly Review* 45 (1991): 161, 169.

28. Ibid., 161.

29. Ibid., 162.

30. Ibid., 170.

31. Walter J. Hollenweger, "An Introduction to Pentecostalisms," *Journal of Beliefs and Values* 25, no. 2 (August 2004): 126.

32. John Dillenberger, *From Fallow Fields to Hallowed Halls: A Theologian's Journey* (Santa Rosa, Calif.: Polebridge Press, 2004), 86.

33. Rick Bragg, *All Over But The Shoutin'* (New York: Vintage, 1997), xiii.

34. Delmore Schwartz, *Selected Poems of Delmore Schwartz: Summer Knowledge* (New York: New Directions, 1967), 9.

35. Ronald L. Grimes, *Marrying & Burying, Rites of Passage in a Man's Life* (Boulder: Westview Press, 1995), 63.

36. C.S. Lewis, *The Allegory of Love* (New York: Oxford University Press, 1936), 1.

37. R.R. Marett, *The Threshold of Religion* (London: Methuen, 1914), xxxi.

38. Richard Crouter, editor, *Schleiermacher on Religion, Speeches to its Cultured Despisers* (Cambridge: Cambridge University Press, 2003), 22.

39. William James, *The Varieties of Religious Experience* (New York: Touchstone, 2004 [1902]), 319.

40. Ibid., 372.

41. Gerald T. Sheppard, "Word and Spirit: Scripture in the Pentecostal Tradition, Part 2," *Agora* 2, no. 1: 14-15.

42. "It's Real, It's Real."

43. Alan Jackson, Kane Kieran, "Ill Go On Loving You," *High Mileage*, Arista, 1998.

44. Alan Jackson, "Precious Memories, *Arista*, 2006.

45. Cone, *God of the Opressed*, 111.

46. Anita Maria Leopold and Jeppe Sinding Jensen, (eds) *Syncretism in Religion: A Reader* (London: Equinox, 2004), x.

47. Ernest Sutherland Bates, *American Faith, Its Religious, Political, and Economic Foundations* (New York: W.W. Norton & Company, Inc., 1940), 34.

48. Ibid., 43-44.

49. Roland H. Bainton, "The Left Wing of the Reformation," *The Journal of Religion* 21, no .2 (April 1941): 126.

50. Ibid., 129.

51. Ibid.

52. Bates, *American Faith,* 55-56.

53. Bainton, "The Left Wing," 129-130.

54. Ibid., 131.

55. Ibid., 132.

56. Ibid., 134.

57. Bill J. Leonard "Contemporary Spirituality in Historical Perspective," *Review & Expositor* 76:2 (Spring 1979), 248.

58. F. Ernest Stoeffler, *The Rise of Evangelical Pietism* (Leiden: E.J. Brill, 1965), 23.

59. Harvey G. Cox, Jr., "Some Personal Reflections on Pentecostalism" *Pneuma: The Journal of the Society for Pentecostal Studies* 15, no. 1 (Spring 1993),: 30.

60. Ibid.

61. Sydney E. Ahlstrom, *A Religious History of the American People* (New Haven: Yale University Press, 1973), 236.

62. Stoeffler, *Rise of Evangelical Pietism*, 16.

63. Ibid., 19.

64. Ibid., 21.

65. Ibid., 22.

66. David Martin, *On Secularization: Towards A Revised General Theory* (Aldershot: Ashgate Publishing, 2005), 144.

67. Theodore M. Steeman, "Church, Sect, Mysticism, Denomination: Periodological Aspects of Troeltsch's Types*," Sociological Analysis* 36, no. 3 (1975): 199-200.

68. Charles H. Barfoot and Gerald T. Sheppard, "Prophetic vs. Priestly Religion: The Changing role of Women Clergy in Classical Pentecostal Churches, " *Review of Religious Research* 22, no. 1 (September 1980): 10.

69. Ibid., 11.

70. Ibid., 14.

71. Wendy S. McDowell, "Past, Present, & Future Tense.*" Harvard Divinity School, News and Events.* http:hds.harvard.edu/news/article_archive_archive/cox_hollywood.html.

72. Ernst Troeltsch, *The Social Teachings of the Christian Churches*, vol. l, trans. Olive Wyon, (New York: MacMillian, 1949), 381.

73. George O. Carney, "Country Music and the Radio: A Historical Geographic Assessment," *Rocky Mountain Social Science Journal* 2 (April 1974): 19. See also Larry Eskridge, "Slain By The Music," *Christian Century,* March 7, 2006, 18-20.

74. Ellis Nassour, "Hag's Song Reflect Life," *Music City News* 13 (August 1975): 8.

75. Charles F. Gritzner, "Country Music: A Reflection of Popular Culture" *Journal of Popular Culture* 11, no. 4 (Spring 1978): 857.

76. Ibid., 860-861.

77. Miriam Longino, "Hearing Ourselves in Country Music," *American Visions,* 13, no. 3 (June/July 1998): 24.

78. Keith Whitley, "Hard Livin'," *LA to Miami,* RCA, 1986; Alan Jackson, "Monday Morning Church," *What I Do*, Arista, 2004.

79. Willie Nelson, "Hands on the Wheel," *Red-Headed Stranger*, Sony, 1975.

80. Harvey G. Cox, Jr., *The Seduction of the Spirit, The Use and Misuse of People's Religion* (New York: Simon and Schuster, 1973), 144.

81. James, *Varieties*, 3.

82. Catherine L. Albanese, editor, *American Spiritualities, A Reader* (Bloomington: Indiana University Press, 2001), 179.

83. John E. Minor, "The Mantle of Elijah: Nineteenth-century Pentecostalism and Twentieth-century Pentecostalism," *Proceedings of the Wesley Historical Society* 43 (1982): 141-49.

84. Nathan O. Hatch, "The Puzzle of American Methodism," *Church History* 63, no. 2 (1994): 189.

85. David Martin, *Pentecostalism: The World Their Parish* (Malden, Massa.: Blackwell, 2002), 8-9.

86. Ibid., 167.

87. Roger Finke and Rodney Stark, *The Churching of America 1776-2005, Winners and Losers in Our Religious Economy* (New Brunswick, N.J.: Rutgers University Press, 2005), 113.

88. Gilbert T. Rowe, *The Meaning of Methodism* (Nashville: Cokesbury Press, 1926).

89. David Hempton, *Methodism: Empire of the Spirit* (New Haven: Yale University Press, 2005), 9.

90. Conrad Cherry, *Hurrying Toward Zion, Universities, Divinity Schools, and American Protestantism* (Bloomington: Indiana University Press, 1995), 19.

91. Ibid., 20.

92. Cushing Strout, *The New Hevens and New Earth: Political Religion in America.* (New York: Harper and Row, 1974), 106.

93. Cherry, *Zion,* 20.

94. Ibid.

95. Ibid.

96. Ibid., 1.

97. *Word and Work,* August 10, 1918.

98. *TBridal Call,* February 1921.

99. Aimee Semple McPherson, "Methodism and Pentecost," *Pentecostal Evangel,* January 8, 1921.

100. Ibid.

101. Ibid.

102. Hempton, *Methodism,* 191.

103. Ibid., 208-209.

104. W. J. Hollenweger, "Theology of the New World, The Religion of the Poor is not a Poor Religion," *Expository Times* 97, no. 8 (May 1976): 228.

105. Ibid.

106. Walter J. Hollenweger, *The Pentecostals* (Peabody, Mass.: Hendrickson, 1988), 270.

107. Hempton, *Methodism,* 56.

108. Morton Kelsey, *Myth, History and Faith* (New York: Paulist Press, 1974),

112.

109. H. Richard Niebuhr, *The Social Sources of Denominationalism* (New York: Meridian Books, 1970), 32.

110. Ibid., 32-33.

111. Ibid., 33.

112. Hollenweger, "Theology of the New World," 231.

113. Richard A. Baer, Jr., "Quaker Silence, Catholic Liturgy and Pentecostal Glossolalia—Some Functional Similarities," in *Perspectives on the New Pentecostalism*, ed. Russell P. Spittler (Grand Rapids: Baker Books, 1976), 163.

114. Hollenweger, "Theology of the New World," 231.

115. Hollenweger, "Pentecostalisms," 131.

116. Walter J. Hollenweger, "My Pilgrimage in Mission." www.hollenwegercenter.net/.

117. Nils Bloch-Hoell, *The Pentecostal Movement: Its Origin, Development, and Distinctive Character* (Oslo: Universitetsforlaget, 1964), 13.

118. Ibid., 13.

119. Robert Baird, *Religion in America* (New York: Harper and Brothers, 1844), 213.

120. Ibid., 135.

121. Ibid., 321.

122. *Apostolic Faith*, November, 1906.

123. Ibid..

124. Ibid.

125. Jonathan R. Baer, "Perfectly Empowered Bodies: Divine Healing in Modernizing America" (PhD. diss., Yale University, 2002), 16.

126. Ibid., 34.

127. Edwin S. Gaustad and Leigh E. Schmidt, *The Religious History of America*, Revised Edition (San Francisco: HarperSanFrancisco, 2002), 282.

128. Ibid.

129. Baer, ""Perfectly Empowered Bodies," Abstract.

130. Russell P. Spittler, "Are Pentecostals and Charismatics Fundamentalists?" in *Charismatic Christianity as a Global Culture*, ed. Karla Poewe(Columbia, S.C.: University of South Carolina Press, 1994), 110.

131. Baer, "Perfectly Empowered Bodies," 303.

132. Spittler, "Pentecostal and Charismatics," 109.

133. Charles Reynolds Brown, *Faith and Health* (New York: Thomas Y. Crowell, 1910), 148, 24.

134. Ibid., 56-58.

135. Ibid., 63.

136. Ibid., 34-35.

137. Charles Reynolds Brown, *Being Made Over* (New York: Harper & Brothers, 1939), 1-2.

138. Sandra Tamar Frankiel, *California's Spiritual Frontiers, Religious Alternatives in Anglo-Protestantism, 1859-1910* (Berkeley: University of California Press, 1988), 83,

85.

139. R. Andrew Chestnut, *Born Again In Brazil: The Pentecostal Boom and the Pathogens of Poverty* (New Brunswick, New Jersey: Rutgers University Press, 1997), 3.

140. Ibid.

141. Ibid., 5, 167.

142. Ibid., 5-6.

143. Harvey G. Cox, Jr., *Fire From Heaven, The Rise of Pentecostal Spirituality and the Reshaping of Religion in the Twenty-first Century* (Reading, Mass.: Addison-Wesley, 1995), 101-102.

144. Karla Poewe, ed., *Charismatic Christianity as a Global Culture* (Columbia, S.C.: University of South Carolina Press, 1994), 13.

145. Ibid., 1.

146. "Pentecostalism's Global Language: An Inteview with Walter J. Hollenweger," *Christian History Magazine* 17, no. 2 (Spring 1998): 42.

147. See Harvey G. Cox, Jr., *The Seduction of the Spirit* (New York: Simon and Schuster, 1973), 190.

148. Martin, *Pentecostalism*, 176.

149. Roger E. Olson, "Pentecostalism's Dark Side," *The Christian Century*, March 7, 2006, 27-30.

150. I Corinthians 1: 26-29.

151. Lap Yan Kung, "Outpouring of the Spirit" A Reflection on Pentecostals' Identity," *Asian Journal of Pentecostal Studies* 4, no. 1 (2001): 3-4.

152. "Charismatic Movement," *Encyclopedia of Religion and Society,* ed. William H. Swatos, Jr., Hartford Institute for Religion Research, http://hirr.hartsem.edu/ency/cmovement.

153. Niebuhr, *Social Sources*, 6.

154. "Pentecostalism's Global Language," Hollenweger, 42.

155. Robert T. Handy, "American Religious History: Some Bibliographical Trends," *Union Seminary Quarterly Review* 34, no. 4 (Summer 1979): 250.

156. Tomoko Masuzawa, *In Search of Dreamtime: The Quest for the Origin of Religion* (Chicago: University of Chicago Press, 1993), 71-72.

157. Crouter, *Schleiermacher*, 50.

158. Ibid., 58.

159. James, *Varieties*, 363.

160. Ibid., 141.

161. Ibid., 372.

162. Ibid., 23.

163. Ibid., 24.

164. Ibid., 7.

165. Ibid., 249, 251.

166. Max Weber, *The Sociology of Religion*, trans. Ephraim Fischoff (Boston: Beacon Press, 1964), 104.

167. Ibid.

168. James, *Varieties*, 7.

169. Silvia Anne Sheafer, *Aimee Semple McPherson* (Philadelphia: Chelsea House, 2004), viii.

170. *Blind Gary Davis, Harlem Street Singer*, Prestige/Bluesville, 1993.

BIBLIOGRAPHY

Abernathy, Bob and William Bole. *The Life of Meaning: Reflections on Faith, Doubt, and Repairing the World.* New York: Seven Stories Press, 2007.

Adamic, Louis. "Aimee McPherson's Great Faith Factory." *The Truth About Aimee Semple McPherson:* Girard, Kansas: Haldeman-Julius Company, no date.

Aikman, David. *Jesus in Beijing: How Chrisianity is Transforming China and Changing the Global Balance of Power.* Washington, D.C.: Regnery Pub., 2003.

Albanese, Catherine L. *America Religions, and Religion.* Belmont: California, Wadsworth Pub., 1999.

———. editor. *American Spiritualities: A Reader.* Bloomington: Indiana University Press, 2001.

Alexander, Estrelda Y. *Limited Liberty, The Legacy of Four Pentecostal Women Pioneers.* Cleveland: Pilgrim Press, 2008.

Allen, A.A. *Born to Lose, Bound to Win: An Autobiography.* New York:Doubleday, 1970.

Allen, Lexie. *God's Man of Faith and Power: The Life Story of A.A. Allen.* Hereford, Arizona: A.A. Allen Publications, 1954.

Alstrom, Sidney E. *A Religious History of the America*s. New Haven: Yale University Press, 1972.

Anderson, Allan H. and Walter J. Hollenweger. *Pentecostals After a Century: Global Perspectives on a Movement in Transition.* Sheffield: Sheffield Academic Press, 1999.

Anderson, Robert Mapes. *Vision of the Disinherited, the Making of American Pentecostalism.* New York: Oxford University Press, 1979.

Angelus Temple Pictorial Review. Los Angeles: International Church of Foursquare Gospel, c. 1931.

Antoun, Richard T. *Understanding Fundamentalism,* 2nd ed. Lanham, Maryland: Rowman & Littlefield, 2008.

Assemblies of God Northern California and Nevada District Council, Inc. *Chronicle of the Past Fifty Years.* San Jose: Pruntree Graphics, 1971.

Atlas, James. *Delmore Schwartz: The Life of an American Poet*. New York: Farrar, Straus and Giroux, 1977.

Austin, Alvyn. *Aimee Semple McPherson*. Dan Mills, Ontario: Fitzhenry & Whiteside, 1980.

Babbie, Earl R. *Science and Morality in Medicine: A Survey of Medical Educators*. Berkeley: University of California Press, 1970.

Bach, Marcus. *Report to Protestants: A Personal Investigation of the Weakness, Need, Vision and Great Potential of Protestants Today*. Indianapolis: Bobbs-Merrill, 1948.

———. *Strange Sects and Curious Cults*. New York: Dodd, Mead, 1961.

———. *They Have Found A Faith*. Indianapolis: Bobbs-Merrill, 1946.

Bainton, Roland Herbert. *The Age of the Reformation*. Malabar, Fla: R.E. Krieger, 1985.

Baird, Robert. *Religión in America*. New York: Harper & Brothers, 1844.

Baranczak, Stanislaw, and Clare Cavanaugh, eds. *Polish Poetry of the Last Two Decades of Communist Rule*. Evanston, Illinois: Northwestern University Press, 1992.

Baritz, Loren. *The Culture of the Twenties*. Indianapolis: Bobbs-Merrill, 1970.

Bartleman, Frank. *Another Wave Rolls In* (formerly *What Really Happened at Azusa Street*), edited by John Walker and John G. Myers. Monroeville, Pa.: Whitaker Books, 1980.

———. *Witness to Pentecost: The Life of Frank Bartleman*. New York: Garland, 1985.

Bastide, Roger. *Social Origins of Religion*. Minneapolis: University of Minnesota Press, 2003.

Bates, Ernest Sutherland. *American Faith: Its Religious, Political, and Economic Foundations*. New York: W.W. Norton, 1940.

Baur, John E. *The Health Seekers of Southern California, 1870-1900*. San Marino, California: Huntington Library, 1959.

Baxter, Betty. *The Betty Baxter Story*. Tulsa: Reverend Don Heidt, publisher, 1951.

Bell, Roy E. *LIFE Bible College Notes*. Volume 4, Homiletics, Los Angeles: n.d.

Bellah, Robert N., Richard Madsen, William Sullivan, Ann Swidler, and Stephen

M. Tipton. *Habits of the Heart : Individualism and Commitment in American Life.* Berkeley: University of California Press, 1985.

Benton, F. Weber. *Semitropic California, The Garden of the World.* Los Angeles: Benton & Company, 1914.

Berger, Peter L. *The Sacred Canopy: Elements of a Sociological Theory of Religion.* New York: Anchor Books, 1990.

Bloch-Hoell, Nils. *The Pentecostal Movement: Its Origin, Development, and Distinctive Character.* London: Allen & Unwin, 1964.

Blumhofer, Edith L. *Pentecost in My Soul, Explorations in the Meaning of Pentecostal Experience in the Early Assemblies of God.* Springfield, Missouri: Gospel Publishing House, 1989.

—————. *The Assemblies of God, A Popular History.* Springfield, Missouri: Radiant Books, 1985.

Bond, Ervin. *Percy Bowden: Born to be a Frontier Lawman.* Douglas, Arizona: 1976.

Bradbury, Malcolm, and David Palmer, eds. *The American Novel and the Nineteen Twenties.* London: Edward Arnold, 1971.

Bradley, Benjamin C. *Conversations with Kennedy.* New York: W.W. Norton, 1975.

Bragg, Rick. *The Prince of Frogtown.* New York: Knopf, 2008.

—————. *Being Made Over.* New York: Harper, 1939.

—————. *Faith and Health.* New York: Thomas Y. Crowell, 1910.

Brown, Charles Reynolds. *My Own Yesterdays.* New York: Century Co., 1931.

Bruccoli, Matthew J. *Some Sort of Epic Grandeur: The Life of F. Scott Fitzgerald.* New York: Harcourt Brace Jovanovich, 1981.

Bunyan, John. *The Pilgrim's Progress from This World to That Which is to Come.* London: J. Mawman, 1816.

Burkett, Randall K. *Garveyism as a Religious Movement: The Institutionalization of a Black Civil Religion.* Metuchen, N.J.: Scarecrow Press, 1978.

Burnett, Gene M. *Florida's Past: People and Events that Shaped the State.* Englewood, Florida: Pineapple Press, 1986.

Burtchaell, James Tunstead. *The Dying of the Light: The Disengagement of Colleges and Universities From Their Christian Churches*. Grand Rapids: Eerdmans 1998.

Butler, Jonathan M. *Softly and Tenderly Jesus is Calling: Heaven and Hell in American Revivalism, 1870-1920*. Brooklyn: Carlson Pub., 1991.

Capote, Truman. *In Cold Blood: A True Account of a Multiple Murder and its Consequences*. New York: Random House, 1965.

Carr, Harry. *Los Angeles: City of Dreams*. New York: D. Appleton-Century, 1935.

Caughey, John and Laree Caughey. *Los Angeles: Biography of a City*. Berkeley: University of California Press, 1976.

Cherry, Conrad. *Hurrying Toward Zion: Universities, Divinity Schools, and American Protestantism*. Bloomington: Indiana University Press, 1995.

Chesnut, R. Andrew. *Born Again in Brazil: The Pentecostal Boom and the Pathogens of Poverty*. New Brunswick, N.J.: Rutgers University Press, 1997.

Church of England. *Liberal Evangelicalism An Interpretation*. London: Hodder & Stoughton, 1923.

Clemmons, Ithiel C. *Bishop C.H. Mason and the Roots of the Church of God in Christ*. Bakersfield: Pneuma Life Publishing, 1996.

Cone, James H. *God of the Oppressed*. New York: Seabury Press, 1975.

———. *My Soul Looks Back*. Maryknoll, New York: Orbis Books, 1986.

Connelley, William E. *History of Kansas State and People*. Chicago: The American Historical Society, Inc., 1928.

Connor, Linda H., and Geoffrey Samule, eds. *Healing Powers and Modernity*. Westport, Conn.: Bergin & Garvey, 2000.

Conway, Daniel W. and K.E.Gover. *Soren Kierkegaard: Critical Assessments of Leading Philosophers*. London: Taylor & Francis, 2002.

Cook, Glen A. *The Azusa Street Meeting, Some High Lights of this Outpouring*. Los Angeles: published by the author, no date.

Corrigan, John and Winthrop S Hudson. *Religion in America*, 7ᵗʰ edition. Upper Saddle River, N.J.: Prentice-Hall, 2004.

Costigan, Edward P. *Papers of Edward P. Costigan Relating to the Progressive Movement in Colorado, 1902-1917*. Boulder, University of Colorado Press, 1941.

Cowles, Edward S., M.D. *Religion and Medicine in the Church*. New York: Macmillan, 1925.

Cox, Harvey Gallagher. *Fire From Heaven: The Rise of Pentecostal Spirituality and the Reshaping of Religion in the Twenty-First Century*. Reading, Mass.: Addison-Wesley Pub., 1995.

―――. *The Seduction of the Spirit: The Use and Misuse of People's Religion*. New York: Simon and Schuster, 1973.

Cox, Raymond L. "Aimee Semple McPherson." Unpublished manuscript, International Church of the Foursquare Gospel Archives, Los Angeles.

―――. "Guilty Until Proven Innocent." Unpublished manuscript, International Church of the Foursquare Gospel Archives, Los Angeles.

Cronin, William, George A. Miles, and Jay Gitlin, eds. *Under an Open Sky: Rethinking America's Western Past*. New York: W.W. Norton, 1992.

Cross, Whitney R. *The Burned-Over District: The Social and Intellectual History of Enthusiastic Religion in Western New York: 1800-1850*. New York, Harper & Row, 1965.

Crouter, Richard, ed. *Schleiermacher on Religion: Speeches to Its Cultured Despisers*. Cambridge: Cambridge University Press, 2003.

Dayton, Donald W. *Discovering an Evangelical Heritage*. New York: Harper & Row, 1976.

―――, ed. *Witness to Pentecost: The Life of Frank Bartleman*. New York: Garland Publishing, Inc., 1985.

De Caro, Louis. *Our Heritage: The Christian Church of North America*. Sharon, Pa: Christian Church, 1977.

Dempster, Murray. *The Globalization of Pentecostalism: A Religion Made To Travel*. Irvine, Calif.: Regnum, 1999.

Deverell, William Francis. *Whitewashed Adobe: The Rise of Los Angeles and The Remaking of its Mexican Past*. Berkeley: University of California Press, 2004.

Dillenberger, John. *From Fallowed Fields to Hallowed Halls: A Theologian's Journey*. Santa Rosa, Calif.: Polebridge Press, 2004.

Dorchester, Daniel. *Christianity in the United States from the First Settlement Down to the Present Time*. New York: Phillips & Hunt, 1888.

Dorsett, Lyle W. *The Queen City, A History of Denver*. Boulder: Pruett, 1977.

Dunlap, Carol. *California People*. Salt Lake City: Gibbs M. Smith, 1982.

Dwyer, Walter W. *The Churches' Handbook for Spiritual Healing*. New York: Ascension Press, 1965.

Eliot, T.S. *Four Quartets*. New York: Harcourt, Brace, 1943.

Engh, Michael E. *Frontier Faiths: Church, Temple and Synagogue in Los Angeles, 1846-1888*. Albuquerque: University of New Mexico Press, 1992.

Etulain, Richard W., ed. *The American Literary West*. Manhattan, Kan., Sunflower University Press, 1980.

————, ed. *Western Lives: A Biographical History of The American West*. Albuquerque, University of New Mexico Press, 2004.

Jerry Falwell, ed., *The Fundamentalist Phenomenon: The Resurgence of Conservative Christianity*. Garden City: Doubleday, 1981.

Fante, John. *Ask the Dust*. Santa Barbara: Black Sparrow Press, 1980.

Federal Council of the Churches of Christ in America. *Annual Report, 1918*. New York: Missionary Education Movement of the United States and Canada, 1918.

Federal Writers' Project of the Works Progress Administration for the State of California. *A Guide to the Golden State*. New York: Hastings House, 1939.

Fenton, Frank. *A Place In the Sun*. New York: Random House, 1942.

Ferguson, Charles W. *The Confusion of Tongues: A Review of Modern Isms*. New York: Doubleday, 1928.

Finke, Roger and Rodney Stark. *The Churching of America, 1776-2005: Winners and Losers in our Religious Economy.* New Brunswick, N.J.: Rutgers University Press, 2005.

First Baptist Church, San Jose, California. *Diamond Jubilee History.* San Jose: First Baptist Church, 1925.

First Congregational Church of Lodi, California. *Seventy-Five Years in Lodi: A History of the First Congregational Church of Lodi, California, 1872-1947.* Lodi: First Congregational Church, 1947.

First Congregational Church of Oakland, California. *"Charles R. Brown, Remembered."* Oakland: First Congregational Church, no date.

First Congregational Church, San Francisco. *Reverend James Logan Gordon: An Appraisal and Appreciation.* San Francisco: First Congregational Church: 1930.

First Congregational Church of Santa Rosa, California. *Annals of 1915.* Santa Rosa: First Congregational Church, 1915.

Fitzgerald, F. Scott. *Scott Fitzgerald: Letters to His Daughter.* New York: Scribner's, 1965.

———. *The Great Gatsby.* New York: Scribner's, 1953.

———. *The Last Tycoon.* New York: Scribner's, 1941.

Flamming, Douglas. *Bound for Freedom: Black Los Angeles in Jim Crow America.* Berkeley: University of California Press, 2005.

Foursquare Favorites. Los Angeles: Echo Park Evangelistic Association, 1927.

Fox, Richard Wightman. *Trials of Intimacy: Love and Loss in the Beecher-Tilton Scandal.* Chicago: University of Chicago Press, 1999.

Fradkin, Philip L. *The Great Earthquake and Firestorms of 1906: How San Francisco Nearly Destroyed Itself.* Berkeley: University of California Press, 2005.

Frankiel, Tamar. *California's Spiritual Frontiers: Religious Alternatives to Anglo-Protestantism, 1850-1910.* Berkeley: University of California Press,1988.

Frost, Robert. *Mountain Interval.* New York: H.Holt, 1921.

Fuller, Daniel P. *Give the Winds a Mighty Voice: The Story of Charles E. Fuller.* Waco, Texas: Word Books, 1972.

Fulop, Timothy Earl, and Albert J. Raboteau, eds. *African-American Religion: Interpretive Essays in History and Culture.* New York: Routledge,1997.

Gaustad, Edwin S., and Leigh F. Schmidt. *The Religious History of America, Revised Edition.* San Francisco: Harper, San Francisco: 2002.

Gifford, Sanford. *The Emmanuel Movement: (Boston, 1904-1929): The Origins of Group Treatment and the Assault on Lay Psychotherapy.* Cambridge, Mass.: Harvard University Press, 1998.

Goben, John. *Aimee, The Gospel Gold Digger.* Los Angeles: John Goben, 1932.

Goff, James R. Fields. *White Unto Harvest: Charles F. Parham and the Missionary Origins of Pentecostalism.* Fayetteville: University of Arkansas Press, 1988.

Goss, Ethel. *The Winds of God.* New York: Comet Books, 1958.

Gray, James Henry. *The Roar of the Twenties.* Toronto: Macmillan, 1975.

Grimes, Ronald L. *Marrying and Burying: Rites of Passage in a Man's Life.* Boulder: Westview Press, 1995.

Guedalla, Philip. *Conquistador: American Fantasia.* New York: Harper & Brothers, 1928.

Hackett, David G. *Religion and American Culture: A Reader.* New York: Routledge, 1995.

Haldeman-Julius, E. *The Truth About Aimee Semple McPherson.* Girard, Kan.: Haldeman-Julius, no date.

Hall, Gordon Langley. *The Sawdust Trail: The Story of American Evangelism.* Philadelphia: Macrae Smith Co., 1964.

Halpern, Stephen Mark. *Looking Back: Modern America In Historical Perspective.* Chicago: Rand, McNally, 1975.

Hammond, George P., "The Search for the Fabulous in the Settlement of the Southwest." In *New Spain's Far Northern Frontier: Essays on Spain in the American West, 1540-1821* edited by David J. Weber, 17-33. Albuquerque: University of New Mexico, 1979.

Haskell, George W. *The Southern California of Congregationalism*. San Bernardino, published by the author, no date.

Haugk, Kenneth C. *Antagonists in the Church*. Minneapolis: Augsburg Fortress, 1988.

Heilbrun, Carolyn G. *Writing a Woman's Life*. New York: Norton, 1988.

Hempton, David. *Methodism: Empire of the Spirit*. New Haven: Yale University Press, 2005.

Henn, Richard. *The History of Asbury First United Methodist Church*, 5th Edition. Rochester: Asbury First United Methodist Church, 2001.

Hepp, John Henry, IV. *The Middle-Class City: Transforming Space and Time in Philadelphia, 1876-1926*. Philadelphia: University of Pennsylvania Press, 2003.

Hickson, James Moore. *Heal the Sick*. New York. Dutton, 1929.

Hill, Laurance L. *La Reina, Los Angeles in Three Centuries*. Los Angeles: Security Trust and Savings Bank, 1929.

Hoch-Smith, Judith, and Anita Spring, eds. *Women in Ritual and Symbolic Roles*. New York: Plenum Press, 1978.

Hollenweger, Walter J. *Pentecostalism: Origins and Developments Worldwide*. Peabody, Mass.: Hendrickson, 1997.

———. *The Pentecostals*. London: SCM, 1972.

Hoover, Herbert. *The Memoirs of Herbert Hoover: The Cabinet and the Presidency, 1920-1933*. New York: MacMillian,1952.

Howard Presbyterian Church, San Francisco: California. "Session Minutes, April 26, 1922." San Francisco Theological Seminary Archives.

Howard Presbyterian Church, San Francisco: California. "Session Minutes, December 13, 1922. San Francisco Theological Seminary Archives.

Hudson, Winthrop S. *Religion in America: An Historical Account of the Development of American Religious Life*, 2nd ed. New York: Scribner's, 1973.

Irwin, Will. *The City That Was*. New York: B.W. Huebsch, 1906.

James, William. *The Varieties of Religious Experience*. New York: Touchstone, 2004 [1902].

John-Steiner, Vera. *Notebooks of the Mind: Explorations of Thinking*. Albuquerque: University of New Mexico Press, 1985.

Keen, Sam. *To A Dancing God*. New York: Harper & Row, 1970.

Kelsey, Morton T. *Myth, History, and Faith: The Remythologizing of Christianity*. New York: Paulist Press, 1974.

Kohlenberger, John R. *All About Bibles*. New York: Oxford University Press, 1985.

Larsen, Charles. *The Good Fight: The Life and Times of Ben B. Lindsey*. Chicago, Quadrangle Books, 1972.

Latham, A.O. *History of the McKendree Methodist Episcopal Church of Washington, D.C., 1845-1935*. Washington, D.C.: McKendree Methodist Episcopal Church, 1935.

Leckie, Robert. *The Wars of America*. New York: Harper & Row, 1981.

Leighton, Isabel, ed. *The Aspirin Age, 1919-1941*. New York: Simon and Schuster, 1949.

Leopold, Anita Maria and Jeppe Sinding Jensen, eds. *Syncretism in Religion: A Reader*. London: Equinox, 2004.

Lewis, C.S. *The Allegory of Love: A Study in Medieval Tradition*. Oxford: Oxford University Press, 1959.

Lindvall, Terry. *Sanctuary Cinema: Origins of the Christian Film Industry*. New York: New York University Press, 2007.

Lippy, Charles H., ed. *Twentieth-Century Shapers of American Popular Religion*. New York: Greenwood Press, 1989.

Los Angeles City Directories, 1924, 1925, 1927-42.
Los Angeles County Book of Records, Book 51.

Mackay, John A. *Ecumenics: The Science of The Church Universal*. Englewood Cliffs, N.J.: Prentice Hall, 1964.

MacKenzie, Kenneth. *Our Physical Heritage in Christ*. New York: Fleming H. Revell, 1923.

MacRobert, Iain. *The Black Roots and White Racism of Early Pentecostalism In the USA*. Houndmills, Hampshire: Macmillan Press, 1988.

Magee, Charles H. *Antics of Aimee: The Poetical Tale of a Kidnapped Female*. Los Angeles: published by the author, 1927.

Marett, R.R. *The Threshold of Religion*. London: Methuen, 1914.

Marsden, George M. *The Soul of the American University: From Protestant Establishment to Established Nonbelief*. New York: Oxford University Press, 1994.

Martin, David. *On Secularization: Towards a Revised General Theory*. Aldershot: Ashgate, 2005

————. *Pentecostalism: The World Their Parish*. Oxford. Blackwell, 2002.

Martin, Larry E. *The Life and Ministry of William J. Seymour: And a History of the Azusa Street Revival*. Joplin, Mo.: Christian Life Books, 1999.

Martin, Robert Francis. *Hero of the Heartland: Billy Sunday and the Transformation of American Society, 1862-1935*. Bloomington: Indiana University Press, 2002.

Marty, Martin E. *Modern American Religion, Volume 1: The Irony of it All, 1893-1919*. Chicago, University of Chicago Press, 1986.

————. *Modern American Religion, Volume 2: The Noise of Conflict, 1919-1941*. Chicago, University of Chicago Press, 1997.

Masuzawa, Tomoko. *In Search of Dreamtime: The Quest for the Origin of Religion*. Chicago, University of Chicago Press, 1993.

Mathews, Hubert C. *Hubert: Here, There, and Yonder*. Springfield, Mo: published by the author, 1976.

Mavity, Nancy Barr. *Sister Aimee*. Garden City: Doubleday, 1931.

May, Henry Farnham. *Ideas, Faiths, and Feelings: Essays on American Intellectual and Religious History*. New York: Oxford University Press, 1983.

McCawley, William. *The First Angelinos: The Gabrielino Indians of Los Angeles*. Banning, Calif.: Malki Museum Press, 1996.

McGerr, Michael E. *A Fierce Discontent: The Rise and Fall of the Progressive Movement in America, 1870-1920*. New York: Free Press, 2003.

McLoughlin, William Gerald. *Billy Sunday Was His Real Name*. Chicago: University of Chicago Press, 1955.

McPherson, Aimee Semple. "A Short Autobiography." Unpublishd manuscript. Los Angeles: International Church of Foursquare Gospel Archives, no date.

———. "Class Notes on Book of Acts." Los Angeles: LIFE Bible College, no date.

———. "Class Notes on Homiletics." Los Angeles: LIFE Bible College, no date.

———. *Give Me My Own God*. New York: H.C. Kinsey, 1936.

———. *In the Service of the King*. New York: Boni and Liveright, 1927.

———. "Life Story." Unpublished manuscript. Los Angeles: International Church of Foursquare Gospel Archives, no date.

———. "Practical Christianity." Sermon, Los Angeles: International Church Foursquare Gospel Archives, no date.

———. "Rebekah at the Well," Sermon. Los Angeles: Foursquare Gospel Publications, no date.

———. *The Narrow Line or Is Mrs. McPherson Pentecostal?* Los Angeles: Foursquare Gospel Publications, no date.

———. *The Personal Testimony of Aimee Semple McPherson*. Los Angeles: Foursquare Publications, Inc., 1928.

———. *This Is That*. Los Angeles: Bridal Call Publishing House, 1919.

———. *This Is That*. Los Angeles: Echo Park Evangelistic Association, Inc., 1923.

———. *What's the Matter With the Churches, The Preacher, The Pew, The Seminary, The Old-Time Religion?* Los Angeles: Echo Park Evangelistic Association, 1928.

McWilliams, Carey. *Southern California Country*. New York: Duell, Sloan & Pearce, 1946.

———. "Sunlight In My Soul," In *The Aspirin Age 1919-1941*, edited by Isabel Leighton, 50–80. New York: Simon & Schuster, 1949.

———. *The Education of Carey McWilliams*. New York: Simon and Schuster, 1978.

Mead, Sidney Earl. *The Nation With the Soul of a Church*. New York: Harper & Row, 1975.

Melcon, Alice Kesone. *California in Fiction*. Berkeley: California Library Association, 1961.

Mencken, H.L. *A Mencken Chrestomathy*. New York: Knopf, 1949.

———. H.L. *Mencken on Religion*. Amherst, N.Y.: Prometheus Books, 2002.

Messenger, Troy. *Holy Leisure: Recreation and Religion in God's Square Mile*. Minneapolis: University of Minnesota Press, 1999.

Miller, Donald E. *Global Pentecostalism: The New Face of Christian Social Engagement*. Berkeley: University of California Press, 2007.

———. *Reinventing American Protestantism: Christianity in The New Millennium*. Berkeley: University of California Press, 1997.

Moore, R. Laurence. *Religious Outsiders and the Making of Americans*. New York: Oxford University Press, 1986.

Newman, John Henry. *An Essay on the Development of Christian Doctrine*. Westminister, Md.: Christian Classics, 1968.

Niebuhr, H. Richard. *The Social Sources of Denominationalism*. New York: Meridian Books, 1960.
Noll, Mark A. *The Old Religion in a New World: The History of North American Christianity*. Grand Rapids: Eerdmans, 2002.

O'Neill, Michael. *Poems of W.B. Yeats: A Sourcebook*. New York: Routledge, 2004.

O'Neill, William L., ed. *Echoes of Revolt: The Masses, 1911-1917*. Chicago: Quadrangle Books, 1966.

Orlando, Guido. "Trouble Shooter in Paradise." Unpublished manuscript, author's possession.

Overacker, Ingrid. *The African American Church Community in Rochester, New York: 1900-1940*. Rochester: University of Rochester Press, 1998.

Parham, Charles F. *The Sermons of Charles F. Parham*. New York: Garland, 1985.

Parsons, Edward Lambe. *A Quarter Century, 1915-1940, Diocese of California*. Austin, Texas: Episcopal Church Historical Society, 1958.

Patterson, Eric, and Edmund Rybarczyk. *The Future of Pentecostalism in the United States*. Lanham, Md.: Lexington Books, 2007.

Perkins, Jonathan Ellsworth. *Pentecostalism on the Washboard*. Fort Worth: published by the author, 1939.

Peters, James E. *Prevailing Westerlies (The Pentecostal Heritage of Maine): The Story of How the Pentecostal Fire Spread From Topeka, Kansas, to Houston to Los Angeles to Bangor*. Shippensburg, Pa.: Destiny Image, 1988.

Piepkorn, Arthur Carl. *Profiles in Belief, The Religious Bodies of the United States and Canada, Vol. 3, Holiness and Pentecostal*. San Francisco: Harper & Row, 1979.

Pitt, Leonard. *The Decline of the Californios: A Social History of the Spanish-Speaking Californians, 1846-1890*. Berkeley: University of California Press,1966.

Poewe, Karla, Editor. *Charismatic Christianity As a Global Culture*. Columbia: University of South Carolina Press, 1994.

Porterfield, Amanda. *Healing in the History of Christianity*. New York: Oxford University Press, 2005.

Price, Charles S. *...And Signs Followed: Life Story of Charles S. Price*. Plainfield, N.Y.: Logos International, 1972.

———. *The Great Physician*. Oakland: DeMontport Press, 1924.

Price, Lynne. *Theology Out of Place: A Theological Biography of Walter J. Hollenweger*. London: Sheffield Academic Press, 2003.

Publicity Department, Equitable Branch, Security Trust & Savings Bank. *El Pueblo: Los Angeles Before the Railroads*. Los Angeles: Equitable Branch of the Security Trust and Savings Bank, 1928.

Pullman, Steven. *Foul Demons, Come Out! The Rhetoric of Twentieth-Century American Faith Healing*. Westport, Conn.: Praeger, 1999.

Raboteau, Albert J. *A Fire in the Bones: Reflections on African-American Religious History.* Boston: Beacon Press, 1995.

———. *Slave Religion: The "Invisible Institution" in the Antebellum South.* New York: Oxford University Press, 1978.

Rarsson, Flora. *My Best Men Are Women.* London: Hodder and Stoughton, 1974.

Rawlyk, George A. and Mark A. Noll, eds. *Amazing Grace: Evangelicalism in Australia, Britain, Canada, and the United States.* Montreal: McGill-Queens University Press, 1994.

Rediger, G. Lloyd. *Clergy Killers.* Louisville, Ky.: Westminister John Knox Press, 1997.

Richardson, Peter. *American Prophet: The Life and Work of Carey McWilliams.* Ann Arbor: University of Michigan Press, 2005.

Robeck, Cecil M., Jr. *The Azusa Street Mission and Revival.* Nashville: Thomas Nelson, Inc., 2006.

Roberts, Oral. *The Fourth Man.* Garden City, N.Y.: Country Life Press, 1951.

Robins, R.G., and A.J. Tomlinson: *Plainfolk Modernist.* New York: Oxford University Press, 2004.

Robinson, Judith. *Working Miracles: The Drama and Passion of Aimee Semple McPherson.* Canmore, Alberta: Altitude Publishing, 2006.

Rodeheaver, Homer A. *Twenty Years With Billy Sunday.* Nashville: Cokesbury, 1936.

Rogers, Darrin J. *Northern Harvest: Pentecostalism in North Dakota.* Bismark: North Dakota District Council, 2003.

Rowe, Gilbert T. *The Meaning of Methodism.* Nashville: Cokesbury Press, 1926.

Ruether, Rosemary, and Eleanor McLaughlin. *Women of Spirit: Female Leadership in the Jewish and Christian Traditions.* New York: Simon and Schuster, 1979.

Salter, Roberta Star Semple. "Harold Stewart McPherson." Unpublished manuscript, 1979.

———. "James Kennedy, Father of Aimee Semple McPherson." Unpublished manuscript, no date.

————. "The Story of My Mother's Life." Illustrated sermon, August 7, 1932. Los Angelese: International Church of Foursquare Gospel Archives.

Schwartz, Delmore. *Selected Poems of Delmore Schwartz: Summer Knowledge*. New York: New Directions, 1967.

Scofield, Sandra. *Occasions of Sin: A Memoir*. New York: W.W. Norton, 2004.

Selden, Willian K. *Princeton Theological Seminary: A Narrative History*. Princeton: Princeton University Press, 1992.

Sernett, Milton C. *African America Religious History: A Documentary Witness*. Durham: Duke University Press, 1999.

Sheafer, Silvia Anne. *Aimee Semple McPherson*. Philadelphia, Chelsea House, 2004.

Shuler, Robert Pierce . *McPhersonism: A Study of Healing Cults and Modern Day Tongues Movements*, 2nd ed. Los Angeles: J.R. Spencer, 1924.

————. *Miss X*. Los Angeles: published by the author, no date.

————. *What New Doctrine Is This?* Nashville: Abington, 1946.

Shuster, Robert, ed. *The Papers of William and Helen Sunday, 1882-1974*. Wheaton College, The Billy Graham Center, Section l, Scrapbooks, reel 25.

Singleton, Gregory H. *Religion in the City of Angeles: American Protestant Culture and Urbanization, Los Angeles: 1850-1930*. Ann Arbor: U.M.I. Research Press, 1979.

Sitton, Tom, and William Francis Deverell, eds. *Metropolis in the Making: Los Angeles in the 1920s*. Berkeley: University of California Press, 2001.

Sloan, Douglas. *Faith and Knowledge: Mainline Protestantism and American Higher Education*. Louisville, Ky.: Westminister John Knox Press, 1994.

Smith, Timothy Lawrence. *Called Unto Holiness: The Story of the Nazarenes*. Kansas City: Nazarene Publishing House, 1962.

————. *Revivalism and Social Reform in Mid-Nineteenth-Century America*. New York: Abingdon Press, 1957.

Soper, Brittany. *The Gillette Family*. Rochester, N.Y: Speaking Stones, 2006.

Spittler, Russell Paul, ed. *Perspectives on the New Pentecostalism*. Grand Rapids: Baker Book House, 1976.

Stanley, Susie Cunningham. *Feminist Pillar of Fire: The Life of Alma White*. Cleveland: Pilgrim Press, 1993.

Stoeffler, F. Ernest. *Continental Pietism and Early American Christianity*. Grand Rapids: Eerdmans, 1976.

———. *German Pietism During the Eighteenth Century*. Lieden: E.J. Brill, 1973.

———. *The Rise of Evangelical Pietism*. Leiden: E.J. Brill, 1965.

Stout, Harry S. *The Divine Dramatist: George Whitefield and the Rise of Modern Evangelism*. Grand Rapids: Eerdmans, 1991.

Stout, Harry S., and D.G. Hart, eds. *New Directions in American Religious History*. New York: Oxford University Press, 1997.

Strout, Cushing. *The New Heavens and New Earth: Political Religion in America*. New York: Harper and Row, 1974.

Sullivan, George. *Unknown God*. Los Angeles: published by the author, 1928.

Susman, Warren. *Culture as History: The Transformation of American Society in the Twentieth Century*. New York: Pantheon Books, 1984.

Sutton, Matthew Avery. *Aimee Semple McPherson and the Resurrection of Christian America*. Cambridge, Mass.: Harvard University Press, 2007.

Swatos, William H., Jr., ed. "Charismatic Movement," In *Encyclopedia of Religion and Society*. Hartford Institute for Religion Research, Hartford Seminary. hirr. hartsem.edu/ency/cmovement 3/21/2007.

Sweet, William Warren. *Methodism in American History*. New York: Methodist Book Concern, 1933.

Swigart, William R. *Biography of Spring Street in Los Angeles*. Los Angeles: published by the author, 1945.

Szasz, Ferenc Morton. *Religion in the Modern American West*. Tucson: University of Arizona Press, 2000.

————. *The Divided Mind of Protestant America, 1880-1930*. Birmingham: University of Alabama Press, 1982.

Thomas, James E. *A Look at Los Angeles in the 20ᵗʰ Century*. Sacramento: Johnson Publishing Company, 1963.

Thomas, Lately. *The Vanishing Evangelist: The Aimee Semple McPherson Kidnaping Affair*. New York: Viking Press, 1959.

Thompson, James J., Jr. *Tried as by Fire: Southern Baptists and the Religious Controverises of the 1920s*. Macon, Ga.: Mercer University Press, 1982.

Towner, W.K. *Church Notes, 1921*. Los Angeles: International Church of the Four-square Archives.

Troeltsch, Ernst. *The Social Teachings of the Christian Churches, Vol. 1*. Translated by Olive Wyon. New York: MacMillian, 1949.

Tweed, Thomas A., ed. *Retelling U.S. Religious History*. Berkeley: University of California Press, 1997.

Unification Theological Seminary. *Toward Our Third Century*. Barrytown, N.Y: Unification Theological Seminary, 1976.

Valdez, A.C., Sr., and James F. Scheer., *Fire on Azusa Street: An Eyewitness Account*. Costa Mesa: Gist Publications, 1980.

Warner, Wayne E. *Kathryn Kuhlman: The Woman Behind the Miracles*. Ann Arbor:Servant Publishers, 1993.

————. *The Woman Evangelist: The Life and Times of Charismatic Evangelist Maria B. Woodworth-Etter*. Metuchen, N.J.: Scarecrow Press, 1986.

Weaver, John D. *El Pueblo Grande: A Non-Fiction Book About Los Angeles*. Los Angeles: Ward Ritchie Press, 1973.

Weber, David J., ed. *New Spain's Far Northern Frontier, Essays on Spain in the American West, 1540-1821*. Albuquerque, University of New Mexico, 1979.

Weber, Max. *The Sociology of Religion*. Translated by Sphraim Fischoff. Boston: Beacon Press, 1964.

Wells, Carl Douglas. *The Changing City Church*. Los Angeles: University of Southern California Press, 1934.

Wessel, Helen, editor. *The Autobiography of Charles G. Finney.* Minneapolis: Bethany Fellowship, 1977.

West, Cornel, and Eddie S. Glaude. *African American Religious Thought: An Anthology.* Louisville, Ky.: Westminster John Knox Press, 2003.

Wilhoit, Bert H. *Rody: Memories of Homer Rodeheaver.* Greensville, S.C.: Bob Jones University, 2000.

Williams, Tennessee, *Tennessee Williams Memoirs.* Garden City, N.J.: Doubleday, 1975.

Wolfe, Thomas. *Look Homeward Angel: A Story of the Buried Life.* New York: Modern Library, 1929.

Worcester, Elwood. *Life's Adventure, The Story of a Varied Career.* New York: Scribner's, 1932.

Worsfold, J.E. *A History of Charismatic Movements in New Zealand.* Bradford, UK: Julian Literature Trust, 1974

Writers' Program (Calif.) . *Los Angeles: A Guide to the City and Its Environs.* New York: Hastings House, 1941.

Journals

Armstrong, Karen. "Is Immortality Important?" *Harvard Divinity Bulletin*, 34, no. 1 (2006): 20-28.

Austin, Herbert D. "New Light on the Name of California." *The Quarterly Historical Society of Southern California*,12, no. 3 (1923): 29-31.

Bainton, Roland H. "The Left Wing of the Reformation." *Journal of Religion* 21, no. 2 (1941): 124-134.

Barfoot, Charles H., and Gerald T. Sheppard. "Prophetic vs. Priestly Religion: The Changing Role of Women Clergy in Classical Pentecostal Churches." *Review of Religious Research* 22, no. 1 (1980): 2-16.

Barnes, Joseph W. "The City's Golden Age." *Rochester History*, 35, no. 2 (973): 1-24.

Bluemel, C.S. "Faith Healers: With Special Reference to Aimee Semple McPherson." *Colorado Medicine*, July 1921, 143-46.

Blumhofer, Edith. "The Finished Work of Calvary: William H. Durham and a Doctrinal Controversy." *Assemblies of God Heritage* 3, no. 3 (1983): 9-11.

Bois, Jules. "The New Religions of America." *The Forum* 63, no. 2 (1925):145-55.

Bynum, Lindley. "Los Angeles in 1854-5: The Diary of Rev. James Woods." *Quarterly Historical Society of Southern California* 23, no. 2 (1941): 65-86.

Carey, George O. "Country Music and the Radio: A Historical Geographic Assessment." *Rocky Mountain Social Science Journal* 2 (1974): 19.

Christiansen, Larry D. "Henceforth and Forever: Aimee and Douglas." *Cochise Quarterly*, 8-9, no. 3-4 (1977, 1978): 3-62.

Clark, David L. "Miracles for a Dime—from Chautauqua Tent to Radio Station With Sister Aimee." *California History* 47, no. 4 (1978-79): 354-63.

Clayton, Allen L. "Another Side of Oneness Controversy," Letters From Our Readers, *Assemblies of God Heritage* 6, no. 1(1985-1986): 15.

Cochran, Joseph Wilson. "The Church and the Working Man." *Annals of the American Academy of Political and Social Science* 30, no. 3, (1907): 13-27.

Cox, Harvey. "Into the Age of Miracles: Culture, Religion and the Market Revolution." *World Policy Journal* 14, no. 1 (1997): 87-95.

———. "Some Personal Reflections on Pentecostalism." *Pneuma: The Journal of the Society for Pentecostal Studies* 15, no. 1 (1993): 29-34.

Cunningham, Raymond J. "The Emmanuel Movement: A Variety of American Religious Experience." *American Quarterly* 14, no. l, (1961): 499-513.

DeGraaf, Lawrence B. "The City of Black Angels: The Emergence of the Los Angeles Ghetto, 1890-1930." *Pacific Historical Review* 39, no. 3 (1970): 323-52.

Dickin, Janice. " 'Take Up Thy Bed and Walk': Aimee Semple McPherson and Faith Healing." *Canadian Bulletin of Medical History* 17 (2000): 137-53.

Ebeling, Harry. "Aimee S. McPherson: Evangelist of the City." *Western Speech* 21, no. 3 (1957), 153-59.

Enloe, Tim. "Dr. Charles S. Price." *Assemblies of God Heritage*, 2008, 4-13.

Ernst, Elden. "The Emergence of California in American Religious Hisoriography." *Religion and American Culture* 11, no. 1 (2001): 31-52.

Etulain, Richard W. "The American Literary West and Its Interpreters: The Rise of a New Historiography." *Pacific Historical Review* 45, no. 3 (1976): 311-48.

Fox, Richard Wightman. "The Culture of Liberal Protestant Progressivism, 1875-1925." *Journal of Interdisciplinary History* 23, no. 3 (1993): 639-60.

Guthrie, Stewart E. "Review of *Shamanism, The Neural Ecology of Consciousness and Healing* by Michael Winkelman." *Journal of Ritual Studies* 18, no. 1 (2004): 96-118.

Etulain, Richard W. "The American Literary West and Its Interpreters: The Rise of a New Historiography." *Pacific Historical Review* 45, no. 3 (1976): 311-48.

Gohr, Glenn. "The Ministry of Ben Mahan, A Man of Prayer and Conviction." *Assemblies of God Heritage* 14, no 4 (1994 95): 6 9, 34 35.

Gritzner, Charles F. "Country Music: A Reflection of Popular Culture." *Journal of Popular Culture* 11, no 4 (1978): 857-64.

Hackett, David G. "Forum: American Religion and Class with contributions by David G. Hackett, Laurie F. Maffly-Kipp, R. Laurence Moore, and Leslie Woodcock Tentler." *Religion and American Culture* 15, no. 1 (2005): 1-30.

Handy, Robert T. "American Religious History: Some Bibliographical Trends." *Union Seminary Quarterly Review* 34, no. 4 (1979): 249- 51.

Hollenweger, Walter J. "An Introduction to Pentecostalisms." *Journal of Beliefs and Values* 25, no. 2 (2004): 127-37.

———. "Theology of the New World, The Religion of the Poor is not a Poor Religion." *Expository Times* 87, no. 8 (976): 228-32.

Hatch, Nathan O. "The Puzzle of American Methodism." *Church History* 63, no. 2 (1994): 175-89.

Kung, Lap Yan. "Outpouring of the Spirit: A Reflection on Pentecostals' Identity." *Asian Journal of Pentecostal Studies* 4, no. 1 (2001): 3-19.

Lawrence, Margaret Morgan. "Creativity and the Family." *Gender & Psychoanalysis* 4 (1999): 399-412.

609

Leonard, Bill J. "Contemporary Spirituality in Historical Perspective." *Review & Expositor* 76, no. 2 (1979): 241-55.

Longino, Miriam. "Hearing Ourselves in Country Music." *American Visions,* 13, no. 3 (1998): 24.

Mack, Phyllis. "Women as Prophets during the English Civil War." *Feminist Studies,* 8, no. 1 (1982): 19-45.

Martin, David. "Rescripting Spiritual Autobiography." *Exchange* 35, no 1 (2006): 92-101.

McGee, Gary B. "The Pentecostal Movement and Assemblies of God Theology." *Assemblies of God Heritage,* 14, no. 1 (1994): 24-29.

McLoughlin, William G. "Aimee Semple McPherson: 'Your Sister in the King's Glad Service.' " *Journal of Popular Culture* 3 (1967): 213-29.

McKelvey, Blake. "A Panoramic Review of Rochester's History." *Rochester History* 11, no. 12 (1949): 1-24.

———. "A Sesquicentennial Review of Rochester's History." *Rochester History* 24, no. 3 (1962): 1-40.

———. "Civic Medals Awarded Posthumously." *Rochester History* 22, no. 2 (1960): 11-24.

———. "Economic Stages in the Growth of Rochester." *Rochester History* 3, no 4 (1941): 1-24.

———. "Susan B. Anthony." *Rochester History* 7, no. 2 (1945): 1-24.
———. "Rochester in Retrospect and Prospect, *Rochester History* 23, no. 3 (1961): 1-28.

———. "Walter Rauschenbusch's Rochester." *Rochester History* 14, no. 4 (1952): 1-27.

———. "Woman's Rights in Rochester, A Century of Progress." *Rochester History* 10, nos. 2-3 (1948): 1-24.
Minor, John E. "The Mantle of Elihah: Nineteenth-century Pentecostalism and Twentieth century Pentecostalism." *Proceedings of the Wesley Historical Society* 43 (1982): 141-49.

Murphy, Cullen. "Protestantism and the Evengelicals." *The Wilson Quarterly* 5, no.

4(1981): 105-19.

Orsi, Robert A. "Is the Study of Lived Religion Irrelevant to the World We Live In?" *Journal for the Scientific Study of Religion* 42, no. 2 (2003): 169-74.

Parsons, Edward L. "Bishop Parsons Recalls Memories of Dean James Wilmer Gresham." *Pacific Churchman*, May 1951: 2,13.

"Pentecostalism's Global Language: An Interview with Walter J. Hollenweger." *Christian History Magazine* 17, no. 2 (1998): 42

Perkins, Dexter. "Rochester One Hundred Years Ago." *Rochester History* 1, no. 3 (1939): 1-24.

Perry, H. Francis. "The Workingman's Alienation From the Church." *American Journal of Sociology* 4, no. 5 (899): 621-29.

Piper, John F., Jr. "The American Churches in World War I." *Journal of the Academy of Religion* 38, no. 2 (1970): 147-55.

Reinders, Robert C. "Training for a Prophet: The West Coast Missions of John Alexander Dowie, 1888-1890." *Pacific Historian* 30, no. 1 (1986): 3-8.

Rhomberg, Chris. "White Nativism and Urban Politics: The 1920s Ku Klux Klan in Oakland, California." *Journal of American Ethnic History* 17, no. 2 (1998): 39-56.

Robeck, Cecil M., Jr. "The Earliest Pentecostal Mission of Los Angeles."*Assemblies of God Heritage* 3, no. 3 (1983): 3-4, 12.

Romer, Margaret. "The Story of Los Angeles." *Journal of the West* 3, no. 1(1964): 1-39.

Sheppard, Gerald T. "Word and Spirit: Scripture in the Pentecostal Tradition, Part 2." *Agora* 2, no 1: 5-33.

Smith, George G. "Parson's Progress to California." *Quarterly Historical Society of Southern California* 21, no 2-3 (1939): 45-78.

Steeman, Theodore M. "Chruch, Sect, Mysticism, Denomination: Periodological Aspects of Troeltsch's Types," *Sociological Analysis* 36, no. 3 (1975), 181-204.

Thomas, William Miller. "The Canadian Jerusalem, Part 2." *Assemblies of God Heritage*11, no. 4 (1991-92), 22-25.

Tinney, James S. "William J. Seymour: Father of Modern-Day Pentecostalism." *Journal of the Interdenominational Theological Center* 4, no. 1 (1976): 34-44.

Wacker, Grant. "Travail of a Broken Family: Evangelical Responses to Pentecostalism in America, 1906-1916." *Journal of Ecclesiastical History* 47, no. 3 (1996): 505-28.

Warner, Wayne. "The 1913 Worldwide Camp Meeting." *Assemblies of God Heritage* 3, no. 1 (1983): 1, 4-5.

Weston, William J. "Princeton and Union: The Dialogue of Pluralism." *UnionSeminary Quarterly Review* 45 (1991): 155-75.

Wilson, Everett A. "Robert J. Craig's Glad Tidings and the Realization of a Vision for 100,000 Souls." *Assemblies of God Heritage* 8, no. 2 (1988): 9-11, 19.

Wilson, Leslie. "The Rise of the Golden City, Los Angeles in the Twentieth Century." Review Essay, *Journal of Urban History* 30, no. 2 (2004): 275-88.

Articles

Armstrong, Chris. "Embrace Your Innter Pentecostal." *Christianity Today*, September 2006.

Bonham, Chad. "Oral Roberts Praises ORU Leaders." *Charisma*, April, 2009.

Burlingame, George. "How Religious is the City of Los Angeles?" *Los Angeles Times*, August 28, 1927.

Campbell, Edward. "Aimee at Work Saving Souls." *Haldeman-Julius Monthly*, February 1926.

Carr, Harry. "Lancer." *Los Angeles Times*, May 21,1926.

Comstock, Sarah. "Aimee Semple McPherson, Primadona of Revivalism." *Harper's Monthly Magazine*, December, 1927.

Cox, Raymond L. "Revival in Denver." http://www/geocities/ruinum/denver.htm.
———. "The Greatest Nine Days, Revival in Boston." http://www.geocities.com/runim/boston.htm.

Daggett, Mabel Potter. "Are There Modern Miracles?" *The Ladies Home Journal*, June 1923.

Douthat, Ross. "The 100 Most Influential Americans of All Time." *The Atlantic*, December, 2006.

Eskridge, Larry. "Slain By The Music." *Christian Century*, March 7, 2006.

"Faith Healers: Getting Back Double From God." *Time*, March 7, 1969.

Fitzgerald, F. Scott. "Echoes of the Jazz Age." *Scribner's Magazine*, November 1931.

Friedman, Bruce Jay. "One for the Books." Review of Al Silverman, The Time of Their Lives, The Golden Age of Great American Publishers, Their Editors and Authors. *The New York Times*, September 14, 2008.

Goodman, Mark. "The Radio Act of 1927 as a Product of Progressivism." http://www.scripps.ohiou.edu/mediahistory/mhmjour2-Z.htm.

Hedgepeth, William. "Brother A.A. Allen on the Gospel Trail: He Feels, He Heals & He Turns You On With God." *Look,* October 7, 1969.

Hilliker, Jim. "History of KFSG: Pioneer Los Angeles Christian Station Stops Broadcasting after 79 Years." http://members.aol.com/jeff560/kfsg.html.

Hollenweger, Walter J. "My Pilgrimage in Mission." wwhollenwegercenter.net.

Johnson, Burke. "The Reappearance of Aimee Semple McPherson, How It Was, From the People Who Where There." *Arizona*, June 22, 1969.

Lange, Robert E., Andrea Sarzynski, Mark Muro. "Moutain Megas: America's Newest Metropolitan Places and a Federal Partnership to Help Them Prosper." *Brookings Institution*, July 20, 2008. http://www.brookings/edu./reports/2008/0720-mountainmegas-sarzynski.aspx.

Lawrence, B.F. "Apostolic Faith Restored, A History of the Present Latter Rain-Outpouring of the Holy Spirit Known as the Apostolic or Pentecostal Movement." *Weekly Evangel*, March 18, 1916.

McDowell, Wendy S. "Past, Present, & Future Tense." *Harvard Divinity School, News and Events*. http://www.hds.harvard.edu/news/articlearchive/cox_hollywood.html.

McPherson, Aimee Semple. "Methodism and Pentecost." *Pentecostal Evangel,* January 8, 1921.

"Mrs. McPherson Is A Type." *Christian Century*, August 12, 1926.

Mencken, H.L. "Two Enterprising Ladies." *The American Mercury*, 13:49 (January, 1928), 507.

Morris, B.J. "The Revivals of Aimee Semple McPherson." *Pacific Christian Advocate* October 5, 1921, 4-7, 10.

Narvarez, Alfonso A. "Guido Orlando, 80, Press Agent Who Devised Outlandish-Stunts." *New York Times*, May 28, 1988.

Nassour, Ellis. "Hag's Songs Reflect Life." *Music City News*, 13, August, 1975.

Olsen, Roger E. "Pentecostalism's Dark Side." *Christian Century*, March 7, 2006.

Reisem, Richard O. "The Man Who Invented The Five-Day Work Week." *Epitaph Newsletter*. http://www.lib/rochester.edu/index.cfm?PAGE+3093

Rodriquez, Richard. "Paradise Lost: California Has Always Been the Last Chance for Eden on the American Continent." *Los Angeles Times*, March 30, 1997.

Shribman, David M. "Review of *American Sermons: The Pilgrims to Martin Luther King, Jr.*" *Wall Street Journal*, April 23, 1999.

Silver, Allison. "Writing the Good Life." *New York Times*, November 8, 1981.

Updike, John. "Famous Aimee, The Life of Aimee Semple McPherson." *New Yorker*, April 30, 2007.

Van Allen, Jennie. "Her Greatest Miracle." *Los Angeles Times*, June 16, 1926.

Waggoner, W.R. "Admit Miracles are Performed by M'Pherson." *Arkansas City Traveler*, May 16, 1922.

Wilson, Lewis. "An Early Pioneer in Pentecostal Education." *Vanguard Magazine*, Winter, 2006.

Zikmund, Barbara Brown. "Kathryn Kuhlman: The Woman Behind the Miracles." *Christian Century*, August 2, 1995.

Dissertations & Theses

Baer, Jonathan R. "Perfectly Empowered Bodies: Divine Healing in Modernizing America." Ph.D. diss., Yale University, 2002.

Bond, J. Max. "The Negro in Los Angeles." Ph.D. diss., University of Southern California, 1936.

Deno, Vivian Eilythisa. "Holy Ghost Nation: Race, Gender and Working-Class Pentecostalism, 1906-1926." Ph.D. diss., University of California, Irvine, 2002.

Eskridge, Larry K. "Only Believe: Paul Rader and the Chicago Gospel Tabernacle, 1922-1933." M.A. thesis, University of Maryland, 1985.

Haskell, George William. "Formative Factors in the Life and Thought of Southern California Congregationalism, 1850-1908." Ph.D. diss., University of Southern California, 1947.

Jeffrey, Robert S. "The History of Douglas, Arizona." M.A. thesis, University of Arizona, 1951.

Guillow, Lawrence E. "The Origins of Race Relations in Los Angeles, 1820-1880: A Multi-Ethnic Study." Ph.D. diss., Arizona State University, 1996.

Kenyon, Howard Nelson. "An Analysis of Racial Separation Within the Early Pentecostal Movement." M.A. thesis, Baylor University, 1978.

Lacour, Lawrence Lealand. "A Study of the Revival Method in America, 1920-1955, With Special Reference to Billy Sunday, Aimee Semple McPherson and Billy Graham." Ph.D. diss., Northwestern University, 1956.

Nelson, Douglas J. "For Such a Time as This: The Story of Bishop W.J. Seymour and the Azusa Street Revival." Ph.D. diss., University of Birmingham, U.K, 1981.

Overacker, Ingrid. "And the Work was Accomplished: The African-American Church Community in Rochester, New York." Ph.D. diss., University of Rochester, 1995.

Reed, David Arthur. "Origins and Development of the Theology of Oneness Pentecostalism in the United States." Ph.D. diss., Boston University 1978.

Sanders, Rufus Gene William. "The Life of William Joseph Seymour: Black Father of the Twentieth Century Pentecostal Movement." Ph.D. diss., Bowling Green State University, 2000.

Still, Mark Summer. " 'Fighting Bob' Shuler, Fundamentalist and Reformer." Ph.D. diss., Claremont Graduate School, 1988.

Swartz, David R. "Left Behind: The Evangelical Left and the Limits of Evangelical Politics, 1965-1988." Ph.D. diss., University of Notre Dame, 2008.

INDEX

Page numbers in *italics* refer to illustrations. The abbreviation ASM is used for Aimee Semple McPherson